5/18/07

Hi Rich &

ENJOYED SEEING YOU
BOTH AGAIN...
Take care,

Dan

Wisdom of the Ages
At Your Fingertips

Wisdom of the Ages
At Your Fingertips

Provides easy access to timeless knowledge from over 1,000 of history's greatest American, European and Asian Minds. Over 6,500 carefully selected quotations, sayings and ideas, some quite rare, are intuitively organized into 81 major subjects. Each subject is consistently divided into 7 sections.

Compiled by: A. L. Linall, Jr.

Edited by: Barry Fetter and Monique Lenain-Fetter

The wisdom of the wise and the experience of ages
may be preserved by quotation.

Disraeli (1804-1881)

The superior man acquaints himself with many
sayings of antiquity and many deeds of the past,
in order to strengthen his character thereby.

I Ching (B.C. 1150?)

PREFACE

Desirable Quotation Qualities

Do not say a little in many words but a great deal in a few.

Pythagoras (B.C. 582-507)

Sixty percent of the quotations in this book are two lines or less.

* * * * * * * * *

*That writer does the most, who gives his reader the most
knowledge, and takes from him the least time.*

Colton (1780-1832)

There are millions of quotations. Quantity is not synonymous with
quality. The best book doesn't always have the most pages. Few movie
critics think the longest film is the best.

* * * * * * * * *

*Whatever we well understand we express clearly,
and words flow with ease.*

Nicholas Boileau (1636-1711)

Lack of clarity is more often the fault of the author or the editor than
any failing on the part of the reader.

* * * * * * * * *

*It is with books as with men: a very small number play a
great part, the rest are lost in the multitude.*

Voltaire (1694-1778)

Unusual Features Of This Book

"Wisdom of the Ages" differs from other books of quotations in three significant ways. The major subjects come from systems of knowledge that have reached us from antiquity. Each subject is consistently divided into seven sections. And, more quotations than usual come from non-western and ancient sources.

* * * * * * * * *

MAJOR SUBJECTS FROM ANTIQUITY - The 81 Major Subjects used in this book come from systems of knowledge that have reached us from antiquity. Arranged alphabetically, these common denominators allow us to group related minor subjects together. For example, the major subject of CHARACTER includes minor subjects such as Dignity, Ethics, Honor, Integrity and Reputation. This arrangement results in fewer subjects, and enables you to find what you're looking for in one place. Although most subjects like ANGER, BEAUTY, COURAGE, HOPE, TRUTH, POWER etc. will be familiar, we'd like to call your attention to the subjects of CREATION, THE ETERNAL, SOUL and NON-BEING which are not usually covered in other quotation books. The Subject List is on the following pages and the Subject Finder Index in the back of the book.

We see then how far the monuments of wit and learning are
more durable than the monuments of power, or of the hands.
For have not some books continued twenty-five hundred years
or more, without the loss of a syllable or letter; during
which time infinite palaces, temples, castles, and cities
have been decayed and demolished?

Bacon (1561-1626)

* * * * * * * *

ALL SUBJECTS HAVE 7 SECTIONS – Each major subject is consistently divided into the following seven sections: Essence, Opposites, Insight, Positive, Negative, Advice and Potpourri. This organizational technique helps you understand the subject better and communicate more effectively. Here's why. Quotations make every one more authoritative. They add another voice to your writing or speeches. But to be really effective, the quotation has to reinforce your point of view. Sections, such as Positive, Negative, Advice, etc., allow you to read 80% fewer quotes and yet still find the best quote for your purpose. Also, when reading a complete subject – which we strongly recommend – they give you a more complete understanding. The Section List is on the following pages.

When a man's knowledge is not in order, the more of it he has the greater will be his confusion.

Herbert Spencer (1820-1903)

* * * * * * * * *

MORE NON-WESTERN AND ANCIENT CONTENT - Now you can see what different religions and major traditions say about the same subject. Roughly 50% of quotations come from native English speakers and about 50% were translated from other languages. Almost 65% of the quotations come from before 1776; 28% before 1,000 A.D.

The oldest books are still only just out to those who have not read them.

Samuel Butler (1835-1902)

But as the world, harmoniously confused, Where order in variety we see; And where, tho' all things differ, all agree.

Pope (1688-1744

How to Use This Book

Read one complete subject – any subject. You will see how *"Wisdom of the Ages"* differs from other books of quotations by reading at least one complete subject. Then, take a look at the Section List.

Plan of the Book

The subjects are arranged alphabetically. Each subject is divided into seven sections. Within each section the oldest quotations appear first. The Subject List and Section List are in the front; the Subject Finder Index and Author Index with biographical snapshots are in the back of the book. (See the Table of Contents.)

The focus of this book is to provide an overview of major topics of interest to discerning readers.   Since a high percentage of the entries are translations from non-English sources book names are not included.

Miscellaneous

This is the hardcopy edition of a computer program by the same name in use on six continents. Details on this and our other programs are available at: **www.quotations.com**.

CONTENTS

SUBJECT LIST

SECTION LIST

CHAPTER SUBJECT ORGANIZATION

A   Every subject is divided into the following seven sections:

1. Essence   - Root, Heart.

2. Opposites   - Balance, Change, Paradoxes.

3. Insight   - Perspective, Viewpoint.

4. Positive   - Aspects, Influences, Presence, Qualities, and Virtues.

5. Negative   - Aspects, Influences, Absence, Qualities, and Vices.

6. Advice   - Strategy, Suggestions, Helpful Information.

7. Potpourri   - Poetry, Verse, Humor, Flowers and Weeds.

This organization enables the user to readily locate all items of a particular type. However, since each section has both an individual and a collective meaning, the best results will be obtained by reading each subject from 1 to 7.

B.   Within each section individual quotes are arranged chronologically by the source's date of birth. The oldest quote is listed first. Undated proverbs come last.

ACTIVITY
Action, Deeds and Energy

1. ESSENCE

1   It is a descending stream of pure activity which is the
     dynamic force of the universe.
                              Kabbalah (B.C. 1200?-700? A.D.)

2   Action is the product of the Qualities inherent in Nature.
                              Bhagavad Gita (c. B.C. 400)

3   Action is eloquence.
                              Shakespeare (1564-1616)

4   The end of man is action, and not thought,
     though it be of the noblest.
                              Carlyle (1795-1881)

5   Our deeds determine us, as much as we determine our deeds.
                              George Eliot (1819-1880)

6   Action is coarsened thought;
     thought becomes concrete, obscure, and unconscious.
                              Henri Frederic Amiel (1821-1881)

7   Everything is energy in motion.
                              Pir Vilayat Inayat Khan (born 1916)

2. OPPOSITES

8   As one acts and conducts himself, so does he become.
     The doer of good becomes good.
     The doer of evil becomes evil.
     One becomes virtuous by virtuous action, bad by bad action.
                              Upanishads (c. B.C. 800)

9   One who sees inaction in action, and action in inaction,
     is intelligent among men.
                              Bhagavad Gita (c. B.C. 400)

10   The secret of the magic of life consists in using action in
     order to attain non-action. One must not wish to leap over
     everything and penetrate directly.
                              Lu Yen (fl. 800 A.D.)

11   Desire and force between them are responsible for all our
      actions; desire causes our voluntary acts, force our
      involuntary.

                                              Pascal (1623-1662)

12   The deed is everything,
      the glory is naught.

                                              Goethe (1749-1832)

13   The more we do, the more we can do;
      the more busy we are, the more leisure we have.

                                              Hazlitt (1778-1830)

14   Deliberate with caution, but act with decision;
      and yield with graciousness, or oppose with firmness.

                                              Colton (1780-1832)

15   Our acts make or mar us,
      we are the children of our own deeds.

                                              Victor Hugo (1802-1885)

16   Action may not always bring happiness;
      but there is no happiness without action.

                                              Disraeli (1804-1881)

17   Think like a man of action, act like a man of thought.
                                  Henri Louis Bergson (1859-1941)

18   Action without study is fatal.
      Study without action is futile.

                                              Mary Beard (1876-1958)

3. INSIGHT

19   This universe is a trinity and this is made of name, form,
      and action. The source of all actions is the body, for it
      is by the body that all actions are done. The body is
      behind all actions, even as the Eternal is behind the body.
                                              Upanishads (c. B.C. 800)

20   Knowledge, the object of knowledge and the knower
        are the three factors which motivate action;
      the senses, the work and the doer
        comprise the threefold basis of action.
                                              Bhagavad Gita (c. B.C. 400)

21   All human actions have one or more of these seven causes:
      chance, nature, compulsions, habit, reason, passion, desire.
                                              Aristotle (B.C. 384-322)

22   Our actions are like the terminations of verses,
      which we rhyme as we please.
                              La Rochefoucauld (1613-1680)

23   The actions of men are the best interpreters of their
      thoughts.
                              John Locke (1632-1704)

24   Words may show a man's wit but actions his meaning.
                              Franklin (1706-1790)

25   Action hangs, as it were, "dissolved" in speech, in thoughts
      whereof speech is the shadow; and precipitates itself
      therefrom. The kind of speech in a man betokens the kind of
      action you will get from him.
                              Carlyle (1795-1881)

26   Every man feels instinctively that all the beautiful
      sentiments in the world weigh less than a single
      lovely action.
                              James Lowell (1819-1891)

27   The great end of life is not knowledge but action.
                              Thomas Huxley (1825-1895)

28   It is the mark of a good action that it appears inevitable
      in retrospect.
                              Robert Louis Stevenson (1850-1895)

29   According to real, exact knowledge, one force, or two
      forces, can never produce a phenomenon. The presence
      of a third force is necessary, for it is only with the
      help of a third force that the first two can produce
      what may be called a phenomenon, no matter in what sphere.
                              Gurdjieff (1873-1949)

30   Actions are the seed of Fate
      Deeds grow into Destiny.
                              A. L. Linall, Jr. (born 1947)

31   To talk goodness is not good...
      Only to do it is.
                              Chinese Proverb

4. POSITIVE

32   To be doing good deeds is man's most glorious task.
                              Sophocles (B.C. 495-406)

33   A tree is known by its fruit; a man by his deeds.
A good deed is never lost; he who sows courtesy reaps
friendship, and he who plants kindness gathers love.

           Basil (329-379 A.D.)

34   Good actions ennoble us, we are the sons of our own deeds.

           Cervantes (1547-1616)

35   How far that little candle throws his beams!
So shines a good deed in a naughty world.

           Shakespeare (1564-1616)

36   A good action is never lost;
it is a treasure laid up and guarded for the doer's need.

           Pedro Calderon (1600-1681)

37   Action is the highest perfection and drawing forth of the
utmost power, vigor, and activity of man's nature.

           Robert South (1634-1716)

38   Well done is better than well said.

           Franklin (1706-1790)

39   Act well at the moment,
and you have performed a good action for all eternity.

           Lavater (1741-1801)

40   Thought and theory must precede all salutary action;
yet action is nobler in itself than either thought or
theory.

           Wordsworth (1770-1850)

41   It is well to think well; it is divine to act well.

           Horace Mann (1796-1859)

42   Action is greater than writing. A good man is a nobler
object of contemplation than a great author. There are but
two things worth living for: to do what is worthy of being
written; and to write what is worthy of being read; and the
greater of these is the doing.

           Albert Pike (1809-1891)

43   But the good deed, through the ages
  Living in historic pages,
Brighter grows and gleams immortal,
  Unconsumed by moth or rust.

           Longfellow (1807-1882)

44   Active natures are rarely melancholy.
Activity and sadness are incompatible.

           Bovee (1820-1904)

5. NEGATIVE

45   Heaven never helps the men who will not act.
                                    Sophocles (B.C. 495-406)

46   Just as a flower which seems beautiful and has colour but
      no perfume, so are the fruitless words of the man who
      speaks them but does them not.
                              The Dhammapada (c. B.C. 300)

47   Men do not value a good deed unless it brings a reward.
                                    Ovid (B.C. 43-18 A.D.)

48   We should often be ashamed of our very best actions,
      if the world only saw the motives which caused them.
                              La Rochefoucauld (1613-1680)

49   Thinking is easy, acting is difficult,
      and to put one's thoughts into action
      is the most difficult thing in the world.
                                    Goethe (1749-1832)

50   He who considers too much will perform little.
                                    Schiller (1759-1805)

51   When a man has not a good reason for doing a thing,
      he has one good reason for letting it alone.
                                    Walter Scott (1771-1832)

52   Mark this well, ye proud men of action!
      ye are, after all, nothing but unconscious instruments
      of the men of thought.
                                    Heine (1797-1856)

53   We have only to change the point of view
      and the greatest action looks mean.
                                    Thackeray (1811-1863)

54   Words without actions are the assassins of idealism.
                              Herbert Hoover (1874-1964)

55   There is nothing so useless as doing efficiently that which
      should not be done at all.
                              Peter F. Drucker (born 1909)

6. ADVICE

56   One should act in consonance with the way of heaven and
earth, which is enduring and eternal. The superior man
perseveres long in his course, adapts to the times, but
remains firm in his direction and correct in his goals.

I Ching (B.C. 1150?)

57   The superior man acts before he speaks,
and afterwards speaks according to his action.

Confucius (B.C. 551-479)

58   Do not do what is already done.

Terence (B.C. 185-159)

59   We should not be so taken up in the search for truth,
as to neglect the needful duties of active life;
for it is only action that gives a true value
and commendation to virtue.

Cicero (B.C. 106-43)

60   What one has, one ought to use: and whatever he does
he should do with all his might.

Cicero (B.C. 106-43)

61   To do an evil act is base.
To do a good one without incurring danger, is common enough.
But it is part of a good man to do great and noble deeds
though he risks everything in doing them.

Plutarch (46-120 A.D.)

62   Be great in act, as you have been in thought.

Shakespeare (1564-1616)

63   Attempt the end, and never stand to doubt;
Nothing's so hard but search will find it out.

Robert Herrick (1591-1674)

64   The shortest answer is doing.

Herbert (1593-1632)

65   Do not wait for extraordinary circumstances to do good
action; try to use ordinary situations.

Richter (1763-1825)

66   Let us, if we must have great actions, make our own so. All
action is of infinite elasticity, and the least admits of
being inflated with celestial air, until it eclipses the sun
and moon.

Emerson (1803-1882)

67 Speak out in acts; the time for words has passed,
and only deeds will suffice.

John Greenleaf Whittier (1807-1892)

68 This is a world of action,
and not for moping and droning in.

Charles Dickens (1812-1870)

69 Trust no future, however pleasant!
 Let the dead past bury its dead!
Act, - act in the living Present!
 Heart within and God overhead.

Longfellow (1807-1882)

70 For purposes of action nothing is more useful than
narrowness of thought combined with energy of will.

Henri Frederic Amiel (1821-1881)

71 Our only true course is to let the motive for action be in
the action itself, never in its reward; not to be incited
by the hope of the result, nor yet indulge a propensity for
inertness.

H. P. Blavatsky (1831-1891)

72 It is not good enough for things to be planned - they still
have to be done; for the intention to become a reality,
energy has to be launched into operation.

Pir Vilayat Inayat Khan (born 1916)

73 Better do a good deed near at home
than go far away to burn incense.

Chinese Proverb

7. POTPOURRI

74   When a man dies, what does not leave him?
   The voice of a dead man goes into fire, his breath into
wind, his eyes into the sun, his mind into the moon, his
hearing into the quarters of heaven, his body into the
earth, his spirit into space, the hairs of his head into
plants, and his blood and semen are placed in water, what
then becomes of this person?
   What remains is action. It's quality becomes fate.
Verily, one becomes good by good action, bad by bad action.

Upanishads (c. B.C. 800)

75   That deed is not well done of which a man must repent,
      and the reward of which he receives crying and with a
      tearful face. No, that deed is well done of which a man
      does not repent, and the reward of which he receives gladly
      and cheerfully.

                                    The Dhammapada (c. B.C. 300)

76   A wise man guides his own course of action;
      The fool follows another's direction,
      When an old dog barks, the others run,
      And this for no reason at all.

                                    Saskya Pandita (1182-1251)

77   For as one star another far exceeds,
      So souls in heaven are placed by their deeds.

                                    Robert Greene (1558?-1592)

78   And future deeds crowded round us
      as the countless stars in the night.

                                    Goethe (1749-1832)

79   Each morning sees some task begun,
        Each evening sees it close;
      Something attempted, something done,
        Has earned a night's repose.

                                    Longfellow (1807-1882)

80   Action is the last resource of those who know not how
      to dream.

                                    Oscar Wilde (1854-1900)

ANGER

Fury, Hatred, Malice, Rage and Wrath

1. ESSENCE

81   Hatred is inveterate anger.
> Cicero (B.C. 106-43)

82   Anger is momentary madness.
> Horace (B.C. 65-8)

83   Hatreds are the cinders of affection.
> Walter Raleigh (1552-1618)

84   To be angry is to revenge the faults of others on ourselves.
> Pope (1688-1744)

85   Hatred is self-punishment.
> Hosea Ballou (1771-1852)

86   Anger is a wind which blows out the lamp of the mind.
> Robert G. Ingersoll (1833-1899)

2. OPPOSITES

87   He who is slow to anger has great understanding,
     but he who has a hasty temper exalts folly.
> Proverbs (B.C. 1000?-200?)

88   Anger begins with folly, and ends with repentance.
> Pythagoras (B.C. 582-507)

89   For hatred does not cease by hatred at any time:
     hatred ceases by love - this is an old rule.
> The Dhammapada (c. B.C. 300)

90   An angry man opens his mouth and shuts his eyes.
> Cato the Elder (B.C. 234-149)

91   He that will be angry for anything
     will be angry for nothing.
> Sallust (B.C. 86-34)

92   If anger proceeds from a great cause, it turns to fury;
     if from a small cause, it is peevishness;
     and so is always either terrible or ridiculous.
> Jeremy Taylor (1613-1667)

93   Whatever is begun in anger, ends in shame.

Franklin (1706-1790)

94   I was angry with my friend;
      I told my wrath, my wrath did end.
      I was angry with my foe;
      I told it not, my wrath did grow.

William Blake (1757-1828)

95   Most men know what they hate,
      few know what they love.

Colton (1780-1832)

96   The intoxication of anger, like that of the grape,
      shows us to others, but hides us from ourselves.

Colton (1780-1832)

3. INSIGHT

97   Anyone can become angry - that is easy,
      but to be angry with the right person, to the right degree,
      at the right time, for the right purpose,
      and in the right way - that is not easy.

Aristotle (B.C. 384-322)

98   Whom men fear they hate,
      and whom they hate, they wish dead.

Quintus Ennius (B.C. 239?-169?)

99   Like fragile ice anger passes away in time.

Ovid (B.C. 43-18 A.D.)

100   Anger, though concealed, is betrayed by the countenance.

Seneca (B.C. 3-65 A.D.)

101   Anger may repast with thee for an hour,
      but not repose for a night;
      the continuance of anger is hatred,
      the continuance of hatred turns malice.
      That anger is not warrantable which hath seen two suns.

Quarles (1592-1644)

102   We are almost always guilty of the hate we encounter.

Vauvenargues(1715-1747)

103   Hatred is active, and envy passive dislike;
      there is but one step from envy to hate.

Goethe (1749-1832)

104   If you hate a person, you hate something in him that is part
       of yourself. What isn't part of ourselves doesn't disturb
       us.
                                          Hermann Hesse (1877-1962)

4. POSITIVE

105   He who holds back rising anger like a rolling chariot, him
       I call a real driver; other people are but holding the reins
                                          The Dhammapada (c. B.C. 300)

106   I never work better than when I am inspired by anger;
       for when I am angry, I can write, pray, and preach well,
       for then my whole temperament is quickened, my understanding
       sharpened, and all mundane vexations and temptations depart.
                                          Martin Luther (1483-1546)

107   Now hatred is by far the longest pleasure;
       Men love in haste, but they detest at leisure.
                                          Byron (1788-1824)

108   A good indignation brings out all one's powers.
                                          Emerson (1803-1882)

109   Anger is a great force. If you control it, it can be
       transmuted into a power which can move the whole world.
                                          Sivananda (born 1887)

110   Passionate hatred can give meaning and purpose to an empty
       life.
                                          Eric Hoffer (1902-1983)

5. NEGATIVE

111   As the whirlwind in its fury teareth up trees,
       and deformeth the face of nature, or as an earthquake
       in its convulsions overturneth whole cities;
       so the rage of an angry man throweth mischief around him.
                                          Akhenaton? (c. B.C. 1375)

112   There is such malice in men as to rejoice in misfortunes
       and from another's woes to draw delight.
                                          Terence (B.C. 185-159)

113   An angry man is again angry with himself
       when he returns to reason.
                                          Publilius Syrus (fl. B.C. 42)

114   There is no medicine to cure hatred.
                                          Publilius Syrus (fl. B.C. 42)

115   Malice drinks one half of its own poison.

                         Seneca (B.C. 3-65 A.D.)

116   Anger, if not restrained, is frequently more hurtful to
       us than the injury that provokes it.

                         Seneca (B.C. 3-65 A.D.)

117   The hatred of relatives is the most violent.

                         Tacitus (55-117 A.D.)

118   He whose anger causes no fear,
       Who can confer no benefit when pleased,
       Who can neither destroy nor subjugate,
       What good is such a man's anger?

                  Nagarjuna (c. 100-200 A.D.)

119   How much more grievous are the consequences of anger
       than the causes of it.

                 Marcus Aurelius (121-180 A.D.)

120   When our hatred is violent, it sinks us even beneath those
       we hate.

                 La Rochefoucauld (1613-1680)

121   Hatred is something peculiar. You will always find it
       strongest and most violent where there is the lowest
       degree of culture.

                 Goethe (1749-1832)

122   Hatred is the vice of narrow souls; they feed it with all
       their littleness, and make it the pretext of base tyrannies.

                 Balzac (1799-1850)

123   Hatred is the coward's revenge for being intimidated.

                 G. B. Shaw (1856-1950)

124   The tendency of aggression is an innate, independent,
       instinctual disposition in man...it constitutes the most
       powerful obstacle to culture.

                 Sigmund Freud (1856-1939)

125   We must interpret a bad temper as a sign of inferiority.

                 Alfred Adler (1870-1937)

6. ADVICE

126   Indulge not thyself in the passion of Anger; it is whetting
       a sword to wound thine own breast, or murder thy friend.

                 Akhenaton? (c. B.C. 1375)

127   Anger will never disappear so long as thoughts of resentment
       are cherished in the mind. Anger will disappear just as
       soon as thoughts of resentment are forgotten.
                                           Buddha (B.C. 568-488)

128   When anger rises, think of the consequences.
                                           Confucius (B.C. 551-479)

129   Take care that no one hates you justly.
                                           Publilius Syrus (fl. B.C. 42)

130   The greatest remedy for anger is delay.
                                           Seneca (B.C. 3-65 A.D.)

131   Oppose not rage while rage is in its force,
       but give it way a while and let it waste.
                                           Shakespeare (1564-1616)

132   Beware of him that is slow to anger; anger, when it is long
       in coming, is the stronger when it comes, and the longer
       kept. Abused patience turns to fury.
                                           Quarles (1592-1644)

133   Act nothing in a furious passion.
       It's putting to sea in a storm.
                                           Thomas Fuller (1608-1661)

134   Think when you are enraged at any one, what would probably
       become your sentiments should he die during the dispute.
                                           William Shenstone (1714-1763)

135   When angry, count ten before you speak,
       if very angry, a hundred.
                                           Thomas Jefferson (1743-1826)

136   To rule one's anger is well; to prevent it is better.
                                           Tryon Edwards (1809-1894)

137   If you have written a clever and conclusive,
       but scathing letter, keep it back till the next day,
       and it will very often never go at all.
                                           Lubbock (1834-1913)

7. POTPOURRI

138   Anger, which, far sweeter than trickling drops of honey,
       rises in the bosom of a man like smoke.
                                           Homer (c. B.C. 700)

139   When a man dwells on the objects of sense, he creates an
attraction for them; attraction develops into desire, and
desire breeds anger.

Bhagavad Gita (c. B.C. 400)

140   Although you may spend your life killing,
You will not exhaust all your foes.
But if you quell your own anger,
Your real enemy will be slain.

Nagarjuna (c. 100-200 A.D.)

141   In rage deaf as the sea; hasty as fire.

Shakespeare (1564-1616)

142   The brain may devise laws for the blood;
but a hot temper leaps o'er a cold decree:
such a hare is madness the youth, to skip
over the meshes of good counsel, the cripple.

Shakespeare (1564-1616)

143   Heaven has no rage like love to hatred turned,
Nor Hell a fury like a woman scorned.

William Congreve (1670-1729)

144   Are you angry that others disappoint you?
Remember you cannot depend on yourself.

Franklin (1706-1790)

145   Hate is ravening vulture beaks
descending on a place of skulls.

Amy Lowell (1874-1925)

146   When one God dwells in all living beings, then why do you
hate others? Why do you frown at others? Why do you become
indignant towards others? Why do you use harsh words? Why
do you try to rule and domineer over others? Why do you
exploit folly? Is this not sheer ignorance? Get wisdom and
rest in peace.

Sivananda (born 1887)

BEAUTY
Form and Grace

1. ESSENCE

147 Beauty - the adjustment of all parts proportionately so that one cannot add or subtract or change without impairing the harmony of the whole.
Leon Battista Alberti (1404-1472)

148 Beauty is the purgation of superfluities.
Michelangelo (1474-1564)

149 Beauty is a harmonious relation between something in our nature and the quality of the object which delights us.
Pascal (1623-1662)

150 The ideal of beauty is simplicity and tranquility.
Goethe (1749-1832)

151 Grace is the beauty of form under the influence of freedom.
Schiller (1759-1805)

152 Beauty is the promise of happiness.
Stendhal (1783-1842)

153 Beauty is truth, truth beauty.
Keats (1795-1821)

154 Beauty itself is but the sensible image of the Infinite.
George Bancroft (1800-1891)

155 Beauty is the mark God sets on virtue.
Emerson (1803-1882)

156 Beauty is the index of a larger fact than wisdom.
Oliver Wendell Holmes (1809-1894)

157 The essence of the beautiful is unity in variety.
Felix Mendelssohn (1809-1847)

2. OPPOSITES

158 When the people of the world all know beauty as beauty,
   There arises the recognition of ugliness.
When they all know the good as good,
   There arises the recognition of evil.
Therefore: Being and non-being produce each other.
Lao-Tzu (fl. B.C. 600)

159 The criterion of true beauty is that it increases on
examination; if false, that it lessens.

Greville (1554-1628)

160 To give pain is the tyranny;
to make happy, the true empire of beauty.

Richard Steele (1672-1729)

161 Grace has been defined as the outward expression of the
inward harmony of the soul.

Hazlitt (1778-1830)

162 The beautiful seems right by force of beauty,
and the feeble wrong because of weakness.

Elizabeth B. Browning (1806-1861)

163 Beauty is the power by which a woman charms a lover and
terrifies a husband.

Ambrose Bierce (1842-1914?)

164 The beauty of the world has two edges, one of laughter,
one of anguish, cutting the heart asunder.

Virginia Woolf (1882-1941)

165 Beauty is the wisdom of women.
Wisdom is the beauty of men.

Chinese Proverb

3. INSIGHT

166 Heat cannot be separated from fire,
or beauty from The Eternal.

Dante (1265-1321)

167 All kinds of beauty do not inspire love;
there is a kind which only pleases the sight,
but does not captivate the affections.

Cervantes (1547-1616)

168 Beauty is the bait which with delight
allures man to enlarge his kind.

Edmund Spenser (1552-1599)

169 The best part of beauty is that which no picture
can express.

Bacon (1561-1626)

170 There is no excellent beauty that hath not some
strangeness in the proportion.

Bacon (1561-1626)

171 Beauty is nature's brag, and must be shown in courts,
at feasts, and high solemnities, where most may wonder
at the workmanship.

Milton (1608-1674)

172 That which is striking and beautiful is not always good;
but that which is good is always beautiful.

Ninon de L'Enclos (1620-1705)

173 Variety of uniformities makes complete beauty.

Christopher Wren (1632-1723)

174 There is nothing that makes its way more directly to the
soul than beauty.

Addison (1672-1719)

175 Beauty is an outward gift, which is seldom despised,
except by those to whom it has been refused.

Gibbon (1737-1794)

176 Beauty is a manifestation of secret natural laws,
which otherwise would have been hidden from us forever.

Goethe (1749-1832)

177 Grace is in garments, in movements, in manners; beauty in
the nude, and in forms. This is true of bodies; but when
we speak of feelings, beauty is in their spirituality, and
grace in their moderation.

Joubert (1754-1824)

178 Truth exists for the wise, beauty for the feeling heart.

Schiller (1759-1805)

179 The beautiful rests on the foundations of the necessary.

Emerson (1803-1882)

180 We ascribe beauty to that which is simple;
which has not superfluous parts;
which exactly answers its ends.

Emerson (1803-1882)

181 In life, as in art, the beautiful moves in curves.

Bulwer-Lytton (1803-1873)

182 The beauty that addresses itself to the eyes
is only the spell of the moment;
the eye of the body is not always that of the soul.

George Sand (1804-1876)

183   Beauty is not caused, - it is;
       Chase it and it ceases,
       Chase it not and it abides...

                               Emily Dickinson (1830-1886)

4. POSITIVE

184   When virtue and modesty enlighten her charms, the lustre of
       a beautiful woman is brighter than the stars of heaven,
       and the influence of her power it is in vain to resist.

                               Akhenaton? (c. B.C. 1375)

185   What is beautiful is good,
       and who is good will soon be beautiful.

                                    Sappho (fl. B.C. 600)

186   Personal beauty is a greater recommendation
       than any letter of reference.

                               Aristotle (B.C. 384-322)

187   Even virtue is fairer when it appears in a beautiful person.

                                    Vergil (B.C. 70-19)

188   For, when with beauty we can virtue join,
       We paint the semblance of a form divine.

                               Matthew Prior (1664-1721)

189   Beauty attracts us men; but if, like an armed magnet it
       is pointed, beside, with gold and silver, it attracts
       with tenfold power.

                                    Richter (1763-1825)

190   Who doth not feel, until his failing sight
       Faints into dimness with its own delight,
       His changing cheek, his sinking heart confess,
       The might - the majesty of Loveliness?

                                    Byron (1788-1824)

191   A thing of beauty is a joy forever,
       Its loveliness increases; it will never
       Pass into nothingness.

                                    Keats (1795-1821)

192   A beautiful form is better than a beautiful face;
       it gives a higher pleasure than statues or pictures;
       it is the finest of the fine arts.

                                    Emerson (1803-1882)

193   The soul, by an instinct stronger than reason,
ever associates beauty with truth.

Tuckerman (1813-1871)

194   Beauty is power; a smile is its sword.

Charles Reade (1814-1884)

195   Beauty is a form of genius - is higher, indeed, than genius,
as it needs no explanation. It is of the great facts in the
world like sunlight, or springtime, or the reflection in
dark water of that silver shell we call the moon.

Oscar Wilde (1854-1900)

5. NEGATIVE

196   Beauty is a short-lived tyranny.

Socrates (B.C. 469-399)

197   Nothing is beautiful from every point of view.

Horace (B.C. 65-8)

198   Rare is the union of beauty and purity.

Juvenal (40-125 A.D.)

199   Beauty - a deceitful bait with a deadly hook.

John Lyly (1554-1606)

200   Beauty is but a vain and doubtful good;
  A shining gloss that fadeth suddenly;
A flower that dies when first it 'gins to bud;
  A brittle glass that's broken presently;
A doubtful good, a gloss, a glass, a flower,
  Lost, faded, broken, dead within an hour.

Shakespeare (1564-1616)

201   Beauty is but a flower
Which wrinkles will devour;
Brightness falls from the air;
Queens have died young and fair;
Dust hath closed Helen's eye.

Thomas Nashe (1567-1601)

202   Gaze not on beauty too much, lest it blast thee;
nor too long, lest it blind thee;
nor too near, lest it burn thee.
If thou like it, it deceives thee;
if thou love it, it disturbs thee;
if thou hunt after it, it destroys thee.
If virtue accompany it, it is the heart's paradise;
if vice associate it, it is the soul's purgatory.
It is the wise man's bonfire, and the fool's furnace.

Quarles (1592-1644)

203   In beauty, faults conspicuous grow;
        The smallest speck is seen in snow.

                                        Gay (1688-1732)

204   Beauties in vain their pretty eyes may roll;
        charms strike the sight, but merit wins the soul.

                                        Pope (1688-1744)

205   Beauty and folly are old companions.

                                        Franklin (1706-1790)

206   Beauty and sadness always go together.
        Nature thought beauty too rich to go forth
        Upon the earth without a meet alloy.

                                George MacDonald (1824-1905)

207   What a strange illusion it is to suppose
        that beauty is goodness.

                                        Leo Tolstoy (1828-1910)

208   Beauty is all very well at first sight; but who ever
        looks at it when it has been in the house three days?

                                        G. B. Shaw (1856-1950)

209   Beauty, more than bitterness
        Makes the heart break.

                                        Sara Teasdale (1884-1933)

210   Beauty is unbearable, drives us to despair, offering us for
        a minute the glimpse of an eternity that we should like to
        stretch out over the whole of time.

                                        Albert Camus (1913-1960)

6. ADVICE

211   Trust not too much to an enchanting face.

                                        Vergil (B.C. 70-19)

212   Remember if you marry for beauty, thou bindest thyself all
        thy life for that which perchance, will neither last nor
        please thee one year: and when thou hast it, it will be to
        thee of no price at all.

                                        Walter Raleigh (1552-1618)

213   Gather ye rose-buds while ye may,
        Old Time is still a-flying:
        And this same flower that smiles today,
        Tomorrow will be dying.

                                        Robert Herrick (1591-1674)

214   A man should hear a little music, read a little poetry,
      and see a fine picture every day of his life,
      in order that worldly cares may not obliterate the sense
      of the beautiful which God has implanted in the human soul.
                                              Goethe (1749-1832)

215   There's beauty all around our paths, if but our
      watchful eyes can trace it 'midst familiar things,
      and through their lowly guise.
                                       Felicia Hemans (1794-1835)

216   Though we travel the world over to find the beautiful,
      we must carry it with us or we find it not.
                                             Emerson (1803-1882)

217   Remember that the most beautiful things in the world
      are the most useless; peacocks and lilies, for instance.
                                         John Ruskin (1819-1900)

218   Walk on a rainbow trail; walk on a trail of song,
      and all about you will be beauty.
      There is a way out of every dark mist, over a rainbow trail.
                                                    Navajo Song

7. POTPOURRI

219   When the candles are out all women are fair.
                                        Plutarch (46-120 A.D.)

220   O, thou art fairer than the evening air clad in the
      beauty of a thousand stars.
                                 Christopher Marlowe (1564-1593)

221   There's no use being young without being beautiful,
      and no use being beautiful without being young.
                                   La Rochefoucauld (1613-1680)

222   Beauty, like ice, our footing does betray;
      Who can tread sure on the smooth, slippery way:
      Pleased with the surface, we glide swiftly on,
      And see the dangers that we cannot shun.
                                              Dryden (1631-1700)

223   'Tis not a lip, or eye, we beauty call,
      But the joint force and full result of all.
                                                Pope (1688-1744)

224   Her air, her manners, all who saw admired;
       Courteous though coy, and gentle though retired;
       The joy of youth and health her eyes displayed,
       And ease of heart her every look conveyed.

                                  George Crabbe (1754-1832)

225   Not more the rose, the queen of flowers,
       Outblushes all the bloom of bower,
       Than she unrivall'd grace discloses;
       The sweetest rose, where all are roses.

                                Thomas Moore (1779-1852)

226   She walks in beauty like the night
       Of cloudless climes and starry skies;
       And all that's best of dark and bright
       Meet in her aspect and in her eyes:
       Thus mellowed to that tender light
       Which heaven to gaudy day denies.

                                Byron (1788-1824)

227   Loveliest of lovely things are they
       On earth, that soonest pass away.
       The rose that lives its little hour
       Is prized beyond the sculptured flower.

                     William Cullen Bryant (1794-1878)

228   She is not fair to outward view
       As many maidens be;
       Her loveliness I never knew
       Until she smiled on me:
       Oh! then I saw her eye was bright,
       A well of love, a spring of light.

                     Hartley Coleridge (1796-1849)

229   Sunsets are so beautiful that they almost seem as if we
       were looking through the gates of Heaven.

                              Lubbock (1834-1913)

CHANGE
Cycles and Mutability

1. ESSENCE

230   Everything changes, nothing remains without change.
Buddha (B.C. 568-488)

231   All things change, nothing perishes.
Ovid (B.C. 43-18 A.D.)

232   In all things there is a law of cycles.
Tacitus (55-117 A.D.)

233   We must all obey the great law of change.
It is the most powerful law of nature.
Burke (1729-1797)

2. OPPOSITES

234   We are negative in our relationships with that which is of
a higher potential than we are; and we are positive in our
relationships with that which has a lower potential. This
is a relationship which is in a perpetual state of flux, and
which varies at every separate point at which we make our
innumerable contracts with our environment.
Kabbalah (B.C. 1200?-700? A.D.)

235   There is nothing permanent except change.
Heraclitus (B.C. 535-475)

236   The seen is the changing,
the unseen is the unchanging.
Plato (B.C. 427?-347?)

237   As the blessings of health and fortune have a beginning,
so they must also find an end. Everything rises but to
fall, and increases but to decay.
Sallust (B.C. 86-34)

238   The misery which follows pleasure
Is the pleasure which follows misery.
The pleasure and misery of mankind
Revolve like a wheel.
Nagarjuna (c. 100-200 A.D.)

239   The end of all motion is its beginning; for it terminates
      at no other end save its own beginning from which it begins
      to be moved and to which it tends ever to return, in order
      to cease and rest in it.
                                    Joannes Scotus Erigena (815?-877? A.D.)

240   Still ending, and beginning still.
                                                Cowper (1731-1800)

241   In this world of change, nothing which comes stays,
      and nothing which goes is lost.
                                          Anne Swetchine (1782-1857)

242   Change is inevitable...Change is constant.
                                              Disraeli (1804-1881)

243   The appearance and disappearance of the Universe are
      pictured as an outbreathing and inbreathing of "the Great
      Breath," which is eternal, and which, being Motion, is
      one of the three aspects of the Absolute - Abstract Space
      and Duration being the other two.
                                        H. P. Blavatsky (1831-1891)

3. INSIGHT

244   The atom, being for all practical purposes the stable unit
      of the physical plane, is a constantly changing vortex of
      reactions.
                                      Kabbalah (B.C. 1200?-700? A.D.)

245   The universe is moved by a power which cycles endlessly from
      day to day. Such greatness endures for all time. As in
      heaven, so on earth.
                                            I Ching (B.C. 1150?)

246   As when rivers flowing towards the ocean find there final
      peace, their name and form disappear, and people speak only
      of the ocean, even so the different forms of the seer of all
      flows towards the Spirit and find there final peace, their
      name and form disappear and people speak only of Spirit.
                                          Upanishads (c. B.C. 800)

247   At the dawning of that day all objects in manifestation
      stream forth from the Unmanifest, and when evening falls
      they are dissolved into It again. The same multitude of
      beings, which have lived on earth so often, all are
      dissolved as the night of the universe approaches, to issue
      forth anew when morning breaks. Thus is it ordained.
                                        Bhagavad Gita (c. B.C. 400)

248   In human life there is constant change of fortune;
and it is unreasonable to expect an exemption from the
common fate. Life itself decays, and all things are
daily changing.

Plutarch (46-120 A.D.)

249   The customs and fashions of men change like leaves on the
bough, some of which go and others come.

Dante (1265-1321)

250   It is not strange that even our loves should change
with our fortunes.

Shakespeare (1564-1616)

251   There is such a thing as a general revolution which changes
the taste of men as it changes the fortunes of the world.

La Rochefoucauld (1613-1680)

252   The world goes up and the world goes down,
And the sunshine follows the rain;
And yesterday's sneer and yesterday's frown
Can never come over again.

Charles Kingsley (1819-1875)

253   All things must change to something new,
to something strange.

Longfellow (1807-1882)

254   It is the greatest mistake to think that man is always one
and the same. A man is never the same for long. He is
continually changing. He seldom remains the same even for
half an hour.

Gurdjieff (1873-1949)

255   To change and change for the better are two different things
German Proverb

4. POSITIVE

256   The way of the Creative works through change and transformation, so that each thing receives its true nature
and destiny and comes into permanent accord with the
Great Harmony: this is what furthers and what perseveres.

I Ching (B.C. 1150?)

257   A rolling stone can gather no moss.

Publilius Syrus (fl. B.C. 42)

258   Since 'tis Nature's law to change,
Constancy alone is strange.

John Wilmot (1647-1680)

259   To-day is not yesterday: we ourselves change; how can our
       Works and Thoughts, if they are always to be the fittest,
       continue always the same? Change, indeed is painful;
       yet ever needful; and if Memory have its force and worth,
       so also has Hope.

                                        Carlyle (1795-1881)

260   The true past departs not, no truth or goodness realized
       by man ever dies, or can die; but all is still here, and,
       recognized or not, lives and works through endless change.

                                        Carlyle (1795-1881)

261   To live is to change,
       and to be perfect is to have changed often.

                              John Henry Newman (1801-1890)

262   When to the Permanent is sacrificed the Mutable, the prize
       is thine: the drop returneth whence it came. The Open
       Path leads to the changeless change - Non-Being, the
       glorious state of Absoluteness, the Bliss past human
       thought.

                                 H. P. Blavatsky (1831-1891)

263   The search for static security - in the law and elsewhere -
       is misguided. The fact is security can only be achieved
       through constant change, adapting old ideas that have
       outlived their usefulness to current facts.

                              William O. Douglas (1898-1980)

5. NEGATIVE

264   Keep what you have; the known evil is best.

                                       Plautus (B.C. 254-184)

265   He despises what he sought; and he seeks that which he
       lately threw away.

                                         Horace (B.C. 65-8)

266   Believe, if thou wilt, that mountains change their place,
       but believe not that man changes his nature.

                                  Mohammed (570-632 A.D.)

267   He that will not apply new remedies must expect new evils.

                                        Bacon (1561-1626)

268   Then rose the seed of Chaos, and of Night,
       To blot out order and extinguish light.

                                         Pope (1688-1744)

269 What I possess I would gladly retain. Change amuses the
mind, yet scarcely profits.

Goethe (1749-1832)

270 They are the weakest-minded and the hardest-hearted men
that most love change.

John Ruskin (1819-1900)

271 Humanity is moving in a circle. In one century it destroys
everything it creates in another, and the progress in
mechanical things of the past hundred years has proceeded
at the cost of losing many other things which perhaps were
much more important for it.

Gurdjieff (1873-1949)

6. ADVICE

272 Change is certain. Peace is followed by disturbances;
departure of evil men by their return. Such recurrences
should not constitute occasions for sadness but realities
for awareness, so that one may be happy in the interim.

I Ching (B.C. 1150?)

273 Man must be prepared for every event of life,
for there is nothing that is durable.

Menander (B.C. 342-291)

274 No sensible man ever imputes inconsistency to another
for changing his mind.

Cicero (B.C. 106-43)

275 Observe constantly that all things take place by change,
and accustom thyself to consider that the nature of the
Universe loves nothing so much as to change the things which
are, and to make new things like them.

Marcus Aurelius (121-180 A.D.)

276 Perfection is immutable. But for things imperfect,
change is the way to perfect them.

Owen Feltham (1602-1668)

277 Weep not that the world changes - did it keep a stable,
changeless state, it were cause indeed to weep.

William Cullen Bryant (1794-1878)

278 Slumber not in the tents of your fathers.
The world is advancing.

Giuseppe Mazzini (1805-1872)

279   To act and act wisely when the time for action comes, to
      wait and wait patiently when it is time for repose, put man
      in accord with the rising and falling tides (of affairs),
      so that with nature and law at his back, and truth and
      beneficence as his beacon light, he may accomplish wonders.
      Ignorance of this law results in periods of unreasoning
      enthusiasm on the one hand, and depression on the other.
      Man thus becomes the victim of the tides when he should be
      their Master.

                                        H. P. Blavatsky (1831-1891)

7. POTPOURRI

280   Force never moves in a straight line, but always in a curve
      vast as the universe, and therefore eventually returns
      whence it issued forth, but upon a higher arc, for the
      universe has progressed since it started.

                                        Kabbalah (B.C. 1200?-700? A.D.)

281   So many great nobles, things, administrations,
      So many high chieftains, so many brave nations,
      So many proud princes, and power so splendid,
      In a moment, a twinkling, all utterly ended.

                                        Jacopone (c. 1230-1306)

282   The ever-whirling wheele
      Of Change, to which all mortal things doth sway.

                                        Edmund Spenser (1552-1599)

283   See dying vegetables life sustain,
      See life dissolving vegetate again;
      All forms that perish other forms supply;
      By turns we catch the vital breath and die.

                                        Pope (1688-1744)

284   Ships, wealth, general confidence,-
      All were his;
      He counted them at break of day,
      And when the sun set! where were they.

                                        Byron (1788-1824)

285   Life may change, but it may fly not;
      Hope may vanish, but can die not;
      Truth be veiled, but still it burneth;
      Love repulsed, - but it returneth.

                                        Shelley (1792-1822)

286   Nature gives to every time and season some beauties of its
      own; and from morning to night, as from the cradle to the
      grave, it is but a succession of changes so gentle and easy
      that we can scarcely mark their progress.

Charles Dickens (1812-1870)

287   But the nearer the dawn the darker the night,
      And by going wrong all things come right;
      Things have been mended that were worse,
      And the worse, the nearer they are to mend.

Longfellow (1807-1882)

288   That rivers flow into the sea
      Is loss and waste, the foolish say,
      Nor know that back they find their way
      Unseen, to where they want to be.

Arthur Clough (1819-1861)

289   Time fleeth on, Youth soon is gone,
      Naught earthly may abide; Life seemeth fast,
      But may not last - It runs as runs the tide.

Leland (1824-1903)

290   The old believe everything;
      the middle-aged suspect everything;
      the young know everything.

Oscar Wilde (1854-1900)

CHARACTER
Dignity, Ethics, Honor, Integrity and Reputation

1. ESSENCE

291   Character is destiny.
>> Heraclitus (B.C. 535-475)

292   Dignity does not consist in possessing honors,
but in deserving them.
>> Aristotle (B.C. 384-322)

293   Character is simply habit long continued.
>> Plutarch (46-120 A.D.)

294   Reputation is what men and women think of us;
character is what God and angels know of us.
>> Paine (1737-1809)

295   Character, in great and little things, means carrying
through what you feel able to do.
>> Goethe (1749-1832)

296   Character is a perfectly educated will.
>> Novalis (1772-1801)

297   Character is that which can do without success.
>> Emerson (1803-1882)

298   Character - a reserved force which acts directly by
presence, and without means.
>> Emerson (1803-1882)

299   Character is not cut in marble; it is not something solid
and unalterable. It is something living and changing...
>> George Eliot (1819-1880)

2. OPPOSITES

300   Honour is the inner garment of the Soul; the first thing put
on by it with the flesh, and the last it layeth down at its
separation from it.
>> Akhenaton? (c. B.C. 1375)

301   A man should endeavor to be as pliant as a reed,
yet as hard as cedar-wood.
>> The Talmud (B.C. 500?-400? A.D.)

302 To enjoy the things we ought, and to hate the things we
ought, has the greatest bearing on excellence of character.
Aristotle (B.C. 384-322)

303 An excellent man, like precious metal,
Is in every way invariable;
A villain, like the beams of a balance,
Is always varying, upwards and downwards.
Saskya Pandita (1182-1251)

304 He that has light within his own clear breast
May sit in the centre, and enjoy bright day:
But he that hides a dark soul and foul thoughts
Benighted walks under the mid-day sun;
Himself his own dungeon.
Milton (1608-1674)

305 Talent is nurtured in solitude; character is formed in the
stormy billows of the world.
Goethe (1749-1832)

306 Strong characters are brought out by change of situation,
and gentle ones by permanence.
Richter (1763-1825)

307 A mans' character is the reality of himself;
his reputation, the opinion others have formed about him;
character resides in him, reputation in other people;
that is the substance, this is the shadow.
Beecher (1813-1878)

308 All men are alike in their lower natures;
it is in their higher characters that they differ.
Bovee (1820-1904)

309 It is better to deserve honors and not have them
than to have them and not deserve them.
Mark Twain (1835-1910)

310 Man consists of two parts: essence and personality.
Essence in man is what is his own. Personality in man
is what is "not his own." "Not his own" means what has
come from outside, what he has learned, or reflects, all
traces of exterior impressions left in the memory and in the
sensations, all words and movements that have been learned,
all feelings created by imitation.
Gurdjieff (1873-1949)

311   Good character is like a rubber ball -
          Thrown down hard - it bounces right back.
       Good reputation is like a crystal ball -
          Thrown for gain - shattered and cracked.
A. L. Linall, Jr. (born 1947)

312   Practice no vice because it's trivial...
       Neglect no virtue because it's so.
Chinese Proverb

3. INSIGHT

313   As the shadow waiteth on the substance,
       even so true honour attendeth upon goodness.
Akhenaton? (c. B.C. 1375)

314   Many individuals have, like uncut diamonds,
       shining qualities beneath a rough exterior.
Juvenal (40-125 A.D.)

315   Not to be cheered by praise,
       Not to be grieved by blame,
       But to know thoroughly ones own virtues or powers
       Are the characteristics of an excellent man.
Saskya Pandita (1182-1251)

316   Every one is the son of his own works.
Cervantes (1547-1616)

317   Life every man holds dear; but the dear man holds honor
       far more precious dear than life.
Shakespeare (1564-1616)

318   True dignity is never gained by place,
       and never lost when honors are withdrawn.
Philip Massinger (1583-1640)

319   The discipline of desire is the background of character.
John Locke (1632-1704)

320   Honor is like an island, rugged and without shores;
       we can never re-enter it once we are on the outside.
Nicholas Boileau (1636-1711)

321   It is in men as in soils where sometimes there is a vein
       of gold which the owner knows not of.
Swift (1667-1745)

322   Be your character what it will, it will be known;
       and nobody will take it upon your word.
Chesterfield (1694-1773)

323   The integrity of men is to be measured by their conduct,
       not by their professions.

                                            Junius (1740-1818)

324   Action, looks, words, steps, form the alphabet by which you
       may spell character.

                                            Lavater (1741-1801)

325   A man never shows his own character so plainly as by his
       manner of portraying another's.

                                            Richter (1763-1825)

326   Our own heart, and not other men's opinion, form our true
       honor.

                                    Samuel Coleridge (1772-1834)

327   It is with trifles, and when he is off guard, that a man
       best reveals his character.

                                    Schopenhauer (1788-1860)

328   The measure of a man's real character is what he would do
       if he knew he would never be found out.

                                            Macaulay (1800-1859)

329   Characters do not change. - Opinions alter, but characters
       are only developed.

                                            Disraeli (1804-1881)

330   Character is like a tree and reputation like its shadow.
       The shadow is what we think of it;
       the tree is the real thing.

                                            Lincoln (1809-1865)

331   Reputation is only a...candle, of wavering and uncertain
       flame, and easily blown out, but it is the light by which
       the world looks for and finds merit.

                                    James Lowell (1819-1891)

332   Your character will be what you yourself choose to make it.

                                            Lubbock (1834-1913)

333   Character is the result of two things:
       Mental attitude and the way we spend our time.

                                    Elbert Hubbard (1859-1915)

334   If you create an act, you create a habit.
       If you create a habit, you create a character.
       If you create a character, you create a destiny.

                                    Andre Maurois (1885-1967)

335   Good character is not formed in a week or a month. It is
      created little by little, day by day. Protracted and
      patient effort is needed to develop good character.

                                        Sivananda (born 1887)

336   Integrity has no need of rules.

                                   Albert Camus (1913-1960)

4. POSITIVE

337   As a plain garment best adorneth a beautiful woman, so a
      decent behaviour is the best ornament of inner wisdom.

                                 Akhenaton? (c. B.C. 1375)

338   The best man in his dwelling loves the earth.
         In his heart, he loves what is profound.
         In his associations, he loves humanity.
         In his words, he loves faithfulness.
         In government, he loves order.
         In handling affairs, he loves competence.
         In his activities, he loves timeliness.
         It is because he does not compete that he is
           without reproach.

                                    Lao-Tzu (fl. B.C. 600)

339   To be fond of learning is near to wisdom;
      to practice with vigor is near to benevolence;
      and to be conscious of shame is near to fortitude.
      He who knows these three things
      knows how to cultivate his own character.

                                Confucius (B.C. 551-479)

340   What is honorable is also safest.

                                   Livy (B.C. 59-17 A.D.)

341   The highest of characters, in my estimation,
      is as ready to pardon the moral errors of mankind,
      as if he were every day guilty of some himself;
      and at the same time as cautious of committing a fault
      as if he never forgave one.

                           Pliny the Younger (62-113 A.D.)

342   The purest treasure mortal time afford
      Is spotless reputation; that away,
      Men are but gilded loam or painted clay.

                                  Shakespeare (1564-1616)

343   In all the affairs of this world, so much reputation is,
      in reality, so much power.

                               John Tillotson (1630-1694)

344   Character is higher than intellect. A great soul will be
      strong to live as well as think.
                                                    Emerson (1803-1882)

345   Property may be destroyed and money may lose its purchasing
      power; but, character, health, knowledge and good judgement
      will always be in demand under all conditions.
                                                    Roger Babson (1875-1967)

346   Clear conscience never fears midnight knocking.
                                                    Chinese Proverb

5. NEGATIVE

347   To disregard what the world thinks of us is not only
      arrogant but utterly shameless.
                                                    Cicero (B.C. 106-43)

348   No one ever lost his honor, except he who had it not.
                                                    Publilius Syrus (fl. B.C. 42)

349   How difficult it is to save the bark of reputation from
      the rocks of ignorance.
                                                    Francesco Petrarch (1304-1374)

350   The qualities we have do not make us so ridiculous as
      those which we affect to have.
                                                    La Rochefoucauld (1613-1680)

351   Honor is but an empty bubble.
                                                    Dryden (1631-1700)

352   Those who quit their proper character to assume what does
      not belong to them, are for the greater part ignorant of
      both the character they leave and of the character they
      assume.
                                                    Burke (1729-1797)

353   No change of circumstances can repair a defect of character.
                                                    Emerson (1803-1882)

354   Honor is simply the morality of superior men.
                                                    H. L. Mencken (1880-1956)

355   A man without ethics is a wild beast loosed upon this world.
                                                    Manly P. Hall (born 1901)

6. ADVICE

356 Be thou incapable of change in that which is right, and
men will rely upon thee. Establish unto thyself principles
of action; and see that thou ever act according to them.
First know that thy principles are just, and then be thou
inflexible in the path of them.

Akhenaton? (c. B.C. 1375)

357 Be upright in thy whole life; be content in all its changes;
so shalt thou make thy profit out of all occurrences; so
shall everything that happeneth unto thee be the source of
praise.

Akhenaton? (c. B.C. 1375)

358 The superior man acquaints himself with many
sayings of antiquity and many deeds of the past,
in order to strengthen his character thereby.

I Ching (B.C. 1150?)

359 The stages of the Noble Path are: Right View, Right
Thought, Right Speech, Right Behavior, Right Livelihood,
Right Effort, Right Mindfulness and Right Concentration.

Buddha (B.C. 568-488)

360 Do not appease thy fellow in his hour of anger; do not
comfort him while the dead is still laid out before him;
do not question him in the hour of his vow; and do not
strive to see him in his hour of misfortune.

The Talmud (B.C. 500?-400? A.D.)

361 The way to gain a good reputation is to endeavor to be
what you desire to appear.

Socrates (B.C. 469-399)

362 Let not a man do what his sense of right bids him not to
do, nor desire what it forbids him to desire. This is
sufficient. The skillful artist will not alter his
measures for the sake of a stupid workman.

Mencius (B.C. 371-288)

363 In honorable dealing you should consider what you intended,
not what you said or thought.

Cicero (B.C. 106-43)

364 Let honor be to us as strong an obligation as necessity is
to others.

Pliny the Elder (23-79 A.D.)

365   Everyone ought to bear patiently the results of his own
      conduct.

                                    Phaedrus (fl. 25 A.D.)

366   When about to commit a base deed, respect thyself,
      though there is no witness.

                                    Ausonius (310-395 A.D.)

367   When a chivalrous man makes an oath, he is faithful to it,
      and when he attains power, he spares his enemy.

                                    'Ali (600-661 A. D.)

368   Honour and shame from no condition rise;
      Act well your part, there all the honour lies.

                                    Pope (1688-1744)

369   Say not you know another entirely till you have divided an
      inheritance with him.

                                    Lavater (1741-1801)

370   Human improvement is from within outward.

                                    Froude (1818-1894)

371   By constant self-discipline and self-control you can develop
      greatness of character.

                                    Grenville Kleiser (1868-1953)

372   Adhere To - Faith, Unity, Sacrifice.
      Avoid - Back-biting, Falsehood and Crookedness.
      Admire - Frankness, Honesty and Large-heartedness.
      Control - Tongue, Temper and Tossing of the mind.
      Cultivate - Cosmic Love, Forgiveness and Patience.
      Hate - Lust, Anger and Pride.

                                    Sivananda (born 1887)

373   Faced with crisis, the man of character falls back on
      himself. He imposes his own stamp of action, takes
      responsibility for it, makes it his own.

                                    Charles De Gaulle (1890-1970)

374   If you stand straight
      Do not fear a crooked shadow.

                                    Chinese Proverb

7. POTPOURRI

375   As fire when thrown into water is cooled down and put out,
      so also a false accusation when brought against a man of
      the purest and holiest character, boils over and is at
      once dissipated, and vanishes.

                                    Cicero (B.C. 106-43)

376   They attack the one man with their hate and their shower of
       weapons. But he is like some rock which stretches into
       the vast sea and which, exposed to the fury of the winds
       and beaten against by the waves, endures all the violence
       and threats of heaven and sea, himself standing unmoved.
                                                 Vergil (B.C. 70-19)

377   In all thy humours, whether grave or mellow,
       Thou art such a touchy, testy, pleasant fellow;
       Hast so much wit, and mirth, and spleen about thee,
       That there's no living with thee, or without thee.
                                              Martial (43-104 A.D.)

378   O reputation! dearer far than life,
       Thou precious balsam, lovely, sweet of smell,
       Whose cordial drops once spilt by some rash hand,
       Not all the owner's care, nor the repenting toil
       Of the rude spiller, ever can collect
       To its first purity and native sweetness.
                                         Walter Raleigh (1552-1618)

379   O, he sits high in all the people's hearts;
       And that which would appear offence in us,
       His countenance, like richest alchemy,
       Will change to virtue and to worthiness.
                                          Shakespeare (1564-1616)

380   Of Manners gentle, of Affections mild;
       In Wit a man; Simplicity, a child.
                                                 Pope (1688-1744)

381   Zealous, yet modest; innocent, though free;
       Patient of toil; serene amidst alarms;
       Inflexible in faith; invincible in arms.
                                         James Beattie (1735-1803)

382   I have but one system of ethics for men and for nations -
       to be grateful, to be faithful to all engagements and under
       all circumstances, to be open and generous, promoting in the
       long run even the interests of both.
                                      Thomas Jefferson (1743-1826)

383   The reason firm, the temperate will.
       Endurance, foresight, strength and skill.
                                          Wordsworth (1770-1850)

384   The louder he talked of his honor
       the faster we counted our spoons.
                                             Emerson (1803-1882)

COURAGE
Bravery, Daring, Heroism and Valor

1. ESSENCE

385 Courage consists not in hazarding without fear,
but being resolutely minded in a just cause.
Plutarch (46-120 A.D.)

386 True bravery is shown by performing without witness
what one might be capable of doing before all the world.
La Rochefoucauld (1613-1680)

387 Courage consists not in blindly overlooking danger,
but in seeing it, and conquering it.
Richter (1763-1825)

388 Self-truth is the essence of heroism.
Emerson (1803-1882)

389 Courage - a perfect sensibility of the measure of danger,
and a mental willingness to endure it.
William T. Sherman (1820-1891)

390 Courage is resistance to fear, mastery of fear,
not absence of fear.
Mark Twain (1835-1910)

391 Courage is fear holding on a minute longer.
George S. Patton (1885-1945)

2. OPPOSITES

392 The wicked flee when no one pursues,
but the righteous are bold as a lion.
Proverbs (B.C. 1000?-200?)

393 He who is brave in daring will be killed.
He who is brave in not daring will live.
Of these two, one is advantageous and one is harmful.
Who knows why Heaven dislikes what it dislikes?
Even the sage considers it a difficult question...
Lao-Tzu (fl. B.C. 600)

394 There is a wide difference between true courage and a mere
contempt of life.
Cato the Elder (B.C. 234-149)

395   No man can be brave who thinks pain the greatest evil;
       nor temperate, who considers pleasure the highest good
                                              Cicero (B.C. 106-43)

396   Courage leads to heaven; fear, to death.
                                              Seneca (B.C. 3-65 A.D.)

397   Courage stands halfway between cowardice and rashness,
       one of which is a lack, the other an excess, of courage.
                                              Plutarch (46-120 A.D.)

398   A timid person is frightened before a danger, a coward
       during the time, and a courageous person afterwards.
                                              Richter (1763-1825)

399   Courage is fire, and bullying is smoke.
                                              Disraeli (1804-1881)

400   Courage enlarges, cowardice diminishes resources.
       In desperate straits the fears of the timid
       aggravate the dangers that imperil the brave.
                                              Bovee (1820-1904)

401   The more thou dost advance, the more thy feet pitfalls will
       meet. The Path that leadeth on is lighted by one fire-
       the light of daring burning in the heart. The more one
       dares, the more he shall obtain. The more he fears, the
       more that light shall pale - and that alone can guide.
                                              H. P. Blavatsky (1831-1891)

402   The paradox of courage is that a man must be a little
       careless of his life in order to keep it.
                                              G. K. Chesterton (1874-1936)

3. INSIGHT

403   Say not that honour is the child of boldness, nor believe
       thou that the hazard of life alone can pay the price of it:
       it is not to the action that it is due, but to the manner
       of performing it.
                                              Akhenaton? (c. B.C. 1375)

404   I count him braver who overcomes his desires than him who
       conquers his enemies; for the hardest victory is over self.
                                              Aristotle (B.C. 384-322)

405   A man of courage is also full of faith.
                                              Cicero (B.C. 106-43)

406   Fortune can take away riches, but not courage.
                                              Seneca (B.C. 3-65 A.D.)

407   A true knight is fuller of bravery in the midst,
      than in the beginning of danger.

                              Philip Sidney (1554-1586)

408   Most men have more courage than even they themselves
      think they have.

                              Greville (1554-1628)

409   We can never be certain of our courage until we have
      faced danger.

                              La Rochefoucauld (1613-1680)

410   Courage from hearts and not from numbers grows.

                              Dryden (1631-1700)

411   It is in great dangers that we see great courage.

                              Jean Francois Regnard (1655-1709)

412   Courage is poorly housed that dwells in numbers;
      the lion never counts the herd that are about him,
      nor weighs how many flocks he has to scatter.

                              Aaron Hill (1685-1750)

413   One man with courage makes a majority.

                              Andrew Jackson (1767-1845)

414   The courage we desire and prize is not the courage to die
      decently, but to live manfully.

                              Carlyle (1795-1881)

415   All brave men love;
      for he only is brave who has affections to fight for,
      whether in the daily battle of life,
      or in physical contests.

                              Nathaniel Hawthorne (1804-1864)

4. POSITIVE

416   A decent boldness ever meets with friends.

                              Homer (c. B.C. 700)

417   Courage conquers all things: it even gives strength
      to the body.

                              Ovid (B.C. 43-18 A.D.)

418   Fortune and love favor the brave.

                              Ovid (B.C. 43-18 A.D.)

419   There is nothing in the world so much admired as a man
      who knows how to bear unhappiness with courage.
                                          Seneca (B.C. 3-65 A.D.)

420   True courage is cool and calm.
      The bravest of men have the least of a brutal, bullying
      insolence, and in the very time of danger are found the most
      serene and free.
                                          Shaftesbury III (1671-1713)

421   The brave love mercy, and delight to save.
                                          Gay (1688-1732)

422   Courage and modesty are the most unequivocal of virtues,
      for they are of a kind that hypocrisy cannot imitate;
      they too have this quality in common,
      that they are expressed by the same color.
                                          Goethe (1749-1832)

423   Heroism - the divine relation which, in all times,
      unites a great man to other men.
                                          Carlyle (1795-1881)

424   There is always safety in valor.
                                          Emerson (1803-1882)

425   You will never do anything in this world without courage.
      It is the greatest quality of the mind next to honor.
                                          James L. Allen (1849-1925)

426   Courage is the first of human qualities because it is the
      quality which guarantees all the others.
                                          Winston Churchill (1874-1965)

5. NEGATIVE

427   To see what is right, and not do it, is want of courage,
      or of principle.
                                          Confucius (B.C. 551-479)

428   The human race afraid of nothing,
      rushes on through every crime.
                                          Horace (B.C. 65-8)

429   Take away ambitions and vanity, and where will be your
      heroes and patriots?
                                          Seneca (B.C. 3-65 A.D.)

430   Valor hath its bounds, as well as other virtues, which once
transgressed, the next step is into the territories of vice,
so that, by having too large a proportion of this heroic
virtue...may unawares run into temerity, obstinacy, and
folly.

Montaigne (1533-1592)

431   He who loses wealth loses much;
he who loses a friend loses more;
but he that loses his courage loses all.

Cervantes (1547-1616)

432   Valor employed in an ill quarrel, turns to cowardice;
and virtue then puts on foul vice's vizor.

Philip Massinger (1583-1640)

433   Valor that parleys is near yielding.

Herbert (1593-1632)

434   The more wit the less courage.

Thomas Fuller (1608-1661)

435   No man is a hero to his valet.

Cornuel (1614-1694)

436   Who combats bravely is not therefore brave:
He dreads a deathbed like the meanest slave.

Pope (1688-1744)

437   Personal courage is really a very subordinate virtue...
in which we are surpassed by the lower animals.

Schopenhauer (1788-1860)

438   It is an error to suppose that courage means courage in
everything. Most people are brave only in the dangers
to which they accustom themselves, either in imagination
or practice.

Bulwer-Lytton (1803-1873)

6. ADVICE

439   Never ask the gods for life set free from grief,
but ask for courage that endureth long.

Menander (B.C. 342-291)

440   The burden which is well borne becomes light.

Ovid (B.C. 43-18 A.D.)

441   No one reaches a high position without daring.

Publilius Syrus (fl. B.C. 42)

442   The brave and bold persist even against fortune;
      the timid and cowardly rush to despair though fear alone.
                                          Tacitus (55-117 A.D.)

443   Aspire rather to be a hero than merely appear one.
                                          Baltasar Gracian (1601-1658)

444   Rest not! Life is sweeping by; go and dare before you die.
      Something mighty and sublime, leave behind to conquer time.
                                          Goethe (1749-1832)

445   A hero is no braver than an ordinary man,
      but he is braver five minutes longer.

                                          Emerson (1803-1882)

446   Nurture your minds with great thoughts,
      to believe in the heroic makes heroes.
                                          Disraeli (1804-1881)

447   Write on your doors the saying wise and old.
      "Be bold!" and everywhere - "Be bold;
      Be not too bold!" Yet better the excess
      Than the defect; better the more than less...
                                          Longfellow (1807-1882)

7. POTPOURRI

448   As a rock on the seashore he standeth firm, and the dashing
      of the waves disturbeth him not. He raiseth his head like
      a tower on a hill, and the arrows of fortune drop at his
      feet. In the instant of danger, the courage of his heart
      sustaineth him; and the steadiness of his mind beareth him
      out.
                                          Akhenaton? (c. B.C. 1375)

449   O friends, be men; so act that none may feel ashamed to
      meet the eyes of other men. Think each one of his children
      and his wife, his home, his parents, living yet or dead.
      For them, the absent ones, I supplicate, and bid you rally
      here, and scorn to fly.
                                          Homer (c. B.C. 700)

450   And what he greatly thought, he nobly dared.
                                          Homer (c. B.C. 700)

451   Valour, glory, firmness, skill, generosity, steadiness in
      battle and ability to rule - these constitute the duty of a
      soldier. They flow from his own nature.
                                          Bhagavad Gita (c. B.C. 400)

452 Courage in danger is half the battle.

Plautus (B.C. 254-184)

453 Go on and increase in valor, O boy!
this is the path to immortality.

Vergil (B.C. 70-19)

454 That's a valiant flea that dares eat his breakfast on the
lip of a lion.

Shakespeare (1564-1616)

455 He either fears his fate too much,
  Or his deserts are small,
That dares not put it to the touch,
  To gain or lose it all.

James Graham (1612-1650)

456 He was a bold man that first ate an oyster.

Swift (1667-1745)

457 Tender handed stroke a nettle,
And it stings you for your pains;
Grasp it like a man of mettle,
And it soft as silk remains.

Aaron Hill (1685-1750)

458 A light supper, a good night's sleep, and a fine morning
have often made a hero of the same man who, by indigestion,
a restless night, and a rainy morning, would have proved
a coward.

Chesterfield (1694-1773)

459 The prudent see only the difficulties, the bold only the
advantages, of a great enterprise; the hero sees both;
diminishes the former and makes the latter preponderate,
and so conquers.

Lavater (1741-1801)

460 No man is a hero to his valet. This is not because the hero
is no hero, but because the valet is a valet.

Hegel (1770-1831)

461 The hero is not fed on sweets,
Daily his own heart he eats;
Chambers of the great are jails,
And head-winds right for royal sails.

Emerson (1803-1882)

462   One who never turned his back but marched breast forward,
         never doubted clouds would break,
    Never dreamed, though right were worsted,
         wrong would triumph,
    Held we fall to rise, are baffled to fight better,
         sleep to wake.

Robert Browning (1812-1889)

463   In the world's broad field of battle,
        In the bivouac of Life,
    Be not like dumb, driven cattle!
        Be a hero in the strife.

Longfellow (1807-1882)

464   Stand upright, speak thy thoughts, declare
    The truth thou hast, that all may share;
    Be bold, proclaim it everywhere:
    They only live who dare.

Lewis Morris (1835-1907)

465   A man not perfect, but of heart
        So high, of such heroic rage,
    That even his hopes became a part
        Of earth's eternal heritage.

Richard Gilder (1844-1909)

466   Out of the night that covers me,
        Black as the pit from pole to pole,
    I thank whatever gods may be
        For my unconquerable soul.

William Henley (1849-1903)

COVETOUSNESS
Envy, Greed, Jealousy, Lust and Selfishness

1. ESSENCE

467   Envy is the adversary of the fortunate.
Epictetus (50-138 A.D.)

468   From covetousness anger proceeds; from covetousness lust
is born; from covetousness come delusion and perdition.
Covetousness is the cause of sin.
The Hitopadesa (600?-1100? A.D.)

469   Desire of having is the sin of covetousness.
Shakespeare (1564-1616)

470   Jealousy is the fear or apprehension of superiority;
envy our uneasiness under it.
William Shenstone (1714-1763)

471   Covetousness is a sort of mental gluttony, not confined to
money, but greedy of honor and feeding on selfishness.
Chamfort (1741-1794)

472   Jealousy - magnifier of trifles.
Schiller (1759-1805)

473   Envy is littleness of soul.
Hazlitt (1778-1830)

474   Selfishness is not living as one wishes to live.
It is asking others to live as one wishes to live.
Oscar Wilde (1854-1900)

2. OPPOSITES

475   The things which belong to others please us more,
and that which is ours, is more pleasing to others.
Publilius Syrus (fl. B.C. 42)

476   The lust of avarice has so totally seized upon mankind
that their wealth seems rather to possess them
than they possess their wealth.
Pliny the Elder (23-79 A.D.)

477   True it is that covetousness is rich, modesty starves.
Phaedrus (fl. 25 A.D.)

478   In plain truth, it is not want, but rather abundance,
       that creates avarice.
                                   Montaigne (1533-1592)

479   Our envy always lasts longer than the happiness of those we
       envy.
                              La Rochefoucauld (1613-1680)

480   Covetousness is both the beginning and the end of the
       devil's alphabet - the first vice in corrupt nature that
       moves, and the last which dies.
                                 Robert South (1634-1716)

481   Envy will merit, as its shade pursue,
       but like a shadow, proves the substance true.
                                         Pope (1688-1744)

482   Envy ought to have no place allowed it in the heart of man;
       for the goods of this present world are so vile and low that
       they are beneath it; and those of the future world are so
       vast and exalted that they are above it.
                                       Colton (1780-1832)

483   The same people who can deny others everything
       are famous for refusing themselves nothing.
                                  Leigh Hunt (1784-1859)

484   Selfishness is the only real atheism;
       aspiration, unselfishness, the only real religion.
                             Israel Zangwill (1864-1926)

3. INSIGHT

485   There is no calamity greater than lavish desires.
       There is no greater guilt than discontentment.
       And there is no greater disaster than greed.
       He who is contented with contentment is always contented.
                                   Lao-Tzu (fl. B.C. 600)

486   Of all the worldly passions, lust is the most intense.
       All other worldly passions seem to follow in its train.
                                 Buddha (B.C. 568-488)

487   Just as a tree, though cut down, can grow again and again
       if its roots are undamaged and strong, in the same way if
       the roots of craving are not wholly uprooted sorrows will
       come again and again.
                          The Dhammapada (c. B.C. 300)

488   Envy, like flame, soars upwards.
                             Livy (B.C. 59-17 A.D.)

489   Envy assails the noblest: the winds howl around the
       highest peaks.

                                         Ovid (B.C. 43-18 A.D.)

490   Envy always implies conscious inferiority wherever it
       resides.

                                      Pliny the Elder (23-79 A.D.)

491   Lust of power is the most flagrant of all passions.
                                          Tacitus (55-117 A.D.)

492   He that is jealous is not in love.

                                      Augustine (354-430 A.D.)

493   Envy is ever joined with the comparing of a man's self;
       and where there is no comparison, no envy.

                                           Bacon (1561-1626)

494   Excess of wealth is cause of covetousness.
                               Christopher Marlowe (1564-1593)

495   Envy, like the worm, never runs but to the fairest fruit;
       like a cunning bloodhound, it singles out the fattest deer
       in the flock.

                                   Francis Beaumont (1584-1616)

496   In jealousy there is more self-love than love.
                              La Rochefoucauld (1613-1680)

497   Jealousy lives upon doubts, it becomes madness or ceases
       entirely as soon as we pass from doubt to certainty.
                              La Rochefoucauld (1613-1680)

498   Poverty wants some, luxury many, and avarice all things.
                               Abraham Cowley (1618-1667)

499   The envious will die, but envy never.

                                      Moliere (1622-1673)

500   The covetous man heaps up riches, not to enjoy them,
       but to have them.

                                   John Tillotson (1630-1694)

501   Nature is content with little; grace with less;
       but lust with nothing.

                                   Matthew Henry (1662-1714)

502   If we did but know how little some enjoy of the great things
that they possess, there would not be much to envy in the
world.

                                          Young (1683-1765)

503   Avarice is generally the last passion of those lives of
which the first part has been squandered in pleasure, and
the second devoted to ambition.

                                     Johnson (1709-1784)

504   A man is called selfish, not for pursuing his own good,
but for neglecting the neighbor's.

                            Richard Whately (1787-1863)

505   The deepest principle in human nature is the craving to be
appreciated.

                          William James (1842-1910)

4. POSITIVE

506   The soul of man is infinite in what it covets.

                             Ben Jonson (1572-1637)

507   Though we take from a covetous man all his treasure, he has
yet one jewel left; you cannot bereave him of his
covetousness.

                                     Milton (1608-1674)

508   Jealousy is, in some sort, rational and just; it aims at
the preservation of a good which belongs, or which we think
belongs, to us; whereas envy is a frenzy that cannot
endure, even in idea, the good of others.

                     La Rochefoucauld (1613-1680)

509   Misers are very kind people:
they amass wealth for those who wish their death.

                 Leszczynski Stanislaus (1677-1766)

510   Fools may our scorn, not envy raise,
for envy is a kind of praise.

                                     Gay (1688-1732)

511   Envy, to which the ignoble mind's a slave,
Is emulation in the learned or brave.

                                   Pope (1688-1744)

512   Avarice, the spur of industry.

                           David Hume (1711-1776)

513   Envy, among other ingredients, has a mixture of the love of justice in it. We are more angry at undeserved than at deserved good fortune.

Hazlitt (1778-1830)

514   It is astonishing how well men wear when they think of no one but themselves.

Bulwer-Lytton (1803-1873)

515   Bare-faced covetousness was the moving spirit of civilization from the first dawn to the present day...

Friedrich Engels (1820-1895)

516   Selfishness is the dynamo of our economic system...which may range from mere petty greed to admirable types of self-expression.

Felix Frankfurter (1882-1965)

5. NEGATIVE

517   An immoderate desire of riches is a poison lodged in the mind. It contaminates and destroys everything that was good in it. It is no sooner rooted there, than all virtue, all honesty, all natural affection, fly before the face of it.

Akhenaton? (c. B.C. 1375)

518   The heart of the envious is gall and bitterness; his tongue spitteth venom; the success of his neighbour breaketh his rest. He sitteth in his cell repining; and the good that happeneth to another, is to him an evil. Hatred and malice feed upon his heart, and there is no rest in him.

Akhenaton? (c. B.C. 1375)

519   Can a man carry fire in his bosom
    and his clothes not be burned?
Or can one walk upon hot coals
    and his feet not be scorched?
So is he who goes in to his neighbor's wife;
    none who touches her will go unpunished.

Proverbs (B.C. 1000?-200?)

520   An envious man waxeth lean with the fatness of his neighbors. Envy is the daughter of pride, the author of murder and revenge, the beginner of secret sedition, and the perpetual tormenter of virtue. Envy is the filthy slime of the soul; a venom, a poison, or quicksilver which consumeth the flesh, and drieth up the marrow of the bones.

Socrates (B.C. 469-399)

521   As iron is eaten by rust, so are the envious consumed
       by envy.

                            Antisthenes (fl. B.C. 444)

522   Those who are envious and mischievous, who are the lowest
       among men, are cast by Me into the ocean of material
       existence, into various demoniac species of life.

                            Bhagavad Gita (c. B.C. 400)

523   The avaricious man is like the barren sandy ground of the
       desert which sucks in all the rain and dew with greediness,
       but yields no fruitful herbs or plants for the benefit of
       others.

                            Zeno (B.C. 335?-264)

524   Four things does a reckless man gain who covets his
       neighbor's wife - demerit, an uncomfortable bed, thirdly,
       punishment, and lastly, hell.

                            The Dhammapada (c. B.C. 300)

525   Avarice, in old age, is foolish; for what can be more
       absurd than to increase our provisions for the road the
       nearer we approach to our journey's end?

                            Cicero (B.C. 106-43)

526   The envious man grows lean at the success of his neighbor.

                            Horace (B.C. 65-8)

527   The miser acquires, yet fears to use his gains.

                            Horace (B.C. 65-8)

528   The miser is as much in want of what he has
       as of what he has not.

                            Publilius Syrus (fl. B.C. 42)

529   Lust is an enemy to the purse, a foe to the person,
       a canker to the mind, a corrosive to the conscience,
       a weakness of the wit, a besotter of the senses,
       and, finally, a mortal bane to all the body.

                            Pliny the Elder (23-79 A.D.)

530   Some men make fortunes, but not to enjoy them; for, blinded
       by avarice, they live to make fortunes.

                            Juvenal (40-125 A.D.)

531   When men are full of envy they disparage everything,
       whether it be good or bad.

                            Tacitus (55-117 A.D.)

532   As a moth gnaws a garment, so doth envy consume a man.

                            Chrysostom (347-407 A.D.)

533 Nothing can allay the rage of biting envy.

Claudianus (365?-408? A.D.)

534 Though an avaricious man possesses wealth,
An envious man possesses another's goods,
And an ill-minded man possesses his learning-
None of these can produce lasting pleasure.

Saskya Pandita (1182-1251)

535 Envy is like a fly that passes all a body's sounder parts,
and dwells upon the sores.

George Chapman (1557-1634)

536 Every other sin hath some pleasure annexed to it, or will
admit of an excuse: envy alone wants both.

Robert Burton (1576-1640)

537 The virtues are lost in self-interest
as rivers are lost in the sea.

La Rochefoucauld (1613-1680)

538 Avarice is insatiable and is always pushing on for more.

L'Estrange (1616-1704)

539 Covetousness, by a greediness of getting more,
deprives itself of the true end of getting;
it loses the enjoyment of what it had got.

Thomas Sprat (1635-1713)

540 Avarice is always poor, but poor by her own fault.

Johnson (1709-1784)

541 The selfish man suffers more from his selfishness than he
from whom that selfishness withholds some important
benefit.

Emerson (1803-1882)

542 No man is more cheated than the selfish man.

Beecher (1813-1878)

543 Covetousness has for its mother unlawful desire, for its
daughter injustice, and for its friend violence.

Arabian Proverb

6. ADVICE

544 Attribute not the good actions of another to bad causes:
thou canst not know his heart; but the world will know by
this that thine is full of envy.

Akhenaton? (c. B.C. 1375)

545   Thou shalt not covet thy neighbor's house, thou shalt not
covet thy neighbor's wife, nor his manservant, nor his
maidservant, nor his ox, nor his ass, nor anything that is
thy neighbor's.

Exodus (B.C. 1200?)

546   Form no covetous desire, so that the demon of greediness
may not deceive thee, and the treasure of the world may
not be tasteless to thee.

Zoroaster (B.C. 628?-551?)

547   Do not overrate what you have received, nor envy others.
He who envies others does not obtain peace of mind.

Buddha (B.C. 568-488)

548   The demon of worldly desires is always seeking chances to
deceive the mind. If a viper lives in your room and you
wish to have a peaceful sleep, you must first chase it out.

Buddha (B.C. 568-488)

549   Refrain from covetousness, and thy estate shall prosper.

Plato (B.C. 427?-347?)

550   As fire is covered by smoke, as a mirror is covered by dust,
or as an embryo is covered by the womb, similarly the living
entity is covered by different degrees of lust which veils
real knowledge and is never satisfied. Therefore regulate
the senses in the beginning and slay this destroyer of
knowledge and self-realization.

Bhagavad Gita (c. B.C. 400)

551   If you wish to remove avarice you must remove its mother,
luxury.

Cicero (B.C. 106-43)

552   Expel avarice, the mother of all wickedness, who, always
thirsty for more, opens wide her jaws for gold.

Claudianus (365?-408? A.D.)

553   An enemy to whom you show kindness becomes your friend,
excepting lust, the indulgence of which increases its
enmity.

Saadi (1184-1291)

554   The greatest harm that you can do unto the envious,
is to do well.

John Lyly (1554-1606)

555   Envy not greatness: for thou makest thereby
Thyself the worse, and so the distance greater.

Herbert (1593-1632)

556   All jealousy must be strangled in its birth, or time will
soon make it strong enough to overcome the truth.

William Davenant (1605-1668)

557   Do not believe that lust can ever be killed out if gratified
or satiated, for this is an abomination inspired by
illusion. It is by feeding vice that it expands and waxes
strong, like to the worm that fattens on the blossom's
heart.

H. P. Blavatsky (1831-1891)

558   Selfishness is the greatest sin. It constrains the heart.
It separates man from man. It makes him greedy. It is the
root of all evils and sufferings. Destroy selfishness
through selfless service, charity, generosity and love.

Sivananda (born 1887)

7. POTPOURRI

559   He that visits the sick in hopes of a legacy, but is never
so friendly in all other cases, I look upon him as being no
better than a raven that watches a weak sheep only to peck
out its eyes.

Seneca (B.C. 3-65 A.D.)

560   Surely, those who swallow the property of the orphans
unjustly, swallow nothing but fire into their bellies,
and they shall soon enter into the flaming fire.

Koran (c. 651 A.D.)

561   Arise, fair sun, and kill the envious moon,
Who is already sick and pale with grief,
That thou her maid art far more fair than she:
Be not her maid, since she is envious.

Shakespeare (1564-1616)

562   Hoards after hoards his rising raptures fill;
Yet still he sighs, for hoards are wanting still.

Goldsmith (1728-1774)

563   O, Jealousy, thou ugliest fiend of hell! thy deadly venom
preys on my vitals, turns the healthful hue of my fresh
cheek to haggard sallowness, and drinks my spirit up.

Hannah More (1745-1833)

564 Despite those titles, power, and pelf,
The wretch, concentred all in self,
Living, shall forfeit fair renown,
And, doubly dying, shall go down
To the vile dust from whence he sprung,
Unwept, unhonoured and unsung.

Walter Scott (1771-1832)

565 Envy is the deformed and distorted offspring of egotism;
and when we reflect on the strange and disproportioned
character of the parent, we cannot wonder at the perversity
and waywardness of the child.

Hazlitt (1778-1830)

566 Yet he was jealous, though he did not show it,
For jealousy dislikes the world to know it.

Byron (1788-1824)

CREATION

Nature, Fertility and Art

1. ESSENCE

567   ...The last vibration of the seventh eternity thrills
through infinitude. The mother swells, expanding from
within without, like the bud of the lotus.
     The vibration sweeps along, touching with its swift
wing the whole universe and the germ that dwelleth in darkness: the darkness that breathes over the slumbering waters
of life...
     Darkness radiates light, and light drops one solitary
ray into the mother-deep. The ray shoots through the
virgin egg. The ray causes the eternal egg to thrill, and
drop the non-eternal germ, which condenses into the
world-egg...

Book of Dzyan (B.C. 3000?)

568   These are the ten spheres of existence out of nothing.
From the spirit of the living God emanated air, from the
air, water, from the water, fire or ether, from the ether,
the height and the depth, the East and West, the North
and South.

Sepher Yezirah (B.C. 2000?-600 A.D.)

569   In the beginning God created the Heaven and the earth. And
the earth was without form, and void; and darkness was upon
the face of the deep. And the Spirit of God moved upon the
face of the waters. And God said, Let there be light, and
there was light.

Genesis (B.C. 1200?)

570   This is the truth: As from a fire aflame thousands of
sparks come forth, even so from the Creator an infinity
of beings have life and to him return again.

Upanishads (c. B.C. 800)

571   As a spider emits and draws in its thread,
As plants arise on the earth,
As the hairs of the head and body from a living person,
So from The Eternal arises everything here.

Upanishads (c. B.C. 800)

572   Before God manifested Himself, when all things were still
hidden in Him...He began by forming an imperceptible point;
that was His own thought. With this thought He then began
to construct a mysterious and holy form...the Universe.

Zohar (120?-1200? A.D.)

573   Nature is the glass reflecting God, as by the sea reflected
      is the sun, too glorious to be gazed on in his sphere.
                                             Young (1683-1765)

574   Nature is but a name for an effect whose cause is God.
                                             Cowper (1731-1800)

575   Nature is the time-vesture of God that reveals him to the
      wise, and hides him from the foolish.
                                             Carlyle (1795-1881)

576   What is art? Nature concentrated.
                                             Balzac (1799-1850)

577   Nature is a mutable cloud which is always and never the
      same.
                                             Emerson (1803-1882)

578   For Art is Nature made by man
      To Man the interpreter of God.
                                             Owen Meredith (1831-1891)

2. OPPOSITES

579   Father-Mother spin a web whose upper end is fastened to
      spirit - the light of the one darkness - and the lower one
      to its shadowy end, matter; and this web is the universe
      spun out of the two substances made in one...
                                             Book of Dzyan (B.C. 3000?)

580   The decade of existence out of nothing has its end linked
      to its beginning and its beginning linked to its end,
      just as the flame is wedded to the live coal; because the
      Lord is one and there is not a second one, and before one
      what wilt thou count?
                                             Sepher Yezirah (B.C. 2000?-600 A.D.)

581   In wisdom and understanding we have the archetypal Positive
      and Negative, the primordial Maleness and Femaleness,
      established while "countenance beheld not countenance" and
      manifestation was incipient. It is from these primary Pairs
      of Opposites that the Pillars of the Universe spring,
      between which is woven the web of Manifestation.
                                             Kabbalah (B.C. 1200?-700? A.D.)

582   The Creative knows the great beginnings.
      The Receptive completes the finished things.
                                             I Ching (B.C. 1150?)

583   The Creative, in a state of rest, is one,
and in a state of motion it is straight;
therefore it creates that which is great.
  The Receptive is closed in a state of rest,
and in a state of motion it opens;
therefore it creates that which is vast.

                  I Ching (B.C. 1150?)

584   The Nameless is the origin of Heaven and Earth;
The Named is the mother of all things.
Therefore let there always be non-being
  so we may see their subtlety,
And let there always be being so we may see their outcome.
The two are the same,
But after they are produced, they have different names.
They both may be called deep and profound.
Deeper and more profound,
The door of all subtleties!

                Lao-Tzu (fl. B.C. 600)

585   There are two aspects in Nature: the perishable and the
imperishable. All life in this world belongs to the former,
the unchanging element belongs to the latter.

                Bhagavad Gita (c. B.C. 400)

586   Emanation is the Resulting displayed from the Unresulting,
the Finite from the Infinite, the Manifold and Composite
from the Perfect Single and Simple, Potentiality from that
which is Infinite Power and Act, the mobile from that which
is perennially permanent; and therefore in a more imperfect
and diminished mode than His Infinite Perfection is.

                Zohar (120?-1200? A.D.)

587   Surely God causes the seed and the stone to sprout;
He brings forth the living from the dead,
and He is the bringer forth of the dead from the living.

                Koran (c. 651 A.D.)

588   The point appeared in the circle, yet wasn't.
Rather, it was the circle, traversed by the point.
To one who has completed the circle,
  the point exists on the circumference.
The whole world I said is His imagination,
  then I saw: His imagination is Himself.

                Ni'matullah Wali (1331-1431?)

589   In nature things move violently to their place,
and calmly in their place.

                Bacon (1561-1626)

590   For Art may err, but Nature cannot miss.

                                     Dryden (1631-1700)

591   The double law of attraction and radiation or of sympathy
and antipathy, of fixedness and movement, which is the
principle of Creation, and the perpetual cause of life.

                               Albert Pike (1809-1891)

592   The soil, in return for her service, keeps the tree
tied to her; the sky asks nothing and leaves it free.

                        Rabindranath Tagore (1861-1941)

593   Art is the stored honey of the human soul,
gathered on wings of misery and travail.

                        Theodore Dreiser (1871-1945)

594   Art is a lie that makes us realize truth.

                        Pablo Picasso (1881-1973)

3. INSIGHT

595   ...The eternal vital power builds them in the likeness
of older worlds, placing them on the Imperishable Centres.
     How does he build them? He collects the fiery dust.
He makes balls of fire, runs through them, and round them,
infusing life thereinto, then sets them into motion; some
one way, some the other way. They are cold, he makes them
hot. They are dry, he makes them moist. They shine, he
fans and cools them. Thus he acts from one twilight to the
other, during Seven Eternities.

                        Book of Dzyan (B.C. 3000?)

596   The appearance of the ten spheres out of manifestation
is like a flash of lightning, being without an end, His
word is in them, when they go and return; they run by
His order like a whirlwind and humble themselves before
His throne.

                    Sepher Yezirah (B.C. 2000?-600 A.D.)

597   Polarity is the principle that runs through the whole of
creation, and is, in fact, the basis of manifestation.
Polarity really means the flowing of force from a sphere
of high pressure to a sphere of low pressure; high and low
being always relative terms. Every sphere of energy needs
to receive the stimulus of an influx of energy at higher
pressure, and to have an output into a sphere of lower
pressure. The source of all energy is the Great Unmanifest,
and it makes its own way down the levels, changing its form
from one to the other, till it is finally "earthed" in
matter.

                    Kabbalah (B.C. 1200?-700? A.D.)

598   The pure impulse of dynamic creation is formless; and being
       formless, the creation it gives rise to can assume any and
       every form.
                                            Kabbalah (B.C. 1200?-700? A.D.)

599   Great indeed is the sublimity of the Creative, to which
       all beings owe their beginning and which permeates all
       heaven.
                                                   I Ching (B.C. 1150?)

600   The cosmos comes forth from The Eternal, and moves
       In Him. With His power it reverberates,
       Like thunder crashing in the sky. Those who
       Realize Him pass beyond the sway of death.
                                              Upanishads (c. B.C. 800)

601   The spirit of the valley never dies.
         It is called the subtle and profound female.
       The gate of the subtle and profound female
         Is the root of Heaven and Earth.
       It is continuous, and seems to be always existing.
       Use it and you will never wear it out.
                                               Lao-Tzu (fl. B.C. 600)

602   The Eternal generates the One.
       The One generates the Two.
       The Two generates the Three.
       The Three generates all things.
       All things have darkness at their back
       and strive towards the light,
       and the flowing power gives them harmony.
                                               Lao-Tzu (fl. B.C. 600)

603   Painting is silent poetry, and poetry is painting that
       speaks.
                                            Simonides (B.C. 556?-468?)

604   A picture is a poem without words.
                                            Confucius (B.C. 551-479)

605   The aim of art is to represent not the outward appearance
       of things, but their inward significance.
                                              Aristotle (B.C. 384-322)

606   Nothing which we can imagine about Nature is incredible.
                                            Pliny the Elder (23-79 A.D.)

607   The perfection of art is to conceal art.
                                            Quintilian (35-90 A.D.)

608 Nature never says one thing, Wisdom another.
Juvenal (40-125 A.D.)

609 God has made all things out of nothing: because...even
though the world has been made of some material, that
very same material has been made out of nothing.
Augustine (354-430 A.D.)

610 Art, as far as it is able, follows nature, as a pupil
imitates his master; thus your art must be, as it were,
God's grandchild.
Dante (1265-1321)

611 Nature never breaks her own laws.
Leonardo Da Vinci (1452-1519)

612 The true work of art is but a shadow of
the divine perfection.
Michelangelo (1474-1564)

613 When one is painting one does not think.
Raphael Sanzio (1483-1520)

614 We call that against nature which cometh against custom.
But there is nothing, whatsoever it be, that is not
according to nature.
Montaigne (1533-1592)

615 Now nature is not at variance with art, nor art with nature,
they being both servants of his providence: art is the
perfection of nature; were the world now as it was the
sixth day, there were yet a chaos; nature hath made one
world, and art another. In brief, all things are
artificial; for nature is the art of God.
Thomas Browne (1605-1682)

616 Nature imitates herself. A grain thrown into good ground
brings forth fruit; a principle thrown into a good mind
brings forth fruit. Everything is created and conducted by
the same Master: the root, the branch, the fruits - the
principles, the consequences.
Pascal (1623-1662)

617 The highest problem of any art is to cause by appearance the
illusion of a higher reality.
Goethe (1749-1832)

618   The ordinary true, or purely real, cannot be the object of
       the arts. - Illusion on a ground of truth, that is the
       secret of the fine arts.
                                              Joubert (1754-1824)

619   The ideal should never touch the real;
       When nature conquers, Art must then give way.
                                              Schiller (1759-1805)

620   Light is the first of painters. There is no object so foul
       that intense light will not make it beautiful.
                                              Emerson (1803-1882)

621   Art is the effort of man to express the ideas which nature
       suggests to him of a power above nature, whether that power
       be within the recesses of his own being, or in the Great
       First Cause of which nature, like himself, is but the
       effect.
                                              Bulwer-Lytton (1803-1873)

622   ... a first cause, eternal, all-wise, almighty and
       holy, is the origin and the centre of the whole universe,
       from whom gradually all beings emanated. Thought, speech
       and action are an inseparable unity in the divine being.
                                              Isidor Kalisch (1810-1886)

623   The object of art is to crystallize emotion into thought,
       and then fix it in form.
                                              Francois Delsarte (1811-1871)

624   Art is a man's nature; nature is God's art.
                                              Bailey (1816-1902)

625   All art does but consist in the removal of surplusage.
                                              Walter Pater (1839-1894)

626   Art is not a thing; it is a way.
                                              Elbert Hubbard (1859-1915)

627   A work of art is a corner of creation seen through a
       temperament.
                                              Emile Zola (1840-1902)

628   The process of creation never stops, although, on a plane-
       tary scale, growth proceeds so slowly that if we reckon it
       in our time planetary conditions can be regarded as
       permanent for us.
                                              Gurdjieff (1873-1949)

629   What was any art but a mould in which to imprison for a
       moment the shining, elusive element which is life itself.
                                        Willa Cather (1876-1947)

630   Art does not reproduce the visible;
       rather it makes it visible.
                                        Paul Klee (1879-1940)

4. POSITIVE

631   THE CREATIVE works sublime success,
       Furthering through perseverance.
                                        I Ching (B.C. 1150?)

632   Surely there is something in the unruffled calm of nature
       that overawes our little anxieties and doubts: the sight of
       the deep-blue sky, and the clustering stars above, seem to
       impart a quiet in the mind.
                                        Jonathan Edwards (1703-1758)

633   Nature goes on her way, and all that to us seems an
       exception is really according to order.
                                        Goethe (1749-1832)

634   Art is the right hand of Nature. The latter has only given
       us being, the former has made us men.
                                        Schiller (1759-1805)

635   Art is more godlike than science.
       Science discovers; art creates.
                                        John Opie (1761-1807)

636   Nature pleases, attracts, delights, merely because it is
       nature. We recognize in it an Infinite Power.
                                        Karl Wilhelm Humboldt (1767-1835)

637   Nature never did betray the heart that loved her.
                                        Wordsworth (1770-1850)

638   For what has made the sage or poet write
       But the fair paradise of Nature's light.
                                        Keats (1795-1821)

639   Nature, like a kind and smiling mother, lends herself to our
       dreams and cherishes our fancies.
                                        Victor Hugo (1802-1885)

640   Nothing is rich but the inexhaustible wealth of nature.
       She shows us only surfaces, but she is million fathoms
       deep.
                                        Emerson (1803-1882)

641   Art is a human activity having for its purpose the
transmission to others of the highest and best feelings
to which men have risen.

Leo Tolstoy (1828-1910)

642   Art is unquestionably one of the purest and highest elements
in human happiness. It trains the mind through the eye, and
the eye through the mind. As the sun colors flowers, so
does art color life.

Lubbock (1834-1913)

643   Art comes to you posing frankly to give nothing but the
highest quality to your moments as they pass.

Walter Pater (1839-1894)

644   Art is the great stimulus to life.

Nietzsche (1844-1900)

645   Art is like a border of flowers along the course of
civilization.

Lincoln Steffens (1866-1936)

5. NEGATIVE

646   All art, all education, can be merely a supplement
to nature.

Aristotle (B.C. 384-322)

647   Nature abhors annihilation.

Cicero (B.C. 106-43)

648   Nature too unkind;
That made no medicine for a troubled mind!

Beaumont and Fletcher (c. 1600)

649   Ah! would that we could at once paint with the eyes!
In the long way, from the eye, through the arm to the
pencil, how much is lost!

Gotthold Lessing (1729-1781)

650   Art is difficult, transient is her reward.

Schiller (1759-1805)

651   Nature, red in tooth and claw.

Alfred Tennyson (1809-1892)

652   Nature has no principles. She furnishes us with no reason
to believe that human life is to be respected. Nature, in
her indifference, makes no distinction between good and
evil.

Anatole France (1844-1924)

653   Without art, the crudeness of reality would make the world
       unbearable.

                                                    G. B. Shaw (1856-1950)

654   There is nothing but art. Art is living. To attempt to
       give an object of art life by dwelling on its historical,
       cultural, or archaeological association is senseless.

                                          Somerset Maugham (1874-1965)

6. ADVICE

655   In order for a creation to be possible there must first be a
       contraction, a concentration of all energies at a center.
       Then, an expansion must occur; the gathered energies must
       be sent forth in concentrated form as a ray or beam of
       energy.

                                        Kabbalah (B.C. 1200?-700? A.D.)

656   Let us permit nature to have her way; she understands her
       business better than we do.

                                               Montaigne (1533-1592)

657   Nature, to be commanded, must be obeyed.

                                                   Bacon (1561-1626)

658   And hark! how blithe the thristle sings!
          He, too, is no mean preacher:
       Come forth into the light of things,
          Let Nature be your teacher.

                                           Wordsworth (1770-1850)

659   Whatever you are from nature, keep to it; never desert your
       own line of talent. Be what nature intended you for, and
       you will succeed; be anything else, and you will be ten
       thousand times worse than nothing.

                                           Sydney Smith (1771-1845)

660   Help Nature and work on with her; and Nature will regard
       thee as one of her creators and make obeisance. And she
       will open wide before thee the portals of her secret
       chambers, lay bare before thy gaze the treasures hidden in
       the depths of her pure virgin bosom.

                                        H. P. Blavatsky (1831-1891)

7. POTPOURRI

661   Before the visible universe was formed its mold was cast.
This mold was called the Archetype, and the Archetype was in
the Supreme Mind long before the process of creation began.
Beholding the Archetypes, the Supreme Mind become enamored
with Its own thought; so, taking the Word as a mighty
hammer, It gouged out caverns in primordial space and cast
the form of the spheres in the Archetypical mold, at the
same time sowing in the newly fashioned bodies the seeds of
living things. The darkness below, receiving the hammer of
the Word, was fashioned into an orderly universe.

The Divine Pymander (BC 2500?-200 AD?)

662   Ten are the numbers out of nothing, and not the number nine,
ten and not eleven. Comprehend this great wisdom, understand this knowledge, inquire into it and ponder on it,
render it evident and lead the Creator back to His throne
again.

Sepher Yezirah (B.C. 2000?-600 A.D.)

663   Casteth he his eye towards the clouds, findeth he not the
heavens full of his wonders? Looketh he down to the earth,
doth not the worm proclaim "Less than omnipotence could
not have formed me!"

Akhenaton? (c. B.C. 1375)

664   In the beginning the Golden Embryo arose. Once he was born,
he was the one lord of creation. He held in place the earth
and this sky. He who gives life, who gives strength, whose
command all the gods, his own, obey; his shadow is immortality - and death.

Rig Veda (B.C. 1200-900?)

665   The Receptive is all-potential, but inert. The Creative is
pure energy, limitless and tireless, but incapable of doing
anything except radiate off into space if left to its own
devices. But when the Creative acts upon the Receptive, its
energy is gathered up and set to work. When the Receptive
receives the impulse of the Creative, all her latent
capacities are energized.

Kabbalah (B.C. 1200?-700? A.D.)

666   From the ONE LIFE formless and Uncreate, proceeds the
Universe of lives. First was manifested from the Deep
(Chaos) cold luminous fire (gaseous light?) which formed
the curds in Space. (Irresolvable nebulae, perhaps?)
...These fought, and a great heat was developed by the
encountering and collision, which produced rotation. Then
came the first manifested MATERIAL...

Book of Dzyan Commentary (B.C. 1000?)

667   All beings return at the close of every cosmic cycle into the realm of Nature, which is a part of Me, and at the beginning of the next I send them forth again. With the help of Nature, again and again I pour forth the whole multitude of beings, whether they will or no, for they are ruled by My Will.

Bhagavad Gita (c. B.C. 400)

668   In those vernal seasons of the year when the air is calm and pleasant, it were an injury and sullenness against nature not to go out and see her riches, and partake in her rejoicing with heaven and earth.

Milton (1608-1674)

669   Man's rich with little, were his judgement true;
Nature is frugal, and her wants are few;
These few wants answer'd bring sincere delights;
But fools create themselves new appetites.

Young (1683-1765)

670   Slave to no sect, who takes no private road,
But looks through Nature up to Nature's God.

Pope (1688-1744)

671   Nature I loved, and next to Nature, Art.

Landor (1775-1864)

672   'Tis to create, and in creating live
A being more intense, that we endow
With form our fancy, gaining as we give
The life we image.

Byron (1788-1824)

673   The man, who has seen the rising moon break out of the clouds at midnight, has been present like an archangel at the creation of light and of the world.

Emerson (1803-1882)

674   The counterfeit and counterpart
Of Nature reproduced in art.

Longfellow (1807-1882)

675   Art is the child of Nature; yes,
her darling child in whom we trace
The features of the mother's face,
Her aspect and her attitude.

Longfellow (1807-1882)

676   Once, when the days were ages,
         And the old Earth was young,
      The high gods and the sages
      From Nature's golden pages
         Her open secrets wrung.

                                        Richard Stoddard (1825-1903)

CUNNING

Deceit, Dishonesty, Lying, Treachery, Treason, Disgrace and Shame

1. ESSENCE

677 We take cunning for a sinister or crooked wisdom.
Bacon (1561-1626)

678 Cunning...is but the low mimic of wisdom.
Bolingbroke (1678-1751)

679 Cunning is the art of concealing our own defects,
and discovering other people's weaknesses.
Hazlitt (1778-1830)

680 Dishonesty is a forsaking of permanent for temporary
advantages.
Bovee (1820-1904)

2. OPPOSITES

681 Deadly poisons are concealed under sweet honey.
Ovid (B.C. 43-18 A.D.)

682 In the mind of the wicked there is one thing; in their
discourse another; their conduct is another. In the heart,
in the speech, and in the conduct of the magnanimous there
is one and the same thing.
The Hitopadesa (600?-1100? A.D.)

683 Treason doth never prosper: what's the reason?
Why if it prosper, none dare call it treason.
John Harrington (1561-1612)

684 It is as easy to deceive one's self without perceiving it,
as it is difficult to deceive others without their finding
it out.
La Rochefoucauld (1613-1680)

685 Cunning to wisdom is as an ape to man.
William Penn (1614-1718)

686 Half the truth is often a great lie.
Franklin (1706-1790)

687 Falsehood is susceptible of an infinity of combinations,
but truth has only one mode of being.
Rousseau (1712-1778)

688 A liar begins with making falsehood appear like truth,
and ends with making truth itself appear like falsehood.
William Shenstone (1714-1763)

689 We are never deceived; we deceive ourselves.
Goethe (1749-1832)

690 The weak in courage is strong in cunning.
William Blake (1757-1828)

691 Fraud and falsehood only dread examination.
Truth invites it.
Thomas Cooper (1759-1839)

692 Falsehood is cowardice, - truth is courage.
Hosea Ballou (1771-1852)

693 And, after all, what is a lie? 'Tis but
The truth in masquerade.
Byron (1788-1824)

694 White lies are but the ushers to black ones.
Frederick Marryat (1792-1848)

695 His honour rooted in dishonour stood,
And faith unfaithful kept him falsely true.
Alfred Tennyson (1809-1892)

696 The cruelest lies are often told in silence.
Robert Louis Stevenson (1850-1895)

697 Truth is the safest lie.
Jewish Proverb

698 Thy secret is thy prisoner if thou keepest it;
thou art its prisoner if thou divulgest it.
Chinese Proverb

3. INSIGHT

699 If the Great Way perishes
there will morality and duty.
When cleverness and knowledge arise
great lies will flourish.
When relatives fall out with one another
there will be filial duty and love.
When states are in confusion
there will be faithful servants.
Lao-Tzu (fl. B.C. 600)

700   A lie never lives to be old.
                                        Sophocles (B.C. 495-406)

701   Knowledge without justice ought to be called cunning rather
      than wisdom.
                                        Plato (B.C. 427?-347?)

702   No wise man ever thought that a traitor should be trusted.
                                        Cicero (B.C. 106-43)

703   Treachery, though at first very cautious,
      in the end betrays itself.
                                        Livy (B.C. 59-17 A.D.)

704   You are in a pitiable condition if you have to conceal what
      you wish to tell.
                                        Publilius Syrus (fl. B.C. 42)

705   One crime is concealed by the commission of another.
                                        Seneca (B.C. 3-65 A.D.)

706   For whoever contemplates a crime is guilty of the deed.
                                        Juvenal (40-125 A.D.)

707   If one is plotting evil,
      He always uses pleasant words.
      When a hunter sees the game,
      He sings a sweet song to lure it.
                                        Nagarjuna (c. 100-200 A.D.)

708   One who deceives will always find those who allow themselves
      to be deceived.
                                        Machiavelli (1469-1527)

709   No man was ever so much deceived by another as by himself.
                                        Greville (1554-1628)

710   Cunning and treachery are the offspring of incapacity.
                                        La Rochefoucauld (1613-1680)

711   The fox puts off all with a jest.
                                        L'Estrange (1616-1704)

712   All deception in the course of life is indeed nothing else
      but a lie reduced to practice, and falsehood passing from
      words into things.
                                        Robert South (1634-1716)

713 Cunning leads to knavery. - It is but a step from one to the
other, and that very slippery. - Only lying makes the
difference; add that to cunning, and it is knavery.
La Bruyere (1645-1696)

714 Cunning has effect from the credulity of others.
It requires no extraordinary talents to lie and deceive.
Johnson (1709-1784)

715 Falsehood is never so successful as when she baits her hook
with truth, and no opinions so fastly misled us as those
that are not wholly wrong, as no timepieces so effectually
deceive the wearer as those that are sometimes right.
Colton (1780-1832)

716 Treason is like diamonds;
there is nothing to be made by the small trader.
Douglas Jerrold (1803-1857)

717 There is no lie that many men will not believe;
there is no man who does not believe many lies;
and there is no man who believes only lies.
John Sterling (1806-1844)

718 Sin has many tools, but a lie is the handle which fits them
all.
Oliver Wendell Holmes (1809-1894)

719 No one can disgrace us but ourselves.
Josiah Holland (1819-1881)

720 The very cunning conceal their cunning;
the indifferently shrew boast of it.
Bovee (1820-1904)

721 A lie can travel half way around the world while the truth
is putting on its shoes.
Mark Twain (1835-1910)

4. POSITIVE

722 Shame greatly hurts or greatly helps mankind.
Homer (c. B.C. 700)

723 Shame is an ornament to the young;
a disgrace to the old.
Aristotle (B.C. 384-322)

724 Shame may restrain what law does not prohibit.
Seneca (B.C. 3-65 A.D.)

725 A goodly apple rotten at the heart;
O, what a goodly outside falsehood hath!
Shakespeare (1564-1616)

726 Any fool can tell the truth, but it requires a man of some
sense to know how to lie well.
Samuel Butler (1612-1680)

727 Whatever disgrace we may have deserved, it is almost always
in our power to re-establish our character.
La Rochefoucauld (1613-1680)

728 It is double pleasure to deceive the deceiver.
La Fontaine (1621-1695)

729 If there were no falsehood in the world, there would be no
doubt; if there were no doubt, there would be no inquiry;
if no inquiry, no wisdom, no knowledge, no genius.
Landor (1775-1864)

730 Cunning is the natural and universal defense of the weak
against the violence of the strong.
Macaulay (1800-1859)

731 Foxes are so cunning
Because they are not strong.
Emerson (1803-1882)

732 Men, like musical instruments, seem made to be played upon.
Bovee (1820-1904)

733 The best liar is he who makes the smallest amount of lying
go the longest way.
Samuel Butler (1835-1902)

734 A little inaccuracy sometimes saves tons of explanation.
Saki (1870-1916)

735 Lying is an indispensable part of making life tolerable.
Bergen Evans (born 1904)

5. NEGATIVE

736 The heart of the hypocrite is hid in his breast;
he masketh his words in the semblance of truth,
while the business of his life is only to deceive.
Akhenaton? (c. B.C. 1375)

737 For he who speaks untruth withers like a tree to the roots.
Upanishads (c. B.C. 800)

738   Hateful to me as are the gates of hell,
Is he who, hiding one thing in his heart,
Utters another.

Homer (c. B.C. 700)

739   If people become accustomed to lying, they will uncon-
sciously commit every possible wrong deed. Before they
can act wickedly they must lie, and once they begin to
lie they will act wickedly with unconcern.

Buddha (B.C. 568-488)

740   For one who has been honored, dishonor is worse than death.

Bhagavad Gita (c. B.C. 400)

741   Disgrace is immortal, and living even when one thinks
it dead.

Plautus (B.C. 254-184)

742   Lying is a most disgraceful vice; it first despises God,
and then fears men.

Plutarch (46-120 A.D.)

743   To tell a falsehood is like the cut of a saber;
for though the wound may heal, the scar of it will remain.

Saadi (1184-1291)

744   The gain of lying is, not to be trusted by any,
nor to be believed when we speak the truth.

Walter Raleigh (1552-1618)

745   Though those who are betrayed do feel the treason
sharply, yet the traitor stands in worse case of woe.

Shakespeare (1564-1616)

746   Where trust is greatest, there treason is in its most
horrid shape.

Dryden (1631-1700)

747   He who tells a lie is not sensible how great a task he
undertakes; for he must invent twenty more to maintain that
one.

Pope (1688-1744)

748   Trickery and treachery are the practices of fools that have
not wits enough to be honest.

Franklin (1706-1790)

749 Deceivers are the most dangerous members of society. They
trifle with the best parts of our nature, and violate the
most sacred obligations.

George Crabbe (1754-1832)

750 Not the least misfortune in a prominent falsehood is the
fact that tradition is apt to repeat it for truth.

Hosea Ballou (1771-1852)

751 The first and worst of all frauds is to cheat oneself.

Bailey (1816-1902)

752 The liar's punishment is not in the least that he is not
believed, but that he cannot believe anyone else.

G. B. Shaw (1856-1950)

6. ADVICE

753 So near is falsehood to truth that a wise man would do well
not to trust himself on the narrow edge.

Cicero (B.C. 106-43)

754 He who does not prevent a crime when he can, encourages it.

Seneca (B.C. 3-65 A.D.)

755 Who is not sure of his memory should not attempt lying.

Montaigne (1533-1592)

756 We should do by our cunning as we do by our courage,
always have it ready to defend ourselves,
never to offend others.

Greville (1554-1628)

757 Watchfulness is the only guard against cunning. Be intent
on his intentions. Many succeed in making others do their
own affairs, and unless you possess the key to their motives
you may at any moment be forced to take their chestnuts out
of the fire to the damage of your own fingers.

Baltasar Gracian (1601-1658)

758 Trust not in him that seems a saint.

Thomas Fuller (1608-1661)

759 How can we expect another to keep our secret if we cannot
keep it ourselves.

La Rochefoucauld (1613-1680)

760 Distrust all those who love you extremely upon a very slight
acquaintance and without any visible reason.

Chesterfield (1694-1773)

761   I deny the lawfulness of telling a lie to a sick man for
fear of alarming him; you have no business with consequences
you are to tell the truth.

Johnson (1709-1784)

762   Do not talk about disgrace from a thing being known,
when disgrace is, that the thing should exist.

William Falconer (1732-1769)

763   I have known a vast quantity of nonsense talked about bad
men not looking you in the face. Don't trust that
conventional idea. Dishonesty will stare honesty out of
countenance any day in the week, if there is anything to be
got by it.

Charles Dickens (1812-1870)

7. POTPOURRI

764   O fool, fool! the pains which thou takest to hide what thou
art, are far more than would make thee what thou wouldst
seem; and the children of wisdom shall mock at thy cunning
when, in the midst of security, thy disguise is stripped
off, and the finger of derision shall point thee to scorn.

Akhenaton? (c. B.C. 1375)

765   And oftentimes, to win us to our harm,
The instruments of darkness tell us truths,
Win us with honest trifles, to betrays
In deepest consequence.

Shakespeare (1564-1616)

766   We trust our secrets to our friends,
but they escape from us in love.

La Bruyere (1645-1696)

767   Is there not some chosen curse,
Some hidden thunder in the stores of heaven,
Red with uncommon wrath, to blast the man
Who owes his greatness to his country's ruin?

Addison (1672-1719)

768   It is the just decree of Heaven that a traitor never sees
his danger till his ruin is at hand.

Metastasio (1698-1782)

769   Three may keep a secret if two of them are dead.

Franklin (1706-1790)

770 Some have learnt many Tricks of sly Evasion,
Instead of Truth they use Equivocation,
And eke it out with mental Reservation,
Which is to good Men an Abomination.

Franklin (1706-1790)

771 Round numbers are always false.

Johnson (1709-1784)

772 A great lie is like a great fish on dry land; it may fret
and fling, and make a frightful bother, but it cannot hurt
you. You have only to keep still and it will die of itself.

George Crabbe (1754-1832)

773 O, what a tangled web we weave
when first we practise to deceive!

Walter Scott (1771-1832)

774 Oh, colder than the wind that freezes
Founts, that but now in sunshine play'd,
Is that congealing pang which seizes
The trusting bosom, when betray'd.

Thomas Moore (1779-1852)

775 Mary, I believed thee true,
And I was blest in thus believing;
But now I mourn that ever I knew
A girl so fair and so deceiving.

Thomas Moore (1779-1852)

776 Falsehoods not only disagree with truths,
but usually quarrel among themselves.

Daniel Webster (1782-1852)

777 You can fool some of the people all of the time,
and all of the people some of the time,
but you cannot fool all of the people all of the time.

Lincoln? (1809-1865)

778 A traitor is good fruit to hang from the boughs of the
tree of liberty.

Beecher (1813-1878)

779 Spies are of no use nowadays. Their profession is over.
The newspapers do their work instead.

Oscar Wilde (1854-1900)

780 We (Communist Party) must be ready to employ trickery, deceit, law-breaking, withholding and concealing truth. We can and must write in the language which sows among the masses hate, revulsion, scorn, and the like, toward those who disagree with us.

Nikolai Lenin (1870-1924)

DANGER
Enemies, Jeopardy, Risk and Peril

1. ESSENCE

781   Every man is his own chief enemy.

Anacharsis (fl. B.C. 600)

782   Our enemies are our outward consciences.

Shakespeare (1564-1616)

783   As soon as there is life there is danger.

Emerson (1803-1882)

2. OPPOSITES

784   The space in a needle's eye is sufficient for two friends, but the whole world is scarcely big enough to hold two enemies.

Solomon Ibn Gabirol (1021?-1053)

785   Perils commonly ask to be paid on pleasures.

Bacon (1561-1626)

786   Out of this nettle, danger, we pluck this flower, safety.

Shakespeare (1564-1616)

787   There is no person who is not dangerous for some one.

Marie de Sevigne (1626-1696)

788   Be assured those will be thy worst enemies, not to whom thou hast done evil, but who have done evil to thee. And those will be thy best friends, not to whom thou hast done good, but who have done good to thee.

Lavater (1741-1801)

789   A malicious enemy is better than a clumsy friend.

Anne Swetchine (1782-1857)

790   I destroy my enemy when I make him my friend.

Lincoln (1809-1865)

791   Two dangers constantly threaten the world: order and disorder.

Paul Valery (1871-1945)

792   Biggest profits mean gravest risks.

Chinese Proverb

3. INSIGHT

793   The responses of human beings vary greatly under dangerous
circumstances. The strong man advances boldly to meet them
head on. The weak man grows agitated. But the superior man
stands up to fate, endures resolutely in his inner certainty
of final success, and bides his time until the onset of
reassuring odds.

I Ching (B.C. 1150?)

794   Know the enemy and know yourself;
   in a hundred battles you will never be in peril.
When you are ignorant of the enemy but know yourself,
   your chances of winning or losing are equal.
If ignorant both of your enemy and of yourself,
   you are certain in every battle to be in peril.

Sun Tzu (fl. c. B.C. 500)

795   The wise man does not expose himself needlessly to danger,
since there are few things for which he cares sufficiently;
but he is willing, in great crises to give even his life-
knowing that under certain conditions it is not worth while
to live.

Aristotle (B.C. 384-322)

796   There is no gathering the rose without being pricked by the
thorns.

Pilpay (B.C. 300?)

797   Man is never watchful enough against dangers that threaten
him every hour.

Horace (B.C. 65-8)

798   Constant exposure to dangers will breed contempt for them.

Seneca (B.C. 3-65 A.D.)

799   The mere apprehension of a coming evil has put many into a
situation of the utmost danger.

Lucan (39-65 A.D.)

800   Method is more important than strength,
   when you wish to control your enemies.
By dropping golden beads near a snake,
   a crow once managed
To have a passerby kill the snake
   for the beads.

Nagarjuna (c. 100-200 A.D.)

801   It is the enemy whom we do not suspect
who is the most dangerous.

Fernando Rojas (1465?-1541?)

802   There is no little enemy.

>   Franklin (1706-1790)

803   A merely fallen enemy may rise again, but the reconciled
        one is truly vanquished.

>   Schiller (1759-1805)

804   If we could read the secret history of our enemies we
        should find in each man's life sorrow and suffering enough
        to disarm all hostility.

>   Longfellow (1807-1882)

805   You can discover what your enemy fears most
        by observing the means he uses to frighten you.

>   Eric Hoffer (1902-1983)

4. POSITIVE

806   Men of sense often learn from their enemies. It is from
        their foes, not their friends, that cities learn the lesson
        of building high walls and ships of war; and this lesson
        saves their children, their homes, and their properties.

>   Aristophanes (B.C. 448-380)

807   Some men are more beholden to their bitterest enemies
        than to friends who appear to be sweetness itself.
        The former frequently tell the truth, but the latter never.

>   Cato the Younger (B.C. 95-46)

808   Danger, the spur of all great minds.

>   George Chapman (1557-1634)

809   Many have had their greatness made for them by their
        enemies.

>   Baltasar Gracian (1601-1658)

810   Our enemies come nearer the truth in the opinions they
        form of us than we do in our opinion of ourselves.

>   La Rochefoucauld (1613-1680)

811   Great perils have this beauty, that they bring to light
        the fraternity of strangers.

>   Victor Hugo (1802-1885)

812   Everything is sweetened by risk.

>   Alexander Smith (1830-1867)

813   All centuries are dangerous, it is the business of the
future to be dangerous. It must be admitted that there
is a degree of instability which is inconsistent with
civilization. But, on the whole, the great ages have
been the unstable ages.

Alfred North Whitehead (1861-1947)

814   Behold the turtle. He makes progress only when he sticks
his neck out.

James B. Conant (1893-1978)

5. NEGATIVE

815   The worst enemy is one that fears the gods.

Aeschylus (B.C. 525-456)

816   Even if the son of his enemy speaks sweetly,
The wise man remains on guard.
A poisonous leaf retains its potency,
And can cause injury at any time.

Nagarjuna (c. 100-200 A.D.)

817   If you have no enemies, it is a sign fortune has forgot you.

Thomas Fuller (1608-1661)

818   Dangers bring fears, and fears more dangers bring.

Richard Baxter (1615-1691)

819   Whatever the number of a man's friends, there will be times
in his life when he has one too few; but if he has only
one enemy, he is lucky indeed if he has not one too many.

Bulwer-Lytton (1803-1873)

820   We each have some dominant defect, by which the enemy can
grasp us. In some it is vanity, in others indolence, in
most egotism. Let a cunning and evil spirit possess himself
of this, and you are lost.

Albert Pike (1809-1891)

6. ADVICE

821   A person in danger should not try to escape at one stroke.
He should first calmly hold his own, then be satisfied
with small gains, which will come by creative adaptations.

I Ching (B.C. 1150?)

822   If thine enemy be hungry, give him bread to eat.

Proverbs (B.C. 1000?-200?)

823   The world is always burning, burning with the fire of greed,
anger and ignorance; one should flee from such dangers as
soon as possible.

> Buddha (B.C. 568-488)

824   Observe your enemies, for they first find out your faults.

> Antisthenes (fl. B.C. 444)

825   Let us carefully observe those good qualities wherein our
enemies excel us; and endeavor to excel them, by avoiding
what is faulty, and imitating what is excellent in them.

> Plutarch (46-120 A.D.)

826   If we must fall, we should boldly meet the danger.

> Tacitus (55-117 A.D.)

827   Whoever benefits his enemy
With straightforward intention
That man's enemies will soon
Fold their hands in devotion.

> Nagarjuna (c. 100-200 A.D.)

828   In time of danger it is proper to be alarmed until danger be
near at hand; but when we perceive that danger is near, we
should oppose it as if we were not afraid.

> The Hitopadesa (600?-1100? A.D.)

829   O wise man, wash your hands of that friend who associates
with your enemies.

> Saadi (1184-1291)

830   Wise men say nothing in dangerous times.

> John Selden (1584-1654)

831   Let the fear of a danger be a spur to prevent it;
he that fears not, gives advantage to the danger.

> Quarles (1592-1644)

832   In fighting and in everyday life you should be determined
though calm. Meet the situation without tenseness yet not
recklessly, your spirit settled yet unbiased...An elevated
spirit is weak and a low spirit is weak. Do not let the
enemy see your spirit.

> Miyamoto Musashi (1584-1645)

833   Beware of meat twice boiled,
and an old foe reconciled.

> Franklin (1706-1790)

834   It is better to meet danger than to wait for it. He that
       is on a lee shore, and foresees a hurricane, stands out
       to sea and encounters a storm to avoid a shipwreck.

                                                    Colton (1780-1832)

835   Danger - if you meet it promptly and without flinching -
       you will reduce the danger by half. Never run away from
       anything. Never!

                                          Winston Churchill (1874-1965)

7. POTPOURRI

836   Man should observe the strictest self-restraint and reserve
       in dangerous times. In this way he incurs neither injury
       from antagonists with designs on pre-eminence nor
       obligations to others.

                                                  I Ching (B.C. 1150?)

837   There's nothing like the sight of an old enemy down on his
       luck.

                                           Euripides (B.C. 480-406)

838   It is better to do thine own duty, however lacking in merit,
          than to do that of another, even though efficiently.
       It is better to die doing one's own duty,
          for to do the duty of another is fraught with danger.

                                        Bhagavad Gita (c. B.C. 400)

839   You are dealing with a work full of dangerous hazard, and
       you are venturing upon fires overlaid with treacherous ashes

                                                Horace (B.C. 65-8)

840   Send danger from the east unto the west,
       So honor cross it from the north to south.

                                        Shakespeare (1564-1616)

841   O'er the ice the rapid skater flies,
          With sport above and death below,
       Where mischief lurks in gay disguise
          Thus lightly touch and quickly go.

                                     Pierre Charles Roy (1683-1764)

842   During the first period of a man's life the greatest danger
       is: not to take the risk. When once the risk has really
       been taken, then the greatest danger is to risk too much.

                                        Kierkegaard (1813-1855)

843   The world is large when its weary leagues two loving
          hearts divide;
       But the world is small when your enemy is loose on the
          other side.

                                        John O'Reilly (1844-1890)

DEATH
Dying and Mortality

1. ESSENCE

844   For dust thou art, and unto dust shalt thou return.

> Genesis (B.C. 1200?)

845   Even as a caterpillar, when coming to an end of a blade of
grass, reaches out to another blade of grass and draws
itself over to it, in the same way the Soul, leaving the
body and unwisdom behind, reaches out to another body and
draws itself over to it.

> Upanishads (c. B.C. 800)

846   Then shalt dust return to the earth as it was:
and the spirit shall return unto God who gave it.

> Ecclesiastes (B.C. 300?)

847   That last day does not bring extinction to us,
but change of place.

> Cicero (B.C. 106-43)

848   We begin to die as soon as we are born,
and the end is linked to the beginning.

> Manilius (fl. 100 A.D.)

849   Death is the golden key that opens the palace of eternity.

> Milton (1608-1674)

850   Death is the veil which those who live call life;
They sleep, and it is lifted.

> Shelley (1792-1822)

851   Death is the dropping of the flower that the fruit may
swell.

> Beecher (1813-1878)

2. OPPOSITES

852   The Father is the Giver of Life; but the Mother is the
Giver of Death, because her womb is the gate of ingress
to matter, and through her life is ensouled to form,
and no form can be either infinite or eternal.
Death is implicit in birth.

> Kabbalah (B.C. 1200?-700? A.D.)

853   There are two ways of passing from this world -
      one in light and one in darkness.
      When one passes in light, he does not come back;
      but when one passes in darkness, he returns.
                              Bhagavad Gita (c. B.C. 400)

854   Pale death, with impartial step, knocks at the hut of
      the poor and the towers of kings.
                                   Horace (B.C. 65-8)

855   It is as natural to die as to be born; and to a little
      infant, perhaps, the one is as painful as the other.
                                  Bacon (1561-1626)

856   The stroke of death is as a lover's pinch,
      Which hurts and is desired.
                             Shakespeare (1564-1616)

857   And I still onward haste to my last night;
      Time's fatal wings do ever forward fly;
      So every day we live, a day we die.
                           Thomas Campion (1567-1620)

858   One short sleep past, we wake eternally,
      And Death shall be no more; Death, thou shalt die.
                               John Donne (1572-1632)

859   Men fear death, as if unquestionably the greatest evil,
      and yet no man knows that it may not be the greatest good.
                           William Mitford (1744-1827)

860   Is death the last step?
      No, it is the final awakening.
                             Walter Scott (1771-1832)

861   For I say, this is death and the sole death,
      When a man's loss comes to him from his gain,
      Darkness from light, from knowledge ignorance,
      And lack of love from love made manifest.
                           Robert Browning (1812-1889)

862   Living is death; dying is life.
      We are not what we appear to be.
      On this side of the grave we are exiles, on that citizens;
      on this side orphans, on that children;
      on this side captives, on that freemen...
                                 Beecher (1813-1878)

863   Life is the jailer, death the angel sent to draw the
      unwilling bolts and set us free.
                            James Lowell (1819-1891)

864   Life is a dream walking
       Death is a going home.

                                              Chinese Proverb

3. INSIGHT

865   Involvement in a form is the beginning of the death of
       life. It is a straightening and a limiting; a binding
       and a constricting. Form checks life, thwarts it, and
       yet enables it to organize. Seen from the point of view
       of free-moving force, incarceration in a form is extinction.
       Form disciplines force with a merciless severity.

                                 Kabbalah (B.C. 1200?-700? A.D.)

866   Remember the men of old passed away,
       those of days to come will also pass away:
       a mortal ripens like corn and like corn is born again.

                                       Upanishads (c. B.C. 800)

867   No evil is honorable: but death is honorable;
       therefore death is not evil.

                                         Zeno (B.C. 335?-264)

868   Few cross the river of time and are able to reach non-being.
       Most of them run up and down only on this side of the river.
       But those who when they know the law follow the path of the
       law, they shall reach the other shore and go beyond the
       realm of death.

                                 The Dhammapada (c. B.C. 300)

869   The life of the dead is placed in the memory of the living.

                                        Cicero (B.C. 106-43)

870   Nobody dies prematurely who dies in misery.

                                   Publilius Syrus (fl. B.C. 42)

871   Death is sometimes a punishment, sometimes a gift;
       to many it has come as a favor.

                                      Seneca (B.C. 3-65 A.D.)

872   Strange - is it not? - that of the myriads who
       Before us passed the door of Darkness through,
       Not one returns to tell us of the road
       Which to discover we must travel too.

                                   Omar Khayyam (fl. 1100)

873   The fear of death is worse than death.

                                   Robert Burton (1576-1640)

874   The birds of the air die to sustain thee; the beasts of the
field die to nourish thee; the fishes of the sea die to
feed thee. Our stomachs are their common sepulcher. Good
God! with how many deaths are our poor lives patched up!
how full of death is the life of momentary man!

Quarles (1592-1644)

875   Neither the sun nor death can be looked at with a steady eye

La Rochefoucauld (1613-1680)

876   It is impossible that anything so natural, so necessary,
and so universal as death, should ever have been designed by
Providence as an evil to mankind.

Swift (1667-1745)

877   Death, so called, is a thing which makes men weep,
And yet a third of life is passed in sleep.

Byron (1788-1824)

878   We sometimes congratulate ourselves at the moment of waking
from a troubled dream; it may be so the moment after death.

Nathaniel Hawthorne (1804-1864)

879   We look at death through the cheap-glazed windows of the
flesh, and believe him the monster which the flawed and
cracked glass represents him.

James Lowell (1819-1891)

880   Man has the possibility of existence after death. But
possibility is one thing and the realization of the
possibility is quite a different thing.

Gurdjieff (1873-1949)

881   A man's dying is more the survivors' affair than his own.

Thomas Mann (1875-1955)

4. POSITIVE

882   This is thy present world, said the Flame to the Spark.
Thou art myself, my image, and my shadow. I have clothed
myself in thee, and thou art my vehicle to the day, "Be
with us," when thou shalt re-become myself and others,
thyself and me.

Book of Dzyan (B.C. 3000?)

883   Death may be the greatest of all human blessings.

Socrates (B.C. 469-399)

884   He whom the gods love dies young,
while he is in health,
has his senses and his judgments sound.

Plautus (B.C. 254-184)

885   Thou fool, what is sleep but the image of death?
Fate will give an eternal rest.

                                     Ovid (B.C. 43-18 A.D.)

886   This day, which thou fearest as thy last,
is the birthday of eternity.

                                   Seneca (B.C. 3-65 A.D.)

887   The gods conceal from men the happiness of death,
that they may endure life.

                                   Lucan (39-65 A.D.)

888   Not by lamentations and mournful chants ought we to
celebrate the funeral of a good man, but by hymns,
for in ceasing to be numbered with mortals he enters
upon the heritage of a diviner life.

                                   Plutarch (46-120 A.D.)

889   Death is a release from the impressions of the senses,
and from desires that make us their puppets,
and from the vagaries of the mind,
and from the hard service of the flesh.

                                   Marcus Aurelius (121-180 A.D.)

890   As a well-spent day brings happy sleep,
so a life well spent brings happy death.

                                   Leonardo Da Vinci (1452-1519)

891   Death, they say, acquits us of all obligations.

                                   Montaigne (1533-1592)

892   Death is the cure for all diseases.

                                   Thomas Browne (1605-1682)

893   We should weep for men at their birth, not at their death.

                                   Montesquieu (1689-1755)

894   I look upon death to be as necessary to our constitution as
sleep. We shall rise refreshed in the morning.

                                   Franklin (1706-1790)

895   Death is a commingling of eternity with time; in the death
of a good man, eternity is seen looking through time.

                                   Goethe (1749-1832)

896   That which is so universal as death must be a benefit.

                                   Schiller (1759-1805)

897   The darkness of death is like the evening twilight;
it makes all objects appear more lovely to the dying.

                                   Richter (1763-1825)

898 Death gives us sleep, eternal youth, and immortality.

Richter (1763-1825)

899 Death is the liberator of him whom freedom cannot release,
the physician of him whom medicine cannot cure,
and the comforter of him whom time cannot console.

Colton (1780-1832)

900 How wonderful is death!
Death and his brother sleep.

Shelley (1792-1822)

901 But life is sweet, though all that makes it sweet
Lessen like sound of friends' departing feet;
And Death is beautiful as feet of friend
Coming with welcome at our journey's end.

James Lowell (1819-1891)

902 Nothing can happen more beautiful than death.

Walt Whitman (1819-1892)

903 There is no death! the stars go down
To rise upon some other shore,
And bright in Heaven's jeweled crown,
They shine for ever more.

John McCreery (1835-1906)

904 Death is delightful. Death is dawn,
The waking from a weary night
Of fevers unto truth and light.

Joaquin Miller (1839-1913)

905 The essential part of our being can only survive if the
transient part dissolves. Death is a condition of survival.
That which has been gained must be eternalized, and can only
be eternalized by being transmuted, by passing through death
into eternal life. This is the meaning of Resurrection.

Pir Vilayat Inayat Khan (born 1916)

5. NEGATIVE

906 The path of immortality is hard, and only a few find it.
The rest await the Great Day when the wheels of the universe
shall be stopped and the immortal sparks shall escape from
the sheaths of substance. Woe unto those who wait, for
they must return again, unconscious and unknowing, to the
seed-ground of stars, and await a new beginning.

The Divine Pymander (BC 2500?-200 AD?)

907   O how small a portion of earth will hold us when we
      are dead, who ambitiously seek after the whole world
      while we are living.

                                         Philip II (B.C. 382-336)

908   Death alone discloses how insignificant
      are the puny bodies of men.

                                         Juvenal (40-125 A.D.)

909   It is not death, it is dying that alarms me.

                                         Montaigne (1533-1592)

910   Ah, what a sign it is of evil life,
      Where death's approach is seen so terrible!

                                         Shakespeare (1564-1616)

911   If some men died and others did not,
      death would indeed be a most mortifying evil.

                                         La Bruyere (1645-1696)

912   The Fear of Death often proves Mortal, and sets People on
      Methods to save their Lives, which infallibly destroy them.

                                         Addison (1672-1719)

913   A dying man can do nothing easy.

                                         Franklin (1706-1790)

914   To neglect, at any time, preparation for death, is to sleep
      on our post at a siege; to omit it in old age, is to sleep
      at an attack.

                                         Johnson (1709-1784)

915   Death is the tyrant of the imagination. His reign is in
      solitude and darkness, in tombs and prisons, over weak
      hearts and seething brains. He lives, without shape or
      sound, a phantasm, inaccessible to sight or touch, - a
      ghastly and terrible apprehension.

                                         Barry Cornwall (1787-1874)

916   Whatever crazy sorrow saith,
      No life that breathes with human breath
      Has ever truly longed for death.

                                         Alfred Tennyson (1809-1892)

917   There is no such thing as death.
        In nature nothing dies.
      From each sad remnant of decay
        Some forms of life arise.

                                         Charles Mackay (1814-1889)

6. ADVICE

918   Labour not after riches first, and think thou afterwards
wilt enjoy them. He who neglecteth the present moment,
throweth away all that he hath. As the arrow passeth
through the heart, while the warrior knew not that it was
coming; so shall his life be taken away before he knoweth
that he hath it.

Akhenaton? (c. B.C. 1375)

919   Trust not your own powers till the day of your death.

The Talmud (B.C. 500?-400? A.D.)

920   But learn that to die is a debt we must all pay.

Euripides (B.C. 480-406)

921   Death is as sure for that which is born,
  as birth is for that which is dead.
Therefore grieve not for what is inevitable.

Bhagavad Gita (c. B.C. 400)

922   He who knows that this body is like froth,
and has learnt that it is as unsubstantial as a mirage,
will break the flower-pointed arrow of illusion,
and never see the king of death.

The Dhammapada (c. B.C. 300)

923   It is uncertain in what place death may await thee;
therefore expect it in any place.

Seneca (B.C. 3-65 A.D.)

924   Let death be daily before your eyes, and you will never
entertain any abject thought, nor too eagerly covet
anything.

Epictetus (50-138 A.D.)

925   Despise not death, but welcome it,
for Nature wills it like all else.

Marcus Aurelius (121-180 A.D.)

926   At the moment of death there will appear to you, swifter
than lightning, the luminous splendour of the colourless
light of Emptiness, and that will surround you on all sides.
Terrified, you will flee from the radiance...Try to submerge
yourself in that light, giving up all belief in a separate
self, all attachment to your illusory ego. Recognize that
the boundless Light of this true Reality is your own true
self, and you shall be saved!

Tibetan Book of the Dead (c. 780 A.D.)

927 Do not be frightened or bewildered by the luminous,
brilliant, very sharp and clear light of supreme wisdom...
Be drawn to it...take refuge in it...Do not take pleasure in
the soft light...Do not be attracted to it or yearn for it.
It is an obstacle blocking the path of liberation.
Tibetan Book of the Dead (c. 780 A.D.)

928 If you don't know how to die, don't worry;
Nature will tell you what to do on the spot, fully and
adequately. She will do this job perfectly for you;
don't bother your head about it.
Montaigne (1533-1592)

929 Let no man fear to die, we love to sleep all,
And death is but the sounder sleep.
Francis Beaumont (1584-1616)

930 If life must not be taken too seriously -
then so neither must death.
Samuel Butler (1612-1680)

7. POTPOURRI

931 Life that breathes now lies still and yet moves fast, rush-
ing but firmly fixed in the midst of the resting places.
The life of the dead one wanders as his nature wills.
The immortal comes from the same womb as the mortal.
Rig Veda (B.C. 1200-900?)

932 Your lost friends are not dead, but gone before,
    Advanced a stage or two upon that road
Which you must travel in the steps they trod.
Aristophanes (B.C. 448-380)

933 Before long, alas! this body will lie on the earth,
despised, without understanding, like a useless log.
The Dhammapada (c. B.C. 300)

934 I have lived, and I have run the course
which fortune allotted me;
and now my shade shall descend illustrious to the grave.
Vergil (B.C. 70-19)

935 Property is unstable, and youth perishes in a moment.
Life itself is held in the grinning fangs of Death,
Yet men delay to obtain release from the world.
Alas, the conduct of mankind is surprising.
Nagarjuna (c. 100-200 A.D.)

936   Oh you who have been removed from God in his solitude
      by the abyss of time, how can you expect to reach him
      without dying?
                                   al-Hallaj (c. 858-922 A.D.)

937   I died a mineral, and became a plant.
      I died a plant and rose an animal.
      I died an animal and I was man.
      Why should I fear? When was I less by dying?
                             Jalal-Uddin Rumi (1207-1273)

938   Now I am about to take my last voyage,
      a great leap in the dark.
                             Thomas Hobbes (1588-1679)

939   This man is freed from servile bands,
        Of hope to rise, or fear to fall;
      Lord of himself, though not of lands,
        And leaving nothing, yet hath all.
                             Robert Herrick (1591-1674)

940   He was exhaled; his great Creator drew
      His spirit, as the sun the morning dew.
                             Dryden (1631-1700)

941   The prince who kept the world in awe,
      The judge whose dictate fix'd the law;
      The rich, the poor, the great, the small,
      Are levelled; death confounds 'em all.
                             Gay (1688-1732)

942   As man, perhaps, the moment of his breath,
      Receives the lurking principle of death,
      The young disease, that must subdue at length,
      Grows with his growth, and strengthens with his strength.
                             Pope (1688-1744)

943   Would you extend your narrow span,
      And make the most of life you can;
      Would you, when medicines cannot save,
      Descend with ease into the grave;
      Calmly retire, like evening light,
      And cheerful bid the world good night?
                             Voltaire (1694-1778)

944   Then with no fiery throbbing pain,
        No cold gradations of decay,
      Death broke at once the vital chain,
        And freed his soul the nearest way.
                             Johnson (1709-1784)

945   All flesh is grass, and all its glory fades
Like the fair flower dishevelled in the wind;
Riches have wings, and grandeur is a dream;
The man we celebrate must find a tomb,
And we that worship him, ignoble graves.

                        Cowper (1731-1800)

946   Like the dew on the mountain,
    Like the foam on the river,
Like the bubble on the fountain,
    Thou art gone, and for ever!

                   Walter Scott (1771-1832)

947   First our pleasures die - and then
Our hopes, and then our fears - and when
These are dead, the debt is due,
Dust claims dust - and we die too.

                      Shelley (1792-1822)

948   The sweet calm sunshine of October, now
    Warms the low spot; upon its grassy mould
The purple oak-leaf falls; the birchen bough
    Drops its bright spoil like arrow-heads of gold.

        William Cullen Bryant (1794-1878)

949   To every man upon this earth
    Death cometh soon or late,
And how can man die better
    Than facing fearful odds,
For the ashes of his fathers
    And the temples of his gods?

                   Macaulay (1800-1859)

950   When a great man dies,
for years the light he leaves behind him,
lies on the paths of men.

                  Longfellow (1807-1882)

951   Because I could not stop for Death,
He kindly stopped for me;
The carriage held but just ourselves
And Immortality.

             Emily Dickinson (1830-1886)

952   Dying is a wild night and a new road.

             Emily Dickinson (1830-1886)

953   And I hear from the outgoing ship in the bay
        The song of the sailors in glee:
    So I think of the luminous footprints that bore
        The comfort o'er dark Galilee,
    And wait for the signal to go to the shore,
        To the ship that is waiting for me.

                              Bret Harte (1836-1902)

954   Out of the chill and the shadow,
        Into the thrill and the shine;
    Out of the dearth and the famine,
        Into the fullness divine.

                   Margaret Sangster (1838-1912)

DECREASE

Aging, Autumn, Decay, Decline and Twilight

1. ESSENCE

955   Age carries all things away, even the mind.

Vergil (B.C. 70-19)

956   Old age is an incurable disease.

Seneca (B.C. 3-65 A.D.)

957   All human things are subject to decay.

Dryden (1631-1700)

958   Old age is an island surrounded by death.

Juan Montalvo (1832-1889)

2. OPPOSITES

959   Old things are always in good repute,
       present things in disfavor.

Tacitus (55-117 A.D.)

960   As we grow old we become both more foolish and more wise.
La Rochefoucauld (1613-1680)

961   We hope to grow old, yet we fear old age; that is,
       we are willing to live, and afraid to die.

La Bruyere (1645-1696)

962   Every man desires to live long; but no man would be old.
Swift (1667-1745)

963   As we advance in life the circle of our pains enlarges,
       while that of our pleasures contracts.

Anne Swetchine (1782-1857)

964   Heaven gives our days of failing strength
         Indemnifying fleetness
       And those of youth a seeming length
         Proportioned to their sweetness.

Thomas Hood (1798-1845)

965   Forty is the old age of youth; fifty the youth of old age.
Victor Hugo (1802-1885)

966   Youth is fair, a graceful stag,
Leaping, playing in a park
Age is gray, a toothless hag,
Stumbling in the dark.

Isaac L. Peretz (1852-1915)

967   The young feel tired at the end of an action;
The old at the beginning.

T. S. Eliot (1888-1965)

3. INSIGHT

968   Old people have fewer diseases than the young,
but their diseases never leave them.

Hippocrates (B.C. 460-370)

969   No one is so old as to think he cannot live one more year.

Cicero (B.C. 106-43)

970   Old age is by nature rather talkative.

Cicero (B.C. 106-43)

971   Nature hath appointed twilight as a bridge to pass us out of
day into night.

Thomas Fuller (1608-1661)

972   Few persons know how to be old.

La Rochefoucauld (1613-1680)

973   Man can have only a certain number of teeth, hair and ideas;
there comes a time when he necessarily loses his teeth,
hair and ideas.

Voltaire (1694-1778)

974   Age makes us not childish, as some say;
it finds us still true children.

Goethe (1749-1832)

975   Winter, which strips the leaves from around us,
makes us see the distant regions they formerly concealed;
so does old age rob us of our enjoyments,
only to enlarge the prospect of eternity before us.

Richter (1763-1825)

976   Autumn wins you best by this, its mute
Appeal to sympathy for its decay.

Robert Browning (1812-1889)

977   I've never known a person to live to be one hundred and be
remarkable for anything else.

Josh Billings (1815-1885)

978   To know how to grow old is the master work of wisdom,
       and one of the most difficult chapters
       in the great art of living.

                        Henri Frederic Amiel (1821-1881)

4. POSITIVE

979   A graceful and honorable old age is the childhood of
       immortality.

                                Pindar (B.C. 518?-438)

980   Old age has a great sense of calm and freedom. When the
       passions have relaxed their hold and have escaped, not
       from one master, but from many.

                              Plato (B.C. 427?-347?)

981   It is not by muscle, speed, or physical dexterity that great
       things are achieved, but by reflection, force of character,
       and judgment; in these qualities old age is usually not
       only not poorer, but is even richer.

                               Cicero (B.C. 106-43)

982   Old age, especially an honoured old age, has so great
       authority, that this is of more value than all the pleasures
       of youth.

                               Cicero (B.C. 106-43)

983   As for old age, embrace and love it. It abounds with
       pleasure if you know how to use it. The gradually declining
       years are among the sweetest in a man's life, and I maintain
       that, even when they have reached the extreme limit, they
       have their pleasure still.

                            Seneca (B.C. 3-65 A.D.)

984   Even in decline, a virtuous man
       Increases the beauty of his behavior.
       A burning stick, though turned to the ground,
       Has its flame drawn upwards.

                          Saskya Pandita (1182-1251)

985   Old wood best to burn, old wine to drink,
       old friends to trust, and old authors to read.

                                Bacon (1561-1626)

986   No Spring nor Summer Beauty hath such grace
       As I have seen in one Autumnal face.

                            John Donne (1572-1632)

987   The evening of a well-spent life brings its lamps with it.

                              Joubert (1754-1824)

988   Men, like peaches and pears, grow sweet a little while
      before they begin to decay.
                              Oliver Wendell Holmes (1809-1894)

989   Age, like distance lends a double charm.
                              Oliver Wendell Holmes (1809-1894)

990   Grow old along with me!
      The best is yet to be,
      The last of life, for which the first was made.
                                    Robert Browning (1812-1889)

991   For age is opportunity no less
      Than youth itself, though in another dress,
      And as the evening twilight fades away
      The sky is filled with stars, invisible by day.
                                        Longfellow (1807-1882)

992   Age is not all decay; it is the ripening, the swelling,
      of the fresh life within, that withers and bursts the husk.
                                George MacDonald (1824-1905)

993   Who soweth good seed shall surely reap;
      The year grows rich as it groweth old,
      And life's latest sands are its sands of gold!
                                    Julia Ripley Dorr (1825-1913)

994   How beautifully leaves grow old.
      How full of light and colour are their last days.
                                    John Burroughs (1837-1921)

5. NEGATIVE

995   The man reaches his declining years and recalls the
      transitoriness of life. Instead of enjoying the
      ordinary pleasures while they last, he groans in
      melancholy.
                                        I Ching (B.C. 1150?)

996   What else is an old man but voice and shadow?
                                    Euripides (B.C. 480-406)

997   Old age is, so to speak, the sanctuary of ills:
      they all take refuge in it.
                                    Antiphanes (B.C. 388-311)

998   Nothing is more dishonorable than an old man, heavy with
      years, who has no other evidence of his having lived long
      except his age.
                                    Seneca (B.C. 3-65 A.D.)

999   Whoever saw old age that did not applaud the past and
       condemn the present?

                                          Montaigne (1533-1592)

1000   Men of age object too much, consult too long,
       adventure too little, repent too soon,
       and seldom drive business home to the full period,
       but content themselves with a mediocrity of success.

                                              Bacon (1561-1626)

1001   And so from hour to hour we ripe and ripe,
       And then from hour to hour we rot and rot;
       And thereby hangs a tale.

                                        Shakespeare (1564-1616)

1002   Old age is a tyrant, which forbids the pleasure of youth
       on pain of death.

                                   La Rochefoucauld (1613-1680)

1003   No skill or art is needed to grow old;
       the trick is to endure it.

                                             Goethe (1749-1832)

1004   Thus pleasures fade away;
       Youth, talents, beauty, thus decay,
       And leave us dark, forlorn, and gray.

                                      Walter Scott (1771-1832)

1005   What is the worst of woes that wait on age?
         What stamps the wrinkle deeper on the brow?
       To view each loved one blotted from life's page,
         And be alone on earth as I am now.

                                              Byron (1788-1824)

1006   Nature abhors the old, and old age seems the only disease;
       all others run into this one.

                                           Emerson (1803-1882)

1007   Few envy the consideration enjoyed by the eldest inhabitant.
                                           Emerson (1803-1882)

1008   What makes old age hard to bear is not the failing of one's
       faculties, mental and physical, but the burden of one's
       memories.

                                  Somerset Maugham (1874-1965)

6. ADVICE

1009   Those who search beyond the natural limits will retain good
hearing and clear vision, their bodies will remain light and
strong, and although they grow old in years they will remain
able-bodied and flourishing; and those who are able-bodied
can govern to great advantage.

Huang Ti (B.C. 2700?-2600?)

1010   Great effort is required to arrest decay and restore vigor.
One must exercise proper deliberation, plan carefully before
making a move, and be alert in guarding against relapse
following a renaissance.

I Ching (B.C. 1150?)

1011   It is always in season for old men to learn.

Aeschylus (B.C. 525-456)

1012   You must become an old man in good time
if you wish to be an old man long.

Cicero (B.C. 106-43)

1013   Discern of the coming on of years, and think not to do the
same things still; for age will not be defied.

Bacon (1561-1626)

1014   No wise man ever wished to be younger.

Swift (1667-1745)

1015   To be happy, we must be true to nature and carry our age
along with us.

Hazlitt (1778-1830)

1016   If wrinkles must be written upon your brows, let them not be
written upon the heart. The spirit should not grow old.

James Garfield (1831-1881)

1017   All objects of this world are perishable. This body is
subject to decay and death. Remembrance of this will wean
your mind from the sensual pleasures and turn it inwards
in awakening a sense of reality in the Unseen and the
Invisible.

Sivananda (born 1887)

7. POTPOURRI

1018   A green old age, unconscious of decay
That proves the hero born in better days.

Homer (c. B.C. 700)

1019   The mind of age is like a lamp
      Whose oil is running thin;
   One moment it is shining bright,
      Then darkness closes in.

Kalidasa (fl. c. 450 A.D.)

1020   Have you not a moist eye, a dry hand, a yellow cheek,
   a white beard, a decreasing leg, an increasing belly?
   Is not your voice broken, your wind short, your chin double,
   your wit single, and every part about you blasted with
   antiquity? And will you yet call yourself young?

Shakespeare (1564-1616)

1021   He that loves a rosy cheek,
      Or a coral lip admires,
   Or from star-like eyes doth seek
      Fuel to maintain his fires;
   As old Time makes these decay,
      So his flames must waste away.

Thomas Carew (1595?-1639)

1022   The sun, when he from noon declines,
   and with abated heat less fiercely shines;
   seems to grow milder as he goes away.

Dryden (1631-1700)

1023   An age that melts with unperceiv'd decay,
   And glides in modest innocence away.

Johnson (1709-1784)

1024   Thus fares it still in our decay,
      And yet the wiser mind
   Mourns less for what age takes away
      Than what it leaves behind.

Wordsworth (1770-1850)

1025   All that's bright must fade,
      The brightest still the fleetest;
   All that's sweet was made
      But to be lost when sweetest.

Thomas Moore (1779-1852)

1026   Every season hath its pleasures;
      Spring may boast her flowery prime,
   Yet the vineyard's ruby treasures
      Brighten Autumn's sob'rer time.

Thomas Moore (1779-1852)

1027   Years steal fire from the mind, as vigor from the limb;
        And life's enchanted cup but sparkles near the brim.

                                        Byron (1788-1824)

1028   The first forty years of life give us the text;
        the next thirty supply the commentary on it.

                                        Schopenhauer (1788-1860)

1029   The melancholy days have come, the saddest of the year,
        Of wailing winds, and naked woods, and meadows brown
        and sear.

                                        William Cullen Bryant (1794-1878)

1030   Fires that shook me once, but now to silent ashes
            fall'n away,
        Cold upon the dead volcano sleeps the gleam of
            dying day.

                                        Alfred Tennyson (1809-1892)

1031   How far the gulf-stream of our youth may flow
        Into the arctic regions of our lives,
        Where little else than life itself survives.

                                        Longfellow (1807-1882)

1032   My experience is that as soon as people are old enough to
        know better, they don't know anything at all.

                                        Oscar Wilde (1854-1900)

1033   Twilight, a timid fawn, went glimmering by,
        And Night, the dark-blue hunter, followed fast.

                                        George W. Russell (1867-1935)

1034   Senescence begins
        And middle age ends,
        The day your descendents,
        Outnumber your friends.

                                        Ogden Nash (1902-1971)

DOUBT
Despair, Pessimism and Suspicion

1. ESSENCE

1035   Doubt is the father of invention.

                                                          Galileo (1564-1642)

1036   Doubt is the vestibule through which all must pass before
       they can enter into the temple of wisdom.

                                               Colton (1780-1832)

1037   Despair is the conclusion of fools.

                                           Disraeli (1804-1881)

1038   Who never doubted, never half believed.
       Where doubt is, there truth is - it is her shadow.

                                              Bailey (1816-1902)

1039   Doubt is the opposite of belief.

                                            Bovee (1820-1904)

1040   Life is doubt, and faith without doubt is nothing but death.
                         Miguel de Unamuno (1864-1936)

1041   Doubt is the key to knowledge.

                                            Persian Proverb

2. OPPOSITES

1042   True wisdom is less presuming than folly.
       The wise man doubteth often, and changeth his mind;
       the fool is obstinate, and doubteth not;
       he knoweth all things but his own ignorance.

                                Akhenaton? (c. B.C. 1375)

1043   It is as hard for the good to suspect evil
       as it is for the bad to suspect good.

                                   Cicero (B.C. 106-43)

1044   In contemplation, if a man begins with certainties
        he shall end in doubts;
       but if he be content to begin with doubts,
        he shall end in certainties.

                                  Bacon (1561-1626)

1045   Despair is the damp of hell,
       as joy is the serenity of heaven.

                            John Donne (1572-1632)

1046 Industry pays debts, despair increases them.

Franklin (1706-1790)

1047 The natural cause of the human mind is certainly from credulity to skepticism.

Thomas Jefferson (1743-1826)

1048 Can that which is the greatest virtue in philosophy, doubt, be in religion what the priests term it, the greatest of sins?

Bovee (1820-1904)

1049 Great doubts
  deep wisdom...
Small doubts
  little wisdom.

Chinese Proverb

3. INSIGHT

1050 Suspicion amongst thoughts are like bats amongst birds, they never fly by twilight.

Bacon (1561-1626)

1051 He that knows nothing doubts nothing.

Herbert (1593-1632)

1052 Suspicion follows close on mistrust.

Gotthold Lessing (1729-1781)

1053 We know accurately only when we know little, with knowledge doubt increases.

Goethe (1749-1832)

1054 Skepticism means not intellectual doubt alone, but moral doubt.

Carlyle (1795-1881)

1055 Doubt comes in at the window when inquiry is denied at the door.

Benjamin Jowett (1817-1893)

1056 There is no rule more invariable than that we are paid for our suspicions by finding what we suspect.

Thoreau (1817-1862)

4. POSITIVE

1057 There is one safeguard known generally to the wise, which is an advantage and security to all, but especially to democracies as against despots - suspicion.

Demosthenes (B.C. 384-322)

1058   Modest doubt is called the beacon of the wise.
                                Shakespeare (1564-1616)

1059   If you would be a real seeker after truth, it is necessary
        that at least once in your life you doubt, as far as
        possible, all things.
                                Rene Descartes (1596-1650)

1060   Doubt is an incentive to truth,
        and patient inquiry leadeth the way.
                                Hosea Ballou (1771-1852)

1061   There lives more faith in honest doubt,
        Believe me, than in half the creeds.
                                Alfred Tennyson (1809-1892)

1062   To have doubted one's own first principles is the mark of a
        civilized man.
                                Oliver Wendell Holmes (1809-1894)

1063   Doubt, indulged and cherished, is in danger of becoming
        denial; but if honest, and bent on thorough investigation,
        it may soon lead to full establishment of the truth.
                                Tryon Edwards (1809-1894)

1064   Doubt, the essential preliminary of all improvement and
        discovery, must accompany the stages of man's onward
        progress. The faculty of doubting and questioning, without
        which those of comparison and judgment would be useless, is
        itself a divine prerogative of the reason.
                                Albert Pike (1809-1891)

1065   An honest man can never surrender an honest doubt.
                                Walter Malone (1866-1915)

1066   Men become civilized, not in proportion to their willingness
        to believe, but in proportion to their readiness to doubt.
                                H. L. Mencken (1880-1956)

5. NEGATIVE

1067   There is nothing more dreadful than the habit of doubt.
        Doubt separates people. It is a poison that disintegrates
        friendships and breaks up pleasant relations. It is a
        thorn that irritates and hurts; it is a sword that kills.
                                Buddha (B.C. 568-488)

1068   Neither in this world nor elsewhere is there any happiness
        in store for him who always doubts.
                                Bhagavad Gita (c. B.C. 400)

1069   There is no greater folly in the world than for a man to
        despair.

Cervantes (1547-1616)

1070   Our doubts are traitors, and make us lose the good we oft
        might win by fearing to attempt.

Shakespeare (1564-1616)

1071   To doubt is worse than to have lost; And to despair
        is but to antedate those miseries that must fall on us.

Philip Massinger (1583-1640)

1072   Always to think the worst, I have ever found to be the
        mark of a mean spirit and a base soul.

Bolingbroke (1678-1751)

1073   Suspicion is no less an enemy to virtue than to happiness.

Johnson (1709-1784)

1074   Despair is a mental state which exaggerates not only our
        misery but also our weakness.

Vauvenargues(1715-1747)

1075   Suspicion is a heavy armor,
        and with its own weight impedes more than protects.

Byron (1788-1824)

1076   The fearful Unbelief is unbelief in yourself.

Carlyle (1795-1881)

1077   A person who doubts himself is like a man who would enlist
        in the ranks of his enemies and bear arms against himself.
        He makes his failure certain by himself being the first
        person to be convinced of it.

Alexandre Dumas (1802-1870)

1078   There is no sadder sight than a young pessimist.

Mark Twain (1835-1910)

1079   Pessimism is the one ism which kills the soul.

John Buchan (1875-1940)

6. ADVICE

1080   When you doubt, abstain.

Zoroaster (B.C. 628?-551?)

1081   Never despair, but if you do, work on in despair.

Terence (B.C. 185-159)

1082   There is nothing makes a man suspect much, more than to know
        little, and therefore men should remedy suspicion by
        procuring to know more, and not keep their suspicions in
        smother.

                                                    Bacon (1561-1626)

1083   A certain amount of distrust is wholesome, but not so
        much of others as of ourselves; neither vanity nor
        conceit can exist in the same atmosphere with it.

                                            Suzanne Necker (1739-1794)

1084   Doubt, of whatever kind, can be ended by Action alone.

                                                    Carlyle (1795-1881)

1085   Doubt whom you will, but never yourself.

                                                    Bovee (1820-1904)

1086   The important thing is not to stop questioning.

                                                    Einstein (1879-1955)

7. POTPOURRI

1087   Suspicions that the mind, of itself, gathers, are but
        buzzes; but suspicions that are artificially nourished
        and put into men's heads by the tales and whisperings
        of others, have stings.

                                                    Bacon (1561-1626)

1088   Suspicion may be no fault, but showing it may be a great one

                                            Thomas Fuller (1608-1661)

1089   I'll trust him no further than I can fling him.

                                                    John Ray (1627-1705)

1090   There was a castle called Doubting Castle,
        the owner whereof was Giant Despair.

                                            John Bunyan (1628-1688)

1091   If the Sun and Moon should doubt
        They'd immediately Go out.

                                            William Blake (1757-1828)

1092   There is no despair so absolute as that which comes with the
        first moments of our first great sorrow, when we have not
        yet known what it is to have suffered and be healed, to have
        despaired and have recovered hope.

                                            George Eliot (1819-1880)

1093   A pessimist is a man who thinks everybody as nasty as
        himself, and hates them for it.

                                              G. B. Shaw (1856-1950)

1094   Pessimist: One who, when he has the choice of two evils,
        chooses both.

                                          Oscar Wilde (1854-1900)

ENTHUSIASM
Ambition, Initiative and Zeal

1. ESSENCE

1095   Ambition's like a circle on the water,
Which never ceases to enlarge itself,
'Till by broad spreading it disperses to nought.
Shakespeare (1564-1616)

1096   Earnestness is enthusiasm tempered by reason.
Pascal (1623-1662)

1097   The sense of this word among the Greeks affords the noblest
definition of it: enthusiasm signifies God in us.
Germaine De Stael (1766-1817)

1098   Initiative is doing the right thing without being told.
Victor Hugo (1802-1885)

1099   Enthusiasm is the mother of effort...
Emerson (1803-1882)

1100   Enthusiasm...the sustaining power of all great action.
Samuel Smiles (1812-1904)

2. OPPOSITES

1101   Though ambition in itself is a vice,
yet it is often the parent of virtues.
Quintilian (35-90 A.D.)

1102   One often passes from love to ambition,
but one rarely returns from ambition to love.
La Rochefoucauld (1613-1680)

1103   The ambitious deceive themselves when they propose an end
to their ambition; for that end, when attained, becomes a
means.
La Rochefoucauld (1613-1680)

1104   Zeal is fit for wise men, but flourishes chiefly among
fools.
John Tillotson (1630-1694)

1105   I prefer the errors of enthusiasm to the indifference of
wisdom.
Anatole France (1844-1924)

3. INSIGHT

1106   Ambition is so powerful a passion in the human breast
        that however high we reach we are never satisfied.
                                        Machiavelli (1469-1527)

1107   The very substance of the ambitious is merely the shadow
        of a dream.
                                        Shakespeare (1564-1616)

1108   Like dogs in a chain, birds in a cage, or squirrels in a
        wheel, ambitious men still climb and climb, with great
        labor, and incessant anxiety, but never reach the top.
                                        Robert Burton (1576-1640)

1109   Ambition is like love, impatient both of delays and rivals.
                                        John Denham (1615-1668)

1110   Ambition makes the same mistake concerning power
        that avarice makes concerning wealth.
        She begins by accumulating power as a means to happiness,
        and she finishes by continuing to accumulate it as an end.
                                        Colton (1780-1832)

1111   Every production of genius must be the production of
        enthusiasm.
                                        Disraeli (1804-1881)

1112   Ambition is not what man does...
        but what man would do.
                                        Robert Browning (1812-1889)

1113   Experience shows that success is due less to ability
        than to zeal. The winner is he who gives himself to
        his work body and soul.
                                        Charles Buxton (1823-1871)

1114   Perpetual inspiration is as necessary to the life of good-
        ness, holiness and happiness as perpetual respiration is
        necessary to animal life.
                                        Andrew Bonar Law (1858-1923)

4. POSITIVE

1115   He who possesses the source of Enthusiasm
        Will achieve great things.
        Doubt not. You will gather friends around you
        As a hair clasp gathers the hair.
                                        I Ching (B.C. 1150?)

1116   To be ambitious of true honor, of the true glory and
        perfection of our natures, is the very principle and
        incentive of virtue.

                                    Philip Sidney (1554-1586)

1117   Ambition and love are the wings to great deeds.

                                    Goethe (1749-1832)

1118   All noble enthusiasms pass through a feverish stage,
        and grow wiser and more serene.

                                    Channing (1780-1842)

1119   Every great and commanding moment in the annals of the world
        is the triumph of some enthusiasm.

                                    Emerson (1803-1882)

1120   Nothing is so contagious as enthusiasm; it moves stones, it
        charms brutes. Enthusiasm is the genius of sincerity and
        truth accomplishes no victories without it.

                                    Bulwer-Lytton (1803-1873)

1121   It's faith in something and enthusiasm for something that
        makes life worth living.

                                    Oliver Wendell Holmes (1809-1894)

1122   Ambition is the germ from which all growth of nobleness
        proceeds.

                                    Thomas English (1819-1902)

1123   Enthusiasm is the inspiration of everything great.
        Without it no man is to be feared, and with it none
        despised.

                                    Bovee (1820-1904)

1124   Fires can't be made with dead embers, nor can enthusiasm be
        stirred by spiritless men. Enthusiasm in our daily work
        lightens effort and turns even labor into pleasant tasks.

                                    Stanley Baldwin (1867-1947)

5. NEGATIVE

1125   The ambitious will always be first in the crowd; he presseth
        forward, he looketh not behind him. More anguish is it to
        his mind to see one before him, than joy to leave thousands
        at a distance.

                                    Akhenaton? (c. B.C. 1375)

1126   Ambition destroys its possessor.

                                    The Talmud (B.C. 500?-400? A.D.)

1127   It is the constant fault and inseparable evil quality of
       ambition that it never looks behind it.
                                           Seneca (B.C. 3-65 A.D.)

1128   Zeal without knowledge is the sister of folly.
                                           John Davies (1570-1626)

1129   Ambition, a proud covetousness, or a dry thirst of honour,
       a great torture of the mind, composed of envy, pride, and
       covetousness, a gallant madness, one defines it a pleasant
       poison.
                                           Robert Burton (1576-1640)

1130   A slave has but one master; the ambitious man has as many
       masters as there are persons whose aid may contribute to the
       advancement of his fortune.
                                           La Bruyere (1645-1696)

1131   Ambition - A lust that is never quenched,
       grows more inflamed and madder by enjoyment.
                                           Thomas Otway (1652-1685)

1132   Ambition is a vice which often puts men upon doing the
       meanest offices; so climbing is performed in the same
       posture with creeping.
                                           Swift (1667-1745)

1133   There is no greater sign of a general decay of virtue in a
       nation, than a want of zeal in its inhabitants for the
       good of their country.
                                           Addison (1672-1719)

1134   There is no zeal blinder than that which is inspired with a
       love of justice against offenders.
                                           Henry Fielding (1707-1754)

1135   Ambition breaks the ties of blood,
       and forgets the obligations of gratitude.
                                           Walter Scott (1771-1832)

1136   Ambition has but one reward for all:
       A little power, a little transient fame;
       A grave to rest in, and a fading name!
                                           William Winter (1836-1917)

1137   Ambition: An overmastering desire to be vilified by
       enemies while living and made ridiculous by friends when
       dead.
                                           Ambrose Bierce (1842-1914?)

6. ADVICE

1138   Through zeal knowledge is gotten, through lack of zeal
knowledge is lost; let a man who knows this double path of
gain and loss thus place himself that knowledge may grow.
Buddha (B.C. 568-488)

1139   If you wish to reach the highest, begin at the lowest.
Publilius Syrus (fl. B.C. 42)

1140   Fling away ambition; by that sin fell the angels:
how can man then, the image of his Maker, hope to win by it?
Shakespeare (1564-1616)

1141   Be always displeased at what thou art,
if thou desire to attain to what thou art not;
for where thou hast pleased thyself, there thou abidest.
Quarles (1592-1644)

1142   Our ambition should be to rule ourselves, the true kingdom
for each one of us; and true progress is to know more, and
be more, and to do more.
Lubbock (1834-1913)

7. POTPOURRI

1143   Too low they build who build beneath the stars.
Young (1683-1765)

1144   To be happy at home is the ultimate result of all
ambition, the end to which every enterprise and labor
tends, and of which every desire prompts the prosecution.
Johnson (1709-1784)

1145   Ambition is an idol, on whose wings
Great minds are carried only to extreme;
To be sublimely great or to be nothing.
Robert Southey (1774-1843)

1146   Enthusiasm is the leaping lightning, not to be measured by
the horse-power of the understanding.
Emerson (1803-1882)

1147   Zealots have an idol, to which they consecrate themselves
high-priests, and deem it holy work to offer sacrifices
of whatever is most precious.
Nathaniel Hawthorne (1804-1864)

EVIL

Cruelty, Sin, Vice and Wickedness

1. ESSENCE

1148   Evil is simply misplaced force. It can be misplaced in
time, like the violence that is acceptable in war is
unacceptable in peace. It can be misplaced in space, like
a burning coal on the rug rather than the fireplace. Or
it can be misplaced in proportion, like an excess of love
can make us overly sentimental, or a lack of love can make
us cruel and destructive. It is in things such as these
that evil lies, not in a personal Devil who acts as an
Adversary.

Kabbalah (B.C. 1200?-700? A.D.)

1149   All cruelty springs from weakness.

Seneca (B.C. 3-65 A.D.)

1150   Sin is essentially a departure from God.

Martin Luther (1483-1546)

1151   Evil has no substance of its own, but is only the defect,
excess, perversion, or corruption of that which has
substance.

John Henry Newman (1801-1890)

1152   What is evil? - Whatever springs from weakness.

Nietzsche (1844-1900)

2. OPPOSITES

1153   The only good is knowledge and the only evil is ignorance.

Socrates (B.C. 469-399)

1154   They who are ashamed of what they ought not to be,
  and are not ashamed of what they ought to be,
such men, embracing false doctrines, enter the evil path.
They who fear when they ought not to fear,
  and fear not when they ought to fear,
such men, embracing false doctrines, enter the evil path.

The Dhammapada (c. B.C. 300)

1155   Bad men hate sin through fear of punishment;
good men hate sin through their love of virtue.

Juvenal (40-125 A.D.)

1156   To overcome evil with good is good,
to resist evil by evil is evil.

Mohammed (570-632 A.D.)

1157 The evil man is like a pot of clay,
easily breaking, but reunited with difficulty;
whilst a good man is like a jar of gold,
hard to break and quickly to be joined again.

The Hitopadesa (600?-1100? A.D.)

1158 The greatest evils, are from within us; and from ourselves
also we must look for the greatest good.

Jeremy Taylor (1613-1667)

1159 Vice stings us even in our pleasures,
but virtue consoles us even in our pains.

Cowper (1731-1800)

1160 The cruelty of the weak is more dreadful than that of the
strong.

Lavater (1741-1801)

1161 Evil is a form of good, of which the results are not
immediately manifest.

Balzac (1799-1850)

1162 The first lesson of history, is, that evil is good.

Emerson (1803-1882)

1163 Preventives of evil are far better than remedies;
cheaper and easier of application, and surer in result.

Tryon Edwards (1809-1894)

1164 Evil and good are God's right hand and left.

Bailey (1816-1902)

1165 He who does evil that good may come, pays a toll to the
devil to let him into heaven.

Hare & Charles (c. 1830)

1166 Sin may open bright as the morning,
but it will end dark as night.

Thomas Talmage (1832-1902)

1167 Evil exists to glorify the good. Evil is negative good.
It is a relative term. Evil can be transmuted into good.
What is evil to one at one time, becomes good at another
time to somebody else.

Sivananda (born 1887)

3. INSIGHT

1168 To see and listen to the wicked is already the beginning
of wickedness.

Confucius (B.C. 551-479)

1169   Evil events from evil causes spring.

Aristophanes (B.C. 448-380)

1170   There is wickedness in the intention of wickedness,
       even though it be not perpetrated in the art.

Cicero (B.C. 106-43)

1171   There are a thousand forms of evil; there will be a
       thousand remedies.

Ovid (B.C. 43-18 A.D.)

1172   The way to wickedness is always through wickedness.

Seneca (B.C. 3-65 A.D.)

1173   No one ever reached the worst of a vice at one leap.

Juvenal (40-125 A.D.)

1174   Through no amount of effort can a naturally wicked man
       Be turned into an honest one.
       However long you boil water,
       It is impossible to make it burn like fire.

Saskya Pandita (1182-1251)

1175   He that falls into sin is a man;
       that grieves at it may be a saint;
       that boasteth of it is a devil.

Thomas Fuller (1608-1661)

1176   Sin first is pleasing, then it grows easy, then delightful,
       then frequent, then habitual, then confirmed; then the man
       is impenitent, then he is obstinate, then he is resolved
       never to repent, and then he is ruined.

Robert Leighton (1611-1684)

1177   No man is clever enough to know all the evil he does.

La Rochefoucauld (1613-1680)

1178   Wickedness may prosper for awhile, but in the long run,
       he that sets all the knaves at work will pay them.

L'Estrange (1616-1704)

1179   Most of the evils of life arise from man's being unable to
       sit still in a room.

Pascal (1623-1662)

1180   The dread of evil is a much more forcible principle of human
       actions than the prospect of good.

John Locke (1632-1704)

1181   What maintains one vice would bring up two children.

                                          Franklin (1706-1790)

1182   The lives of the best of us are spent in choosing between
      evils.

                                            Junius (1740-1818)

1183   Sin puts on that which tempteth to destruction.
      It has been said that sin is like the bee,
      with honey in its mouth, but a sting in its tail.

                                 Hosea Ballou (1771-1852)

1184   This is the course of every evil deed, that, propagating
      still it brings forth evil.

                         Samuel Coleridge (1772-1834)

1185   If evil is inevitable, how are the wicked accountable?
      Nay, why do we call men wicked at all?
      Evil is inevitable, but is also remediable.

                            Horace Mann (1796-1859)

1186   Moral Evil is Falsehood in actions;
        as Falsehood is Crime in words.
      Injustice is the essence of Falsehood;
        and every false word is an injustice.
      Injustice is the death of the Moral Being,
        as Falsehood is the poison of the Intelligence.

                            Albert Pike (1809-1891)

1187   There are a thousand hacking at the branches of evil
      to one who is striking at the root.

                             Thoreau (1817-1862)

1188   The belief in a supernatural source of evil is not
      necessary; men alone are quite capable of every wickedness.

                         Joseph Conrad (1857-1934)

1189   One may say that evil does not exist for subjective man at
      all, that there exist only different conceptions of good.
      Nobody ever does anything deliberately in the interests of
      evil, for the sake of evil. Everybody acts in the interests
      of good, as he understands it. But everybody understands
      it in a different way. Consequently men drown, slay, and
      kill one another in the interests of good.

                          Gurdjieff (1873-1949)

1190   Evil is unspectacular and always human
      And shares our bed and eats at our own table.

                        W. H. Auden (1907-1973)

1191 Sin is hoping for another life and...eluding the implacable
grandeur of this life.

Albert Camus (1913-1960)

1192 Mankind fears an evil man
But heaven does not.

Chinese Proverb

4. POSITIVE

1193 The best known evil is the most tolerable.

Livy (B.C. 59-17 A.D.)

1194 The sun shines even on the wicked.

Seneca (B.C. 3-65 A.D.)

1195 Much that we call evil is really good in disguises;
and we should not quarrel rashly with adversities not yet
understood, nor overlook the mercies often bound up in them.

Thomas Browne (1605-1682)

1196 The vices enter into the composition of the virtues,
as poisons into that of medicines.
Prudence collects, arranges, and uses them
beneficially against the ills of life.

La Rochefoucauld (1613-1680)

1197 We sometimes learn more from the sight of evil than from
an example of good; and it is well to accustom ourselves
to profit by the evil which is so common, while that which
is good is so rare.

Pascal (1623-1662)

1198 There is this good in real evils, - they deliver us,
while they last, from the petty despotism of all
that were imaginary.

Colton (1780-1832)

1199 The world loves a spice of wickedness.

Longfellow (1807-1882)

1200 It is some compensation for great evils that they enforce
great lessons.

Bovee (1820-1904)

5. NEGATIVE

1201 The fool who does evil to a man who is good, to a man who
is pure and free from sin, the evil returns to him like the
dust thrown against the wind.

The Dhammapada (c. B.C. 300)

1202   Bad conduct soils the finest ornament more than filth.
                                    Plautus (B.C. 254-184)

1203   What has this unfeeling age of ours left untried,
        what wickedness has it shunned?
                                    Horace (B.C. 65-8)

1204   Cruelty is fed, not weakened by tears.
                                    Publilius Syrus (fl. B.C. 42)

1205   Vice is contagious, and there is no trusting the sound and
        the sick together.
                                    Seneca (B.C. 3-65 A.D.)

1206   A few vices are sufficient to darken many virtues.
                                    Plutarch (46-120 A.D.)

1207   Who though he has been born a man
          yet gives himself to evil ways,
        More foolish is he than the fool
          who fills with vomit, urine, dung
        Golden vessels jewel-adorned -
          harder man's birth to gain than these.
                                    Nagarjuna (c. 100-200 A.D.)

1208   Men never do evil so completely and cheerfully as when
        they do it from religious conviction.
                                    Pascal (1623-1662)

1209   The happiness of the wicked passes away like a torrent.
                                    Jean Baptiste Racine (1639-1699)

1210   If you do what you should not,
        you must bear what you would not.
                                    Franklin (1706-1790)

1211   Physical evils destroy themselves, or they destroy us.
                                    Rousseau (1712-1778)

1212   The only thing necessary for the triumph of evil
        is for good men to do nothing.
                                    Burke (1729-1797)

1213   Men scanning the surface count the wicked happy; they see
        not the frightful dreams that crowd a bad man's pillow.
                                    Tupper (1810-1889)

1214   It is almost impossible systematically to constitute a
       natural moral law. Nature has no principles. She furnishes
       us with no reason to believe that human life is to be
       respected. Nature, in her indifference, makes no
       distinction between good and evil.
                                           Anatole France (1844-1924)

6. ADVICE

1215   If a man possesses a repentant spirit his sins will
       disappear, but if he has an unrepentant spirit his
       sins will continue and condemn him for their sake forever.
                                               Buddha (B.C. 568-488)

1216   Keep far way from an evil neighbor, do not associate with
       the wicked, and do not shrug off all thought of calamity.
                                     The Talmud (B.C. 500?-400? A.D.)

1217   The gates of hell are three: lust, wrath and avarice.
       They destroy the Self. Avoid them.
                                       Bhagavad Gita (c. B.C. 400)

1218   Let no man think lightly of evil, saying in his heart,
       it will not come to stay with me. Even by the falling of
       water-drops a water-pot is filled; the fool becomes full
       of evil, even if he gather it little by little.
                                     The Dhammapada (c. B.C. 300)

1219   Every evil in the bud is easily crushed:
       as it grows older, it becomes stronger.
                                           Cicero (B.C. 106-43)

1220   If thou wishest to get rid of thy evil propensities,
       thou must keep far from evil companions.
                                        Seneca (B.C. 3-65 A.D.)

1221   Be not overcome of evil, but overcome evil with good.
                                          Romans (c. 56 A.D.)

1222   O ye men! Eat of the produce of the earth things that are
       lawful and pure, and follow not the footsteps of the
       evil-one; surely, he is an enemy to you clear.
                                           Koran (c. 651 A.D.)

1223   Association with corrupt people is a pain,
       the cure of which is separating yourself from them.
                                     Abu Ali Katib (fl. c. 940)

1224   When better choices are not to be had,
       We needs must take the seeming best of bad.
                                   Samuel Daniel (1562?-1619)

1225   Each year, one vicious habit rooted in time
ought to make the worst man good.

Franklin (1706-1790)

1226   Let no man be sorry he has done good, because others have
done evil! If a man has acted right, he has done well,
though alone; if wrong, the sanction of all mankind will
not justify him.

Henry Fielding (1707-1754)

1227   The doing evil to avoid an evil cannot be good.

Samuel Coleridge (1772-1834)

1228   For every evil under the sun,
There is a remedy, or there is none;
If there be one, try and find it,
If there is none, never mind it.

Hazlitt (1778-1830)

1229   Between two evils, choose neither; between two goods,
choose both.

Tryon Edwards (1809-1894)

1230   The true rule in determining to embrace or reject anything
is not whether it have any evil in it, but whether it have
more of evil than of good. There are few things wholly evil
or wholly good.

Lincoln (1809-1865)

1231   Strive with thy thoughts unclean before they overpower thee.
Use them as they will thee, for if thou sparest them and
they take root and grow, know well, these thoughts will
overpower and kill thee. Beware! Suffer not their shadow
to approach. For it will grow, increase in size and power,
and then this thing of darkness will absorb thy being before
thou hast well realized the black foul monster's presence.

H. P. Blavatsky (1831-1891)

7. POTPOURRI

1232   The butcher relenteth not at the bleating of the lamb;
neither is the heart of the cruel moved with distress. But
the tears of the compassionate are sweeter than dew-drops,
falling from roses on the bosom of spring.

Akhenaton? (c. B.C. 1375)

1233   If Jupiter hurled his thunderbolt as often as men sinned,
he would soon be out of thunderbolts.

Ovid (B.C. 43-18 A.D.)

1234   In whatever manner you fashion a wicked man,
It is impossible to make his nature good.
You may wash charcoal with zeal,
But you will not make it white.

Saskya Pandita (1182-1251)

1235   Capricious, wanton, bold, and brutal lust
Is meanly selfish; when resisted, cruel;
And, like the blast of pestilential winds,
Taints the sweet bloom of nature's fairest forms.

Milton (1608-1674)

1236   When our vices leave us, we flatter ourselves with the
idea that we have left them.

La Rochefoucauld (1613-1680)

1237   Vice is a monster so frightful mien,
As to be hated needs but to be seen;
Yet too oft, familiar with her face,
We first endure, then pity, then embrace.

Pope (1688-1744)

1238   Scarcely anything awakens attention like a tale of cruelty.
The writer of news never fails to tell how the enemy
murdered children and ravished virgins.

Johnson (1709-1784)

1239   I would not enter in my list of friends,
Who needlessly sets foot upon a worm.
An inadvertent step may crush the snail
That crawls at evening in the public path,
But he has the humanity, forewarned,
Will tread aside, and let the reptile live.

Cowper (1731-1800)

1240   Evils in the journey of life are like the hills which alarm
travelers on their road. - Both appear great at a distance,
but when we approach them we find they are far less
insurmountable than we had conceived.

Colton (1780-1832)

1241   There are times when it would seem as if God fished with a
line, and the Devil with a net.

Anne Swetchine (1782-1857)

1242   But, by all thy nature's weakness,
   Hidden faults and follies known,
Be thou, in rebuking evil,
   Conscious of thine own.

John Greenleaf Whittier (1807-1892)

1243   Wild animals never kill for sport. Man is the only one to
       whom the torture and death of his fellow creatures is
       amusing in itself.

                                          Froude (1818-1894)

1244   It is a proof of our natural bias to evil, that
       in all things good, gain is harder and slower than loss;
       but in all things bad or evil, getting is quicker
       and easier than getting rid of them.

                                    Hare & Charles (c. 1830)

1245   Vice is waste of life. Poverty, obedience, and celibacy
       are the canonical vices.

                                      G. B. Shaw (1856-1950)

1246   The very emphasis of the commandment: Thou shalt not kill,
       makes it certain that we are descended from an endlessly
       long chain of generations of murderers, whose love of murder
       was in their blood as it is perhaps also in ours.

                                 Sigmund Freud (1856-1939)

1247   It is a sin to believe evil of others,
       but it is seldom a mistake.

                                 H. L. Mencken (1880-1956)

1248   Virtuous ten years - still not enough.
       Evil one day - too much already.

                                           Chinese Proverb

FAILURE
Defeat and Error

1. ESSENCE

1249   Men do not fail; they give up trying.
Elihu Root (1845-1937)

1250   Failure - The man who can tell others what to do and how to
       do it, but never does it himself.
Elbert Hubbard (1859-1915)

2. OPPOSITES

1251   People in their handlings of affairs often fail when they
          are about to succeed.
       If one remains as careful at the end as he was at the
          beginning, there will be no failure.
Lao-Tzu (fl. B.C. 600)

1252   There are some defeats more triumphant than victories.
Montaigne (1533-1592)

1253   One seldom rushes into a single error. Rushing into the
       first one, one always does too much. Hence one usually
       commits another; and this time does too little.
Nietzsche (1844-1900)

1254   In this world there are only two tragedies. One is not
       getting what one wants, and the other is getting it. The
       last is much the worst; the last is a real tragedy!
Oscar Wilde (1854-1900)

3. INSIGHT

1255   Defeat ensues when others interfere with the authority
       of the chosen leader. Divided command is often fatal.
I Ching (B.C. 1150?)

1256   Few things are impracticable in themselves. It is for want
       of application, rather than of means, that men fail.
La Rochefoucauld (1613-1680)

1257   There are few, very few, that will own themselves in a
       mistake.
Swift (1667-1745)

1258   Failure is more frequently from want of energy than want
       of capital.
Daniel Webster (1782-1852)

1259   He only is exempt from failures who makes no efforts.
                                          Richard Whately (1787-1863)

1260   A failure establishes only this,
        that our determination to succeed was not strong enough.
                                          Bovee (1820-1904)

1261   The only real failure in life
        is not to be true to the best one knows.
                                          Farrar (1831-1903)

1262   Show me a thoroughly satisfied man - and I will show
        you a failure.
                                          Thomas A. Edison (1847-1931)

1263   A lost battle is a battle one thinks one has lost.
                                          Ferdinand Foch (1851-1929)

1264   Experience is the name everyone gives to his mistakes.
                                          Oscar Wilde (1854-1900)

1265   No man is a failure who is enjoying life.
                                          William Feather (born 1888)

1266   If the first words fail...
        Ten thousand will not then avail.
                                          Chinese Proverb

4. POSITIVE

1267   What is defeat? Nothing but education;
        nothing but the first step to something better.
                                          Wendell Phillips (1811-1884)

1268   How far high failure overleaps the bound of low successes.
                                          Lewis Morris (1835-1907)

1269   "All honor to him who shall win the prize,"
          The world has cried for a thousand years;
        But to him who tries and fails and dies,
          I give great honor and glory and tears.
                                          Joaquin Miller (1839-1913)

1270   Sometimes a noble failure serves the world as faithfully
        as a distinguished success.
                                          Edward Dowden (1843-1913)

1271   There is something good in all seeming failures. You are
        not to see that now. Time will reveal it. Be patient.
                                          Sivananda (born 1887)

1272   It is often the failure who is the pioneer of new lands,
       new undertakings, and new forms of expression.
                                        Eric Hoffer (1902-1983)

1273   Good people are good because they've come to wisdom through
       failure.
                                      William Saroyan (1908-1981)

5. NEGATIVE

1274   There are five things which no one is able to accomplish
       in this world:
         first, to cease growing old when he is growing old;
         second, to cease being sick;
         third, to cease dying;
         fourth, to deny dissolution when there is dissolution;
         fifth, to deny non-being.
                                       Buddha (B.C. 568-488)

1275   The only safety for the conquered is to expect no safety.
                                         Vergil (B.C. 70-19)

1276   Misfortunes one can endure - they come from outside, they
       are accidents. But to suffer for one's own faults - Ah!
       there is the sting of life.
                                      Oscar Wilde (1854-1900)

1277   Man is not made for defeat.
                                   Ernest Hemingway (1898-1961)

1278   Victory has a hundred fathers but defeat is an orphan.
                                 Galeazzo Ciano (1903-1944)

6. ADVICE

1279   Help yourself, and Heaven will help you.
                                      La Fontaine (1621-1695)

1280   Defeat should never be a source of discouragement,
       but rather a fresh stimulus.
                                      Robert South (1634-1716)

1281   The surest way not to fail is to determine to succeed.
                                   Richard Sheridan (1751-1816)

1282   Ill-health, of body or of mind, is defeat...Health alone
       is victory. Let all men, if they can manage it, contrive
       to be healthy!
                                        Carlyle (1795-1881)

1283   The greatest mistake you can make in life is to be
continually fearing you will make one.

Elbert Hubbard (1859-1915)

1284   Conquer thyself. Till thou hast done this, thou art
but a slave; for it is almost as well to be subjected
to another's appetite as to thine own.

Richard E. Burton (1861-1940)

1285   Believe and act as if it were impossible to fail.

Charles Kettering (1876-1958)

1286   Do not brood over your past mistakes and failures as this
will only fill your mind with grief, regret and depression.
Do not repeat them in the future.

Sivananda (born 1887)

7. POTPOURRI

1287   Behold prosperity, how sweetly she flattereth thee; how
insensibly she robbeth thee of thy strength and thy
vigour! Though thou has been constant in ill fortune,
though thou has been invincible in distress; yet by her
thou art conquered: not knowing that thy strength returneth
not again; and yet that thou again mayst need it.

Akhenaton? (c. B.C. 1375)

1288   What though the field be lost?
All is not lost; the unconquerable will,
And study of revenge, immortal hate
And courage never to submit or yield,
And what else is not to be overcome.

Milton (1608-1674)

1289   There are few people who are more often in the wrong
than those who cannot endure to be thought so.

La Rochefoucauld (1613-1680)

1290   Not in the clamor of the crowded street,
Not in the shouts and plaudits of the throng,
But in ourselves, are triumph and defeat.

Longfellow (1807-1882)

1291   Greatly begin! Though thou have time
But for a line, be that sublime-
Not failure, but low aim is crime.

James Lowell (1819-1891)

1292   We are the doubles of those whose way
        Was festal with fruits and flowers;
    Body and brain we were sound as they,
        But the prizes were not ours.

Richard E. Burton (1861-1940)

FAME

Glory and Illusion

1. ESSENCE

1293   Fame is the perfume of heroic deeds.

                                              Socrates (B.C. 469-399)

1294   Worldly fame is but a breath of wind that blows now this
       way, and now that, and changes name as it changes direction.

                                               Dante (1265-1321)

1295   Fame is like a river, that beareth up things light and
       swollen, and drowns things weighty and solid.

                                             Bacon (1561-1626)

1296   Fame is the echo of actions, resounding them to the world,
       save that the echo repeats only the last part, but fame
       relates all, and often more than all.

                                        Thomas Fuller (1608-1661)

1297   Fame is the thirst of youth.

                                             Byron (1788-1824)

1298   The dog barks; the Caravan passes.

                                             Arabian Proverb

2. OPPOSITES

1299   Glory, like a shadow, flieth from him who pursueth it; but
       it followeth at the heels of him who would fly from it;
       if thou courtest it without merit, thou shalt never attain
       unto it; if thou deservest it, though thou hidest thyself,
       it will never forsake thee.

                                      Akhenaton? (c. B.C. 1375)

1300   There is no less danger from great fame than from infamy.

                                    Tacitus (55-117 A.D.)

1301   Good fame is like fire; when you have kindled
       you may easily preserve it; but if you extinguish it,
       you will not easily kindle it again.

                                      Bacon (1561-1626)

1302   Death makes no conquest of this conqueror:
       For now he lives in fame, though not in life.

                                  Shakespeare (1564-1616)

1303   Even those who write against fame wish for the fame of
       having written well, and those who read their works desire
       the fame of having read them.
                                        Pascal (1623-1662)

1304   Renown is a source of toil and sorrow;
       obscurity is a source of happiness.
                                        Von Mosheim (1694-1755)

1305   Fame is what you have taken, character is what you give.
       When to this truth you awaken, then you begin to live.
                                        Bayard Taylor (1825-1878)

1306   Fame is an illusive thing - here today, gone tomorrow.
       The fickle, shallow mob raises its heroes to the pinnacle
       of approval today and hurls them into oblivion tomorrow
       at the slightest whim; cheers today, hisses tomorrow;
       utter forgetfulness in a few months.
                                        Henry Miller (1891-1980)

3. INSIGHT

1307   The world, indeed, is like a dream and the treasures of
       the world are an alluring mirage! Like the apparent
       distances in a picture, things have no reality in them-
       selves, but they are like heat haze.
                                        Buddha (B.C. 568-488)

1308   I am not concerned that I am not known,
       I seek to be worthy to be known.
                                        Confucius (B.C. 551-479)

1309   Toil, says the proverb, is the sire of fame.
                                        Euripides (B.C. 480-406)

1310   True glory takes root, and even spreads; all false
       pretences, like flowers, fall to the ground;
       nor can any counterfeit last long.
                                        Cicero (B.C. 106-43)

1311   Glory is like a circle in the water, which never ceaseth to
       enlarge itself, till, by broad spreading, it disperse to
       naught.
                                        Shakespeare (1564-1616)

1312   The glories of our birth and state
       Are shadows, not substantial things.
                                        James Shirley (1596-1666)

1313   Fame is no plant that grows on mortal soil.
                                        Milton (1608-1674)

1314   What is fame? The advantage of being known by people of
        whom you yourself know nothing, and for whom you care as
        little.

                              Leszczynski Stanislaus (1677-1766)

1315   And what is Fame? the Meanest have their Day,
        The Greatest can but blaze, and pass away.

                                              Pope (1688-1744)

1316   Wood burns because it has the proper stuff in it; and a man
        becomes famous because he has the proper stuff in him.

                                           Goethe (1749-1832)

1317   Fame, we may understand is no sure test of merit, but
        only a probability of such: it is an accident, not a
        property of a man.

                                          Carlyle (1795-1881)

1318   Fame comes only when deserved, and then is as inevitable
        as destiny, for it is destiny.

                                       Longfellow (1807-1882)

1319   Men think highly of those who rise rapidly in the world;
        whereas nothing rises quicker than dust, straw, and
        feathers.

                                    Hare & Charles (c. 1830)

1320   Illusion is an element which enters into all finite things,
        for everything that exists has only a relative, not an
        absolute, reality, since the appearance which the hidden
        phenomenon assumes for any observer depends upon his power
        of cognition.

                                    H. P. Blavatsky (1831-1891)

1321   Fame usually comes to those who are thinking about something
        else.

                                Oliver W. Holmes, Jr. (1841-1935)

1322   The day will come when everyone will be famous for fifteen
        minutes.

                                    Andy Warhol (born 1930)

4. POSITIVE

1323   Glory follows virtue as if it were its shadow.

                                         Cicero (B.C. 106-43)

1324   The love of glory gives an immense stimulus.

                                       Ovid (B.C. 43-18 A.D.)

1325   It is pleasing to be pointed at with the finger and to have
       it said, "There goes the man."

                                                    Persius (34-62 A.D.)

1326   Of all the possessions of this life fame is the noblest;
       when the body has sunk into the dust
       the great name still lives.

                                                    Schiller (1759-1805)

1327   Let us not disdain glory too much; nothing is finer, except
       virtue. - The height of happiness would be to unite both in
       this life.

                                                Chateaubriand (1768-1848)

1328   Fame, they tell you, is air; but without air there is no
       life for any; without fame there is none for the best.

                                                    Landor (1775-1864)

1329   Fame is the inheritance not of the dead, but of the living.
       It is we who look back with lofty pride to the great names
       of antiquity.

                                                    Hazlitt (1778-1830)

1330   Though fame is smoke, its fumes are frankincense to human
       thoughts.

                                                    Byron (1788-1824)

1331   Fame is that which is known to exist by the echo of its
       footsteps through congenial minds.

                                                Anna Jameson (1794-1860)

1332   Fame lulls the fever of the soul, and makes
       Us feel that we have grasp'd an immortality.

                                            Joaquin Miller (1839-1913)

5. NEGATIVE

1333   Glory drags all men along, low as well as high,
       bound captive at the wheels of her glittering car.

                                                    Horace (B.C. 65-8)

1334   It is a wretched thing to live on the fame of others.

                                                    Juvenal (40-125 A.D.)

1335   I do not like the man who squanders life for fame;
       give me the man who living makes a name.

                                                    Martial (43-104 A.D.)

1336   The love of fame is the last weakness which even the wise
       resign.
                                            Tacitus (55-117 A.D.)

1337   And what after all is everlasting fame? All together vanity
                                    Marcus Aurelius (121-180 A.D.)

1338   All fame is dangerous: Good, bringeth Envy; Bad, Shame.
                                    Thomas Fuller (1608-1661)

1339   Men's fame is like their hair, which grows after they are
       dead, and with just as little use to them.
                                    George Villiers (1628-1687)

1340   Fame has also this great drawback, that if we pursue it,
       we must direct our lives so as to please the fancy of men.
                                    Spinoza (1632-1677)

1341   There is not in the world so toilsome a trade as the
       pursuit of fame; life concludes before you have so much
       as sketched your work.
                                    La Bruyere (1645-1696)

1342   What's fame? a fancy'd life in other's breath.
       A thing beyond us, even before our death.
                                            Pope (1688-1744)

1343   What a heavy burden is a name that has become too famous.
                                    Voltaire (1694-1778)

1344   Fame is but the breath of people,
       and that often unwholesome.
                                            Rousseau (1712-1778)

1345   The paths of glory lead but to the grave.
                                    Thomas Gray (1716-1771)

1346   Glory, built on selfish principles, is shame and guilt.
                                            Cowper (1731-1800)

1347   Celebrity is the chastisement of merit
       and the punishment of talent.
                                            Chamfort (1741-1794)

1348   How men long for celebrity! Some would willingly sacrifice
       their lives for fame, and not a few would rather be known
       by their crimes than not known at all.
                                    John Sinclair (1754-1835)

1349 Fame and power are the objects of all men. Even their
partial fruition is gained by very few; and that, too,
at the expense of social pleasure, health, conscience, life.
Disraeli (1804-1881)

1350 Fame is not just. She never finely or discriminatingly
praises, but coarsely hurrahs.
Thoreau (1817-1862)

1351 Even the best things are not equal to their fame.
Thoreau (1817-1862)

1352 Fame - a few words upon a tombstone, and the truth of those
not to be depended on.
Bovee (1820-1904)

1353 A celebrity is one who is known to many persons he is
glad he doesn't know.
H. L. Mencken (1880-1956)

1354 Fame is the penalty of success.
Jealousy is the penalty of fame.
Sivananda (born 1887)

6. ADVICE

1355 True glory consists in doing what deserves to be written;
in writing what deserves to be read; and in so living as to
make the world happier and better for our living in it.
Pliny the Elder (23-79 A.D.)

1356 All the fame you should look for in life
is to have lived it quietly.
Montaigne (1533-1592)

1357 The fame of great men ought always to be estimated by the
means used to acquire it.
La Rochefoucauld (1613-1680)

1358 Avoid popularity; it has many snares, and no real benefit.
William Penn (1614-1718)

1359 Of present fame think little, and of future less; the
praises that we receive after we are buried, like the
flowers that are strewed over our grave, may be gratifying
to the living, but they are nothing to the dead...
Colton (1780-1832)

1360 He who would acquire fame must not show himself afraid of
censure. The dread of censure is the death of genius.
William Simms (1806-1870)

1361 The veil of illusion cannot be lifted by a mere decision
of reason, but demands the most thoroughgoing and persevering preparation consisting in the full payment of all debts
to life.

C. G. Jung (1875-1961)

7. POTPOURRI

1362 The life, which others pay, let us bestow,
And give to fame what we to nature owe.

Homer (c. B.C. 700)

1363 She (Fame) walks on the earth, and her head is concealed in
the clouds.

Vergil (B.C. 70-19)

1364 All your renown is like the summer flower that blooms and
dies; because the sunny glow which brings it forth, soon
slays with parching power.

Dante (1265-1321)

1365 There have been as great souls unknown to fame as any of
the most famous.

Franklin (1706-1790)

1366 He that pursues fame with just claims, trusts his happiness
to the winds; but he that endeavors after it by false merit,
has to fear, not only the violence of the storm, but the
leaks of his vessel.

Johnson (1709-1784)

1367 O Fame! if I e'er took delight in thy praises,
'Twas less for the sake of thy high-sounding phrases,
Than to see the bright eyes of the dear one discover
The thought that I was not unworthy to love her.

Byron (1788-1824)

1368 Thou hast a charmed cup, O Fame!
  A draught that mantles high,
And seems to lift this earthly frame
  Above mortality.
Away! to me -a woman- bring
Sweet water from affection's spring.

Felicia Hemans (1794-1835)

1369 Fame is a vapor, popularity an accident, riches take wings,
those who cheer today will curse tomorrow, only one thing
endures - character.

Horace Greeley (1811-1872)

1370   Lives of great men all remind us
            We can make our lives sublime,
        And, departing, leave behind us
            Footprints on the sands of time.

                                        Longfellow (1807-1882)

1371   Fame is a bee
        It has a song-
        It has a sting-
        Ah, too, it has a wing.

                                    Emily Dickinson (1830-1886)

1372   Don't part with your illusions. When they are gone you
        may still exist, but you have ceased to live.
                                        Mark Twain (1835-1910)

1373   It is dangerous to let the public behind the scenes. They
        are easily disillusioned and then they are angry with you,
        for it was the illusion they loved.
                                    Somerset Maugham (1874-1965)

1374   Riches: A dream in the night...
        Fame: A gull floating on water.
                                        Chinese Proverb

FAMILY

Ancestry, Children, Fathers, Motherhood and Parents

1. ESSENCE

1375   The family is the nucleus of civilization.

                        Will Durant (1885-1981)

2. OPPOSITES

1376   A family is a place where minds come in contact with one
another. If these minds love one another the home will be
as beautiful as a flower garden. But if these minds get
out of harmony with one another it is like a storm that
plays havoc with the garden.

                        Buddha (B.C. 568-488)

1377   If we could trace our descendants, we should find all slaves
to come from princes, and all princes from slaves.

                        Seneca (B.C. 3-65 A.D.)

1378   Children sweeten labors; but they make misfortunes more
bitter.

                        Bacon (1561-1626)

1379   Children wish fathers looked but with their eyes;
fathers that children with their judgment looked;
and either may be wrong.

                        Shakespeare (1564-1616)

1380   The child is father of the man.

                        Wordsworth (1770-1850)

1381   Every man is his own ancestor, and every man is his
own heir. He devises his own future, and he inherits
his own past.

                        Frederick Henry Hedge (1805-1890)

1382   Many children, many cares; no children, no felicity.
                        Bovee (1820-1904)

1383   All happy families resemble one another;
every unhappy family is unhappy in its own way.
                        Leo Tolstoy (1828-1910)

1384   When a father gives to his son, both laugh;
when a son gives to his father, both cry.

                        Jewish Proverb

3. INSIGHT

1385 It is of no consequence of what parents a man is born,
      so he be a man of merit.
                                        Horace (B.C. 65-8)

1386 Some men by ancestry are only the shadow of a mighty name.
                                        Lucan (39-65 A.D.)

1387 It is a wise father that knows his own child.
                                        Shakespeare (1564-1616)

1388 Those who depend on the merits of their ancestors may be
      said to search in the roots of the tree for those fruits
      which the branches ought to produce.
                                        Isaac Barrow (1630-1677)

1389 There must always be a struggle between a father and son,
      while one aims at power and the other at independence.
                                        Johnson (1709-1784)

1390 The future destiny of the child is always the work of the
      mother.
                                        Napoleon (1769-1821)

1391 There are fathers who do not love their children;
      there is no grandfather who does not adore his grandson.
                                        Victor Hugo (1802-1885)

1392 Men are what their mothers made them.
                                        Emerson (1803-1882)

1393 Mother is the name for God in the lips and hearts of
      children.
                                        Thackeray (1811-1863)

1394 There is no friendship, no love, like that of the parent
      for the child.
                                        Beecher (1813-1878)

1395 Where does the family start? It starts with a young man
      falling in love with a girl - no superior alternative has
      yet been found.
                                        Winston Churchill (1874-1965)

1396 The family you come from isn't as important as the family
      you're going to have.
                                        Ring Lardner (1885-1933)

4. POSITIVE

1397　What gift has Providence bestowed on man that is so dear
　　　　to him as his children?

　　　　　　　　　　　　　　　　　　Cicero (B.C. 106-43)

1398　Who is not attracted by bright and pleasant children,
　　　　to prattle, to creep, and to play with them?

　　　　　　　　　　　　　　　　Epictetus (50-138 A.D.)

1399　Children are poor men's riches.

　　　　　　　　　　　　　　　　John Ray (1627-1705)

1400　The happiest moments of my life have been the few which I
　　　　have passed at home in the bosom of my family.

　　　　　　　　　　　　　　Thomas Jefferson (1743-1826)

1401　In the family where the father rules secure, there dwells
　　　　the peace which thou wilt in vain seek for elsewhere in
　　　　the wide world outside.

　　　　　　　　　　　　　　　　　　Goethe (1749-1832)

1402　To make a happy fire-side clime
　　　　　　To weans and wife,
　　　　That's the true pathos and sublime
　　　　　　Of human life.

　　　　　　　　　　　　　　　Robert Burns (1759-1796)

1403　Where children are, there is the golden age.

　　　　　　　　　　　　　　　　Novalis (1772-1801)

1404　Call not that man wretched, who whatever ills he suffers,
　　　　has a child to love.

　　　　　　　　　　　　　　Robert Southey (1774-1843)

1405　A father may turn his back on his child, brothers and
　　　　sisters may become inveterate enemies, husbands may desert
　　　　their wives, wives their husbands. But a mother's love
　　　　endures through all.

　　　　　　　　　　　　　Washington Irving (1783-1859)

1406　Nor need we power or splendour,
　　　　　Wide hall or lordly dome;
　　　　The good, the true, the tender-
　　　　　These form the wealth of home.

　　　　　　　　　　　　　　　Sarah J. Hale (1788-1879)

1407　A happy family is but an earlier heaven.

　　　　　　　　　　　　　　John Bowring (1792-1872)

1408　Children are living jewels dropped unsustained from heaven.
　　　　　　　　　　　　　　Robert Pollok (1798-1827)

1409   Nature's loving proxy, the watchful mother.
                                   Bulwer-Lytton (1803-1873)

1410   Children are the keys of paradise.
                                   Richard Stoddard (1825-1903)

1411   A child is a beam of sunlight from the Infinite and Eternal,
       with possibilities of virtue and vice- but as yet unstained.
                                   Lyman Abbott (1835-1922)

1412   For unflagging interest and enjoyment, a household of
       children, if things go reasonably well, certainly all
       other forms of success and achievement lose their
       importance by comparison.
                                   Theodore Roosevelt (1858-1919)

5. NEGATIVE

1413   Few sons attain the praise
       Of their great sires and most their sires disgrace.
                                   Homer (c. B.C. 700)

1414   He who boasts of his descent, praises the deeds of another.
                                   Seneca (B.C. 3-65 A.D.)

1415   When your eyes are fixed in the stare of unconsciousness,
       And your throat coughs the last gasping breath -
       As one dragged in the dark to a great precipice -
       What assistance are a wife and child?
                                   Nagarjuna (c. 100-200 A.D.)

1416   He that hath a wife and children hath given hostages to
       fortune; for they are impediments to great enterprises,
       either of virtue or mischief.
                                   Bacon (1561-1626)

1417   Some people seem compelled by unkind fate to parental
       servitude for life. There is no form of penal servitude
       worse than this.
                                   Samuel Butler (1612-1680)

1418   Parents wonder why the streams are bitter, when they
       themselves have poisoned the fountain.
                                   John Locke (1632-1704)

1419   It is only shallow-minded pretenders who either make
       distinguished origin a matter of personal merit,
       or obscure origin a matter of personal reproach.
                                   Daniel Webster (1782-1852)

1420   Pride of origin, whether high or low, springs from the same
        principle in human nature; one is but the positive, the
        other the negative, pole of a single weakness.
                                            James Lowell (1819-1891)

1421   Relations are simply a tedious pack of people who haven't
        got the remotest knowledge of how to live, nor the smallest
        instinct about when to die.
                                            Oscar Wilde (1854-1900)

1422   The first half of our lives is ruined by our parents and the
        second half by our children.
                                            Clarence Darrow (1857-1938)

1423   I have certainly known more men destroyed by the desire to
        have a wife and child and to keep them in comfort than I
        have seen destroyed by drink and harlots.
                                            Yeats (1865-1939)

6. ADVICE

1424   A proper balance must be struck between indulgence and
        severity. However, severity, despite occasional mistakes,
        is preferable to a lack of discipline.
                                            I Ching (B.C. 1150?)

1425   Train up a child in the way he should go and when he is old,
        he will not depart from it.
                                            Wisdom of Solomon (c. B.C. 200)

1426   It is fortunate to come of distinguished ancestry. - It is
        not less so to be such that people do not care to inquire
        whether you are of high descent or not.
                                            La Bruyere (1645-1696)

1427   Children have more need of models than of critics.
                                            Joubert (1754-1824)

1428   It is better to be the builder of our own name than to be
        indebted by descent for the proudest gifts known to the
        books of heraldry.
                                            Hosea Ballou (1771-1852)

1429   To bring up a child in the way he should go, travel that way
        yourself once in a while.
                                            Josh Billings (1815-1885)

1430   A torn jacket is soon mended;
        but hard words bruise the heart of a child.
                                            Longfellow (1807-1882)

1431   Do not confine your children to your own learning,
        for they were born in another time.

                                                        Chinese Proverb

7. POTPOURRI

1432   The voice of parents is the voice of gods, for to their
        children they are heaven's lieutenants.

                                                        Shakespeare (1564-1616)

1433   The man who has nothing to boast of but his illustrious
        ancestry is like a potato, - the only good belonging to him
        is underground.

                                                        Thomas Overbury (1581-1613)

1434   Behold the child, by nature's kindly law,
        pleased with a rattle, tickled with a straw.

                                                        Pope (1688-1744)

1435   Who ran to help me when I fell,
        And would some pretty story tell,
        Or kiss the place to make it well?
        My Mother.

                                                        Anne Taylor (1782-1866)

1436   Youth fades; love droops; the leaves of friendship fall;
        a mother's secret hope outlives them all!
                                                        Oliver Wendell Holmes (1809-1894)

1437   When I was a boy of fourteen, my father was so ignorant
        I could hardly stand to have the old man around.
        But when I got to be twenty-one,
        I was astonished at how much he had learned in seven years.
                                                        Mark Twain (1835-1910)

1438   The bravest battle that ever was fought;
            Shall I tell you where and when?
        On the maps of the world you will find it not;
            It was fought by the mothers of men.
                                                        Joaquin Miller (1839-1913)

1439   If you cannot get rid of the family skeleton,
        you may as well make it dance.

                                                        G. B. Shaw (1856-1950)

1440   Children begin by loving their parents.
        After a time they judge them.
        Rarely, if ever, do they forgive them.

                                                        Oscar Wilde (1854-1900)

1441   If I were hanged on the highest hill,
        Mother o' mine, O mother o' mine!
        I know whose love would follow me still,
        Mother o' mine, O mother o' mine!

Kipling (1865-1936)

1442   Children aren't happy with nothing to ignore,
        And that's what parents were created for.

Ogden Nash (1902-1971)

1443   God could not be everywhere, and therefore he made mothers.

Jewish Proverb

1444   An ounce of mother is worth a pound of clergy.

Spanish Proverb

FATE

Chance, Destiny, Fortune and Luck

1. ESSENCE

1445 The wheel of fortune turns round incessantly, and who can
say to himself, "I shall to-day be uppermost."
Confucius (B.C. 551-479)

1446 Fate is the endless chain of causation, whereby things are;
the reason or formula by which the world goes on.
Zeno (B.C. 335?-264)

1447 It is fortune, not wisdom, that rules man's life.
Cicero (B.C. 106-43)

1448 Fortune is a shadow upon a wall.
Geoffrey Chaucer (1340-1400)

1449 It is not in the stars to hold our destiny but in ourselves;
we are underlings.
Shakespeare (1564-1616)

1450 Fate is nothing but the deeds committed in a prior state of
existence.
Emerson (1803-1882)

1451 The wheel goes round and round,
And some are up and some are on the down,
And still the wheel goes round.
Josephine Pollard (1843-1892)

1452 Luck is tenacity of purpose.
Elbert Hubbard (1859-1915)

1453 Throw a lucky man into the sea,
and he will come up with a fish in his mouth.
Arabian Proverb

2. OPPOSITES

1454 A man's felicity consists not in the outward and visible
blessing of fortune, but in the inward and unseen
perfections and riches of the mind.
Anacharsis (fl. B.C. 600)

1455   Birth goes with death. Fortune goes with misfortune.
        Bad things follow good things. Men should realize these.
        Foolish people dread misfortune and strive after good
        fortune, but those who seek Enlightenment must transcend
        both of them and be free of the worldly attachments.
                                              Buddha (B.C. 568-488)

1456   Fortune is never permanently...adverse or favorable;
        one sees her veering from one mood to the other.
                                              Herod I (B.C. 73-4)

1457   The fates lead the willing, and drag the unwilling.
                                              Seneca (B.C. 3-65 A.D.)

1458   Fortune gives too much to many, enough to none.
                                              Martial (43-104 A.D.)

1459   That which is not allotted - the hand cannot reach,
        and what is allotted - will find you wherever you may be.
                                              Saadi (1184-1291)

1460   Ill Fortune never crushed that man whom good Fortune
        deceived not.
                                              Bacon (1561-1626)

1461   The less we deserve good fortune, the more we hope for it.
                                              Moliere (1622-1673)

1462   The power of fortune is confessed only by the miserable,
        for the happy impute all their success to prudence or merit.
                                              Swift (1667-1745)

1463   Every night and every morn
        Some to misery are born;
        Every morn and every night
        Some are born to sweet delight.
                                              William Blake (1757-1828)

1464   It sounds like stories from the land of spirits,
        If any man obtain that which he merits,
        Or any merit that which he obtains.
                                              Samuel Coleridge (1772-1834)

1465   Destiny has two ways of crushing us -
        by refusing our wishes and by fulfilling them.
                                              Henri Frederic Amiel (1821-1881)

3. INSIGHT

1466   It is wrong to think that misfortunes come from the east
or from the west; they originate within one's own mind.
Therefore, it is foolish to guard against misfortunes from
the external world and leave the inner mind uncontrolled.

Buddha (B.C. 568-488)

1467   No man has perpetual good fortune.

Plautus (B.C. 254-184)

1468   Men are seldom blessed with good fortune and good sense
at the same time.

Livy (B.C. 59-17 A.D.)

1469   Fortune is brittle as glass, and when she is most refulgent,
she is often most unexpectedly broken.

Publilius Syrus (fl. B.C. 42)

1470   A lucky man is rarer than a white crow.

Juvenal (40-125 A.D.)

1471   This body, full of faults,
Has yet one great quality:
Whatever it encounters in this temporal life
Depends upon one's actions.

Nagarjuna (c. 100-200 A.D.)

1472   Everything that exists is in a manner the seed of that which
will be.

Marcus Aurelius (121-180 A.D.)

1473   The Moving Finger writes; and having writ,
Moves on; nor all your Piety nor Wit
Shall lure it back to cancel half a Line,
Nor all your Tears wash out a Word of it.

Omar Khayyam (fl. 1100)

1474   He who owes least to fortune is in the strongest position.

Machiavelli (1469-1527)

1475   Fortune is a woman, and therefore friendly to the young,
who with audacity command her.

Machiavelli (1469-1527)

1476   Fortune is like the market, where, many times,
if you can stay a little, the price will fall.

Bacon (1561-1626)

1477   Men at some time are masters of their fates.

Shakespeare (1564-1616)

1478   Every one is the architect of his own fortune.
Mathurin Regnier (1573-1613)

1479   Heaven from all creatures hides the book of fate.
Pope (1688-1744)

1480   He that waits upon Fortune, is never sure of a Dinner.
Franklin (1706-1790)

1481   Human life is more governed by fortune than by reason.
David Hume (1711-1776)

1482   Fortune is ever seen accompanying industry.
Goldsmith (1728-1774)

1483   Man supposes that he directs his life and governs his
actions, when his existence is irretrievably under the
control of destiny.
Goethe (1749-1832)

1484   There is no such thing as chance; and what seem to us
merest accident springs from the deepest source of destiny.
Schiller (1759-1805)

1485   Shallow men believe in luck,
wise and strong men in cause and effect.
Emerson (1803-1882)

1486   Chance happens to all, but to turn chance to account is
the gift of few.
Bulwer-Lytton (1803-1873)

4. POSITIVE

1487   Fortune truly helps those who are of good judgment.
Euripides (B.C. 480-406)

1488   Happy the man who can endure the highest
and the lowest fortune.
He, who has endured such vicissitudes with equanimity,
has deprived misfortune of its power.
Seneca (B.C. 3-65 A.D.)

1489   Whatever the universal nature assigns to any man at any time
is for the good of that man at that time.
Marcus Aurelius (121-180 A.D.)

1490 The way of fortune is like the milkyway in the sky; which
is a number of small stars, not seen asunder, but giving
light together: so it is a number of little and scarce
discerned virtues, or rather faculties and customs, that
make men fortunate.

Bacon (1561-1626)

1491 Chance corrects us of many faults that reason would not know
how to correct.

La Rochefoucauld (1613-1680)

1492 To be thrown upon one's own resources is to be cast into the
very lap of fortune: for our faculties then undergo a
development and display an energy of which they were
previously unsusceptible.

Franklin (1706-1790)

1493 The best fortune that can fall to a man is that which
corrects his defects and makes up for his failings.

Goethe (1749-1832)

5. NEGATIVE

1494 Toil is the lot of all, and bitter woe
The fate of many.

Homer (c. B.C. 700)

1495 Fortune is not on the side of the faint-hearted.

Sophocles (B.C. 495-406)

1496 A strict belief in fate is the worst of slavery,
imposing upon our necks an everlasting lord and tyrant,
whom we are to stand in awe of night and day.

Epicurus (B.C. 341-270)

1497 When fortune favors a man too much, she makes him a fool.

Publilius Syrus (fl. B.C. 42)

1498 Whatever fortune has raised to a height,
she has raised only to cast it down.

Seneca (B.C. 3-65 A.D.)

1499 They are raised on high that they may be dashed to
pieces with a greater fall.

Claudianus (365?-408? A.D.)

1500 Although men flatter themselves with their great actions,
they are not so often the result of a great design as of
chance.

La Rochefoucauld (1613-1680)

1501   Chance is a word void of sense;
        nothing can exist without a cause.

                                      Voltaire (1694-1778)

1502   Fortune! There is no fortune; all is trial, or punishment,
        or recompense, or foresight.

                                      Voltaire (1694-1778)

1503   We do not know what is really good or bad fortune.

                                  Rousseau (1712-1778)

1504   Man, be he who he may, experiences a last piece of
        good fortune and a last day.

                                  Goethe (1749-1832)

1505   Destiny - A tyrant's authority for crime and a fool's
        excuse for failure.

                          Ambrose Bierce (1842-1914?)

1506   Diseases are often cured
        Never fate.

                                    Chinese Proverb

6. ADVICE

1507   See that prosperity elate not thine heart above measure;
        neither depress thy mind unto the depths, because fortune
        beareth hard against thee. Her smiles are not stable,
        therefore build not thy confidence upon them; her frowns
        endureth not forever, therefore let hope teach thee patience

                          Akhenaton? (c. B.C. 1375)

1508   Great progress and success can be realized. But spring
        does not last forever, and the favorable trend will reverse
        itself in due time. The wise man foresees evil and handles
        its threat accordingly.

                          I Ching (B.C. 1150?)

1509   People naturally fear misfortune and long for good fortune,
        but if the distinction is carefully studied, misfortune
        often turns out to be good fortune and good fortune to be
        misfortune. The wise man learns to meet the changing
        circumstances of life with an equitable spirit, being
        neither elated by success nor depressed by failure.

                          Buddha (B.C. 568-488)

1510   Chance never helps those who do not help themselves.

                          Sophocles (B.C. 495-406)

1511 Persevere: It is fitting, for a better fate
      awaits the afflicted.
                                    Vergil (B.C. 70-19)

1512 If matters go badly now, they will not always be so.
                                    Horace (B.C. 65-8)

1513 Chance is always powerful. - Let your hook be always cast;
      in the pool where you least expect it, there will be a fish.
                                    Ovid (B.C. 43-18 A.D.)

1514 Depend not on fortune, but on conduct.
                                    Publilius Syrus (fl. B.C. 42)

1515 We are sure to get the better of fortune if we do
      but grapple with her.
                                    Seneca (B.C. 3-65 A.D.)

1516 If fortune favors you do not be elated;
      if she frowns do not despond.
                                    Ausonius (310-395 A.D.)

1517 'Tis writ on Paradise's gate
      "Woe to the dupe that yields to Fate!"
                                    Hafiz (1325?-1390?)

1518 If a man look sharply and attentively,
      he shall see Fortune: for though she be blind,
      yet she is not invisible.
                                    Bacon (1561-1626)

1519 What fates impose, that men must needs abide;
      It boots not to resist both wind and tide.
                                    Shakespeare (1564-1616)

1520 There is tide in the affairs of men, which, taken at the
      flood, leads on to fortune; omitted, all the voyage of
      their life is bound in shallows and in miseries; on such a
      full sea we are now afloat; and we must take the current
      when it serves, or lose our ventures.
                                    Shakespeare (1564-1616)

1521 Whether in favor or in humiliation, be not dismayed. Let
      your eyes leisurely look at the flowers blooming and
      falling in your courtyard. Whether you leave or retain
      your position, take no care. Let your mind wander with
      the clouds folding and unfolding beyond the horizon.
                                    Hung Tzu-ch'eng (1593-1665)

1522   We should manage our fortune as we do our health - enjoy it
        when good, be patient when it is bad, and never apply
        violent remedies except in an extreme necessity.
                                    La Rochefoucauld (1613-1680)

1523   It is a madness to make Fortune the mistress of events,
        because in herself she is nothing, but is ruled by Prudence.
                                    Dryden (1631-1700)

1524   Industry, perseverance, and frugality make fortune yield.
                                    Franklin (1706-1790)

1525   Chance generally favors the prudent.
                                    Joubert (1754-1824)

1526   Intellect annuls fate. So far as a man thinks, he is free.
                                    Emerson (1803-1882)

7. POTPOURRI

1527   No living man can send me to the shades
        Before my time; no man of woman born,
        Coward or brave, can shun his destiny.
                                    Homer (c. B.C. 700)

1528   Death and life have their determined appointments;
        riches and honors depend upon heaven.
                                    Confucius (B.C. 551-479)

1529   Wherever the fates lead us let us follow.
                                    Vergil (B.C. 70-19)

1530   The lofty pine is oftenest shaken by the winds;
          High towers fall with a heavier crash;
        And the lightning strikes the highest mountain.
                                    Horace (B.C. 65-8)

1531   Two fates still hold us fast,
        A future and a past;
        Two vessels' vast embrace
        Surrounds us - Time and Space.
                                    Ma'Arri (973-1057 A.D.)

1532   The bad fortune of the good
          turns their faces up to heaven;
        the good fortune of the bad
          bows their heads down to the earth.
                                    Saadi (1184-1291)

1533   Fortune, the great commandress of the world,
        Hath divers ways to advance her followers:
        To some she gives honor without deserving;
        To other some, deserving without honor;
        Some wit, some wealth, - and some, wit without wealth;
        Some wealth without wit; some nor wit nor wealth.
                           George Chapman (1557-1634)

1534   Will Fortune never come with both hands full,
        But write her fair words still in foulest letters?
        She either gives a stomach, and no food;
        Such are the poor, in health: or else a feast,
        And takes away the stomach; such are the rich,
        That have abundance, and enjoy it not.
                           Shakespeare (1564-1616)

1535   'Tis Fate that flings the dice,
        And as she flings
        Of kings makes peasants,
        And of peasants kings.
                           Dryden (1631-1700)

1536   But blind to former as to future fate,
        What mortal knows his pre-existent state?
                           Pope (1688-1744)

1537   Fate steals along with silent tread,
        Found oftenest in what least we dread;
        Frowns in the storm with angry brow,
        But in the sunshine strikes the blow.
                         Cowper (1731-1800)

1538   All are architects of Fate,
        Working in these walls of Time;
        Some with massive deeds and great,
        Some with ornaments of rhyme.
                         Longfellow (1807-1882)

1539   The wheel of the Good Law moves swiftly on. It grinds by
        night and day. The worthless husks it drives from out
        the golden grain, the refuse from the flour. The hand of
        fate guides the wheel; the revolutions mark the beatings
        of the heart of manifestation
                         H. P. Blavatsky (1831-1891)

1540   Fortune knocks at every man's door once in a life, but
        in a good many cases the man is in a neighboring saloon
        and does not hear her.
                         Mark Twain (1835-1910)

1541   I do not know beneath what sky
      Nor on what seas shall be thy fate;
   I only know it shall be high,
      I only know it shall be great.

Richard Hovey (1869-1900)

1542   He either fears his fate too much,
      Or his deserts are small,
   That dares not put it to the touch
      To gain or lose it all.

Donald Marquis (1878-1937)

FEAR

Anxiety, Dread, Horror, Panic, Terror and Worry

1. ESSENCE

1543 Fear makes men believe the worst.
Curtius-Rufus (fl. 100 A.D.)

1544 Worry, the interest paid by those who borrow trouble.
George Washington (1732-1799)

1545 What are fears but voices airy?
Whispering harm where harm is not.
And deluding the unwary
Til the fatal bolt is shot!
Wordsworth (1770-1850)

1546 Fear always springs from ignorance.
Emerson (1803-1882)

1547 A panic is sudden desertion of us, and a going over to the
enemy of our imagination.
Bovee (1820-1904)

2. OPPOSITES

1548 Favour and disgrace are like fear.
Favour is in a higher place, and disgrace in a lower place.
When you win them you are like being in fear,
and when you lose them you are also like being in fear.
So favour and disgrace are like fear.
Lao-Tzu (fl. B.C. 600)

1549 Valor grows by daring, fear by holding back.
Publilius Syrus (fl. B.C. 42)

1550 Fearfulness, contrary to all other vices, maketh a man think
the better of another, the worse of himself.
Philip Sidney (1554-1586)

1551 To fear the foe, since fear oppresseth strength,
Gives in your weakness strength unto your foe.
Shakespeare (1564-1616)

1552 He that fears you present, will hate you absent.
Thomas Fuller (1608-1661)

1553 From a distance it is something; and nearby it is nothing.
La Fontaine (1621-1695)

1554 The man who fears nothing is not less powerful
than he who is feared by every one.

Schiller (1759-1805)

3. INSIGHT

1555 Nothing in the affairs of men is worthy of great anxiety.

Plato (B.C. 427?-347?)

1556 No one loves the man whom he fears.

Aristotle (B.C. 384-322)

1557 We fear things in proportion to our ignorance of them.

Livy (B.C. 59-17 A.D.)

1558 Everyone wishes that the man whom he fears would perish.

Ovid (B.C. 43-18 A.D.)

1559 For it is not death or hardship that is a fearful thing,
but the fear of death and hardship.

Epictetus (50-138 A.D.)

1560 Even the bravest men are frightened by sudden terrors.

Tacitus (55-117 A.D.)

1561 Where fear is present, wisdom cannot be.

Lactantius (260-340 A.D.)

1562 Present fears are less than horrible imaginings.

Shakespeare (1564-1616)

1563 We often pretend to fear what we really despise,
and more often despise what we really fear.

Colton (1780-1832)

1564 There is great beauty in going through life without anxiety
or fear. Half our fears are baseless, and the other half
discreditable.

Bovee (1820-1904)

1565 We often hear of people breaking down from overwork,
but in nine out of ten they are really suffering from
worry or anxiety.

Lubbock (1834-1913)

1566 Fear is the mother of morality.

Nietzsche (1844-1900)

1567   Our instinctive emotions are those that we have inherited
        from a much more dangerous world, and contain, therefore,
        a larger portion of fear than they should.
                                            Bertrand Russell (1872-1970)

1568   The only thing we have to fear is fear itself.
                                            Franklin D. Roosevelt (1882-1945)

1569   I have never yet met a healthy person who worried very
        much about his health, or a really good person who worried
        much about his own soul.
                                            Haldane (1892-1964)

1570   Fear comes from uncertainty. When we are absolutely
        certain, whether of our worth or worthlessness, we are
        almost impervious to fear. Thus a feeling of utter
        unworthiness can be a source of courage.
                                            Eric Hoffer (1902-1983)

4. POSITIVE

1571   Just as courage imperils life, fear protects it.
                                            Leonardo Da Vinci (1452-1519)

1572   Fear is implanted in us as a preservative from evil;
        but its duty, like that of other passions,
        is not to overbear reason, but to assist it.
        It should not be suffered to tyrannize
        in the imagination, to raise phantoms of horror,
        or to beset life with supernumerary distresses.
                                            Johnson (1709-1784)

1573   Early and provident fear is the mother of safety.
                                            Burke (1729-1797)

1574   Better to be despised for too anxious apprehensions
        than ruined by too confident a security.
                                            Burke (1729-1797)

1575   Fear is the mother of foresight.
                                            Henry Taylor (1800-1886)

1576   Good men have the fewest fears.
        He has but one great fear who fears to do wrong;
        he has a thousand who has overcome it.
                                            Bovee (1820-1904)

1577   A good scare is worth more to a man than good advice.
                                            Edgar W. Howe (1853-1937)

5. NEGATIVE

1578   As the ostrich when pursued hideth his head, but forgetteth
        his body; so the fears of a coward expose him to danger.
                                        Akhenaton? (c. B.C. 1375)

1579   Fear is not a lasting teacher of duty.
                                        Cicero (B.C. 106-43)

1580   In extreme danger fear feels no pity.
                                        Julius Caesar (B.C. 102-44)

1581   Fear is proof of a degenerate mind.
                                        Vergil (B.C. 70-19)

1582   The mind that is anxious about the future is miserable.
                                        Seneca (B.C. 3-65 A.D.)

1583   There is no passion so contagious as that of fear.
                                        Montaigne (1533-1592)

1584   Fear follows crime and is its punishment.
                                        Voltaire (1694-1778)

1585   In morals what begins in fear usually ends in wickedness;
        in religion what begins in fear usually ends in fanaticism.
        Fear, either as a principle or a motive, is the beginning of
        all evil.
                                        Anna Jameson (1794-1860)

1586   Worry - A god, invisible but omnipotent. It steals the
        bloom from the cheek and lightness from the pulse; it takes
        away the appetite, and turns the hair gray.
                                        Disraeli (1804-1881)

1587   Anxiety does not empty tomorrow of its sorrows,
        but only empties today of its strength.
                                        Charles Spurgeon (1834-1892)

1588   Depression, gloom, pessimism, despair, discouragement, these
        slay ten human beings to every one murdered by typhoid,
        influenza, diabetes or pneumonia. If tuberculosis is the
        great white plague, then fear is the great black plague.
                                        Gilbert Murray (1866-1957)

1589   There is perhaps nothing so bad and so dangerous in life
        as fear.
                                        Jawaharial Nehru (1889-1964)

6. ADVICE

1590 Who sees all beings in his own Self, and his own Self in all
      beings, loses all fear.
                                        Upanishads (c. B.C. 800)

1591 Suffer no anxiety, for he who is a sufferer of anxiety
      becomes regardless of enjoyment of the world and the
      spirit, and contraction happens to his body and soul.
                                        Zoroaster (B.C. 628?-551?)

1592 The whole secret of existence is to have no fear.
      Never fear what will become of you, depend on no one.
      Only the moment you reject all help are you freed.
                                        Buddha (B.C. 568-488)

1593 Do not be anxious about tomorrow, for tomorrow will be
      anxious for itself. Let the day's own trouble be
      sufficient for the day.
                                        Jesus (B.C. 6?-30? A.D.)

1594 An anthill increases by accumulation.
      Medicine is consumed by distribution.
      That which is feared lessens by association.
      This is the thing to understand.
                                        Nagarjuna (c. 100-200 A.D.)

1595 It is not death that a man should fear,
      but he should fear never beginning to live.
                                        Marcus Aurelius (121-180 A.D.)

1596 What is not to be, will not be; if it is to be, it cannot
      be otherwise; why do you not drink this antidote that
      destroys the poison of care?
                                        The Hitopadesa (600?-1100? A.D.)

1597 Nothing is to be feared but fear.
                                        Bacon (1561-1626)

1598 Things done well and with a care,
      exempt themselves from fear.
                                        Shakespeare (1564-1616)

1599 Things without remedy, should be without regard;
      what is done, is done.
                                        Shakespeare (1564-1616)

1600   Fear nothing but what thy industry may prevent;
        be confident of nothing but what fortune cannot defeat;
        it is no less folly to fear what is impossible to be avoided
        than to be secure when there is a possibility to be
        deprived.

Quarles (1592-1644)

1601   Do not anticipate trouble, or worry about what may never
        happen. Keep in the sunlight.

Franklin (1706-1790)

1602   They can conquer who believe they can. He has not learned
        the first lesson of life who does not every day surmount a
        fear.

Emerson (1803-1882)

1603   As a cure for worrying, work is better than whiskey.

Thomas A. Edison (1847-1931)

1604   When one is in fear he should appear to be fearless. One
        should seem to be trustful while really mistrusting others.
        Such a man is never ruined.

Sivananda (born 1887)

7. POTPOURRI

1605   He who knows Self as the enjoyer of
        The honey from the flowers of the senses,
        Ever present within, ruler of time,
        Goes beyond fear. For this Self is Supreme!

Upanishads (c. B.C. 800)

1606   When one has the feeling of dislike for evil, when one
        feels tranquil, one finds pleasure in listening to good
        teachings; when one has these feelings and appreciates
        them, one is free of fear.

Buddha (B.C. 568-488)

1607   I am frightened at seeing all the footprints directed
        towards thy den, and none returning.

Horace (B.C. 65-8)

1608   Cowards die many times before their deaths;
        The valiant never taste of death but once.
        Of all the wonders that I yet have heard,
        It seems to me most strange that men should fear,
        Seeing that death, a necessary end,
        Will come when it will come.

Shakespeare (1564-1616)

1609   I could a tale unfold whose lightest word
Would harrow up thy soul, freeze thy young blood,
Make thy two eyes, like stars, start from their spheres,
Thy knotted and combined locks to part
And each particular hair to stand on end,
Like quills upon the fretful porcupine.

Shakespeare (1564-1616)

1610   Huge and mighty forms that do not live
Like living men, moved slowly through the mind
By day, and were a trouble to my dreams.

Wordsworth (1770-1850)

1611   Like one, that on a lonesome road
Doth walk in fear and dread,
And having once turned round, walks on.
And turns once more his head;
Because he knows a frightful fiend
Doth close behind him tread.

Samuel Coleridge (1772-1834)

1612   Fear at my heart, as at a cup,
My life-blood seemed to sip!

Samuel Coleridge (1772-1834)

1613   Oh, fear not in a world like this,
And thou shalt know ere long,
Know how sublime a thing it is
To suffer and be strong.

Longfellow (1807-1882)

1614   I, a stranger and afraid
In a world I never made.

A. E. Housman (1859-1936)

FOLLY
Fools, Ignorance and Nonsense

1. ESSENCE

1615   Ignorance is the night of the mind,
a night without moon or star.

Confucius (B.C. 551-479)

1616   Not to understand what is good and bad,
Not to remember a kindness one has received,
Not to marvel at what one has clearly perceived -
These are the characteristics of a foolish man.

Saskya Pandita (1182-1251)

1617   Folly is wisdom spun too fine.

Franklin (1706-1790)

1618   A fool may be known by six things:
anger, without cause; speech, without profit;
change, without progress; inquiry without object;
putting trust in a stranger, and mistaking foes for friends.

Arabian Proverb

2. OPPOSITES

1619   The fool is not always unfortunate, nor the wise man always
successful; yet never has a fool thorough enjoyment; never
was a wise man wholly unhappy.

Akhenaton? (c. B.C. 1375)

1620   When a wise man is advised of his errors, he will reflect
on and improve his conduct. When his misconduct is pointed
out, a foolish man will not only disregard the advice but
rather repeat the same error.

Buddha (B.C. 568-488)

1621   If a fool be associated with a wise man even all his life,
he will perceive the truth as little as a spoon perceives
the taste of soup. If an intelligent man be associated for
only one minute with a wise man, he will soon perceive the
truth, as the tongue perceives the taste of soup.

The Dhammapada (c. B.C. 300)

1622   Those who wish to appear wise among fools,
among the wise seem foolish.

Quintilian (35-90 A.D.)

1623   The foolish are like ripples on water,
    For whatsoever they do is quickly effaced;
    But the righteous are like carvings upon stone,
    For their smallest act is durable.
Nagarjuna (c. 100-200 A.D.)

1624   Wise men have more to learn of fools than fools of wise men.
Montaigne (1533-1592)

1625   Young men think old men are fools;
    but old men know young men are fools.
George Chapman (1557-1634)

1626   The fool doth think he is wise,
    but the wise man knows himself to be a fool.
Shakespeare (1564-1616)

1627   A learned fool is more foolish than an ignorant fool.
Moliere (1622-1673)

1628   Folly enlarges men's desires
    while it lessens their capacities.
Robert South (1634-1716)

1629   There are more fools than wise men; and even in wise
    men, more folly than wisdom.
Chamfort (1741-1794)

1630   There is nothing in life so irrational, that good sense
    and chance may not set it to rights; nothing so rational,
    that folly and chance may not utterly confound it.
Goethe (1749-1832)

1631   The wise man has his follies no less than the fool;
     but herein lies the difference -
    The follies of the fool are known to the world,
     but are hidden from himself;
    The follies of the wise man are known to himself,
     but hidden from the world.
Colton (1780-1832)

1632   What the fool does in the end,
    the wise man does in the beginning.
Spanish Proverb

3. INSIGHT

1633   Even a fool, when he holdeth his peace, is counted wise.
Proverbs (B.C. 1000?-200?)

1634   There is a foolish corner even in the brain of the sage.

Aristotle (B.C. 384-322)

1635   It is the characteristic of folly to discern the faults of
others and forget its own.

Cicero (B.C. 106-43)

1636   Who are a little wise the best fools be.

John Donne (1572-1632)

1637   He who lives without committing any folly is not so
wise as he thinks.

La Rochefoucauld (1613-1680)

1638   A fool can ask more questions than the wisest can answer.

Swift (1667-1745)

1639   Very often, say what you will, a knave is only a fool.

Voltaire (1694-1778)

1640   The first degree of folly is to conceit one's self wise;
the second to profess it; the third to despise counsel.

Franklin (1706-1790)

1641   There is nothing by which men display their character so
much as in what they consider ridiculous...Fools and
sensible men are equally innocuous. It is in the half fools
and the half wise that the great danger lies.

Goethe (1749-1832)

1642   Prejudice is the child of ignorance.

Hazlitt (1778-1830)

1643   Folly loves the martyrdom of Fame.

Byron (1788-1824)

1644   There are many more fools in the world than there are
knaves, otherwise the knaves could not exist.

Bulwer-Lytton (1803-1873)

1645   The ultimate result of shielding men from the effects of
folly is to fill the world with fools.

Herbert Spencer (1820-1903)

1646   If fifty million people say a foolish thing,
it is still a foolish thing.

Anatole France (1844-1924)

4. POSITIVE

1647   It's a good thing to be foolishly gay once in a while.

Horace (B.C. 65-8)

1648   The folly of one man is the fortune of another;
        for no man prospers so suddenly as by others' errors.

Bacon (1561-1626)

1649   Silence is the wit of fools.

La Bruyere (1645-1696)

1650   The fool is happy that he knows no more.

Pope (1688-1744)

1651   The fool is like those people who think themselves
        rich with little.

Vauvenargues(1715-1747)

1652   Thou Graybeard, old Wisdom, mayst boast of thy treasures;
            Give me with young Folly to live;
        I grant thee thy calm-blooded, time-settled pleasures;
            But Folly has raptures to give.

Robert Burns (1759-1796)

1653   Let us be thankful for the fools. But for them the rest
        of us could not succeed.

Mark Twain (1835-1910)

5. NEGATIVE

1654   Greed, lust, fear, anger, misfortune, unhappiness, all
        are derived from foolishness. Thus, foolishness is the
        greatest of poisons.

Buddha (B.C. 568-488)

1655   Ignorance, the product of darkness, stupefies the senses in
        all embodied beings, binding them by the chains of folly,
        indolence and lethargy.

Bhagavad Gita (c. B.C. 400)

1656   A fool contributes nothing worth hearing and takes offense
        at everything.

Aristotle (B.C. 384-322)

1657   The fool who knows his foolishness, is wise at least so
        far. But a fool who thinks himself wise, he is called a
        fool indeed.

The Dhammapada (c. B.C. 300)

1658   To stumble twice against the same stone,
       is a proverbial disgrace.

Cicero (B.C. 106-43)

1659   In other living creatures ignorance of self is nature;
       in man it is vice.

Boethius (480?-524)

1660   Alas! we see that the small have always suffered
       for the follies of the great.

La Fontaine (1621-1695)

1661   Want and sorrow are the wages that folly earns for
       itself, and they are generally paid.

Christian Schubart (1739-1791)

1662   Of all thieves fools are the worst;
       they rob you of time and temper.

Goethe (1749-1832)

1663   The greatest of faults, I should say, is to be conscious of
       none.

Carlyle (1795-1881)

1664   None but a fool is always right.

Hare & Charles (c. 1830)

1665   No folly is more costly than the folly of intolerant
       idealism.

Winston Churchill (1874-1965)

1666   Those who identify themselves with the body and have no
       soul-consciousness, are utterly ignorant, though they may
       possess University degrees. Man speaks of his glory and
       achievements. It is all vanity. At the bottom of it all
       are sex, food, indolence and ignorance.

Sivananda (born 1887)

1667   Any fool can criticize, condemn and complain -
       and most fools do.

Dale Carnegie (1888-1955)

6. ADVICE

1668   He's a Fool that cannot conceal his Wisdom.

Franklin (1706-1790)

1669   I am always afraid of a fool; one cannot be sure he is
       not a knave.

Hazlitt (1778-1830)

1670   It is a great piece of folly to sacrifice the inner for the
        outer man.

                                    Schopenhauer (1788-1860)

1671   No man really becomes a fool until he stops asking questions
                                    Charles P. Steinmetz (1865-1923)

1672   The greatest lesson in life is to know that even fools are
        right sometimes.

                                    Winston Churchill (1874-1965)

7. POTPOURRI

1673   He who through the error of attachment loves his body,
        abides wandering in darkness, sensible and suffering the
        things of death, but he who realizes that the body is but
        the tomb of his soul, rises to immortality.

                                    The Divine Pymander (BC 2500?-200 AD?)

1674   What lies beyond life shines not to those who are childish,
        or careless, or deluded by wealth. "This is the only world:
        there is no other," they say; and thus they go from death
        to death.

                                    Upanishads (c. B.C. 800)

1675   "These sons belong to me, and this wealth belongs to me";
        with such thoughts a fool is tormented. He himself does
        not belong to himself; how much less sons and wealth?

                                    The Dhammapada (c. B.C. 300)

1676   For take thy balance if thou be so wise,
        And weigh the wind that under heaven doth blow;
        Or weigh the light that in the east doth rise;
        Or weigh the thought that from man's mind doth flow.

                                    Edmund Spenser (1552-1599)

1677   What can be more foolish than to think that all this rare
        fabric of heaven and earth could come by chance,
        when all the skill of art is not able to make an oyster!

                                    Jeremy Taylor (1613-1667)

1678   A fool always finds some greater fool to admire him.

                                    Nicholas Boileau (1636-1711)

1679   Exactness is the sublimity of fools.

                                    Fontenelle (1657-1757)

1680   A fool and his words are soon parted;
        a man of genius and his money.

                                    William Shenstone (1714-1763)

1681   What a fool he must be who thinks that his El Dorado is
        anywhere but where he lives.

                                              Thoreau (1817-1862)

1682   Young people tell what they are doing,
        old people what they have done
        and fools what they wish to do.

                                                  French Proverb

FREEDOM

Democracy, Independence and Liberty

1. ESSENCE

1683   No man is free who cannot command himself.
                              Pythagoras (B.C. 582-507)

1684   Liberty consists in the power of doing that which is
       permitted by the law.
                                   Cicero (B.C. 106-43)

1685   Who then is free?
       The wise man who can command himself.
                                   Horace (B.C. 65-8)

1686   Freedom is the right to live as we wish.
                              Epictetus (50-138 A.D.)

1687   Liberty, then, about which so many volumes have been written
       is, when accurately defined, only the power of acting.
                              Voltaire (1694-1778)

1688   The sovereignty of one's self over one's self is called
       Liberty.
                              Albert Pike (1809-1891)

1689   Freedom - to walk free and own no superior.
                              Walt Whitman (1819-1892)

1690   Freedom is the emancipation from the arbitrary rule of other
       men.
                              Mortimer Adler (born 1902)

2. OPPOSITES

1691   Man is born free, yet he is everywhere in chains.
                              Rousseau (1712-1778)

1692   None are more hopelessly enslaved
       than those who falsely believe they are free.
                              Goethe (1749-1832)

1693   The shepherd drives the wolf from the sheep's throat,
       for which the sheep thanks the shepherd as his liberator,
       while the wolf denounces him for the same act as the
       destroyer of liberty.
                              Lincoln (1809-1865)

1694   Freedom is the ferment of freedom. The moistened sponge
        drinks up water greedily; the dry one sheds it.
                                    Oliver Wendell Holmes (1809-1894)

1695   Only necessity understood, and bondage to the highest
        is identical with true freedom.
                                    William James (1842-1910)

1696   Liberty has restraints but not frontiers.
                                    Lloyd George (1863-1945)

1697   What a curious phenomenon it is that you can get men to die
        for the liberty of the world who will not make the little
        sacrifice that is needed to free themselves from their
        own individual bondage.
                                    Bruce Barton (1886-1967)

1698   No man was ever endowed with a right without being at the
        same time saddled with a responsibility.
                                    Gerald W. Johnson (born 1890)

1699   Communism destroys democracy.
        Democracy can also destroy Communism.
                                    Andre Malraux (1901-1976)

1700   The basic test of freedom is perhaps less in what we are
        free to do than in what we are free not to do.
                                    Eric Hoffer (1902-1983)

1701   We first have to find the way of freedom from involvement
        before we can introduce freedom in involvement.
                                    Pir Vilayat Inayat Khan (born 1916)

3. INSIGHT

1702   The secret of Happiness is Freedom,
        and the secret of Freedom, Courage.
                                    Thucydides (B.C. 460-400)

1703   Democracy arose from men's thinking that if they are equal
        in any respect, they are equal absolutely.
                                    Aristotle (B.C. 384-322)

1704   Freedom is not being a slave to any circumstance, to any
        constraint, to any chance; it means compelling Fortune to
        enter the lists on equal terms.
                                    Seneca (B.C. 3-65 A.D.)

1705   Is any man free except the one
        who can pass his life as he pleases?
                                    Persius (34-62 A.D.)

1706 Liberty is given by nature even to mute animals.
Tacitus (55-117 A.D.)

1707 Only that thing is free which exists by the necessities of
its own nature, and is determined in its actions by itself
alone.
Spinoza (1632-1677)

1708 The true character of liberty is independence,
maintained by force.
Voltaire (1694-1778)

1709 A country cannot subsist well without liberty,
nor liberty without virtue.
Rousseau (1712-1778)

1710 Abstract liberty, like other mere abstractions, is not
to be found.
Burke (1729-1797)

1711 He is the freeman whom the truth makes free,
and all are slaves beside.
Cowper (1731-1800)

1712 Liberty, according to my metaphysics...is a self-determining
power in an intellectual agent. It implies thought and
choice and power.
John Adams (1735-1826)

1713 Enslave the liberty of but one human being and the liberties
of the world are put in peril.
William Garrison (1805-1879)

1714 The only freedom which deserves the name
is that of pursuing our own good, in our own way,
so long as we do not attempt to deprive others of theirs,
or impede their efforts to obtain it.
John Stuart Mill (1806-1873)

1715 Freedom exists only where people take care of the
government.
Woodrow Wilson (1856-1924)

1716 Liberty is not merely a privilege to be conferred;
it is a habit to be acquired.
Lloyd George (1863-1945)

1717 Democracy is the worst system devised by the wit of man,
except for all the others.
Winston Churchill (1874-1965)

1718   Perfect freedom is reserved for the man who lives by his own
        work and in that work does what he wants to do.
                                        Robin G. Collingwood (1889-1943)

1719   When people are free to do as they please, they usually
        imitate each other.
                                        Eric Hoffer (1902-1983)

1720   Democracy is a process, not a static condition. It is
        becoming, rather than being. It can easily be lost, but
        never is fully won. Its essence is eternal struggle.
                                        William H. Hastie (1904-1976)

4. POSITIVE

1721   Governing sense, mind and intellect, intent on liberation,
        free from desire, fear and anger, the sage is forever free.
                                        Bhagavad Gita (c. B.C. 400)

1722   In the light of his vision he has found his freedom:
        his thoughts are peace, his words are peace
        and his work is peace.
                                        The Dhammapada (c. B.C. 300)

1723   What is so beneficial to the people as liberty,
        which we see not only to be greedily sought after by men,
        but also by beasts, and to be preferred to all things.
                                        Cicero (B.C. 106-43)

1724   Freedom all solace to man gives:
        He lives at ease that freely lives.
                                        John Barbour (1320-1395)

1725   Liberty is one of the most precious gifts which heaven has
        bestowed on man; with it we cannot compare the treasures
        which the earth contains or the sea conceals; for liberty,
        as for honor, we can and ought to risk our lives; and, on
        the other hand, captivity is the greatest evil that can
        befall man.
                                        Cervantes (1547-1616)

1726   Countries are well cultivated,
        not as they are fertile, but as they are free.
                                        Montesquieu (1689-1755)

1727   Freedom hath a thousand charms to show,
        That slaves however contented never know.
                                        Cowper (1731-1800)

1728 Liberty, when it begins to take root,
is a plant of rapid growth.

George Washington (1732-1799)

1729 Perfect freedom is as necessary to the health and vigor
of commerce as it is to the health and vigor of citizenship.

Patrick Henry (1736-1799)

1730 Can anything be so elegant as to have few wants,
and to serve them one's self?

Emerson (1803-1882)

1731 Freedom is the last, best hope of earth.

Lincoln (1809-1865)

1732 What light is to the eyes - what air is to the lungs -
what love is to the heart, liberty is to the soul of man.

Robert G. Ingersoll (1833-1899)

1733 Freedom is the open window through which pours the sunlight
of the human spirit and human dignity.

Herbert Hoover (1874-1964)

1734 There are two good things in life -
freedom of thought and freedom of action.

Somerset Maugham (1874-1965)

5. NEGATIVE

1735 No man is free who is a slave to the flesh.

Seneca (B.C. 3-65 A.D.)

1736 No nation ancient or modern ever lost the liberty of freely
speaking, writing, or publishing their sentiments, but
forthwith lost their liberty in general and became slaves.

John Peter Zenger (1697-1746)

1737 Those who would give up essential liberty to purchase a
little temporary safety deserve neither liberty nor safety.

Franklin (1706-1790)

1738 But what is liberty without wisdom, and without virtue?
It is the greatest of all possible evils;
for it is folly, vice, and madness,
without tuition or restraint.

Burke (1729-1797)

1739 Those who expect to reap the blessings of freedom must,
like men, undergo the fatigue of supporting it.

Paine (1737-1809)

1740 The wish to be independent of all men, and not to be under
      obligation to any one is the sure sign of a soul without
      tenderness.

                                            Joubert (1754-1824)

1741 Liberty is slow fruit. It is never cheap;
      it is made difficult because freedom is the accomplishment
      and perfectness of man.

                                            Emerson (1803-1882)

1742 The man who seeks freedom for anything but freedom's self is
      made to be a slave.

                            Alexis De Tocqueville (1805-1859)

1743 The policy of Russia is changeless...Its methods, its
      tactics, its maneuvers may change, but the polar star of its
      policy - world domination - is a fixed star.

                                          Karl Marx (1818-1883)

1744 Not free from what, but free for what?

                                        Nietzsche (1844-1900)

1745 Liberty means responsibility.
      That is why most men dread it.

                                          G. B. Shaw (1856-1950)

1746 If a nation values anything more than freedom, it will lose
      its freedom: and the irony of it is that if it is comfort
      or money that it values more, it will lose that, too.

                                  Somerset Maugham (1874-1965)

1747 The death of democracy is not likely to be an assassination
      from ambush. It will be a slow extinction from apathy,
      indifference, and undernourishment.

                            Robert Maynard Hutchins (1899-1977)

1748 Communism is the death of the soul. It is the organization
      of total conformity - in short, of tyranny - and it is
      committed to making tyranny universal.

                                  Adlai E. Stevenson (1900-1965)

1749 Man is condemned to be free; because once thrown into the
      world, he is responsible for everything he does.

                                    Jean-Paul Sartre (1905-1980)

1750 ...while they (Communists) preach the supremacy of the state
      and predict its eventual domination of all peoples on Earth,
      they are the focus of evil in the modern world...

                                      Ronald Reagan (born 1911)

6. ADVICE

1751 Freedom is the sure possession of those alone who have the
courage to defend it.

Pericles (B.C. 495-429)

1752 Men well governed should seek after no other liberty,
for there can be no greater liberty than a good government.

Walter Raleigh (1552-1618)

1753 Free people, remember this maxim: We may acquire liberty,
but it is never recovered if it is once lost.

Rousseau (1712-1778)

1754 Let all your views in life be directed to a solid,
however moderate, independence; without it no man can be
happy, nor even honest.

Junius (1740-1818)

1755 Our liberty depends on freedom of the press,
and that cannot be limited without being lost.

Thomas Jefferson (1743-1826)

1756 Yes! to this thought I hold with firm persistence;
The last result of wisdom stamps it true;
He only earns his freedom and existence
Who daily conquers them anew.

Goethe (1749-1832)

1757 Let us not be unmindful that liberty is power, that the
nation blessed with the largest portion of liberty must in
proportion to its numbers be the most powerful nation upon
earth.

John Quincy Adams (1767-1848)

1758 Liberty will not descend to a people;
a people must raise themselves to liberty; it is
a blessing that must be earned before it can be enjoyed.

Colton (1780-1832)

1759 Whoever will be free must make himself free.
Freedom is no fairy gift to fall into a man's lap.
What is freedom?
To have the will to be responsible for one's self.

Max Stirner (1806-1856)

1760 You can only protect your liberties in this world by
protecting the other man's freedom. You can only be free if
I am free.

Clarence Darrow (1857-1938)

1761   To enjoy freedom we have to control ourselves.
                              Virginia Woolf (1882-1941)

1762   If the fires of freedom and civil liberties burn low in
        other lands, they must be made brighter in our own...If in
        other lands the eternal truths of the past are threatened by
        intolerance, we must provide a safe place for their
        perpetuation.
                          Franklin D. Roosevelt (1882-1945)

1763   By All Resources Realize Yourself...
        Fetters fall off of themselves
        when the knowledge of self is gained.
                              A. L. Linall, Jr. (born 1947)

1764   The saving man becomes the free man.
                                    Chinese Proverb

7. POTPOURRI

1765   Happiness follows sorrow, sorrow follows happiness, but
        when one no longer discriminates happiness and sorrow, a
        good deal and a bad deed, one is able to realize freedom.
                              Buddha (B.C. 568-488)

1766   The traveller has reached the end of the journey!
        In the freedom of the Infinite he is free from all sorrows,
        the fetters that bound him are thrown away,
        and the burning fever of life is no more.
                          The Dhammapada (c. B.C. 300)

1767   Such being the happiness of the times,
        that you may think as you wish,
        and speak as you think.
                                Tacitus (55-117 A.D.)

1768   How happy is he born and taught,
          That serveth not another's will;
        Whose armour is his honest thought,
          And simple truth his utmost skill!
                              Henry Wotton (1568-1639)

1769   If I have freedom in my love,
          And in my soul am free,-
        Angels alone that soar above,
          Enjoy such liberty.
                          Richard Lovelace (1618-1657)

1770 I am as free as nature first made man,
   Ere the base laws of servitude began,
   When wild in woods the noble savage ran.

            Dryden (1631-1700)

1771 Liberty is to the collective body,
   what health is to every individual body.
   Without health no pleasure can be tasted by man;
   without liberty, no happiness can be enjoyed by society.

            Bolingbroke (1678-1751)

1772 The tree of liberty must be refreshed from time to time
   with the blood of patriots and tyrants. It is its natural
   manure.

            Thomas Jefferson (1743-1826)

1773 How does the Meadow flower its bloom unfold?
    Because the lovely little flower is free
   Down to its root, and in that freedom bold.

            Wordsworth (1770-1850)

1774 When Freedom from her mountain height
    Unfurled her standard to the air.
   She tore the azure robe of night,
    And set the stars of glory there.

            Joseph Drake (1795-1820)

1775 Of old sat Freedom on the heights
    The thunders breaking at her feet:
   Above her shook the starry lights;
    She heard the torrents meet.

            Alfred Tennyson (1809-1892)

1776 If a man does not keep pace with his companions,
   perhaps it is because he hears a different drummer.
   Let him step to the music which he hears,
   however measured or far away.

            Thoreau (1817-1862)

1777 His brow is wet with honest sweat
    He earns what'er he can,
   And looks the whole world in the face,
    For he owes not any man.

            Longfellow (1807-1882)

1778 We Americans...bear the ark of liberties of the world.

            Herman Melville (1819-1891)

1779   It is by the goodness of God that in our country
        we have those three unspeakably precious things:
        freedom of speech, freedom of conscience,
        and the prudence never to practice either.

                                        Mark Twain (1835-1910)

1780   All we have of freedom - all we use or know -
        This our fathers bought for us, long and long ago.

                                        Kipling (1865-1936)

FRIENDSHIP
Friends

1. ESSENCE

1781   Friendship is composed of a single soul inhabiting two bodies.

Aristotle (B.C. 384-322)

1782   What is thine is mine, and all mine is thine.

Plautus (B.C. 254-184)

1783   A friend is, as it were, a second self.

Cicero (B.C. 106-43)

1784   Friendship is Love without his wings!

Byron (1788-1824)

2. OPPOSITES

1785   It is better to decide between our enemies than our friends;
for one of our friends will most likely become our enemy;
but on the other hand, one of your enemies
will probably become your friend.

Bias (fl B.C. 600)

1786   He who hath many friends, hath none.

Aristotle (B.C. 384-322)

1787   To give counsel as well as to take it
is a feature of true friendship.

Cicero (B.C. 106-43)

1788   It may be doubtful, at first,
Whether a person is an enemy or friend.
Meat, if not properly digested, becomes poison;
But poison, if used rightly, may turn medicinal.

Saskya Pandita (1182-1251)

1789   Words are easy, like the wind;
Faithful friends are hard to find.

Shakespeare (1564-1616)

1790   That friendship will not continue to the end
which is begun for an end.

Quarles (1592-1644)

1791   He who has not the weakness of friendship
has not the strength.

Joubert (1754-1824)

1792 Every friend is to the other a sun, and a sunflower also.
He attracts and follows.

Richter (1763-1825)

1793 Our most intimate friend is not he to whom we show the
worst, but the best of our nature.

Nathaniel Hawthorne (1804-1864)

3. INSIGHT

1794 The rule of friendship means there should be mutual
sympathy between them, each supplying what the other
lacks and trying to benefit the other, always using
friendly and sincere words.

Buddha (B.C. 568-488)

1795 Friendship is the only thing in the world concerning the
usefulness of which all mankind are agreed.

Cicero (B.C. 106-43)

1796 As the yellow gold is tried in fire, so the faith
of friendship must be seen in adversity.

Ovid (B.C. 43-18 A.D.)

1797 Friendship always benefits; love sometimes injures.

Seneca (B.C. 3-65 A.D.)

1798 The mind is lowered through association with inferiors.
With equals it attains equality; and with superiors,
superiority.

The Hitopadesa (600?-1100? A.D.)

1799 A friend who cannot at a pinch remember a thing or two that
never happened is as bad as one who does not know how to
forget.

Samuel Butler (1612-1680)

1800 Rare as is true love, true friendship is rarer.

La Fontaine (1621-1695)

1801 The more we love our friends, the less we flatter them;
it is by excusing nothing that pure love shows itself.

Moliere (1622-1673)

1802 Two persons cannot long be friends if they cannot
forgive each other's little failings.

La Bruyere (1645-1696)

1803   Friendship's the privilege of private men;
       for wretched greatness knows no blessing so substantial.
                                           Nahum Tate (1652-1715)

1804   True friendship is a plant of slow growth,
       and must undergo and withstand the shocks of adversity,
       before it is entitled to the appellation.
                                     George Washington (1732-1799)

1805   The qualities of your friends will be those of your enemies,
       cold friends, cold enemies; half friends, half enemies;
       fervid enemies, warm friends.
                                           Lavater (1741-1801)

1806   True friendship is like sound health,
       the value of it is seldom known until it be lost.
                                           Colton (1780-1832)

1807   The condition which high friendship demands is ability
       to do without it.
                                           Emerson (1803-1882)

1808   A true friend is somebody who can make us do what we can.
                                           Emerson (1803-1882)

1809   The language of friendship is not words but meanings.
                                           Thoreau (1817-1862)

1810   False friends are like our shadow, keeping close to us
       while we walk in the sunshine, but leaving us the instant
       we cross into the shade.
                                           Bovee (1820-1904)

1811   Friendship is almost always the union of a part of one mind
       with the part of another; people are friends in spots.
                                     George Santayana (1863-1952)

4. POSITIVE

1812   Secret forces are bringing compatible spirits together.
       If the man permits himself to be led by this ineffable
       attraction, good fortune will come his way. When deep
       friendships exist, formalities and elaborate preparations
       are not necessary.
                                           I Ching (B.C. 1150?)

1813   Life has no blessing like a prudent friend.
                                     Euripides (B.C. 480-406)

1814   There is nought better than to be
With noble souls in company:
There is nought dearer than to wend
With good friends faithful to the end.
This is the love whose fruit is sweet;
Therefore to bide therein is meet.

Mahabharata (c. B.C. 400)

1815   It is not so much our friends' help that helps
as the confidence of their help.

Epicurus (B.C. 341-270)

1816   Friendship improves happiness and abates misery,
by the doubling of our joy and the dividing of our grief.

Cicero (B.C. 106-43)

1817   Friendship is the shadow of the evening,
which increases with the setting sun of life.

La Fontaine (1621-1695)

1818   Poor is the friendless master of a world;
a world in purchase of a friend is gain.

Young (1683-1765)

1819   Friendship, peculiar boon of Heaven,
The noble mind's delight and pride,
To men and angels only given,
To all the lower world denied.

Johnson (1709-1784)

1820   A friend may well be reckoned the masterpiece of nature.

Emerson (1803-1882)

1821   The ornament of a house is the friends who frequent it.

Emerson (1803-1882)

1822   Friendship is the only cement that will ever hold the
world together.

Woodrow Wilson (1856-1924)

1823   With true friends...even water drunk together is sweet
enough.

Chinese Proverb

5. NEGATIVE

1824   The joys that spring from external associations bring pain;
they have their beginnings and their endings. The wise man
does not rejoice in them.

Bhagavad Gita (c. B.C. 400)

1825   Every man can tell how many goats or sheep he possesses,
       but not how many friends.

                                           Cicero (B.C. 106-43)

1826   He who pursues people for what they can give,
       And yet pays no heed to those who have offered much,
       Is like the man who thinks only of the butter to come,
       And pays no heed to what has already been churned.

                                    Nagarjuna (c. 100-200 A.D.)

1827   Friends are thieves of time.

                                             Bacon (1561-1626)

1828   He that wants money, means, and content
       is without three good friends.

                                       Shakespeare (1564-1616)

1829   Whenever Fortune sends Disasters to our Dearest Friends,
       Although we outwardly may grieve,
       We oft are laughing in our sleeve.

                                  La Rochefoucauld (1613-1680)

1830   There have been fewer friends on earth than kings.

                                     Abraham Cowley (1618-1667)

1831   Nothing more dangerous than a friend without discretion;
       even a prudent enemy is preferable.

                                       La Fontaine (1621-1695)

1832   If all men knew what each said of the other, there would
       not be four friends in the world.

                                            Pascal (1623-1662)

1833   An open foe may prove a curse,
       But a pretended friend is worse.

                                               Gay (1688-1732)

1834   The most fatal disease of friendship is gradual decay,
       or dislike hourly increased by causes too slender for
       complaint, and too numerous for removal.

                                           Johnson (1709-1784)

1835   Give me the avowed, the erect, and manly foe,
       Bold I can meet, perhaps may turn the blow;
       But of all plagues, good Heaven, thy wrath can send,
       Save, save, oh save me from the candid friend!

                                    George Canning (1770-1827)

1836   The most violent friendships soonest wear themselves out.

                                            Hazlitt (1778-1830)

1837   Our very best friends have a tincture of jealousy even
        in their friendship; and when they hear us praised by others
        will ascribe it to sinister and interested motives if they
        can.
                                              Colton (1780-1832)

1838   Rely on your own Self, your own inner spiritual strength.
        Stand on your own feet. Do not depend on money, friends or
        any one. When the friends are put to test, they will desert
        you.
                                           Sivananda (born 1887)

1839   People become friends and enemies from consideration of gain
        and loss. Self-interest plays a very prominent part. Self-
        interest is very powerful. It can turn a friend into an
        enemy in no time and an enemy also into a friend. There is
        no such thing in existence as a friend or an enemy.
                                           Sivananda (born 1887)

1840   Friendship of officials...
        Thin as their papers.
                                                 Chinese Proverb

6. ADVICE

1841   Expect not a friendship with him who hath injured thee:
        he who suffereth the wrong, may forgive it; but he who doth
        it never will it be well with him.
                                         Akhenaton? (c. B.C. 1375)

1842   Friends are as companions on a journey, who ought to aid
        each other to persevere in the road to a happier life.
                                       Pythagoras (B.C. 582-507)

1843   A good friend who points out mistakes and imperfections
        and rebukes evil is to be respected as if he reveals a
        secret of hidden treasure.
                                          Buddha (B.C. 568-488)

1844   Be more prompt to go to a friend in adversity
        than in prosperity.
                                            Chilo (fl. B.C. 560)

1845   Never contract friendship with a man that is not better
        than thyself.
                                        Confucius (B.C. 551-479)

1846   Join the company of lions rather than assume
        the lead among foxes.
                                  The Talmud (B.C. 500?-400? A.D.)

1847   Be slow to fall into friendship; but when thou art in,
continue firm and constant.

Socrates (B.C. 469-399)

1848   Do not have evil-doers for friends,
     do not have low people for friends:
have virtuous people for friends,
     have for friends the best of men.

The Dhammapada (c. B.C. 300)

1849   Foresake not an old friend, for the new is not comparable
unto him. A new friend is as new wine: when it is
old thou shalt drink it with pleasure.

Ecclesiasticus (B.C. 200?)

1850   Reprove your friends in secret, praise them openly.

Publilius Syrus (fl. B.C. 42)

1851   Purchase not friends by gifts; when thou ceasest to
give, such will cease to love.

Thomas Fuller (1608-1661)

1852   It is more shameful to distrust our friends than to be
deceived by them.

La Rochefoucauld (1613-1680)

1853   Be not the fourth friend of him who had three before
and lost them.

Lavater (1741-1801)

1854   Friendship requires deeds.

Richter (1763-1825)

1855   Go often to the house of thy friend,
weeds choke the unused path.

Emerson (1803-1882)

1856   The only way to have a friend is to be one.

Emerson (1803-1882)

1857   One of the surest evidences of friendship that one
individual can display to another is telling him gently of a
fault. If any other can excel it, it is listening to such a
disclosure with gratitude, and amending the error.

Bulwer-Lytton (1803-1873)

1858   Never do a wrong thing to make a friend or to keep one.

Robert E. Lee (1807-1870)

1859   A man cannot be said to succeed in this life
        who does not satisfy one friend.

                                        Thoreau (1817-1862)

1860   If a friend is in trouble, don't annoy him by asking if
        there is anything you can do. Think up something
        appropriate and do it.

                                        Edgar W. Howe (1853-1937)

1861   Do not use a hatchet to remove a fly from your friend's
        forehead.

                                        Chinese Proverb

7. POTPOURRI

1862   Two friends, two bodies with one soul inspired.

                                        Homer (c. B.C. 700)

1863   The amity that wisdom knits not, folly may easily untie.

                                        Shakespeare (1564-1616)

1864   Then come the wild weather, come sleet or come snow,
        We will stand by each other, however it blow.

                                        Simon Dach (1605-1659)

1865   There are three faithful friends: an old wife, an old dog,
        and ready money.

                                        Franklin (1706-1790)

1866   Not until you become a stranger to yourself
        Will you be able to make acquaintance with the Friend.

                                        Nur 'Ali Shah (died 1797)

1867   Friendship is no plant of hasty growth;
        Tho' planted in esteem's deep fixed soil,
        The gradual culture of kind intercourse
        Must bring it to perfection.

                                        Joanna Baillie (1762-1851)

1868   Nothing so fortifies a friendship as a belief on the part
        of one friend that he is superior to the other.

                                        Balzac (1799-1850)

1869   A day for toil, an hour for sport,
        but for a friend is life too short.

                                        Emerson (1803-1882)

1870   Yes, we must ever be friends;
        and of all who offer you friendship
        Let me be ever the first, the truest,
        the nearest and dearest!
                                            Longfellow (1807-1882)

1871   The holy passion of Friendship is of so sweet and steady
        and loyal and enduring a nature that it will last through
        a whole lifetime, if not asked to lend money.
                                            Mark Twain (1835-1910)

1872   Instead of loving your enemies,
        treat your friends better.
                                            Edgar W. Howe (1853-1937)

1873   He hasn't an enemy in the world,
        and none of his friends like him.
                                            Oscar Wilde (1854-1900)

1874   There are some people who are very resourceful
        At being remorseful,
        And who apparently feel the best way to make friends
        Is to do something terrible and then make amends.
                                            Ogden Nash (1902-1971)

GENIUS

Creativity, Imagination, Invention, Originality and Talent

1. ESSENCE

1875   Creativity comes from awakening and directing men's higher
natures, which originate in the primal depths of the universe and are appointed by Heaven.

I Ching (B.C. 1150?)

1876   Genius is eternal patience.

Michelangelo (1474-1564)

1877   Imagination is the eye of the soul.

Joubert (1754-1824)

1878   Genius is essentially creative;
it bears the stamp of the individual who possesses it.

Germaine De Stael (1766-1817)

1879   Genius is the power of lighting one's own fire.

John Foster (1770-1843)

1880   Genius is a promontory jutting out into the infinite.

Victor Hugo (1802-1885)

1881   Originality is simply a pair of fresh eyes.

Thomas Higginson (1823-1911)

1882   Genius is initiative on fire.

Holbrook Jackson (1874-1948)

2. OPPOSITES

1883   Genius always gives its best at first; prudence, at last.

Lavater (1741-1801)

1884   It is the great triumph of genius to make the common appear
novel.

Goethe (1749-1832)

1885   Genius does what it must, talent does what it can.

Bulwer-Lytton (1803-1873)

1886   Talent repeats, genius creates.
Talent is a cistern; genius a fountain.

Edwin Whipple (1819-1886)

1887   Nature is the master of talents;
       genius is the master of nature.

                              Josiah Holland (1819-1881)

1888   Genius makes its observations in short-hand;
       talent writes them out at length.

                                    Bovee (1820-1904)

1889   Doing easily what others find difficult is talent;
       doing what is impossible for talent is genius.

                        Henri Frederic Amiel (1821-1881)

1890   To do great work a man must be very idle
       as well as very industrious.

                              Samuel Butler (1835-1902)

1891   Inventing is a combination of brains and materials.
       The more brains you use, the less material you need.

                           Charles Kettering (1876-1958)

1892   Talent is what you possess; genius is what possesses you.

                            Malcolm Cowley (born 1898)

3. INSIGHT

1893   Genius must be born, and never can be taught.

                                   Dryden (1631-1700)

1894   When a true genius appears in the world you may know him by
       this sign, that the dunces are all in confederacy against
       him.

                                    Swift (1667-1745)

1895   The merit of great men is not understood, but by those who
       are formed to be such themselves; genius speaks only to
       genius.

                        Leszczynski Stanislaus (1677-1766)

1896   Genius is independent of situation.

                            Charles Churchill (1731-1764)

1897   Everyone is a genius at least once a year;
       a real genius has his original ideas closer together.

                          Georg Lichtenberg (1742-1799)

1898   Everything has been thought of before, but the problem is
       to think of it again.

                                   Goethe (1749-1832)

1899   The lamp of genius burns quicker than the lamp of life.

                                  Schiller (1759-1805)

1900   Talent, lying in the understanding, is often inherited;
genius, being the action of reason and imagination,
rarely or never.

Samuel Coleridge (1772-1834)

1901   Genius is the gold in the mine;
talent is the miner who works and brings it out.

Marguerite Blessington (1789-1849)

1902   Great geniuses have the shortest biographies.
Their cousins can tell you nothing about them.

Emerson (1803-1882)

1903   There are geniuses in trade as well as in war, or state,
or letters; and the reason why this or that man is fortunate
is not to be told. It lies in the man: that is all anybody
can tell you about it.

Emerson (1803-1882)

1904   To believe your own thought, to believe that what is true
for you in your private heart is true for all men - that is
genius.

Emerson (1803-1882)

1905   He is the greatest artist who has embodied, in the sum of
his works, the greatest number of the greatest ideas.

John Ruskin (1819-1900)

1906   Genius - To know without having learned;
to draw just conclusions from unknown premises;
to discern the soul of things.

Ambrose Bierce (1842-1914?)

1907   Genius is one per cent inspiration and ninety-nine
per cent perspiration.

Thomas A. Edison (1847-1931)

1908   True genius resides in the capacity for evaluation of
uncertain, hazardous, and conflicting information.

Winston Churchill (1874-1965)

1909   The principal mark of genius is not perfection but
originality, the opening of new frontiers.

Arthur Koestler (1905-1983)

4. POSITIVE

1910   The honors of genius are eternal.

Propertius (B.C. 50-16)

1911   There is no genius free from some tincture of madness.
Seneca (B.C. 3-65 A.D.)

1912   The poets' scrolls will outlive the monuments of stone.
Genius survives; all else is claimed by death.
Edmund Spenser (1552-1599)

1913   Imagination disposes of everything; it creates beauty,
justice, and happiness, which is everything in this world.
Pascal (1623-1662)

1914   The first and last thing required of genius is the love
of truth.
Goethe (1749-1832)

1915   Imagination rules the world.
Napoleon (1769-1821)

1916   The drafts which true genius draws upon posterity, although
they may not always be honored so soon as they are due, are
sure to be paid with compound interest in the end.
Colton (1780-1832)

1917   All good things which exist are the fruits of originality.
John Stuart Mill (1806-1873)

1918   Dead he is not, but departed, - for the artist never dies.
Longfellow (1807-1882)

1919   Imagination is more important than knowledge.
Einstein (1879-1955)

1920   There is the happiness which comes from creative effort.
The joy of dreaming, creating, building, whether in painting
a picture, writing an epic, singing a song, composing a
symphony, devising new invention, creating a vast industry.
Work is the great redeemer. It has therapeutic value. It
brings happiness.
Henry Miller (1891-1980)

1921   Geniuses are the luckiest of mortals because what they must
do is the same as what they most want to do.
W. H. Auden (1907-1973)

5. NEGATIVE

1922   If people knew how hard I have to work to gain my mastery
it wouldn't seem wonderful at all.
Michelangelo (1474-1564)

1923   Originality is nothing but judicious imitation.

Voltaire (1694-1778)

1924   The richest genius, like the most fertile soil, when
uncultivated, shoots up into the rankest weeds.

David Hume (1711-1776)

1925   He who has imagination without learning
has wings but no feet.

Joubert (1754-1824)

1926   Fortune has rarely condescended to be the companion
of genius.

Isaac D'Israeli (1766-1848)

1927   The imagination is of so delicate a texture that even words
wound it.

Hazlitt (1778-1830)

1928   In every work of genius we recognize our own rejected
thoughts; they come back to us with a certain alienated
majesty.

Emerson (1803-1882)

1929   The artists must be sacrificed to their art. Like the bees,
they must put their lives into the sting they give.

Emerson (1803-1882)

1930   Talent is often to be envied, and genius very commonly to be
pitied. It stands twice the chance of the other of dying in
a hospital, in jail, in debt, in bad repute. It is a
perpetual insult to mediocrity; its every word is a
trespass against somebody's vested ideas.

Oliver Wendell Holmes (1809-1894)

1931   For precocity some great price is always demanded sooner or
later in life.

Margaret Fuller (1810-1850)

1932   Genius and its rewards are briefly told:
A liberal nature and a niggardly doom,
A difficult journey to a splendid tomb.

John Forster (1812-1876)

1933   Genius unexerted is no more genius than a bushel of acorns
is a forest of oaks.

Beecher (1813-1878)

1934   Men of genius are often dull and inert in society, as a
       blazing meteor when it descends to earth, is only a stone.
                                           Longfellow (1807-1882)

1935   Genius may be almost defined as the faculty of acquiring
       poverty.
                                           Edwin Whipple (1819-1886)

1936   In the republic of mediocrity, genius is dangerous.
                                           Robert G. Ingersoll (1833-1899)

1937   The public is wonderfully tolerant.
       It forgives everything except genius.
                                           Oscar Wilde (1854-1900)

6. ADVICE

1938   Beware of dissipating your powers; strive constantly to
       concentrate them. Genius thinks it can do whatever it sees
       others doing, but it is sure to repent every ill-judged
       outlay.
                                           Goethe (1749-1832)

1939   For a man to achieve all that is demanded of him
       he must regard himself as greater than he is.
                                           Goethe (1749-1832)

1940   The three indispensables of genius are understanding, feel-
       ing, and perseverance. The three things that enrich genius
       are contentment of mind, the cherishing of good thoughts,
       and exercising the memory.
                                           Robert Southey (1774-1843)

1941   Where we cannot invent, we may at least improve;
       we may give somewhat of novelty to that which was old;
       condensation to that which was diffuse, perspicuity to that
       which was obscure, and currency to that which was recondite.
                                           Colton (1780-1832)

1942   The human body is the magazine of inventions, the patent
       office, where are the models from which every hint is
       taken. All the tools and engines on earth are only
       extensions of its limbs and senses.
                                           Emerson (1803-1882)

1943   Only an inventor knows how to borrow, and every man is
       or should be an inventor.
                                           Emerson (1803-1882)

1944   Every man who observes vigilantly and resolves steadfastly
       grows unconsciously into genius.

                                          Bulwer-Lytton (1803-1873)

7. POTPOURRI

1945   The lunatic, the lover and the poet
       Are of imagination all compact.

                                          Shakespeare (1564-1616)

1946   Sometimes men come by the name of genius in the same way
       that certain insects come by the name of centipede -
       not because they have a hundred feet, but because most
       people can't count above fourteen.

                                          Georg Lichtenberg (1742-1799)

1947   If we can advance propositions both true and new, these are
       our own by right of discovery; and if we can repeat what
       is old, more briefly and brightly than others, this also
       becomes our own, by right of conquest.

                                          Colton (1780-1832)

1948   Genius lasts longer than Beauty. That accounts for the fact
       that we all take such pains to over-educate ourselves.

                                          Oscar Wilde (1854-1900)

1949   Originality does not consist in saying what no one has
       ever said before, but in saying exactly what you think
       yourself.

                                          James Stephens (1882-1950)

1950   When I am finishing a picture I hold a God made object up to
       it - a rock, a flower, the branch of a tree or my hand - as
       a kind of final test. If the painting stands up beside a
       thing man cannot make, the painting is authentic. If
       there's a clash between the two, it is bad art.

                                          Marc Chagall (born 1887)

GOODNESS
Charity, Kindness and Mercy

1. ESSENCE

1951   Every good act is charity. A man's true wealth hereafter
is the good that he does in this world to his fellows.
Mohammed (570-632 A.D.)

1952   Goodness is beauty in its best estate.
Christopher Marlowe (1564-1593)

1953   Kindness is the golden chain by which society is bound
together.
Goethe (1749-1832)

1954   An act of goodness is of itself an act of happiness.
No reward coming after the event can compare with the
sweet reward that went with it.
Maurice Maeterlinck (1862-1949)

1955   Goodness is love in action. It is noble to be good.
Goodness is the greatest virtue. Every good deed is a grain
of seed for immortality or eternal life.
Sivananda (born 1887)

2. OPPOSITES

1956   The higher the sun ariseth, the less shadow doth he cast;
even so the greater is the goodness, the less doth it
covet praise; yet cannot avoid its rewards in honours.
Akhenaton? (c. B.C. 1375)

1957   If you wish to be good, first believe that you are bad.
Epictetus (50-138 A.D.)

1958   He who receives a good turn should never forget it;
he who does one should never remember it.
Pierre Charron (1541-1603)

1959   Good and evil, we know, in the field of this world grow up
together almost inseparably.
Milton (1608-1674)

1960   Whatever mitigates the woes or increases the happiness of
others - this is my criterion of goodness.
And whatever injures society at large, or any individual,
in it - this is my measure of iniquity.
Robert Burns (1759-1796)

1961   A good person can put himself in the place of a bad person
more easily than a bad person can put himself in the place
of a good person.

Richter (1763-1825)

1962   He that is good will infallibly become better, and he that
is bad will as certainly become worse; for vice, virtue,
and time are three things that never stand still.

Colton (1780-1832)

1963   We are rich only through what we give,
and poor only through what we refuse.

Anne Swetchine (1782-1857)

1964   As the purse is emptied the heart is filled.

Victor Hugo (1802-1885)

1965   Giving is true having.

Charles Spurgeon (1834-1892)

1966   Kindness is a language which the deaf can hear and the blind
can read.

Mark Twain (1835-1910)

1967   Should not the giver be thankful that the receiver received?
Is not giving a need? Is not receiving, mercy?

Nietzsche (1844-1900)

1968   If you always give
You will always have.

Chinese Proverb

3. INSIGHT

1969   As the branches of a tree return their sap to the root, from
whence it arose; as a river poureth its streams to the sea,
whence its spring was supplied; so the heart of a grateful
man delighteth in returning a benefit received.

Akhenaton? (c. B.C. 1375)

1970   Heaven endows man with innate goodness.
Instinctive devotion to this spirit leads to success,
though conscious purpose jeopardizes nature's innocence.
But even with instinctive sincerity,
action must be in accord with the will of heaven.

I Ching (B.C. 1150?)

1971   The highest goodness is like water.
Water benefits all things and does not compete.
It stays in the lowly places which others despise.
Therefore it is near The Eternal.

Lao-Tzu (fl. B.C. 600)

1972   That gift which is given out of duty, at the proper time
       and place, to a worthy person, and without expectation of
       return, is considered to be charity in the mode of goodness.
                                          Bhagavad Gita (c. B.C. 400)

1973   A real man is he whose goodness is a part of himself.
                                          Mencius (B.C. 371-288)

1974   Wherever there is a human being there is an opportunity
       for a kindness.
                                          Seneca (B.C. 3-65 A.D.)

1975   Confidence in the goodness of another is good proof of
       one's own goodness.
                                          Montaigne (1533-1592)

1976   I have found men more kind than I expected, and less just.
                                          Johnson (1709-1784)

1977   As freely as the firmament embraces the world,
       or the sun pours forth impartially his beams,
       so mercy must encircle both friend and foe.
                                          Schiller (1759-1805)

1978   No good book, or good thing of any sort,
       shows its best face at first.
                                          Carlyle (1795-1881)

1979   There is many a good man to be found under a shabby hat.
                                          Chinese Proverb

4. POSITIVE

1980   As the rose breatheth sweetness from its own nature,
       so the heart of a benevolent man produceth good works.
                                          Akhenaton? (c. B.C. 1375)

1981   Kindness in words creates confidence.
       Kindness in thinking creates profoundness.
       Kindness in giving creates love.
                                          Lao-Tzu (fl. B.C. 600)

1982   Loving kindness is greater than laws;
       and the charities of life are more than all ceremonies.
                                          The Talmud (B.C. 500?-400? A.D.)

1983   Kindness gives birth to kindness.
                                          Sophocles (B.C. 495-406)

1984   Just as a man who has long been far away is welcomed with
        joy on his safe return by his relatives, well-wishers and
        friends; in the same way the good works of a man in his
        life welcome him in another life, with the joy of a friend
        meeting a friend on his return.
                                        The Dhammapada (c. B.C. 300)

1985   A good disposition I far prefer to gold;
        for gold is the gift of fortune;
        goodness of disposition is the gift of nature.
        I prefer much rather to be called good than fortunate.
                                        Plautus (B.C. 254-184)

1986   Men in no way approach so nearly to the gods
        as in doing good to men.
                                        Cicero (B.C. 106-43)

1987   Charity suffereth long and is kind; charity envieth not;
        charity vaunteth not itself, is not puffed up.
                                        I Corinthians (50?-100? A.D.)

1988   If you disclose your alms, even then it is well done,
        but if you keep them secret, and give them to the poor,
        then that is better still for you;
        and this wipes off from you some of your evil deeds.
                                        Koran (c. 651 A.D.)

1989   If you lend money, it is uncertain
            Whether you shall be repaid;
        But if you bestow alms, though they be small,
            Your return will be a hundred-fold.
                                        Saskya Pandita (1182-1251)

1990   Among the attributes of God, although they are all equal,
        mercy shines with even more brilliancy than justice.
                                        Cervantes (1547-1616)

1991   Of all virtues and dignities of the mind,
        goodness is the greatest, being the character of the Deity;
        and without it, man is a busy, mischievous, wretched thing.
                                        Bacon (1561-1626)

1992   It is heaven upon earth to have a man's mind move in
        charity, rest in providence and turn upon the poles
        of truth.
                                        Bacon (1561-1626)

1993   Good, the more communicated, more abundant grows.
                                        Milton (1608-1674)

1994   Kindness in ourselves is the honey that blunts the sting
of unkindness in another.

Landor (1775-1864)

1995   A kind heart is a fountain of gladness,
making everything in its vicinity freshen into smiles.

Washington Irving (1783-1859)

1996   He who loves goodness harbors angels, reveres reverence,
and lives with God.

Emerson (1803-1882)

1997   Wise sayings often fall on barren ground;
but a kind word is never thrown away.

Arthur Helps (1813-1875)

1998   Goodness is the only investment which never fails.

Thoreau (1817-1862)

1999   No man or woman of the humblest sort can really be strong,
gentle and good, without the world being better for it,
without somebody being helped and comforted by the very
existence of that goodness.

Phillips Brooks (1835-1893)

5. NEGATIVE

2000   Charity performed at an improper place and time and given to
unworthy persons without respect and with contempt is
charity in the mode of ignorance.

Bhagavad Gita (c. B.C. 400)

2001   It is not goodness to be better than the very worst.

Seneca (B.C. 3-65 A.D.)

2002   With gifts, you may gather your enemies about you.
When giving nothing, even your own family will leave.

Saskya Pandita (1182-1251)

2003   I know and love the good, yet ah! the worst pursue.

Francesco Petrarch (1304-1374)

2004   There is no man so good who, were he to submit all his
thoughts and actions to the law, whould not deserve
hanging ten times in his life.

Montaigne (1533-1592)

2005   No man deserves to be praised for his goodness unless he has
the strength of character to be wicked. All other goodness
is generally nothing but indolence or impotence of will.

La Rochefoucauld (1613-1680)

2006 The spirit of the world has four kinds of spirits
diametrically opposed to charity: resentment, aversion,
jealousy, and indifference.

Jacques Benigue Bossuet (1627?-1704)

2007 Look around the habitable world, how few
Know their own good, or knowing it, pursue.

Dryden (1631-1700)

2008 Better is the enemy of good.

Voltaire (1694-1778)

2009 He who waits to do a great deal of good at once,
will never do anything.

Johnson (1709-1784)

2010 Posthumous charities are the very essence of selfishness
when bequeathed by those who, even alive, would part with
nothing.

Colton (1780-1832)

2011 I hate the giving of the hand unless the whole man
accompanies it.

Emerson (1803-1882)

2012 If you're naturally kind, you attract a lot of people you
don't like.

William Feather (born 1888)

6. ADVICE

2013 Let the stronger man give to the man whose need is greater;
let him gaze upon the lengthening path of life. For riches
roll like the wheels of a chariot, turning from one to
another.

Rig Veda (B.C. 1200-900?)

2014 All strangers and beggars are from God,
and a gift, though small, is precious.

Homer (c. B.C. 700)

2015 Be good, be kind, be humane, and charitable; love your
fellows; console the afflicted; pardon those who have
done you wrong.

Zoroaster (B.C. 628?-551?)

2016 Treat those who are good with goodness,
And also treat those who are not good with goodness.
  Thus goodness is attained.
Be honest to those who are honest,
And be also honest to those who are not honest.
  Thus honesty is attained...

Lao-Tzu (fl. B.C. 600)

2017 Love thy neighbor as thyself: Do not to others what thou
wouldst not wish be done to thyself: Forgive injuries.
Forgive thy enemy, be reconciled to him, give him
assistance, invoke God in his behalf.

Confucius (B.C. 551-479)

2018 Make haste and do what is good;
keep your mind away from evil.
If a man is slow in doing good,
his mind finds pleasure in evil.

The Dhammapada (c. B.C. 300)

2019 It is kindness to immediately refuse
what you intend to deny.

Publilius Syrus (fl. B.C. 42)

2020 We should give as we would receive, cheerfully, quickly, and
without hesitation; for there is no grace in a benefit that
sticks to the fingers.

Seneca (B.C. 3-65 A.D.)

2021 Ask thyself, daily, to how many ill-minded persons thou hast
shown a kind disposition.

Marcus Aurelius (121-180 A.D.)

2022 Do all the good you can, By all the means you can,
In all the ways you can, In all the places you can,
At all the times you can, To all the people you can,
As long as ever you can.

John Wesley (1703-1791)

2023 Do good to thy Friend to keep him,
to thy enemy to gain him.

Franklin (1706-1790)

2024 To cultivate kindness is a valuable part of the business
of life.

Johnson (1709-1784)

2025 Be charitable and indulgent to every one but thyself.

Joubert (1754-1824)

2026 To be good, we must do good; and by doing good we take a
sure means of being good, as the use and exercise of the
muscles increase their power.

Tryon Edwards (1809-1894)

2027   There is so much good in the worst of us,
        And so much bad in the best of us,
        That it hardly becomes any of us
        To talk about the rest of us.

Edward Hoch (1849-1925)

7. POTPOURRI

2028   Goodness is the race which God hath set him to run, and
        happiness the goal; which none can arrive at till he hath
        finished his course, and received his crown in the mansions
        of eternity.

Akhenaton? (c. B.C. 1375)

2029   Of all that is good, sublimity is supreme.
        Succeeding is the coming together of all that is beautiful.
        Furtherance is the agreement of all that is just.
        Perseverance is the foundation of all actions.

I Ching (B.C. 1150?)

2030   Never are noble spirits
        Poor while their like survive;
        Pure love has gems to render,
        And virtue wealth to give.
        Never is lost or wasted
        The goodness of the good...

Mahabharata (c. B.C. 400)

2031   Prayer carries us half-way to God, fasting brings us to the
        door of his palace, and alms-giving procures us admission.

Koran (c. 651 A.D.)

2032   The desire of power in excess caused the angels to fall;
        the desire of knowledge in excess caused man to fall;
        but in charity there is no excess,
        neither can angel or man come in danger by it.

Bacon (1561-1626)

2033   That best portion of a good man's life,
        His little nameless, unremembered acts
        Of kindness and of love.

Wordsworth (1770-1850)

2034   He was so good he would pour rose-water on a toad.

Douglas Jerrold (1803-1857)

2035   There is dew in one flower and not in another, because one
       opens its cup and takes it in, while the other closes
       itself, and the drops run off. God rains His goodness and
       mercy as widespread as the dew, and if we lack them, it is
       because we will not open our hearts to receive them.
                                                   Beecher (1813-1878)

2036   If I knew...that a man was coming to my house with the
       conscious design of doing me good, I should run for my life.
                                                   Thoreau (1817-1862)

2037   For the cause that lacks
       The wrong that needs resistance,
       For the future in the distance,
       And the good that I can do.
                                           George Banks (1821-1881)

2038   There's no dearth of kindness
          In this world of ours;
       Only in our blindness
          We gather thorns for flowers.
                                           Gerald Massey (1828-1907)

2039   Let not the fierce sun dry one tear of pain before thyself
       hast wiped it from the sufferer's eye.
                                           H. P. Blavatsky (1831-1891)

2040   Life is mostly froth and bubble;
       two things stand like stone:
       kindness in another's trouble,
       courage in our own.
                                           Adam Gordon (1833-1870)

2041   The word good has many meanings. For example, if a man were
       to shoot his grandmother at a range of five hundred yards,
       I should call him a good shot, but not necessarily a good
       man.
                                           G. K. Chesterton (1874-1936)

2042   One may not doubt that, somehow Good
       Shall come of Water and of Mud;
       And sure, the reverent eye must see
       A purpose in Liquidity.
                                           Rupert Brooke (1887-1915)

GROWTH

Evolution, Gain, Increase, Morning, Progress, Spring and Youth

1. ESSENCE

2043   All men's gains are the fruit of venturing.
                                    Herodotus (B.C. 484-425)

2044   Growth is the only evidence of life.
                              John Henry Newman (1801-1890)

2045   Spring - An experience in immortality.
                                    Thoreau (1817-1862)

2046   Youth is a quality, not a matter of circumstances.
                              Frank Lloyd Wright (1869-1959)

2. OPPOSITES

2047   The way of heaven is to diminish the prosperous and
       augment the needy. The superior man gains without boasting.
                                    I Ching (B.C. 1150?)

2048   Youth is the best time to be rich,
       and the best time to be poor.
                                    Euripides (B.C. 480-406)

2049   He who seeks for gain, must be at some expense.
                                    Plautus (B.C. 254-184)

2050   Sometimes the best gain is to lose.
                                    Herbert (1593-1632)

2051   Youth, what man's age is like to be, doth show;
       We may our ends by our beginnings know.
                                    John Denham (1615-1668)

2052   An old young man, will be a young old man.
                                    Franklin (1706-1790)

2053   Progress has not followed a straight ascending line,
       but a spiral with rhythms of progress and retrogression,
       of evolution and dissolution.
                                    Goethe (1749-1832)

2054   Every street has two sides, the shady side and the sunny.
       When two men shake hands and part, mark which of the two
       takes the sunny side; he will be the younger man of the two.
                                    Bulwer-Lytton (1803-1873)

2055 The art of progress is to preserve order amid change
      and to preserve change amid order.
                              Alfred North Whitehead (1861-1947)

2056 Climb mountains to see lowlands.
                                              Chinese Proverb

3. INSIGHT

2057 Every phase of evolution commences by being in a state of
      unstable force and proceeds through organization to
      equilibrium. Equilibrium having been achieved, no further
      development is possible without once more oversetting the
      stability and passing through a phase of contending forces.
                              Kabbalah (B.C. 1200?-700? A.D.)

2058 A tree trunk the size of a man
      grows from a blade as thin as a hair.
      A tower nine stories high
      is built from a small heap of earth.
      A journey of a thousand miles
      starts in front of your feet.
      Whosoever acts spoils it.
      Whosoever keeps loses it.
                                        Lao-Tzu (fl. B.C. 600)

2059 Youth holds no society with grief.
                                      Euripides (B.C. 480-406)

2060 Childhood shows the man, as morning shows the day.
                                            Milton (1608-1674)

2061 Just as the twig is bent the tree is inclined.
                                              Pope (1688-1744)

2062 At 20 years of age the will reigns;
      At 30 the wit;
      At 40 the judgment.
                                          Franklin (1706-1790)

2063 Everyone believes in his youth that the world really began
      with him, and that all merely exists for his sake.
                                            Goethe (1749-1832)

2064 Youth is to all the glad season of life; but often only by
      what it hopes, not by what it attains, or what it escapes.
                                            Carlyle (1795-1881)

2065   If spring came but once in a century, instead of once a
year, or burst forth with the sound of an earthquake, and
not in silence, what wonder and expectation there would be
in all hearts to behold the miraculous change!

Longfellow (1807-1882)

2066   All growth depends upon activity. There is no development
physically or intellectually without effort, and effort
means work.

Calvin Coolidge (1872-1933)

2067   The evolution of man is the evolution of his consciousness,
    and 'consciousness' cannot evolve unconsciously.
The evolution of man is the evolution of his will,
    and 'will' cannot evolve involuntarily.
The evolution of man is the evolution of his power of doing,
    and 'doing' cannot be the result of things which 'happen.'

Gurdjieff (1873-1949)

2068   All progress has resulted from people who took unpopular
positions.

Adlai E. Stevenson (1900-1965)

2069   The purpose of learning is growth, and our minds, unlike
our bodies, can continue growing as we continue to live.

Mortimer Adler (born 1902)

2070   Enough shovels of earth..........................a mountain.
Enough pails of water..............................a river.

Chinese Proverb

4. POSITIVE

2071   Those who have high thoughts are ever striving;
they are not happy to remain in the same place.
Like swans that leave their lake and rise into the air,
they leave their home and fly for a higher home.

The Dhammapada (c. B.C. 300)

2072   That age is best which is the first
When youth and blood are warmer.

Robert Herrick (1591-1674)

2073   Sweet spring, full of sweet days and roses,
a box where sweets compacted lie.

Herbert (1593-1632)

2074   The morning hour has gold in its mouth.

Franklin (1706-1790)

2075   The morning of life is like the dawn of day,
        full of purity, of imagery, and harmony.
                                        Chateaubriand (1768-1848)

2076   Youth, with swift feet, walks onward in the way;
        the land of joy lies all before his eyes.
                                        Bulwer-Lytton (1803-1873)

2077   Youth is the trustee of prosperity.
                                        Disraeli (1804-1881)

2078   The morning pouring everywhere, its golden glory on the air.
                                        Longfellow (1807-1882)

2079   How beautiful is youth! how bright it gleams
        with its illusions, aspirations, dreams!
        Book of Beginnings, Story without End,
        Each maid a heroine, and each man a friend!
                                        Longfellow (1807-1882)

2080   The grandest of all laws is the law of progressive
        development. Under it, in the wide sweep of things, men
        grow wiser as they grow older, and societies better.
                                        Bovee (1820-1904)

2081   The need of expansion is as genuine an instinct in man as
        the need in a plant for the light, or the need in man
        himself for going upright...The love of liberty is simply
        the instinct in man for expansion.
                                        Matthew Arnold (1822-1888)

5. NEGATIVE

2082   An evil gain equals a loss.
                                        Publilius Syrus (fl. B.C. 42)

2083   It is the failing of youth not to be able to restrain its
        own violence.
                                        Seneca (B.C. 3-65 A.D.)

2084   Youthful rashness skips like a hare over the meshes of
        good counsel.
                                        Shakespeare (1564-1616)

2085   The greatest part of mankind employ their first years
        to make their last miserable.
                                        La Bruyere (1645-1696)

2086   No gain without pains.
                                        Franklin (1706-1790)

2087   The self-conceit of the young is the great source of those
        dangers to which they are exposed.

                                          Hugh Blair (1718-1800)

2088   Everybody wants to be somebody; nobody wants to grow.

                                          Goethe (1749-1832)

2089   Spring makes everything young again except man.

                                          Richter (1763-1825)

2090   Consider what heavy responsibility lies upon you in your
        youth, to determine, among realities, by what you will be
        delighted, and, among imaginations, by whose you will be
        led.

                                          John Ruskin (1819-1900)

2091   Unless a tree has borne blossoms in spring,
        you will vainly look for fruit on it in autumn.

                                          Hare & Charles (c. 1830)

2092   Growing is not easy, plain sailing business that it is
        commonly supposed to be: it is hard work - harder than any
        but a growing boy can understand; it requires attention,
        and you are not strong enough to attend to your bodily
        growth and to your lessons too.

                                          Samuel Butler (1835-1902)

6. ADVICE

2093   Within the earth, wood grows:
        The image of Pushing Upward.
        Thus the superior man of devoted character
        Heaps up small things
        In order to achieve something high and great.

                                          I Ching (B.C. 1150?)

2094   The perfecting of one's self is the fundamental base of all
        progress and all moral development.

                                          Confucius (B.C. 551-479)

2095   As I approve of a youth that has something of the old man
        in him, so I am no less pleased with an old man that has
        something of the youth. He that follows this rule may be
        old in body, but can never be so in mind.

                                          Cicero (B.C. 106-43)

2096   Let this be an example for the acquisition of all knowledge,
        virtue, and riches. By the fall of drops of water, by
        degrees, a pot is filled.

                                          The Hitopadesa (600?-1100? A.D.)

2097 By depending on the great,
The small may rise high.
See: the little plant ascending the tall tree
Has climbed to the top.

Saskya Pandita (1182-1251)

2098 The true way to gain much, is never to desire to gain too
much. He is not rich that possesses much, but he that
covets no more; and he is not poor that enjoys little, but
he that wants too much.

Francis Beaumont (1584-1616)

2099 Everywhere in life, the true question is not what we gain,
but what we do.

Carlyle (1795-1881)

2100 The heights by great men reached and kept
Were not attained by sudden flight,
But they, while their companions slept,
Were toiling upward in the night.

Longfellow (1807-1882)

2101 ...all good growth is slow growth.

William J. Gaynor (1849-1913)

2102 A change of being cannot be brought about by any rites.
Rites can only mark an accomplished transition. And it is
only in pseudo-esoteric systems in which there is nothing
else except these rites, that they begin to attribute to
the rites an independent meaning...Inner growth, a change
of being, depends entirely upon the work which a man must do
on himself.

Gurdjieff (1873-1949)

2103 The key to growth is the introduction of higher dimensions
of consciousness into our awareness.

Pir Vilayat Inayat Khan (born 1916)

7. POTPOURRI

2104 The spark hangs from the flame by the finest thread of
eternal vital power. It journeys through the Seven Worlds
of illusion. It stops in the first, and is a metal and a
stone; it passes into the second and behold - a plant;
the plant whirls through seven changes and becomes a sacred
animal. From the combined attributes of these, the thinker
is formed...

Book of Dzyan (B.C. 3000?)

2105   The Breath becomes a stone; the stone, a plant; the plant,
an animal; the animal, a man; the man, a spirit; and the
spirit, a god.

Kabbalah (B.C. 1200?-700? A.D.)

2106   In saffron-colored mantle, from the tides of ocean rose
the morning to bring light to gods and men.

Homer (c. B.C. 700)

2107   For lo, the winter is past, the rain is over and gone;
the flowers appear on the earth; the time of the singing
of birds is come, and the voice of the turtledove is heard
in our land.

Song of Solomon (B.C. 500?-200?)

2108   Yet Ah, that Spring should vanish with the Rose.
   That Youth's sweet-scented manuscript should close!
The Nightingale that in the branches sang
   Ah whence and whither flown again, who knows?

Omar Khayyam (fl. 1100)

2109   As when the golden sun salutes the morn,
And, having gilt the ocean with his beams,
Gallops the zodiac in his glistening coach,
And overlooks the highest-peering hills.

Shakespeare (1564-1616)

2110   See! led by Morn, with dewy feet,
Apollo mounts his golden seat,
   Replete with seven-fold fire;
While, dazzled by his conquering light,
Heaven's glittering host and awful night
   Submissively retire.

Thomas Taylor (1758-1835)

2111   The morn is up again, the dewy morn,
with breath all incense, and with cheek all bloom,
laughing the clouds away with playful scorn,
and glowing into day.

Byron (1788-1824)

2112   I was always an early riser. Happy the man who is! Every
morning day comes to him with a virgin's love, full of
bloom and freshness. The youth of nature is contagious,
like the gladness of a happy child.

Bulwer-Lytton (1803-1873)

2113   An acorn is not an oak tree when it is sprouted. It must go
through long summers and fierce winters; it has to endure
all that frost and snow and side-striking winds can bring
before it is a full grown oak. These are rough teachers;
but rugged schoolmasters make rugged pupils. So a man is
not a man when he is created; he is only begun. His manhood
must come with years.

Beecher (1813-1878)

2114   All common things, each day's events,
        That with the hour begin and end,
    Our pleasures and our discontents,
        Are rounds by which we may ascend.
                      Longfellow (1807-1882)

2115   There is no time like Spring,
        When life's alive in everything,
    Before new nestlings sing,
    Before cleft swallows speed their journey back
    Along the trackless track.
                Christina Rossetti (1830-1894)

2116   When the hounds of spring are on winter's traces,
    The mother of months in meadow or plain
    Fill the shadows and windy places
    With lisp of leaves and ripple of rain.
                     Swinburne (1837-1909)

2117   Slow buds the pink dawn like a rose
        From out night's gray and cloudy sheath;
    Softly and still it grows and grows,
        Petal by petal, leaf by leaf.
                  Susan Coolidge (1845-1905)

2118   When I am grown to man's estate
    I shall be very proud and great.
    And tell the other girls and boys
    Not to meddle with my toys.
              Robert Louis Stevenson (1850-1895)

2119   Why build these cities glorious
        If man unbuilded goes?
    In vain we build the world unless
        The builder also grows.
                Edwin Markham (1852-1940)

2120   The splendid discontent of God
        With chaos, made the world...
    And from the discontent of man
        The world's best progress springs.
            Ella Wheeler Wilcox (1855-1919)

2121   I sing the first green leaf upon the bough,
        The tiny kindling flame of emerald fire,
    The stir amid the roots of reeds, and how
        The sap will flush the briar.
                Clinton Scollard (1860-1932)

HAPPINESS
Contentment and Joy

1. ESSENCE

2122   Where there is joy there is creation. Where there is no joy
there is no creation: know the nature of joy.
Upanishads (c. B.C. 800)

2123   Happiness is unrepented pleasure.
Socrates (B.C. 469-399)

2124   Happiness is the absence of the striving for happiness.
Chuang-tzu (fl. B.C. 350)

2125   Happiness is the light on the water.
The water is cold and dark and deep.
William Maxwell (1676-1744)

2126   Happiness consists more in small conveniences of pleasures
that occur every day, than in great pieces of good fortune
that happen but seldom to a man in the course of his life.
Franklin (1706-1790)

2127   Happiness is not being pained in body or troubled in mind.
Thomas Jefferson (1743-1826)

2128   Happiness? That's nothing more than good health and a poor
memory.
Albert Schweitzer (1875-1965)

2129   Happiness is the interval between periods of unhappiness.
Donald Marquis (1878-1937)

2. OPPOSITES

2130   Contentment is natural wealth; luxury, artificial poverty.
Socrates (B.C. 469-399)

2131   The nonpermanent appearance of happiness and distress, and
their disappearance in due course, are like the appearance
and disappearance of summer and winter seasons.
Bhagavad Gita (c. B.C. 400)

2132   A highly learned man has two sources of happiness:
Either he abandons all earthly interests
Or else he possesses much which could be abandoned.
Nagarjuna (c. 100-200 A.D.)

2133   Contentment consisteth not in adding more fuel,
       but in taking away some fire.

                                      Thomas Fuller (1608-1661)

2134   False happiness renders men stern and proud,
          and that happiness is never communicated.
       True happiness renders them kind and sensible,
          and that happiness is always shared.

                                      Montesquieu (1689-1755)

2135   The most happy man is he who knows how to bring into
       relation the end and beginning of his life.

                                            Goethe (1749-1832)

2136   There is this difference between happiness and wisdom,
       that he that thinks himself the happiest man really is so;
       but he that thinks himself the wisest is generally the
       greatest fool.

                                            Colton (1780-1832)

2137   The foolish man seeks happiness in the distance;
       The wise grows it under his feet.

                                   James Oppenheim (1882-1932)

2138   The bringers of joy have always been the children of sorrow.
                                 Hazrat Inayat Khan (1882-1927)

2139   Happiness is like a sunbeam, which the least shadow
       intercepts, while adversity is often as the rain of spring.

                                                Chinese Proverb

3. INSIGHT

2140   Indecision regarding the choice among pleasures temporarily
       robs a man of inner peace. After due reflection, he attains
       joy by turning away from the lower pleasures and seeking the
       higher ones.

                                          I Ching (B.C. 1150?)

2141   We think a happy life consists in tranquility of mind.

                                         Cicero (B.C. 106-43)

2142   You traverse the world in search of happiness,
       which is within the reach of every man.
       A contented mind confers it on all.

                                          Horace (B.C. 65-8)

2143   Happiness hath he who renounces this cycle of being, which
       is utterly unsubstantial and overwhelmed by the pains of
       birth, death, old age and disease.

                               The Hitopadesa (600?-1100? A.D.)

2144   Silence is the perfectest herald of joy.
       I were but little happy if I could say how much.
                                           Shakespeare (1564-1616)

2145   A great obstacle to happiness is to expect too much
       happiness.
                                           Fontenelle (1657-1757)

2146   Three grand essentials to happiness in this life are
       something to do, something to love, and something
       to hope for.
                                           Addison (1672-1719)

2147   If one only wished to be happy, this could be easily
       accomplished; but we wish to be happier than other people,
       and this is always difficult, for we believe others to be
       happier than they are.
                                           Montesquieu (1689-1755)

2148   Thus happiness depends, as Nature shows,
       Less on exterior things than most suppose.
                                           Cowper (1731-1800)

2149   Our greatest happiness does not depend on the condition of
       life in which chance has placed us, but is always the result
       of a good conscience, good health, occupation, and freedom
       in all just pursuits.
                                           Thomas Jefferson (1743-1826)

2150   Happiness is a ball after which we run wherever it rolls,
       and we push it with our feet when it stops.
                                           Goethe (1749-1832)

2151   To be happy is not the purpose of our being,
       but to deserve happiness.
                                           Fichte (1762-1814)

2152   We are no longer happy as soon as we wish to be happier.
                                           Landor (1775-1864)

2153   Happiness grows at our own firesides,
       and is not to be picked in stranger's gardens.
                                           Douglas Jerrold (1803-1857)

2154   Tranquil pleasures last the longest;
       we are not fitted to bear long the burden of great joys.
                                           Beecher (1813-1878)

2155   Objects we ardently pursue bring little happiness when
       gained; most of our pleasures come from unexpected sources.
                                           Herbert Spencer (1820-1903)

2156   Be it jewel or toy,
       Not the prize gives the joy,
       But the striving to win the prize.

                              Owen Meredith (1831-1891)

2157   It is not how much we have, but how much we enjoy,
       that makes happiness.

                              Charles Spurgeon (1834-1892)

2158   The greatest happiness you can have is knowing that you do
       not necessarily require happiness.

                              William Saroyan (1908-1981)

4. POSITIVE

2159   Thousands of candles can be lighted from a single candle,
       and the life of the candle will not be shortened.
       Happiness never decreases by being shared.

                              Buddha (B.C. 568-488)

2160   Better than power over all the earth, better than going to
       heaven and better than dominion over the worlds is the joy
       of the man who enters the river of life that leads to
       Non-Being.

                              The Dhammapada (c. B.C. 300)

2161   What is there given by the gods
       more desirable than a happy hour?

                              Catullus (B.C. 84?-54?)

2162   Happiness seems made to be shared.

                              Pierre Corneille (1606-1684)

2163   Joy descends gently upon us like the evening dew,
       and does not patter down like a hailstorm.

                              Richter (1763-1825)

2164   Joys too exquisite to last,
       and yet more exquisite when past.

                              James Montgomery (1771-1854)

2165   Happiness and virtue rest upon each other;
       the best are not only the happiest,
       but the happiest are usually the best.

                              Bulwer-Lytton (1803-1873)

2166   He who has no wish to be happier is the happiest of men.
                              William R. Alger (1822-1905)

2167 Happiness makes up in height for what it lacks in length.
Robert Frost (1875-1963)

5. NEGATIVE

2168 No one can be said to be happy until he is dead.
Solon (B.C. 639-559)

2169 We take greater pains to persuade others that we are happy
than in endeavoring to think so ourselves.
Confucius (B.C. 551-479)

2170 Whoever does not regard what he has as most ample wealth,
is unhappy, though he be master of the world.
Epicurus (B.C. 341-270)

2171 Joys do not stay, but take wing and fly away.
Martial (43-104 A.D.)

2172 One kind of happiness is to know exactly at what point to be
miserable.
La Rochefoucauld (1613-1680)

2173 Happiness is nothing if it is not known,
and very little if it is not envied.
Johnson (1709-1784)

2174 The best advice on the art of being happy is about as easy
to follow as advice to be well when one is sick.
Anne Swetchine (1782-1857)

2175 There is even a happiness that makes the heart afraid.
Thomas Hood (1798-1845)

2176 Unquestionably, it is possible to do without happiness;
it is done involuntarily by nineteen-twentieths of mankind.
John Stuart Mill (1806-1873)

2177 Capacity for joy
Admits temptation.
Elizabeth B. Browning (1806-1861)

2178 The rays of happiness, like those of light,
are colorless when unbroken.
Longfellow (1807-1882)

2179 A lifetime of happiness! It would be hell on earth.
G. B. Shaw (1856-1950)

2180   As the ivy twines around the oak, so do misery and
        misfortune encompass the happiness of man. Felicity,
        pure and unalloyed, is not a plant of earthly growth;
        her gardens are the skies.

                                        Richard E. Burton (1861-1940)

6. ADVICE

2181   If thou be industrious to procure wealth, be generous in
        the disposal of it. Man never is so happy as when he giveth
        happiness unto another.

                                        Akhenaton? (c. B.C. 1375)

2182   He who, before he leaves his body, learns to surmount the
        promptings of desire and anger is a saint and is happy.

                                        Bhagavad Gita (c. B.C. 400)

2183   Avoid greatness; in a cottage there may be more real
        happiness than kings or their favorites enjoy.

                                        Horace (B.C. 65-8)

2184   There is only one way to happiness and that is to cease
        worrying about things which are beyond the power of our
        will.

                                        Epictetus (50-138 A.D.)

2185   The happiness of your life depends upon the quality of your
        thoughts: therefore, guard accordingly, and take care that
        you entertain no notions unsuitable to virtue and reasonable
        nature.

                                        Marcus Aurelius (121-180 A.D.)

2186   Know then this truth, enough for man to know
        Virtue alone is happiness below.

                                        Pope (1688-1744)

2187   To have joy one must share it.
        Happiness was born a twin.

                                        Byron (1788-1824)

2188   Happiness in this world, when it comes, comes incidentally.
        Make it the object of pursuit, and it leads us a wild-goose
        chase, and is never attained.

                                        Nathaniel Hawthorne (1804-1864)

2189   No matter what looms ahead, if you can eat today, enjoy
        the sunlight today, mix good cheer with friends today,
        enjoy it and bless God for it. Do not look back on
        happiness - or dream of it in the future. You are only
        sure of today; do not let yourself be cheated out of it.

                                        Beecher (1813-1878)

2190   There is no end of craving. Hence contentment alone is the
best way to happiness. Therefore, acquire contentment.

Sivananda (born 1887)

7. POTPOURRI

2191   The wise realizing through meditation the timeless Self,
beyond all perception, deep in the cave of the heart
leave pleasure and pain far behind.
The man who knows he is neither body nor mind,
but the eternal Self, divine principle of existence,
finds the source of all joy and lives in joy abiding.

Upanishads (c. B.C. 800)

2192   Happiness is brief.
It will not stay.
God batters at its sails.

Euripides (B.C. 480-406)

2193   The loss of wealth is loss of dirt,
As sages in all times assert;
The happy man's without a shirt.

John Heywood (1497?-1580?)

2194   What can be happier than for a man,
conscious of virtuous acts, and content with liberty,
to despise all human affairs?

Shakespeare (1564-1616)

2195   Human happiness seems to consist in three ingredients;
action, pleasure and indolence. And though these
ingredients ought to be mixed in different proportions,
according to the disposition of the person, yet no one
ingredient can be entirely wanting without destroying in
some measure the relish of the whole composition.

David Hume (1711-1776)

2196   From trial he wins his spirits light,
From busy day the peaceful night;
Rich, from the very want of wealth,
In heaven's best treasures - peace and health.

Thomas Gray (1716-1771)

2197   Existence is a strange bargain. Life owes us little;
we owe it everything. The only true happiness
comes from squandering ourselves for a purpose.

Cowper (1731-1800)

2198   There's a hope for every woe,
        And a balm for every pain,
        But the first joys of our heart
        Come never back again!

Robert Gilfillan (1798-1850)

2199   The Greeks said grandly in their tragic phrase,
        "Let no one be called happy till his death;"
         to which I would add,
        "Let no one, till his death be called unhappy."

Elizabeth B. Browning (1806-1861)

2200   One by one (bright gifts from heaven)
           Joys are sent thee here below;
        Take them readily when given,
           Ready, too, to let them go.

Adelaide Procter (1825-1864)

2201   All human joys are swift of wing,
           For heaven doth so allot it;
        That when you get an easy thing,
           You find you haven't got it.

Eugene Field (1850-1895)

HEALTH
Moderation, Safety and Temperance

1. ESSENCE

2202   Moderation is the silken string running through the pearl-
chain of all virtues.

> Thomas Fuller (1608-1661)

2203   Health consists with Temperance alone.

> Pope (1688-1744)

2204   Health is not a condition of matter, but of Mind.

> Mary Baker Eddy (1821-1910)

2. OPPOSITES

2205   Heaven's way is indeed like the bending of a bow.
When the string is high, bring it down.
When it is low, raise it up.
When it is excessive, reduce it.
When it is insufficient, supplement it.
The Way of Heaven reduces the excessive,
And supplements the insufficient...

> Lao-Tzu (fl. B.C. 600)

2206   Health, beauty, vigor, riches, and all the other things
called goods, operate equally as evils to the vicious and
unjust, as they do as benefits to the just.

> Plato (B.C. 427?-347?)

2207   Health is no other (as the learned hold)
But a just measure both of Heat and Cold.

> Robert Herrick (1591-1674)

2208   Abstinence is as easy to me as temperance would be
difficult.

> Johnson (1709-1784)

2209   Moderation in temper is always a virtue;
but moderation in principle is always a vice.

> Paine (1737-1809)

2210   The poorest man would not part with health for money,
but the richest would gladly part with all their money for
health.

> Colton (1780-1832)

2211   There is moderation even in excess.

> Disraeli (1804-1881)

2212   Every human being is the author of his own health or
        disease.

                                              Sivananda (born 1887)

3. INSIGHT

2213   The blessings, O man! of thy external part, are health,
        vigour, and proportion. The greatest of these is health.
        What health is to the body, even that is honesty to the
        Soul.

                                            Akhenaton? (c. B.C. 1375)

2214   To hold and fill to overflowing
          Is not as good as to stop in time.
        Sharpen a knife-edge to its very sharpest,
          And the edge will not last long.
        When gold and diamonds fill your hall,
          You will not be able to keep them.
        To be proud with honor and wealth
          Is to cause one's own downfall.
        Withdraw as soon as your work is done.
          Such is Heaven's Way.

                                              Lao-Tzu (fl. B.C. 600)

2215   In everything the middle course is best: all things in
        excess bring trouble to men.

                                              Plautus (B.C. 254-184)

2216   There is a mean in all things; and, moreover, certain
        limits on either side of which right cannot be found.

                                                 Horace (B.C. 65-8)

2217   Moderation is the center wherein all philosophies, both
        human and divine, meet.

                                            Joseph Hall (1574-1656)

2218   Moderation, which consists in an indifference about little
        things, and in a prudent and well-proportioned zeal about
        things of importance, can proceed from nothing but true
        knowledge, which has its foundation in self-acquaintance.

                                              Chatham (1708-1778)

2219   Moderation is the inseparable companion of wisdom, but
        with it genius has not even a nodding acquaintance.

                                                Colton (1780-1832)

2220   What a searching preacher of self-command is the varying
        phenomenon of health.

                                              Emerson (1803-1882)

4. POSITIVE

2221   Her name is Health: she is the daughter of Exercise, who
        begot her on Temperance. The rose blusheth on her cheeks,
        the sweetness of the morning breatheth from her lips; joy,
        tempered with innocence and modesty, sparkleth in her eyes
        and from the cheerfulness of her heart she singeth as she
        walketh.

                                            Akhenaton? (c. B.C. 1375)

2222   Sound health is the greatest of gifts;
        contentedness, the greatest of riches;
        trust, the greatest of qualities;
        enlightenment, the greatest happiness.

                                            Buddha (B.C. 568-488)

2223   Who loves the golden mean is safe from the poverty of a
        tenement, is free from the envy of a palace.

                                            Horace (B.C. 65-8)

2224   Safety lies in the middle course.

                                            Ovid (B.C. 43-18 A.D.)

2225   Temperance is reason's girdle, and passion's bride,
        the strength of the soul, and the foundation of virtue.

                                            Jeremy Taylor (1613-1667)

2226   To learn moderation is the essence of sound sense and real
        wisdom.

                                            Jacques Benigue Bossuet (1627-1704)

2227   Health is the soul that animates all the enjoyments of life,
        which fade and are tasteless without it.

                                            William Temple (1628-1699)

2228   He knows to live who keeps the middle state.

                                            Pope (1688-1744)

2229   Temperance and labor are the two best physicians of man;
        labor sharpens the appetite, and temperance prevents from
        indulging to excess.

                                            Rousseau (1712-1778)

2230   True happiness springs from moderation.

                                            Goethe (1749-1832)

2231   Only actions give life strength; only moderation gives
        it a charm.

                                            Richter (1763-1825)

2232   Moderation is the key of lasting enjoyment.

Hosea Ballou (1771-1852)

2233   The first wealth is health.

Emerson (1803-1882)

2234   The choicest pleasures of life lie within the ring of
        moderation.

Tupper (1810-1889)

2235   Moderation is the secret of survival.

Manly P. Hall (born 1901)

5. NEGATIVE

2236   Everything that exceeds the bounds of moderation has an
        unstable foundation.

Seneca (B.C. 3-65 A.D.)

2237   Without health life is not life; it is only a state of
        languor and suffering - an image of death.

Rabelais (1490-1553)

2238   Preserving the health by too strict a regimen is a
        wearisome malady.

La Rochefoucauld (1613-1680)

2239   Men have made a virtue of moderation to limit the ambition
        of the great, and to console people of mediocrity for their
        want of fortune and of merit.

La Rochefoucauld (1613-1680)

2240   He's a Fool that makes his Doctor his Heir.

Franklin (1706-1790)

2241   Health is so necessary to all the duties, as well as
        pleasures of life, that the crime of squandering it is
        equal to the folly.

Johnson (1709-1784)

2242   People who are always taking care of their health are like
        misers, who are hoarding a treasure which they have never
        spirit enough to enjoy.

Sterne (1713-1768)

2243   Objection, evasion, distrust and irony are signs of health.
        Everything absolute belongs to pathology.

Nietzsche (1844-1900)

2244   Moderation is a fatal thing. Nothing succeeds like excess.
Oscar Wilde (1854-1900)

6. ADVICE

2245   The secret of health for both mind and body is not to
mourn for the past, not to worry about the future, or
not to anticipate troubles, but to live the present moment
wisely and earnestly.
Buddha (B.C. 568-488)

2246   It is best to rise from life as from a banquet,
neither thirsty nor drunken.
Aristotle (B.C. 384-322)

2247   To live long, it is necessary to live slowly.
Cicero (B.C. 106-43)

2248   Kill neither men, nor beasts, nor yet the food which goes
into your mouth. For if you eat living food, the same will
quicken you, but if you kill your food, the dead food will
kill you also. For life comes only from life, and from
death always comes death...And our bodies become what your
foods are, even as your spirits, likewise, become what your
thoughts are...Eat nothing, therefore, which a stronger fire
than the fire of life has killed. Wherefore, prepare and
eat all fruits of trees, and all grasses of the fields, and
all milk of beasts good for eating. For all these are fed
and ripened by the fire of life; all are the gift of the
angels of our Earthly Mother. But eat nothing to which only
the fire of death gives savor, for such is of Satan.
Jesus (B.C. 6?-30? A.D.)

2249   To wish to be well is a part of becoming well.
Seneca (B.C. 3-65 A.D.)

2250   Fortify yourself with moderation; for this is an
impregnable fortress.
Epictetus (50-138 A.D.)

2251   Strive to preserve your health; and in this you will better
succeed in proportion as you keep clear of the physicians,
for their drugs are a kind of alchemy concerning which there
are no fewer books than there are medicines.
Leonardo Da Vinci (1452-1519)

2252   There is a wisdom in this beyond the rules of physic:
a man's own observation what he finds good of and what
he finds hurt of is the best physic to preserve health.
Bacon (1561-1626)

2253 Use, do not abuse; nether abstinence nor excess ever
renders man happy.

Voltaire (1694-1778)

2254 Be sober and temperate, and you will be healthy.

Franklin (1706-1790)

2255 Eat to live, not live to eat.

Franklin (1706-1790)

2256 Regularity in the hours of rising and retiring, perseverance
in exercise, adaptation of dress to the variations of
climate, simple and nutritious aliment, and temperance in
all things are necessary branches of the regimen of health.

Lydia Sigourney (1791-1865)

2257 He who would keep himself to himself should imitate the
dumb animals, and drink water.

Bulwer-Lytton (1803-1873)

2258 Refuse to be ill. Never tell people you are ill; never own
it to yourself. Illness is one of those things which a man
should resist on principle at the onset.

Bulwer-Lytton (1803-1873)

2259 Never hurry; take plenty of exercise; always be cheerful,
and take all the sleep you need, and you may expect to be
well.

James F. Clarke (1810-1888)

2260 The sum of the whole is this: walk and be happy; walk and
be healthy. The best way to lengthen out our days is to
walk steadily and with a purpose.

Charles Dickens (1812-1870)

2261 Drinking water neither makes a man sick, nor in debt,
nor his wife a widow.

John Neale (1818-1866)

2262 The requisites of health are plain enough; regular habits,
daily exercise, cleanliness, and moderation in all things -
in eating as well as in drinking - would keep most people
well.

Lubbock (1834-1913)

2263 Health is a gift, but you have to work to keep it.

Elbert Hubbard (1859-1915)

7. POTPOURRI

2264   Use no medicine in an illness
        Incurred through no fault of your own.
        It will pass of itself.

                                        I Ching (B.C. 1150?)

2265   The man who makes everything that leads to happiness
        depends upon himself, and not upon other men, has adopted
        the very best plan for living happily. This is the man
        of moderation, the man of manly character and of wisdom.

                                        Plato (B.C. 427?-347?)

2266   The foods that prolong life and increase purity, vigour,
        health, cheerfulness, and happiness are those that are
        delicious, soothing, substantial and agreeable. ... Foods
        that are bitter, sour, salt, over-hot, pungent, dry and
        burning produce unhappiness, repentance and disease.

                                        Bhagavad Gita (c. B.C. 400)

2267   Comport thyself in life as at a banquet. If a plate is
        offered thee, extend thy hand and take it moderately; if it
        be withdrawn, do not detain it. If it come not to thy side,
        make not thy desire loudly known, but wait patiently till it
        be offered thee. Use the same moderation towards thy wife
        and thy children, toward honors and riches.

                                        Epictetus (50-138 A.D.)

2268   The common ingredients of health and long life are:
            Great temperance, open air,
            Easy labor, little care.

                                        Philip Sidney (1554-1586)

2269   Nor love, nor honour, wealth nor power,
        Can give the heart a cheerful hour
        When health is lost, be timely wise;
        With health all taste of pleasure flies.

                                        Gay (1688-1732)

2270   When I go into my garden with a spade, and dig a bed, I
        feel such an exhilaration and health that I discover that
        I have been defrauding myself all this time in letting
        others do for me what I should have done with my own hands.

                                        Emerson (1803-1882)

2271   Joy, temperance, and repose,
        slam the door on the doctor's nose.

                                        Longfellow (1807-1882)

HOPE
Belief, Confidence, Faith and Optimism

1. ESSENCE

2272   Hopes are but the dreams of those who are awake.
                                        Pindar (B.C. 518?-438)

2273   It is hope which maintains most of mankind.
                                        Sophocles (B.C. 495-406)

2274   Man is made by his belief. As he believes, so he is.
                                        Bhagavad Gita (c. B.C. 400)

2275   Confidence is that feeling by which the mind embarks on
       great and honourable courses with a sure hope and trust
       in itself.
                                        Cicero (B.C. 106-43)

2276   Hope is the pillar that holds up the world.
                                        Pliny the Elder (23-79 A.D.)

2277   Faith is the substance of things hoped for,
       the evidence of things not seen.
                                        Hebrews (50?-100? A.D.)

2278   The roots of faith rest in Understanding,
       the synthetic principle of consciousness.
                                        H. P. Blavatsky (1831-1891)

2. OPPOSITES

2279   Nothing is so firmly believed as what we least know.
                                        Montaigne (1533-1592)

2280   Hope is a good breakfast, but it is a bad supper.
                                        Bacon (1561-1626)

2281   Hope and fear are inseparable.
                                        La Rochefoucauld (1613-1680)

2282   The beginning of faith is the beginning of fruitfulness;
       but the beginning of unbelief, however glittering, is empty.
                                        Goethe (1749-1832)

2283   Hope is brightest when it dawns from fears.
                                        Walter Scott (1771-1832)

2284   You do not believe, you only believe that you believe.
                                        Samuel Coleridge (1772-1834)

2285 Credulity is the man's weakness, but the child's strength.
Charles Lamb (1775-1834)

2286 Belief consists in accepting the affirmations of the soul;
unbelief, in denying them.
Emerson (1803-1882)

2287 A believer is a bird in a cage, a free-thinker is an eagle
parting the clouds with tireless wing.
Robert G. Ingersoll (1833-1899)

3. INSIGHT

2288 Things which you don't hope happen more frequently
than things which you do hope.
Plautus (B.C. 254-184)

2289 You believe that easily which you hope for earnestly.
Terence (B.C. 185-159)

2290 Where belief is painful, we are slow to believe.
Ovid (B.C. 43-18 A.D.)

2291 Vows begin when hope dies.
Leonardo Da Vinci (1452-1519)

2292 How many things served us yesterday for articles of faith,
which to-day are fables to us!
Montaigne (1533-1592)

2293 We are inclined to believe those we do not know,
because they have never deceived us.
Johnson (1709-1784)

2294 The hours we pass with happy prospects in view
are more pleasing than those crowded with fruition.
Goldsmith (1728-1774)

2295 No iron chain, or outward force of any kind,
could ever compel the soul of man to believe or disbelieve
Carlyle (1795-1881)

2296 Man is, properly speaking, based upon hope,
he has no other possession but hope;
this world of his is emphatically the place of hope.
Carlyle (1795-1881)

2297 Faith begins where Reason sinks exhausted.
Albert Pike (1809-1891)

2298 The only faith that wears well and holds its color in all
weathers is that which is woven of conviction.

James Lowell (1819-1891)

4. POSITIVE

2299 Hope is the only good which is common to all men;
those who have nothing more possess hope still.

Thales (B.C. 625?-547?)

2300 On a long journey of human life, faith is the best of
companions; it is the best refreshment on the journey;
and it is the greatest property.

Buddha (B.C. 568-488)

2301 Faith removes greed, fear and pride;
it teaches courtesy and wins respect;
it frees one from the bondage of circumstances;
it gives one courage to meet hardship;
it gives one power to overcome temptation;
faith enables one to keep one's deeds bright and pure;
and it enriches the mind with wisdom.

Buddha (B.C. 568-488)

2302 If a man has faith and has virtue, then he has true glory
and treasure. Wherever that man may go, there he will be
held in honour.

The Dhammapada (c. B.C. 300)

2303 True hope is swift, and flies with swallow's wings:
Kings it makes gods, and meaner creatures kings.

Shakespeare (1564-1616)

2304 Hope and patience are two sovereign remedies for all,
the surest reposals, the softest cushions to lean on
in adversity.

Robert Burton (1576-1640)

2305 However deceitful hope may be,
yet she carries us on pleasantly to the end of life.

La Rochefoucauld (1613-1680)

2306 Hope! of all ills that men endure,
The only cheap and universal cure.

Abraham Cowley (1618-1667)

2307 Whatever enlarges hope will also exalt courage.

Johnson (1709-1784)

2308   Hope is itself a species of happiness,
       and perhaps the chief happiness which this world affords.
                                        Johnson (1709-1784)

2309   Hope is the best part of our riches. What sufficeth it that
       we have great wealth in our pockets, if we have not the
       hope of heaven in our souls?
                                        Bovee (1820-1904)

2310   It is always easier to believe than to deny.
       Our minds are naturally affirmative.
                                        John Burroughs (1837-1921)

2311   He who has health, has hope;
       and he who has hope, has everything.
                                        Arabian Proverb

5. NEGATIVE

2312   Much knowledge of divine things is lost to us through
       want of faith.
                                        Heraclitus (B.C. 535-475)

2313   Hope of ill gain is the beginning of loss.
                                        Democritus (B.C. 490-360)

2314   Nothing is so easy as to deceive one's self;
       for what we wish, that we readily believe.
                                        Demosthenes (B.C. 384-322)

2315   Confidence is nowhere safe.
                                        Vergil (B.C. 70-19)

2316   Hope is such a bait, it covers any hook.
                                        Ben Jonson (1572-1637)

2317   Hope! fortune's cheating lottery
       Where for one prize a thousand blanks there are.
                                        Abraham Cowley (1618-1667)

2318   He that lives on hopes will die fasting.
                                        Franklin (1706-1790)

2319   When there is no hope, there can be no endeavor.
                                        Johnson (1709-1784)

2320   Hope is a flatterer, but the most upright of all parasites;
       for she frequents the poor man's hut, as well as the
       palace of his superior.
                                        William Shenstone (1714-1763)

2321   Have you not observed that faith is generally strongest
        in those whose character may be called the weakest?
                                    Germaine De Stael (1766-1817)

2322   Hope is a delusion; no hand can grasp a wave or a shadow.
                                    Victor Hugo (1802-1885)

2323   I suppose it can be truthfully said that hope is the only
        universal liar who never loses his reputation for veracity.
                                    Robert G. Ingersoll (1833-1899)

2324   Convictions are more dangerous enemies of truth than lies.
                                    Nietzsche (1844-1900)

6. ADVICE

2325   Be of good hope in the face of death. Believe in this one
        truth for certain, that no evil can befall a good man either
        in life or death, and that his fate is not a matter of
        indifference to the gods.
                                    Socrates (B.C. 469-399)

2326   A strong mind always hopes, and has always cause to hope.
                                    Polybius (B.C. 203?-120)

2327   One does not have to believe everything one hears.
                                    Cicero (B.C. 106-43)

2328   It is best to hope only for things possible and probable;
        he that hopes too much shall deceive himself at last,
        especially if his industry does not go along with his hopes;
        for hope without action is a barren undoer.
                                    Owen Feltham (1602-1668)

2329   In the Affairs of the World Men are saved,
        not by Faith but by the Want of it.
                                    Franklin (1706-1790)

2330   In all things it is better to hope than to despair.
                                    Goethe (1749-1832)

2331   I can tell you, honest friend, what to believe:
        believe life; it teaches better than book or orator.
                                    Goethe (1749-1832)

2332   Better trust all and be deceived,
          And weep that trust, and that deceiving,
        Than doubt one heart that, if believed,
          Had blessed one's life with true believing.
                                    Francis Anne Kemble (1809-1893)

2333   Our belief at the beginning of a doubtful undertaking is
        the one thing that assures the successful outcome of any
        venture.

                                    William James (1842-1910)

7. POTPOURRI

2334   The miserable hath no other medicine but only hope.
                                    Shakespeare (1564-1616)

2335   He that lives in hope dances without music.
                                    Herbert (1593-1632)

2336   Hope springs eternal in the human breast;
        Man never is, but always to be blest.

                                    Pope (1688-1744)

2337   For modes of faith let graceless zealots fight,
        His can't be wrong whose life is in the right.

                                    Pope (1688-1744)

2338   Hope, like the gleaming taper's light,
            Adorns and cheers our way;
        And still, as darker grows the night,
            Emits a brighter ray.

                                    Goldsmith (1728-1774)

2339   I steer my bark with hope in the head, leaving fear astern.
                                    Thomas Jefferson (1743-1826)

2340   Hopes, what are they? - Beads of morning
            Strung on slender blades of grass;
        Or a spider's web adorning
            In a straight and treacherous pass.

                                    Wordsworth (1770-1850)

2341   Hope is a prodigal young heir, and experience is his
        banker, but his drafts are seldom honored since there is
        often a heavy balance against him, because he draws largely
        on a small capital and is not yet in possession.

                                    Colton (1780-1832)

2342   Hope is a pleasant acquaintance, but an unsafe friend.
        Hope is not the man for your banker, though he may do for a
        travelling companion.

                                    Haliburton (1796-1865)

2343   Whose faith has centre everywhere,
        Nor cares to fix itself to form.

                                    Alfred Tennyson (1809-1892)

2344   The setting of a great hope is like the setting of the sun.
        The brightness of our life is gone.

                                        Longfellow (1807-1882)

2345   Faith is a fine invention
            For gentlemen who see;
        But Microscopes are prudent
            In an emergency.

                                        Emily Dickinson (1830-1886)

2346   Under the storm and the cloud today,
            and today the hard peril and pain -
        tomorrow the stone shall be rolled away,
            for the sunshine shall follow the rain.

                                        Joaquin Miller (1839-1913)

2347   Optimism is a kind of heart stimulant -
        the digitalis of failure.

                                        Elbert Hubbard (1859-1915)

2348   We do not stray out of all worlds into the ever silent;
        We do not raise our hands to the void for things beyond
        hope.

                                        Rabindranath Tagore (1861-1941)

HUMILITY
Humbleness, Modesty and Sacrifice

1. ESSENCE

2349 Humility is the solid foundation of all virtues.
Confucius (B.C. 551-479)

2350 Modesty is the color of virtue.
Diogenes (B.C. 412-323)

2351 Modesty is the citadel of beauty and virtue.
Demades (B.C. 380-318)

2352 Lowliness is the base of every virtue,
And he who goes the lowest builds the safest.
Bailey (1816-1902)

2353 Humility is to make a right estimate of oneself.
Charles Spurgeon (1834-1892)

2354 Life is a long lesson in humility.
James Matthew Barrie (1860-1937)

2. OPPOSITES

2355 The sage wears clothes of coarse cloth but carries jewels
   in his bosom;
He knows himself but does not display himself;
He loves himself but does not hold himself in high esteem.
Thus he rejects the latter and takes the former.
Lao-Tzu (fl. B.C. 600)

2356 When possessed of wealth or learning,
Low people become proud.
But even when doubly honored,
The wise become more humble.
Nagarjuna (c. 100-200 A.D.)

2357 The beloved of the Almighty are:
   the rich who have the humility of the poor,
   and the poor who have the magnanimity of the rich.
Saadi (1184-1291)

2358 It is easier to sacrifice great than little things.
Montaigne (1533-1592)

2359 It is what we give up, not what we lay up, that adds to our
lasting store.
Hosea Ballou (1771-1852)

2360 The Devil did grin, for his darling sin
Is pride that apes humility.
Samuel Coleridge (1772-1834)

2361 We cannot think too highly of our nature,
nor too humbly of ourselves.
Colton (1780-1832)

2362 The more humble a man is before God,
the more he will be exalted;
the more humble he is before man,
the more he will get rode roughshod.
Josh Billings (1815-1885)

2363 The higher a man is in grace,
the lower he will be in his own esteem.
Charles Spurgeon (1834-1892)

3. INSIGHT

2364 Modesty is at the core of the man's being and reveals
itself in his outward behavior.
I Ching (B.C. 1150?)

2365 I have three precious things which I hold fast and prize.
The first is gentleness; the second is frugality; the
third is humility, which keeps me from putting myself before
others. Be gentle and you can be bold; be frugal and you
can be liberal; avoid putting yourself before others and
you can become a leader among men.
Lao-Tzu (fl. B.C. 600)

2366 Humble things become the humble.
Horace (B.C. 65-8)

2367 Modesty once extinguished knows not how to return.
Seneca (B.C. 3-65 A.D.)

2368 Modesty is to merit, what shade is to figures in a picture;
it gives it strength and makes it stand out.
La Bruyere (1645-1696)

2369 To be humble to Superiors is Duty, to Equals Courtesy,
to Inferiors Nobleness.
Franklin (1706-1790)

2370   The boughs that bear most hang lowest.

                                            David Garrick (1716-1779)

2371   Humility does not consist in hiding our talents and virtues,
        in thinking ourselves worse and more ordinary than we are,
        but in possessing a clear knowledge of all that is lacking
        in us and in not exalting ourselves for that which we have..

                                            Lacordaire (1802-1861)

2372   I believe the first test of a truly great man is in his
        humility.

                                            John Ruskin (1819-1900)

4. POSITIVE

2373   The unassuming youth seeking instruction with humility
        gains good fortune.

                                            I Ching (B.C. 1150?)

2374   Humble station is the basis of honor.
        The low is the foundation of the high.

                                            Lao-Tzu (fl. B.C. 600)

2375   What can be found equal to modesty, uncorrupt faith,
        the sister of justice, and undisguised truth?

                                            Horace (B.C. 65-8)

2376   Modesty is a sweet song-bird no open cage-door can tempt to
        flight.

                                            Hafiz (1325?-1390?)

2377   Sense shines with a double luster when it is set in
        humility. An able and yet humble man is a jewel worth a
        kingdom.

                                            William Penn (1614-1718)

2378   Humility makes great men twice honourable.

                                            Franklin (1706-1790)

2379   Modesty seldom resides in a breast that is not
        enriched with nobler virtues.

                                            Goldsmith (1728-1774)

2380   He who does not think too much of himself
        is much more esteemed than he imagines.

                                            Goethe (1749-1832)

2381   Modesty is a shining light;
        it prepares the mind to receive knowledge,
        and the heart for truth.

                                            Guizot (1787-1874)

2382   Humility, like darkness, reveals the heavenly lights.
Thoreau (1817-1862)

5. NEGATIVE

2383   Modesty is of no use to a beggar.
Homer (c. B.C. 700)

2384   It is hard, indeed, to feel humble, to know respect and
honor, to get rid of all attachments, to keep pure in
thought and deed, and to become wise.
Buddha (B.C. 568-488)

2385   It is often found that modesty and humility not only do no
good, but are positively hurtful, when they are shown to the
arrogant who have taken up a prejudice against you, either
from envy or from any other cause.
Machiavelli (1469-1527)

2386   One may be humble out of pride.
Montaigne (1533-1592)

2387   False modesty is the refinement of vanity.
It is a lie.
La Bruyere (1645-1696)

2388   If man makes himself a worm he must not complain when he is
trodden on.
Immanuel Kant (1724-1804)

2389   Modesty is the lowest of the virtues, and is a confession
of the deficiency it indicates. He who undervalues himself
is justly overvalued by others.
Hazlitt (1778-1830)

2390   Never to talk about oneself is a very refined form of
hypocrisy.
Nietzsche (1844-1900)

6. ADVICE

2391   Manifest plainness,
Embrace simplicity,
Reduce selfishness,
Have few desires.
Lao-Tzu (fl. B.C. 600)

2392   Be of an exceedingly humble spirit,
for the end of man is the worm.
The Talmud (B.C. 500?-400? A.D.)

2393   Demand not that events should happen as you wish, but wish
them to happen as they do, and you will go on well.

                                              Epictetus (50-138 A.D.)

2394   A modesty in delivering our sentiments leaves us a liberty
of changing them without blushing.

                                    Thomas Wilson (1525?-1581)

2395   Be wise; soar not too high to fall,
but stoop to rise.

                                  Philip Massinger (1583-1640)

2396   Search others for their virtues, and thyself for thy vices.

                                    Thomas Fuller (1608-1661)

2397   A modest man never talks of himself.

                                    La Bruyere (1645-1696)

2398   O be very sure
That no man will learn anything at all,
Unless he first will learn humility.

                                  Owen Meredith (1831-1891)

2399   Be humble, if thou would'st attain to Wisdom.
Be humbler still, when Wisdom thou hast mastered.

                                  H. P. Blavatsky (1831-1891)

2400   Bear all and do nothing
Hear all and say nothing
Abandon all and be nothing.

                              Hazrat Inayat Khan (1882-1927)

2401   Be humble as the blade of grass that is being trodden
underneath the feet. The little ant tastes joyously the
sweetness of honey and sugar. The mighty elephant trembles
in pain under the agony of sharp goad.

                              Sivananda (born 1887)

7. POTPOURRI

2402   I have offended God and mankind because my work didn't
reach the quality it should have.

                              Leonardo Da Vinci (1452-1519)

2403   After crosses and losses men grow humbler and wiser.

                              Franklin (1706-1790)

2404   The bird of wisdom flies low, and seeks her food under
hedges; the eagle himself would be starved if he always
soared aloft and against the sun.

                              Landor (1775-1864)

2405 Humility, that low, sweet root,
      From which all heavenly virtues shoot.

Thomas Moore (1779-1852)

2406 At least I have the modesty to admit that lack of modesty
      is one of my failings.

Hector Berlioz (1803-1869)

2407 Good taste is the modesty of the mind;
      that is why it cannot be either imitated or acquired.

Emile de Girardin (1806-1881)

2408 The violet droops its soft and bashful brow,
      But from its heart sweet incense fills the air;
      So rich within - so pure without - art thou,
      With modest mien and soul of virtue rare.

Frances Osgood (1811-1850)

2409 In the world's audience hall, the simple blade of grass sits
      on the same carpet with the sunbeams, and the stars of
      midnight.

Rabindranath Tagore (1861-1941)

2410 The tumult and the shouting dies;
        The Captains and the Kings depart:
      Still stands Thine ancient sacrifice,
        An humble and a contrite heart.
      Lord God of Hosts, be with us yet,
        Lest we forget - lest we forget!

Kipling (1865-1936)

INERTIA

Boredom, Idleness, Indolence, Laziness, Procrastination and Sloth

1. ESSENCE

2411   Idleness is the holiday of fools.

                                 Chesterfield (1694-1773)

2412   Idleness is the Dead Sea that swallows all virtues.

                                 Franklin (1706-1790)

2413   Indolence is the sleep of the mind.

                                 Vauvenargues(1715-1747)

2414   Procrastination is the art of keeping up with yesterday.

                                 Donald Marquis (1878-1937)

2. OPPOSITES

2415   To be idle is a short road to death
       and to be diligent is a way of life;
       foolish people are idle,
       wise people are diligent.

                                 Buddha (B.C. 568-488)

2416   To-morrow I will live, the fool does say:
       to-day itself's too late; the wise lived yesterday.

                                 Martial (43-104 A.D.)

2417   Indolence of which a man is conscious, and indolence of
       which he is unconscious, are a thousand miles apart.
       Unconscious indolence is real indolence; conscious
       indolence is not complete indolence, because there is still
       some clarity in it... Unconscious indolence is like a
       sickness without symptoms; it is not noticed.

                                 Lu Yen (fl. 800 A.D.)

2418   Sloth makes all things difficult, but industry all easy;
       and he that riseth late must trot all day, and shall scarce
       overtake his business at night; while laziness travels so
       slowly that poverty soon overtakes him.

                                 Franklin (1706-1790)

2419   An idler is a watch that wants both hands;
       As useless if it goes as when it stands.

                                 Cowper (1731-1800)

2420 Necessity is the constant scourge of the lower classes,
      ennui of the higher ones.

                              Schopenhauer (1788-1860)

2421 Sow kindly acts and thou shalt reap their fruition.
      Inaction in a deed of mercy becomes an action in a deadly
      sin.

                              H. P. Blavatsky (1831-1891)

3. INSIGHT

2422 Thou seest how sloth wastes the sluggish body,
      as water is corrupted unless it moves.

                                Ovid (B.C. 43-18 A.D.)

2423 While we are postponing, life speeds by.

                               Seneca (B.C. 3-65 A.D.)

2424 Surely man was not created to be an idle fellow; he was not
      set in this universal orchard to stand still as a tree.

                              Thomas Dekker (1577-1632)

2425 Of all our faults, the one that we excuse most easily
      is idleness.

                           La Rochefoucauld (1613-1680)

2426 Sloth, like rust, consumes faster than labor wears,
      while the key often used is always bright.

                                 Franklin (1706-1790)

2427 Too much idleness, I have observed, fills up a man's time
      much more completely, and leaves him less his own master,
      than any other sort of employment whatsoever.

                                    Burke (1729-1797)

2428 There is no progress whatever. Everything is just the same
      as it was thousands, and tens of thousands, of years ago.
      The outward form changes. The essence does not change. Man
      remains just the same

                              Gurdjieff (1873-1949)

2429 Rivers and mountains may change...
      Human nature never.

                                    Chinese Proverb

4. POSITIVE

2430 Never do to-day what you can put off till to-morrow.
      Delay may give clearer light as to what is best to be done.
                              Aaron Burr (1756-1836)

2431   There is, by God's grace, an immeasurable distance between
       late and too late.

       Anne Swetchine (1782-1857)

2432   Where duty is plain delay is both foolish and hazardous;
       where it is not, delay may be both wisdom and safety.

       Tryon Edwards (1809-1894)

2433   Periods of wholesome laziness, after days of energetic
       effort, will wonderfully tone up the mind and body. It does
       not involve loss of time, since after a day of complete rest
       and quietness you will return to your regular occupation
       with renewed interest and vigor.

       Grenville Kleiser (1868-1953)

5. NEGATIVE

2434   The slothful man is a burden to himself, his hours hang
       heavy on his head; he loitereth about, and knoweth not what
       he would do.

       Akhenaton? (c. B.C. 1375)

2435   The man who procrastinates struggles with ruin.

       Hesiod (B.C. 800?)

2436   He who knoweth the precepts by heart,
          but faileth to practice them,
       Is like unto one who lighteth a lamp
          and then shutteth his eyes.

       Nagarjuna (c. 100-200 A.D.)

2437   Iron rusts from disuse, stagnant water loses its purity, and
       in cold weather becomes frozen; even so does inaction sap
       the vigors of the mind.

       Leonardo Da Vinci (1452-1519)

2438   Procrastination brings loss, delay danger.

       Erasmus (1466-1536)

2439   In delay we waste our lights in vain; like lamps by day.

       Shakespeare (1564-1616)

2440   Absence of occupation is not a rest;
       a mind quite vacant is a mind distressed.

       Cowper (1731-1800)

2441   The procrastinator is not only indolent and weak but
       commonly false too; most of the weak are false.

       Lavater (1741-1801)

2442 Life is a short day; but it is a working day. Activity may
lead to evil, but inactivity cannot lead to good.
Hannah More (1745-1833)

2443 Nature knows no pause in progress and development,
and attaches her curse to all inaction.
Goethe (1749-1832)

2444 Indolence and stupidity are first cousins.
Antoine de Rivaroli (1753-1801)

2445 The man who never alters his opinion is like standing water,
and breeds reptiles of the mind.
William Blake (1757-1828)

2446 Idleness is emptiness;
the tree in which the sap is stagnant, remains fruitless.
Hosea Ballou (1771-1852)

2447 Ennui has made more gamblers than avarice, more drunkards
than thirst, and perhaps as many suicides as despair.
Colton (1780-1832)

2448 There is no remedy for time misspent;
No healing for the waste of idleness,
Whose very languor is a punishment
Heavier than active souls can feel or guess.
Aubrey De Vere (1814-1902)

2449 The foolish and the dead alone never change their opinions.
James Lowell (1819-1891)

2450 The only horrible thing in the world is ennui. That is
the one sin for which there is no forgiveness.
Oscar Wilde (1854-1900)

2451 It is only a step from boredom to disillusionment,
which leads naturally to self-pity,
which in turn ends in chaos.
Manly P. Hall (born 1901)

6. ADVICE

2452 Flee sloth, for the indolence of the soul is the decay of
the body.
Cato the Younger (B.C. 95-46)

2453 That destructive siren, sloth, is ever to be avoided.
Horace (B.C. 65-8)

2454   Life is not long, and too much of it must not pass in idle
       deliberation how it shall be spent.

                                                    Johnson (1709-1784)

2455   When it is time to turn over in bed, it is time to turn out.
                                                    Wellington (1769-1852)

7. POTPOURRI

2456   We excuse our sloth under the pretext of difficulty.
                                                    Quintilian (35-90 A.D.)

2457   By the streets of "by and by", one arrives at the house
       of "never".

                                                    Cervantes (1547-1616)

2458   To-morrow, and to-morrow, and to-morrow, creeps in this
       petty pace from day to day; to the last syllable of
       recorded time; and all our yesterdays have lighted fools
       the way to dusty death.

                                                    Shakespeare (1564-1616)

2459   Procrastination is the thief of time:
       Year after year it steals, till all are fled,
       And to the mercies of a moment leaves
       The vast concerns of an eternal scene.

                                                    Young (1683-1765)

2460   Fix'd like a plant on his peculiar spot,
       To draw nutrition, propagate and rot.

                                                    Pope (1688-1744)

2461   Society is now one polished horde,
       Formed of two mighty tribes, the Bores and the Bored.
                                                    Byron (1788-1824)

2462   How dull it is to pause, to make an end,
       To rust unburnish'd, not to shine in use!
       As tho' to breathe were life!

                                                    Alfred Tennyson (1809-1892)

2463   In idle dreams I like to rest
       preferring the unmanifest.

                                                    Monique Louise De Nelle (born 1945)

JUDGMENT
Decision, Fire, Heaven and Hell

1. ESSENCE

2464   Heaven means to be one with God.
Confucius (B.C. 551-479)

2465   Heaven is not the wide blue sky but the place where
corporeality is begotten in the house of the Creative.
Lu Yen (fl. 800 A.D.)

2466   Heaven, the treasury of everlasting joy.
Shakespeare (1564-1616)

2467   Hell is the full knowledge of the truth when truth, resisted
long, is sworn our foe, and calls eternity to do her right.
Young (1683-1765)

2468   By heaven we understand a state of happiness
infinite in degree, and endless in duration.
Franklin (1706-1790)

2469   A perpetual holiday is a good working definition of hell.
G. B. Shaw (1856-1950)

2470   Hell is not to love anymore.
Georges Bernanos (1888-1948)

2. OPPOSITES

2471   The choice must be made between the path of public acclaim
and the path of obscurity and introspection. Each person
must make their own choice.
I Ching (B.C. 1150?)

2472   Heaven but the Vision of fulfilled Desire.
And Hell the Shadow from a Soul on fire.
Omar Khayyam (fl. 1100)

2473   Men's judgements are a parcel of their fortunes; and
things outward do draw the inward quality after them.
Shakespeare (1564-1616)

2474   It is not alone what we do, but also what we do not do,
for which we are accountable.
Moliere (1622-1673)

2475 Hell was built on spite, and Heaven on pride.

Pope (1688-1744)

2476 In our judgment of human transactions, the law of optics is
reversed; we see the most indistinctly the objects which
are close around us.

Richard Whately (1787-1863)

2477 The majority of men are subjective toward themselves and
objective toward all others, terribly objective sometimes,
but the real task is in fact to be objective toward oneself
and subjective toward all others.

Kierkegaard (1813-1855)

2478 The very thing that men think they have got the most of,
they have got the least of; and that is judgment.

Josh Billings (1815-1885)

2479 We judge ourselves by what we feel capable of doing,
while others judge us by what we have already done.

Longfellow (1807-1882)

2480 Nothing is farther than earth from heaven;
nothing is nearer than heaven to earth.

Hare & Charles (c. 1830)

2481 It took me forty years on earth
    To reach this sure conclusion:
There is no Heaven but clarity,
    No Hell except confusion.

Jan Struther (1901-1953)

2482 A wise man makes his own decisions,
an ignorant man follows the public opinion.

Chinese Proverb

3. INSIGHT

2483 As the kindled fire consumes the fuel, so in the flame of
wisdom the embers of action are burnt to ashes.

Bhagavad Gita (c. B.C. 400)

2484 The nature of all men is so formed that they see and
discriminate in the affairs of others, much better than
in their own.

Terence (B.C. 185-159)

2485 What came from the earth returns back to the earth,
and the spirit that was sent from heaven, again carried
back, is received into the temple of heaven.

Lucretius (B.C. 99-55)

2486   The love of heaven makes one heavenly.
                                Shakespeare (1564-1616)

2487   Everyone complains of his memory;
       no one complains of his judgement.
                             La Rochefoucauld (1613-1680)

2488   Knowledge is the treasure, but judgment is the treasurer
       of a wise man.
                                William Penn (1614-1718)

2489   Men are not to be judged by their looks, habits, and
       appearances; but by the character of their lives and
       conversations, and by their works.
                                L'Estrange (1616-1704)

2490   Self-love and the love of the world constitute hell.
                                Swedenborg (1688-1772)

2491   It is with our judgments as our watches,
       none go just alike, yet each believes his own.
                                Pope (1688-1744)

2492   I mistrust the judgment of every man in a case in which
       his own wishes are concerned.
                                Wellington (1769-1852)

2493   How little do they see what really is, who frame their
       hasty judgment upon that which seems.
                                Robert Southey (1774-1843)

2494   We do not judge men by what they are in themselves, but
       by what they are relatively to us.
                                Anne Swetchine (1782-1857)

2495   Whatsoever a man soweth, that, and not something else, shall
       he reap. That which we are doing, good or evil, grave or
       gay, that which we do to-day and shall do to-morrow; each
       thought, each feeling, each action, each event; every pass-
       ing hour, every breathing moment; all are contributing to
       form the character, according to which we are to be judged.
                                Albert Pike (1809-1891)

2496   It is an eternal law that man cannot be redeemed by a power
       external to himself.
                                H. P. Blavatsky (1831-1891)

2497   It does not take much strength to do things, but it
       requires great strength to decide on what to do.
                                Elbert Hubbard (1859-1915)

2498 A mountain is composed of tiny grains of earth. The ocean
is made up of tiny drops of water. Even so, life is but an
endless series of little details, actions, speeches and
thoughts...And the consequences whether good or bad of even
the least of them are far-reaching.

Sivananda (born 1887)

4. POSITIVE

2499 The Way of Heaven does not compete,
And yet it skillfully achieves victory.
It does not speak, and yet it skillfully responds to things.
It comes to you without your invitation.
It is not anxious about things and yet it plans well.
Heaven's net is indeed vast.
Though its meshes are wide, it misses nothing.

Lao-Tzu (fl. B.C. 600)

2500 As the touchstone which tries gold, but is not itself tried
by the gold; such is he, who has the standard of judgment.

Epictetus (50-138 A.D.)

2501 A right judgment draws us a profit from all things we see.

Shakespeare (1564-1616)

2502 The generous who is always just, and the just who is always
generous, may, unannounced, approach the throne of heaven.

Lavater (1741-1801)

2503 There is nothing more to be esteemed than a manly firmness
and decision of character. I like a person who knows his
own mind and sticks to it; who sees at once what is to be
done in given circumstances and does it.

Hazlitt (1778-1830)

5. NEGATIVE

2504 There are demon-haunted worlds, regions of utter darkness.
Whoever in life denies the Spirit falls into that darkness
of death.

Upanishads (c. B.C. 800)

2505 He who says what is not goes to hell; he also who, having
done a thing, says I have not done it. After death both
are equal: they are men with evil deeds in the next world.

The Dhammapada (c. B.C. 300)

2506 The way of sinners is made plain with stones,
but at the end thereof is the pit of hell.

Ecclesiasticus (B.C. 200?)

2507 The ascent from earth to heaven is not easy.
Seneca (B.C. 3-65 A.D.)

2508 And where two raging fires meet together,
They do consume the thing that feeds their fury.
Shakespeare (1564-1616)

2509 We sometimes see a fool possessed of talent,
but never of judgment.
La Rochefoucauld (1613-1680)

2510 The more one judges, the less one loves.
Balzac (1799-1850)

2511 Heaven might be defined as the place which men avoid.
Thoreau (1817-1862)

2512 There is no more miserable human being than one in whom
nothing is habitual but indecision.
William James (1842-1910)

2513 Only our concept of time makes it possible for us to speak
of the Day of Judgment by that name; in reality it is a
summary court in perpetual session.
Franz Kafka (1883-1924)

2514 Maybe this world is another planet's Hell.
Aldous Huxley (1894-1963)

2515 The safest road to Hell is the gradual one - the gentle
slope, soft underfoot, without sudden turnings, without
milestones, without signposts.
C. S. Lewis (1898-1963)

6. ADVICE

2516 Examine the contents, not the bottle.
The Talmud (B.C. 500?-400? A.D.)

2517 Mark well three things and thou wilt not fall into the
clutches of sin: Know what is above thee - an eye that
sees, an ear that hears, and all thine actions recorded
in the book.
The Talmud (B.C. 500?-400? A.D.)

2518 Judge a tree from its fruit; not from the leaves.
Euripides (B.C. 480-406)

2519   Men must be decided on what they will not do, and then
       they are able to act with vigor in what they ought to do.
                                         Mencius (B.C. 371-288)

2520   Speak the truth, do not yield to anger; give, if thou art
       asked for little; by these three steps thou wilt go near
       the gods.
                                    The Dhammapada (c. B.C. 300)

2521   Judge not, that ye be not judged. For with what judgment
       ye judge, ye shall be judged; and with what measure ye
       mete, it shall be measured to you again.
                                      Jesus (B.C. 6?-30? A.D.)

2522   In judging of others a man laboreth in vain, often erreth,
       and easily sinneth; but in judging and examining himself,
       he always laboreth fruitfully.
                                    Thomas A. Kempis (1380-1471)

2523   Give every man thy ear, but few thy voice;
       Take each man's censure, but reserve thy judgment.
                                        Shakespeare (1564-1616)

2524   Give your decisions, never your reasons; your decisions may
       be right, your reasons are sure to be wrong.
                                        Mansfield (1705-1793)

2525   When confronted with two courses of action I jot down on a
       piece of paper all the arguments in favor of each one -
       then on the opposite side I write the arguments against each
       one. Then by weighing the arguments pro and con and
       canceling them out, one against the other, I take the course
       indicated by what remains.
                                        Franklin (1706-1790)

2526   Be sure you are right, then go ahead.
                                    David Crockett (1786-1836)

2527   To reach the port of Heaven we must sail sometimes with the
       wind and sometimes against it. But we must sail, and not
       drift or lie at anchor.
                              Oliver Wendell Holmes (1809-1894)

2528   When once a decision is reached and execution is the order
       of the day, dismiss absolutely all responsibility and care
       about the outcome.
                                    William James (1842-1910)

2529   To get to heaven we must take it with us.
                                    Henry Drummond (1851-1897)

2530   Depend upon yourself. Make your judgement trustworthy by
       trusting it. You can develop good judgement as you do the
       muscles of your body - by judicious, daily exercise. To be
       known as a man of sound judgement will be much in your
       favor.

                                        Grenville Kleiser (1868-1953)

2531   I shall tell you a great secret, my friend. Do not wait for
       the last judgment, it takes place every day.

                                        Albert Camus (1913-1960)

2532   One must be aware that one is continually being tested in
       what one wishes most in order to make clear whether one's
       heart is on earth or in heaven.

                                        Pir Vilayat Inayat Khan (born 1916)

7. POTPOURRI

2533   For the Lord thy God is a consuming fire, even a jealous
       God.

                                        Deuteronomy (B.C. 1200?-800?)

2534   Into deep darkness fall those who follow action.
       Into deeper darkness fall those who follow knowledge.
       There are worlds of no joy, regions of utter darkness.
       To those worlds go after death those who in their unwisdom
       have not wakened up to light.

                                        Upanishads (c. B.C. 800)

2535   The descent to hell is easy; the gates stand open night
       and day; but to reclimb the slope, and escape to the upper
       air, this is labor.

                                        Vergil (B.C. 70-19)

2536   He who does not try a remedy
       For the disease of going to hell
       What will he do when he reaches that place
       Where there is no cure to be found?

                                        Nagarjuna (c. 100-200 A.D.)

2537   Every soul is subject to the trial of Transmigration...
       An individual does not know that he is called for assessment
       before entering this World as well as after leaving it. He
       does not know how many transformations and esoteric trials
       he has to pass through...and that souls revolve like a stone
       shot from a sling.

                                        Zohar (120?-1200? A.D.)

2538   When the Heaven is rent asunder, and when the stars are
        scattered, and when the seas are let loose, and when the
        tombs are turned upside-down, the soul shall know what
        it hath done and left undone.

                                            Koran (c. 651 A.D.)

2539   Lo! the Day of Decision is appointed - the day when there
        shall be a blowing of the trumpet, and ye shall come in
        troops, and the heavens shall be opened, and be full of
        gates, and the mountains shall be removed, and turn into
        mist.

                                            Koran (c. 651 A.D.)

2540   You are now before the King of the Dead. In vain will you
        try to lie, and to deny or conceal the evil deeds you have
        done. The Judge holds up before you the shining mirror of
        action, wherein all your deeds are reflected...The mirror in
        which the King of the Dead seems to read your past is your
        own memory, and also his judgment is your own. It is you
        yourself who pronounce your own judgment, which in its turn
        determines your next rebirth.

                                Tibetan Book of the Dead (c. 780 A.D.)

2541   Whoever has done good in the main has spirit-energy that is
        pure and clear when death comes. It passes out by the upper
        openings of mouth and nose. The pure and light energy rises
        upward and floats up to heaven and becomes shadow-spirit.
         But if, during life, the primal spirit was used by the
        conscious spirit for avarice, folly, desire, and lust, and
        committed all sorts of sins, then in the moment of death
        the spirit-energy is turbid and confused...it crystallizes
        downward, sinks down to hell, and becomes a demon...

                                            Lu Yen (fl. 800 A.D.)

2542   I would not give one moment of heaven for all the joy and
        riches of the world, even if it lasted for thousands
        and thousands of years.

                                        Martin Luther (1483-1546)

2543   The trumpet! the trumpet! the dead have all heard;
        Lo, the depths of the stone-covered charnels are stirred:
        From the sea, from the land, from the south and the north.
        The vast generations of man are come forth.
                                        Henry H. Milman (1791-1868)

2544   It is not beyond the tomb, but in life itself, that we are
        to seek for the mysteries of death. Salvation or reproba-
        tion begins here below, and the terrestrial world too has
        its Heaven and its Hell. Always, even here below, virtue
        is rewarded; always, even here below, vice is punished...
                                        Albert Pike (1809-1891)

2545 Once to every man and nation comes the moment to decide,
In the strife of Truth with Falsehood, for the good or
evil side.

James Lowell (1819-1891)

2546 We see but dimly through the mists and vapors;
Amid these earthly damps
What seem to us but sad, funeral tapers
May be heaven's distant lamps.

Longfellow (1807-1882)

2547 Of the delights of this world man cares most for sexual
intercourse, yet he has left it out of his heaven.

Mark Twain (1835-1910)

2548 Who seeks for Heaven alone to save his soul
May keep the path, but will not reach the goal;
While he who walks in love may wander far,
Yet God will bring him where the blessed are.

Henry Van Dyke (1852-1933)

2549 For when the One Great Scorer comes
To write against your name,
He marks - not that you won or lost -
But how you played the game.

Grantland Rice (1880-1954)

JUSTICE

Equality and Rights

1. ESSENCE

2550   What is justice? - To give every man his own.

Aristotle (B.C. 384-322)

2551   Justice renders to every one his due.

Cicero (B.C. 106-43)

2552   Justice is truth in actions.

Disraeli (1804-1881)

2. OPPOSITES

2553   The love of justice in most men is only the fear of
suffering injustice.

La Rochefoucauld (1613-1680)

2554   Justice without force is powerless;
force without justice is tyrannical.

Pascal (1623-1662)

2555   Justice is the first virtue of those who command,
and stops the complaints of those who obey.

Denis Diderot (1713-1784)

2556   Justice without strength, or strength without justice;
fearful misfortunes!

Joubert (1754-1824)

2557   That which is unjust can really profit no one;
that which it just can really harm no one.

Henry George (1839-1897)

2558   The law of cause and effect is inexorable and unrelenting.
   You reap a harvest of suffering, poverty, pain and sorrow,
because you have sown the seed of evil in the past.
   You reap a harvest of plenty and bliss owing to your
sowing seeds of good.

Sivananda (born 1887)

2559   I would remind you that extremism in the defence of liberty
is no vice. And let me remind you also that moderation in
pursuit of justice is no virtue.

Barry Goldwater (born 1909)

3. INSIGHT

2560 A just man is not one who does no ill,
   But he, who with the power, has not the will.
Philemon (B.C. 361-262)

2561 Justice consists in doing no injury to men;
   decency in giving them no offense.
Cicero (B.C. 106-43)

2562 Fidelity is the sister of justice.
Horace (B.C. 65-8)

2563 Equality is the share of every one at their advent upon
   earth, and equality is also theirs when placed beneath it.
Ninon de L'Enclos (1620-1705)

2564 The sentiment of justice is so natural, so universally
   acquired by all mankind, that it seems to be independent of
   all law, all party, all religion.
Voltaire (1694-1778)

2565 Whenever a separation is made between liberty and justice,
   neither, in my opinion, is safe.
Burke (1729-1797)

2566 Justice is the bread of the nation;
   it is always hungry for it.
Chateaubriand (1768-1848)

2567 Justice delayed, is justice denied.
William Gladstone (1809-1898)

2568 To hear patiently, to weigh deliberately and dispassion-
   ately, and to decide to impartially; these are the chief
   duties of a Judge.
Albert Pike (1809-1891)

2569 I do not see why we should not be as just to an ant as to a
   human being.
Charles Kingsley (1819-1875)

2570 It is not who is right, but what is right,
   that is of importance.
Thomas Huxley (1825-1895)

2571 The whole history of the world is summed up in the fact
   that, when nations are strong, they are not always just,
   and when they wish to be just, they are no longer strong.
Winston Churchill (1874-1965)

2572   It is the spirit and not the form of law that keeps justice
        alive.
                                        Earl Warren (1891-1974)

4. POSITIVE

2573   How invincible is justice if it be well spoken.
                                        Cicero (B.C. 106-43)

2574   Justice, though moving with tardy pace,
        has seldom failed to overtake the wicked in their flight.
                                        Horace (B.C. 65-8)

2575   Justice is an unassailable fortress, built on the brow of a
        mountain which cannot be overthrown by the violence of
        torrents, nor demolished by the force of armies.
                                        Koran (c. 651 A.D.)

2576   Only the actions of the just
        smell sweet and blossom in the dust.
                                        James Shirley (1596-1666)

2577   To be perfectly just is an attribute of the divine nature;
        to be so to the utmost of our abilities, is the glory of
        man.
                                        Addison (1672-1719)

2578   Justice is the great interest of man on earth. It is the
        ligament which holds civilized beings and civilized nations
        together.
                                        Daniel Webster (1782-1852)

2579   A man is a little thing while he works by and for himself;
        but when he gives voice to the rules of love and justice,
        he is godlike.
                                        Emerson (1803-1882)

2580   Above all other things is justice.
        Success is a good thing; wealth is good also;
        honor is better, but justice excels them all.
                                        David Dudley Field (1805-1894)

2581   Knowledge is convertible into power, and axioms into rules
        of utility and duty. But knowledge itself is not Power.
        Wisdom is Power; and her Prime Minister is Justice,
        which is the perfected law of Truth.
                                        Albert Pike (1809-1891)

2582   The proof of a thing's being right is that it has power
        over the heart; that it excites us, wins us, or helps us.
                                        John Ruskin (1819-1900)

5. NEGATIVE

2583   There is a point at which even justice does injury.
                                    Sophocles (B.C. 495-406)

2584   He who commits injustice is ever made more wretched
        than he who suffers it.
                                    Plato (B.C. 427?-347?)

2585   There is no cruder tyranny than that which is perpetuated
        under the shield of law and in the name of justice.
                                    Montesquieu (1689-1755)

2586   So far is it from being true that men are naturally equal,
        that no two people can be half an hour together but one
        shall acquire an evident superiority over the other.
                                    Johnson (1709-1784)

2587   It is untrue that equality is a law of nature. Nature has
        no equality. Its sovereign law is subordination and
        dependence.
                                    Vauvenargues(1715-1747)

2588   He who is only just is cruel.
        Who on earth could live were all judged justly?
                                    Byron (1788-1824)

2589   Justice without wisdom is impossible.
                                    Froude (1818-1894)

2590   There is no such thing as justice - in or out of court.
                                    Clarence Darrow (1857-1938)

2591   Injustice is relatively easy to bear;
        what stings is justice.
                                    H. L. Mencken (1880-1956)

6. ADVICE

2592   If thou suffer injustice, console thyself;
        the true unhappiness is in doing it.
                                    Democritus (B.C. 490-360)

2593   Justice, being destroyed, will destroy;
        being preserved, will preserve;
        it must never therefore be violated.
                                    Manu (c. B.C. 200)

2594   Equal rights for all, special privileges for none.
                                    Thomas Jefferson (1743-1826)

2595   One man's word is no man's word;
        we should quietly hear both sides.

                                        Goethe (1749-1832)

2596   Stand with anybody that stands right while he is right
        and part with him when he goes wrong.

                                        Lincoln (1809-1865)

2597   Keep justice, keep generosity, yielding to neither singly.
                                        Tupper (1810-1889)

2598   We win justice quickest by rendering justice
        to the other party.

                                        Gandhi (1869-1948)

2599   If we are to keep our democracy,
        there must be one commandment:
        "Thou shalt not ration justice."

                                        Learned Hand (1872-1961)

7. POTPOURRI

2600   Eye for eye, tooth for tooth, hand for hand, foot for foot.
                                        Exodus (B.C. 1200?)

2601   A clear-cut case meets with difficulty because of a tendency
        to be lenient. The man must be as true as gold and as
        impartial as the mean.

                                        I Ching (B.C. 1150?)

2602   All men are by nature equal, made all of the same earth by
        one Workman; and however we deceive ourselves, as dear unto
        God is the poor peasant as the mighty prince.

                                        Plato (B.C. 427?-347?)

2603   Just are the ways of God,
        And justifiable to men.

                                        Milton (1608-1674)

2604   All Nature is but art unknown to thee;
        All chance direction, which thou canst not see;
        All discord, harmony not understood;
        All partial evil, universal good;
        And spite of pride, in erring reason's spite,
        One truth is clear, Whatever is is right.

                                        Pope (1688-1744)

2605   Justice is as strictly due between neighbor nations, as
        between neighbor citizens. A highwayman is as much a robber
        when he plunders in a gang, as when single; and a nation
        that makes an unjust war is only a great gang of robbers.
                                                Franklin (1706-1790)

2606   Justice is my being allowed to do whatever I like.
        Injustice is whatever prevents my doing so.
                                                Johnson (1709-1784)

2607   Your levellers wish to level down as far as themselves,
        but they cannot bear levelling up to themselves.
                                                Johnson (1709-1784)

2608   Freedom of religion, freedom of the press, freedom of person
        under protection of habeas corpus; and trial by juries
        impartially selected, these principles form the bright
        constellation which has gone before us, and guided our
        steps through an age of revolution and reformation.
                                        Thomas Jefferson (1743-1826)

2609   Prompt sense of equality! to thee belongs
        The swift redress of unexamined wrongs!
        Eager to serve, the cause perhaps untried,
        But always apt to choose the suffering side.
                                            Hannah More (1745-1833)

2610   I will be as harsh as truth
        and as uncompromising as justice.
                                        William Garrison (1805-1879)

2611   Man is unjust, but God is just; and finally justice
        Triumphs.
                                            Longfellow (1807-1882)

2612   Judging from the main portions of the history of the world,
        so far, justice is always in jeopardy.
                                        Walt Whitman (1819-1892)

2613   Within me justice saith: Men are not equal; neither shall
        they become so.
                                            Nietzsche (1844-1900)

2614   When a man wants to murder a tiger, he calls it sport;
        When the tiger wants to murder him, he calls it ferocity.
        The distinction between crime and justice is no greater.
                                            G. B. Shaw (1856-1950)

LEARNING

Education, Experience, Study and Teaching

1. ESSENCE

2615 Learning is a kind of natural food for the mind.
Cicero (B.C. 106-43)

2616 From one learn all.
Vergil (B.C. 70-19)

2617 Each day is the scholar of yesterday.
Publilius Syrus (fl. B.C. 42)

2618 Education: A debt due from present to future generations.
George Peabody (1795-1869)

2619 Education is the instruction of the intellect in the laws
of Nature.
Thomas Huxley (1825-1895)

2620 Teaching is the art of awakening the natural curiosity of
young minds for the purpose of satisfying it afterwards.
Anatole France (1844-1924)

2621 Education is the transmission of civilization.
Will Durant (1885-1981)

2622 Experience is not what happens to a man.
It is what a man does with what happens to him.
Aldous Huxley (1894-1963)

2. OPPOSITES

2623 The good man is the teacher of the bad,
And the bad is the material from which the good may learn.
He who does not value the teacher,
Or greatly care for the material,
Is greatly deluded although he may be learned.
Such is the essential mystery.
Lao-Tzu (fl. B.C. 600)

2624 Learning without thought is labor lost;
thought without learning is perilous.
Confucius (B.C. 551-479)

2625 The roots of education are bitter, but the fruit is sweet.
Aristotle (B.C. 384-322)

2626 It is impossible for a man to learn what he thinks he
already knows.

Epictetus (50-138 A.D.)

2627 If you desire ease, forsake learning.
If you desire learning, forsake ease.
How can a man at ease acquire knowledge,
And how can an earnest student enjoy ease?

Nagarjuna (c. 100-200 A.D.)

2628 Learning makes the wise wiser and the fool more foolish.

John Ray (1627-1705)

2629 Learning is like mercury, one of the most powerful and
excellent things in the world in skillful hands;
in unskillful, the most mischievous.

Pope (1688-1744)

2630 He that studies only men, will get the body of knowledge
without the soul; and he that studies only books, the soul
without the body. He that to what he sees, adds
observation, and to what he reads, reflection, is on the
right road to knowledge, provided that in scrutinizing
the hearts of others, he neglects not his own.

Colton (1780-1832)

2631 It is only when we forget all our learning that we begin
to know.

Thoreau (1817-1862)

2632 The chief object of education is not to learn things
but to unlearn things.

G. K. Chesterton (1874-1936)

2633 Sixty years ago I knew everything; now I know nothing;
education is a progressive discovery of our own ignorance.

Will Durant (1885-1981)

2634 Lessons are not given, they are taken.

Cesare Pavese (1908-1950)

3. INSIGHT

2635 The great teacher who skillfully waits to be questioned may
be compared to a bell when it is struck. Struck with a
small hammer, it gives a small sound; struck with a great
one, it gives a great sound. But let it be struck leisurely
and properly, and it gives out all the sound of which it is
capable.

Confucius (B.C. 551-479)

2636   Iron sharpens iron; scholar, the scholar.
                                    The Talmud (B.C. 500?-400? A.D.)

2637   The most effective kind of education is that a child
        should play amongst lovely things.
                                    Plato (B.C. 427?-347?)

2638   We have need of very little learning to have a good mind.
                                    Montaigne (1533-1592)

2639   Reading maketh a full man; conference a ready man;
        and writing an exact man.
                                    Bacon (1561-1626)

2640   Crafty men condemn studies, simple men admire them,
        and wise men use them.
                                    Bacon (1561-1626)

2641   You cannot teach a man anything; you can only help him to
        find it within himself.
                                    Galileo (1564-1642)

2642   Some men grow mad by studying much to know,
        But who grows mad by studying good to grow.
                                    Franklin (1706-1790)

2643   The supreme end of education is expert discernment in all
        things - the power to tell the good from the bad, the
        genuine from the counterfeit, and to prefer the good and the
        genuine to the bad and the counterfeit.
                                    Johnson (1709-1784)

2644   The aim of education should be to teach us rather how to
        think, than what to think - rather to improve our minds, so
        as to enable us to think for ourselves, than to load the
        memory with the thoughts of other men.
                                    James Beattie (1735-1803)

2645   A college education shows a man how little other people
        know.
                                    Haliburton (1796-1865)

2646   The secret of education is respecting the pupil.
                                    Emerson (1803-1882)

2647   Seeing much, suffering much, and studying much, are the
        three pillars of learning.
                                    Disraeli (1804-1881)

2648   The best education in the world is that got by struggling
        to get a living.
                                    Wendell Phillips (1811-1884)

2649   There are three schoolmasters for everybody that will employ
        them - the senses, intelligent companions, and books.
                                            Beecher (1813-1878)

2650   To know how to suggest is the great art of teaching.
                                    Henri Frederic Amiel (1821-1881)

2651   Reading and writing, arithmetic and grammar do not
        constitute education, any more than a knife, fork and spoon
        constitute a dinner.
                                            Lubbock (1834-1913)

2652   Education does not consist merely in studying languages and
        learning a number of facts. It is something very different
        from, and higher than, mere instruction. Instruction shores
        up for future use, but education sows seed which will bear
        fruit, some thirty, sixty, some one hundred fold.
                                            Lubbock (1834-1913)

2653   Education is what survives when what has been learnt has
        been forgotten.
                                        B. F. Skinner (born 1904)

4. POSITIVE

2654   The noblest employment of the mind of man, is the study of
        the works of his Creator.
                                        Akhenaton? (c. B.C. 1375)

2655   To live a single day and hear a good teaching is better
        than to live a hundred years without knowing such teaching.
                                        Buddha (B.C. 568-488)

2656   The rules aimed at in the Great College were:
          the prevention of evil before it was manifested;
          the timeliness of instruction when it was required; the
          suitability of the lessons in adaptation to circumstances;
          and the good influence of example to all those concerned.
        From these four things the Great Teaching flourishes.
                                        Confucius (B.C. 551-479)

2657   There are more men ennobled by study than by nature.
                                        Cicero (B.C. 106-43)

2658   Instruction enlarges the natural powers of the mind.
                                        Horace (B.C. 65-8)

2659   Only the educated are free.

                                          Epictetus (50-138 A.D.)

2660   The teachings of elegant sayings
       Should be collected when one can.
       For the supreme gift of words of wisdom,
       Any price will be paid.

                                          Nagarjuna (c. 100-200 A.D.)

2661   Histories make men wise; poets, witty; the mathematics,
       subtle; natural philosophy, deep; morals, grave; logic
       and rhetoric, able to contend.

                                          Bacon (1561-1626)

2662   Learning makes a man fit company for himself.

                                          Young (1683-1765)

2663   There is an unspeakable pleasure attending the life of
       a voluntary student.

                                          Goldsmith (1728-1774)

2664   Education is the cheap defence of nations.

                                          Burke (1729-1797)

2665   The true purpose of education is to cherish and unfold
       the seed of immortality already sown within us; to develop,
       to their fullest extent, the capacities of every kind
       with which the God who made us has endowed us.

                                          Anna Jameson (1794-1860)

2666   Education alone can conduct us to that enjoyment which is,
       at once, best in quality and infinite in quantity.

                                          Horace Mann (1796-1859)

2667   The true teacher defends his pupils against his own
       personal influence.

                                          Amos B. Alcott (1799-1888)

2668   The teacher is like the candle which lights others in
       consuming itself.

                                          Giovanni Ruffini (1807-1881)

2669   Education is leading human souls to what is best, and
       making what is best out of them; and these two objects are
       always attainable together, and by the same means; the
       training which makes men happiest in themselves also makes
       them most serviceable to others.

                                          John Ruskin (1819-1900)

2670   Knowledge increases in proportion to its use -
        that is, the more we teach the more we learn.
                                                H. P. Blavatsky (1831-1891)

2671   Learning is weightless...
        Treasure you always carry easily.
                                                            Chinese Proverb

5. NEGATIVE

2672   There is the love of knowing without the love of learning;
        the beclouding here leads to dissipation of mind.
                                                Confucius (B.C. 551-479)

2673   The learning and knowledge that we have, is, at the most,
        but little compared with that of which we are ignorant.
                                                Plato (B.C. 427?-347?)

2674   As a man can drink water from any side of a full tank,
        so the skilled theologian can wrest from any scripture
        that which will serve his purpose.
                                                Bhagavad Gita (c. B.C. 400)

2675   Much study is a weariness of the flesh.
                                                Ecclesiastes (B.C. 300?)

2676   Suffering is but another name for the teaching of
        experience, which is the parent of instruction and the
        schoolmaster of life.
                                                Horace (B.C. 65-8)

2677   Since learned men have appeared, good men have become rare.
                                                Seneca (B.C. 3-65 A.D.)

2678   All wish to be learned, but no one is willing to pay the
        price.
                                                Juvenal (40-125 A.D.)

2679   He who learns, and makes no use of his learning, is a beast
        of burden with a load of books. - Does the ass comprehend
        whether he carries on his back a library or a bundle of
        faggots?
                                                Saadi (1184-1291)

2680   I perceive all the professors of exoteric knowledge
            to be full of learning with no application -
        Day and night wasting their lives, pursuing
            discussion, chatter, and empty disputation.
                                                Ni'matullah Wali (1331-1431?)

2681   It is the worst of madness to learn what has to be
       unpleasant.

                                            Erasmus (1466-1536)

2682   As plants are suffocated and drowned with too much moisture,
       and lamps with too much oil, so is the active part of the
       understanding with too much study.

                                            Montaigne (1533-1592)

2683   Studies teach not their own use; that is a wisdom without
       them and above them, won by observation.

                                            Bacon (1561-1626)

2684   He that was only taught by himself
       had a fool for his master.

                                            Ben Jonson (1572-1637)

2685   Learning, that cobweb of the brain,
       Profane, erroneous, and vain.

                                            Samuel Butler (1612-1680)

2686   To be proud of learning, is the greatest ignorance.

                                            Jeremy Taylor (1613-1667)

2687   Much reading is an oppression of the mind, and extinguishes
       the natural candle, which is the reason there are so many
       senseless scholars in the world.

                                            William Penn (1614-1718)

2688   Words are but wind; and learning is nothing but words;
       ergo, learning is nothing but wind.

                                            Swift (1667-1745)

2689   He not only overflowed with learning, but stood in the
       slop.

                                            Sydney Smith (1771-1845)

2690   One of the benefits of a college education
       is to show the boy its little avail.

                                            Emerson (1803-1882)

2691   It is a thousand times better to have common sense without
       education than to have education without common sense.

                                            Robert G. Ingersoll (1833-1899)

2692   Never learn to do anything: if you don't learn, you'll
       always find someone else to do it for you.

                                            Mark Twain (1835-1910)

2693   The surest way to corrupt a young man is to teach him to
       esteem more highly those who think alike than those who
       think differently.

                                        Nietzsche (1844-1900)

2694   Education is an admirable thing, but it is well to remember
       from time to time that nothing that is worth knowing can be
       taught.

                                        Oscar Wilde (1854-1900)

2695   A learned man is an idler who kills time by study.

                                        G. B. Shaw (1856-1950)

2696   He who can does. He who can't, teaches.

                                        G. B. Shaw (1856-1950)

2697   There is nothing so stupid as an educated man,
       if you get off the thing he was educated in.

                                        Will Rogers (1879-1935)

6. ADVICE

2698   Learn that the advantage lieth not in possessing good
       things, but in the knowing the use of them.

                                        Akhenaton? (c. B.C. 1375)

2699   If I am walking with two other men, each of them will serve
       as my teacher. I will pick out the good points of the one
       and imitate them, and the bad points of the other and
       correct them in myself.

                                        Confucius (B.C. 551-479)

2700   The elements of instruction should be presented to the
       mind in childhood, but not with any compulsion.

                                        Plato (B.C. 427?-347?)

2701   What we have to learn to do, we learn by doing.

                                        Aristotle (B.C. 384-322)

2702   Study what thou art
       Whereof thou art a part
       What thou knowest of this art
       This is really what thou art.
       All that is without thee also is within.

                                        Solomon Trismosin (fl. 1580)

2703   Men must be taught as if you taught them not,
       And things unknown propos'd as things forgot.

                                        Pope (1688-1744)

2704 Wear your learning like your watch, in a private pocket;
and do not pull it out and strike it merely to show that
you have one.

Chesterfield (1694-1773)

2705 Let the great book of the world be your principle study.

Chesterfield (1694-1773)

2706 Learn that the present hour alone is man's.

Johnson (1709-1784)

2707 Life teaches us to be less severe with ourselves and others.

Goethe (1749-1832)

2708 There is no easy method of learning difficult things. The
method is to close the door, give out that you are not at
home, and work.

De Maistre (1754-1821)

2709 To waken interest and kindle enthusiasm is the sure way to
teach easily and successfully.

Tryon Edwards (1809-1894)

2710 As turning the logs will make a dull fire burn,
so changes of studies a dull brain.

Longfellow (1807-1882)

2711 Perhaps the most valuable result of all education is the
ability to make yourself do the thing you have to do, when
it ought to be done, whether you like it or not.

Thomas Huxley (1825-1895)

2712 Those who have not distinguished themselves at school need
not on that account be discouraged. The greatest minds do
not necessarily ripen the quickest.

Lubbock (1834-1913)

2713 The study of oneself must go side by side with the study of
the fundamental laws of the universe. The laws are the
same everywhere and on all planes. But the very same laws
manifesting themselves in different worlds, that is, under
different conditions, produce different phenomena.

Gurdjieff (1873-1949)

2714 Never regard study as a duty but as an enviable opportunity
to learn to know the liberating influence of beauty in the
realm of the spirit for your own personal joy and to the
profit of the community to which your later works belong.

Einstein (1879-1955)

2715   ...Be for ever a student. He and he alone is an old man who
        feels that he has learnt enough and has need for no more
        knowledge.

                                              Sivananda (born 1887)

2716   Teachers open the door...
        You enter by yourself.

                                                   Chinese Proverb

7. POTPOURRI

2717   He who knoweth not what he ought to know, is a brute beast
        among men; he that knoweth no more than he hath need of,
        is a man among brute beasts; and he that knoweth all that
        may be known, is as a God among men.

                                          Pythagoras (B.C. 582-507)

2718   The monuments of wit and learning are more durable than the
        monuments of power, or of the hands. For have not the
        verses of Homer continued twenty-five hundred years, or
        more, without the loss of a syllable or letter; during
        which time infinite palaces, temples, castles, cities have
        been decayed and demolished?

                                              Bacon (1561-1626)

2719   I can easier teach twenty what were good to be done,
        than be one of the twenty to follow my own teaching.

                                          Shakespeare (1564-1616)

2720   The bookful blockhead, ignorantly read,
        With loads of learned lumber in his head,
        With his own tongue still edifies his ears,
        And always list'ning to himself appears.

                                              Pope (1688-1744)

2721   Delightful task! to rear the tender Thought,
        To teach the young Idea how to shoot,
        To pour the fresh Instruction o'er the Mind,
        To breathe the enlivening Spirit, and to fix
        The generous Purpose in the glowing breast.

                                       James Thomson (1700-1748)

2722   And still they gazed, and still the wonder grew,
        That one small head should carry all it knew.

                                          Goldsmith (1728-1774)

2723   I've studied new Philosophy
And Jurisprudence, Medicine
And even, alas, Theology
From end to end with labor keen;
And here, poor fool; with all my lore
I stand no wiser than before.

Goethe (1749-1832)

2724   He might have been a very clever man by nature, but he had
laid so many books on his head that his brain could not
move.

Robert Hall (1764-1831)

2725   One impulse from a vernal wood
     May teach you more of man,
Of moral evil and of good,
     Than all the sages can.

Wordsworth (1770-1850)

2726   The languages, especially the dead,
     The sciences, and most of all the abstruse,
The arts, at least all such as could be said
     To be the most remote from common use,
In all these he was much and deeply read.

Byron (1788-1824)

2727   Unknown to her the rigid rule,
     The dull restraint, the chiding frown
The weary torture of the school,
     The taming of wild nature down.

John Greenleaf Whittier (1807-1892)

2728   Learn to live, and live to learn,
Ignorance like a fire doth burn,
Little tasks make large return.

Bayard Taylor (1825-1878)

LIFE
Being and Manifestation

1. ESSENCE

2729   Life comes from the Spirit. Even as a man casts a shadow,
so the Spirit casts the shadow of life, and, as a shadow of
former lives, a new life comes to this body.
Upanishads (c. B.C. 800)

2730   As leaves on the trees, such is the life of man.
Homer (c. B.C. 700)

2731   Our days upon earth are a shadow.
Job (B.C. 400?)

2732   Life is a pure flame,
and we live by an invisible sun within us.
Thomas Browne (1605-1682)

2733   Life is rather a state of embryo, a preparation for life;
a man is not completely born till he has passed through
death.
Franklin (1706-1790)

2734   Life is the childhood of our immortality.
Goethe (1749-1832)

2735   Life is but thought.
Samuel Coleridge (1772-1834)

2736   One life - a little gleam of Time between two Eternities.
Carlyle (1795-1881)

2737   Life is a progress and not a station.
Emerson (1803-1882)

2738   The experience of life consists of the experience
which the spirit has of itself in matter and as matter,
in mind and as mind, in emotion, as emotion, etc.
Pir Vilayat Inayat Khan (born 1916)

2. OPPOSITES

2739   It is between the two polarizing aspects of manifestation -
the Supernal Father and the Supernal Mother - that the web
of Life is woven; souls going back and forth between them
like a weaver's shuttle. In our individual lives, in our
physiological rhythms, and in the history of the rise and
fall of nations, we observe the same rhythmic periodicity.
Kabbalah (B.C. 1200?-700? A.D.)

2740   Who knoweth if to die be but to live,
       And that called life by mortals be but death?
                                    Euripides (B.C. 480-406)

2741   Life is easy to live for a man who is without shame, bold
       after the fashion of a crow, a mischief-maker, an insulting,
       arrogant, and dissolute fellow.
          But life is hard to live for a modest man, who is free
       from attachment, unassuming, spotless, and of clear vision.
                                    The Dhammapada (c. B.C. 300)

2742   O life! long to the wretched, short to the happy.
                                    Publilius Syrus (fl. B.C. 42)

2743   If you live according to nature, you never will be poor;
       if according to the world's caprice, you will never be rich.
                                    Seneca (B.C. 3-65 A.D.)

2744   We are always beginning to live, but are never living.
                                    Manilius (fl. 100 A.D.)

2745   I came like Water, and like Wind I go.
                                    Omar Khayyam (fl. 1100)

2746   Life is a lying dream, he only wakes
       Who casts the World aside.
                                    Seami Motokiyo (1363-1444)

2747   Like bubbles on the sea of matter borne,
       They rise, they break, and to that sea return.
                                    Pope (1688-1744)

2748   All that is alive tends toward color, individuality,
          specificity, effectiveness, and opacity.
       All that is done in life inclines toward knowledge,
          abstraction, generality, transfiguration, and transparency.
                                    Goethe (1749-1832)

2749   Life can only be understood backwards;
       but it must be lived forwards.
                                    Kierkegaard (1813-1855)

2750   Love is sunshine, hate is shadow,
       Life is checkered shade and sunshine.
                                    Longfellow (1807-1882)

2751   Half my life is full of sorrow,
          Half of joy, still fresh and new;
       One of these lives is a fancy,
          But the other one is true.
                                    Adelaide Procter (1825-1864)

2752   We have two lives:
       The soul of man is like the rolling world,
       One half in day, the other dipt in night;
       The one has music and the flying cloud,
       The other, silence and the wakeful stars.
                                   Alexander Smith (1830-1867)

2753   Life imitates Art far more than Art imitates Life.
                                     Oscar Wilde (1854-1900)

2754   At birth we come
       At death we go...
       Bearing nothing.
                                             Chinese Proverb

3. INSIGHT

2755   Whatsoever quits the non-manifest, becomes active life;
       it is drawn into the vortex of the ONE, which is neither
       Spirit nor Matter, both being the absolute life, latent.
                                     Book of Dzyan (B.C. 3000?)

2756   As the ocean giveth rise to springs, whose water
       return again into its bosom through the rivers,
       so runneth thy life force from the heart outwards,
       and so returneth into its place again.
                                     Akhenaton? (c. B.C. 1375)

2757   Rhythm is the basis of life, not steady forward progress.
       The forces of creation, destruction, and preservation have
       a whirling, dynamic interaction.
                                   Kabbalah (B.C. 1200?-700? A.D.)

2758   A mortal lives not through that breath that flows in and
       that flows out. The source of his life is another and this
       causes the breath to flow.
                                     Upanishads (c. B.C. 800)

2759   The Eternal is veiled by the real. The Spirit of life is
       The Eternal. Name and form are the real, and by them the
       Spirit is veiled.
                                     Upanishads (c. B.C. 800)

2760   Whosoever knows others is clever.
       Whosoever knows himself is wise.
       Whosoever conquers others has force.
       Whosoever conquers himself is strong.
       Whosoever asserts himself has will-power.
       Whosoever is contented is rich.
       Whosoever does not lose his place has duration.
       Whosoever does not perish in death lives.
                                     Lao-Tzu (fl. B.C. 600)

2761   Man is a microcosm, or little world, as possessing in
        miniature all the qualities found on a great scale in the
        Universe; by his reason and intelligence partaking of the
        Divine Nature: and by his faculty of changing aliments into
        other substances, of growing, and reproducing himself,
        partaking of elementary Nature.

                                    Pythagoras (B.C. 582-507)

2762   Ignorant people see life as either existence or
        non-existence, but wise men see it beyond both existence
        and non-existence to something that transcends them both;
        this is an observation of the Middle Way.

                                    Buddha (B.C. 568-488)

2763   The end of life is to be like God, and the soul following
        God will be like him.

                                    Socrates (B.C. 469-399)

2764   No one has lived a short life who has performed his duties
        with unblemished character.

                                    Cicero (B.C. 106-43)

2765   Nor has he spent his life badly who has passed it
        in privacy.

                                    Horace (B.C. 65-8)

2766   This body is not a home, but an inn;
        and that only for a short time.

                                    Seneca (B.C. 3-65 A.D.)

2767   As is a tale, so is life:
        not how long it is, but how good it is, is what matters.

                                    Seneca (B.C. 3-65 A.D.)

2768   Everything is the product of one universal creative effort.
        There is nothing dead in Nature. Everything is organic and
        living, and therefore the whole world appears to be a living
        organism.

                                    Paracelsus (1493-1541)

2769   Life is like music, it must be composed by ear, feeling and
        instinct, not by rule. Nevertheless one had better know
        the rules, for they sometimes guide in doubtful cases,
        though not often.

                                    Samuel Butler (1612-1680)

2770   Life is a quarry, out of which we are to mold and chisel
        and complete a character.

                                    Goethe (1749-1832)

2771   Life, like the waters of the seas, freshens only when it
       ascends toward heaven.

       Richter (1763-1825)

2772   Life is short, and time is swift;
       Roses fade, and shadows shift.

       Ebenezer Elliott (1781-1849)

2773   Life is a language in which certain truths are conveyed to
       us; if we could learn them in some other way, we should
       not live.

       Schopenhauer (1788-1860)

2774   A well-written life is almost as rare as a well-spent one.

       Carlyle (1795-1881)

2775   Life is a succession of lessons which must be lived to
       be understood.

       Emerson (1803-1882)

2776   Life is what we make it, and the world is what we make it.
       The eyes of the cheerful and of the melancholy man are fixed
       upon the same creation; but very different are the aspects
       which it bears to them.

       Albert Pike (1809-1891)

2777   We sleep, but the loom of life never stops
       and the pattern which was weaving when the sun went down
       is weaving when it comes up to-morrow.

       Beecher (1813-1878)

2778   Repetition is the reality and the seriousness of life.

       Kierkegaard (1813-1855)

2779   Life is the continuous adjustment of external relations.

       Herbert Spencer (1820-1903)

2780   The value of life itself cannot be estimated.

       Nietzsche (1844-1900)

2781   In three words I can sum up everything I've learned about
       life. It goes on.

       Robert Frost (1875-1963)

2782   A little work, a little sleep, a little love and it is
       all over.

       Mary Rinehart (1876-1958)

2783   Life is like a game of cards. The hand that is dealt you
        represents determinism; the way you play it is free will.
                                        Jawaharial Nehru (1889-1964)

2784   Human life is as evanescent as the morning dew
        or a flash of lightning.
                                        Akutagawa Ryunosuke (1892-1927)

2785   At any given moment, life is completely senseless.
        But viewed over a period, it seems to reveal itself
        as an organism existing in time, having a purpose,
        trending in a certain direction.
                                        Aldous Huxley (1894-1963)

2786   ...What has been gained by incarnation can only really have
        been gained if it has been eternalized: If it survives the
        transiency of our fragile existence, if the essence of the
        essence is drawn from all those aspects of creation which
        are subject to change and decay, just as the essence of the
        flower is drawn by the bees for honey.
                                        Pir Vilayat Inayat Khan (born 1916)

2787   Man's life...
        Candle in the wind
        Frost on the tiles.
                                        Chinese Proverb

4. POSITIVE

2788   Life precedes form, and life survives the last atom of form.
        Through the countless rays proceeds the life-ray,
        the one, like a thread through many jewels.
                                        Book of Dzyan (B.C. 3000?)

2789   As the eye of morning to the lark, as the shade of evening
        to the owl, as the honey to the bee, or as the carcass to
        the vulture; even such is life unto the heart of man.
        Though bright, it dazzleth not; though obscure it displea-
        seth not; though sweet it cloyeth not; though corrupt, it
        forbiddeth not; yet who is he that knoweth its true value?
                                        Akhenaton? (c. B.C. 1375)

2790   On life's journey faith is nourishment, virtuous deeds are
        a shelter, wisdom is the light by day and right mindfulness
        is the protection by night. If a man lives a pure life
        nothing can destroy him; if he has conquered greed nothing
        can limit his freedom.
                                        Buddha (B.C. 568-488)

2791   Life is short, yet sweet.

Euripides (B.C. 480-406)

2792   All that a man hath will he give for his life.

Job (B.C. 400?)

2793   Life, if thou knowest how to use it, is long enough.

Seneca (B.C. 3-65 A.D.)

2794   A good man doubles the length of his existence;
       to have lived so as to look back with pleasure
       on our past existence is to live twice.

Martial (43-104 A.D.)

2795   Man contains all that is above in heaven and below upon
       earth, the celestial as well as the terrestrial creatures;
       it is for this reason that The Eternal chose Man as His
       Divine manifestation. No World could exist before Adam
       came into being, for the human figure contains all things,
       and all that exists is by virtue of it.

Zohar (120?-1200? A.D.)

2796   The good life is the healthful life, the merry life.
       Life is health, joy, laughter.

Jean Bodin (1530-1596)

2797   The finest lives, in my opinion, are those who rank in
       the common model, and with the human race, but without
       miracle, without extravagance.

Montaigne (1533-1592)

2798   That life is long which answers life's great end.

Young (1683-1765)

2799   One hour of life, crowded to the full with glorious action,
       and filled with noble risks, is worth whole years of those
       mean observances of paltry decorum.

Walter Scott (1771-1832)

2800   Every man's life is a fairy tale, written by God's fingers.

Hans Christian Anderson (1802-1875)

2801   No life that breathes with human breath
       Has ever truly longed for death.

Alfred Tennyson (1809-1892)

2802   We live in deeds, not years:
       In thoughts, not breaths;
       In feelings, not in figures on a dial.
       We should count time by heart-throbs. He most lives
       Who thinks most, feels the noblest, acts the best.

Bailey (1816-1902)

2803   There is no wealth but life.

> John Ruskin (1819-1900)

2804   Life has loveliness to sell,
       All beautiful and splendid things,
       Blue waves whitened on a cliff,
       Soaring fire that sways and sings
       And children's faces looking up
       Holding wonder like a cup.

> Sara Teasdale (1884-1933)

5. NEGATIVE

2805   Life is short, the art long, opportunity fleeting,
       experience treacherous, judgment difficult.

> Hippocrates (B.C. 460-370)

2806   No man enjoys the true taste of life, but he who
       is ready and willing to quit it.

> Seneca (B.C. 3-65 A.D.)

2807   Nature has given man no better thing than shortness of life.

> Pliny the Elder (23-79 A.D.)

2808   Those who speak ill of the spiritual life,
       Although they come and go by day,
       Are like the smith's bellows:
       They take breath but are not alive.

> Nagarjuna (c. 100-200 A.D.)

2809   Know that the life of this world is but a game and pastime
       and show and boast among you; and multiplying riches and
       children is like rain, whose vegetation delighteth the
       infidels - then they wither away, and thou seest them all
       yellow, and they become chaff.

> Koran (c. 651 A.D.)

2810   O threats of Hell and Hopes of Paradise!
       One thing at least is certain - This Life flies;
       One thing is certain and the rest is Lies;
       The Flower that once has bloomed for ever dies.

> Omar Khayyam (fl. 1100)

2811   Life is as tedious as a twice told tale
       Vexing the dull ear of a drowsy man.

> Shakespeare (1564-1616)

2812 Human affairs are like a chess-game: only those who do
   not take it seriously can be called good players.
   Life is like an earthen pot: only when it is shattered,
   does it manifest its emptiness.
                              Hung Tzu-ch'eng (1593-1665)

2813 Who breathes must suffer; and who thinks must mourn;
   And he alone is bless'd who ne'er was born.
                              Matthew Prior (1664-1721)

2814 Life is a tragedy wherein we sit as spectators for a while
   and then act our part in it.
                              Swift (1667-1745)

2815 Our days begin with trouble here, our life is but a span,
   And cruel death is always near, so frail a thing is man.
                              New England Primer (c. 1690)

2816 Human life is everywhere in a state in which much is to be
   endured, and little to be enjoyed.
                              Johnson (1709-1784)

2817 Life is a malady in which sleep soothes us every sixteen
   hours; it is a palliation; death is the remedy.
                              Chamfort (1741-1794)

2818 A useless life is an early death.
                              Goethe (1749-1832)

2819 Those who complain of the shortness of life, let it slide
   by them without wishing to seize and make the most of its
   golden moments.
                              Hazlitt (1778-1830)

2820 Life is a waste of wearisome hours,
    Which seldom the rose of enjoyment adorns,
   And the heart that is soonest awake to the flowers,
    Is always the first to be touch'd by the thorns.
                              Thomas Moore (1779-1852)

2821 Through life's road, so dim and dirty,
   I have dragged to three and thirty;
   What have these years left to me?
   Nothing, except thirty-three.
                              Byron (1788-1824)

2822 Youth is a blunder;
   Manhood a struggle;
   Old Age a regret.
                              Disraeli (1804-1881)

2823   The mass of men lead lives of quiet desperation.
                                    Thoreau (1817-1862)

2824   The basic fact about human existence is not that it is
        a tragedy, but that it is a bore.
                                    H. L. Mencken (1880-1956)

2825   Life is an unanswered question, but let's still believe
        in the dignity and importance of the question.
                                    Tennessee Williams (1911-1983)

2826   If there is a sin against life, it lies perhaps less in
        despairing of it than in hoping for another and evading the
        implacable grandeur of the one we have.
                                    Albert Camus (1913-1960)

6. ADVICE

2827   The union of the Word and the Mind
        produces that mystery which is called Life...
        Learn deeply of the Mind and its mystery,
        for therein lies the secret of immortality.
                                    The Divine Pymander (BC 2500?-200 AD?)

2828   We should live as though our life would be both long and
        short.
                                    Bias (fl B.C. 600)

2829   It is impossible to live pleasurably without living
        prudently, honorably, and justly; or to live prudently,
        honorably, and justly, without living pleasurably.
                                    Epicurus (B.C. 341-270)

2830   For if a man live many years, let him rejoice in them all;
        but let him remember that the days of darkness will be
        many. All that comes is vanity.
                                    Ecclesiastes (B.C. 300?)

2831   Enter by the narrow gate; for the gate is wide and the
        way is easy, that leads to destruction, and those who
        enter by it are many. For the gate is narrow and the way
        is hard, that leads to life, and those who find it are few.
                                    Jesus (B.C. 6?-30? A.D.)

2832   One should count each day a separate life.
                                    Seneca (B.C. 3-65 A.D.)

2833   The art of living is more like that of wrestling than of
        dancing. The main thing is to stand firm and be ready for
        an unforeseen attack.
                                    Marcus Aurelius (121-180 A.D.)

2834   Learn to live well, that thou may'st die so too;
        To live and die is all we have to do.

                                  John Denham (1615-1668)

2835   To make good use of life,
        one should have in youth the experience of advanced years,
        and in old age the vigor of youth.

                       Leszczynski Stanislaus (1677-1766)

2836   Would you live with ease,
        Do what you ought, and not what you please.

                                     Franklin (1706-1790)

2837   Reflect that life, like every other blessing,
        Derives its value from its use alone.

                                    Johnson (1709-1784)

2838   To execute great things, one should live as though one
        would never die.

                              Vauvenargues(1715-1747)

2839   Plunge boldly into the thick of life! Each lives it,
        not to many is it known; and seize it where you will,
        it is interesting.

                                   Goethe (1749-1832)

2840   Life is divided into three terms - that which was, which is,
        and which will be. Let us learn from the past to profit by
        the present, and from the present to live better in the
        future.

                              Wordsworth (1770-1850)

2841   The fraction of life can be increased in value not so much
        by increasing your numerator as by lessening your
        denominator. Nay, unless my Algebra deceives me, unity
        itself divided by zero will give infinity.

                                  Carlyle (1795-1881)

2842   This span of life was lent for lofty duties, not for
        selfishness; not to be wiled away for aimless dreams,
        but to improve ourselves, and serve mankind.

                               Aubrey De Vere (1814-1902)

2843   Live neither in the present nor the future, but in the
        eternal. The giant weed (of evil) cannot flower there;
        this blot upon existence is wiped out by the very atmosphere
        of eternal thought.

                               H. P. Blavatsky (1831-1891)

2844   The great use of life is to spend it for something that
        will outlast it.

                                        William James (1842-1910)

2845   For life is the mirror of king and slave,
            'Tis just what we are and do;
        Then give to the world the best you have,
            And the best will come back to you.

                                        Madeline Bridges (1844-1920)

2846   Let your life lightly dance on the edges of Time
        like dew on the tip of a leaf.

                                        Rabindranath Tagore (1861-1941)

2847   I worked for a menial's hire,
            Only to learn, dismayed,
        That any wage I had asked of Life,
            Life would have gladly paid.

                                        Jessie Rittenhouse (1869-1948)

2848   Serenity, regularity, absence of vanity,
        Sincerity, simplicity, veracity, equanimity,
        Fixity, non-irritability, adaptability,
        Humility, tenacity, integrity, nobility, magnanimity,
            charity, generosity, purity.
        Practise daily these eighteen "ities"
        You will soon attain immortality.

                                        Sivananda (born 1887)

7. POTPOURRI

2849   ...The root of life was in every drop of the ocean of
        immortality, and the ocean was radiant light, which was
        fire, and heat, and motion. Darkness vanished and was no
        more; it disappeared in its own essence, the body of fire
        and water, or father and mother...

                                        Book of Dzyan (B.C. 3000?)

2850   Life is the fire that burns and the sun that gives light.
        Life is the wind and the rain and the thunder in the sky.
        Life is matter and is earth, what is and what is not,
        and what beyond is in Eternity.

                                        Upanishads (c. B.C. 800)

2851   He who knows wrath, knows pride; he who knows pride, knows
deceit; he who knows deceit, knows greed; he who knows
greed, knows love; he who knows love, knows hate; he who
knows hate, knows delusion; he who knows delusion, knows
conception; he who know conception, knows birth; he who
knows birth, knows death; he who knows death, knows hell;
he who knows hell, knows animal existence; he who knows
animal existence, knows pain. Therefore, a wise man
should avoid wrath, pride, deceit, greed, love, hate,
delusion, conception, birth, death, hell, animal existence,
and pain.

Nagarjuna (c. 100-200 A.D.)

2852   But helpless Pieces of the Game He plays
Upon this Checker-board of Nights and Days;
Hither and thither moves, and checks, and slays,
And one by one back in the Closet lays.

Omar Khayyam (fl. 1100)

2853   For in and out, above, about, below,
'Tis nothing but a Magic Shadow-show,
   Play'd in a Box whose Candle is the Sun,
Round which we Phantom Figures come and go.

Omar Khayyam (fl. 1100)

2854   That everything throughout the world,
   everywhere, end to end,
Is but a reflection of a ray
   cast from the face of The Friend.

Ni'matullah Wali (1331-1431?)

2855   Life's but a walking shadow, a poor player
That struts and frets his hour upon the stage
And then is heard no more: it is a tale
Told by an idiot, full of sound and fury,
Signifying nothing.

Shakespeare (1564-1616)

2856   Our life so fast away doth slide
   As doth an hungry eagle through the wind;
Or as a ship transported with the tide,
   Which in their passage leave no print behind.

John Davies (1570-1626)

2857   A little rule, a little sway,
A sunbeam in a winter's day,
Is all the proud and mighty have
Between the cradle and the grave.

John Dyer (1700-1758)

2858   Thus at the flaming forge of life
           Our fortunes must be wrought;
        Thus on its sounding anvil shaped
           Each burning deed and thought!

                                        Longfellow (1807-1882)

2859   Life is real! Life is earnest!
           And the grave is not its goal;
        Dust thou art, to dust returnest,
           Was not spoken of the soul.

                                        Longfellow (1807-1882)

2860   Life is a magic vase filled to the brim; so made that you
        cannot dip into it nor draw from it; but it overflows into
        the hand that drops treasures into it - drop in malice and
        it overflows hate; drop in charity and it overflows love.
                                        John Ruskin (1819-1900)

2861   We are the voices of the wandering wind,
        Which moan for rest and rest can never find;
        Lo! as the wind is so is mortal life,
        A moan, a sigh, a sob, a storm, a strife.

                                        Edwin Arnold (1832-1904)

2862   I want to be thoroughly used up when I die, for the harder
        I work, the more I live. Life is no brief candle for me.
        It is a sort of splendid torch which I have got hold of for
        a moment, and I want to make it burn as brightly as possible
        before handing it on to future generations.

                                        G. B. Shaw (1856-1950)

2863   One should absorb the color of life,
        but one should never remember its details.

                                        Oscar Wilde (1854-1900)

2864   Welcome, O life! I go to encounter for the millionth time
        the reality of experience and to forge in the smithy of my
        soul the uncreated conscience of my race.

                                        James Joyce (1882-1941)

2865   Life is short. Time is fleeting. Realize the Self.
        Purity of the heart is the gateway to God.
        Aspire. Renounce. Meditate.
        Be good; do good.
        Be kind; be compassionate.
        Inquire, know Thyself.

                                        Sivananda (born 1887)

LOVE

Courtship, Heart and Romance

1. ESSENCE

2866   Love in its essence is spiritual fire.
> Swedenborg (1688-1772)

2867   Love is a canvas furnished by Nature and embroidered by imagination.
> Voltaire (1694-1778)

2868   Love is the emblem of eternity:
it confounds all notion of time:
effaces all memory of a beginning, all fear of an end.
> Germaine De Stael (1766-1817)

2869   Love is the essence of God.
> Emerson (1803-1882)

2870   Love is but another name for that inscrutable presence by which the soul is connected with humanity.
> William Simms (1806-1870)

2871   Love is energy of life.
> Robert Browning (1812-1889)

2872   Love is space and time measured by the heart.
> Marcel Proust (1871-1922)

2. OPPOSITES

2873   A heat full of coldness, a sweet full of bitterness, a pain full of pleasantness, which maketh thoughts have eyes, and hearts, and ears; bred by desire, nursed by delight, weaned by jealousy, killed by dissembling, buried by ingratitude; and this is love.
> John Lyly (1554-1606)

2874   O what a heaven is love! O what a hell!
> Thomas Dekker (1577-1632)

2875   As love increases, prudence diminishes.
> La Rochefoucauld (1613-1680)

2876   The more we love the nearer we are to hate.
> La Rochefoucauld (1613-1680)

2877 Pains of love be sweeter far
Than all other pleasures are.

Dryden (1631-1700)

2878 So weak thou art that fools thy power despise;
And yet so strong, thou triumph'st o'er the wise.

Swift (1667-1745)

2879 Mysterious love, uncertain treasure,
Hast thou more of pain or pleasure!
Endless torments dwell about thee:
Yet who would live, and live without thee!

Addison (1672-1719)

2880 Love is the history of a woman's life;
it is an episode in man's.

Germaine De Stael (1766-1817)

2881 In her first passion woman loves her lover;
In all others, all she loves is love.

Byron (1788-1824)

2882 It is an ancient story
Yet is it ever new.

Heine (1797-1856)

2883 Pure love and suspicion cannot dwell together: at the door
where the latter enters, the former makes its exit.

Alexandre Dumas (1802-1870)

2884 The reason why all men honor love is because it looks up,
and not down; aspires and not despairs.

Emerson (1803-1882)

2885 The sweetest joy, the wildest woe is love.

Bailey (1816-1902)

2886 There is nothing in this world so sweet as love,
and next to love, the sweetest thing is hate.

Longfellow (1807-1882)

2887 It is ever the invisible that is the object of our
profoundest worship. With the lover it is not the seen
but the unseen that he muses upon.

Bovee (1820-1904)

2888 Men always want to be a woman's first love -
Women like to be a man's last romance.

Oscar Wilde (1854-1900)

2889   Man begins by loving love and ends by loving a woman.
Woman begins by loving a man and ends by loving love.
Remy de Gourmont (1858-1915)

2890   The one thing we can never get enough of is love.
And the one thing we never give enough is love.
Henry Miller (1891-1980)

2891   In love the paradox occurs that two things become one and
yet remain two.
Erich Fromm (1900-1980)

3. INSIGHT

2892   He is not a lover who does not love forever.
Euripides (B.C. 480-406)

2893   Love will make men dare to die for their beloved -
love alone; and women as well as men.
Plato (B.C. 427?-347?)

2894   Lovers' quarrels are the renewal of love.
Terence (B.C. 185-159)

2895   Greater love hath no man than this, that a man lay down
his life for his friends.
Jesus (B.C. 6?-30? A.D.)

2896   Pleasant fragrances of the breezes of love blow from the
lovers even thought they might conceal it. The effects of
these breezes bear witness to them even if they disguise it
and are apparent even if they hide it.
Abu Ali Katib (fl. c. 940)

2897   They do not love that do not show their love.
John Heywood (1497?-1580?)

2898   Nuptial love maketh mankind; friendly love perfecteth it;
but wanton love corrupteth and embaseth it.
Bacon (1561-1626)

2899   Where love is great, the littlest doubts are fear;
When little fears grow great, great love grows there.
Shakespeare (1564-1616)

2900   The breath of divine knowledge is the bellows of divine
love, and the flame of divine love is the perfection of
divine knowledge.
Quarles (1592-1644)

2901 Love that is not madness is not love.

Pedro Calderon (1600-1681)

2902 When the heart is still agitated by the remains of a
passion, we are more ready to receive a new one than when
we are entirely cured.

La Rochefoucauld (1613-1680)

2903 The pleasure of love is in loving. We are happier in the
passion we feel than in that which we excite.

La Rochefoucauld (1613-1680)

2904 For all true love is grounded on esteem.

George Villiers (1628-1687)

2905 Love is a passion
Which kindles honor into noble acts.

Dryden (1631-1700)

2906 Love reckons hours for months, and days for years;
and every little absence is an age.

Dryden (1631-1700)

2907 Love begins with love.

La Bruyere (1645-1696)

2908 Courtship is to marriage, as a very witty prologue
to a very dull play.

William Congreve (1670-1729)

2909 Courtship consists in a number of quiet attentions, not so
pointed as to alarm, nor so vague as not to be understood.

Sterne (1713-1768)

2910 Love is like what is called the Milky Way in heaven,
a brilliant mass formed by thousands of little stars,
of which each perhaps is nebulous.

Stendhal (1783-1842)

2911 Love is not altogether a delirium,
yet it has many points in common therewith.
I call it rather a discerning of the infinite in the finite-
of the ideal made real.

Carlyle (1795-1881)

2912 There are no little events with the heart. It magnifies
everything; it places in the same scales the fall of an
empire of fourteen years and the dropping of a woman's
glove, and almost always the glove weighs more than the
empire.

Balzac (1799-1850)

2913   The motto of chivalry is also the motto of wisdom;
       to serve all, but love only one.

                                         Balzac (1799-1850)

2914   Love is like a hunter, who cares not for the game when once
       caught, which he may have pursued with the most intense and
       breathless eagerness. Love is strongest in pursuit;
       friendship in possession.

                                        Emerson (1803-1882)

2915   Life is a sleep, love is a dream;
       and you have lived if you have loved.

                                       De Musset (1810-1857)

2916   It is difficult to know at what moment love begins;
       it is less difficult to know that it has begun.

                                      Longfellow (1807-1882)

2917   As the rays come from the sun, and yet are not the sun,
       even so our love and pity, though they are not God,
       but merely a poor, weak image and reflection of him,
       yet from him alone they come.

                                Charles Kingsley (1819-1875)

2918   There are three kinds of love, - unselfish, mutual, and
       selfish. The unselfish love is of the highest kind. The
       lover only minds the welfare of the beloved and does not
       care for his own sufferings. In mutual love the lover not
       only wants the happiness of his beloved but has an eye
       towards his own happiness also. It is middling. The
       selfish love is the lowest. It only looks towards its own
       happiness, no matter whether the beloved suffers weal
       or woe.

                                    Ramakrishna (1836-1886)

2919   Love is eternal - the aspect may change, but not the
       essence. There is the same difference in a person before
       and after he is in love as there is in an unlighted lamp
       and one that is burning. The lamp was there and was a good
       lamp, but now it is shedding light too, and that is its real
       function. And love makes one calmer about many things,
       and that way, one is more fit for one's work.

                                Vincent Van Gogh (1853-1890)

4. POSITIVE

2920   The little space within the heart is as great as this vast
       universe. The heavens and the earth are there, and the sun,
       and the moon, and the stars; fire and lightning and winds
       are there; and all that now is and all that is not: for
       the whole universe is in Him and He dwells within our heart.

                                   Upanishads (c. B.C. 800)

2921   If one has love in battle one is victorious.
        If one has it in defense one is invincible.
        Whom Heaven wants to save him he protects through love.
                                        Lao-Tzu (fl. B.C. 600)

2922   Love is the crowning grace of humanity, the holiest right of
        the soul, the golden link which binds us to duty and truth,
        the redeeming principle that chiefly reconciles the heart to
        life, and is prophetic of eternal good.
                                        Francesco Petrarch (1304-1374)

2923   Love is an image of God, and not a lifeless image,
        but the living essence of the divine nature
        which beams full of all goodness.
                                        Martin Luther (1483-1546)

2924   My bounty is as boundless as the sea,
        My love as deep; the more I give to thee
        The more I have, for both are infinite.
                                        Shakespeare (1564-1616)

2925   For thy sweet love remembered such wealth brings
        That then I scorn to change my state with kings.
                                        Shakespeare (1564-1616)

2926   A smooth and steadfast mind,
          Gentle thoughts and calm desires,
        Hearts with equal love combined,
          Kindle never-dying fires.
                                        Thomas Carew (1595?-1639)

2927   Mutual love, the crown of all our bliss.
                                        Milton (1608-1674)

2928   The greatest pleasure of life is love.
                                        William Temple (1628-1699)

2929   Love, then, hath every bliss in store;
        'Tis friendship, and 'tis something more.
        Each other every wish they give;
        Not to know love is not to live.
                                        Gay (1688-1732)

2930   Love and desire are the spirit's wings to great deeds.
                                        Goethe (1749-1832)

2931   Love has power to give in a moment what toil can scarcely
        reach in an age.
                                        Goethe (1749-1832)

2932   Paradise is always where love dwells.

Richter (1763-1825)

2933   There is nothing half so sweet in life
       as love's young dreams.

Thomas Moore (1779-1852)

2934   To love deeply in one direction makes us more loving in all
       others.

Anne Swetchine (1782-1857)

2935   Yes, Love indeed is light from heaven;
         A spark of that immortal fire
       With angels shared, by Allah given
         To lift from earth our low desire.

Byron (1788-1824)

2936   True love is eternal, infinite, and always like itself.
       It is equal and pure, without violent demonstrations:
       it is seen with white hairs and is always young in the heart

Balzac (1799-1850)

2937   Life is the flower of which love is the honey.

Jean Baptiste Alphonse Karr (1808-1890)

2938   He who for love hath undergone
         The worst that can befall,
       Is happier thousandfold than one
         Who never loved at all.

Richard Milnes (1809-1885)

2939   A loving heart is the truest wisdom.

Charles Dickens (1812-1870)

2940   The heart is wiser than the intellect.

Josiah Holland (1819-1881)

2941   Ah, how skillful grows the hand
         That obeyeth Love's command!
       It is the heart and not the brain
         That to the highest doth attain,
       And he who followeth Love's behest
         Far excelleth all the rest.

Longfellow (1807-1882)

2942   Love is infallible; it has no errors, for all errors are
       the want of love.

Andrew Bonar Law (1858-1923)

2943   Love expects no reward. Love knows no fear. Love Divine
        gives - does not demand. Love thinks no evil; imputes no
        motive. To Love is to share and serve.

                                        Sivananda (born 1887)

2944   The way of heaven can be known and experienced through
        the heart.

                                        Manly P. Hall (born 1901)

5. NEGATIVE

2945   He whom love touches not walks in darkness.

                                        Plato (B.C. 427?-347?)

2946   He who falls in love meets a worse fate
        than he who leaps from a rock.

                                        Plautus (B.C. 254-184)

2947   Everybody in love is blind.

                                        Propertius (B.C. 50-16)

2948   Love is a thing full of anxious fears.

                                        Ovid (B.C. 43-18 A.D.)

2949   Love and dignity cannot share the same abode.

                                        Ovid (B.C. 43-18 A.D.)

2950   True love hates and will not bear delay.

                                        Seneca (B.C. 3-65 A.D.)

2951   Love is the tyrant of the heart; it darkens
        Reason, confounds discretion; deaf to Counsel
        It runs a headlong course to desperate madness.

                                        John Ford (1586-1640)

2952   The reason why lovers are never weary of one another is
        this - they are always talking of themselves.

                                        La Rochefoucauld (1613-1680)

2953   If we judge of love by most of its results,
        it resembles hatred more than friendship.

                                        La Rochefoucauld (1613-1680)

2954   O tyrant love, when held by you,
        We may to prudence bid adieu.

                                        La Fontaine (1621-1695)

2955   The first sigh of love is the last of wisdom.

                                        Antoine Bret (1717-1792)

2956   Yes, loving is a painful thrill
       And not to love more painful still;
       But oh, it is the worst of pain,
       To love and not be lov'd again.

                           Thomas Moore (1779-1852)

2957   Let none think to fly the danger
       For soon or late love is his own avenger.

                                Byron (1788-1824)

2958   Love is a pearl of purest hue,
          But stormy waves are round it;
       And dearly may a woman rue,
          The hour that she found it.

                       Letitia Landon (1802-1838)

2959   Never self-possessed, or prudent, love is all abandonment.

                             Emerson (1803-1882)

2960   No man, or woman, was ever cured of love by discovering the
       falseness of his or her lover. The living together for
       three long, rainy days in the country has done more to
       dispel love than all the perfidies in love that have ever
       been committed.

                          Arthur Helps (1813-1875)

2961   I cannot love as I have loved,
          And yet I know not why;
       It is the one great woe of life
          To feel all feeling die.

                               Bailey (1816-1902)

2962   Laurel is green for a season,
          and love is sweet for a day;
       But love grows bitter with treason,
          and laurel outlives not May.

                            Swinburne (1837-1909)

2963   When a man has once loved a woman he will do anything for
       her except continue to love her.
                          Oscar Wilde (1854-1900)

2964   When one is in love one begins by deceiving oneself,
       one ends by deceiving others.
       That is what the world calls romance.
                          Oscar Wilde (1854-1900)

2965   Love is an ocean of emotions,
       entirely surrounded by expenses.
                         Thomas Dewar (1864-1930)

2966   The great tragedy of life is not that men perish,
        but that they cease to love.

                                Somerset Maugham (1874-1965)

2967   And if I loved you Wednesday,
            Well, what is that to you?
        I do not love you Thursday -
            So much is true.

                                    Edna Millay (1892-1950)

6. ADVICE

2968   In the spring of thy youth, in the morning of thy days, when
        the eyes of man gaze on thee with delight, and nature
        whispereth in thine ear the meaning of their looks; Ah!
        hear with caution their seducing words, guard well thy
        heart, nor listen to their soft persuasions.

                                    Akhenaton? (c. B.C. 1375)

2969   If thou wishest to put an end to love,
        attend to business (love yields to employment);
        then thou wilt be safe.

                                        Ovid (B.C. 43-18 A.D.)

2970   If you wished to be loved, love.

                                    Seneca (B.C. 3-65 A.D.)

2971   In love, as in war, a fortress that parleys is half taken.
                                Margaret of Valois (1553-1615)

2972   If you would be loved, love and be lovable.

                                        Franklin (1706-1790)

2973   He who cannot love must learn to flatter.

                                            Goethe (1749-1832)

2974   Do proper homage to thine idol's eyes;
        But not too humbly, or she will despise
        Thee and thy suit, though told in moving tropes;
        Disguise even tenderness, if thou art wise.

                                            Byron (1788-1824)

2975   Who are wise in love, love most, say least.
                                Alfred Tennyson (1809-1892)

2976   'Tis better to have loved and lost than never to have
        loved at all.

                                Alfred Tennyson (1809-1892)

2977   It is best to love wisely, no doubt;
        but to love foolishly is better than not to be able to love
        at all.

                                                    Thackeray (1811-1863)

2978   Do not be afraid of showing your affection. Be warm and
        tender, thoughtful and affectionate. Men are more helped
        by sympathy, than by service; love is more than money, and
        a kind word will give more pleasure than a present.

                                                    Lubbock (1834-1913)

7. POTPOURRI

2979   Fear not to swear; the winds carry the perjuries of lovers
        without effect over land and sea, thanks to Jupiter. The
        father of the gods himself has denied effect to what foolish
        lovers in their eagerness have sworn.

                                                    Tibullus (B.C. 49-19)

2980   Divine is love, and scorneth worldly pelf,
        And can be bought with nothing but with self.

                                                    Walter Raleigh (1552-1618)

2981   Were beauty under twenty locks kept fast,
        Yet love breaks through and picks them all at last.

                                                    Shakespeare (1564-1616)

2982   Doubt thou the stars are fire!
        Doubt that the sun doth move;
        Doubt truth to be a liar;
        But never doubt I love.

                                                    Shakespeare (1564-1616)

2983   They are but beggars that can count their worth,
        But my true love is grown to such excess,
        I cannot sum up half my sum of wealth.

                                                    Shakespeare (1564-1616)

2984   Follow a shadow, it still flies you,
            Seem to fly, it will pursue:
        So court a mistress, she denies you:
            Let her alone, she will court you.
        Say are not women truly, then,
            Styled but the shadows of men?

                                                    Ben Jonson (1572-1637)

2985   So dear I love him,
        that with him all deaths I could endure,
        that without him live no life.

                                                    Milton (1608-1674)

2986   It is with true love as it is with ghosts;
       everyone talks of it, but few have seen it.
                                    La Rochefoucauld (1613-1680)

2987   Love, free as air, at sight of human ties,
       Spreads his light wings, and in a moment flies.
                                              Pope (1688-1744)

2988   What is life, when wanting love?
          Night without a morning;
       Love's the cloudless summer sun,
          Nature gay adorning.
                                    Robert Burns (1759-1796)

2989   Love is the idler's occupation, the warrior's relaxation,
       and the sovereign's ruination.
                                          Napoleon (1769-1821)

2990   Love rules the court, the camp, the grove,
       And men below, and saints above:
       For love is heaven, and heaven is love.
                                       Walter Scott (1771-1832)

2991   All thoughts, all passions, all delights,
          Whatever stirs this mortal frame,
       All are but ministers of Love,
          And feed his sacred flame.
                                 Samuel Coleridge (1772-1834)

2992   Come live in my heart, and pay no rent.
                                    Samuel Lover (1797-1868)

2993   A ruddy drop of manly blood
          The surging sea outweighs;
       The world uncertain comes and goes,
          The lover rooted stays.
                                          Emerson (1803-1882)

2994   And on her lover's arm she leant,
          And round her waist she felt it fold,
       And far across the hills they went
          In that new world which is the old.
                                 Alfred Tennyson (1809-1892)

2995   I love thee, I love but thee,
       With a love that shall not die
          Till the sun grows cold,
          And the stars are old.
       And the leaves of the Judgement Book unfold!
                                    Bayard Taylor (1825-1878)

2996   And my heart springs up anew,
        Bright and confident and true,
        And the old loves comes to meet me
        in the dawning and the dew.
                                        Robert Louis Stevenson (1850-1895)

2997   The night has a thousand eyes, And the day but one;
        Yet the light of the bright world dies, With the dying sun.
        The mind has a thousand eyes, And the heart but one;
        Yet the light of a whole life dies, When love is done.
                                                    Bourdillon (1852-1921)

2998   Yet each man kills the thing he loves,
          By each let this be heard,
        Some do it with a bitter look,
          Some with a flattering word.
        The coward does it with a kiss,
          The brave man with a sword!
                                                Oscar Wilde (1854-1900)

2999   Wine come in at the mouth
        And love comes in at the eye;
        That's all we shall know for truth
        Before we grow old and die.
                                                        Yeats (1865-1939)

3000   The heart of a man to the heart of a maid -
          Light of my tents, be fleet -
        Morning awaits at the end of the world,
          And the world is all at our feet.
                                                      Kipling (1865-1936)

3001   Sing, for faith and hope are high -
          None so true as you and I -
        Sing the Lover's Litany:
          "Love like ours can never die!"
                                                      Kipling (1865-1936)

MARRIAGE
Union and Unity

1. ESSENCE

3002   Marriage is not a matter of two halves but of four quarters,
(male-active, male-passive, female-passive, and female-
active) uniting in balanced harmony of reciprocal
fecundation.
                                        Kabbalah (B.C. 1200?-700? A.D.)

3003   Matrimony - the high sea for which no compass has yet
been invented.
                                        Heine (1797-1856)

3004   Marriage - a community consisting of a master, a mistress,
and two slaves - making in all two.
                                        Ambrose Bierce (1842-1914?)

3005   Marriage is one long conversation, checkered by disputes.
                                        Robert Louis Stevenson (1850-1895)

3006   The ritual of marriage is not simply a social event;
it is a crossing of threads in the fabric of fate.
Many strands bring the couple and their families together
and spin their lives into a fabric that is woven on their
children.
                                        Portuguese-Jewish Wedding Ceremony

2. OPPOSITES

3007   Unity can only be manifested by the Binary. Unity itself
and the idea of Unity are already two.
                                        Kabbalah (B.C. 1200?-700? A.D.)

3008   Of earthly goods, the best is a good wife;
A bad, the bitterest curse of human life.
                                        Simonides (B.C. 556?-468?)

3009   The land of marriage has this peculiarity: that strangers
are desirous of inhabiting it, while its natural
inhabitants would willingly be banished from it.
                                        Montaigne (1533-1592)

3010   Maids want nothing but husbands, and when they have them,
they want everything.
                                        Shakespeare (1564-1616)

3011   The calmest husbands make the stormiest wives.
                                        Thomas Dekker (1577-1632)

3012 Men should keep their eyes wide open before marriage,
and half shut afterward.

Madeleine Scuderi (1608-1701)

3013 Thus grief still treads upon the heels of pleasure,
Marry'd in haste, we may repent at leisure.

William Congreve (1670-1729)

3014 Men dream in courtship, but in wedlock wake.

Pope (1688-1744)

3015 Where there's marriage without love,
there will be love without marriage.

Franklin (1706-1790)

3016 Marriage has many pains, but celibacy has no pleasures.

Johnson (1709-1784)

3017 In the opinion of the world marriage ends all, as it does in
a comedy. - The truth is precisely the reverse; it begins
all.

Anne Swetchine (1782-1857)

3018 Love-making is radical, while marriage is conservative.

Eric Hoffer (1902-1983)

3019 Love is the dawn of marriage,
and marriage is the sunset of love.

French Proverb

3. INSIGHT

3020 A close bond is possible only between two persons.
A group of three engenders jealousy.

I Ching (B.C. 1150?)

3021 From of old the things that have acquired unity are these:
Heaven by unity has become clear;
Earth by unity has become steady;
The Spirit by unity has become spiritual;
The Valley by unity has become full;
All things by unity have come into existence.

Lao-Tzu (fl. B.C. 600)

3022 All things appear and disappear because of the concurrence
of causes and conditions. Nothing ever exists entirely
alone; everything is in relation to everything else.

Buddha (B.C. 568-488)

3023   When without any apparent cause a young wife, pulling her
       old husband by the hair and hugging him unmercifully,
       kisses him, there will be a reason for it.
                            The Hitopadesa (600?-1100? A.D.)

3024   We're like the sea, people our waves;
       Necessarily we are associated with everyone.
                            Ni'matullah Wali (1331-1431?)

3025   The wedlocks of minds will be greater than that of bodies.
                            Erasmus (1466-1536)

3026   A good marriage (if any there be) refuses the conditions
       of love and endeavors to present those of amity.
                            Montaigne (1533-1592)

3027   One year of Joy, another of Comfort, the rest of Content,
       make the married Life happy.
                            Thomas Fuller (1608-1661)

3028   Society is the union of men but not men themselves;
       the citizen may perish, but man remains.
                            Montesquieu (1689-1755)

3029   Marriage is the only adventure open to the timid.
                            Voltaire (1694-1778)

3030   We must, indeed, all hang together,
       or most assuredly we shall hang separately.
                            Franklin (1706-1790)

3031   I believe it will be found that those who marry late
       are best pleased with their children, and those who marry
       early with their partners.
                            Johnson (1709-1784)

3032   In married life three is company and two is none.
                            Oscar Wilde (1854-1900)

3033   A man who marries a woman to educate her falls into the same
       fallacy as the woman who marries a man to reform him.
                            Elbert Hubbard (1859-1915)

3034   A man may be a fool and not know it, but not if he is
       married.
                            H. L. Mencken (1880-1956)

4. POSITIVE

3035 Honour not thy wife the less, because she is in thy power;
and despise him that hath said, "Wouldst thou love her less?
marry her!" What hath put her into thy power, but her
confidence in thy virtue? Shouldst thou love her less,
for being more obliged to her?

Akhenaton? (c. B.C. 1375)

3036 Unity requires a collective moral force, together with a
great leader. Ancestors unite the clan, and heaven unites
nature. With unity the time is right for great deeds.

I Ching (B.C. 1150?)

3037 Happy and thrice happy are they who enjoy an uninterrupted
union, and whose love, unbroken by any complaints, shall
not dissolve until the last day.

Horace (B.C. 65-8)

3038 Where there is unity there is always victory.

Publilius Syrus (fl. B.C. 42)

3039 When many work together for a goal,
Great things may be accomplished.
It is said a lion cub was killed
By a single colony of ants.

Saskya Pandita (1182-1251)

3040 No happiness is like unto it, no love so great as that of
man and wife, no such comfort as a sweet wife.

Robert Burton (1576-1640)

3041 The joys of marriage are the heaven on earth,
Life's paradise, great princess, the soul's quiet,
Sinews of concord, earthly immortality,
Eternity of pleasures.

John Ford (1586-1640)

3042 Love is often a fruit of marriage.

Moliere (1622-1673)

3043 Two persons who have chosen each other out of all the
species with a design to be each other's mutual comfort and
entertainment have, in that action, bound themselves to be
good-humored, affable, discreet, forgiving, patient, and
joyful, with respect to each other's frailties and
perfections, to the end of their lives.

Addison (1672-1719)

3044   Marriage is the most natural state of man, and...the state
        in which you will find solid happiness.

                                        Franklin (1706-1790)

3045   Marriage is the best state for man in general; and every
        man is a worse man in proportion as he is unfit for the
        married state.

                                        Johnson (1709-1784)

3046   No jealousy their dawn of love overcast,
            Nor blasted were their wedded days with strife;
        Each season looked delightful as it past,
            To the fond husband and the faithful wife.

                                        James Beattie (1735-1803)

3047   Union does everything when it is perfect. - It satisfies
        desires, simplifies needs, foresees the wishes, and
        becomes a constant fortune.

                                        Senancour (1770-1846)

3048   In the career of female fame, there are few prizes to be
        obtained which can vie with the obscure state of a beloved
        wife, or a happy mother.

                                        Jane Porter (1776-1850)

3049   But happy they, the happiest of their kind!
        Whom gentler stars unite, and in one fate
        Their Hearts, their Fortunes, and their Beings blend.

                                        James B. V. Thomson (1834-1882)

3050   All humanity is one undivided and indivisible family, and
        each one of us is responsible for the misdeeds of all the
        others. I cannot detach myself from the wickedest soul.

                                        Gandhi (1869-1948)

3051   A good marriage is that in which each appoints the other
        guardian of his solitude. Once the realization is accepted
        that even between the closest human beings infinite
        distances continue to exist, a wonderful living side by side
        can grow up, if they succeed in loving the distance between
        them which makes it possible for each to see the other whole
        and against a wide sky.

                                        Rilke (1875-1926)

5. NEGATIVE

3052   As to marriage or celibacy, let a man take which course he
        will, he will be sure to repent.

                                        Socrates (B.C. 469-399)

3053   Marriage, to tell the truth, is an evil, but it is a
        necessary evil.

                                    Menander (B.C. 342-291)

3054   Marriage is a covenant which hath nothing free but the
        entrance.

                                    Montaigne (1533-1592)

3055   A man finds himself seven years older the day after his
        marriage.

                                    Bacon (1561-1626)

3056   One was never married, and that's his hell;
        another is, and that's his plague.

                                    Robert Burton (1576-1640)

3057   Suspicion, Discontent, and Strife,
        Come in for Dowrie with a Wife.

                                    Robert Herrick (1591-1674)

3058   There may be good, but there are no pleasant marriages.
                                    La Rochefoucauld (1613-1680)

3059   There are few women so perfect that their husbands do not
        regret having married them at least once a day.

                                    La Bruyere (1645-1696)

3060   Every man plays the fool once in his life, but to
        marry is playing the fool all one's life long.

                                    William Congreve (1670-1729)

3061   Oh! how many torments lie in the small circle of a wedding
        ring.

                                    Colley Cibber (1671-1757)

3062   It destroys one's nerves to be amiable every day to the
        same human being.

                                    Isaac D'Israeli (1766-1848)

3063   Marriage resembles a pair of shears, so joined that they
        cannot be separated; often moving in opposite directions,
        yet always punishing any one who comes between them.

                                    Sydney Smith (1771-1845)

3064   Marriage is a feast where the grace is sometimes better
        than the feast.

                                    Colton (1780-1832)

3065   The boredom of married life is inevitably the death
        of love whenever love has preceded marriage.

                                    Stendhal (1783-1842)

3066   So heavy is the chain of wedlock that it needs two to carry
it, and sometimes three.

                       Alexandre Dumas (1802-1870)

3067   Of all sexual aberrations, chastity is the strangest.

                       Anatole France (1844-1924)

3068   Men marry because they are tired, women because they are
curious: both are disappointed.

                       Oscar Wilde (1854-1900)

3069   How marriage ruins a man! It is as demoralizing as ciga-
rettes, and far more expensive.

                       Oscar Wilde (1854-1900)

6. ADVICE

3070   Remember thou art man's reasonable companion, not the slave
of his passion; the end of thy being is not merely to
gratify his loose desire, but to assist him in the toils of
life, to soothe him with thy tenderness, and recompense his
care with soft endearments.

                       Akhenaton? (c. B.C. 1375)

3071   When thou findest sensibility of heart, joined with softness
of manners, an accomplished mind, with a form agreeable to
thy fancy, take her home to thy house; she is worthy to be
thy friend, thy companion in life, the wife of thy bosom.

                       Akhenaton? (c. B.C. 1375)

3072   If you would marry suitably, marry your equal.

                       Ovid (B.C. 43-18 A.D.)

3073   What therefore God hath joined together
let not man put asunder.

                       Matthew (50?-100? A.D.)

3074   The happiness of married life depends upon making small
sacrifices with readiness and cheerfulness.

                       John Selden (1584-1654)

3075   First get an absolute conquest over thyself, and then thou
wilt easily govern thy wife.

                       Thomas Fuller (1608-1661)

3076   If you would have the nuptial union last,
let virtue be the bond that ties it fast.

                       Nicholas Rowe (1674-1718)

3077   If you wish to ruin yourself, marry a rich wife.

Jules Michelet (1798-1874)

3078   One should believe in marriage as in the immortality of the
soul.

Balzac (1799-1850)

3079   Marriage is a great responsibility. Do not trust altogether
to, or be beguiled by, the eye, for marriages are not to be
contracted by the hands and eye, but with reason and the
heart.

Lubbock (1834-1913)

3080   Let there be spaces in your togetherness.

Kahlil Gibran (1883-1931)

3081   Don't marry for money, you can borrow it cheaper.

Scottish Proverb

7. POTPOURRI

3082   Water, everywhere over the earth, flows to join together.
A single natural law controls it. Each human is a member
of a community and should work within it.

I Ching (B.C. 1150?)

3083   He who experiences the unity of life sees his own Self in
all beings, and all beings in his own Self, and looks on
everything with an impartial eye.

Bhagavad Gita (c. B.C. 400)

3084   To understand a holy unity, examine the flame rising from a
candle. We see at first two kinds of light, one glistening
white and one blue or black. The white light is above and
rises in a straight line, the blue or black light is beneath
and appears to be the source of the white; yet the two
lights are so closely united they form one single flame.
But the source formed by the blue or black light is, in
turn, attached to the wick under it. The white light never
changes, it always remains white; but several shades are
distinguishable in the lower light. Moreover, the lower
light moves in two opposite directions; above, it is
connected to the white light, and below, it is attached to
the burning matter; this matter continually consumes itself
and rises toward the upper light. It is thus that all that
is, reunites with the one unity.

Zohar (120?-1200? A.D.)

3085   Men are April when they woo,
        December when they wed,
        and maids are May when they are maids,
        but the sky changes when they are wives.
                                        Shakespeare (1564-1616)

3086   Tho' marriage be a lottery in which there are a wondrous
        many blanks, yet there is one inestimable lot in which
        the only heaven on earth is written.
                                        John Vanbrugh (1666-1726)

3087   Under this window in stormy weather
        I marry this man and woman together;
        Let none but Him who rules the thunder
        Put this man and woman asunder.
                                        Swift (1667-1745)

3088   I know not which lives more unnatural lives,
        Obeying husbands, or commanding wives.
                                        Franklin (1706-1790)

3089   You cannot pluck roses without fear of thorns,
        Nor enjoy a fair wife without danger of horns.
                                        Franklin (1706-1790)

3090   A good wife is like the ivy which beautifies the building to
        which it clings, twining its tendrils more lovingly as time
        converts the ancient edifice into a ruin.
                                        Johnson (1709-1784)

3091   Man is lyrical, woman epic, marriage dramatic.
                                        Novalis (1772-1801)

3092   All comedies are ended by a marriage.
                                        Byron (1788-1824)

3093   When a husband and wife have got each other,
        the devil only knows which has got the other.
                                        Balzac (1799-1850)

3094   The moment a woman marries, some terrible revolution happens
        in her system; all her good qualities vanish, presto, like
        eggs out of a conjuror's box. 'Tis true that they appear on
        the other side of the box, but for the husband they are gone
        forever.
                                        Bulwer-Lytton (1803-1873)

3095   You know, my Friends, with what a brave Carouse
      I made a Second Marriage in my house;
        Divorced old barren Reason from my Bed,
      And took the Daughter of the Vine to Spouse.
                 Edward FitzGerald (1809-1883)

3096   Thou shalt not separate thy being from BEING, and the rest,
      but merge the Ocean in the deep, the drop within the Ocean.
                 H. P. Blavatsky (1831-1891)

3097   The whole world is strewn with snares, traps, gins and
      pitfalls for the capture of men by women.
                 G. B. Shaw (1856-1950)

3098   One should always be in love. That is the reason one should
      never marry.
                 Oscar Wilde (1854-1900)

3099   There is nothing in the world like the devotion of a married
      woman. It is a thing no married man knows anything about.
                 Oscar Wilde (1854-1900)

3100   A man marries to have a home, but also because he doesn't
      want to be bothered with sex and all that sort of thing.
                 Somerset Maugham (1874-1965)

3101   The only real happy folk are married women and single men.
                 H. L. Mencken (1880-1956)

3102   A deaf husband and a blind wife are always a happy couple.
                 Danish Proverb

MEDITATION

Contemplation, Reflection, Self-Examination and Solitude

1. ESSENCE

3103   Meditation is the soul's perspective glass...
Owen Feltham (1602-1668)

3104   Meditation is the tongue of the soul
and the language of our spirit.
Jeremy Taylor (1613-1667)

3105   Meditation has been defined as "the cessation of active
eternal thought."
H. P. Blavatsky (1831-1891)

3106   Meditation is the dissolution of thoughts in Eternal
awareness or Pure consciousness without objectification,
knowing without thinking, merging finitude in infinity.
Sivananda (born 1887)

3107   Meditation consists in conducting consciousness beyond the
point where it is the consciousness of a finite body or a
finite mind, transferring the focus from level to level
without losing its continuity or form.
Pir Vilayat Inayat Khan (born 1916)

2. OPPOSITES

3108   Whosoever is delighted in solitude,
is either a wild beast or a god.
Plato (B.C. 427?-347?)

3109   As rain breaks through an ill-thatched house,
passion will break through an unreflecting mind.
As rain does not break through a well-thatched house,
passion will not break through a well-reflecting mind.
The Dhammapada (c. B.C. 300)

3110   That he was never less at leisure than when at leisure;
nor that he was never less alone than when alone.
Cicero (B.C. 106-43)

3111   In solitude, be a multitude to thyself.
Tibullus (B.C. 49-19)

3112   Eagles we see fly alone; and they are but sheep which
always herd together.
Philip Sidney (1554-1586)

3113   If from society we learn to live,
        it is solitude should teach us how to die.

                                        Byron (1788-1824)

3114   Reflection is a flower of the mind, giving out wholesome
        fragrance; but revelry is the same flower, when rank and
        running to seed.

                                        Tupper (1810-1889)

3. INSIGHT

3115   The sage, who is living outside the routine of the world,
        contemplates his own character, not as an isolated ego
        manifestation, but in relation to the laws of life.
        He judges freedom from blame to be the highest good.

                                        I Ching (B.C. 1150?)

3116   When the mind is silent, beyond weakness or non-
        concentration, then it can enter into a world which is far
        beyond the mind: the highest End.

                                        Upanishads (c. B.C. 800)

3117   The mind is restless, turbulent, obstinate, and very strong.
        To subdue it is more difficult than controlling the wind,
        but it is possible by constant practice and attachment.
        He who strives by right means is assured of success.

                                        Bhagavad Gita (c. B.C. 400)

3118   If an eye never falls asleep,
        All dreams will by themselves cease:
        If the mind retains its absoluteness,
        The ten thousand things are of one suchness.

                                        Seng-T'San (540?-606 A.D.)

3119   If the thoughts are absolutely tranquil the heavenly heart
        can be seen. The heavenly heart lies between sun and moon
        (i.e. between the two eyes). It is the home of the inner
        light. To make light circulate is the deepest and most
        wonderful secret. The light is easy to move, but difficult
        to fix. If it is made to circulate long enough, then it
        crystallizes itself; that is the natural spirit body...

                                        Lu Yen (fl. 800 A.D.)

3120   Meditation is the life of the soul; action is the soul of
        meditation; honor is the reward of action: so meditate,
        that thou mayst do; so do, that thou mayst purchase honor;
        for which purchase, give God the glory.

                                        Quarles (1592-1644)

3121   A drop of water has the tastes of the water of the seven
seas: there is no need to experience all the ways of
worldly life. The reflections of the moon on one thousand
rivers are from the same moon: the mind must be full of
light.

                          Hung Tzu-ch'eng (1593-1665)

3122   Leisure and solitude are the best effect of riches, because
the mother of thought. Both are avoided by most rich men,
who seek company and business, which are signs of being
weary of themselves.

                          William Temple (1628-1699)

3123   One can acquire everything in solitude but character.

                          Stendhal (1783-1842)

3124   Solitude, though it may be silent as light, is like light,
the mightiest of agencies; for solitude is essential to
man. All men come into this world alone; all leave it
alone.

                          Thomas De Quincey (1785-1859)

3125   In solitude, where we are least alone.

                          Byron (1788-1824)

3126   It is easy in the world to live after the world's opinion-
it is easy in solitude to live after your own; but the
great man is he who, in the midst of the world, keeps with
perfect sweetness the independence of solitude.

                          Emerson (1803-1882)

3127   Adoration is an activity of the loving, but still separate,
individuality. Contemplation is the state of union with
the divine Ground of all being. The highest prayer is the
most passive...For the less there is of self, the more there
is of God.

                          Aldous Huxley (1894-1963)

3128   It is a matter of incorporating higher dimensions of
awareness into a total picture without blacking out the
lower levels.

                          Pir Vilayat Inayat Khan (born 1916)

4. POSITIVE

3129   The quiet and solitary man apprehends the inscrutable.
He seeks nothing, holds to the mean, and remains free
from entanglements.

                          I Ching (B.C. 1150?)

3130 Meditation is in truth higher than thought. The earth seems
to rest in silent meditation; and the waters and the
mountains and the sky and the heavens seem all to be in
meditation. Whenever a man attains greatness on this earth,
he has his reward according to his meditation.

Upanishads (c. B.C. 800)

3131 The sun makes the day bright, the moon makes the night
beautiful, as armament adds to the dignity of a soldier;
so the quiet meditation distinguishes the seeker for
Enlightenment.

Buddha (B.C. 568-488)

3132 By meditation upon light and upon radiance, knowledge of
the spirit can be reached and thus peace can be achieved.

Patanjali (B.C. 500?)

3133 The soul who meditates on the Self is content to serve the
Self and rests satisfied within the Self; there remains
nothing more for him to accomplish.

Bhagavad Gita (c. B.C. 400)

3134 The reflections on a day well spent furnish us with joys
more pleasing than ten thousand triumphs.

Thomas A. Kempis (1380-1471)

3135 When holy and devout religious men
Are at their beads, 'tis hard to draw them thence;
So sweet is zealous contemplation.

Shakespeare (1564-1616)

3136 Solitude is sometimes best society, and short retirement
urges sweet return.

Milton (1608-1674)

3137 One self-approving hour whole years out-weighs
Of stupid starers of loud huzzas.

Pope (1688-1744)

3138 Solitude is the best nurse of wisdom.

Sterne (1713-1768)

3139 Conversation enriches the understanding,
but solitude is the school of the genius.

Gibbon (1737-1794)

3140 The contemplation of truth and beauty is the proper object
for which we were created, which calls forth the most
intense desires of the soul, and of which it never tires.

Hazlitt (1778-1830)

3141 The attachment to solitude is the surest preservative
from the ills of life.

Albert Pike (1809-1891)

3142 I love to be alone. I never found the companion that was so
companionable as solitude.

Thoreau (1817-1862)

3143 Solitude is as needful to the imagination
as society is wholesome for the character.

James Lowell (1819-1891)

3144 When he has ceased to hear the many, he may discern the
One - the inner sound which kills the outer.

H. P. Blavatsky (1831-1891)

3145 Solitude is the most comprehensive of rights, and the right
most valued by civilized men.

Louis D. Brandeis (1856-1941)

3146 Solitude is the beginning of all freedom.

William O. Douglas (1898-1980)

5. NEGATIVE

3147 It is not good that the man should be alone.

Genesis (B.C. 1200?)

3148 I used to spend whole days without food and whole nights
without sleep in order to meditate. But I made no progress.
Study, I found, was better.

Confucius (B.C. 551-479)

3149 The life that is unexamined is not worth living.

Plato (B.C. 427?-347?)

3150 Meditation is not for him who eats too much, nor for him who
eats not at all; not for him who is overmuch addicted to
sleep, nor for him who is always awake.

Bhagavad Gita (c. B.C. 400)

3151 As a grass-blade, if badly grasped, cuts the arm,
badly-practised asceticism leads to hell.

The Dhammapada (c. B.C. 300)

3152 Hardly one man in ten knows himself.

Plautus (B.C. 254-184)

3153   A soul without reflection, like a pile
       Without inhabitant, to ruin runs.

                                        Young (1683-1765)

3154   Solitude excludes pleasure, and does not always secure
       peace.

                                     Johnson (1709-1784)

3155   O solitude, where are the charms
          That sages have seen in thy face?
       Better dwell in the midst of alarms,
          Than reign in this horrible place.

                                      Cowper (1731-1800)

3156   They only babble who practise not reflection.
       I shall think; and thought is silence.

                              Richard Sheridan (1751-1816)

3157   That which happens to the soil when it ceases to be
       cultivated, happens to man himself when he foolishly
       forsakes society for solitude; the brambles grow up
       in his desert heart.

                           Antoine de Rivaroli (1753-1801)

6. ADVICE

3158   Listen within yourself and look into the infinitude of
       Space and Time. There can be heard the songs of the
       Constellations, the voices of the Numbers, and the
       harmonies of the Spheres.

                        The Divine Pymander (BC 2500?-200 AD?)

3159   Contemplate thy powers, contemplate thy wants and thy
       connections; so shalt thou discover the duties of life,
       and be directed in all thy ways.

                                   Akhenaton? (c. B.C. 1375)

3160   Taking as a bow the great weapon of this Scripture,
       One should put upon it an arrow sharpened by meditation.
       Stretching it with a thought directed to the essence of
         That,
       Penetrate the Imperishable as the mark, my friend.

                                   Upanishads (c. B.C. 800)

3161   Let no sleep fall upon thy eyes till thou hast thrice re-
       viewed the transactions of the past day. Where have I turn-
       ed aside from rectitude? What have I been doing? What have
       I left undone, which I ought to have done? Begin thus from
       the first act, and proceed; and, in conclusion, at the ill
       which thou hast done, be troubled, and rejoice for the good.

                                 Pythagoras (B.C. 582-507)

3162   The point of the teachings is to control your own mind.
        Restrain your mind from greed, and you will keep your
        body right, your mind pure and your words faithful. Always
        thinking of the transiency of your life, you will be able
        to desist from greed and anger and will be able to avoid
        all evils.
                                                    Buddha (B.C. 568-488)

3163   The superior man will watch over himself when he is alone.
        He examines his heart that there may be nothing wrong there,
        and that he may have no cause of dissatisfaction with
        himself.
                                                Confucius (B.C. 551-479)

3164   Man, know thyself.
                                                Socrates (B.C. 469-399)

3165   Those who are interested in self-realization, in terms of
        mind and sense control, offer the functions of all the
        senses, as well as the vital force (breath), as oblations
        into the fire of the controlled mind.
                                            Bhagavad Gita (c. B.C. 400)

3166   We should every night call ourselves to an account:
        What infirmity have I mastered to-day? what passions
        opposed? what temptation resisted? what virtue acquired?
        Our vices will abate of themselves if they be brought every
        day to the shrift.
                                                Seneca (B.C. 3-65 A.D.)

3167   Forget not on every occasion to ask thyself, is this not
        one of the unnecessary things?
                                            Marcus Aurelius (121-180 A.D.)

3168   Abandon the crowd of distractions and confusions, and rest
        in the boundless state without grasping or disturbance;
        firm in two practices: visualization and complete, at this
        time of meditation, one-pointed, free from activity.
        Fall not into the power of confused emotions.
                                        Tibetan Book of the Dead (c. 780 A.D.)

3169   To concentrate the seed flower (spiritual embryo formed by
        light) of the human body above in the eyes, that is the
        great key of the human body. Children take heed! If for a
        day you do not practice meditation, this light streams out,
        who knows wither? If you only meditate for a quarter of an
        hour, by it you can do away with the ten thousand eons and a
        thousand births. All methods end in quietness. This
        marvelous magic cannot be fathomed.
                                                    Lu Yen (fl. 800 A.D.)

3170   Seated in a desert place, exempt from passion, master of his
        senses, let man represent to himself this spirit, one and
        infinite, without allowing his thoughts to stray elsewhere.
        Considering the visible universe as annihilated in spirit,
        let a man, pure through intelligence, constantly contemplate
        the One Spirit, as he might contemplate luminous ether.
                                                Sankara (c. 900 A.D.)

3171   Make it thy business to know thyself,
        which is the most difficult lesson in the world.
                                                Cervantes (1547-1616)

3172   Go to your bosom;
        Knock there, and ask your heart what it doth know.
                                                Shakespeare (1564-1616)

3173   By all means use some time to be alone.
                                                Herbert (1593-1632)

3174   'Tis greatly wise to talk with our past hours;
        And ask them what report they bore to heaven:
        And how they might have borne more welcome news.
                                                Young (1683-1765)

3175   There is one art of which man should be master,
        the art of reflection.
                                                Samuel Coleridge (1772-1834)

3176   Thou hast to reach that fixity of mind in which no breeze,
        however strong, can waft an earthly thought within. "Ere
        the gold flame can burn with steady light, the lamp must
        stand well guarded in a spot free from all wind." Exposed
        to shifting breeze, the jet will flicker and the quivering
        flame cast shades deceptive, dark and everchanging, on the
        Soul's white shrine.
                                                H. P. Blavatsky (1831-1891)

3177   Make no violent effort to control the mind, but rather allow
        it to run along for a while, and exhaust its efforts. It
        will take advantage of the opportunity and will jump around
        like an unchained monkey at first, until it gradually slows
        down and looks to you for orders. It may take some time to
        tame the mind, but each time you try it will come round to
        you in a shorter time.
                                                Sivananda (born 1887)

7. POTPOURRI

3178   Wake up with one mind, my friends, and kindle the fire,
you many who share the same nest. Make your thoughts
harmonious; stretch them on the loom; make a ship whose
oars will carry us across...

Rig Veda (B.C. 1200-900?)

3179   The wind blows over the earth:
The image of CONTEMPLATION.
Thus the kings of old visited the regions of the world,
Contemplated the people,
And gave them instruction.

I Ching (B.C. 1150?)

3180   Though one sits in meditation in a particular place,
the Self in him can exercise its influence far away.
Though still, it moves everywhere...
The Self cannot be known by anyone who desists not
from unrighteous ways, controls not his senses,
stills not his mind, and practices not meditation.

Upanishads (c. B.C. 800)

3181   The method used by the ancients for escaping from the world
consisted in melting out completely the slag of darkness in
order to return to the purely creative. This is nothing
more than a reduction of the anima (consciousness) and a
completion of the animus (spirit). And the circulation of
the inner light is the magical means of reducing the dark,
and gaining mastery over the anima (consciousness).

Lu Yen (fl. 800 A.D.)

3182   I study myself more than any other subject;
it is my metaphysic, and my physic.

Montaigne (1533-1592)

3183   Thrice happy he, who by some shady grove,
    Far from the clamorous world, doth live his own;
    Though solitary, who is not alone,
But doth converse with that eternal love.

William Drummond (1585-1649)

3184   Far in a wild, unknown to public view,
From youth to age a reverend hermit grew;
The moss his bed, the cave his humble cell,
His food the fruits, his drink the crystal well,
Remote from man, with God he pass'd the days;
Prayer all his business, all his pleasure praise.

Thomas Parnell (1679-1717)

3185   O sacred solitude! divine retreat!
        Choice of the prudent! envy of the great!
        By thy pure stream, or in thy waving shade,
        We court fair wisdom, that celestial maid.

                                          Young (1683-1765)

3186   They flash upon that inward eye
        Which is the bliss of solitude.

                                     Wordsworth (1770-1850)

3187   She dwelt among the untrodden ways
           Beside the springs of Dove,
        A maid whom there were none to praise
           And very few to love.

                                     Wordsworth (1770-1850)

3188   I love tranquil solitude
        And such society
        As is quiet, wise, and good.

                                          Shelley (1792-1822)

3189   We must certainly acknowledge that solitude is a fine thing;
        but it is a pleasure to have some one who can answer,
        and to whom we can say, from time to time,
        that solitude is a fine thing.

                                          Balzac (1799-1850)

MIRTH

Humor, Jesting, Laughter, Merriment and Smiles

1. ESSENCE

3190   Humor - Its essence is love; it issues not in laughter, but
        in still smiles, which lie far deeper.

        Carlyle (1795-1881)

3191   Humor is wit and love.

        Thackeray (1811-1863)

3192   Laughter is the sensation of feeling good all over,
        and showing it principally on one spot.

        Josh Billings (1815-1885)

3193   Incongruity is the mainspring of laughter.

        Max Beerbohm (1872-1956)

2. OPPOSITES

3194   An ounce of mirth is worth a pound of sorrow.

        Richard Baxter (1615-1691)

3195   It was the saying of an ancient sage that humor was the
        only test of gravity, and gravity of humor.

        Shaftesbury III (1671-1713)

3196   Good humor is the health of the soul, sadness is its poison.

        Leszczynski Stanislaus (1677-1766)

3197   The vulgar only laugh, but never smile; whereas well-bred
        people often smile, but seldom laugh.

        Chesterfield (1694-1773)

3198   A laugh is worth a hundred groans in any market.

        Charles Lamb (1775-1834)

3199   Man is the only animal that laughs and weeps;
        for he is the only animal that is struck by the difference
        between what things are and what they might have been.

        Hazlitt (1778-1830)

3200   Smiles form the channel of a future tear.

        Byron (1788-1824)

3201   In a natural state, tears and laughter go hand in hand;
        for they are twin-born. Like two children sleeping in one
        cradle, when one wakes and stirs, the other wakes also.

        Beecher (1813-1878)

3202   Whenever you find Humor, you find Pathos close by its side.
                                        Edwin Whipple (1819-1886)

3203   The secret source of Humor itself is not joy but sorrow.
       There is no humor in heaven.
                                          Mark Twain (1835-1910)

3204   Laughter is not a bad beginning for a friendship, and
       it is the best ending for one.
                                          Oscar Wilde (1854-1900)

3205   Humour is the contemplation of the finite from the point of
       view of the infinite.
                                Christian Morgenstern (1871-1914)

3206   Humour is emotional chaos remembered in tranquility.
                                    James G. Thurber (1894-1961)

3. INSIGHT

3207   Even in laughter the heart is sorrowful; and the end
       of mirth is heaviness.
                                     Proverbs (B.C. 1000?-200?)

3208   For a man learns more quickly and remembers more easily
       that which he laughed at, than that which he approves and
       than that which he approves and reveres.
                                             Horace (B.C. 65-8)

3209   Man is the only creature endowed with the power of laughter;
       is he not also the only one that deserves to be laughed at?
                                           Greville (1554-1628)

3210   A jest's prosperity lies in the ear of him that hears it,
       Never in the tongue of him that makes it.
                                        Shakespeare (1564-1616)

3211   The jest which is expected is already destroyed.
                                          Johnson (1709-1784)

3212   Men show their characters in nothing more clearly
       than in what they think laughable.
                                            Goethe (1749-1832)

3213   Fun I love, but too much fun is of all things the most
       loathsome. Mirth is better than fun, and happiness is
       better than mirth.
                                     William Blake (1757-1828)

3214 How much lies in laughter:
      the cipher key, wherewith we decipher the whole man!
                                        Carlyle (1795-1881)

3215 To provoke laughter without joining in it greatly
      heightens the effect.
                                        Balzac (1799-1850)

3216 Laughter is day, and sobriety is night; a smile is the
      twilight that hovers gently between both, more bewitching
      than either.
                                        Beecher (1813-1878)

3217 Something of a person's character may be discovered by
      observing when and how he smiles. Some people never smile;
      they merely grin.
                                        Bovee (1820-1904)

3218 Laugh and the world laughs with you,
      Weep and you weep alone;
      For the sad old earth must borrow its mirth,
      But has trouble enough of its own.
                                Ella Wheeler Wilcox (1855-1919)

3219 Life does not cease to be funny when people die,
      any more than it ceases to be serious when people laugh.
                                        G. B. Shaw (1856-1950)

3220 The total absence of humour from the Bible is one of the
      most singular things in all literature.
                            Alfred North Whitehead (1861-1947)

3221 Laughter relieves us of superfluous energy, which, if it
      remained unused, might become negative, that is, poison.
      We always have plenty of this poison in us. Laughter is the
      antidote. But this antidote is necessary only so long as we
      are unable to use all the energy for useful work.
                                        Gurdjieff (1873-1949)

4. POSITIVE

3222 A merry heart doeth good like a medicine.
                                Proverbs (B.C. 1000?-200?)

3223 Jesters do often prove prophets.
                                Shakespeare (1564-1616)

3224 What sunshine is to flowers, smiles are to humanity.
      They are but trifles, to be sure,
      but, scattered along life's pathway,
      the good they do is inconceivable.
                                        Addison (1672-1719)

3225   The man that loves and laughs must sure do well.

Pope (1688-1744)

3226   Honest good humor is the oil and wine of a merry meeting,
and there is no jovial companionship equal to that where
the jokes are rather small, and the laughter abundant.

Washington Irving (1783-1859)

3227   Laughter is one of the very privileges of reason, being
confined to the human species.

Leigh Hunt (1784-1859)

3228   Humor has justly been regarded as the finest perfection
of poetic genius.

Carlyle (1795-1881)

3229   No man who has once heartily and wholly laughed can be
altogether irreclaimably depraved.

Carlyle (1795-1881)

3230   A good laugh is sunshine in a house.

Thackeray (1811-1863)

3231   The human race has only one really effective weapon
and that is laughter.

Mark Twain (1835-1910)

3232   That older and greater church to which I belong; the church
where the oftener you laugh the better, because by laughter
only can you destroy evil without malice, and affirm good
fellowship without mawkishness.

G. B. Shaw (1856-1950)

3233   It is a great loss to a man when he cannot smile and laugh.
Laughing is the best tonic to keep one healthy.

Sivananda (born 1887)

5. NEGATIVE

3234   Laughter has its source in some kind of meanness or
deformity.

Cicero (B.C. 106-43)

3235   A laugh costs too much when bought at the expense of virtue.

Quintilian (35-90 A.D.)

3236   A bitter jest, when it comes too near the truth,
leaves a sharp sting behind it.

Tacitus (55-117 A.D.)

3237   Unseasonable mirth always turns to sorrow.

Cervantes (1547-1616)

3238   Laughter is the hiccup of a fool.

                                     John Ray (1627-1705)

3239   Madness, we fancy, gave an ill-timed birth
         To a grinning laughter and to frantic mirth.

                             Matthew Prior (1664-1721)

3240   Some people are commended for a giddy kind of good humor,
         which is no more a virtue than drunkenness.

                                        Pope (1688-1744)

3241   Thou canst not joke an enemy into a friend,
         but thou may'st a friend into an enemy.

                                 Franklin (1706-1790)

3242   The most completely lost of all days is that on which
         one has not laughed.

                               Chamfort (1741-1794)

3243   No one is more profoundly sad than he who laughs too much.
                                   Richter (1763-1825)

3244   The man who cannot laugh is not only fit for treasons,
         stratagems, and spoils, but his whole life is already a
         treason and a stratagem.

                                   Carlyle (1795-1881)

3245   No, you never get any fun
         Out of the things you haven't done.

                               Ogden Nash (1902-1971)

6. ADVICE

3246   It better befits a man to laugh at life
         than to lament over it.

                               Seneca (B.C. 3-65 A.D.)

3247   Be merry if you are wise.

                               Martial (43-104 A.D.)

3248   Frame thy mind to mirth and merriment, which bars a thousand
         harms, and lengthens life.

                               Shakespeare (1564-1616)

3249   Laugh not too much; the witty man laughs least:
         For wit is news only to ignorance.
         Less at thine own things: lest in the jest
         Thy person share, and thy conceit advance.

                               Herbert (1593-1632)

3250   One should take good care not to grow too wise
for so great a pleasure of life as laughter.

                         Addison (1672-1719)

3251   Laugh at your friends, and if your friends are sore;
So much the better, you may laugh the more.

                         Pope (1688-1744)

3252   If you want to make people weep, you must weep yourself.
If you want to make people laugh, your face must remain
serious.

                  Giovanni G. Casanova (1725-1798)

3253   Be not affronted at a joke. If one throw salt at thee,
thou wilt receive no harm, unless thou art raw.

                        Junius (1740-1818)

3254   Beware of him who hates the laugh of a child.

                        Lavater (1741-1801)

3255   Mirth is God's medicine. Everybody ought to bathe in it.
Grim care, moroseness, anxiety, - all this rust of life,
ought to be scoured off by the oil of mirth. It is better
than emery. Every man ought to rub himself with it.

                      Beecher (1813-1878)

7. POTPOURRI

3256   To laugh, if but for an instant only, has never been
granted to man before the fortieth day from his birth,
and then it is looked upon as a miracle of precocity.

                    Pliny the Elder (23-79 A.D.)

3257   I have observed, that in comedy, the best actor plays the
part of the droll, while some scrub rogue is made the hero,
or fine gentleman. So, in this farce of life, wise men pass
their time in mirth, whilst fools only are serious.

                    Bolingbroke (1678-1751)

3258   Old Times have bequeathed us a precept:
  To be merry and wise,
  but who has been able to observe it?

                      Johnson (1709-1784)

3259   When the green woods laugh with the voice of joy,
And the dimpling stream runs laughing by;
When the air does laugh with our merry wit,
And the green hill laughs with the noise of it.

                  William Blake (1757-1828)

3260   Let us have Wine and Women, Mirth and Laughter;
        Sermons and soda-water the day after.

                                        Byron (1788-1824)

3261   My mirth can laugh and talk, but cannot sing:
        My grief finds harmonies in everything.

                                James B. V. Thomson (1834-1882)

3262   Laughter is an internal convulsion, producing a distortion
        of the features and accompanied by inarticulate noises.

                                    Ambrose Bierce (1842-1914?)

3263   A joke is an epigram on the death of a feeling.

                                        Nietzsche (1844-1900)

3264   The smile that flickers on baby's lips when he sleeps-
        does anybody know where it was borne?
        Yes, there is a rumor that a young pale beam of a crescent
        moon touched the edge of a vanishing autumn cloud, and there
        the smile was first born in the dream of a dew-washed
        morning.

                                Rabindranath Tagore (1861-1941)

3265   Everything is funny as long as it is happening to somebody
        else.

                                    Will Rogers (1879-1935)

NON-BEING

Darkness, Emptiness, Nothingness, Silence and Space

1. ESSENCE

3266   The eternal parent wrapped in her ever invisible robes had slumbered once again for seven eternities.

Time was not, for it lay asleep in the infinite bosom of duration.

Universal mind was not, for there were no celestial beings to contain it.

The seven ways to bliss were not. The great causes of misery were not, for there was no one to produce and get ensnared by them.

Darkness alone filled the boundless all, for father, mother and son were once more one, and the son had not awakened yet for the new wheel, and his pilgrimage thereon.

Book of Dzyan (B.C. 3000?)

3267   In the first age of the gods, existence was born from non-existence.

Rig Veda (B.C. 1200-900?)

3268   All things in the world come from being.
And being comes from non-being.

Lao-Tzu (fl. B.C. 600)

3269   At the dawning of that day all objects in manifestation stream forth from the Unmanifest, and when evening falls they are dissolved into It again. In truth, therefore, there is the Eternal Unmanifest, which is beyond and above the Unmanifest Spirit of Creation, which is never destroyed when all these beings perish.

Bhagavad Gita (c. B.C. 400)

3270   It began of nothing and in nothing it ends.

Gallus (B.C. 70-26)

3271   ...And the still deeper secret of the secret:
The land that is nowhere, that is the true home...

Chang Po-tuan (fl. 1000 A.D.)

3272   Silence is the mother of Truth.

Disraeli (1804-1881)

3273   ...The limitless ocean of negative light does not proceed from a centre, for it is centreless, but it concentrates a centre.

Samuel L. Mathers (1850?-1918)

2. OPPOSITES

3274   The causes of existence had been done away with;
       the visible that was, and the invisible that is,
       rested in eternal non-being - the one being.
                                          Book of Dzyan (B.C. 3000?)

3275   Wherefrom do all these worlds come? They come from space.
       All beings arise from space, and into space they return:
       space is indeed their beginning, and space is their final
       end.
                                          Upanishads (c. B.C. 800)

3276   Wherever there is light, there is shadow; wherever there
       is length, there is shortness; wherever there is white,
       there is black. Just like these, as the self-nature of
       things can not exist alone, they are called non-substantial.
                                          Buddha (B.C. 568-488)

3277   That which is not, shall never be;
       that which is, shall never cease to be.
       To the wise, these truths are self-evident.
                                          Bhagavad Gita (c. B.C. 400)

3278   When the Holy One who created the Universe wished to reveal
       its hidden aspect, the light within the darkness, He showed
       how things were intermingled. Thus out of darkness comes
       light and from the concealed comes the revealed. In the
       same manner does good emerge from evil and mercy from
       justice, since they too are intertwined.
                                          Zohar (120?-1200? A.D.)

3279   Silence is one great art of conversation.
                                          Hazlitt (1778-1830)

3280   Under all speech that is good for anything
          there lies a silence that is better,
       Silence is deep as Eternity;
          speech is shallow as Time.
                                          Carlyle (1795-1881)

3. INSIGHT

3281   He (The Eternal) created a reality out of nothing, called
       the nonentity into existence and hewed, as it were,
       colossal pillars from intangible air.
                                          Sepher Yezirah (B.C. 2000?-600 A.D.)

3282   Cosmic night, the sinking of manifestation into a state of
        rest, comes about when the forth-rushing expansive force
        of creation is interlocked and stabilized into equilibrium.
                                    Kabbalah (B.C. 1200?-700? A.D.)

3283   The softest things in the world
          overcome the hardest things in the world.
        Non-being penetrates that in which there is no space.
        Through this I know the advantage of taking no action.
        Few in the world can understand teaching without words
          and the advantage of taking no action.
                                            Lao-Tzu (fl. B.C. 600)

3284   Silence is learned by the many misfortunes of life.
                                            Seneca (B.C. 3-65 A.D.)

3285   There is an eloquent silence: it serves sometimes to
        approve, sometimes to condemn; there is a mocking silence;
        there is a respectful silence.
                                    La Rochefoucauld (1613-1680)

3286   What is called the spirit of the void is where there is
        nothing. It is not included in man's knowledge. Of course
        the void is nothingness. By knowing things that exist, you
        can know that which does not exist. That is the void.
          People in this world look at things mistakenly, and think
        that what they do not understand must be the void. This is
        not the true void. It is bewilderment...
          Polish the twofold spirit heart and mind, and sharpen the
        twofold perception and sight. When your spirit is not in
        the least clouded, when the clouds of bewilderment clear
        away, there is the true void...
          In the void is virtue, and no evil. Wisdom has existence,
        principle has existence, the Way has existence, spirit is
        nothingness.
                                    Miyamoto Musashi (1584-1645)

3287   None preaches better than the ant, and she says nothing.
                                            Franklin (1706-1790)

3288   Our noisy years seem moments in the being of the
        eternal silence.
                                            Wordsworth (1770-1850)

3289   Three things are ever silent:
        Thought, Destiny, and the Grave.
                                            Bulwer-Lytton (1803-1873)

3290   ...In a seed, the tree which may spring from it is hidden;
       it is in a condition of potential existence; is there;
       but it will not admit definition. How much less, then,
       will those seeds which that tree in its turn may yield.
                                    Samuel L. Mathers (1850?-1918)

3291   The finest command of language is often shown by saying
       nothing.
                                         Roger Babson (1875-1967)

3292   When the tree falls
       The shadow flies.
                                                   Chinese Proverb

4. POSITIVE

3293   The sage manages affairs without action
       And spreads doctrines without words.
       All things arise, and he does not turn away from them.
       He produces them, but does not take possession of them.
       He acts, but does not rely on his own ability.
       He accomplishes his task, but does not claim credit for it.
       It is precisely because he does not claim credit
          that his accomplishment remains with him.
                                         Lao-Tzu (fl. B.C. 600)

3294   If a word be worth a nickel, silence is worth two.
                                    The Talmud (B.C. 500?-400? A.D.)

3295   Nothing is more useful than silence.
                                         Menander (B.C. 342-291)

3296   Health is the greatest possession.
       Contentment is the greatest treasure.
       Confidence is the greatest friend.
       Non-being is the greatest joy.
                                    The Dhammapada (c. B.C. 300)

3297   Silence at the proper season is wisdom, and better than any
       speech.
                                         Plutarch (46-120 A.D.)

3298   The world would be happier if men had the same capacity
       to be silent that they have to speak.
                                         Spinoza (1632-1677)

3299   Silence is the genius of the fool
       and one of the virtues of the wise.
                                         Bonnard (1744-1784)

3300 There is a silence, the child of love, which expresses
everything, and proclaims more loudly than the tongue
is able to do.
Vittorio Alfieri (1749-1803)

3301 The temple of our purest thoughts is silence.
Sarah J. Hale (1788-1879)

3302 Silence is the element in which great things fashion
themselves together; that at length they may emerge,
full formed and majestic, into the delights of life,
which they are thenceforth to rule.
Carlyle (1795-1881)

3303 Silence provokes no man's envy, and wounds no man's self-
love.
Bulwer-Lytton (1803-1873)

3304 Silence is the universal refuge, the sequel to all dull
discourses and all foolish acts, a balm to our every
chagrin, as welcome after satiety as after disappointment.
Thoreau (1817-1862)

3305 Silence, when nothing need be said, is the eloquence of
discretion.
Bovee (1820-1904)

3306 But let me silent be:
For silence is the speech of love,
The music of the sphere above.
Richard Stoddard (1825-1903)

3307 I have noticed that nothing I never said ever did me any
harm.
Calvin Coolidge (1872-1933)

5. NEGATIVE

3308 We cannot conceive of matter being formed of nothing,
since things require a seed to start from...
Therefore there is not anything which returns to nothing,
but all things return dissolved into their elements.
Lucretius (B.C. 99-55)

3309 Slight is the merit of keeping silence on a matter, on the
other hand serious is the guilt of talking on things
whereon we should be silent.
Ovid (B.C. 43-18 A.D.)

3310   Nothing can be born of nothing,
       nothing can be resolved into nothing.

                                           Persius (34-62 A.D.)

3311   Nothing proceeds from nothingness,
       as also nothing passes away into non-existence.
                                           Marcus Aurelius (121-180 A.D.)

3312   There is no reply so sharp as silent contempt.
                                           Montaigne (1533-1592)

3313   An horrid stillness first invades the ear,
       And in that silence we the tempest fear.

                                           Dryden (1631-1700)

3314   Nothing's new, and nothing's true, and nothing matters.
                                           Sidney Morgan (1789-1859)

3315   A life of nothing's nothing worth,
       From that first nothing ere his birth,
       To that last nothing under earth.

                                           Alfred Tennyson (1809-1892)

6. ADVICE

3316   Clay is molded to form a cup,
           But it is on its non-being that the utility of the cup
             depends.
       Doors and windows are cut out to make a room,
           But it is on its non-being that the utility of the room
             depends.
       Therefore turn being into advantage, and turn non-being into
             utility.

                                           Lao-Tzu (fl. B.C. 600)

3317   It is better either to be silent, or to say things of more
       value than silence. Sooner throw a pearl at hazard than an
       idle or useless word; and do not say a little in many
       words, but a great deal in a few.

                                           Pythagoras (B.C. 582-507)

3318   Choose silence of all virtues, for by it you hear
       other men's imperfections, and conceal your own.

                                           Zeno (B.C. 335?-264)

3319   The first virtue is to restrain the tongue; he approaches
       nearest to the gods who knows how to be silent, even though
       he is in the right.

                                           Cato the Younger (B.C. 95-46)

3320   Silence is the safest course for any man to adopt who
        distrusts himself.
                                    La Rochefoucauld (1613-1680)

3321   Let us be silent, that we may hear the whispers of the gods.
                                           Emerson (1803-1882)

3322   Be silent and safe - silence never betrays you.
                                       John O'Reilly (1844-1890)

7. POTPOURRI

3323   Darkness which may be felt.
                                          Exodus (B.C. 1200?)

3324   The Eternal is the intensest form of existence, pure being
        unlimited by form or reaction; but it is existence of
        another type than that to which we are accustomed, and
        therefore it appears to us as non-existence because it
        conforms to none of the requirements we are accustomed to
        think of as determining existence.
                              Kabbalah (B.C. 1200?-700? A.D.)

3325   The Imperishable - It is not coarse, not fine,
        not short, not long, not glowing like fire, not adhesive
        like water, without shadow and without darkness, without
        air and without space, without stickiness intangible,
        odorless, tasteless, without eye, without ear, without
        voice, without wind, without energy, without breath, without
        mouth, (without personal or family name, unaging, undying,
        without fear, immortal, stainless, not uncovered, not
        covered), without measure, without inside and without
        outside...
           The Imperishable is the unseen Seer, the unheard Hearer,
        the unthought Thinker, the ununderstood Understander.
        Other than It there is naught that sees...hears...thinks...
        understands. Across this Imperishable is space woven.
                                     Upanishads (c. B.C. 800)

3326   Although one perceives non-existent reality,
        Who can believe in its non-existence?
        How could a painted peacock
        Devour real pearls?
                                  Nagarjuna (c. 100-200 A.D.)

3327   When the light is made to move in a circle,
        all the energies of heaven and earth, of the light and dark,
        are crystallized. That is what is termed seed-like thinking,
        or purification of the energy, or purification of the idea.
        When one begins to apply this magic it is as if,
        in the middle of being, there were non-being.
                                       Lu Yen (fl. 800 A.D.)

3328   Where every something, being blent together
        Turns to a wild of nothing.

                                        Shakespeare (1564-1616)

3329   Dark night that from the eye his function takes,
        The ear more quick of apprehension makes,
        Wherein it doth impair the seeing sense,
        It pays the hearing double recompense.

                                        Shakespeare (1564-1616)

3330   How sweetly did they float upon the wings
        Of silence, through the empty-vaulted night,
        At every fall smoothing the raven-down
        Of darkness till it smiled.

                                        Milton (1608-1674)

3331   Silence, how dead! and darkness, how profound!
        Nor eye, nor list'ning ear, an object finds;
        Creation sleeps. 'Tis as the general pulse
        Of life stood still, and nature made a pause;
        An awful pause! prophetic of her end.

                                        Young (1683-1765)

3332   The waves were dead; the tides were in their grave,
        The Moon, their Mistress, had expired before;
        The winds were wither'd in the stagnant air,
        And the clouds perish'd; darkness had no need
        Of aid from them - she was the Universe.

                                        Byron (1788-1824)

3333   And out of darkness came the hands
        That reach thro' nature, moulding men.

                                        Alfred Tennyson (1809-1892)

3334   Blessed are they who have nothing to say,
        and who cannot be persuaded to say it.

                                        James Lowell (1819-1891)

3335   Silence more musical than any song.

                                        Christina Rossetti (1830-1894)

3336   Why and Wherefore set out one day,
          To hunt for a wild Negation.
        They agreed to meet at a cool retreat
          On the Point of Interrogation.

                                        Oliver Herford (1863-1935)

3337   I have known the silence of the stars and of the sea,
        And the silence of the city when it pauses,
        And the silence of a man and a maid,
        And the silence for which music alone finds the word.

                                        Edgar Lee Masters (1869-1950)

3338   They cannot scare me with their empty spaces
Between stars - on stars void of human races.
I have it in me so much nearer home
To scare myself with my own desert places.

Robert Frost (1875-1963)

OPPOSITION

Adversity, Difficulty, Obstacles, Trials and Trouble

1. ESSENCE

3339   Man is born unto trouble,
as the sparks fly upward.

Job (B.C. 400?)

3340   Gold is tried by fire, brave men by adversity.

Seneca (B.C. 3-65 A.D.)

3341   Adversity has ever been considered the state in which
a man most easily becomes acquainted with himself, then
especially, being free from flatterers.

Johnson (1709-1784)

3342   Adversity is the first path to truth.

Byron (1788-1824)

3343   The diamond cannot be polished without friction,
nor the man perfected without trials.

Chinese Proverb

2. OPPOSITES

3344   Adversity reveals genius, prosperity conceals it.

Horace (B.C. 65-8)

3345   Night brings our troubles to the light rather than banishes
them.

Seneca (B.C. 3-65 A.D.)

3346   Light troubles speak; immense troubles are silent.

Seneca (B.C. 3-65 A.D.)

3347   Prosperity tries the fortunate, adversity the great.

Pliny the Younger (62-113 A.D.)

3348   It is often better to have a great deal of harm happen to
one than a little; a great deal may rouse you to remove
what a little will only accustom you to endure.

Greville (1554-1628)

3349   Prosperity is not without many fears and distastes,
and Adversity is not without comforts and hopes.

Bacon (1561-1626)

3350   Many things difficult to design prove easy to performance.

Johnson (1709-1784)

3351   The trouble is small, the fun is great.

> Goethe (1749-1832)

3352   The block of granite which was an obstacle in the path of
the weak, becomes a steppingstone in the path of the strong.

> Carlyle (1795-1881)

3353   He who has not tasted bitter does not know what sweet is.

> German Proverb

3. INSIGHT

3354   If thou faint in the day of adversity,
thy strength is small.

> Proverbs (B.C. 1000?-200?)

3355   The three things most difficult are:
to keep a secret, to forget an injury,
and to make good use of leisure.

> Chilo (fl. B.C. 560)

3356   Nothing is so difficult but that it may be found out by
seeking.

> Terence (B.C. 185-159)

3357   Prosperity is no just scale; adversity is the only balance
to weigh friends.

> Plutarch (46-120 A.D.)

3358   The flower that follows the sun does so even on cloudy days.

> Robert Leighton (1611-1684)

3359   The coldest bodies warm with opposition;
the hardest sparkle in collision.

> Junius (1740-1818)

3360   The greatest difficulties lie where we are not
looking for them.

> Goethe (1749-1832)

3361   Adversity is sometimes hard upon a man;
but for one man who can stand prosperity,
there are a hundred that will stand adversity.

> Carlyle (1795-1881)

3362   Trials teach us what we are; they dig up the soil, and let
us see what we are made of; they just turn up some of the
ill weeds on to the surface.

> Charles Spurgeon (1834-1892)

3363   The greatest and most important problems of life are all
        in a certain sense insoluble. They must be so because
        they express the necessary polarity inherent in every self-
        regulating system. They can never be solved, but only
        outgrown.
                                               C. G. Jung (1875-1961)

3364   The ultimate measure of a man is not where he stands in
        moments of comfort and convenience, but where he stands at
        times of challenge and controversy.
                                    Martin Luther King, Jr. (1929-1968)

4. POSITIVE

3365   Adversity is the seed of well-doing: it is the nurse of
        heroism and boldness; who that hath enough, will endanger
        himself to have more? who that is at ease, will set his
        life on the hazard?
                                        Akhenaton? (c. B.C. 1375)

3366   Sweet is the remembrance of troubles when you are in safety.
                                        Euripides (B.C. 480-406)

3367   The greater difficulty, the more glory in surmounting it.
        Skillful pilots gain their reputation from storms and
        tempests.
                                        Epicurus (B.C. 341-270)

3368   I attempt a difficult work;
        but there is no excellence without difficulty.
                                        Ovid (B.C. 43-18 A.D.)

3369   Difficulties strengthen the mind, as labor does the body.
                                        Seneca (B.C. 3-65 A.D.)

3370   Difficulties show men what they are.   In case of any
        difficulty remember that God has pitted you against a rough
        antagonist that you may be a conqueror, and this cannot be
        without toil.
                                        Epictetus (50-138 A.D.)

3371   Sweet are the uses of adversity, which, like the toad,
        though ugly and venomous, wears yet a precious jewel in his
        head.
                                        Shakespeare (1564-1616)

3372   That which caused us trial shall yield us triumph; and that
       which made our heart ache shall fill us with gladness. The
       only true happiness is to learn, to advance, and to improve;
       which could not happen unless we had commenced with error,
       ignorance, and imperfection. We must pass through the dark-
       ness, to reach the light.

                                            Albert Pike (1809-1891)

3373   We are always in the forge, or on the anvil; by trials
       God is shaping us for higher things.

                                              Beecher (1813-1878)

3374   Trouble is the next best thing to enjoyment; there is no
       fate in the world so horrible as to have no share in either
       its joys or sorrows.

                                          Longfellow (1807-1882)

3375   In a democracy, the opposition is not only tolerated as
       constitutional, but must be maintained because it is
       indispensable.

                                    Walter Lippmann (1889-1974)

5. NEGATIVE

3376   What does it avail you, if of many thorns
       only one be removed?

                                            Horace (B.C. 65-8)

3377   He knows not his own strength that hath not met adversity.

                                              Bacon (1561-1626)

3378   In the adversity of our best friends we often find
       something which does not displease us.

                                    La Rochefoucauld (1613-1680)

3379   This mournful truth is everywhere confessed,
       Slow rises worth by poverty depressed.

                                            Johnson (1709-1784)

3380   Obstacles are those frightful things you see when you take
       your eyes off the goal.

                                        Hannah More (1745-1833)

3381   Difficulties increase the nearer we approach our goal.

                                              Goethe (1749-1832)

3382   Opposition always inflames the enthusiast,
       never converts him.

                                            Schiller (1759-1805)

3383   A man's worst difficulties begin when he is able to do as
he likes.

Thomas Huxley (1825-1895)

6. ADVICE

3384   Man becomes the master of difficult situations by refusing
the assistance of weak men. He relies on his own strength
of character.

I Ching (B.C. 1150?)

3385   In adversity
It furthers one to be persevering.

I Ching (B.C. 1150?)

3386   Awake, arise! Strive for the Highest, and be in the Light!
Sages say the path is narrow and difficult to tread, narrow
as the edge of a razor.

Upanishads (c. B.C. 800)

3387   The superior man makes the difficulty to be overcome his
first interest; success only comes later.

Confucius (B.C. 551-479)

3388   In the day of prosperity be joyful,
but in the day of adversity consider.

Ecclesiastes (B.C. 300?)

3389   In great straits and when hope is small,
the boldest counsels are the safest.

Livy (B.C. 59-17 A.D.)

3390   In adversity assume the countenance of prosperity,
and in prosperity moderate the temper and desires.

Livy (B.C. 59-17 A.D.)

3391   Few things are impossible to diligence and skill.

Johnson (1709-1784)

3392   Face all difficulties with a smile. Pain is the real eye-
opener and real guide. God is putting you to this severe
test to make you more strong and more powerful. Understand
this secret well. Never be despondent. Ever laugh, jump,
whistle and smile.

Sivananda (born 1887)

7. POTPOURRI

3393 Adversity breaks the inferior man's will but only bends
the superior man's spirit. Outward influence is denied
the great man, who accordingly uses words sparingly but
retains his central position.

I Ching (B.C. 1150?)

3394 This I know - if all men should take their troubles to the
market to barter with their neighbors, not one, when he had
seen the troubles of other men, but would be glad to carry
his own home again.

Herodotus (B.C. 484-425)

3395 Behold a worthy sight, to which the God, turning his
attention to his own work, may direct his gaze.
Behold an equal thing, worthy of a God,
a brave man matched in conflict with evil fortune.

Seneca (B.C. 3-65 A.D.)

3396 Let me embrace thee, sour adversity,
For wise men say it is the wisest course.

Shakespeare (1564-1616)

3397 Aromatic plants bestow
No spicy fragrance while they grow;
But crush'd or trodden to the ground,
Diffuse their balmy sweets around.

Goldsmith (1728-1774)

3398 I love the man that can smile in trouble, that can gather
strength from distress, and grow brave by reflection. 'Tis
the business of little minds to shrink, but he whose heart
is firm, and whose conscience approves his conduct, will
pursue his principles unto death.

Paine (1737-1809)

3399 The fiery trials through which we pass will light us down in
honour or dishonour to the latest generation.

Lincoln (1809-1865)

3400 He who endeavors to serve, to benefit, and improve the
world, is like a swimmer, who struggles against a rapid
current, in a river lashed into angry waves by the winds.
Often they roar over his head, often they beat him back and
baffle him. Most men yield to the stress of the current...
Only here and there the stout, strong heart and vigorous
arms struggle on toward ultimate success.

Albert Pike (1809-1891)

PAIN
Misery and Suffering

1. ESSENCE

3401   Pain is the outcome of sin.

Buddha (B.C. 568-488)

3402   All pain is one malady with many names.

Antiphanes (B.C. 388-311)

3403   It is the lot of man to suffer.

Disraeli (1804-1881)

2. OPPOSITES

3404   For Fate has wove the thread of life with pain
And twins ev'n from the birth are Misery and Man!

Homer (c. B.C. 700)

3405   Pain wastes the Body, Pleasures the Understanding.

Franklin (1706-1790)

3406   Pain and pleasure, like light and darkness,
succeed each other.

Sterne (1713-1768)

3407   Pain may be said to follow pleasure, as its shadow; but
the misfortune is, that the substance belongs to the
shadow, and the emptiness to its cause.

Colton (1780-1832)

3408   In a free country there is much clamor
  with little suffering;
in a despotic state there is little complaint
  but much suffering.

Carnot (1801-1888)

3409   Happiness is not a reward - it is a consequence.
Suffering is not a punishment - it is a result.

Robert G. Ingersoll (1833-1899)

3410   Only one who is in pain really senses nothing but himself;
pleasure does not enjoy itself but something beside itself.

Hannah Arendt (1906-1975)

3. INSIGHT

3411   If all men were to bring their miseries together in one
place, most would be glad to take his own home again rather
than take a portion out of the common stock.
                       Solon (B.C. 639-559)

3412   What is deservedly suffered must be borne with calmness,
but when the pain is unmerited, the grief is resistless.
                       Ovid (B.C. 43-18 A.D.)

3413   The pain of the mind is worse than the pain of the body.
                       Publilius Syrus (fl. B.C. 42)

3414   We have suffered lightly, if we have suffered what we
should weep for.
                       Seneca (B.C. 3-65 A.D.)

3415   He who suffers for love does not suffer,
for all suffering is forgotten.
                       Meister Eckhart (1260-1327)

3416   Other men's pains are easily borne.
                       Cervantes (1547-1616)

3417   Misery loves company.
                       John Ray (1627-1705)

3418   If we are more affected by the ruin of a palace than by the
conflagration of a cottage, our humanity must have formed
a very erroneous estimate of the miseries of human life.
                       Montesquieu (1689-1755)

3419   The mind is seldom quickened to very vigorous operations but
by pain, or the dread of pain. We do not disturb ourselves
with the detection of fallacies which do us no harm.
                       Johnson (1709-1784)

3420   The transformation of pain to aversion is a fundamental law
of the soul.
                       Schiller (1759-1805)

3421   Pain is no evil unless it conquers us.
                       George Eliot (1819-1880)

3422   Pain is no longer pain when it is past.
                       Margaret Preston (1820-1897)

3423   Man is never helped in his suffering by what he thinks for
himself, but only by revelation of a wisdom greater than his
own. It is this which lifts him out of his distress.
                       C. G. Jung (1875-1961)

4. POSITIVE

3424 To suffer, is a necessity entailed upon thy nature, wouldst
thou that miracles should protect thee from its lessons?
or shalt thou repine, because it happeneth unto thee, when
lo! it happeneth unto all? Suffering is the golden cross
upon which the rose of the Soul unfoldeth.

Akhenaton? (c. B.C. 1375)

3425 By suffering comes wisdom.

Aeschylus (B.C. 525-456)

3426 Remember that pain has this most excellent quality:
if prolonged it cannot be severe, and if severe it cannot
be prolonged.

Seneca (B.C. 3-65 A.D.)

3427 Pain itself is not without its alleviations. It is seldom
both violent and long-continued; and its pauses and
intermissions become positive pleasures. It has the power
of shedding a satisfaction over intervals of ease, which
few enjoyments exceed.

William Paley (1743-1805)

3428 The burden of suffering seems a tombstone hung about our
necks, while in reality it is only the weight which is
necessary to keep down the diver while he is hunting for
pearls.

Richter (1763-1825)

3429 Real pain can alone cure us of imaginary ills. We feel a
thousand miseries till we are lucky enough to feel misery.

Samuel Coleridge (1772-1834)

3430 Suffering is the surest means of making us truthful to
ourselves.

Jean Charles Sismondi (1773-1842)

3431 Pain addeth zest unto pleasure,
and teacheth the luxury of health.

Tupper (1810-1889)

3432 Know how sublime a thing it is to suffer and be strong.

Longfellow (1807-1882)

3433 There is nothing the body suffers that the soul may not
profit by.

George Meredith (1828-1909)

3434   Pain is the great teacher of mankind, beneath its breath
        souls develop.

                          Marie von Ebner Eschenbach (1830-1916)

3435   Pain is a sure sign that you are alive.

                                    Elbert Hubbard (1859-1915)

5. NEGATIVE

3436   The world is full of suffering. Birth is suffering, decre-
        pitude is suffering, sickness and death are sufferings. To
        face a man of hatred is suffering, to be separated from a
        beloved one is suffering, to be vainly struggling to satisfy
        one's needs is suffering. In fact, life that is not free
        from desire and passion is always involved with suffering.

                                       Buddha (B.C. 568-488)

3437   To have a stomach and lack meat, to have meat and lack a
        stomach, to lie in bed and cannot rest, are great miseries.

                                  William Camden (1551-1623)

3438   The scourge of life, and death's extreme disgrace,
        The smoke of hell - that monster called Pain.

                                     Philip Sidney (1554-1586)

3439   Why, all delights are vain: but that most vain,
        Which, with pain purchas'd, doth inherit pain.

                                    Shakespeare (1564-1616)

3440   Those who do not feel pain seldom think that it is felt.

                                      Johnson (1709-1784)

3441   Small miseries, like small debts, hit us in so many places,
        and meet us at so many turns and corners, that what they
        want in weight, they make up in number, and render it
        less hazardous to stand the fire of one cannon ball,
        than a volley composed of such a shower of bullets.

                                        Colton (1780-1832)

3442   It is not true that suffering ennobles the character;
        happiness does that sometimes, but suffering for the most
        part, makes men petty and vindictive.

                                Somerset Maugham (1874-1965)

6. ADVICE

3443   If your head or dress caught fire
           in haste you would extinguish it,
        Do likewise with desire -
        Which whirls the wheel of wandering-on
           and is the root of suffering.
        No better thing to do!

                                Nagarjuna (c. 100-200 A.D.)

3444   As an enemy is made more fierce by our flight, so Pain grows proud to see us knuckle under it. She will surrender upon much better terms to those who make head against her.

Montaigne (1533-1592)

3445   Our real blessings often appear to us in the shape of pains, losses and disappointments; but let us have patience, and we soon shall see them in their proper figures.

Addison (1672-1719)

3446   There is nothing too little for so little a creature as man. It is by studying little things that we attain the great knowledge of having as little misery and as much happiness as possible.

Johnson (1709-1784)

3447   The art of life is the art of avoiding pain.

Thomas Jefferson (1743-1826)

3448   Nature knows best, and she says, roar!

Maria Edgeworth (1767-1849)

3449   Work is the grand cure for all maladies and miseries that ever beset mankind - honest work, which you intend getting done.

Carlyle (1795-1881)

3450   We live in a world which is full of misery and ignorance, and the plain duty of each and all of us is to try to make the little corner he can influence somewhat less miserable and somewhat less ignorant than it was before he entered it.

Thomas Huxley (1825-1895)

7. POTPOURRI

3451   The body was created to be subservient to the Soul; while thou afflictest the Soul for the body's pain, behold thou settest the body above it. As the wise afflicteth not himself, because a thorn teareth his garment; so the patient grieveth not his Soul because that which covereth it is injured.

Akhenaton? (c. B.C. 1375)

3452   You purchase pain with all that joy can give, And die of nothing but a rage to live.

Pope (1688-1744)

3453   See the Wretch, that long has tost
     On the thorny bed of Pain,
   At length repair his vigour lost,
     And breathe and walk again.

Thomas Gray (1716-1771)

3454   For there are deeds
   Which have no form, sufferings which have no tongue.

Shelley (1792-1822)

3455   They talk of short-lived pleasures: be it so;
   pain dies as quickly, and lets her weary prisoner go;
   the fiercest agonies have shortest reign.

William Cullen Bryant (1794-1878)

3456   World's use is cold, world's love is vain,
   World's cruelty is bitter bane;
   But is not the fruit of pain.

Elizabeth B. Browning (1806-1861)

3457   Pain has an element of blank; It cannot recollect
   When it began, or if there were a day when it was not.
   It has no future but itself, its infinite realms contain
   Its past, enlightened to perceive new periods of pain.

Emily Dickinson (1830-1886)

3458   To the person with a toothache, even if the world is
   tottering, there is nothing more important than a visit
   to a dentist.

G. B. Shaw (1856-1950)

3459   Nothing begins, and nothing ends,
     That is not paid with moan;
   For we are born in other's pain,
     And perish in our own.

Francis Thompson (1859-1907)

PATIENCE
Endurance, Forbearance and Waiting

1. ESSENCE

3460   Patience is the key to contentment.

Mohammed (570-632 A.D.)

3461   Patience is the art of hoping.

Vauvenargues(1715-1747)

3462   Endurance is patience concentrated.

Carlyle (1795-1881)

3463   Patience is power; with time and patience the mulberry leaf
becomes silk.

Chinese Proverb

2. OPPOSITES

3464   The heavy is the root of the light.
The tranquil is the ruler of the hasty.

Lao-Tzu (fl. B.C. 600)

3465   Patience is bitter, but its fruit is sweet.

Rousseau (1712-1778)

3466   Patience is the support of weakness;
impatience is the ruin of strength.

Colton (1780-1832)

3. INSIGHT

3467   Patience is so like Fortitude, that she seems either her
sister or her daughter.

Aristotle (B.C. 384-322)

3468   The patient in spirit is better that the proud in spirit.

Ecclesiastes (B.C. 300?)

3469   Everything comes if a man will only wait.

Tancred (1076-1112)

3470   How poor are they that have not patience!
What wound did ever heal but by degrees?

Shakespeare (1564-1616)

3471   Patience and time do more than strength or passion.

La Fontaine (1621-1695)

3472   There is one form of hope which is never unwise, and which
       certainly does not diminish with the increase of knowledge.
       In that form it changes its name, and we call it patience.
                                        Bulwer-Lytton (1803-1873)

3473   On the whole, it is patience which makes the final
       difference between those who succeed or fail in all things.
       All the greatest people have it in an infinite degree,
       and among the less, the patient weak ones always conquer
       the impatient strong.
                                        John Ruskin (1819-1900)

3474   Patience, when it is a divine thing, is active, not passive.
                                        James Lowell (1819-1891)

4. POSITIVE

3475   Every misfortune is to be subdued by patience.
                                        Vergil (B.C. 70-19)

3476   There is nothing so disagreeable, that a patient mind cannot
       find some solace for it.
                                        Seneca (B.C. 3-65 A.D.)

3477   There is no road too long to the man
       who advances deliberately and without undue haste;
       there are no honors too distant to the man
       who prepares himself for them with patience.
                                        La Bruyere (1645-1696)

3478   He that can have patience, can have what he will.
                                        Franklin (1706-1790)

3479   To know how to wait is the great secret of success.
                                        De Maistre (1754-1821)

3480   Only those who have the patience to do simple things
       perfectly will acquire the skill to do difficult things
       easily.
                                        Schiller (1759-1805)

3481   It is not necessary for all men to be great in action.
       The greatest and sublimest power is often simple patience.
                                        Horace Bushnell (1802-1876)

3482   If the single man plant himself indomitably on his
       instincts, and there abide,
       the huge world will come round to him.
                                        Emerson (1803-1882)

3483　Patience is a necessary ingredient of genius.

> Disraeli (1804-1881)

3484　Patience with deserving ever winneth due reward.

> Tupper (1810-1889)

3485　Endurance is nobler than strength, and patience than beauty.

> John Ruskin (1819-1900)

5. NEGATIVE

3486　Just as too much charity is the handiwork of a fool,
　　　so too much patience is the hallmark of a coward.

> Kabbalah (B.C. 1200?-700? A.D.)

3487　Patience, when too often outraged, is converted into
　　　madness.

> Valerius Maximus (fl. c. 20 A.D.)

3488　Extreme patience of long-sufferance, if it once come to be
　　　dissolved, produceth most bitter and excessive revenges.

> Montaigne (1533-1592)

3489　That which in mean men we entitle patience, is pale, cold
　　　cowardice in noble breasts.

> Shakespeare (1564-1616)

3490　For there was never yet philosopher
　　　That could endure the toothache patiently.

> Shakespeare (1564-1616)

3491　Let us only suffer any person to tell us his story morning
　　　and evening, but for twelve months, and he will become our
　　　master.

> Burke (1729-1797)

3492　Patience - a minor form of despair disguised as virtue.

> Ambrose Bierce (1842-1914?)

3493　Perhaps there is only one cardinal sin: impatience.
　　　Because of impatience we are driven out of Paradise;
　　　because of impatience we cannot return.

> Franz Kafka (1883-1924)

3494　A little impatience...
　　　Big plans ruined.

> Chinese Proverb

6. ADVICE

3495 When clouds form in the skies we know that rain will follow but we must not wait for it. Nothing will be achieved by attempting to interfere with the future before the time is ripe. Patience is needed.

I Ching (B.C. 1150?)

3496 Have patience and endure;
this unhappiness will one day be beneficial.

Ovid (B.C. 43-18 A.D.)

3497 It is best to bear what can't be altered.

Seneca (B.C. 3-65 A.D.)

3498 What can't be cured must be endured.

Rabelais (1490-1553)

3499 Have patience with all things, but chiefly have patience with yourself. Do not lose courage in considering your own imperfections, but instantly set about remedying them - every day begin the task anew.

Francis de Sales (1567-1622)

3500 If you'd learn patience superfine,
Go you to fish with rod and line.

Herbert (1593-1632)

3501 Beware the fury of a patient man.

Dryden (1631-1700)

3502 Never cut what you can untie.

Joubert (1754-1824)

3503 Adopt the pace of nature, her secret is patience.

Emerson (1803-1882)

3504 There is no great achievement that is not the result of patient working and waiting.

Josiah Holland (1819-1881)

7. POTPOURRI

3505 Wise to resolve, and patient to perform.

Homer (c. B.C. 700)

3506 My patience to his fury, and am arm'd
To suffer, with a quietness of spirit,
the very tyranny and rage of his.

Shakespeare (1564-1616)

3507   My soul, sit thou a patient looker-on;
        judge not the play before the play is done;
        her plot has many changes,
        everyday speaks a new scene,
        the last act crowns the play.

                                    Shakespeare (1564-1616)

3508   With strength and patience all his grievous loads are borne.
        And from the world's rose-bed he only asks a thorn.
                                    William R. Alger (1822-1905)

3509   So now in patience I possess
        My soul year after tedious year,
        Content to take the lowest place
        The place assigned me here.

                                    Christina Rossetti (1830-1894)

3510   Have patience as one who fears no failure, courts no
        success. Fix thy Soul's gaze upon the star whose ray
        thou art, the flaming star that shines within the light-
        less depths of ever-being, the boundless fields of the
        Unknown.

                                    H. P. Blavatsky (1831-1891)

PEACE

Calmness, Harmony, Serenity and Tranquility

1. ESSENCE

3511 Peace comes from within. Do not seek it without.
Buddha (B.C. 568-488)

3512 Peace is an armistice in a war that is continuously going
on.
Thucydides (B.C. 460-400)

3513 Peace is not the absence of war, it is a virtue, a state of
mind, a disposition for benevolence, confidence, and
justice.
Spinoza (1632-1677)

3514 Peace is the evening star of the soul, as virtue is its sun;
and the two are never far apart.
Colton (1780-1832)

2. OPPOSITES

3515 An unjust peace is better than a just war.
Cicero (B.C. 106-43)

3516 Fair peace becomes men;
ferocious anger belongs to beasts.
Ovid (B.C. 43-18 A.D.)

3517 The most disadvantageous peace is better than the most
just war.
Erasmus (1466-1536)

3518 Such subtle covenants shall be made,
Till peace itself is war in masquerade.
Dryden (1631-1700)

3519 Peace is the happy natural state of man;
war is corruption and disgrace.
James Thomson (1700-1748)

3520 You may either win your peace or buy it;
win it by resistance to evil;
buy it by compromise with evil.
John Ruskin (1819-1900)

3521 Whatever foster militarism makes for barbarism;
whatever fosters peace makes for civilization.
Herbert Spencer (1820-1903)

3522 The alternative to peace is not war. It is annihilation.

Raymond Swing (1887-1968)

3. INSIGHT

3523 In seasons of tumult and discord bad men have most power;
mental and moral excellence require peace and quietness.

Tacitus (55-117 A.D.)

3524 A peace is of the nature of a conquest; for then both
parties nobly are subdued, and neither party loser.

Shakespeare (1564-1616)

3525 If we have not peace within ourselves, it is in vain to seek
it from outward sources.

La Rochefoucauld (1613-1680)

3526 If peace cannot be maintained with honor,
it is no longer peace.

John Russell (1792-1878)

3527 Peace is not only better than war, but infinitely more
arduous.

G. B. Shaw (1856-1950)

3528 Vast and fearsome as the human scene has become, personal
contact of the right people, in the right places, at the
right time, may yet have a potent and valuable part to play
in the cause of peace which is in our hearts.

Winston Churchill (1874-1965)

3529 Peace is not merely a vacuum left by the ending of wars. It
is the creation of two eternal principles, justice and
freedom.

James Shotwell (1874-1965)

4. POSITIVE

3530 Richer is one hour of repentance and good works in this
world than all of life of the world to come;
and richer is one hour's calm of spirit in the world to come
than all of life of this world.

The Talmud (B.C. 500?-400? A.D.)

3531 Better than a thousand useless words
is one single word that gives peace.
Better than a thousand useless verses
is one single verse that gives peace.
Better than a hundred useless poems
is one single poem that gives peace.

The Dhammapada (c. B.C. 300)

3532   The excellence of good temper is that you offend no one and
that you endure other people's annoyance without rancor or
seeking retaliation.

                                        Sari al-Saqati (fl. c. 850 A.D.)

3533   When the mind is possessed of reality, it feels tranquil
and joyous even without music or song, and it produces a
pure fragrance even without incense or tea.

                                   Hung Tzu-ch'eng (1593-1665)

3534   Peace hath her victories
No less renowned than war.

                                   Milton (1608-1674)

3535   Peace is such a precious jewel that I would give anything
for it but truth.

                                   Matthew Henry (1662-1714)

3536   The man who consecrates his hours by vigorous effort, and
an honest aim, at once he draws the sting of life and Death;
he walks with nature; and her paths are peace.

                                   Young (1683-1765)

3537   Quiet minds cannot be perplexed or frightened, but go on in
fortune or misfortune at their own private pace, like a
clock during a thunderstorm.

                          Robert Louis Stevenson (1850-1895)

5. NEGATIVE

3538   Everything is changeable, everything appears and disappears;
there is no blissful peace until one passes beyond the
agony of life and death.

                                   Buddha (B.C. 568-488)

3539   A peace may be so wretched as not to be ill exchanged for
war.

                                   Tacitus (55-117 A.D.)

3540   He who does not attempt to make peace
When small discords arise,
Is like the bee's hive which leaks drops of honey -
Soon, the whole hive collapses.

                                Nagarjuna (c. 100-200 A.D.)

3541   Five great enemies to peace inhabit with us: vice, avarice,
ambition, envy, anger, and pride. If those enemies were
to be banished, we should infallibly enjoy perpetual peace.

                              Francesco Petrarch (1304-1374)

3542   Even peace be may purchased at too high a price.

                                                    Franklin (1706-1790)

3543   "Peace upon earth!" was said. We sing it
        And pay a million priests to bring it.
        After two thousand years of mass
        We've got as far as poison-gas.

                                                    Thomas Hardy (1840-1928)

3544   Peace - A period of cheating between two periods of
        fighting.

                                                    Ambrose Bierce (1842-1914?)

6. ADVICE

3545   Peace can be reached through meditation on the knowledge
        which dreams give. Peace can also be reached through
        concentration upon that which is dearest to the heart.

                                                    Patanjali (B.C. 500?)

3546   The self-controlled soul, who moves amongst sense objects,
        free from either attachment or repulsion, he wins eternal
        Peace.

                                                    Bhagavad Gita (c. B.C. 400)

3547   The pursuit, even of the best things, ought to be calm
        and tranquil.

                                                    Cicero (B.C. 106-43)

3548   Remember to preserve a calm soul amid difficulties.

                                                    Horace (B.C. 65-8)

3549   Pursue not the outer entanglements,
        Dwell not in the inner void;
        Be serene in the oneness of things,
        And dualism vanishes by itself.

                                                    Seng-T'San (540?-606 A.D.)

3550   There is nothing so likely to produce peace as to be well
        prepared to meet the enemy.

                                                    George Washington (1732-1799)

3551   Peace, above all things, is to be desired, but blood must
        sometimes be spilled to obtain it on equable and lasting
        terms.

                                                    Andrew Jackson (1767-1845)

3552   In moderating, not in satisfying desires, lies peace.

                                                    Reginald Heber (1783-1826)

3553 Cultivate peace first in the garden of your heart by
      removing the weeds of lust, hatred, greed, selfishness,
      and jealousy. Then only you can manifest it externally.
      Then only, those who come in contact with you, will be
      benefited by your vibrations of peace and harmony.
                                             Sivananda (born 1887)

7. POTPOURRI

3554 To be satisfied with a little, is the greatest wisdom;
      and he that increaseth his riches, increaseth his cares;
      but a contented mind is a hidden treasure,
      and trouble findeth it not.
                                          Akhenaton? (c. B.C. 1375)

3555 Her ways are ways of pleasantness,
      and all her paths are peace.
                                        Proverbs (B.C. 1000?-200?)

3556 The wise should surrender speech in mind, mind in the
      knowing self, the knowing self in the Spirit of the
      universe, and the Spirit of the universe in the Spirit of
      peace.
                                          Upanishads (c. B.C. 800)

3557 O for a lodge in some vast wilderness,
      Some boundless contiguity of shade;
      Where rumor of oppression and deceit,
      Of unsuccessful or successful war,
      Might never reach me more.
                                             Cowper (1731-1800)

3558 Let the world see that this nation can bear prosperity;
      and that her honest virtue in time of peace is equal to
      her bravest valor in time of war.
                                             Paine (1737-1809)

3559 Ne'er saw I, never felt, a calm so deep!
      The river glideth at his own sweet will:
      Dear God! the very houses seem asleep:
      And all that mighty heart is lying still!
                                          Wordsworth (1770-1850)

3560 How calm, -how beautiful comes on
      The still hour, when storms have gone,
      When warring winds have died away
      And clouds, beneath the dancing ray
      Melt off and leave the land and sea,
      Sleeping in bright tranquility.
                                       Thomas Moore (1779-1852)

3561   Peace will come soon and come to stay, and so come as to be
        worth keeping in all future time. It will then have to be
        proved that among free men there can be no successful appeal
        from the ballot to the bullet, and that they who take such
        appeal are sure to lose their cases and pay the cost.

                                            Lincoln (1809-1865)

3562   Here are cool mosses deep,
        And thro' the moss the ivies creep,
        And in the stream the long-leaved flowers weep,
        And from the craggy ledge the poppy hangs in sleep.

                                    Alfred Tennyson (1809-1892)

3563   Buried was the bloody hatchet;
        Buried were all warlike weapons,
        And the war-cry was forgotten.
        Then was peace among the nations.

                                        Longfellow (1807-1882)

PERFECTION
Completion and Excellence

1. ESSENCE

3564   The function of perfection - to make one know one's
imperfection.

Augustine (354-430 A.D.)

3565   Perfection - An imaginary state...distinguished from the
actual by an element known as excellence.

Ambrose Bierce (1842-1914?)

3566   Perfection - Nothing more than a complete adaptation to the
environment; but the environment is constantly changing,
so perfection can never be more than transitory.

Somerset Maugham (1874-1965)

3567   There are two perfect men;
one dead, and the other unborn.

Chinese Proverb

2. OPPOSITES

3568   What is most perfect seems to be incomplete;
But its utility is unimpaired.
What is most full seems to be empty;
But its usefulness is inexhaustible.
What is most straight seems to be crooked.
The greatest skills seems to be clumsy.
The greatest eloquence seems to stutter.
Hasty movement overcomes cold,
But tranquility overcomes heat.
By being greatly tranquil,
One is qualified to be the ruler of the world.

Lao-Tzu (fl. B.C. 600)

3569   How can you expect me to be perfect...
when I am full of contradictions.

Abraham Ibn Ezra (1098-1164)

3570   Trifles make perfection, and perfection is no trifle.

Michelangelo (1474-1564)

3571   Nature has perfections, in order to show that she is the
image of God; and defects, to show that she is only his
image.

Pascal (1623-1662)

3572   A man must be strong enough to mold the peculiarity of his
        imperfections into the perfection of his peculiarities.

Walter Rathenau (1867-1922)

3573   Humanity, divine limitation;
        Divinity, human perfection.

Hazrat Inayat Khan (1882-1927)

3. INSIGHT

3574   He who wherever he goes is attached to no person and to no
        place by ties of flesh; who accepts good and evil alike,
        neither welcoming the one nor shrinking from the other -
        take it that such a one has attained Perfection.

Bhagavad Gita (c. B.C. 400)

3575   Excellence is an art won by training and habituation. We do
        not act rightly because we have virtue or excellence, but we
        rather have those because we have acted rightly. We are
        what we repeatedly do. Excellence, then, is not an act but
        a habit.

Aristotle (B.C. 384-322)

3576   Things perfected by nature are better
        than those finished by art.

Cicero (B.C. 106-43)

3577   A hero is born among a hundred,
        A wise man is found among a thousand,
        But an accomplished one might not be found
        Even among a hundred thousand men.

Nagarjuna (c. 100-200 A.D.)

3578   The true perfection of man lies, not in what man has,
        but in what man is...Nothing should be able to harm a man
        but himself. Nothing should be able to rob a man at all.
        What a man really has is what is in him. What is outside
        of him should be a matter of no importance.

Oscar Wilde (1854-1900)

3579   There is a tricycle in man.
        He knows, he feels and acts.
        He has emotion, intellect and will.
        He must develop head, heart and hand.
        He must have integral development.
        Then alone he can have perfection.

Sivananda (born 1887)

4. POSITIVE

3580   All things are already complete in us. There is no greater
        delight than to be conscious of right within us. If one
        strives to treat others as he would be treated by them, he
        shall not fail to come near the perfect life.

                                    Mencius (B.C. 371-288)

3581   Only the heart without a stain knows perfect ease.

                                    Goethe (1749-1832)

3582   A perfect human being: Man in search of his ideal of
        perfection. Nothing less.

                        Pir Vilayat Inayat Khan (born 1916)

5. NEGATIVE

3583   Excellence when concealed,
        differs but little from buried worthlessness.

                                    Horace (B.C. 65-8)

3584   Whoever thinks a faultless piece to see
        Thinks what ne'er was, nor is, nor shall be.

                                    Pope (1688-1744)

3585   Those who attain to any excellence commonly spend life in
        some one single pursuit, for excellence is not often gained
        upon easier terms.

                                    Johnson (1709-1784)

3586   The surest hindrance of success is to have too high a
        standard of refinement in our own minds, or too high an
        opinion of the judgment of the public. He who is determined
        not to be satisfied with anything short of perfection will
        never do anything to please himself or others.

                                    Hazlitt (1778-1830)

3587   Perfection does not exist. To understand it is the triumph
        of human intelligence; to desire to possess it is the most
        dangerous kind of madness.

                                    De Musset (1810-1857)

3588   If a man should happen to reach perfection in this world,
        he would have to die immediately to enjoy himself.

                                    Josh Billings (1815-1885)

6. ADVICE

3589   Perfection is attained by slow degrees;
        it requires the hand of time.

                                    Voltaire (1694-1778)

3590   Aim at perfection in everything, though in most things it is
unattainable; however, they who aim at it, and persevere,
will come much nearer to it than those whose laziness and
despondency make them give it up as unattainable.

Chesterfield (1694-1773)

3591   To feel much for others and little for ourselves; to
restrain our selfishness and exercise our benevolent
affections, constitute the perfection of human nature.

Adam Smith (1723-1790)

7. POTPOURRI

3592   The seed of God is in us. Given an intelligent and hard-
working farmer, it will thrive and grow up to God, whose
seed it is; and accordingly its fruits will be God-nature.
Pear seeds grow into pear trees, nut seeds into nut trees,
and God seed into God.

Meister Eckhart (1260-1327)

3593   Bachelor's wives and old maid's children are always perfect.

Chamfort (1741-1794)

3594   Hung on the shower that fronts the golden West,
    The rainbow bursts like magic on mine eyes!
In hues of ancient promise there imprest;
    Frail in its date, eternal in its guise.

Charles Turner (1808-1879)

3595   So mild, so merciful, so strong, so good,
So patient, peaceful, loyal, loving, pure.

Longfellow (1807-1882)

3596   The Great Man never loses his child's heart. The infant has
neither the desire nor the ability to appreciate the
sensuous pleasures. It may cry all day and not become
hoarse. Its innocence and its weakness are its strength.
Its inner harmony is undisturbed. Its bodily organs are
perfect; the years add nothing to them, but only develop
their functions, but do not add to them.

C. Spurgeon Medhurst (born 1850?)

PERSEVERANCE
Constancy, Diligence, Persistence and Tenacity

1. ESSENCE

3597   Water continually dropping will wear hard rocks hollow.
Plutarch (46-120 A.D.)

3598   Many strokes, though with a little axe,
Hew down and fell the hardest timbered oak.
Shakespeare (1564-1616)

3599   He who does not tire, tires adversity.
Tupper (1810-1889)

2. OPPOSITES

3600   Those who gave thee a body, furnished it with weakness;
but He who gave thee Soul, armed thee with resolution.
Employ it, and thou art wise; be wise and thou art happy.
Akhcnaton? (c. B.C. 1375)

3601   Good fortune and misfortune take effect through
perseverance. The way of heaven and earth becomes visible
through perseverance. The way of sun and moon become bright
through perseverance. All movements under heaven become
uniform through perseverance.
I Ching (B.C. 1150?)

3602   'Tis known by the name of perseverance in a good cause-
and of obstinacy in a bad one.
Sterne (1713-1768)

3603   The difference between perseverance and obstinacy is:
that one often comes from a strong will,
and the other from a strong won't.
Beecher (1813-1878)

3604   There is no royal road to anything.
One thing at a time, all things in succession.
That which grows fast withers rapidly;
That which grows slowly endures.
Josiah Holland (1819-1881)

3. INSIGHT

3605   Some men give up their designs when they have almost
reached the goal; while others, on the contrary, obtain
a victory by exerting, at the last moment, more vigorous
efforts than before.
Polybius (B.C. 203?-120)

3606   Perseverance is more prevailing than violence; and many
things which cannot be overcome when they are together,
yield themselves up when taken little by little.

Plutarch (46-120 A.D.)

3607   It is with many enterprises as with striking fire; we do
not meet with success except by reiterated efforts, and
often at the instant when we despaired of success.

Francoise de Maintenon (1635-1719)

3608   What we hope ever to do with ease,
we must first learn to do with diligence.

Johnson (1709-1784)

3609   The bird that flutters least is longest on the wing.

Cowper (1731-1800)

3610   There are two ways of attaining an important end: force and
perseverance. Force falls to the lot only of the privileged
few, but austere and sustained perseverance can be practised
by the most insignificant. Its silent power grows
irresistible with time.

Anne Swetchine (1782-1857)

3611   We can do anything we want to do if we stick to it long
enough.

Helen Keller (1880-1968)

4. POSITIVE

3612   As a camel beareth labor, and heat, and hunger, and thirst,
through deserts of sand, and fainteth not; so the fortitude
of a man shall sustain him through all perils.

Akhenaton? (c. B.C. 1375)

3613   Diligence increases the fruit of toil. A dilatory man ever
wrestles with losses.

Hesiod (B.C. 800?)

3614   Endurance is one of the most difficult disciplines, but
it is to the one who endures that the final victory comes.

Buddha (B.C. 568-488)

3615   Happy are those that persevere to the end,
for they shall inherit the earth.

Jesus (B.C. 6?-30? A.D.)

3616 He will reward them, on account of their having persevered,
with a garden and silk dress: reclining therein upon
thrones, they shall not see either the sun or biting cold,
and the shades of the garden shall be close upon them, and
its fruits shall be within easy reach.

Koran (c. 651 A.D.)

3617 Diligence is the mother of good fortune.

Cervantes (1547-1616)

3618 The greatest results in life are usually attained by simple
means and the exercise of ordinary qualities. These may for
the most part be summed up in these two - commonsense and
perseverance.

Owen Feltham (1602-1668)

3619 Great works are performed, not by strength, but by
perseverance. Yonder palace was raised by single stones,
yet you see its height and spaciousness. He that shall walk
with vigor three hours a day will pass in seven years a
space equal to the circumference of the globe.

Johnson (1709-1784)

3620 The nerve that never relaxes, the eye that never blanches,
the thought that never wanders, the purpose that never
wavers - these are the masters of victory.

Burke (1729-1797)

3621 Courage and perseverance have a magical talisman, before
which difficulties disappear and obstacles vanish into air.

John Quincy Adams (1767-1848)

3622 Victory belongs to the most persevering.

Napoleon (1769-1821)

3623 Constancy is the complement of all other human virtues.

Giuseppe Mazzini (1805-1872)

5. NEGATIVE

3624 Perseverance alone does not assure success. No amount
of stalking will lead to game in a field that has none.

I Ching (B.C. 1150?)

3625 Perseverance merits neither blame nor praise; it is only
the duration of our inclinations and sentiments, which we
can neither create nor extinguish.

La Rochefoucauld (1613-1680)

3626   Perseverance - A lowly virtue whereby mediocrity achieves
        an inglorious success.

                                           Ambrose Bierce (1842-1914?)

6. ADVICE

3627   No plain not followed by a slope.
        No going not followed by a return.
        He who remains persevering in danger is without blame.
        Do not complain about this truth;
        Enjoy the good fortune you still possess.

                                                   I Ching (B.C. 1150?)

3628   Prefer diligence before idleness,
        unless you esteem rust above brightness.

                                               Plato (B.C. 427?-347?)

3629   He who labors diligently need never despair;
        for all things are accomplished by diligence and labor.

                                              Menander (B.C. 342-291)

3630   Always at it wins the day.

                                          Thomas E. Watson (1557-1592)

3631   An enterprise, when fairly once begun,
        should not be left till all that ought is won.

                                              Shakespeare (1564-1616)

3632   Resolve to perform what you ought;
        perform without fail what you resolve.

                                                 Franklin (1706-1790)

3633   Never despair; but if you do, work on in despair.

                                                    Burke (1729-1797)

3634   The secret of success is constancy of purpose.

                                                 Disraeli (1804-1881)

3635   Patience and perseverance are essential in the inner fight.
        The higher self's war with the lower self is a great
        struggle. Develop these two virtues to a maximum degree
        and strengthen them by all manner of intelligent discipline
        and constant exercise.

                                             Sivananda (born 1887)

7. POTPOURRI

3636   Through perils both of wind and limb,
        Through thick and thin she followed him.

                                            Samuel Butler (1612-1680)

3637   Diligence is the mother of good luck, and God gives all
       things to industry. Work while it is called to-day, for you
       know not how much you may be hindered by tomorrow. One to-
       day is worth two tomorrows; never leave that till to-morrow
       which you can do to-day.

                                                    Franklin (1706-1790)

3638   No rock so hard but a little wave may beat admission in
       a thousand years.

                                             Alfred Tennyson (1809-1892)

3639   Less good from genius we may find
          Than that from perseverance flowing;
       So have good grist at hand to grind,
          And keep the mill a-going.

                                             Thomas English (1819-1902)

3640   Let us, then, be up and doing,
          With a heart for any fate;
       Still achieving, still pursuing,
          Learn to labour and to wait.

                                                  Longfellow (1807-1882)

3641   Not enjoyment, and not sorrow,
          Is our destined end or way;
       But to act, that each to-morrow
          Finds us further than to-day.

                                                  Longfellow (1807-1882)

3642   Keep right on to the end of the road;
       Keep right on to the end.

                                               Harry Lauder (1870-1950)

PLEASURE

Delight, Enjoyment, Luxury and Novelty

1. ESSENCE

3643   Pleasure is the bait of sin.

                Plato (B.C. 427?-347?)

3644   In everything satiety closely follows the greatest
pleasures.

                Cicero (B.C. 106-43)

3645   Pleasure itself is painful at the bottom.

                Montaigne (1533-1592)

3646   Novelty is the great parent of pleasure.

                Robert South (1634-1716)

3647   Most pleasures, like flowers
when gathered, die.

                Young (1683-1765)

2. OPPOSITES

3648   Good things cease to be good in our wrong enjoyment of
them. What nature meant pure sweets, are then sources
of bitterness to us; from such delights arise pain, from
such joys, sorrows.

                Akhenaton? (c. B.C. 1375)

3649   There is this difference between spiritual and corporal
pleasures, that corporal ones beget a desire before we have
obtained them, and after we have obtained them, a disgust;
but spiritual pleasures, on the contrary, are not cared for
when we have them not, but are desired when we have them.

                Gregory I (540-604)

3650   Follow pleasure, and then will pleasure flee,
Flee pleasure, and pleasure will follow thee.

                John Heywood (1497?-1580?)

3651   We have not an hour of life in which our pleasures relish
not some pain, our sours, some sweetness.

                Philip Massinger (1583-1640)

3652   The honest man takes pains, and then enjoys pleasures;
the knave takes pleasure, and then suffers pain.

                Franklin (1706-1790)

3653   When our pleasures have exhausted us,
       we think that we have exhausted pleasure.
                                    Vauvenargues(1715-1747)

3654   The seeds of repentance are sown in youth by pleasure,
       but the harvest is reaped in age by pain.
                                          Colton (1780-1832)

3655   Pleasure's a sin, and sometimes sin's a pleasure.
                                           Byron (1788-1824)

3656   Simple pleasures are the last refuge of the complex.
                                    Oscar Wilde (1854-1900)

3657   Pleasures are shallow;
       Sorrows deep.
                                           Chinese Proverb

3. INSIGHT

3658   Times of luxury do not last long, but pass away very
       quickly; nothing in this world can be long enjoyed.
                                    Buddha (B.C. 568-488)

3659   The pleasure of all things increases by the same danger that
       should deter it.
                                    Seneca (B.C. 3-65 A.D.)

3660   Pleasure is a necessary reciprocal; no one feels, who does
       not at the same time give it. To be pleased, one must
       please. What pleases you in others will in general please
       them in you.
                                    Chesterfield (1694-1773)

3661   Men seldom give pleasure where they are not
       pleased themselves.
                                       Johnson (1709-1784)

3662   All the great pleasures in life are silent.
                            Georges Clemenceau (1841-1929)

3663   Speed provides the one genuinely modern pleasure.
                                 Aldous Huxley (1894-1963)

4. POSITIVE

3664   Pleasure is the absence of pain in the body and of trouble
       in the soul.
                                    Epicurus (B.C. 341-270)

3665   The pursuit of pleasure
        Is the most pleasant pleasure.

                                        Montaigne (1533-1592)

3666   Mental pleasures never cloy; unlike those of the body,
        they are increased by repetition, approved by reflection,
        and strengthened by enjoyment.

                                        Nathaniel Cotton (1705-1788)

3667   The fruit derived from labor is the sweetest of pleasures.

                                        Vauvenargues(1715-1747)

3668   The love of study, a passion which derives fresh vigor from
        enjoyment, supplies each day and hour with a perpetual
        source of independent and rational pleasure.

                                        Gibbon (1737-1794)

3669   That man is richest whose pleasures are the cheapest.

                                        Thoreau (1817-1862)

3670   The sweetest pleasure is in imparting it.

                                        Bovee (1820-1904)

5. NEGATIVE

3671   Do not look at wine when it is red,
            when it sparkles in the cup
            and goes down smoothly.
        At the last it bites like a serpent,
            and stings like an adder.

                                        Proverbs (B.C. 1000?-200?)

3672   In this ill-smelling, unsubstantial body, which is a
        conglomerate of bone, skin, muscle, marrow, flesh, semen,
        blood, mucus, tears, rheum, feces, urine, wind, bile, and
        phlegm, what is the good of enjoyment of desires?

                                        Upanishads (c. B.C. 800)

3673   From pleasure comes grief, from pleasure comes fear;
        he who is free from pleasure neither sorrows nor fears.

                                        The Dhammapada (c. B.C. 300)

3674   There is no such thing as pure pleasure;
        some anxiety always goes with it.

                                        Ovid (B.C. 43-18 A.D.)

3675   If I give way to pleasure, I must also yield to grief, to
        poverty, to labor, ambition, anger, until I am torn to
        pieces by my misfortunes and my lust.

                                        Seneca (B.C. 3-65 A.D.)

3676   Fire is never satisfied with fuel,
       nor the ocean with rivers,
       nor death with all creatures,
       nor bright-eyed women with men.

                                 The Hitopadesa (600?-1100? A.D.)

3677   Pleasure admitted in undue degree
       Enslaves the will, nor leaves the judgment free.

                                                  Cowper (1731-1800)

3678   Most of the luxuries, and many of the so-called comforts, of
       life are not only not indispensable, but positive hindrances
       to the elevation of mankind.

                                                Thoreau (1817-1862)

3679   Men may scoff, and men may pray,
         But they pay
       Every pleasure with a pain.

                                       William Henley (1849-1903)

3680   All the things I really like to do are either immoral,
       illegal or fattening.

                                   Alexander Woollcott (1887-1943)

6. ADVICE

3681   Consider pleasures as they depart, not as they come.
                                       Aristotle (B.C. 384-322)

3682   If by leaving a small pleasure one sees a great pleasure,
       let a wise man leave the small pleasure, and look to the
       great.
                                   The Dhammapada (c. B.C. 300)

3683   When the idea of any pleasure strikes your imagination, make
       a just computation between the duration of the pleasure and
       that of the repentance that is likely to follow it.
                                       Epictetus (50-138 A.D.)

3684   Choose such pleasures as recreate much and cost little.
                                   Thomas Fuller (1608-1661)

3685   Venture not to the utmost bounds of even lawful pleasures;
       the limits of good and evil join.
                                   Thomas Fuller (1608-1661)

3686   Mistake not. Those pleasures are not pleasures that trouble
       the quiet and tranquility of thy life.
                                     Jeremy Taylor (1613-1667)

3687   What leads to unhappiness, is making pleasure the chief aim.
                                    William Shenstone (1714-1763)

3688   Pleasure soon exhausts us and itself also;
       but endeavor never does.
                                         Richter (1763-1825)

7. POTPOURRI

3689   There is the path of earthly joy, and there is the path of
       earthly pleasure. Both attract the soul. Who follows the
       first comes to good; who follows pleasures reaches not the
       End.
                                    Upanishads (c. B.C. 800)

3690   An intelligent person does not take part in the sources of
       misery, which are due to contact with material senses.
       Such pleasures have a beginning and an end, and so the
       wise man does not delight in them.
                                    Bhagavad Gita (c. B.C. 400)

3691   Fishing is a pleasure of retirement,
       yet the angler has the power to let the fish live or die.
       Chessplaying is an enjoyable pastime,
       yet the players are motivated by the idea of war.
                                    Hung Tzu-ch'eng (1593-1665)

3692   To hide her cares her only art;
       Her pleasure, pleasures to impart.
                                    Thomas Gray (1716-1771)

3693   Pleasures are like poppies spread,
       You seize the flower, its blossom is shed!
       Or like the snowfall in the river,
       A moment white - then melts for ever.
                                    Robert Burns (1759-1796)

3694   There is a pleasure in the pathless woods,
          There is a rapture on the lonely shore,
       There is society where none intrudes
          By the deep Sea, and music in its roar.
                                         Byron (1788-1824)

3695   Let me enjoy the earth no less
       Because the all-enacting Might
       That fashioned forth its loveliness
       Had other aims than my delight.
                                    Thomas Hardy (1840-1928)

3696   Pleasure is frail like a dewdrop, while it laughs it dies.
                                    Rabindranath Tagore (1861-1941)

POWER

Authority, Command, Dominion, Force and Government

1. ESSENCE

3697   Let him that would move the world,
first move himself.
Socrates (B.C. 469-399)

3698   Knowledge and human power are synonymous,
since the ignorance of the cause frustrates the effect.
Bacon (1561-1626)

3699   Government is not reason, it is not eloquence - it is force.
George Washington (1732-1799)

3700   All human power is a compound of time and patience.
Balzac (1799-1850)

3701   Spiritual force is stronger than material force;
thoughts rule the world.
Emerson (1803-1882)

3702   Self-reverence, self-knowledge, self-control,
These three alone lead life to sovereign power.
Alfred Tennyson (1809-1892)

2. OPPOSITES

3703   The great rivers and seas are kings of all mountain streams
  Because they skillfully stay below them.
   That is why they can be their kings.
Therefore, in order to be the superior of the people,
  One must, in the use of words, place himself below them,
And in order to be ahead of the people,
  One must, in one's own person, follow them.
Lao-Tzu (fl. B.C. 600)

3704   Force and not opinion is the queen of the world;
but it is opinion that uses force.
Pascal (1623-1662)

3705   It is better to have a lion at the head of an army of sheep,
than a sheep at the head of an army of lions.
Daniel DeFoe (1660-1731)

3706   Power may justly be compared to a great river; while kept
        within its bounds it is both beautiful and useful, but
        when it overflows its banks, it is then too impetuous to
        be stemmed; it bears down all before it, and brings
        destruction and desolation wherever it comes.
                                        Andrew Hamilton (1676-1741)

3707   To know the pains of power, we must go to those who have it;
        to know its pleasures, we must go to those who seek it:
        the pains of power are real, its pleasures imaginary.
                                        Colton (1780-1832)

3708   There is no king who has not had a slave among his
        ancestors, and no slave who has not had a king among his.
                                        Helen Keller (1880-1968)

3709   Power corrupts the few, while weakness corrupts the many.
                                        Eric Hoffer (1902-1983)

3. INSIGHT

3710   The measure of man is what he does with power.
                                        Pittacus (B.C. 650-570)

3711   The great rulers - the people do not notice their existence;
        The lesser ones - they love and praise them;
        The still lesser ones - they fear them;
        The still lesser ones - they despise them.
                                        Lao-Tzu (fl. B.C. 600)

3712   When the government is non-discriminative and dull,
            The people are contented and generous.
        When the government is searching and discriminative,
            The people are disappointed and contentious.
        Calamity is that upon which happiness depends;
        Happiness is that in which calamity is latent...
                                        Lao-Tzu (fl. B.C. 600)

3713   If one is the master of oneself, one is the resort one can
        depend on; therefore, one should control oneself of all.
                                        Buddha (B.C. 568-488)

3714   The punishment suffered by the wise who refuse to take
        part in the government, is to live under the government
        of bad men.
                                        Plato (B.C. 427?-347?)

3715   Power exercised with violence has seldom been of long
        duration, but temper and moderation generally produce
        permanence in all things.
                                        Seneca (B.C. 3-65 A.D.)

3716   It is an observation no less just than common, that there
        is no stronger test of a man's real character than power
        and authority, exciting as they do every passion, and
        discovering every latent vice.
                                        Plutarch (46-120 A.D.)

3717   Nothing is so weak and unstable as a reputation for power
        not based on force.
                                        Tacitus (55-117 A.D.)

3718   Covenants without swords are but words.
                                        Thomas Hobbes (1588-1679)

3719   Knowledge comes by eyes always open and working hard,
        and there is no knowledge that is not power.
                                        Jeremy Taylor (1613-1667)

3720   It is necessary from the very nature of things that power
        should be a check to power.
                                        Montesquieu (1689-1755)

3721   Power is always gradually stealing away from the many to the
        few, because the few are more vigilant and consistent.
                                        Johnson (1709-1784)

3722   I have never been able to conceive how any rational being
        could propose happiness to himself from the exercise of
        power over others.
                                        Thomas Jefferson (1743-1826)

3723   What government is the best? That which teaches us to
        govern ourselves.
                                        Goethe (1749-1832)

3724   Those who can command themselves command others.
                                        Hazlitt (1778-1830)

3725   Force is all-conquering, but its victories are short-lived.
                                        Lincoln (1809-1865)

3726   It is Genius that gets Power; and its prime lieutenants
        are Force and Wisdom. The unruliest of men bend before
        the leader that has the sense to see and the will to do.
                                        Albert Pike (1809-1891)

3727   Wherever I found a living creature,
        there I found the will to power.
                                        Nietzsche (1844-1900)

3728   Power invariably means both responsibility and danger.
                                    Theodore Roosevelt (1858-1919)

3729   Not one of us knows what effect his life produces, and what
       he gives to others; that is hidden from us and must remain
       so, though we are often allowed to see some little fraction
       of it, so that we may not lose courage. The way in which
       power works is a mystery.
                                    Albert Schweitzer (1875-1965)

3730   Not believing in force is the same as not believing in
       gravitation.
                                    Leon Trotsky (1879-1940)

4. POSITIVE

3731   The great man with vigor should demand the rightness of
       things, timeliness of action, and propriety of method.
       In this way, power does not degenerate into sheer force.
                                    I Ching (B.C. 1150?)

3732   A skillful commander is not overbearing.
       A skillful fighter does not become angry.
       A skillful conqueror does not compete with people.
       One who is skillful in using men puts himself below them.
       This is called the virtue of not-competing.
       This is called the strength to use men.
       This is called matching Heaven,
       The highest principle of old.
                                    Lao-Tzu (fl. B.C. 600)

3733   I know of nothing sublime which is not some modification
       of power.
                                    Burke (1729-1797)

3734   Happy the man who early learns the wide chasm that lies
       between his wishes and his powers!
                                    Goethe (1749-1832)

3735   Power is so characteristically calm, that calmness in itself
       has the aspect of power.
                                    Bulwer-Lytton (1803-1873)

3736   A good intention clothes itself with power.
                                    Emerson (1803-1882)

3737   The spirit of a person's life is ever shedding some
       power, just as a flower is steadily bestowing fragrance
       upon the air.
                                    T. Starr King (1824-1864)

3738   It (government) is neither business nor technology nor
applied science...(It is) one of the subtlest of the arts...
since it is the art of making men live together in peace and
with reasonable happiness.

Felix Frankfurter (1882-1965)

5. NEGATIVE

3739   What is the pay for titles, but flattery? how doth man
purchase power but by being a slave to him who giveth it?

Akhenaton? (c. B.C. 1375)

3740   Power buries those who wield it.

The Talmud (B.C. 500?-400? A.D.)

3741   It is not possible to found a lasting power upon injustice,
perjury, and treachery.

Demosthenes (B.C. 384-322)

3742   There is nothing which power cannot believe of itself,
when it is praised as equal to the gods.

Juvenal (40-125 A.D.)

3743   Power acquired by guilt was never used for a good purpose.

Tacitus (55-117 A.D.)

3744   The tempest uproots not the soft grasses that bow low on
all sides; on the lofty trees it strikes hard. It is
against the mighty that the mighty puts forth his prowess.

The Hitopadesa (600?-1100? A.D.)

3745   He who makes another powerful ruins himself, for he makes
the other so either by shrewdness or force, and both of
these qualities are feared by the one who becomes
powerful.

Machiavelli (1469-1527)

3746   It is a miserable state of mind, to have few things to
desire and many things to fear: and yet that commonly
is the case of Kings.

Bacon (1561-1626)

3747   Power, like lightning, injures before its warning.

Pedro Calderon (1600-1681)

3748   A crown
Golden in show, is but a wreath of thorns;
Brings danger, troubles, cares, and sleepless nights
To him who wears a regal diadem.

Milton (1608-1674)

3749   Authority intoxicates,
        And makes mere sots of magistrates;
        The fumes of it invade the brain,
        And make men giddy, proud, and vain.

                                    Samuel Butler (1612-1680)

3750   Unlimited power corrupts the possessor.

                                    William Pitt (1708-1778)

3751   Government, even in its best state, is but a necessary evil;
        in its worst state, an intolerable one.

                                    Paine (1737-1809)

3752   The higher we rise, the more isolated we become;
        all elevations are cold.

                                    Boufflers (1738-1815)

3753   In framing a government which is to be administered by men
        over men the great difficulty lies in this: You must first
        enable the government to control the governed, and in the
        next place, oblige it to control itself.

                                    Alexander Hamilton (1757-1804)

3754   The world is governed only by self-interest.

                                    Schiller (1759-1805)

3755   The love of liberty is the love of others;
        the love of power is the love of ourselves.

                                    Hazlitt (1778-1830)

3756   Power, like the diamond, dazzles the beholder, and also
        the wearer; it dignifies meanness; it magnifies littleness;
        to what is contemptible, it gives authority;
        to what is low, exaltation.

                                    Colton (1780-1832)

3757   Power will intoxicate the best hearts, as wine the strongest
        heads. No man is wise enough, nor good enough to be trusted
        with unlimited power.

                                    Colton (1780-1832)

3758   He who ascends to mountain tops, shall find
        The loftiest peaks most wrapped in clouds and snow;
        He who surpasses or subdues mankind,
        Must look down on the hate of those below.

                                    Byron (1788-1824)

3759   He hath no power that hath not power to use.

                                    Bailey (1816-1902)

3760   The natural forces crush and destroy man when he
        transgresses them, as they destroy or neutralize
        one another.

                                    John Burroughs (1837-1921)

3761   Power undirected by high purpose spells calamity; and high
        purpose by itself is utterly useless if the power to put
        it into effect is lacking.

                                    Theodore Roosevelt (1858-1919)

3762   Power intoxicates men. It is never voluntarily surrendered.
        It must be taken from them.

                                    James F. Byrnes (1879-1972)

6. ADVICE

3763   O Thou! the favourite of Heaven, whom the sons of men, thy
        equals, have agreed to raise to sovereign power, and set as
        a ruler over themselves; consider the ends and importance
        of their trust, far more than the dignity and height of thy
        station.

                                    Akhenaton? (c. B.C. 1375)

3764   A person must learn to be adaptable and serve others in
        order to rule. Willing followers are not acquired by
        force or cunning but through consistency in doing what is
        human and proper.

                                    I Ching (B.C. 1150?)

3765   Governing a large organization requires timely activity and
        discreet inactivity on the part of the chief executive.
        One must be particularly sensitive to promising
        circumstances, talented men, and the right objectives.

                                    I Ching (B.C. 1150?)

3766   Beware of the ruling powers! for they do not be-friend a
        person except for their own needs: they seem like friends
        when it is to their advantage, but they do not stand by a
        man when he is hard-pressed.

                                    The Talmud (B.C. 500?-400? A.D.)

3767   The greater a man is in power above others, the more he
        ought to excel them in virtue. None ought to govern who is
        not better than the governed.

                                    Publilius Syrus (fl. B.C. 42)

3768   He who has great power should use it lightly.

                                    Seneca (B.C. 3-65 A.D.)

3769   Power is more retained by wary measures than by daring
        counsels.

                                        Tacitus (55-117 A.D.)

3770   A man should live with his superiors as he does with his
        fire: not too near, lest he burn; nor too far off, lest
        he freeze.

                                        Diogenes Laertius (c. 250 A.D.)

3771   He that would govern others, first should be the master
        of himself, richly endowed with depth of understanding and
        height of knowledge.

                                        Philip Massinger (1583-1640)

3772   The king who delegates his power to other's hands
        but ill deserves the crown he wears.

                                        Henry Brooke (1703-1783)

3773   Power is not revealed by striking hard or often,
        but by striking true.

                                        Balzac (1799-1850)

7. POTPOURRI

3774   Of old those who were the best rulers were
           subtly mysterious and profoundly penetrating;
           Too deep to comprehend.
        And because they cannot be comprehended,
           I can only describe them arbitrarily:
           Cautious, like crossing a frozen stream in the winter,
           Alert, like one fearing danger on all sides,
           Reserved, like one visiting,
           Yielding, like ice about to melt,
           Genuine, like a piece of uncarved wood,
           Open and broad, like a valley,
           Merged and undifferentiated, like muddy water.

                                        Lao-Tzu (fl. B.C. 600)

3775   Only one accomplishment is beyond both the power and the
        mercy of the Gods. They cannot make the past as though it
        had never been.

                                        Aeschylus (B.C. 525-456)

3776   If it were in my power, I would be wiser;
        but a newly felt power carries me off in spite of myself;
        love leads me one way, my understanding another.

                                        Ovid (B.C. 43-18 A.D.)

3777   The King said, "The Athenians govern the Greeks;
        I govern the Athenians; you, my wife, govern me; your
        son governs you."

                                        Plutarch (46-120 A.D.)

3778   Hence it happened that all the armed prophets conquered,
all the unarmed perished.

Machiavelli (1469-1527)

3779   He never sold the truth to serve the hour,
Nor paltered with Eternal God for power.

Alfred Tennyson (1809-1892)

3780   Of that Equilibrium between Authority and Individual Action
which constitutes Free Government, be settling on immutable
foundations Liberty with Obedience to Law, Equality with
Subjection to Authority, and Fraternity with Subordination
to the Wisest and the Best: and of that Equilibrium between
the Active Energy of the Will of the Present, expressed by
the Vote of the People, and the Passive Stability and
Permanence of the Will of the Past, expressed in
constitutions of government, written or unwritten, and in
laws and customs, gray with age and sanctified by time,
as precedents and authority.

Albert Pike (1809-1891)

3781   So when a great man dies,
  For years beyond our ken,
The light he leaves behind him lies
  Upon the paths of men.

Longfellow (1807-1882)

3782   A creature of a more exalted kind
Was wanting yet, and therefore was designed;
Conscious of thought, of more capacious breast
For empire formed and fit to rule the rest....

H. P. Blavatsky (1831-1891)

3783   It matters not how strait the gate,
  How charged with punishments the scroll,
I am the master of my fate:
  I am the captain of my soul.

William Henley (1849-1903)

3784   I thought that my invincible power would hold the world
captive, leaving me in a freedom undisturbed. Thus night
and day I worked at the chain with huge fires and cruel hard
strokes. When at last the work was done and the links were
complete and unbreakable, I found that it held me in its
grip.

Rabindranath Tagore (1861-1941)

3785   The King is dead, by millions mourned,
       That bared their heads, or wept, or sighed;
       The dog, that waited for him in vain,
       Has broken its heart, and died.
       So end two lives, and one so small thing-
       It never knew its Master was a King.

                           William H. Davies (1871-1940)

3786   Start a political upheaval and let yourself be caught, and
       you will hang as a traitor. But place yourself at the head
       of a rebellion and gain your point, and all future
       generations will worship you as the Father of their Country.

                           Hendrik Van Loon (1882-1944)

PRIDE

Arrogance, Boasting, Egotism, Vanity and Self-Love

1. ESSENCE

3787   Self love, as it happens to be well or ill conducted,
       constitutes virtue and vice.

La Rochefoucauld (1613-1680)

3788   What is pride? a whizzing rocket
       That would emulate a star.

Wordsworth (1770-1850)

3789   Arrogance is a mixture of impertinence, disobedience,
       indiscipline, rudeness, harshness and a self-assertive
       nature.

Sivananda (born 1887)

3790   Pride is the mask of one's own faults.

Jewish Proverb

2. OPPOSITES

3791   Arrogance means that one knows how to press forward
         but not how to draw back,
       that one knows existence but not annihilation,
       knows something about winning but nothing about losing.

I Ching (B.C. 1150?)

3792   Pride is a virtue, let not the moralist be scandalized,
       pride is also a vice. Pride, like ambition, is sometimes
       virtuous and sometimes vicious, according to the character
       in which it is found, and the object to which it is
       directed.

Greville (1554-1628)

3793   They are proud in their humility,
       proud that they are not proud.

Robert Burton (1576-1640)

3794   Pride does not wish to owe and vanity does not wish to pay.

La Rochefoucauld (1613-1680)

3795   We rise in glory as we sink in pride.

Young (1683-1765)

3796   Pride is increased by ignorance; those assume the most who
       know the least.

Gay (1688-1732)

3797   The infinitely little have a pride infinitely great.

> Voltaire (1694-1778)

3798   It is equally a mistake to hold one's self too high,
or to rate one's self too cheap.

> Goethe (1749-1832)

3799   The truly proud man knows neither superiors nor inferiors.
The first he does not admit of; the last he does not concern
himself about.

> Hazlitt (1778-1830)

3800   There is a paradox in pride: it makes some men ridiculous,
but prevents others from becoming so.

> Colton (1780-1832)

3. INSIGHT

3801   Who is it that affirms most boldly? Who is it that holds
his opinion most obstinately? Ever he who hath most
ignorance; for he also hath most pride.

> Akhenaton? (c. B.C. 1375)

3802   The human mind is prone to pride even when not supported by
power; how much more, then, does it exalt itself when it
has that support.

> Gregory I (540-604)

3803   There is not one wise man in twenty
that will praise himself.

> Shakespeare (1564-1616)

3804   Pride may be allowed to this or that degree, else a man
cannot keep his dignity. In gluttons there must be eating,
in drunkenness there must be drinking; it is not the eating,
nor is it the drinking, that is to be blamed, but the
excess. So in pride.

> John Selden (1584-1654)

3805   Pride, perceiving humility honourable, often borrows her
cloak.

> Thomas Fuller (1608-1661)

3806   Pride will spit in pride's face.

> Thomas Fuller (1608-1661)

3807   Self-love is more cunning than
the most cunning man in the world.

> La Rochefoucauld (1613-1680)

3808 The most amiable people are those who least wound
the self-love of others.

La Bruyere (1645-1696)

3809 Pride is to the character, like the attic to the house
the highest part, and generally the most empty.

Gay (1688-1732)

3810 He that falls in love with himself will have no rivals.

Franklin (1706-1790)

3811 The proud are always most provoked by pride.

Cowper (1731-1800)

4. POSITIVE

3812 When a man gains wealth within,
He shows it with pride without.
When the clouds are full of water,
They move and rumble with thunder.

Saskya Pandita (1182-1251)

3813 Pride which inspires us with so much envy,
serves also to moderate it.

La Rochefoucauld (1613-1680)

3814 This self-love is the instrument of our preservation;
it resembles the provision for the perpetuity of mankind:
- it is necessary, it is dear to us, it gives us pleasure,
and we must conceal it.

Voltaire (1694-1778)

3815 Pride will not act unless it be allowed that it can succeed;
and it will do nothing rather than not do it brilliantly.

Thomas Lynch (1749-1779)

3816 There is a certain noble pride, through which
merits shine brighter than through modesty.

Richter (1763-1825)

3817 The essence of a self-reliant and autonomous culture
is an unshakable egoism.

H. L. Mencken (1880-1956)

5. NEGATIVE

3818 Behold the vain man, and observe the arrogant; he clotheth
himself in rich attire, he walketh in the public street, he
casteth round his eyes, and courteth observation. He
tosseth up his head, and overlooketh the poor; he treateth
his inferiors with insolence, his superiors in return look
down on his pride and folly with laughter.

Akhenaton? (c. B.C. 1375)

3819   Pride goeth before destruction,
       and an haughty spirit before a fall.

                                    Proverbs (B.C. 1000?-200?)

3820   Ignorant of their ignorance, yet wise
       In their own esteem, these deluded men,
       Proud of their vain learning, go round and round
       Like the blind led by the blind. Far beyond
       Their eyes, hypnotized by the world of sense,
       Opens the way to immortality.

                                    Upanishads (c. B.C. 800)

3821   He who stands on tiptoe is not steady.
       He who strides forward does not go.
       He who shows himself is not luminous.
       He who justifies himself is not prominent.
       He who boasts of himself is not given credit.
       He who brags does not endure for long.

                                    Lao-Tzu (fl. B.C. 600)

3822   Arrogance, pride, anger, conceit, harshness and ignorance-
       these qualities belong to those of demonic nature.

                                    Bhagavad Gita (c. B.C. 400)

3823   Small things make base men proud.

                                    Shakespeare (1564-1616)

3824   To be proud and inaccessible is to be timid and weak.

                                    Massillon (1663-1742)

3825   Pride is observed to defeat its own end, by bringing the man
       who seeks esteem and reverence into contempt.

                                    Bolingbroke (1678-1751)

3826   What the weak head with stronger bias rules,
       Is pride, the never-failing vice of fools.

                                    Pope (1688-1744)

3827   Pride that dines on vanity,
       sups on contempt.

                                    Franklin (1706-1790)

3828   In general, pride is at the bottom of all great mistakes.

                                    John Ruskin (1819-1900)

6. ADVICE

3829   Let another praise you, and not your own mouth;
       a stranger, and not your own lips.

                                    Proverbs (B.C. 1000?-200?)

3830   Thou shouldst not become presumptuous through much treasure
and wealth; for in the end it is necessary for thee to
leave all.

Zoroaster (B.C. 628?-551?)

3831   Respect yourself most of all.

Pythagoras (B.C. 582-507)

3832   Those who love themselves must be on constant guard
lest they yield to evil desires.
Once in a lifetime, at least, they should awaken faith,
either in youth, or in middle age, or even in old age.

Buddha (B.C. 568-488)

3833   When young, rejoice in the tranquillity of the old.
However great your glory, be forbearing in your manner.
Boast not of what you know, even when learned.
However high you may rise, be not proud.

Nagarjuna (c. 100-200 A.D.)

3834   And walk not proudly on the earth: verily thou shalt never
cleave the earth, nor reach to the mountains in height!

Koran (c. 651 A.D.)

3835   Do you wish men to speak well of you?
Then never speak well of yourself.

Pascal (1623-1662)

3836   Shun praise. Praise leads to self-delusion. Thy body is
not Self, thy SELF is in itself without a body, and either
praise or blame affects it not.

H. P. Blavatsky (1831-1891)

7. POTPOURRI

3837   If you are truly persevering in virtue,
What is the place of a haughty attitude?
The cow which has no milk will not be purchased,
Even though equipped with a pleasant-sounding bell.

Nagarjuna (c. 100-200 A.D.)

3838   If you wish in this world to advance
Your merits you're bound to enhance;
   You must stir it and stump it,
   And blow your own trumpet,
Or, trust me, you haven't a chance.

William S. Gilbert (1836-1911)

3839   We often boast that we are never bored, but yet we are so
       conceited that we do not perceive how often we bore others.
                                    La Rochefoucauld (1613-1680)

3840   When you begin with so much pomp and show.
       Why is the end so little and so low?
                                    Roscommon (1633?-1685)

3841   Deep is the sea, and deep is hell, but pride mineth deeper;
       it is coiled as a poisonous worm about the foundations of
       the soul.
                                    Tupper (1810-1889)

3842   When flowers are full of heaven-descended dews, they always
       hang their heads; but men hold theirs the higher the more
       they receive, getting proud as they get full.
                                    Beecher (1813-1878)

3843   To love oneself is the beginning of a lifelong romance.
                                    Oscar Wilde (1854-1900)

PRUDENCE

Caution, Discretion, Economy and Vigilance

1. ESSENCE

3844   Prudence is the knowledge of things to be sought,
and those to be shunned.
                                                Cicero (B.C. 106-43)

3845   Prudence consists in the power to recognize the nature of
disadvantages and to take the less disagreeable as good.
                                                Machiavelli (1469-1527)

3846   Prudence is that virtue by which we discern what is proper
to be done under the various circumstances of time and
place.
                                                Milton (1608-1674)

3847   Discretion is the perfection of reason, and a guide to us
in all the duties of life.
                                                La Bruyere (1645-1696)

3848   Caution is the eldest child of wisdom.
                                                Victor Hugo (1802-1885)

3849   Economy does not consist in saving the coal, but in using
the time while it burns.
                                                Emerson (1803-1882)

2. OPPOSITES

3850   Be slow of tongue and quick of eye.
                                                Cervantes (1547-1616)

3851   The prudence of the best heads is often defeated
by the tenderness of the best of hearts.
                                                Henry Fielding (1707-1754)

3852   Without economy none can be rich, and with it few can be
poor.
                                                Johnson (1709-1784)

3853   Mere parsimony is not economy....Expense, and great
expense, may be an essential part of true economy.
                                                Burke (1729-1797)

3854   The one prudence in life is concentration;
the one evil is dissipation.
                                                Emerson (1803-1882)

3855 Prudence is the virtue of the sense. It is the science of
appearances. It is the outmost action of the inward life.

Emerson (1803-1882)

3856 Discretion is the salt, and fancy the sugar of life;
the one preserves, the other sweetens it.

Bovee (1820-1904)

3857 Not he who can extricate himself from difficulties is the
prudent one, but he who cautiously bewares not to intricate
himself.

Chinese Proverb

3. INSIGHT

3858 You will conquer more surely by prudence than by passion.

Publilius Syrus (fl. B.C. 42)

3859 You will soon break the bow if you keep it always stretched.

Phaedrus (fl. 25 A.D.)

3860 Nothing is cheap which is superfluous, for what one does
not need, is dear at a penny.

Plutarch (46-120 A.D.)

3861 We accomplish more by prudence than by force.

Tacitus (55-117 A.D.)

3862 Distrust and caution are the parents of security.

Franklin (1706-1790)

3863 Prudence is a quality incompatible with vice,
and can never be effectively enlisted in its cause.

Burke (1729-1797)

3864 Every step of life shows much caution is required.

Goethe (1749-1832)

3865 Eternal vigilance is the price of liberty.

John Philpot Curran (1750-1817)

3866 Vigilance is not only the price of liberty,
but of success of any sort.

Beecher (1813-1878)

3867 A sound discretion is not so much indicated by never
making a mistake as by never repeating it.

Bovee (1820-1904)

3868   Economy is half the battle of life; it is not so hard to
       earn money as to spend it well.

                                        Charles Spurgeon (1834-1892)

4. POSITIVE

3869   The cautious seldom err.

                                           Confucius (B.C. 551-479)

3870   There is no gain so certain as that which arises from
       sparing what you have.

                                        Publilius Syrus (fl. B.C. 42)

3871   Economy is in itself a source of great revenue.

                                            Seneca (B.C. 3-65 A.D.)

3872   No other protection is wanting,
       providing you are under the guidance of prudence.

                                           Juvenal (40-125 A.D.)

3873   Those who speak with discretion
       Are respected by mankind,
       As the sun, emerging from the shadows,
       By its rays creates great warmth.

                                        Nagarjuna (c. 100-200 A.D.)

3874   If a wise man behaves prudently,
       How can he be overcome by his enemies?
       Even a single man, by right action,
       Can overcome a host of foes.

                                        Saskya Pandita (1182-1251)

3875   Precaution is better than cure.

                                           Edward Coke (1552-1633)

3876   Prevention is the daughter of intelligence.

                                        Walter Raleigh (1552-1618)

3877   Discretion in speech is more than eloquence.

                                               Bacon (1561-1626)

3878   The richest endowments of the mind are temperance, prudence,
       and fortitude. Prudence is a universal virtue, which enters
       into the composition of all the rest; and where she is not,
       fortitude loses its name and nature.

                                        Vincent Voiture (1597-1648)

3879   The first years of man make provision for the last.

                                             Johnson (1709-1784)

3880   Economy is a savings-bank, into which men drop pennies,
        and get dollars in return

                                        Josh Billings (1815-1885)

3881   The careful foot can walk anywhere.

                                        Chinese Proverb

5. NEGATIVE

3882   If one is not extremely careful,
        Somebody may come up from behind and strike him.
        Misfortune.

                                        I Ching (B.C. 1150?)

3883   The injury of prodigality leads to this,
        that he who will not economize will have to agonize.

                                        Confucius (B.C. 551-479)

3884   Too much taking heed is loss.

                                        Herbert (1593-1632)

3885   Great praise is heaped on prudence; yet there is not the
        most insignificant event of which it can make us sure.

                                        La Rochefoucauld (1613-1680)

3886   He that is overcautious will accomplish little.

                                        Schiller (1759-1805)

3887   There is nothing more imprudent than excessive prudence.

                                        Colton (1780-1832)

3888   There can be no economy where there is no efficiency.

                                        Disraeli (1804-1881)

3889   Great ability without discretion comes almost invariably
        to a tragic end.

                                        Leon Gambetta (1838-1882)

3890   Economy is going without something you do want
        in case you should, some day, want something
        which you probably won't want.

                                        Anthony Hawkins (1863-1933)

6. ADVICE

3891   Proceed not to speak or to act before thou hast weighed
        thy words, and examined the tendency of every step thou
        shalt take; so shall disgrace fly far from thee, and in thy
        house shall shame be a stranger; repentance shall not visit
        thee, nor sorrow dwell upon thy cheek in this or many lives
        to come.

                                        Akhenaton? (c. B.C. 1375)

3892   The man does not expose himself needlessly to rebuff
        by pushing forward when the time is not propitious.
        He retreats with kindred souls.

                                              I Ching (B.C. 1150?)

3893   It is a good thing to learn caution by the misfortunes
        of others.

                                        Publilius Syrus (fl. B.C. 42)

3894   The bird alighteth not on the spread net when it beholds
        another bird in the snare. Take warning by the misfortunes
        of others, that others may not take example from you.

                                              Saadi (1184-1291)

3895   Let your own discretion be your tutor:
        suit the action to the word, the word to the action.

                                          Shakespeare (1564-1616)

3896   It is always good
        When a man has two irons in the fire.

                                  Beaumont and Fletcher (c. 1600)

3897   Let prudence always attend your pleasures;
        it is the way to enjoy the sweets of them,
        and not be afraid of the consequences.
        Prudence is the necessary ingredient in all virtues,
        without which they degenerate into folly and excess.

                                       Jeremy Collier (1650-1726)

3898   I recommend you to take care of the minutes,
        for the hours will take care of themselves.

                                      Chesterfield (1694-1773)

3899   Neither trust, nor contend, nor lay wagers, nor lend,
        And you'll have peace to your life's end.

                                          Franklin (1706-1790)

3900   Beware of little expenses; a small leak will sink a great
        ship.

                                          Franklin (1706-1790)

3901   It is a maxim founded on the universal experience of mankind
        that no nation is to be trusted farther than it is bound by
        its interest.

                                  George Washington (1732-1799)

3902   Men are born with two eyes, but with one tongue,
        in order that they should see twice as much as they say.

                                          Colton (1780-1832)

3903   Be cautious, but not too cautious; do not be too much
       afraid of making a mistake; a man who never makes a mistake
       will make nothing.

                                             Lubbock (1834-1913)

3904   You must be vigilant and careful. Do not think that you
       possess all the virtues simply because the opposite of those
       does not manifest themselves in your daily life. Do not get
       false satisfaction.

                                            Sivananda (born 1887)

3905   One should never place trust in one's enemies.
       The basic truth of all treaties is distrust.
       Distrust produces highest good.

                                            Sivananda (born 1887)

3906   Take a second look...
       It costs you nothing.

                                                 Chinese Proverb

7. POTPOURRI

3907   Hear the words of prudence, give heed unto her counsels, and
       store them in thine heart; her maxims are universal, and
       all the virtues lean upon her; she is the guide and the
       mistress of human life.

                                        Akhenaton? (c. B.C. 1375)

3908   Have more than thou showest,
       Speak less than thou knowest,
       Lend less than thou owest,
       Ride more than thou goest...

                                        Shakespeare (1564-1616)

3909   In nature all is managed for the best with perfect frugality
       and just reserve, profuse to none, but bountiful to all;
       never employing on one thing more than enough, but with
       exact economy retrenching the superfluous, and adding force
       to what is principal in everything.

                                        Shaftesbury III (1671-1713)

3910   To balance Fortune by a just expense,
       Join with Economy, Magnificence.

                                                Pope (1688-1744)

3911   For want of a nail the shoe was lost;
       for want of a shoe the horse was lost;
       and for want of a horse the rider was lost;
       being overtaken and slain by the enemy,
       all for want of care about a horse-shoe nail.

                                           Franklin (1706-1790)

3912   To preserve their independence, we must not let our leaders
        load us with perpetual debt. We must make our election
        between economy and liberty, or profusion and servitude.
                                        Thomas Jefferson (1743-1826)

3913   Put your trust in God, my boys, and keep your powder dry.
                                                Blacker (1778-1823)

3914   Before you beat the dog
        Learn his master's name.
                                                    Chinese Proverb

3915   The prudent takes no poison
        even if he possesses the antidote.
                                                    Chinese Proverb

REALIZATION
Thought Becoming Reality

1. ESSENCE

3916   Just as a picture is drawn by an artist, surroundings are
created by the activities of the mind.

                           Buddha (B.C. 568-488)

3917   Ask, and it shall be given you;
      seek, and ye shall find;
         knock, and it shall be opened unto you.
    For every one that asketh receiveth;
      and he that seeketh findeth;
         and to him that knocketh it shall be opened.

                         Jesus (B.C. 6?-30? A.D.)

3918   Our life is what our thoughts make it.

                   Marcus Aurelius (121-180 A.D.)

3919   The act of contemplation creates the thing contemplated.

                   Isaac D'Israeli (1766-1848)

3920   Man is what he believes.

                   Chekhov (1860-1904)

2. OPPOSITES

3921   The mind is its own place, and in itself
Can make a heaven of hell, a hell of heaven.

                   Milton (1608-1674)

3922   If you think about disaster, you will get it.
Brood about death and you hasten your demise.
Think positively and masterfully, with confidence and faith,
and life becomes more secure, more fraught with action,
richer in achievement and experience.

             Edward Rickenbacker (1890-1973)

3. INSIGHT

3923   Such as are thy habitual thoughts, such also will be the
character of thy soul - for the soul is dyed by the
thoughts.

                   Marcus Aurelius (121-180 A.D.)

3924   Thoughts are but dreams till their effects be tried.

                   Shakespeare (1564-1616)

3925   Every separate thought takes shape and becomes
          visible in colour and form.
                                              Liu Hua-Yang (fl. 1794)

3926   A Human Thought is an actual EXISTENCE, and a Force and
          Power, capable of acting upon and controlling matter as
          well as mind.
                                              Albert Pike (1809-1891)

3927   Everything actual must also first have been possible, before
          having actual existence.
                                              Albert Pike (1809-1891)

3928   The greatest events of an age are its best thoughts.
          Thought finds its way into action.
                                              Bovee (1820-1904)

3929   When an idea exclusively occupies the mind, it is
          transformed into an actual physical or mental state.
                                              Sivananda (born 1887)

3930   As above, so below.
          As the Eternal creates Being out of Non-Being,
          So man can weave the threads of the future.
          Visualization and belief in a pattern of reality,
          Activates the creative power of Realization.
                                              A. L. Linall, Jr. (born 1947)

4. POSITIVE

3931   Let a man strive to purify his thoughts. What a man
          thinketh, that is he; this is the eternal mystery.
          Dwelling within himself with thoughts serene,
          he will obtain imperishable happiness.
          Man becomes that of which he thinks.
                                              Upanishads (c. B.C. 800)

3932   If a man's mind becomes pure, his surroundings will also
          become pure.
                                              Buddha (B.C. 568-488)

3933   They can because they think they can.
                                              Vergil (B.C. 70-19)

3934   If one advances confidently in the direction of his dreams,
          and endeavors to live the life which he has imagined,
          he will meet with a success unexpected in common hours.
                                              Thoreau (1817-1862)

3935   It is a funny thing about life; if you refuse to accept
        anything but the best you very often get it.
                                    Somerset Maugham (1874-1965)

5. NEGATIVE

3936   All that we are is the result of what we have thought:
        it is founded on our thoughts, it is made up of our
        thoughts. If a man speaks or acts with an evil thought,
        pain follows him, as the wheel follows the foot of the ox
        that draws the carriage.
                                    The Dhammapada (c. B.C. 300)

3937   Man is only miserable so far as he thinks himself so.
                                    Jacopo Sannazaro (1456-1530)

3938   Strange thoughts beget strange deeds.
                                    Shelley (1792-1822)

3939   Doubt indulged soon becomes doubt realized.
                                    Frances Havergal (1836-1879)

3940   Men die of the diseases which they have studied most...It's
        as if the morbid condition was an evil creature which, when
        it found itself closely hunted, flew at the throat of its
        pursuer.
                                    Arthur Conan Doyle (1859-1930)

6. ADVICE

3941   In all thy undertakings, let a reasonable assurance animate
        thy endeavours; if thou despairest of success, thou shalt
        not succeed.
                                    Akhenaton? (c. B.C. 1375)

3942   A person should contemplate the workings of the universe
        with reverence and introspection. In this way expression is
        given to the effects of these laws upon his own person.
        This is the source of a hidden power.
                                    I Ching (B.C. 1150?)

3943   Garner up pleasant thoughts in your mind, for pleasant
        thoughts make pleasant lives.
                                    John Wilkins (1614-1672)

3944   Be not afraid of life. Believe that life is worth living
        and your belief will help create the fact.
                                    William James (1842-1910)

3945   To get the most out of your life, plant in your mind seeds
       of constructive power that will yield fruitful results.
       Acquire the habit of substituting positive ideas for
       negative ones, and gradually your life will become more and
       more successful.

Grenville Kleiser (1868-1953)

7. POTPOURRI

3946   Think, and be careful what thou art within;
           For there is sin in the desire of sin;
       Think, and be thankful, in a different case;
           For there is grace in the desire of grace.

John Byrom (1692-1763)

3947   Never rail at the world, it is just as we make it,-
           We see not the flower if we sow not the seed;
       And as for ill-luck, why, it's just as we take it,-
           The heart that's in earnest no bars can impede.

Charles Swain (1803-1874)

RESTRICTION
Discipline, Law, Order and Rules

1. ESSENCE

3948   The law is reason from passion.
Aristotle (B.C. 384-322)

3949   Law: an ordinance of reason for the common good,
made by him who has care of the community.
Thomas Aquinas (1225-1274)

3950   Order is Heavens' first law.
Pope (1688-1744)

3951   The law is the last result of human wisdom acting upon
human experience for the benefit of the public.
Johnson (1709-1784)

2. OPPOSITES

3952   Written laws are like spiders' webs, and will like them only
entangle and hold the poor and weak, while the rich and
powerful will easily break through them.
Anacharsis (fl. B.C. 600)

3953   The prince is not above the laws,
but the laws above the prince.
Pliny the Younger (62-113 A.D.)

3954   As laws are necessary that good manners may be preserved,
so there is need of good manners that laws may be
maintained.
Machiavelli (1469-1527)

3955   A stern discipline pervades all nature,
which is a little cruel that it may be very kind.
Edmund Spenser (1552-1599)

3956   The English laws punish vice;
the Chinese laws do more, they reward virtue.
Goldsmith (1728-1774)

3957   It is criminal to steal a purse.
It is daring to steal a fortune.
It is a mark of greatness to steal a crown.
The blame diminishes as the guilt increases.
Schiller (1759-1805)

3958   In civil jurisprudence it too often happens that there is
        so much law, there is no room for justice, and that the
        claimant expires of wrong, in the midst of right,
        as mariners die of thirst in the midst of water.

                                        Colton (1780-1832)

3959   When men are pure, laws are useless;
        when men are corrupt, laws are broken.

                                        Disraeli (1804-1881)

3960   If there were no bad people there would be no good lawyers.
                                        Charles Dickens (1812-1870)

3961   Petty laws breed great crimes.

                                        Ouida (1839-1908)

3962   No man is above the law and no man is below it: nor do we
        ask any man's permission when we ask him to obey it.
                                        Theodore Roosevelt (1858-1919)

3963   When you break the big laws, you do not get liberty;
        you do not even get anarchy. You get the small laws.
                                        G. K. Chesterton (1874-1936)

3964   Laws control the lesser man...
        Right conduct controls the greater one.

                                        Chinese Proverb

3. INSIGHT

3965   Nobody has a more sacred obligation to obey the law than
        those who make the law.
                                        Sophocles (B.C. 495-406)

3966   Laws are silent in the midst of arms.

                                        Cicero (B.C. 106-43)

3967   A desire to resist oppression is implanted in the nature
        of man.
                                        Tacitus (55-117 A.D.)

3968   Fishes live in the sea, as men do a-land;
        the great ones eat up the little ones.

                                        Shakespeare (1564-1616)

3969   Ignorance of the law excuses no man; not that all men
        know the law, but because it is an excuse every man will
        plead, and no man can tell how to confute him.
                                        John Selden (1584-1654)

3970   In law nothing is certain but expense.

Samuel Butler (1612-1680)

3971   Laws in their Original Design are not made to draw Men into
       Crimes, but to prevent Crimes; Laws are Buoys set upon
       dangerous Places under Water, to warn Mankind, that such
       Sands or Rocks are there, and the Language in them is, Come
       here at your Peril.

Daniel DeFoe (1660-1731)

3972   Law should be like death, which spares no one.

Montesquieu (1689-1755)

3973   All are born to observe order,
       but few are born to establish it.

Joubert (1754-1824)

3974   The best way to get a bad law repealed is to enforce it
       strictly.

Lincoln (1809-1865)

3975   Our human laws are but the copies, more or less imperfect,
       of the eternal laws, so far as we can read them.

Froude (1818-1894)

3976   The law is the expression of the will of the strongest for
       the time being, and therefore laws have no fixity, but shift
       from generation to generation.

Brooks Adams (1848-1927)

3977   Few laws are of universal application. It is of the nature
       of our law that it has dealt not with man in general, but
       with him in relationships.

Louis D. Brandeis (1856-1941)

3978   The fewer laws there are in a given world, the nearer it is
       to the will of the Absolute; the more laws there are in a
       given world, the greater the mechanicalness, the further it
       is from the will of the Absolute.

Gurdjieff (1873-1949)

3979   Civilization begins with order, grows with liberty,
       and dies with chaos.

Will Durant (1885-1981)

4. POSITIVE

3980   Law is a form of order, and good law must necessarily mean
       good order.

Aristotle (B.C. 384-322)

3981   Law is intelligence, whose natural function it is to command
       right conduct and forbid wrongdoing.
                                             Cicero (B.C. 106-43)

3982   No evil propensity of the human heart is so powerful that it
       may not be subdued by discipline.
                                          Seneca (B.C. 3-65 A.D.)

3983   That law may be set down as good which is certain in
       meaning, just in precept, convenient in execution,
       agreeable to the form of government, and productive
       of virtue in those that live under it.
                                            Bacon (1561-1626)

3984   A state is better governed which has but few laws,
       and those laws strictly observed.
                                      Rene Descartes (1596-1650)

3985   Mark what unvaried laws preserve each state,
       Laws wise as Nature, and as fixed as Fate.
                                            Pope (1688-1744)

3986   Order is a lovely nymph, the child of Beauty and Wisdom;
       her attendants are Comfort, Neatness, and Activity; her
       abode is the valley of happiness: she is always to be found
       when sought for, and never appears so lovely as when
       contrasted with her opponent, Disorder.
                                           Johnson (1709-1784)

3987   Man must be disciplined, for he is by nature raw and wild.
                                     Immanuel Kant (1724-1804)

3988   Good order is the foundation of all good things.
                                            Burke (1729-1797)

3989   Order is the first requisite of liberty.
                                           Hegel (1770-1831)

3990   Order is the sanity of the mind, the health of the body,
       the peace of the city, the security of the state. As the
       beams to a house, as the bones to the microcosm of man,
       so is order to all things.
                                       Robert Southey (1774-1843)

3991   Liberty exists in proportion to wholesome restraint.
                                      Daniel Webster (1782-1852)

3992   There is no act more moral between men than that of rule
       and obedience.
                                           Carlyle (1795-1881)

3993 All that makes existence valuable to anyone, depends on the
enforcement of restraints upon the actions of other people.
John Stuart Mill (1806-1873)

3994 Just laws are no restraint upon the freedom of the good,
for the good man desires nothing which a just law will
interfere with.
Froude (1818-1894)

3995 Order means light and peace, inward liberty and free command
over one's self; order is power.
Henri Frederic Amiel (1821-1881)

5. NEGATIVE

3996 The more taboos and restrictions there are in the world
 The poorer the people will be....
The more laws and regulations are made prominent,
 The more thieves and robbers there will be.
Lao-Tzu (fl. B.C. 600)

3997 The strictest law sometimes becomes the severest injustice.
Terence (B.C. 185-159)

3998 When the state is most corrupt, then the laws are most
multiplied.
Tacitus (55-117 A.D.)

3999 There is no course of life so weak and sottish as that which
is managed by order, method and discipline.
Montaigne (1533-1592)

4000 There is no worse torture than the torture of laws.
Bacon (1561-1626)

4001 To go to law, is for two persons to kindle a fire at their
own cost to warm others and singe themselves to cinders;
and because they cannot agree as to what is truth and
equity, they will both agree to unplume themselves, that
others may be decorated with their feathers.
Owen Feltham (1602-1668)

4002 In a thousand pounds of law there is not an ounce of love.
John Ray (1627-1705)

4003 Laws are generally not understood by three sorts of persons:
those that make them, those that execute them,
and those that suffer if they break them.
Halifax (1633-1695)

4004   A multitude of laws in a country is like a great number of
       physicians, a sign of weakness and malady.

                                                   Voltaire (1694-1778)

4005   No laws are binding on the human subject which assault the
       body or violate the conscience.

                                          William Blackstone (1723-1780)

4006   He who has no taste for order, will be often wrong in his
       judgement, and seldom considerate or conscientious in his
       actions.

                                                   Lavater (1741-1801)

4007   Every law is an infraction of liberty.

                                          Jeremy Bentham (1748-1832)

4008   All law has for its object to confirm and exalt into a
       system the exploitation of the workers by the ruling class.

                                          Mikhail Bakunin (1814-1876)

4009   Those who are too lazy and comfortable to think for
       themselves and be their own judges obey the laws. Others
       sense their own laws within them.

                                          Hermann Hesse (1877-1962)

4010   Restriction of free thought and free speech is the most
       dangerous of all subversions. It is the one un-American act
       that could most easily defeat us.

                                          William O. Douglas (1898-1980)

4011   Going to law is losing a cow for the sake of a cat.

                                                   Chinese Proverb

6. ADVICE

4012   What is still calm can easily be grasped.
       What is still unmanifest can easily be considered.
       What is still fragile can easily be broken.
       What is still small can easily be scattered.
       Deal with things before they appear.
       Put things in order before disorder arises.

                                                   Lao-Tzu (fl. B.C. 600)

4013   The first virtue, son, if thou wilt learn,
       Is to restrain and keep well thy tongue.

                                          Geoffrey Chaucer (1340-1400)

4014   Set all things in their own peculiar place,
       and know that order is the greatest grace.

                                                   Dryden (1631-1700)

4015   Avoid law suits beyond all things; they influence your
        conscience, impair your health, and dissipate your property.
                                                La Bruyere (1645-1696)

4016   Every actual state is corrupt. Good men must not obey laws
        too well.
                                                Emerson (1803-1882)

4017   There is no man that lives who does not need to be drilled,
        disciplined, and developed into something higher and nobler
        and better than he is by nature.
                                                Beecher (1813-1878)

4018   If we do not discipline ourselves
        the world will do it for us.
                                                William Feather (born 1888)

7. POTPOURRI

4019   Heaven and earth unite to drip sweet dew.
        Without the command of men, it drips evenly over all.
        As soon as there were regulations and institutions, there
          were names (differentiation of things).
        As soon as there are names, know that it is time to stop.
        It is by knowing when to stop that one can be free from
          danger.
                                                Lao-Tzu (fl. B.C. 600)

4020   Nor is there any law more just, than that he who has plotted
        death shall perish by his own plot.
                                                Ovid (B.C. 43-18 A.D.)

4021   The verdict acquits the raven, but condemns the dove.
                                                Juvenal (40-125 A.D.)

4022   And whether you're an honest man, or whether you're a thief,
        Depends on whose solicitor has given me my brief.
                                                William S. Gilbert (1836-1911)

4023   The heavens themselves, the planets and this centre
        Observe degree, priority and place,
        Insisture, course, proportion, season, form,
        Office and custom, in all line of order.
                                                Shakespeare (1564-1616)

4024   It is the bridle and the spur that make a good horse.
                                                Thomas Fuller (1608-1661)

4025   Not chaos-like together crushed and bruised,
       But, as the world, harmoniously confused:
       Where order in variety we see,
       And where tho' all things differ, all agree.

                                                    Pope (1688-1744)

4026   A countryman between two lawyers is like a fish between
       two cats.

                                                Franklin (1706-1790)

4027   God works wonders now and then;
       Behold! a Lawyer, an honest Man!

                                                Franklin (1706-1790)

4028   The plaintiff and defendant in an action at law, are like
       two men ducking their heads in a bucket, and daring each
       other to remain longest under water.

                                                Johnson (1709-1784)

4029   That very law which moulds a tear,
       And bids it trickle from the source,
       That law preserves the earth a sphere,
       And guides the planets in their course.

                                          Samuel Rogers (1763-1855)

4030   The law is a pretty bird, and has charming wings.
       It would be quite a bird of paradise
       if it did not carry such a terrible bill.

                                        Douglas Jerrold (1803-1857)

4031   Laws are essential emanations from the self-poised character
       of God; they radiate from the sun to the circling edge of
       creation. Verily, the mighty Lawgiver hath subjected
       himself unto laws.

                                                 Tupper (1810-1889)

4032   Litigation - A machine which you go into as a pig and come
       out of as a sausage.

                                        Ambrose Bierce (1842-1914?)

4033   The law, in its majestic equality, forbids the rich as well
       as the poor to sleep under bridges, to beg in the streets,
       and to steal bread.

                                          Anatole France (1844-1924)

4034   The net of law is spread so wide,
       No sinner from its sweep may hide.
       Its meshes are so fine and strong,
       They take in every child of wrong.
         O wondrous web of mystery!
         Big fish alone escape from thee!

                                     James Jeffrey Roche (1847-1908)

4035 Our laws make law impossible; our liberties destroy all
freedom; our property is organized robbery; our morality
an impudent hypocrisy; our wisdom is administered by
inexperienced or mal-experienced dupes; our power wielded
by cowards and weaklings; and our honour false in all its
points. I am an enemy of the existing order for good
reasons.

G. B. Shaw (1856-1950)

4036 I know not whether Laws be right,
    Or whether Laws be wrong;
All that we know who lie in jail
    Is that the wall is strong;
And that each day is like a year,
    A year whose days are long.

Oscar Wilde (1854-1900)

4037 Laws should be like clothes. They should be made to fit
the people they are meant to serve.

Clarence Darrow (1857-1938)

4038 The laws of God, the laws of man
He may keep that will and can;
Not I: let God and man decree
Laws for themselves and not for me.

A. E. Housman (1859-1936)

RUIN

Calamity, Disaster, Loss and Poverty

1. ESSENCE

4039   Not he who has little, but he who wishes for more, is poor.
Seneca (B.C. 3-65 A.D.)

4040   The lowest ebb is the turn of the tide.
Longfellow (1807-1882)

2. OPPOSITES

4041   It is more difficult to be well with riches, than to be at
ease under the want of them. Man governeth himself much
easier in poverty than in abundance.
Akhenaton? (c. B.C. 1375)

4042   If the wicked flourished, and thou suffer, be not
discouraged; they are fatted for destruction, thou
art dieted for health.
Thomas Fuller (1608-1661)

4043   And plenty makes us poor.
Dryden (1631-1700)

4044   The poor man must walk to get meat for his stomach,
the rich man to get a stomach to his meat.
Franklin (1706-1790)

4045   Poverty and wealth are comparative sins.
Victor Hugo (1802-1885)

4046   Very few people can afford to be poor.
G. B. Shaw (1856-1950)

4047   People come to poverty in two ways:
accumulating debts and paying them off.
Jewish Proverb

3. INSIGHT

4048   From its beginning, the world has been filled with a
succession of calamities; over and above the unavoidable
facts of illness, decrepitude and death.
Buddha (B.C. 568-488)

4049   If all our misfortunes were laid in one common heap whence everyone must take an equal portion, most people would be contented to take their own and depart.

Socrates (B.C. 469-399)

4050   He is not poor who has the use of necessary things.

Horace (B.C. 65-8)

4051   On the touchstone of misfortune a man discovers the strength of understanding and of spirit in kinsmen, wife, servants, and himself.

The Hitopadesa (600?-1100? A.D.)

4052   A wise man loses nothing, if he but saves himself.

Montaigne (1533-1592)

4053   Poverty is no vice, but an inconvenience.

John Florio (1553?-1625)

4054   Things that are not at all, are never lost.

Christopher Marlowe (1564-1593)

4055   The worst is not
So long as we can say "This is the worst."

Shakespeare (1564-1616)

4056   No man can lose what he never had.

Izaak Walton (1593-1683)

4057   No man is poor who does not think himself so. But if in a full fortune with impatience he desires more, he proclaims his wants and his beggarly condition.

Jeremy Taylor (1613-1667)

4058   Our greatest misfortunes come to us from ourselves.

Rousseau (1712-1778)

4059   Humanity may endure the loss of everything; all its possessions may be torn away without infringing its true dignity - all but the possibility of improvement.

Immanuel von Fichte (1796-1879)

4060   All the great and beneficent operations of Nature are produced by slow and often imperceptible degrees. The work of destruction and devastation only is violent and rapid. The Volcano and the Earthquake, the Tornado and the Avalanche, leap suddenly into full life and fearful energy, and smite with an unexpected blow.

Albert Pike (1809-1891)

4061   It is indeed astonishing how many great men have been poor.
                                                          Lubbock (1834-1913)

4. POSITIVE

4062   When Heaven is about to confer a great office on any man,
       it first disciplines his mind with suffering, and his bones
       and sinews with toil. It exposes him to want and subjects
       him to extreme poverty. It confounds his undertakings.
       By all these methods it stimulates his mind, hardens him,
       and supplies his incompetencies.
                                                     Mencius (B.C. 371-288)

4063   Poverty is the discoverer of all the arts.
                                                  Apollonius (B.C. 257-205)

4064   Calamity is virtue's opportunity.
                                                  Seneca (B.C. 3-65 A.D.)

4065   How wisely fate ordained for human kind
       Calamity! which is the perfect glass,
       Wherein we truly see and know ourselves.
                                            William Davenant (1605-1668)

4066   It may serve as a comfort to us, in all our calamities and
       afflictions, that he that loses anything and gets wisdom by
       it is a gainer by the loss.
                                                  L'Estrange (1616-1704)

4067   He that is down needs fear no fall.
                                               John Bunyan (1628-1688)

4068   Times of general calamity and confusion have ever been
       productive of the greatest minds. The purest ore is
       produced from the hottest furnace, and the brightest
       thunderbolt is elicited from the darkest storm.
                                                     Colton (1780-1832)

4069   The greatest man in history was the poorest.
                                                  Emerson (1803-1882)

4070   Almost all the noblest things that have been achieved in the
       world, have been achieved by poor men; poor scholars, poor
       professional men, poor artisans and artists, poor philoso-
       phers, poets, and men of genius.
                                                  Albert Pike (1809-1891)

4071   It is from the level of calamities, not that of every-day
       life, that we learn impressive and useful lessons.
                                                  Thackeray (1811-1863)

4072   But noble souls, through dust and heat,
        Rise from disaster and defeat
            The stronger.

                                        Longfellow (1807-1882)

4073   When all else is lost,
        the future still remains.

                                        Bovee (1820-1904)

4074   What does not destroy me, makes me strong.
                                        Nietzsche (1844-1900)

4075   Many a good face
        Under a ragged hat.

                                        Chinese Proverb

5. NEGATIVE

4076   Not to be able to bear poverty is a shameful thing, but not
        to know how to chase it away by work is a more shameful
        thing yet.

                                        Pericles (B.C. 495-429)

4077   The real disgrace of poverty is not in owning to the fact
        but in declining to struggle against it.

                                        Thucydides (B.C. 460-400)

4078   Poverty urges us to do and suffer anything that we may
        escape from it, and so leads us away from virtue.

                                        Horace (B.C. 65-8)

4079   Ants do not bend their ways to empty barns,
        so no friend will visit the place of departed wealth.

                                        Ovid (B.C. 43-18 A.D.)

4080   Poverty is shunned and persecuted all over the globe.

                                        Lucan (39-65 A.D.)

4081   They do not easily rise whose abilities are repressed by
        poverty at home.

                                        Juvenal (40-125 A.D.)

4082   Poverty is not dishonorable in itself, but only when it
        comes from idleness, intemperance, extravagance, and folly.

                                        Plutarch (46-120 A.D.)

4083   Poverty is the mother of crime.

                                        Marcus Aurelius (121-180 A.D.)

4084   To mortal men great loads allotted to be;
But of all packs no pack like poverty.

           Robert Herrick (1591-1674)

4085   Poverty often deprives a man of all spirit and virtue;
it is hard for an empty bag to stand upright.

           Franklin (1706-1790)

4086   Poverty is a great enemy to human happiness; it certainly
destroys liberty, and it makes some virtues impracticable,
and others extremely difficult.

           Johnson (1709-1784)

4087   Poverty is the wicked man's tempter, the good man's
perdition, the proud man's curse, the melancholy
man's halter.

           Bulwer-Lytton (1803-1873)

4088   That loss is common would not make
My own less bitter, rather more,
Too common!

           Alfred Tennyson (1809-1892)

4089   Poverty is the openmouthed relentless hell which yawns
beneath civilized society. And it is hell enough.

           Henry George (1839-1897)

4090   The child was diseased at birth - stricken with an
hereditary ill that only the most vital men are able to
shake off. I mean poverty - the most deadly and prevalent
of all diseases.

           Eugene O'Neill (1888-1953)

4091   With money you can call the very gods to help...
Without it not a single man.

           Chinese Proverb

6. ADVICE

4092   Perils, and misfortunes, and want, and pain, and injury, are
more or less the certain lot of every man that cometh into
the world. It behooveth thee, therefore, O child of
calamity! early to fortify thy mind with courage and
patience, that thou mayest support, with a becoming
resolution, thy allotted portion of human evil.

           Akhenaton? (c. B.C. 1375)

4093   Action must be taken at the first signs of disruption or
decay, otherwise disaster will follow as ice-bound water
follows brief autumn frosts.

           I Ching (B.C. 1150?)

4094   He who carries out one good deed acquires one advocate in
        his own behalf, and he who commits one transgression
        acquires one accuser against himself. Repentance and good
        works are like a shield against calamity.
                                    The Talmud (B.C. 500?-400? A.D.)

4095   The consciousness of good intention is the greatest solace
        of misfortunes.
                                    Cicero (B.C. 106-43)

4096   Yield not to misfortunes, but advance all the more
        boldly against them.
                                    Vergil (B.C. 70-19)

4097   When you see a man in distress, recognize him as a fellow
        man.
                                    Seneca (B.C. 3-65 A.D.)

4098   Wise men ne'er sit and wail their loss, but cheerily seek
        how to redress their harms.
                                    Shakespeare (1564-1616)

4099   By the side of honor, humiliation waits.
        When honored, one ought not be high-spirited.
        Behind poverty, prosperity follows.
        When impoverished, why should one by low-spirited.
                                    Hung Tzu-ch'eng (1593-1665)

4100   Life is thickly sown with thorns, and I know no other remedy
        than to pass quickly through them. The longer we dwell on
        our misfortunes, the greater is their power to harm us.
                                    Voltaire (1694-1778)

4101   When any calamity has been suffered the first thing to be
        remembered is, how much has been escaped.
                                    Johnson (1709-1784)

7. POTPOURRI

4102   The ruins of himself! now worn away
        With age, yet still majestic in decay.
                                    Homer (c. B.C. 700)

4103   Whom the gods would destroy they first make mad.
                                    Euripides (B.C. 480-406)

4104   'Tis safer to be that which we destroy
        Than by destruction dwell in doubtful joy.
                                    Shakespeare (1564-1616)

4105 You never find people laboring to convince you that you may
live very happily upon a plentiful income.

> Johnson (1709-1784)

4106 When ancient opinions and rules of life are taken away, the
loss cannot possibly be estimated. From that moment we have
no compass to govern us, nor can we know distinctly to what
port to steer.

> Burke (1729-1797)

4107 A dog starved at his master's gate
Predicts the ruin of the State.

> William Blake (1757-1828)

4108 He went like one that hath been stunned,
  And is of sense forlorn:
A sadder and a wiser man,
  He rose the morrow morn.

> Samuel Coleridge (1772-1834)

4109 But over all things brooding slept
The quiet sense of something lost.

> Alfred Tennyson (1809-1892)

4110 And in the wreck of noble lives
Something immortal still survives.

> Longfellow (1807-1882)

4111 Calamities are of two kinds: misfortune to ourselves,
and good fortune to others.

> Ambrose Bierce (1842-1914?)

4112 Beggars should be abolished. It annoys one to give to them,
and it annoys one not to give to them.

> Nietzsche (1844-1900)

4113 Most people become bankrupt through having invested too
heavily in the prose of life. To have ruined oneself over
poetry is an honor.

> Oscar Wilde (1854-1900)

4114 This is the truth as I see it, my dear,
  Out in the wind and the rain:
They who have nothing have little to fear,
  Nothing to lose or to gain.

> Cawein (1865-1914)

4115 To build it, took one hundred years...
to destroy it, one day.

> Chinese Proverb

SCIENCE
Cause and Effect, Logic, Observation and Reason

1. ESSENCE

4116   Experience is the universal mother of sciences.
Cervantes (1547-1616)

4117   Science is the knowledge of consequences,
and dependence of one fact upon another.
Thomas Hobbes (1588-1679)

4118   Logic is the art of convincing us of some truth.
La Bruyere (1645-1696)

4119   Science when well digested is nothing but good sense and
reason.
Leszczynski Stanislaus (1677-1766)

4120   Men love to wonder, and that is the seed of science.
Emerson (1803-1882)

4121   Science consists in grouping facts so that general laws or
conclusions may be drawn from them.
Charles Darwin (1809-1882)

4122   Science is organized knowledge.
Herbert Spencer (1820-1903)

4123   Science is simply common sense at its best, that is, rigidly
accurate in observation, and merciless to fallacy in logic.
Thomas Huxley (1825-1895)

2. OPPOSITES

4124   Science is the father of knowledge,
but opinion breeds ignorance.
Hippocrates (B.C. 460-370)

4125   The cause is hidden but the effect is evident,
Ovid (B.C. 43-18 A.D.)

4126   Everything in nature is a cause
from which there flows some effect.
Spinoza (1632-1677)

4127   Reason is progressive; instinct is complete;
swift instinct leaps; slow reason feebly climbs.
Young (1683-1765)

4128   Algebra is the metaphysics of arithmetic.
                                            Sterne (1713-1768)

4129   Logic works; metaphysics contemplates.
                                            Joubert (1754-1824)

4130   Grammar is the logic of speech,
       even as logic is the grammar of reason.
                                            Trench (1807-1886)

4131   Science has its nights and its dawns, because it gives the
       intellectual world a life which has its regulated movements
       and its progressive phases. It is with Truths, as with the
       luminous rays: nothing of what is concealed is lost;
       but also, nothing of what is discovered is absolutely new.
                                            Albert Pike (1809-1891)

4132   All things are hidden, obscure and debatable
       if the cause of the phenomena be unknown,
       but everything is clear if this cause be known.
                                            Louis Pasteur (1822-1895)

4133   Logical consequences are the scarecrows of fools
       and the beacons of wise men.
                                            Thomas Huxley (1825-1895)

4134   Science is facts; just as houses are made of stones, so is
       science made of facts; but a pile of stones is not a house
       and a collection of facts is not necessarily science.
                                            Henri Poincare (1854-1912)

4135   Science is what you know, philosophy is what you don't know.
                                            Bertrand Russell (1872-1970)

4136   All exact science is dominated by the idea of approximation.
                                            Bertrand Russell (1872-1970)

4137   A few observations and much reasoning leads to error;
       many observations and a little reasoning to truth.
                                            Alexis Carrel (1873-1944)

4138   Every science begins as philosophy and ends as art.
                                            Will Durant (1885-1981)

4139   Artists treat facts as stimuli for imagination,
       whereas scientists use imagination to coordinate facts.
                                            Arthur Koestler (1905-1983)

4140   He who proves things by experience increases his knowledge;
       he who believes blindly increases his errors.

                                                        Chinese Proverb

3. INSIGHT

4141   Philosophy is the true mother of science.

                                                   Cicero (B.C. 106-43)

4142   When we return to the root, we gain the meaning;
       When we pursue external objects, we lose the reason.
       The moment we are enlightened within,
       We go beyond the voidness of a world confronting us.

                                              Seng-T'San (540?-606 A.D.)

4143   Reason is like an officer when the King appears;
       The officer then loses his power and hides himself.
       Reason is the shadow cast by God; God is the sun.

                                          Jalal-Uddin Rumi (1207-1273)

4144   The men of experiment are like the ant; they only collect
       and use. The reasoners resemble spiders, who make cobwebs
       out of their own substance. But the bee takes a middle
       course; it gathers its material from the flowers of the
       garden and of the field, but transforms and digests it by a
       power of its own.

                                         Leonardo Da Vinci (1452-1519)

4145   Science has its being in a perpetual mental restlessness.

                                           William Temple (1628-1699)

4146   We can only reason from what is; we can reason on
       actualities, but not on possibilities.

                                            Bolingbroke (1678-1751)

4147   Learning is the dictionary, but sense the grammar of science

                                               Sterne (1713-1768)

4148   Logic and metaphysics make use of more tools than all the
       rest of the sciences put together, and they do the least
       work.

                                              Colton (1780-1832)

4149   Art and science have their meeting point in method.

                                         Bulwer-Lytton (1803-1873)

4150   Life is a perpetual instruction in cause and effect.

                                            Emerson (1803-1882)

4151   The theory that can absorb the greatest number of facts,
        and persist in doing so, generation after generation,
        through all changes of opinion and detail, is the one
        that must rule all observation.

                                        John Weiss (1818-1879)

4152   The work of science is to substitute facts for appearances
        and demonstrations for impressions.

                                        John Ruskin (1819-1900)

4153   Reason creates science;
        sentiments and creeds shape history.

                                        Gustave LeBon (1841-1931)

4154   Science, like life, feeds on its own decay. New facts burst
        old rules; then newly divined conceptions bind old and new
        together into a reconciling law.

                                        William James (1842-1910)

4155   Every great advance in science has issued from a new
        audacity of imagination.

                                        John Dewey (1859-1952)

4156   Science is nothing but developed perception, interpreted
        intent, common sense rounded out and minutely articulated.

                                        George Santayana (1863-1952)

4157   Science is the tool of the Western mind and with it more
        doors can be opened than with bare hands. It is part and
        parcel of our knowledge and obscures our insight only when
        it holds that the understanding given by it is the only
        kind there is.

                                        C. G. Jung (1875-1961)

4158   The process of scientific discovery is, in effect, a
        continual flight from wonder.

                                        Einstein (1879-1955)

4159   Truth in science can be defined as the working hypothesis
        best suited to open the way to the next better one.

                                        Konrad Lorenz (born 1903)

4160   Science is the refusal to believe on the basis of hope.

                                        C. P. Snow (1905-1980)

4. POSITIVE

4161   The gods plant reason in mankind, of all good gifts the
        highest.

                                        Sophocles (B.C. 495-406)

4162   Reason is the mistress and queen of all things.

Cicero (B.C. 106-43)

4163   Happy the man who has been able to learn the causes
of things.

Vergil (B.C. 70-19)

4164   Observation, not old age, brings wisdom.

Publilius Syrus (fl. B.C. 42)

4165   Nothing has such power to broaden the mind as the ability to
investigate systematically and truly all that comes under
thy observation in life.

Marcus Aurelius (121-180 A.D.)

4166   General observations drawn from particulars are the jewels
of knowledge, comprehending great store in a little room.

John Locke (1632-1704)

4167   Science is the great antidote to the poison of enthusiasm
and superstition.

Adam Smith (1723-1790)

4168   Science and art belong to the whole world,
and before them vanish the barriers of nationality.

Goethe (1749-1832)

4169   Science is a first-rate piece of furniture for a man's
upper chamber, if he has common sense on the ground floor.

Oliver Wendell Holmes (1809-1894)

4170   The most beautiful thing we can experience is the
mysterious. It is the source of all art and science.
He to whom this emotion is a stranger, who can no longer
pause to wonder and stand rapt in awe, is as good as dead;
his eyes are closed.

Einstein (1879-1955)

4171   The end of science is not to prove a theory,
but to improve mankind.

Manly P. Hall (born 1901)

4172   All science is concerned with the relationship of cause and
effect. Each scientific discovery increases man's ability
to predict the consequences of his actions and thus his
ability to control future events.

Laurence J. Peter (born 1919)

5. NEGATIVE

4173   How can finite grasp infinity?

Dryden (1631-1700)

4174   Reason is a very light rider, and easily shook off.

Swift (1667-1745)

4175   Who reasons wisely is not therefore wise;
His pride in reasoning, not in acting, lies.

Pope (1688-1744)

4176   Many are destined to reason wrongly; others, not to reason
at all; and others, to persecute those who do reason.

Voltaire (1694-1778)

4177   Science has been seriously retarded by the study of what is
not worth knowing, and what is not knowable.

Goethe (1749-1832)

4178   It is common error to infer that things which are
consecutive in order of time have necessarily the relation
of cause and effect.

Jacob Bigelow (1786-1879)

4179   The knowledge of the theory of logic has no tendency
whatever to make men good reasoners.

Macaulay (1800-1859)

4180   We are too much accustomed to attribute to a single cause
that which is the product of several, and the majority of
our controversies come from that.

Justus von Liebig (1803-1873)

4181   Here is the world, sound as a nut, perfect, not the smallest
piece of chaos left, never a stitch nor an end, nor a mark
of haste, or botching, or a second thought; but the theory
of the world is a thing of shreds and patches.

Emerson (1803-1882)

4182   Men are apt to mistake the strength of their feeling for the
strength of their argument. The heated mind resents the
chill touch and relentless scrutiny of logic.

William Gladstone (1809-1898)

4183   Science deals only with phenomena, and is but charlatanism
when it babbles about the powers or causes that produce
these, or what the things are, in essence, of which it gives
us merely the names.

Albert Pike (1809-1891)

4184   Science commits suicide when it adopts a creed.
                                              Thomas Huxley (1825-1895)

4185   Science cannot solve the ultimate mystery of nature. And
        that is because, in the last analysis, we ourselves are part
        of nature and therefore part of the mystery that we are
        trying to solve.
                                              Max Planck (1858-1947)

6. ADVICE

4186   Shun no toil to make yourself remarkable by some one talent.
        Yet do not devote yourself to one branch exclusively.
        Strive to get clear notions about all.
        Give up no science entirely, for all science is one.
                                              Seneca (B.C. 3-65 A.D.)

4187   Although nature commences with reason and ends in experience
        it is necessary for us to do the opposite, that is to
        commence with experience and from this to proceed
        to investigate the reason.
                                              Leonardo Da Vinci (1452-1519)

4188   Art and sciences are not cast in a mould, but are found
        and perfected by degrees, by often handling and polishing.
                                              Montaigne (1533-1592)

4189   An idle reason lessens the weight of the good ones you gave
        before.
                                              Swift (1667-1745)

4190   Sit down before fact as a little child, be prepared to give
        up every preconceived notion, follow humbly wherever and to
        whatever abysses Nature leads, or you shall learn nothing.
                                              Thomas Huxley (1825-1895)

4191   Firstly, gradualness. About this most important condition
        of fruitful scientific work I can never speak without
        emotion. Gradualness, gradualness, gradualness.
                                              Pavlov (1849-1936)

4192   True science teaches, above all, to doubt, and to be
        ignorant.
                                              Miguel de Unamuno (1864-1936)

4193   There must be no barriers to freedom of inquiry. There is
        no place for dogma in science. The scientist is free, and
        must be free to ask any questions, to doubt any assertion,
        to seek for any evidence, to correct any errors.
                                              J. Robert Oppenheimer (1904-1967)

7. POTPOURRI

4194   Rain falls, wind blows, plants bloom, leaves mature
       and are blown away; these phenomena are all interrelated
       with causes and conditions, are brought about by them,
       and disappear as the causes and conditions change.
                                        Buddha (B.C. 568-488)

4195   The science which teacheth arts and handicrafts
       Is merely science for the gaining of a living;
       But the science which teacheth deliverance from worldly
          existence,
       Is not that the true science?
                                        Nagarjuna (c. 100-200 A.D.)

4196   He was in logic a great critic,
       Profoundly skilled in analytic;
       He could distinguish and divide
       A hair 'twixt south and southwest side
       On either which he would dispute,
       Confute, change hands, and still confute.
                                        Samuel Butler (1612-1680)

4197   One science only will one genius fit,
       So vast is art, so narrow human wit.
                                        Pope (1688-1744)

4198   Astronomy is one of the sublimest fields of human
       investigation. The mind that grasps its facts and
       principles receives something of the enlargement and
       grandeur belonging to the science itself. It is a
       quickener of devotion.
                                        Horace Mann (1796-1859)

4199   Every great scientific truth goes through three stages:
          First, people say it conflicts with the Bible.
          Next they say it had been discovered before.
          Lastly, they say they always believed it.
                                        Jean Louis Agassiz (1807-1883)

4200   My kingdom is as wide as the world, and my desire has no
       limit. I go forward always, freeing spirits and weighing
       worlds, without fear, without compassion, without love, and
       without God. Men call me Science.
                                        Gustave Flaubert (1821-1880)

4201   The great tragedy of Science: the slaying of a beautiful
       hypothesis by an ugly fact.
                                        Thomas Huxley (1825-1895)

4202   There is something fascinating about science. One gets such
       wholesome returns of conjectures out of such trifling
       investment of fact.

                                              Mark Twain (1835-1910)

4203   Science is always wrong. It never solves a problem without
       creating ten more.

                                              G. B. Shaw (1856-1950)

4204   Religions die when they are proved to be true.
       Science is the record of dead religions.

                                              Oscar Wilde (1854-1900)

4205   A new scientific truth does not triumph by convincing its
       opponents and making them see the light, but rather because
       its opponents eventually die, and a new generation grows up
       that is familiar with it.

                                              Max Planck (1858-1947)

SEPARATION
Absence, Distance, Farewell and Parting

1. ESSENCE

4206   In farewells we heat above ordinary our affections to
the things we forego.

Montaigne (1533-1592)

4207   A chord, stronger or weaker, is snapped asunder in every
parting, and time's busy fingers are not practised in
re-splicing broken ties. Meet again you may; will it be
in the same way?

Bulwer-Lytton (1803-1873)

4208   In every parting there is an image of death.

George Eliot (1819-1880)

2. OPPOSITES

4209   Not until a person detaches himself from the creation
will he be joined with the Creator.

'Ali (600-661 A. D.)

4210   Absence diminishes little passions and increases great ones,
as the wind extinguishes candles and fans a fire.

La Rochefoucauld (1613-1680)

4211   The absent are never without fault,
nor the present without excuse.

Franklin (1706-1790)

4212   Friendship, like love, is destroyed by long absence,
though it may be increased by short intermissions.

Johnson (1709-1784)

4213   Every parting is a form of death,
as every reunion is a type of heaven.

Tryon Edwards (1809-1894)

3. INSIGHT

4214   Although you may remain somewhere for a long time,
It is certain that you will have to leave;
Whatever may be the manner of parting,
The actual going cannot be avoided.

Nagarjuna (c. 100-200 A.D.)

4215   All flowers will droop in absences of the sun that waked
their sweets.

Dryden (1631-1700)

4216   But fate ordains that dearest friends must part.

Young (1683-1765)

4217   Sometimes, when one person is missing, the whole world seems
depopulated.

Alphonse de Lamartine (1790-1869)

4. POSITIVE

4218   The superior man, when he stands alone, is unconcerned,
And if he has to renounce the world, he is undaunted.

I Ching (B.C. 1150?)

4219   Greater things are believed of those who are absent.

Tacitus (55-117 A.D.)

4220   Parting is such sweet sorrow.

Shakespeare (1564-1616)

4221   Absence doth sharpen love, presence strengthens it; the
one brings fuel, the other blows it till it burns clear.

Thomas Overbury (1581-1613)

4222   Distance sometimes endears friendship, and absence
sweeteneth it - for separation from those we love shows us,
by the loss, their real value and dearness to us.

James Howell (1595-1666)

4223   Let the wind of the spirit blow between your shores. The
great oaks in the forest do not grow in each other's shade.

Kahlil Gibran (1883-1931)

4224   No suffering, no sorrow, no pain will befall the man who has
controlled his anger, who has abandoned his pride, who is
not attached to anything and who calls nothing his own.

Sivananda (born 1887)

5. NEGATIVE

4225   But when he (man) shall have been taken from sight,
he quickly goes also out of mind.

Thomas A. Kempis (1380-1471)

4226   Absence from those we love is self from self -
a deadly banishment.

Shakespeare (1564-1616)

4227   Absence is the death of love.

Pedro Calderon (1600-1681)

4228   Parting is worse than death; it is death of love!

Dryden (1631-1700)

4229   Days of absence, sad and dreary,
         Clothed in sorrow's dark array,
       Days of absence, I am weary;
         She I love is far away.

Rousseau (1712-1778)

4230   Absence in love is like water upon fire;
       a little quickens, but much extinguishes it.

Hannah More (1745-1833)

4231   For in that word, that fatal word, however we promise, hope,
       believe, there breathes despair.

Byron (1788-1824)

4232   That bitter word, which closed all earthly friendships,
       and finished every feast of love - Farewell!

Robert Pollok (1798-1827)

6. ADVICE

4233   Great undertakings cannot succeed during periods of division
       and mutual alienation. The superior man recognizes the
       circumstances, does not become impatient, and sets about
       achieving gradual improvements in small matters.

I Ching (B.C. 1150?)

4234   Let no one be willing to speak ill of the absent.

Propertius (B.C. 50-16)

4235   The logs of wood which move
         down the river together
       Are driven apart by every wave.
       Such inevitable parting
       Should not be the cause of misery.

Nagarjuna (c. 100-200 A.D.)

4236   Let us not be dainty of leave-taking,
       But shift away.

Shakespeare (1564-1616)

4237   Abruptness is an eloquence in parting, when spinning out
       the time is but the weaving of new sorrow.

John Suckling (1609-1642)

4238   Never part without loving words to think of during your
        absence. It may be that you will not meet again in life.
                                                    Richter (1763-1825)

7. POTPOURRI

4239   All the souls created by the activity of God were originally
        one, the male and female portions of them not yet separated,
        existing in conjugal bliss. When they first begin their
        journey to the Below on this earth they do so as male and
        female together. Once arrived, they become separated...A
        man may only find his other half by walking in the way of
        truth. Only then may he have a chance at completion.
                                                    Zohar (120?-1200? A.D.)

4240   Here we part.
        The solitary sail will attempt a flight of a thousand miles,
        The flowing clouds are the dreams of a wandering son,
        The setting sun, the affection of an old friend.
        So you go, waving your hands.
                                                    Li Po (701?-762 A.D.)

4241   What! gone without a word? ay, so true love should do;
        it cannot speak, for truth hath better deeds, than words,
        to grace it.
                                                    Shakespeare (1564-1616)

4242   How like a winter hath my absence been
          From thee, the pleasure of the fleeting year!
        What freezings have I felt, what dark days seen!
          What old December's bareness everywhere.
                                                    Shakespeare (1564-1616)

4243   Ever absent, ever near;
        Still I see thee, still I hear;
        Yet I cannot reach thee, dear!
                                                    Francis Kazinczy (1759-1831)

4244   Fare thee well! and if for ever,
        Still for ever, fare thee well.
                                                    Byron (1788-1824)

4245   When we two parted in silence and tears,
        Half broken-hearted to sever for years,
        Pale grew thy cheek and cold, Colder thy kiss;
        Truly that hour foretold sorrow to this!
                                                    Byron (1788-1824)

4246   Oh hast thou forgotten this day we must part?
        It may be for years and it may be forever;
        Oh why art thou silent, thou voice of my heart?

                                  Julia Crawford (1800-1885)

4247   Distance - the only thing the rich are willing for the poor
        to call theirs, and keep.

                                  Ambrose Bierce (1842-1914?)

4248   She went her unremembering way,
           She went and left in me
        The pang of all the partings gone,
           And partings yet to be.

                                  Francis Thompson (1859-1907)

SICKNESS

Disease, Excess, Madness, Medicine and Physicians

1. ESSENCE

4249   Everything in excess is opposed to nature.
Hippocrates (B.C. 460-370)

4250   A physician is nothing but a consoler of the mind.
Petronius (died 66 A.D.)

4251   The art of medicine consists of amusing the patient while
nature cures the disease.
Voltaire (1694-1778)

4252   Madness is to think of too many things in succession too
fast, or of one thing too exclusively.
Voltaire (1694-1778)

4253   Disease is the retribution of outraged Nature.
Hosea Ballou (1771-1852)

4254   Disease is an experience of so-called mortal mind.
It is fear made manifest on the body.
Mary Baker Eddy (1821-1910)

2. OPPOSITES

4255   Physicians are many in title but very few in reality.
Hippocrates (B.C. 460-370)

4256   Excess generally causes reaction and produces a change in
the opposite direction, whether it be in the seasons,
or in individuals, or in government.
Plato (B.C. 427?-347?)

4257   Men worry over the great number of diseases, while doctors
worry over the scarcity of effective remedies.
Pien Ch'iao (fl. B.C. 255)

4258   Some remedies are worse than the disease.
Publilius Syrus (fl. B.C. 42)

4259   By medicine life may be prolonged, yet death
Will seize the doctor too.
Shakespeare (1564-1616)

4260   The madman who knows that he is mad is close to sanity.
Ruiz de Alarcon (1581-1639)

4261   He who cures a disease may be the skillfullest,
       but he that prevents it is the safest physician.
                                    Thomas Fuller (1608-1661)

4262   Great wits are sure to madness near allied
       And thin partitions do their bounds divide.
                                          Dryden (1631-1700)

4263   Medicine is a science of uncertainty
       and an art of probability.
                                   William Osler (1849-1919)

4264   Before thirty, men seek disease;
       after thirty, disease seeks men.

                                              Chinese Proverb

3. INSIGHT

4265   Misdirected life force is the activity in disease process.
       Disease has no energy save what it borrows from the life
       of the organism. It is by adjusting the life force that
       healing must be brought about, and it is the sun as
       transformer and distributor of primal spiritual energy
       that must be utilized in this process, for life and the
       sun are so intimately connected.
                                 Kabbalah (B.C. 1200?-700? A.D.)

4266   To know that you do not know is the best.
       To pretend to know when you do not know is a disease.
       Only when one recognizes this disease as a disease
       Can one be free from the disease.
       The sage is free from the disease.
       Because he recognized this disease to be disease,
       He is free from it.
                                        Lao-Tzu (fl. B.C. 600)

4267   Medicine is an art, and attends to the nature and
       constitution of the patient, and has principles of action
       and reason in each case.
                                       Plato (B.C. 427?-347?)

4268   Most men are within a finger's breadth of being mad.
                                      Diogenes (B.C. 412-323)

4269   Sickness seizes the body from bad ventilation.
                                       Ovid (B.C. 43-18 A.D.)

4270   Medicine is not only a science; it is also an art. It does
       not consist of compounding pills and plasters; it deals
       with the very processes of life, which must be understood
       before they may be guided.
                                     Paracelsus (1493-1541)

4271   The poets did well to conjoin music and medicine, because
       the office of medicine is but to tune the curious harp of
       man's body.

                                                    Bacon (1561-1626)

4272   In sickness the soul begins to dress herself for
       immortality. And first she unties the strings of vanity
       that make her upper garments cleave to the world and
       sit uneasy.

                                            Jeremy Taylor (1613-1667)

4273   As long as men are liable to die and are desirous to live,
       a physician will be made fun of, but he will be well paid.

                                                La Bruyere (1645-1696)

4274   The canker which the trunk conceals is revealed by the
       leaves, the fruit, or the flower.

                                              Metastasio (1698-1782)

4275   He's the best physician that knows the worthlessness of the
       most medicines.

                                                 Franklin (1706-1790)

4276   It is with disease of the mind, as with those of the body;
       we are half dead before we understand our disorder,
       and half cured when we do.

                                                    Colton (1780-1832)

4277   There can be no excess to love, none to knowledge, none to
       beauty, when these attributes are considered in the purest
       sense.

                                                  Emerson (1803-1882)

4278   A bodily disease which we look upon as whole and entire
       within itself, may, after all, be but a symptom of some
       ailment in the spiritual part.

                                       Nathaniel Hawthorne (1804-1864)

4279   To array a man's will against his sickness is the supreme
       art of medicine.

                                                  Beecher (1813-1878)

4280   Variability is the law of life, and as no two faces are the
       same, so no two bodies are alike, and no two individuals
       react alike and behave alike under the abnormal conditions
       which we know as disease.

                                          William Osler (1849-1919)

4281   The superior doctor prevents sickness;
       The mediocre doctor attends to impending sickness;
       The inferior doctor treats actual sickness.

                                              Chinese Proverb

4. POSITIVE

4282   One gets into situations in life from which it is necessary
       to be a little mad to extricate oneself successfully.
                              La Rochefoucauld (1613-1680)

4283   The feeling of health is acquired only through sickness.
                              Georg Lichtenberg (1742-1799)

4284   I have learned much from disease which life could have never
       taught me anywhere else.
                                        Goethe (1749-1832)

4285   It is in sickness that we most feel the need of that
       sympathy which shows how much we are dependent upon
       one another for our comfort, and even necessities. Thus
       disease, opening our eyes to the realities of life, is an
       indirect blessing.
                                  Hosea Ballou (1771-1852)

4286   A little madness in the Spring
       Is wholesome even for the King.
                              Emily Dickinson (1830-1886)

4287   I reckon being ill as one of the great pleasures of life,
       provided one is not too ill and is not obliged to work
       till one is better.
                              Samuel Butler (1835-1902)

5. NEGATIVE

4288   We cannot employ the mind to advantage when we are filled
       with excessive food and drink.
                                  Cicero (B.C. 106-43)

4289   The body oppressed by excesses, bears down the mind, and
       depresses to the earth any portion of the divine Spirit
       we had been endowed with.
                                    Horace (B.C. 65-8)

4290   All actions beyond the ordinary limits are subject to a
       sinister interpretation.
                                  Montaigne (1533-1592)

4291   Too much noise deafens us; too much light blinds us; too
great a distance, or too much of proximity equally prevents
us from being able to see; too long or too short a discourse
obscures our knowledge of a subject; too much of truth
stuns us.

Pascal (1623-1662)

4292   Doctors prescribe medicine of which they know little
to cure diseases of which they know less
in human beings of which they know nothing.

Voltaire (1694-1778)

4293   The mental disease of the present generation is impatience
of study, contempt of the great masters of ancient wisdom,
and a disposition to rely wholly upon unassisted genius and
natural sagacity.

Johnson (1709-1784)

4294   That dire disease, whose ruthless power
Withers the beauty's transient flower.

Goldsmith (1728-1774)

4295   The excesses of our youth are drafts upon our old age,
payable with interest, about thirty years after the date.

Colton (1780-1832)

4296   Gluttony is the source of all our infirmities and the
fountain of all our diseases. As a lamp is choked by a
superabundance of oil, and a fire extinguished by excess
of fuel, so is the natural health of the body destroyed
by intemperate diet.

Emerson (1803-1882)

4297   Excess always carries its own retribution.

Ouida (1839-1908)

4298   In individuals, insanity is rare, but in groups, parties,
nations and epochs it is the rule.

Nietzsche (1844-1900)

4299   The modern sympathy with invalids is morbid. Illness of any
kind is hardly a thing to be encouraged in others.

Oscar Wilde (1854-1900)

4300   For three things there is no remedy:
  Poverty associated with laziness,
   sickness coupled with old age,
   and enmity mixed with envy.

Chinese Proverb

6. ADVICE

4301   This I consider to be a valuable principle in life:
        Do no thing in excess.

Terence (B.C. 185-159)

4302   The best medicine is the abandonment of desires.

'Ali (600-661 A. D.)

4303   Prevention is better than cure.

Erasmus (1466-1536)

4304   Once a disease has entered the body, all parts which are
        healthy must fight it: not one alone, but all. Because a
        disease might mean their common death. Nature knows this;
        and Nature attacks the disease with whatever help she can
        muster.

Paracelsus (1493-1541)

4305   Against diseases here the strongest fence,
        Is the defensive virtue, abstinence.

Robert Herrick (1591-1674)

4306   The best of all medicines are rest and fasting.

Franklin (1706-1790)

4307   Sickness is a belief, which must be annihilated by the
        divine Mind.

Mary Baker Eddy (1821-1910)

4308   Nine-tenths of our sickness can be prevented by right
        thinking plus right hygiene - nine-tenths of it!
Henry Miller (1891-1980)

4309   To stop drinking...
        Study a drunkard while you are sober.

Chinese Proverb

7. POTPOURRI

4310   Among creatures some lead and some follow.
        Some blow hot and some blow cold.
        Some are strong and some are weak.
        Some may break and some may fall.
        Therefore the sage discards the extremes,
          the extravagant, and the excessive.

Lao-Tzu (fl. B.C. 600)

4311   Extreme remedies are very appropriate for extreme diseases.
Hippocrates (B.C. 460-370)

4312   Lately was Diaulus a doctor, now he is an undertaker,
       What the undertaker now does the doctor too did before.
                                             Martial (43-104 A.D.)

4313   Better to hunt in fields for health unbought,
       Than fee the doctor for a nauseous draught.
       The wise for cure on exercise depend;
       God never made his work for man to mend.
                                             Dryden (1631-1700)

4314   Tell your doctor, that y'are ill
       And what does he, but write a bill,
       Of which you need not read one letter,
       The worse the scrawl, the dose the better.
       For if you knew but what you take,
       Though you recover, he must break.
                                             Matthew Prior (1664-1721)

4315   "Is there no hope?" the sick man said,
       The silent doctor shook his head,
       And took his leave with signs of sorrow,
       Despairing of his fee to-morrow.
                                             Gay (1688-1732)

4316   But nothing is more estimable than a physician who, having
       studied nature from his youth, knows the properties of the
       human body, the diseases which assail it, the remedies which
       will benefit it, exercises his art with caution, and pays
       equal attention to the rich and the poor.
                                             Voltaire (1694-1778)

4317   I know of nothing more laughable than a doctor who does not
       die of old age.
                                             Voltaire (1694-1778)

4318   God heals, and the doctor takes the fee.
                                             Franklin (1706-1790)

4319   The best doctor is the one you run for and can't find.
                                             Denis Diderot (1713-1784)

4320   But when ill indeed,
       Even dismissing the doctor don't always succeed.
                                             George Colman (1762-1836)

4321   Physicians mend or end us;
       but though in health we sneer,
       when sick we call them to attend us,
       without the least propensity to jeer.
                                             Byron (1788-1824)

4322 Some maladies are rich and precious and only to be
acquired by the right of inheritance or purchased
with gold.

Nathaniel Hawthorne (1804-1864)

4323 The universal medicine for the Soul is the Supreme Reason
and Absolute Justice; for the mind, mathematical and
practical Truth; for the body, the Quintessence, a
combination of light and gold.

Albert Pike (1809-1891)

4324 Today I felt pass over me
A breath of wind from the wings of madness.

Baudelaire (1821-1867)

4325 Physician - One upon whom we set our hopes when ill and
our dogs when well.

Ambrose Bierce (1842-1914?)

4326 If the doctor cures, the sun see it;
but if he kills, the earth hides it.

Scottish Proverb

SLEEP
Dreams, Repose, Rest and Unconsciousness

1. ESSENCE

4327   Sleep, the brother of death.

>   Hesiod (B.C. 800?)

4328   Dreams are the wanderings of the spirit though all nine
       heavens and all nine earths.

>   Lu Yen (fl. 800 A.D.)

4329   We are such stuff
          As dreams are made of,
       And our little life
          Is rounded with a sleep.

>   Shakespeare (1564-1616)

4330   All that we see or seem
       Is but a dream within a dream.

>   Edgar Allan Poe (1809-1849)

4331   Dreams are the touchstones of our characters.

>   Thoreau (1817-1862)

2. OPPOSITES

4332   Even as a great fish swims along the two banks of a river,
       first along the eastern bank and then the western bank, in
       the same way the Spirit of man moves along beside his two
       dwellings: this waking world and the land of sleep and
       dreams.

>   Upanishads (c. B.C. 800)

4333   The vigorous are no better than the lazy during one half of
       life, for all men are alike when asleep.

>   Aristotle (B.C. 384-322)

4334   He sleeps well who knows not that he sleeps ill.

>   Publilius Syrus (fl. B.C. 42)

4335   Weariness can snore upon the flint,
       when resty sloth finds the down pillow hard.

>   Shakespeare (1564-1616)

4336   Two gates the silent house of Sleep adorn;
       Of polished ivory this, that of transparent horn:
       True visions through transparent horn arise;
       Through polished ivory pass deluding lies.

>   Dryden (1631-1700)

4337   The bed is a bundle of paradoxes:
        we go to it with reluctance, yet we quit it with regret;
        we make up our minds every night to leave it early,
        but we make up our bodies every morning to keep it late.
                                              Colton (1780-1832)

4338   Our life is two fold: Sleep hath its own world,
        A boundary between the things misnamed
        Death and existence: Sleep hath its own world,
        And a wide realm of wild reality.
                                                Byron (1788-1824)

4339   Sleep - Death without dying - living, but not life.
                                       Edwin Arnold (1832-1904)

4340   I dreamed a thousand new paths...
        I woke and walked my old one.
                                                Chinese Proverb

3. INSIGHT

4341   In dreams the mind beholds its own immensity. What has been
        seen is seen again, and what has been heard is heard again.
        What has been felt in different places or faraway regions
        returns to the mind again. Seen and unseen, heard and
        unheard, felt and not felt, the mind sees all, since the
        mind is all.
                                       Upanishads (c. B.C. 800)

4342   A dream which is not interpreted
        is like a letter which is not read.
                                 The Talmud (B.C. 500?-400? A.D.)

4343   Sleep and deep repose, most like indeed to death's own
        quietness.
                                              Vergil (B.C. 70-19)

4344   Time, motion and wine cause sleep.
                                           Ovid (B.C. 43-18 A.D.)

4345   The eye sees a thing more clearly in dreams
        than the imagination when awake.
                                   Leonardo Da Vinci (1452-1519)

4346   Dreams are the true Interpreters of our Inclinations;
        but there is Art required to sort and understand them.
                                        Montaigne (1533-1592)

4347   Creation sleeps. 'Tis as the general pulse
       Of life stood still, and nature made a pause.

                                          Young (1683-1765)

4348   On every mountain height
       Is rest.

                                          Goethe (1749-1832)

4349   Sleep, riches, and health, are only truly enjoyed after they
       have been interrupted.

                                          Richter (1763-1825)

4350   Dreaming is an act of pure imagination, attesting in all
       men a creative power, which, if it were available in waking,
       would make every man a genius.

                              Frederick Henry Hedge (1805-1890)

4351   Our dreams are as real, while they last, as the occurrences
       of the daytime. We see, hear, feel, act, experience
       pleasure and suffer pain, as vividly and actually in a
       dream as when awake. The occurrences and transactions of a
       year are crowded into the limits of a second: and the dream
       remembered is as real as the past occurrences of life.

                                     Albert Pike (1809-1891)

4352   Without a doubt, consciousness originally arises out of the
       unconscious...It is essential that nothing be taken away
       from the reality of the unconscious and that the figures of
       the unconscious should be understood as active qualities.

                                     C. G. Jung (1875-1961)

4353   The real man lies in the depths of the subconscious.

                                     H. L. Mencken (1880-1956)

4354   Dreams - A microscope through which we look at the hidden
       occurrences in our soul.

                                     Erich Fromm (1900-1980)

4355   ...In dream consciousness...we make things happen by wishing
       them, because we are not only the observer of what we
       experience but also the creator. In our creativity we
       prolong the magic action of the Creator of All in the
       overflow of His imagination, which is all that reality is,
       or ever will be.

                              Pir Vilayat Inayat Khan (born 1916)

4. POSITIVE

4356   The sleep of the body is the sober watchfulness of the
mind and the shutting of my eyes reveals the true Light.
The Divine Pymander (BC 2500?-200 AD?)

4357   There is a Spirit who is awake in our sleep and creates the
wonder of dreams. He is the Spirit of Light, who in truth
is called the Immortal. All the worlds rest on that Spirit
and beyond him no one can go.
Upanishads (c. B.C. 800)

4358   When the soul is in the land of dreams, then all the worlds
belong to the soul. A man can be a great king or even a
wise man and live in conditions high or low. Even as a
great king takes his attendants as he goes about his
dominions, so the soul of man takes the powers of life with
him as he wanders in the land of dreams.
Upanishads (c. B.C. 800)

4359   The sleep of a labouring man is sweet.
Ecclesiastes (B.C. 300?)

4360   O, what is sweeter than when the mind, set free from care,
lays its burden down; and when spent with distant travel,
we come back to our home, and rest our limbs on the
wished-for bed? This, this alone, repays such toils as
these!
Catullus (B.C. 84?-54?)

4361   Sleep, rest of nature, O sleep, most gentle of the
divinities, peace of the soul, thou at whose presence care
disappears, who soothest hearts wearied with daily
employments, and makest them strong again for labour!
Ovid (B.C. 43-18 A.D.)

4362   Blest be...sleep - a cloak to cover all human imaginings,
food to satisfy hunger, water to quench thirst, fire to warm
cold air, cold to temper heat, and, lastly, a coin to buy
whatever we need.
Cervantes (1547-1616)

4363   Come, Sleep: O Sleep! the certain knot of peace,
The baiting place of wit, the balm of woe,
The poor man's wealth, the prisoner's release,
The indifferent judge between the high and low.
Philip Sidney (1554-1586)

4364   Sleep that knits up the ravelled sleeve of care,
        The death of each day's life, sore labour's bath,
        Balm of hurt minds, great nature's second course,
        Chief nourisher in life's feast.

                                    Shakespeare (1564-1616)

4365   Sleep is pain's easiest salve, and doth fulfill all offices
        of death, except to kill.

                                    John Donne (1572-1632)

4366   Sleep is that golden chain that ties health and our bodies
        together.

                                    Thomas Dekker (1577-1632)

4367   For morning dreams, as poets tell, are true.

                                    Michael Bruce (1746-1767)

4368   The long sleep of death closes our scars,
        and the short sleep of life our wounds.
        Sleep is the half of time which heals us.

                                    Richter (1763-1825)

4369   The half hour between waking and rising has all my life
        proved propitious to any task which was exercising my
        invention...It was always when I first opened my eyes that
        the desired ideas thronged upon me.

                                    Walter Scott (1771-1832)

4370   Sleep, to the homeless thou art home;
        the friendless find in thee a friend.

                                    Ebenezer Elliott (1781-1849)

4371   It is a delicious moment, certainly, that of being well
        nestled in bed, and feeling that you shall drop gently to
        sleep. The good is to come, not past...

                                    Leigh Hunt (1784-1859)

4372   Dreams are excursions into the limbo of things,
        a semi-deliverance from the human prison.

                                    Henri Frederic Amiel (1821-1881)

4373   There is more refreshment and stimulation in a nap, even of
        the briefest, than in all the alcohol ever distilled.

                                    Edward Lucas (1868-1938)

5. NEGATIVE

4374   How long will you lie there, O sluggard?
          When will you arise from your sleep?
        A little sleep, a little slumber,

a little folding of the hands to rest,
and poverty will come upon you like a vagabond,
and want like an armed man.

> Proverbs (B.C. 1000?-200?)

4375   Too much rest itself becomes a pain.

> Homer (c. B.C. 700)

4376   Fool, what is sleep but the likeness of icy death?
The fates shall give us a long period of rest.

> Ovid (B.C. 43-18 A.D.)

4377   Dreams are mere productions of the brain,
And fools consult interpreters in vain.

> Swift (1667-1745)

4378   What probing deep
Has ever solved the mystery of sleep?

> Thomas Bailey Aldrich (1836-1907)

4379   Obviously one must hold oneself responsible for the evil
impulses of one's dreams. In what other way can one deal
with them? Unless the content of the dream rightly
understood is inspired by alien spirits, it is part of my
own being.

> Sigmund Freud (1856-1939)

4380   Sleep is perverse as human nature,
Sleep is perverse as a legislature,
Sleep is as forward as hives or goiters,
And where it is least desired, it loiters.

> Ogden Nash (1902-1971)

6. ADVICE

4381   One should rest when it is time to rest and act when it is
time to act. True resting and putting to rest are attained
through the disappearance of the ego, which leads to the
harmony of one's behavior with the laws of the universe.
Resting in principle involves doing that which is right
in every position in which one is placed.

> I Ching (B.C. 1150?)

4382   Take rest; a field that has rested gives a bountiful crop.

> Ovid (B.C. 43-18 A.D.)

4383   A man who values a good night's rest will not lie down with
enmity in his heart, if he can help it.

> Sterne (1713-1768)

4384   Sleep is the interest we have to pay on the capital which is
called in at death; and the higher the rate of interest and
the more regularly it is paid, the further the date of
redemption is postponed.

Schopenhauer (1788-1860)

4385   We cannot always secure sleep. When important decisions
have to be taken, the natural anxiety to come to a right
decision will often keep us awake. Nothing, however, is
more conducive to healthy sleep than plenty of open air.

Lubbock (1834-1913)

4386   It takes a person who is wide awake to make his dream come
true.

Roger Babson (1875-1967)

4387   Try to enjoy the sleepless sleep wherein all the senses and
mind remain in a state of quietude and the intellect ceases
functioning. The sleepless sleep is a super-conscious
state. It is perfect awareness wherein the individual soul
has merged itself into the Supreme Soul. There is no waking
from this sleep.

Sivananda (born 1887)

7. POTPOURRI

4388   When a man is asleep his soul takes the consciousness of the
several senses and goes to rest with them on the Supreme
Spirit who is in the human heart. When all the senses are
quiet the man is said to be asleep. The soul holds the
powers of life - breath, voice, eye, ear, and mind - and
they rest in quietness.

Upanishads (c. B.C. 800)

4389   The eye of man hath not heard, the ear of man hath not seen,
man's hand is not able to taste, his tongue to conceive,
nor his heart to report, what my dream was.

Shakespeare (1564-1616)

4390   Sleep is a death, O make me try,
By sleeping, what it is to die:
And as gently lay my head
On my grave, as now my bed.

Thomas Browne (1605-1682)

4391   Dreams are but interludes, which fancy makes;
When monarch reason sleeps, this mimic wakes.

Dryden (1631-1700)

4392   To all, to each, a fair good-night,
And pleasing dreams, and slumbers light.

Walter Scott (1771-1832)

4393   Visit her, gentle Sleep! with wings of healing,
And may this storm be but a mountain-birth,
May all the stars hang bright above her dwelling,
Silent as though they watched the sleeping Earth!

Samuel Coleridge (1772-1834)

4394   O magic sleep! O comfortable bird,
That broodest o'er the troubled sea of the mind
Till it is hush'd and smooth! O unconfined
Restraint! imprisoned liberty! great key
To golden palaces.

Keats (1795-1821)

4395   Deep into that darkness peering, long I stood there
   wondering, fearing,
Doubting, dreaming dreams no mortal ever dared
   to dream before.

Edgar Allan Poe (1809-1849)

4396   So nature deals with us, and takes away
  Our playthings one by one, and by the hand
   Leads us to rest so gently, that we go,
Scarce knowing if we wish to go or stay,
  Being too full of sleep to understand
   How far the unknown transcends the what we know.

Longfellow (1807-1882)

4397   When to soft Sleep we give ourselves away,
And in a dream as in a fairy bark
Drift on and on through the enchanted dark
To purple daybreak - little thought we pay
To that sweet bitter world we know by day.

Thomas Bailey Aldrich (1836-1907)

4398   All gifts but one the jealous God may keep
From our soul's longing, one he cannot - sleep.
This, though he grudge all other grace to prayer,
This grace his closed hand cannot choose but spare.

Swinburne (1837-1909)

4399   We are the music makers,
  We are the dreamers of dreams,
Wandering by lone sea-breakers,

And sitting by desolate streams-
World-losers and world-forsakers.
On whom the pale moon gleams.
                                    Arthur O'Shaughnessy (1844-1881)

4400   The chambers in the house of dreams
          Are fed with so divine an air,
       That Time's hoary wings grow young therein,
          And they who walk there are most fair.
                                    Francis Thompson (1859-1907)

4401   A thousand creeds and battle cries,
          A thousand warring social schemes,
       A thousand new moralities
          And twenty thousand, thousand dreams.
                                    Alfred Noyes (1880-1958)

4402   If, my dear, you seek to slumber,
       Count of stars an endless number;
       If you still continue wakeful,
       Count the drops that make a lakeful;
       Then, if vigilance yet above you
       Hover, count the times I love you;
       And if slumber still repel you,
       Count the times I do not tell you.
                                    Franklin P. Adams (1881-1960)

4403   Sleep lay upon the wilderness, it lay across the faces of
       nations, it lay like silence on the hearts of sleeping men;
       and low upon lowlands and high upon hills, flowed gently
       sleep, smooth-sliding sleep - sleep - sleep.
                                    Thomas Wolfe (1900-1938)

SORROW

Grief, Melancholy, Sadness and Tears

1. ESSENCE

4404   Tears are the noble language of the eye.
> Robert Herrick (1591-1674)

4405   Tears are the silent language of grief.
> Voltaire (1694-1778)

4406   Melancholy is the pleasure of being sad.
> Victor Hugo (1802-1885)

4407   Sorrow is a form of self-pity.
> John F. Kennedy (1917-1963)

2. OPPOSITES

4408   As joy is not without its alloy of pain,
so neither is sorrow without its portion of pleasure.
> Akhenaton? (c. B.C. 1375)

4409   Let no man ever cleave to things that are pleasant
   or to those that are unpleasant.
Not to see what is pleasant is pain,
   and it is pain to see what is unpleasant.
> The Dhammapada (c. B.C. 300)

4410   The sorrowful dislike the gay, and the gay the sorrowful.
> Horace (B.C. 65-8)

4411   Our days and nights
Have sorrows woven with delights.
> Francois De Malherbe (1555-1628)

4412   Moderate lamentation is the right of the dead;
excessive grief the enemy of the living.
> Shakespeare (1564-1616)

4413   If our inward griefs were seen written on our brow,
how many would be pitied who are now envied!
> Metastasio (1698-1782)

4414   Sorrow never comes too late,
And happiness too swiftly flies.
> Thomas Gray (1716-1771)

4415   Alas! sorrow from happiness is oft evolved.
> Goethe (1749-1832)

4416   Grief is a stone that bears one down,
       but two bear it lightly.

                            Wilhelm Hauff (1802-1825)

4417   We weep when we are born,
       Not when we die!

                    Thomas Bailey Aldrich (1836-1907)

3. INSIGHT

4418   What is the source of sadness, but feebleness of the mind?
       what giveth it power but the want of reason? Rouse thyself
       to the combat, and she quitteth the field before thou
       strikest.

                            Akhenaton? (c. B.C. 1375)

4419   Grief, like a tree, has tears for its fruit.

                            Philemon (B.C. 361-262)

4420   'All is transient.' When one sees this, he is above sorrow.
          This is the clear path.
       'All is sorrow.' When one sees this, he is above sorrow.
          This is the clear path.
       'All is unreal.' When one sees this he is above sorrow.
          This is the clear path.

                     The Dhammapada (c. B.C. 300)

4421   No grief is so acute but that time ameliorates it.

                            Cicero (B.C. 106-43)

4422   Tears are sometimes as weighty as words.

                            Ovid (B.C. 43-18 A.D.)

4423   That grief is light which can take counsel.

                            Seneca (B.C. 3-65 A.D.)

4424   For a man who is contented with little,
       Wealth is inexhaustible.
       He who continually seeks and is never satisfied
       Will experience a constant rain of sorrow.

                        Saskya Pandita (1182-1251)

4425   Our sorrows are like thunder-clouds, which seem black in
       the distance, but grow lighter as they approach.

                            Richter (1763-1825)

4426   We pamper little griefs into great ones,
       and bear great ones as well as we can.

                            Hazlitt (1778-1830)

4427   Earth hath no sorrow that heaven cannot heal.
                          Thomas Moore (1779-1852)

4428   In youth, grief comes with a rush and overflow,
but it dries up, too, like a torrent.
In the winter of life it remains a miserable pool,
resisting all evaporation.
                      Anne Swetchine (1782-1857)

4429   They truly mourn that mourn without a witness.
                              Byron (1788-1824)

4430   There are people who have an appetite for grief;
pleasure is not strong enough and they crave pain.
                      Emerson (1803-1882)

4431   Of all the portions of life it is in the two twilights,
childhood and age, that tears fall with the most
frequency; like the dew at dawn and eve.
                  William R. Alger (1822-1905)

4. POSITIVE

4432   Reflection is the business of man; a sense of his state is
his first duty: but who remembereth himself in joy?
Is it not in mercy then that sorrow is allotted unto us?
                 Akhenaton? (c. B.C. 1375)

4433   There is something pleasurable in calm remembrance of a past
sorrow.
                           Cicero (B.C. 106-43)

4434   The liquid drops of tears that you have shed
Shall come again, transform'd to orient pearl,
Advantaging their loan with interest
Of ten times double gain of happiness.
                    Shakespeare (1564-1616)

4435   The path of sorrow, and that path alone,
leads to the land where sorrow is unknown;
no traveller ever reached that blessed abode
who found not thorns and briars in his road.
                     Cowper (1731-1800)

4436   Sorrow seems sent for our instruction, as we darken the
cages of birds when we would teach them to sing.
                     Richter (1763-1825)

4437   Tears are the softening showers which cause the seed of
heaven to spring up in the human heart.
                   Walter Scott (1771-1832)

4438   Tears hinder sorrow from becoming despair.

                                   Leigh Hunt (1784-1859)

4439   So bright the tear in Beauty's eye,
        Love half regrets to kiss it dry.

                                   Byron (1788-1824)

4440   Grief knits two hearts in closer bonds than happiness ever
        can; and common sufferings are far stronger links than
        common joys.

                 Alphonse de Lamartine (1790-1869)

4441   Man's unhappiness comes of his greatness; it is because
        there is an infinite in him, which, with all his cunning,
        he cannot quite bury under the finite.

                              Carlyle (1795-1881)

4442   There is a joy in sorrow which none but a mourner can know.

                             Tupper (1810-1889)

4443   Night brings out stars as sorrow shows us truths.

                               Bailey (1816-1902)

4444   The soul would have no rainbow had the eyes no tears.
                     John Vance Cheney (1848-1922)

5. NEGATIVE

4445   Be not deceived with fair pretences, nor suppose that sorrow
        healeth misfortune. It is a poison under the colour of a
        remedy; while it pretendeth to draw the arrow from thy
        breast, lo, it plungeth it into thine heart.

                    Akhenaton? (c. B.C. 1375)

4446   Grief tears his heart, and drives him to and fro,
        In all the raging impotence of woe.

                        Homer (c. B.C. 700)

4447   Excess of grief for the deceased is madness; for it is an
        injury to the living, and the dead know it not.
                     Xenophon (B.C. 430-355)

4448   Suppressed grief suffocates, it rages within the breast,
        and is forced to multiply its strength.

                    Ovid (B.C. 43-18 A.D.)

4449   Great grief does not of itself put an end to itself.
                   Seneca (B.C. 3-65 A.D.)

4450   There is no greater grief than to remember days of joy when
        misery is at hand.

                                                    Dante (1265-1321)

4451   Short time seems long in sorrow's sharp sustaining;
        though woe be heavy, yet it seldom sleeps,
        and they who watch, see time how slow it creeps.
                                            Shakespeare (1564-1616)

4452   The most unhappy of all men is he who believes himself
        to be so.
                                            David Hume (1711-1776)

4453   The person who grieves suffers his passion to grow upon him;
        he indulges it, he loves it; but this never happens in the
        case of actual pain, which no man ever willingly endured for
        any considerable time.
                                                    Burke (1729-1797)

4454   It is dangerous to abandon one's self to the luxury of
        grief; it deprives one of courage and even of the wish
        for recovery.
                                    Henri Frederic Amiel (1821-1881)

4455   Two barrels of tears do not heal a bruise.
                                                    Chinese Proverb

6. ADVICE

4456   Grief is natural to the mortal world, and is always about
        thee; pleasure is a guest, and visiteth thee but by thy
        invitation; use well thy mind, and sorrow shall be passed
        behind thee; be prudent, and the visits of joy shall remain
        long with thee.
                                            Akhenaton? (c. B.C. 1375)

4457   Do not vainly lament, but do wonder at the rule of
        transiency and learn from it the emptiness of human
        life. Do not cherish to unworthy desire that the
        changeable might become unchanging.
                                            Buddha (B.C. 568-488)

4458   We should feel sorrow, but not sink under its oppression.
                                            Confucius (B.C. 551-479)

4459   It is some relief to weep;
        grief is satisfied and carried off by tears.
                                            Ovid (B.C. 43-18 A.D.)

4460 If you wish to live a life free from sorrow, think of what
is going to happen as if it had already happened.

Epictetus (50-138 A.D.)

4461 Past sorrows, let us moderately lament them;
For those to come, seek wisely to prevent them.

John Webster (1580?-1634)

4462 Sorrow's best antidote is employment.

Young (1683-1765)

4463 Hide not thy tears; weep boldly, and be proud to give the
flowing virtue manly way; it is nature's mark to know an
honest heart by.

Aaron Hill (1685-1750)

4464 Sorrow is a kind of rust of the soul which every new idea
contributes in its passage to scour away. It is the
putrefaction of stagnant life, and is remedied by exercise
and motion.

Johnson (1709-1784)

4465 If grief is to be mitigated, it must either wear itself out
or be shared.

Anne Swetchine (1782-1857)

4466 If you are melancholy for the first time,
you will find, upon a little inquiry,
that others have been melancholy many times,
and yet are cheerful now.

Leigh Hunt (1784-1859)

4467 Be still, sad heart! and cease repining;
Behind the clouds is the sun still shining;
Thy fate is the common fate of all,
Into each life some rain must fall,
Some days must be dark and dreary.

Longfellow (1807-1882)

4468 Sadness is not an evil. Complain not; what seem to be
sufferings and obstacles are often in reality the mysterious
efforts of nature to help you in your work if you can manage
them properly. Look upon all circumstances with the
gratitude of a pupil. All complaint is a rebellion against
the law of progress.

H. P. Blavatsky (1831-1891)

7. POTPOURRI

4469   Sorrow is invited frequently, pleasure rarely; pain cometh
        of itself, delight must be purchased; grief is unmixed, but
        joy wanteth not its alloy of bitterness. As the soundest
        health is less perceived than the lightest malady, so the
        highest joy toucheth us less deep than the smallest sorrow.
                                        Akhenaton? (c. B.C. 1375)

4470   The deeper the sorrow the less tongue it hath.
                                        The Talmud (B.C. 500?-400? A.D.)

4471   All created beings are unmanifest in their beginning,
        manifest in their interim state, and unmanifest again
        when they are annihilated. So what need is there for
        lamentation?
                                        Bhagavad Gita (c. B.C. 400)

4472   Nothing dries sooner than a tear.
                                        Cicero (B.C. 106-43)

4473   When sorrows come, they come not single spies,
        But in battalions.
                                        Shakespeare (1564-1616)

4474   Weep no more, nor sigh, nor groan,
        Sorrow calls no time that's gone:
        Violets plucked the sweetest rain
        Makes not fresh nor grow again.
                                        John Fletcher (1579-1625)

4475   Words that weep and tears that speak.
                                        Abraham Cowley (1618-1667)

4476   Man alone is born crying, lives complaining, and dies
        disappointed.
                                        William Temple (1628-1699)

4477   The storm of grief bears hard upon his youth,
        And bends him like a drooping flower to earth.
                                        Nicholas Rowe (1674-1718)

4478   Child of mortality, whence comest thou? Why is thy
        countenance sad, and why are thine eyes red with weeping?
                                        Anna Barbauld (1743-1825)

4479   Who never ate his bread in sorrow,
          Who never spent the darksome hours
        Weeping, and watching for the morrow,-
          He knows ye not, ye gloomy Powers.
                                        Goethe (1749-1832)

4480   Sorrows gather around great souls as storms do around
mountains; but, like them, they break the storm and
purify the air of the plain beneath them.

Richter (1763-1825)

4481   Day-thoughts feed nightly dreams;
And sorrow tracketh wrong,
As echo follows song.

Harriet Martineau (1802-1876)

4482   Two aged men, that had been foes for life,
  Met by a grave, and wept - and in those tears
They washed away the memory of their strife;
  Then wept again the loss of all those years.

Frederick Tennyson (1807-1898)

4483   Tears, idle tears, I know not what they mean,
Tears from the depths of some divine despair.

Alfred Tennyson (1809-1892)

4484   Tell me, ye winged winds
  That round my pathway roar,
Know ye not some spot
  Where mortals weep no more?

Charles Mackay (1814-1889)

4485   When I was young, I said to Sorrow,
"Come and I will play with thee!"
He is near me now all day,
And at night returns to say,
"I will come again to-morrow,
I will come and stay with thee."

Aubrey De Vere (1814-1902)

4486   A feeling of sadness and longing, that is not akin to pain,
and resembles sorrow only as the mist resembles the rain.

Longfellow (1807-1882)

4487   Each time we love,
We turn nearer and a broader mark
To that keen archer, Sorrow, and he strikes.

Alexander Smith (1830-1867)

4488   Never a tear bedims the eye
That time and patience will not dry.

Bret Harte (1836-1902)

SOUL
Spirit and Immortality

1. ESSENCE

4489   The Soul is made of consciousness and mind; it is made of
life and vision. It is made of the earth and the waters; it
is made of air and space. It is made of light and darkness;
it is made of desire and peace. It is made of anger and
love; it is made of virtue and vice. It is made of all that
is near; it is made of all that is afar. It is made of all.

                                              Upanishads (c. B.C. 800)

4490   Soul - Something in us that can be without us and will be
after us.

                                       Thomas Browne (1605-1682)

4491   Vital spark of heav'nly flame!

                                       Pope (1688-1744)

4492   Everything here, but the soul of man, is a passing shadow.
The only enduring substance is within.

                                      Channing (1780-1842)

4493   The production of souls is the secret of unfathomable
depth.

                                      Victor Hugo (1802-1885)

4494   Spirit is living, and Life is Spirit, and Life and Spirit
produce all things, but they are essentially one and not
two...

                                  H. P. Blavatsky (1831-1891)

2. OPPOSITES

4495   Doth not the sun harden the clay? Doth it not also soften
the wax? As it is one sun that worketh both, even so it is
one Soul that willeth contrarieties.

                                  Akhenaton? (c. B.C. 1375)

4496   The disembodied spirit is immortal; there is nothing of it
that can grow old or die. But the embodied spirit sees
death on the horizon as soon as its day dawns.

                             Kabbalah (B.C. 1200?-700? A.D.)

4497   The all knowing Self was never born, nor will it die.
Beyond cause and effect, this self is eternal and immutable.
When the body dies, the Self does not die.
If the slayer believes that he can kill,
And the slain believes that he can be killed,
Neither knows the truth.
The eternal Self slays not, nor is ever slain.

                                        Upanishads (c. B.C. 800)

4498   Just as the soul fills the body, so God fills the world.
Just as the soul bears the body, so God endures the world.
Just as the soul sees but is not seen,
  so God sees but is not seen.
Just as the soul feeds the body,
  so God gives food to the world.

                          The Talmud (B.C. 500?-400? A.D.)

4499   I am the resurrection and the life;
he who believes in me, though he die, yet shall he live,
and whoever lives and believes in me shall never die.

                              Jesus (B.C. 6?-30? A.D.)

4500   What springs from earth dissolves to earth again,
and heaven-born things fly to their native seat.

                        Marcus Aurelius (121-180 A.D.)

4501   The soul is created in a place between Time and Eternity:
with its highest powers it touches Eternity,
with its lower Time.

                           Meister Eckhart (1260-1327)

4502   There is nothing strictly immortal, but immortality.
Whatever hath no beginning may be confident of no end.

                         Thomas Browne (1605-1682)

4503   Can it be? matter immortal? and shall spirit die?
above the nobler, shall less nobler rise?
shall man alone, for whom all else revives,
no resurrection know? shall man alone,
imperial man! be sown in barren ground,
less privileged than grain, on which he feeds?

                                Young (1683-1765)

4504   Everywhere the human soul stands between a hemisphere of
light and another of darkness; on the confines of two
everlasting hostile empires, Necessity and Freewill.

                              Carlyle (1795-1881)

4505   From the doctrine of the two Principles, Active and Passive,
       grew that of the Universe, animated by a Principle of
       Eternal Life, and by a Universal Soul, from which every
       isolated and temporary being received at its birth an
       emanation, which, at the death of such being, returned to
       its source.

                                        Albert Pike (1809-1891)

4506   Spirit is the real and eternal;
       matter is unreal and material.

                                   Mary Baker Eddy (1821-1910)

4507   For I never have seen, and never shall see,
       that the cessation of the evidence of existence
       is necessarily evidence of the cessation of existence.

                                        De Morgan (1839-1917)

4508   The Soul is born old, but it grows young;
          that is the comedy of life.
       The Body is born young and grows old;
          that is life's tragedy.

                                     Oscar Wilde (1854-1900)

4509   The Seer is the unchanging, non-dual unity or Soul.
       The seen is the changing, visible universe and the mind.

                                     Sivananda (born 1887)

3. INSIGHT

4510   Spirit is the first differentiation of SPACE; and Matter
       the first differentiation of Spirit. That, which is neither
       Spirit nor matter -that is IT- the Causeless CAUSE of Spirit
       and Matter, which are the Cause of Cosmos. And THAT we call
       the ONE LIFE or the Intra-Cosmic Breath.

                                     Book of Dzyan (B.C. 3000?)

4511   Something is added to thee unlike to what thou seest; some-
       thing animates thy clay higher than all that is the object
       of thy senses. Behold, what is it? Thy body remaineth
       perfect matter after IT is fled, therefore IT is no part of
       it; IT is immaterial, therefore IT is eternal: IT is free
       to act; therefore IT is accountable for its actions.

                                     Akhenaton? (c. B.C. 1375)

4512   The Spirit, without moving, is swifter than the mind;
       the senses cannot reach him: He is ever beyond them.
       Standing still, he overtakes those who run. To the ocean of
       his being, the spirit of life leads the streams of action.

                                     Upanishads (c. B.C. 800)

4513   As the same fire assumes different shapes
       When it consumes objects differing in shape,
       So does the one Self take the shape
       Of every creature in whom he is present.
                                    Upanishads (c. B.C. 800)

4514   'Tis true; 'tis certain; man though dead retains
       Part of himself; the immortal mind remains.
                                         Homer (c. B.C. 700)

4515   All men's souls are immortal,
       but the souls of the righteous are immortal and divine.
                                     Socrates (B.C. 469-399)

4516   The human soul develops up to death.
                                 Hippocrates (B.C. 460-370)

4517   We all have been for all time...and we shall be for all
       time...As the Spirit of our mortal body wanders on in
       childhood, and youth and old age, the Spirit wanders on to
       a new body: of this the sage has no doubts.
                              Bhagavad Gita (c. B.C. 400)

4518   Whatsoever that be within us that feels, thinks, desires,
       and animates, is something celestial, divine, and,
       consequently, imperishable.
                                  Aristotle (B.C. 384-322)

4519   The countenance is the portrait of the soul,
       and the eyes mark its intentions.
                                     Cicero (B.C. 106-43)

4520   All souls must undergo transmigration and the souls of men
       revolve like a stone which is thrown from a sling, so many
       turns before the final release...Only those who have not
       completed their perfection must suffer the wheel of rebirth
       by being reborn into another human body.
                                 Zohar (120?-1200? A.D.)

4521   There is spirit in the soul, untouched by time and flesh,
       flowing from the Spirit, remaining in the Spirit, itself
       wholly spiritual. In this principle is God, ever verdant,
       ever flowering in all the joy and glory of His actual Self.
                              Meister Eckhart (1260-1327)

4522   The soul is a veiled light. This light is triple:
       the pure spirit, the soul or spirit, and the mutable
       mediator. The veil of the soul is the shell of the
       image. The image is double because it reflects a
       light - the good and the evil angel of the soul...
                              Moses Cordouero (1522-1570)

4523 Yet stab at thee who will,
No stab the soul can kill!

Walter Raleigh (1552-1618)

4524 The spirit of man communes with Heaven;
the omnipotence of Heaven resides in man.
Is the distance between Heaven and man very great?

Hung Tzu-ch'eng (1593-1665)

4525 The soul is a fire that darts its rays through all the
senses; it is in this fire that existence consists; all
the observations and all the efforts of philosophers ought
to turn towards this ME, the centre and moving power of our
sentiments and our ideas.

Germaine De Stael (1766-1817)

4526 We are much better believers in immortality than we can
give grounds for. The real evidence is too subtle, or
is higher than we can write down in propositions.

Emerson (1803-1882)

4527 Man only of all earthly creatures, asks, "Can the dead die
forever?" - and the instinct that urges the question is
God's answer to man, for no instinct is given in vain.

Bulwer-Lytton (1803-1873)

4528 The human soul is like a bird that is born in a cage.
Nothing can deprive it of its natural longings, or
obliterate the mysterious remembrance of its heritage.

Epes Sargent (1813-1880)

4529 If thy Soul smiles while bathing in the Sunlight of thy
Life; if thy Soul sings within her chrysalis of flesh and
matter; if thy Soul weeps inside her castle of illusion;
if thy Soul struggles to break the silver thread that
binds her to the MASTER; know that thy Soul is of the earth.

H. P. Blavatsky (1831-1891)

4530 Fire is the most perfect and unadulterated reflection,
in Heaven as on Earth, of the ONE FLAME.
It is Life and Death, the origin and the end of every
material thing. It is divine "Substance."

H. P. Blavatsky (1831-1891)

4531 Our hope of immortality does not come from any religions,
but nearly all religions come from that hope.

Robert G. Ingersoll (1833-1899)

4. POSITIVE

4532   As the moon retaineth her nature, though darkness spread
        itself before her face as a curtain, so the Soul remaineth
        perfect even in the bosom of the fool.

                                    Akhenaton? (c. B.C. 1375)

4533   The Spirit filled all with his radiance. He is incorporeal
        and invulnerable, pure and untouched by evil. He is the
        supreme seer and thinker, immanent and transcendent. He
        placed all things in the path of the Eternal.

                                    Upanishads (c. B.C. 800)

4534   As the sun that beholds the world
            is untouched by earthly impurities,
        so the Spirit that is in all things
            is untouched by external sufferings.

                                    Upanishads (c. B.C. 800)

4535   There is a god within us, and we have intercourse with
        heaven. That spirit comes from abodes on high.

                                    Ovid (B.C. 43-18 A.D.)

4536   The soul has this proof of its divinity:
        that divine things delight in it.

                                    Seneca (B.C. 3-65 A.D.)

4537   'And God created man in His image.'
        It is this image which receives us first when we come
        into this World, it develops with us while we grow and
        accompanies us when we leave the earth. Its source is
        in heaven.

                                    Zohar (120?-1200? A.D.)

4538   'Tis immortality, 'tis that alone,
        Amid life's pains, abasements, emptiness,
        The soul can comfort, elevate, and fill.
        That only, and that amply this performs.

                                    Young (1683-1765)

4539   The soul is indestructible and its activity will continue
        through eternity. It is like the sun, which, to our eyes,
        seems to set at night; but it has in reality only gone to
        diffuse its light elsewhere.

                                    Goethe (1749-1832)

4540   Our dissatisfaction with any other solution is the blazing
        evidence of immortality.

                                    Emerson (1803-1882)

4541 The one thing in the world, of value, is the active soul.
Emerson (1803-1882)

4542 There are souls in this world which have the gift of finding
joy everywhere and of leaving it behind them when they go.
Frederick Faber (1814-1863)

4543 The soul is, of course, the noblest part of man.
Lubbock (1834-1913)

5. NEGATIVE

4544 As a draft-animal is yoked in a wagon,
even so the spirit is yoked in this body.
Upanishads (c. B.C. 800)

4545 This world is indeed in darkness,
and how few can see the light!
Just as few birds can escape from a net,
few souls can fly into the freedom of heaven.
The Dhammapada (c. B.C. 300)

4546 The want of goods is easily repaired,
but the poverty of the soul is irreparable.
Montaigne (1533-1592)

4547 Four thousand volumes of metaphysics will not teach us what
the soul is.
Voltaire (1694-1778)

4548 There are souls which fall from heaven like flowers, but
ere they bloom are crushed under the foul tread of some
brutal hoof.
Richter (1763-1825)

4549 To desire immortality is to desire the eternal perpetuation
of a great mistake.
Schopenhauer (1788-1860)

4550 My mind is incapable of conceiving such a thing as a soul.
I may be in error, and man may have a soul;
but I simply do not believe it.
Thomas A. Edison (1847-1931)

4551 Neither can I believe that the individual survives the death
of his body, although feeble souls harbor such thoughts
through fear or ridiculous egotism.
Einstein (1879-1955)

6. ADVICE

4552   Thinking, understanding, reasoning, willing, call not these
        Soul! They are its actions, but they are not its essence.
                                        Akhenaton? (c. B.C. 1375)

4553   The Spirit is beyond sound and form, without touch and taste
        and perfume. It is eternal, unchangeable, and without
        beginning or end; indeed above reasoning. When
        consciousness of the Spirit manifests itself,
        man becomes free from the jaws of death.
                                        Upanishads (c. B.C. 800)

4554   Know that which pervades the entire body is indestructible.
        No one is able to destroy the imperishable soul.
                                        Bhagavad Gita (c. B.C. 400)

4555   Do not think that man is but flesh, skin, bones and veins;
        far from it! What really makes man is his soul; and the
        things we call skin, flesh, bones and veins are but a
        garment, a cloak; they do not constitute man. When man
        departs this earth, he divests himself of all the veils that
        conceal him.
                                        Zohar (120?-1200? A.D.)

4556   One should leave a single person for the sake of a family;
        for the sake of a village he should abandon a family;
        a village he should renounce for the sake of a country,
        and for the sake of his soul, the earth.
                                        The Hitopadesa (600?-1100? A.D.)

4557   The spirit is smothered, as it were, by ignorance, but
        so soon as ignorance is destroyed, spirit shine forth,
        like the sun when released from clouds.
                                        Sankara (c. 900 A.D.)

4558   I pity men who occupy themselves exclusively with the
        transitory in things and lose themselves in the study of
        what is perishable, since we are here for this very end-
        that we may make the perishable imperishable, which we can
        do only after we have learned how to approach both.
                                        Goethe (1749-1832)

4559   He ne'er is crowned with immortality
        Who fears to follow where airy voices lead.
                                        Keats (1795-1821)

7. POTPOURRI

4560   As the tempest and the thunder affect not the sun or the
stars, but spend their fury on stones and trees below;
so injuries ascend not to the Soul of the great, but waste
themselves on such as are those who offer them.

Akhenaton? (c. B.C. 1375)

4561   The Spirit of the Eternal shot out of his Body like a sheet
of lightning that radiated at once on the billows of the
Seven millions of skies, and my ten splendours were his
limbs.

Zohar (120?-1200? A.D.)

4562   By the Heaven and Him who built it,
by the earth and Him who leveled it,
by the soul and Him who perfected it,
then He taught it the ways of its ruin,
and the way of its safety.

Koran (c. 651 A.D.)

4563   In consequence of possessing diverse attributes, the
Supreme Existence appears manifold, but when the attributes
are annihilated, unity is restored.
In consequence of those diverse attributes, a variety of
names and conditions are supposed proper to the spirit, just
as a variety of tastes and colours are attributed to water.

Sankara (c. 900 A.D.)

4564   I sent my Soul through the Invisible,
Some letter of that After-life spell,
And by and by my Soul returned to me,
And answered "I Myself am Heaven and Hell."

Omar Khayyam (fl. 1100)

4565   Souls perfected on this earth pass on to another station.
After traversing the planets they come to the sun;
they ascend into another universe and recommence their
planetary evolution from world to world and from sun to sun.
In the suns they remember, and in the planets they forget.
The solar lives are the days of eternal life,
and the planetary lives are the nights with their dreams.

Moses Cordouero (1522-1570)

4566   The stars shall fade away, the sun himself
Grow dim with age, and nature sink in years,
But thou shalt flourish in immortal youth,
Unhurt amidst the wars of elements,
The wrecks of matter, and the crush of worlds.

Addison (1672-1719)

4567   Still seems it strange, that thou shouldst live forever?
Is it less strange, that thou shouldst live at all?
This is a miracle; and that no more.

Young (1683-1765)

4568   The soul, uneasy and confined from home,
Rests and expatiates in a life to come.

Pope (1688-1744)

4569   Awake, my soul! stretch every nerve,
  And press with vigour on;
A heavenly race demands thy zeal,
  And an immortal crown.

Philip Doddridge (1702-1751)

4570   I reflected how soon in the cup of desire
  The pearl of the soul may be melted away;
How quickly, alas, the pure sparkle of fire
  We inherit from heaven, may be quenched in the clay.

Thomas Moore (1779-1852)

4571   For the sword outwears its sheath,
And the soul wears out the breast.

Byron (1788-1824)

4572   I feel my immortality oversweep all pains, all tears, all
time, all fears, - and peal, like the eternal thunders of
the deep, into my ears, this truth, - thou livest forever!

Byron (1788-1824)

4573   The soul of man is larger than the sky,
Deeper than ocean, or the abysmal dark
Of the unfathomed centre.

Hartley Coleridge (1796-1849)

4574   We are born for a higher destiny than that of earth.
There is a realm where the rainbow never fades, where
the stars will spread out before us like islands that
slumber on the ocean, and where the beings that pass
before us like shadows, will stay in our presence forever.

Bulwer-Lytton (1803-1873)

4575   Surely God would not have created such a being as man, with
an ability to grasp the infinite, to exist only for a day!
No, no, man was made for immortality.

Lincoln (1809-1865)

4576   Life is the soul's nursery - its training place for the
destinies of eternity.

Thackeray (1811-1863)

4577   Ah, the souls of those that die
      Are but sunbeams lifted higher.

Longfellow (1807-1882)

4578   No, no! The energy of life may be
      Kept on after the grave, but not begun;
      And he who flagg'd not in the earthly strife,
      From strength to strength advancing - only he
      His soul well-knit, and all his battles won,
      Mounts, and that hardly, to eternal life.

Matthew Arnold (1822-1888)

4579   The monuments of the nations are all protests against
      nothingness after death; so are statues and inscriptions;
      so is history.

Lew Wallace (1827-1905)

4580   Immortality - A toy which people cry for,
      And on their knees apply for,
      Dispute, contend and lie for,
        And if allowed
        Would be right proud
      Eternally to die for.

Ambrose Bierce (1842-1914?)

SOUND

Music, Speech and Voice - Eloquence and Song

1. ESSENCE

4581   The voice is nothing but beaten air.
                                    Seneca (B.C. 3-65 A.D.)

4582   Music is nothing else but wild sounds civilized into time
        and tune.
                                    Thomas Fuller (1608-1661)

4583   Eloquence is a painting of the thoughts.
                                    Pascal (1623-1662)

4584   Music is the poetry of the air.
                                    Richter (1763-1825)

4585   Eloquence is the poetry of prose.
                                    William Cullen Bryant (1794-1878)

4586   Music is well said to be the speech of angels.
                                    Carlyle (1795-1881)

4587   Music is the harmonious voice of creation;
        an echo of the invisible world...
                                    Giuseppe Mazzini (1805-1872)

4588   Music is the universal language of mankind.
                                    Longfellow (1807-1882)

4589   Music is the shorthand of emotion.
                                    Leo Tolstoy (1828-1910)

2. OPPOSITES

4590   As empty vessels make the loudest sound,
        so they that have the least wit are the greatest babblers.
                                    Plato (B.C. 427?-347?)

4591   As a vessel is known by the sound, whether it be cracked or
        not; so men are proved, by their speeches, whether they be
        wise or foolish.
                                    Demosthenes (B.C. 384-322)

4592   Talking and eloquence are not the same:
        to speak and to speak well are two things.
        A fool may talk, but a wise man speaks.
                                    Ben Jonson (1572-1637)

4593 As it is the characteristic of great wits to say much in few
words, so it is of small wits to talk much and say nothing.
La Rochefoucauld (1613-1680)

4594 Speech was given to the ordinary sort of men,
whereby to communicate their mind;
but to wise men, whereby to conceal it.
Robert South (1634-1716)

4595 In oratory, the greatest art is to conceal art.
Swift (1667-1745)

4596 What the orators lack in depth, they give you in length.
Montesquieu (1689-1755)

4597 Music should strike fire from the heart of man,
and bring tears from the eyes of woman.
Beethoven (1770-1827)

4598 When you talk, you repeat what you already know;
when you listen, you often learn something.
Jared Sparks (1789-1866)

4599 Our sweetest songs are those which tell of saddest thought.
Shelley (1792-1822)

4600 Where painting is weakest, namely, in the expression of the
highest moral and spiritual ideas, there music is sublimely
strong.
Harriet Beecher Stowe (1811-1896)

4601 Speech is but broken light upon the depth
Of the unspoken.
George Eliot (1819-1880)

4602 Speech is silvern, silence is golden;
speech is human, silence is divine.
German Proverb

3. INSIGHT

4603 Each time a new soul descends in the ocean of the manifested
realm...it generates a vibration which is communicated to
the entire cosmic ocean...Each creature and every so-called
thing (one should say being) is a crystallization of a part
of this symphony of vibrations. Thus we are like a sound
petrified in solid matter and which continues indefinitely
to resound in this matter...and the word became flesh.
Kabbalah (B.C. 1200?-700? A.D.)

4604   The wise ones fashioned speech with their thought,
        sifting it as grain is sifted through a sieve.

                                    Rig Veda (B.C. 1200-900?)

4605   Speech was divided into four parts that the inspired
        priests know. Three parts, hidden in deep secret, humans
        do not stir into action; the fourth part of Speech is what
        men speak.

                                    Rig Veda (B.C. 1200-900?)

4606   Austerity of speech consists in speaking truthfully and
        beneficially and in avoiding speech that offends.

                                    Bhagavad Gita (c. B.C. 400)

4607   He is an eloquent man who can treat humble subjects with
        delicacy, lofty things impressively, and moderate things
        temperately.

                                    Cicero (B.C. 106-43)

4608   Abstruse questions must have abstruse answers.

                                    Plutarch (46-120 A.D.)

4609   It is of eloquence as of a flame; it requires matter to
        feed it, motion to excite it, and it brightens as it burns.

                                    Tacitus (55-117 A.D.)

4610   There is music wherever there is harmony, order, or
        proportion.

                                    Thomas Browne (1605-1682)

4611   True eloquence consists in saying all that is necessary,
        and nothing but what is necessary.

                                    La Rochefoucauld (1613-1680)

4612   Eloquence is to the sublime
        what the part is to the whole.

                                    La Bruyere (1645-1696)

4613   Music resembles poetry:
        In each are nameless graces which no methods teach
        And which a master-hand alone can reach.

                                    Pope (1688-1744)

4614   Music - The one incorporeal entrance into the higher world
        of knowledge which comprehends mankind but which mankind
        cannot comprehend.

                                    Beethoven (1770-1827)

4615   The object of oratory is not truth but persuasion.

                                    Macaulay (1800-1859)

4616 Speech is power: speech is to persuade, to convert,
to compel.

Emerson (1803-1882)

4617 There is no index of character so sure as the voice.

Disraeli (1804-1881)

4618 Talking is like playing on the harp; there is as much in
laying the hands on the strings to stop their vibrations
as in twanging them to bring out their music.

Oliver Wendell Holmes (1809-1894)

4619 All the intelligence and talent in the world can't make a
singer. The voice is a wild thing. It can't be bred in
captivity.

Willa Cather (1876-1947)

4620 Eloquence consists in making the speech comprehensible to
the multitude and agreeable to the learned.

Chinese Proverb

4. POSITIVE

4621 When thunder comes it relieves the tension and promotes
positive action. Music can do the same by making people
enthusiastic and united together. When used to promote good
it brings them closer to heaven.

I Ching (B.C. 1150?)

4622 When the sun and the moon are set and the fire has sunk
down, what is then the light of man? Voice then becomes his
light; and by the voice as his light he rests, goes forth,
does his work and returns. Therefore in truth when a man
cannot see even his own hand, if he hears a voice after that
he wends his way.

Upanishads (c. B.C. 800)

4623 Music produces a kind of pleasure which human nature cannot
do without.

Confucius (B.C. 551-479)

4624 The voice is the flower of beauty.

Zeno (B.C. 335?-264)

4625 Music is the art of the prophets, the only art that can calm
the agitations of the soul...

Martin Luther (1483-1546)

4626 He who sings frightens away his ills.

Cervantes (1547-1616)

4627   Eloquence - The art of saying things in such a way that
       those to whom we speak may listen to them with pleasure.
                                                    Pascal (1623-1662)

4628   The sweetest of all sounds is that of the voice of the
       woman we love.
                                                 La Bruyere (1645-1696)

4629   Music, the greatest good that mortals know,
       And all of heaven we have below.
                                                    Addison (1672-1719)

4630   Music is the only sensual gratification which mankind may
       indulge in to excess without injury to their moral or
       religious feelings.
                                                    Addison (1672-1719)

4631   The music that can deepest reach,
       And cure all ill, is cordial speech.
                                                  Emerson (1803-1882)

4632   Music washes away from the soul the dust of everyday life.
                                          Berthold Auerbach (1812-1882)

4633   There is no feeling, except the extremes of fear and grief,
       that does not find relief in music.
                                              George Eliot (1819-1880)

4634   There is however, a true music of Nature - the song of the
       birds, the whisper of leaves, the ripple of waters upon a
       sandy shore, the wail of wind or sea.
                                                   Lubbock (1834-1913)

4635   After silence, that which comes nearest to expressing the
       inexpressible is music.
                                              Aldous Huxley (1894-1963)

4636   All the sounds of the earth are like music.
                                      Oscar Hammerstein (1895-1960)

5. NEGATIVE

4637   A dog is not considered a good dog
          because he is a good barker.
       A man is not considered a good man
          because he is a good talker.
                                              Chuang-tzu (fl. B.C. 350)

4638   Orators are most vehement when they have the weakest cause,
       as men get on horseback when they cannot walk.
                                                  Cicero (B.C. 106-43)

4639   In labouring to be concise, I become obscure.

Horace (B.C. 65-8)

4640   Talkative people who wish to be loved are hated; when they
desire to please, they bore; when they think they are
admired, they are laughed at; they injure their friends,
benefit their enemies, and ruin themselves.

Plutarch (46-120 A.D.)

4641   The talkative listen to no one, for they are ever speaking.-
And the first evil that attends those who know not how to be
silent, is, that they hear nothing.

Plutarch (46-120 A.D.)

4642   Much talking is the cause of danger.
Silence is the means of avoiding misfortune.
The talkative parrot is shut up in a cage.
Other birds, without speech, fly freely about.

Saskya Pandita (1182-1251)

4643   Man has great power of speech, but the greater part thereof
is empty and deceitful. The animals have little, but that
little is useful and true; and better is a small and certain
thing than a great falsehood.

Leonardo Da Vinci (1452-1519)

4644   The man that hath no music in himself,
Nor is not moved with concord of sweet sounds,
Is fit for treasons, stratagems and spoils.

Shakespeare (1564-1616)

4645   Talking is a disease of age.

Ben Jonson (1572-1637)

4646   It is never so difficult to speak as when we are ashamed
of our silence.

La Rochefoucauld (1613-1680)

4647   It is a sad thing when men have neither the wit to speak
well, nor judgment to hold their tongues.

La Bruyere (1645-1696)

4648   They never taste who always drink;
They always talk who never think.

Matthew Prior (1664-1721)

4649   The secret of being tiresome is in telling everything.

Voltaire (1694-1778)

4650   The spoken discourse may roll on strongly as the great tidal
        wave; but, like the wave, it dies at last feebly on the
        sands. It is heard by few, remembered by still fewer, and
        fades away, like an echo in the mountains, leaving no token
        of power. It is the written human speech, that gave power
        and permanence to human thought.

                                         Albert Pike (1809-1891)

4651   In general those who have nothing to say
        Contrive to spend the longest time in doing it.

                                       James Lowell (1819-1891)

4652   Without music life would be a mistake.

                                            Nietzsche (1844-1900)

4653   The tongue is but three inches long,
        yet it can kill a man six feet high.

                                              Japanese Proverb

4654   The tongue like a sharp knife...
        Kills without drawing blood.

                                               Chinese Proverb

6. ADVICE

4655   Put a bridle on thy tongue; set a guard before thy lips,
        lest the words of thine own mouth destroy thy peace...On
        much speaking cometh repentance, but in silence is safety.

                                     Akhenaton? (c. B.C. 1375)

4656   Hear much; speak little.

                                           Bias (fl B.C. 600)

4657   Whatever words we utter should be chosen with care for
        people will hear them and be influenced by them for good
        or ill.

                                         Buddha (B.C. 568-488)

4658   A superior man is modest in his speech,
        but exceeds in his actions.

                                     Confucius (B.C. 551-479)

4659   Speak briefly and to the point.

                                  Cato the Elder (B.C. 234-149)

4660   We have two ears and only one tongue in order that we may
        hear more and speak less.

                                 Diogenes Laertius (c. 250 A.D.)

4661   Speak only at the proper place and time,
After having given due consideration.
If you utter elegant sayings too often,
Even they lose their value.
Saskya Pandita (1182-1251)

4662   Speak clearly if you speak at all;
carve every word before you let if fall.
Oliver Wendell Holmes (1809-1894)

4663   He who wants to persuade should put his trust, not in the
right argument, but in the right word. The power of sound
has always been greater than the power of sense.
Joseph Conrad (1857-1934)

4664   One of the best ways to persuade others is with your ears-
by listening to them.
Dean Rusk (born 1909)

7. POTPOURRI

4665   Thou, man, alone canst speak. Wonder at thy glorious
prerogative; and pay to Him who gave it to thee a rational
and welcome praise, teaching thy children wisdom,
instructing the offspring of thy loins in piety.
Akhenaton? (c. B.C. 1375)

4666   How sour sweet music is
When time is broke and no proportion kept!
So is it in the music of men's lives.
Shakespeare (1564-1616)

4667   The voice so sweet, the words so fair,
As some soft chime had stroke the air;
And though the sound had parted thence,
Still left an echo in the sense.
Ben Jonson (1572-1637)

4668   When he spoke, what tender words he used!
So softly, that like flakes of feathered snow,
They melted as they fell.
Dryden (1631-1700)

4669   Music hath charms to soothe a savage beast,
To soften rocks, or bend a knotted oak.
I've read that things inanimate have moved,
And as with living souls have been informed
By magic numbers and persuasive sound.
William Congreve (1670-1729)

4670 Music can noble hints impart, engender fury, kindle love,
with unsuspected eloquence can move and manage all the man
with secret art.

Addison (1672-1719)

4671 Tones that sound, and roar and storm about me until I have
set them down in notes.

Beethoven (1770-1827)

4672 The music in my heart I bore,
Long after it was heard no more.

Wordsworth (1770-1850)

4673 There's music in the sighing of a reed;
There's music in the gushing of a rill;
There's music in all things, if men had ears:
Their earth is but an echo of the spheres.

Byron (1788-1824)

4674 The tenor's voice is spoilt by affectation,
And for the bass, the beast can only bellow;
In fact, he had no singing education,
An ignorant, noteless, timeless, tuneless fellow.

Byron (1788-1824)

4675 And music lifted up the listening spirit
Until it walked, exempt from mortal care,
Godlike, o'er the clear billows of sweet sound.

Shelley (1792-1822)

4676 Music once admitted to the soul becomes a sort of spirit,
and never dies; it wanders perturbedly thorough the halls
and galleries of the memory, and is often heard again,
distinct and living as when it first displaced the wavelets
of the air.

Bulwer-Lytton (1803-1873)

4677 So she poured out the liquid music of her voice
to quench the thirst of his spirit.

Nathaniel Hawthorne (1804-1864)

4678 The flowering moments of the mind
Drop half their petals in our speech.

Oliver Wendell Holmes (1809-1894)

4679 Music was a thing of the soul -
a rose-lipped shell that murmured the eternal sea -
a strange bird singing the songs of another shore.

Josiah Holland (1819-1881)

4680　And the night shall be filled with music
　　　　And the cares, that infest the day,
　　　Shall fold their tents, like the Arabs,
　　　　And as silently steal away.

Longfellow (1807-1882)

4681　God sent his Singers upon earth
　　　With songs of sadness and of mirth,
　　　That they might touch the hearts of men,
　　　And bring them back to heaven again.

Longfellow (1807-1882)

4682　That rich celestial music thrilled the air
　　　From hosts on hosts of shining ones, who thronged
　　　Eastward and westward, making bright the night.

Edwin Arnold (1832-1904)

4683　Her ivory hands on the ivory keys
　　　　Strayed in a fitful fantasy
　　　Like the silver gleam when the poplar trees
　　　　Rustle their pale leaves listlessly
　　　Or the drifting foam of a restless sea
　　　　When the waves show their teeth on the flying breeze.

Oscar Wilde (1854-1900)

4684　One dog barks at a shadow...
　　　A hundred bark at his sound.

Chinese Proverb

STRIFE
Argument, Conflict, Discord, Dispute, Quarrel and Rivalry

1. ESSENCE

4685   In quarreling the truth is always lost.
> Publilius Syrus (fl. B.C. 42)

4686   To strive with an equal is dangerous;
with a superior, mad;
with an inferior, degrading.
> Seneca (B.C. 3-65 A.D.)

2. OPPOSITES

4687   Wise men argue causes, and fools decide them.
> Anacharsis (fl. B.C. 600)

4688   The whole concord of this world consists in discords.
> Seneca (B.C. 3-65 A.D.)

4689   In a false quarrel there is no true valor.
> Shakespeare (1564-1616)

4690   There is no dispute managed without passion,
and yet there is scarce a dispute worth a passion.
> Thomas Sherlock (1678-1761)

4691   Strong and bitter words indicate a weak cause.
> Victor Hugo (1802-1885)

4692   Controversy equalizes fools and wise men -
and the fools know it.
> Oliver Wendell Holmes (1809-1894)

4693   If we open a quarrel between the past and the present,
we shall find that we have lost the future.
> Winston Churchill (1874-1965)

3. INSIGHT

4694   Fishes live in the sea, as men do on land:
the great ones eat up the little ones.
> Pericles (B.C. 495-429)

4695   Great affection is often
The cause of violent animosity.
The quarrels of men often arise
From too great a familiarity.
> Saskya Pandita (1182-1251)

4696 No conflict is so severe as his who labors to
subdue himself.

Thomas A. Kempis (1380-1471)

4697 He who establishes his arguments by noise and command shows
that reason is weak.

Montaigne (1533-1592)

4698 Arguments, like children, should be like the subject that
begets them.

Thomas Dekker (1577-1632)

4699 When worthy men fall out, only one of them may be faulty
first; but if the strife continue long, both commonly
become guilty.

Thomas Fuller (1608-1661)

4700 Quarrels would not last long if the fault was only on
one side.

La Rochefoucauld (1613-1680)

4701 A knock-down argument; 'tis but a word and a blow.

Dryden (1631-1700)

4702 Nothing is more certain than that much of the force,
as well as grace, of arguments or instructions
depends on their conciseness.

Pope (1688-1744)

4703 Assertion is not argument; to contradict the statement of
an opponent is not proof that you are correct.

Johnson (1709-1784)

4704 In most quarrels there is a fault on both sides. A quarrel
may be compared to a spark, which cannot be produced
without a flint, as well as steel. Either of them, may
hammer on wood forever; no fire will follow.

Colton (1780-1832)

4705 Neither irony nor sarcasm is argument.

Rufus Choate (1799-1859)

4706 People generally quarrel because they cannot argue.

G. K. Chesterton (1874-1936)

4707 The man who strikes first admits that his ideas have given
out.

Chinese Proverb

4. POSITIVE

4708 It may happen sometimes that a long debate
Becomes the cause of a longer friendship.
Commonly, those who dispute with one another
At last agree.
Saskya Pandita (1182-1251)

4709 He that wrestles with us strengthens our nerves, and
sharpens our skill. Our antagonist is our helper.
Burke (1729-1797)

4710 Everywhere in the Universe, what we call Life and Movement
results from a continual conflict of Forces or Impulses.
Whenever that active antagonism ceases, the immobility and
inertia, which are Death, result.
Albert Pike (1809-1891)

4711 When the fight begins within himself,
a man's worth something.
Robert Browning (1812-1889)

4712 Like the course of the heavenly bodies, harmony in national
life is a resultant of the struggle between contending
forces. In frank expression of conflicting opinion lies the
greatest promise of wisdom in governmental action; and in
suppression lies ordinarily the greatest peril.
Louis D. Brandeis (1856-1941)

4713 Conflict is the gadfly of thought. It stirs us to
observation and memory. It instigates to invention.
It shocks us out of sheeplike passivity, and sets us
at noting and contriving.
John Dewey (1859-1952)

5. NEGATIVE

4714 Better is a dry morsel with quiet
than a house full of feasting with strife.
Proverbs (B.C. 1000?-200?)

4715 If thou continuest to take delight in idle argumentation
thou mayest be qualified to combat with the sophists, but
will never know how to live with men.
Socrates (B.C. 469-399)

4716 If a house be divided against itself,
that house cannot stand.
Mark (50?-100? A.D.)

4717   Argument, as usually managed, is the worst sort of
        conversation, as in books it is generally the worst
        sort of reading.
                                              Swift (1667-1745)

4718   Those who in quarrels interpose,
        Must often wipe a bloody nose.
                                                Gay (1688-1732)

4719   Weakness on both sides is, as we know, the motto of all
        quarrels.
                                           Voltaire (1694-1778)

4720   He that blows the coals in quarrels he has nothing to do
        with has no right to complain if the sparks fly in his
        face.
                                          Franklin (1706-1790)

4721   It is not necessary to understand things in order to argue
        about them.
                                    Beaumarchais (1732-1799)

4722   The pain of dispute exceeds by much its utility.
        All disputation makes the mind deaf;
        and when people are deaf I am dumb.
                                            Joubert (1754-1824)

6. ADVICE

4723   Scorn also to depress thy competitor by any dishonest or
        unworthy method; strive to raise thyself above him only by
        excelling him; so shall thy contest for superiority be
        crowned with honour, if not with success.
                                        Akhenaton? (c. B.C. 1375)

4724   But curb thou the high spirit in thy breast,
        For gentle ways are best, and keep aloof
        From sharp contentions.
                                          Homer (c. B.C. 700)

4725   You should respect each other and refrain from disputes;
        you should not, like water and oil, repel each other,
        but should, like milk and water, mingle together.
                                      Buddha (B.C. 568-488)

4726   In arguing one should meet serious pleading with humor,
        and humor with serious pleading.
                                       Gorgias (B.C. 483-376)

4727   Do not speak harshly to any one; those who are spoken to
       will answer thee in the same way. Angry speech is painful:
       blows for blows will touch thee.

                                   The Dhammapada (c. B.C. 300)

4728   A quarrel is quickly settled when deserted by one party:
       there is no battle unless there be two.

                                        Seneca (B.C. 3-65 A.D.)

4729   Beware of entrance to a quarrel; but being in,
       Bear it, that the opposer may beware of thee.

                                      Shakespeare (1564-1616)

4730   Be calm in arguing; for fierceness makes
       Error a fault, and truth discourtesy.

                                          Herbert (1593-1632)

4731   Don't take the wrong side of an argument just because your
       opponent has taken the right side.

                                   Baltasar Gracian (1601-1658)

4732   In a debate, rather pull to pieces the argument of thy
       antagonist than offer him any of thy own; for thus thou
       wilt fight him in his own country.

                                     Henry Fielding (1707-1754)

4733   There is no good in arguing with the inevitable.
       The only argument available with an east wind
       is to put on your overcoat.

                                       James Lowell (1819-1891)

4734   Desire nothing, Chafe not at fate, nor at Nature's
       changeless laws. But struggle only with the personal,
       the transitory, the evanescent and the perishable.

                                   H. P. Blavatsky (1831-1891)

4735   The unforgivable crime is soft hitting.
       Do not hit at all if it can be avoided;
       but never hit softly.

                                Theodore Roosevelt (1858-1919)

4736   The master-secret in fighting is to strike once,
       but in the right place.

                                     John Snaith (1876-1936)

7. POTPOURRI

4737 Heaven and water go their opposite ways:
The image of CONFLICT.
Thus in all his transactions the superior man
Carefully considers the beginning.

I Ching (B.C. 1150?)

4738 He who knows does not speak;
He who speaks does not know.
He who is truthful is not showy;
He who is showy is not truthful.
He who is virtuous does not dispute;
He who disputes is not virtuous.
He who is learned is not wise;
He who is wise is not learned.
Therefore the sage does not display his own merits.

Lao-Tzu (fl. B.C. 600)

4739 Dissension, like small streams, are first begun,
Scarce seen they rise, but gather as they run:
So lines that from their parallel decline,
More they proceed the more they still disjoin.

Samuel Garth (1670-1719)

4740 Great contest follows, and much learned dust
Involves the combatants; each claiming truth,
And truth disclaiming both.

Cowper (1731-1800)

4741 Discord, a sleepless hag who never dies,
With Snipe-like nose, and Ferret-glowing eyes,
Lean sallow cheeks, long chin with beard supplied,
Poor cracklin joints, and wither'd parchment hide,
As if old Drums, worn out with martial din,
Had clubb'd their yellow Heads to form her Skin.

John Wolcot (1738-1819)

4742 Alas! how light a cause may move
Dissension between hearts that love!
Hearts that the world in vain had tried,
And sorrow but more closely tied;
That stood the storm when waves were rough,
Yet in a sunny hour fall off.

Thomas Moore (1779-1852)

4743 Twas blow for blow, disputing inch by inch,
For one would not retreat, nor t'other flinch.

Byron (1788-1824)

4744 Controversy - A battle in which spittle or ink replace
the...cannon ball.

Ambrose Bierce (1842-1914?)

4745 I dislike arguments of any kind. They are always vulgar,
and often convincing.

Oscar Wilde (1854-1900)

4746 A young Apollo, golden haired,
  Stands dreaming on the verge of strife,
Magnificently unprepared
  For the long littleness of life.

Frances C. Cornford (1886-1960)

SUCCESS

Greatness, Triumph and Victory

1. ESSENCE

4747   To conquer oneself is a greater victory
than to conquer thousands in a battle.

Buddha (B.C. 568-488)

4748   Success is the reward of toil.

Sophocles (B.C. 495-406)

4749   The first and best victory is to conquer self; to be
conquered by self is of all things most shameful and vile.

Plato (B.C. 427?-347?)

4750   Success - keeping your mind awake and your desire asleep.

Moses Ibn Ezra (1060?-1139?)

4751   Success is a result, not a goal.

Gustave Flaubert (1821-1880)

4752   There is only one success -
to be able to spend your life in your own way.

Christopher Morley (1890-1957)

4753   The great are they who attempt the difficult things,
which lesser men avoid.

Indian Proverb

2. OPPOSITES

4754   Prepare for the difficult while it is still easy.
Deal with the big while it is still small.
Difficult undertakings have always started with what's easy.
Great undertakings always started with what is small.
Therefore the sage never strives for the great,
And thereby the great is achieved.

Lao-Tzu (fl. B.C. 600)

4755   The superior man understands what is right;
the inferior man understands what will sell.

Confucius (B.C. 551-479)

4756   Conquered, we conquer.

Plautus (B.C. 254-184)

4757   Yield to him who opposes you;
by yielding you conquer.

Ovid (B.C. 43-18 A.D.)

4758   Victor and vanquished never unite in substantial agreement.
                                           Tacitus (55-117 A.D.)

4759   Perhaps, for worldly success,
        we need virtues that make us loved
        and faults that make us feared.
                                               Joubert (1754-1824)

4760   There is nothing so dreadful as a great victory -
        except a great defeat.
                                             Emerson (1803-1882)

4761   The greatest victory is defeat.
                                           Henrik Ibsen (1828-1906)

4762   Success - To rise from the illusion of pursuit
               to the disillusion of possession.
                                        Elbert Hubbard (1859-1915)

3. INSIGHT

4763   The men who are great live with that which is substantial,
        they do not stay with that which is superficial;
        they abide with realities,
        they remain not with what is showy.
        The one they discard, the other they hold.
                                           Lao-Tzu (fl. B.C. 600)

4764   More will be accomplished, and better, and with more ease,
        if every man does what he is best fitted to do,
        and nothing else.
                                          Plato (B.C. 427?-347?)

4765   The great man is he who does not lose his child-heart. He
        does not think beforehand that his words shall be sincere,
        nor that his acts shall be resolute; he simply abides in
        the right.
                                         Mencius (B.C. 371-288)

4766   He conquers twice who conquers himself in victory.
                                          Shakespeare (1564-1616)

4767   The earnest desire of succeeding is almost always a
        prognostic of success.
                                   Leszczynski Stanislaus (1677-1766)

4768   Success makes success, as money makes money.
                                            Chamfort (1741-1794)

4769   Success usually comes to those who are too busy to be
       looking for it.

> Thoreau (1817-1862)

4770   Victory is a thing of the will.

> Ferdinand Foch (1851-1929)

4771   Success is to be measured not so much by the position that
       one has reached in life as by the obstacles which he has
       overcome while trying to succeed.

> Booker T. Washington (1856-1915)

4772   A man can succeed at almost anything for which he has
       unlimited enthusiasm.

> Charles Schwab (1862-1939)

4773   One beam alone...
       No matter how stout...
       Cannot support a house.

> Chinese Proverb

4. POSITIVE

4774   One's own self conquered is better than all other people;
       not even a god could change into defeat the victory of a
       man who has vanquished himself, and always lives under
       restraint.

> The Dhammapada (c. B.C. 300)

4775   To those who believe and do good deeds,
       for them are gardens beneath which flow rivers.
       This is the great triumph.

> Koran (c. 651 A.D.)

4776   Brave conquerors! for so you are
       That war against your own affections,
       And the huge army of the world's desires.

> Shakespeare (1564-1616)

4777   Success is a rare paint, hides all the ugliness.

> John Suckling (1609-1642)

4778   The talent of success is nothing more than doing what you
       can do well, and doing well whatever you do without thought
       of fame. If it comes at all it will come because it is
       deserved, not because it is sought after.

> Longfellow (1807-1882)

4779   Without victory there is no survival!

> Winston Churchill (1874-1965)

4780   The common idea that success spoils people by making
them vain, egotistic and self-complacent is erroneous;
on the contrary, it makes them for the most part, humble,
tolerant and kind. Failure makes people cruel and bitter.

Somerset Maugham (1874-1965)

5. NEGATIVE

4781   Success has a great tendency to conceal and
throw a veil over the evil deeds of men.

Demosthenes (B.C. 384-322)

4782   Victory is by nature insolent and haughty.

Cicero (B.C. 106-43)

4783   See how does great prosperity
overspreads the mind with darkness.

Seneca (B.C. 3-65 A.D.)

4784   Experience has always shown, and reason also,
that affairs which depend on many seldom succeed.

Francesco Guicciardini (1483-1540)

4785   Success produces confidence;
confidence relaxes industry,
and negligence ruins the reputation
which accuracy had raised.

Ben Jonson (1572-1637)

4786   We triumph without glory
when we conquer without danger.

Pierre Corneille (1606-1684)

4787   Constant success shows us but one side of the world; for,
as it surrounds us with friends, who will tell us only our
merits, so it silences those enemies from whom alone we can
learn our defects.

Colton (1780-1832)

4788   Success is full of promises till men get it; and then it is
as last year's nest, from which the bird has flown.

Beecher (1813-1878)

4789   Success soon palls.
The joyous time is when the breeze first strikes your sails,
and the waters rustle under your bows.

Charles Buxton (1823-1871)

4790   Success is counted sweetest
By those who never succeed.

Emily Dickinson (1830-1886)

4791   Not to the swift, the race:
Not to the strong, the fight:
Not to the righteous, perfect grace:
Not to the wise, the light.

                                     Henry Van Dyke (1852-1933)

6. ADVICE

4792   He will succeed if he remains firm in principle and goes
beyond selfish considerations to mingle freely with those
who do not share his feelings, as well as those who do.

                                     I Ching (B.C. 1150?)

4793   Truth obtains victory, not untruth.
Truth is the way that leads to the regions of light.

                                   Upanishads (c. B.C. 800)

4794   Be a tail to lions rather than a head to jackals.

                          The Talmud (B.C. 500?-400? A.D.)

4795   Our plans miscarry if they have no aim.
When a man does not know what harbor he is making for,
no wind is the right wind.

                                Seneca (B.C. 3-65 A.D.)

4796   If one is intelligent and applies himself well,
What can he not accomplish?
Even small bands of people, I have heard,
Have defeated whole armies.

                          Saskya Pandita (1182-1251)

4797   To climb steep hills requires slow pace at first.

                          Shakespeare (1564-1616)

4798   To win a race, the swiftness of a dart
availeth not without a timely start.

                          La Fontaine (1621-1695)

4799   Presence of mind, and courage in distress,
Are more than armies to procure success.

                                Dryden (1631-1700)

4800   Do not think dishonestly...
Distinguish between gain and loss in worldly matters.
Develop intuitive judgement and understanding for
  everything.
Perceive those things which cannot be seen.
Pay attention even to trifles.
Do nothing which is of no use.

                        Miyamoto Musashi (1584-1645)

4801   Be commonplace and creeping,
        and you attain all things.

                                    Beaumarchais (1732-1799)

4802   Nothing is impossible to the man who can will, and then do;
        this is the only law of success.

                                    Mirabeau (1749-1791)

4803   If you would be well with a great mind,
            leave him with a favorable impression of you;
        if with a little mind,
            leave him with a favorable opinion of himself.

                                    Samuel Coleridge (1772-1834)

4804   If you would hit the mark, you must aim a little above it:
        Every arrow that flies feels the attraction of earth.

                                    Longfellow (1807-1882)

4805   The true road to pre-eminent success in any line
        is to make yourself master of that line.

                                    Andrew Carnegie (1837-1919)

4806   The three great essentials to achieve anything worth-
        while are first, hard work; second, stick-to-itiveness;
        third, common sense.

                                    Thomas A. Edison (1847-1931)

4807   What are the qualities that make for success? Judgement,
        industry, health, and the greatest of these is judgement.

                                    Beaverbrook (1879-1964)

4808   Try not to become a man of success but
        rather try to become a man of value.

                                    Einstein (1879-1955)

4809   The secret of all victory lies in the organization of the
        non-obvious.

                                    Spengler (1880-1936)

4810   I can give you a six-word formula for success:
        "Think things through - then follow through."

                                    Edward Rickenbacker (1890-1973)

7. POTPOURRI

4811   Bit by bit the man achieves success.
        This should be valued but not pushed too far.
        When the moon is full, waning is inevitable.
        Quiescence is in order.

                                    I Ching (B.C. 1150?)

4812   Which does one love more, fame or one's own life?
        Which is more valuable, one's own life or wealth?
        Which is worse, gain or loss?
          Therefore
        He who has lavish desires will spend extravagantly.
        He who hoards most will lose heavily.
        He who is contented suffers no disgrace.
        He who knows when to stop is free from danger.
        Therefore he can long endure.
                                                    Lao-Tzu (fl. B.C. 600)

4813   Despise no man and consider nothing impossible,
          for there is no man who does not have his hour
          and there is no thing that does not have its place.
                                              The Talmud (B.C. 500?-400? A.D.)

4814   To him who knoweth the true nature of things,
            What need is there of a teacher?
        To him who hath recovered from illness,
            What need is there of a physician?
        To him who hath crossed the river,
            What need is there of a boat?
                                              Nagarjuna (c. 100-200 A.D.)

4815   Success, the mark no mortal wit,
        Or surest hand, can always hit:
        For whatsoe'er we perpetrate,
        We do but row, we're steer'd by Fate,
        Which in success oft disinherits,
        For spurious causes, noblest merits.
                                              Samuel Butler (1612-1680)

4816   He that will not stoop for a pin
        will never be worth a pound.
                                              Samuel Pepys (1633-1703)

4817   He that climbs the tall tree has won right to the fruit,
        He that leaps the wide gulf should prevail in his suit.
                                              Walter Scott (1771-1832)

4818   All you need in this life is ignorance and confidence,
        and then success is sure.
                                              Mark Twain (1835-1910)

TASTE

Appreciation, Culture, Refinement, Subtlety and Style

1. ESSENCE

4819   Style is the dress of thoughts.
> Chesterfield (1694-1773)

4820   Taste is, so to speak, the microscope of judgment.
> Rousseau (1712-1778)

4821   Taste is the mind's tact.
> Boufflers (1738-1815)

4822   Taste is the literary conscience of the soul.
> Joubert (1754-1824)

4823   Love of beauty is taste.
> Emerson (1803-1882)

4824   Style is the perfection of good sense.
> John Stuart Mill (1806-1873)

4825   Taste is the feminine of genius.
> Edward FitzGerald (1809-1883)

4826   Tact is the ability to describe others as they see themselves.
> Lincoln (1809-1865)

4827   Culture is to know the best that has been said and thought in the world.
> Matthew Arnold (1822-1888)

4828   Culture is the habit of being pleased with the best and knowing why.
> Henry Van Dyke (1852-1933)

2. OPPOSITES

4829   Too great refinement is false delicacy, and true delicacy is solid refinement.
> La Rochefoucauld (1613-1680)

4830   Between good sense and good taste there is the difference between cause and effect.
> La Bruyere (1645-1696)

4831 The same refinement which brings us new pleasures,
      exposes us to new pains.

                                             Bulwer-Lytton (1803-1873)

4832 Partial culture runs to the ornate;
      extreme culture to simplicity.

                                             Bovee (1820-1904)

4833 Good taste is better than bad taste,
      but bad taste is better than no taste.

                                             Arnold Bennett (1867-1931)

3. INSIGHT

4834 As the soil, however rich it may be,
      cannot be productive without cultivation,
      so the mind without culture
      can never produce good fruit.

                                             Seneca (B.C. 3-65 A.D.)

4835 Whatever are the benefits of fortune, they yet require a
      palate fit to relish and taste them.

                                             Montaigne (1533-1592)

4836 Taste may be compared to that exquisite sense of the
      bee, which instantly discovers and extracts the quintessence
      of every flower, and disregards all the rest of it.

                                             Greville (1554-1628)

4837 The fashion wears out more apparel than the man.

                                             Shakespeare (1564-1616)

4838 People care more about being thought to have good taste
      than about being thought either good, clever or amiable.

                                             Samuel Butler (1612-1680)

4839 Good taste come more from the judgment than from the mind.

                                             La Rochefoucauld (1613-1680)

4840 A well-cultivated mind is, so to speak, made up of all the
      minds of preceding ages; it is only one single mind which
      has been educated during all this time.

                                             Fontenelle (1657-1757)

4841 There is no disputing about taste.

                                             Sterne (1713-1768)

4842 Taste is pursued at a less expense than fashion.

                                             William Shenstone (1714-1763)

4843   Taste depends upon those finer emotions which make the
        organization of the soul.
                                        Joshua Reynolds (1723-1792)

4844   It matters little whether a man be mathematically, or
        philologically, or artistically cultivated, so he be but
        cultivated.
                                        Goethe (1749-1832)

4845   Taste has never been corrupted by simplicity.
                                        Joubert (1754-1824)

4846   Genius creates, and taste preserves.
        Taste is the good sense of genius;
        without taste, genius is only sublime folly.
                                        Chateaubriand (1768-1848)

4847   Culture implies all that which gives the mind possession
        of its own powers; as languages to the critic, telescope
        to the astronomer.
                                        Emerson (1803-1882)

4848   Appreciation, whether of nature, or books, or art, or men,
        depends very much on temperament. What is beauty or genius
        or greatness to one, is far from being so to another.
                                        Tryon Edwards (1809-1894)

4849   Culture, like the kingdom of heaven, lies within us, and not
        in foreign galleries and books.
                                        Randolph S. Bourne (1886-1918)

4. POSITIVE

4850   From the Emperor down to the masses of the people,
        all must consider the cultivation of the person
        the root of everything else.
                                        Confucius (B.C. 551-479)

4851   After a spirit of discernment the next rarest things in the
        world are diamonds and pearls.
                                        La Bruyere (1645-1696)

4852   By appreciation we make excellence in others our own
        property.
                                        Voltaire (1694-1778)

4853   A truly elegant taste is generally accompanied with an
        excellency of heart.
                                        Henry Fielding (1707-1754)

4854   It is in refinement and elegance that the civilized man
differs from the savage.

                                          Johnson (1709-1784)

4855   Delicacy of taste is favorable to love and friendship,
by confining our choice to few people, and making us
indifferent to the company and conversation of the greater
party of men.

                                       David Hume (1711-1776)

4856   Clearness ornaments profound thoughts.

                                   Vauvenargues(1715-1747)

4857   To love one that is great, is almost to be great one's self.

                           Suzanne Necker (1739-1794)

4858   To appreciate the noble is a gain which can never be torn
from us.

                                  Goethe (1749-1832)

4859   That only can with propriety be styled refinement which,
by strengthening the intellect, purifies the manners.

                        Samuel Coleridge (1772-1834)

4860   Refinement creates beauty everywhere. It is the grossness
of the spectator that discovers anything like grossness
in the object.

                                 Hazlitt (1778-1830)

4861   The great law of culture:
Let each become all that he was created capable of being.

                                Carlyle (1795-1881)

4862   Next to excellence is the appreciation of it.

                           Thackeray (1811-1863)

4863   Culture is properly described as the love of perfection;
it is a study of perfection.

                        Matthew Arnold (1822-1888)

4864   The value of culture is its effect on character. It avails
nothing unless it ennobles and strengthens that. Its use is
for life. Its aim is not beauty, but goodness.

                      Somerset Maugham (1874-1965)

4865   Culture is the sum of all the forms of art, of love and of
thought, which, in the course of centuries, have enabled man
to be less enslaved.

                        Andre Malraux (1901-1976)

5. NEGATIVE

4866   Subtlety may deceive you; integrity never will.
Oliver Cromwell (1599-1658)

4867   He who has no opinion of his own, but depends upon the opinion and taste of others, is a slave.
Friedrich Klopstock (1724-1803)

4868   Nothing is more fearful than imagination without taste.
Goethe (1749-1832)

4869   With many readers brilliancy of style passes for affluence of thought; they mistake buttercups in the grass for immeasurable mines of gold under ground.
Longfellow (1807-1882)

4870   It is far more difficult to be simple than to be complicated; far more difficult to sacrifice skill and cease exertion in the proper place, than to expend both indiscriminately.
John Ruskin (1819-1900)

4871   A fashion is nothing but an induced epidemic.
G. B. Shaw (1856-1950)

4872   The more refined one is, the more unhappy.
Chekhov (1860-1904)

4873   Taste is the enemy of creativeness.
Pablo Picasso (1881-1973)

4874   No medicines can cure the vulgar man.
Chinese Proverb

6. ADVICE

4875   Do not become attached to the things you like, do not cherish aversion to the things you dislike. Sorrow, fear and bondage come from one's likes and dislikes.
Buddha (B.C. 568-488)

4876   Cultivation to the mind, is as necessary as food to the body
Cicero (B.C. 106-43)

4877   You will find poetry nowhere unless you bring some with you.
Joubert (1754-1824)

4878   The finest qualities of our nature, like the bloom on fruits, can be preserved only by the most delicate handling.

Thoreau (1817-1862)

4879 Good taste consists first upon fitness.

George Curtiss (1824-1892)

4880 Enhance and intensify one's vision of that synthesis of
truth and beauty which is the highest and deepest reality.

John C. Powys (1872-1963)

7. POTPOURRI

4881 I am very sure that any man of common understanding may,
by culture, care, attention, and labor, make himself whatever he pleases, except a great poet.

Chesterfield (1694-1773)

4882 The poet must be alike polished by an intercourse with the
world as with the studies of taste; one to whom labour is
negligence, refinement a science, and art a nature.

Isaac D'Israeli (1766-1848)

4883 Do not do unto others as you would that they should do unto
you. Their tastes may not be the same.

G. B. Shaw (1856-1950)

4884 Fashion is what one wears oneself. What is unfashionable
is what other people wear.

Oscar Wilde (1854-1900)

THE ETERNAL
God and Creator

1. ESSENCE

4885　There was something undifferentiated and yet complete,
Which existed before heaven and earth.
Soundless and formless, it depends on nothing
　and does not change.
It operates everywhere and is free from danger.
It may be considered the mother of the universe.

Lao-Tzu (fl. B.C. 600)

4886　God is a circle whose center is everywhere,
and its circumference nowhere.

Empedocles (B.C. 495-435)

4887　God is truth and light his shadow.

Plato (B.C. 427?-347?)

4888　The divine essence itself is love and wisdom.

Swedenborg (1688-1772)

4889　All are but parts of one stupendous whole,
Whose body Nature is, and God the soul.

Pope (1688-1744)

4890　Existence is God!

Goethe (1749-1832)

2. OPPOSITES

4891　There are, assuredly, two forms of The Eternal:
the formed and the formless, the mortal and the immortal,
the stationary and the moving, the actual and the yon.

Upanishads (c. B.C. 800)

4892　We look at it and do not see it;
　Its name is The Invisible.
We listen to it and do not hear it;
　Its name is The Inaudible.
We touch it and do not find it;
　Its name is The Subtle (formless).
These three cannot be further inquired into,
And hence merge into one.
Going up high it is not bright,
And coming down low, it is not dark.
Infinite and boundless, it cannot be given any name;

It reverts to nothingness.
This is called shape without shape,
Form without object.
It is The Vague and Elusive.
Meet it and you will not see its head.
Follow it and you will not see its back.
Hold on to The Way of the old in order to master the things
  of the present.
From this one may know the primeval beginning
  (of the universe).
This is called the bond of The Eternal.

Lao-Tzu (fl. B.C. 600)

4893   Of all that is material and all that is spiritual in this
world, know for certain that I am both its origin and
dissolution. There is no true superior to Me. Everything
rests upon Me, as pearls are strung on a thread.

Bhagavad Gita (c. B.C. 400)

4894   I am Alpha and Omega, the beginning and the ending,
saith the Lord.

Revelation (c. 85 A.D.)

4895   The more God is in all things, the more He is outside them.
The more He is within, the more without.

Meister Eckhart (1260-1327)

4896   A God all mercy is a God unjust.

Young (1683-1765)

4897   To Him no high, no low, no great, no small;
He fills, He bounds, connects and equals all!

Pope (1688-1744)

4898   Space is the statue of God.

Joubert (1754-1824)

4899   When the gods were more manlike,
Men were more godlike.

Schiller (1759-1805)

4900   We find God twice - once within, once without us:
within us as an eye, without us as a light.

Richter (1763-1825)

4901   There are, properly speaking, two "ONES" - the One on the
unreachable plane of Absoluteness and Infinity, on which
no speculation is possible, and the Second "One" on the
plane of Emanations. The former can neither emanate nor be
divided, as it is eternal, absolute, and immutable. The
Second, being, so to speak, the reflection of the first One,
can do all this.

H. P. Blavatsky (1831-1891)

3. INSIGHT

4902   There was neither non-existence nor existence then;
         there was neither the realm of space nor the sky beyond.
         There was no distinguishing sign of night nor of day.
         That One breathed, windless, by its own impulse.
         Other than that there was nothing beyond.
         Darkness was hidden by darkness in the beginning;
         with no distinguishing sign, all this was water.
         The life force that was, was covered with emptiness,
         that one arose through the power of heat.
         Desire came upon that one in the beginning;
         that was the first seed of mind.

                                        Rig Veda (B.C. 1200-900?)

4903   He is the one in whose power are the many sources of
         creation, and the root and the flower of all things. The
         Golden Seed, the Creator, was in his mind in the beginning;
         and he saw him born when time began.

                                        Upanishads (c. B.C. 800)

4904   The Eternal is empty (like a bowl),
         It may be used but its capacity is never exhausted.
         It is bottomless, perhaps the ancestor of all things.
         It blunts its sharpness,
         It unties its tangles,
         It softens its light.
         It becomes one with the dusty world.
         Deep and still, it appears to exist forever.
         I do not know whose son it is.
         It seems to have existed before the Lord.

                                        Lao-Tzu (fl. B.C. 600)

4905   God is neither the object of sense, nor subject to passion,
         but invisible, only intelligible, and supremely intelligent.
         In His body He is like the light, and in His soul He
         resembles truth. He is the universal spirit that pervades
         and diffuses itself over all nature...He is the Reason, the
         Life, the Motion of all being.

                                        Pythagoras (B.C. 582-507)

4906   The ignorant think of Me, who am the Unmanifested Spirit,
         as if I were really in human form. They do not understand
         that My Supreme Nature is changeless and most excellent.
         I am not invisible to all, for I am enveloped by the
         illusion of Phenomenon. This deluded world does not know Me
         as the Unborn and the Imperishable.

                                        Bhagavad Gita (c. B.C. 400)

4907   There is something in the nature of things which the mind of
        man, which reason, which human power cannot effect, and
        certainly that which produces this must be better than man.
        What can this be but God?

                                            Cicero (B.C. 106-43)

4908   Call it Nature, Fate, Fortune; all these are names of the
        one and selfsame God.

                                        Seneca (B.C. 3-65 A.D.)

4909   Where one is present, God is the second,
        and where there are two, God is the third.

                                        Mohammed (570-632 A.D.)

4910   That which exists through itself is called The Eternal.
        The Eternal has neither name nor shape. It is the one
        essence, the one primal spirit. Essence and life cannot be
        seen. They are contained in the light of heaven. The light
        of heaven cannot be seen. It is contained in the two eyes.

                                            Lu Yen (fl. 800 A.D.)

4911   The very impossibility in which I find myself to prove that
        God is not, discovers to me his existence.

                                        La Bruyere (1645-1696)

4912   God is the universal substance in existing things.
        He comprises all things. He is the fountain of all being.
        In Him exists everything that is.

                                        Giordano Bruno (1548-1600)

4913   It is easy to understand God as long as you don't try to
        explain him.

                                            Joubert (1754-1824)

4914   God is the poet, men are but the actors.

                                            Balzac (1799-1850)

4915   God enters a private door into every individual.

                                            Emerson (1803-1882)

4916   God is the perfect poet,
        Who in his person acts his own creations.

                                        Robert Browning (1812-1889)

4917   There is no life, truth, intelligence, nor substance in
          matter.
        All is infinite Mind and its infinite manifestation,
          for God is All - in all.
        Spirit is immortal Truth; matter is mortal error.

                                        Mary Baker Eddy (1821-1910)

4918   What is it that ever is?
      Space, the eternal parentless.
    What is it that ever was?
      The Germ in the Root.
    What is it that is ever coming and going?
      The Great Breath.
    Then, there are three Eternals?
      No, the three are one. That which ever is is one,
      that which ever was is one, that which is ever being
      and becoming is also one: and this is Space.

                      H. P. Blavatsky (1831-1891)

4919   God is a reality of spirit...He cannot...be conceived as an
    object, not even as the very highest object. God is not
    to be found in the world of objects.

                    Nicholas Berdyaev (1874-1948)

4920   In Him is an illimitable abyss of glory, and from it there
    goeth forth one little spark which maketh all the glory of
    the sun, and of the moon, and of the stars. Mortal!
    behold how little I know of God; seek not to know more
    of Him, for this is far beyond thy comprehension, however
    wise thou art.

                    Ancient Oracle

4. POSITIVE

4921   Forgetful youth! but know, the Power above
    With ease can save each object of his love;
    Wide as his will, extends his boundless grace.

                    Homer (c. B.C. 700)

4922   The way which is bright appears to be dark.
    The way which goes forward appears to fall backward.
    The way which is level appears uneven.
    Great virtue appears like a valley (hollow).
    Great purity appears like disgrace.
    Far-reaching virtue appears as if insufficient.
    Solid virtue appears as if unsteady.
    True substance appears to be changeable.
    The great square has no corners.
    The great talent is slow to mature.
    Great music sounds faint.
    Great form has no shape.
    The Eternal is hidden and nameless.
    Yet it is The Eternal alone that skillfully provides for all
      and brings them to perfection.

                    Lao-Tzu (fl. B.C. 600)

4923   If hundreds of thousands of suns rose up at once into the
       sky, they might resemble the effulgence of the Supreme
       Person in that universal form.

                                       Bhagavad Gita (c. B.C. 400)

4924   I am the taste in the water, the light of the sun and the
       moon, the sound in the ether, the ability in man, the
       fragrance of the earth, the heat in the fire, the life of
       all that lives, the strength of the strong, the intelligence
       of the intelligent, and the original seed of all existences.

                                       Bhagavad Gita (c. B.C. 400)

4925   There is nothing which God cannot do.

                                               Cicero (B.C. 106-43)

4926   There is a God within us, and we glow when he stirs us.

                                           Ovid (B.C. 43-18 A.D.)

4927   Nothing is void of God; He Himself fills His work.

                                           Seneca (B.C. 3-65 A.D.)

4928   It is one of my favorite thoughts, that God manifests
       himself to mankind in all wise, good, humble, generous,
       great and magnanimous men.

                                              Lavater (1741-1801)

4929   A superintending power to maintain the Universe in its
       course and order.

                                     Thomas Jefferson (1743-1826)

4930   If we look closely at this world, where God seems so
       utterly forgotten, we shall find that it is he, who, after
       all, commands the most fidelity and the most love.

                                       Anne Swetchine (1782-1857)

4931   Nature is too thin a screen; the glory of the omnipresent
       God bursts through everywhere.

                                              Emerson (1803-1882)

4932   There is a realm where there is neither earth nor water,
       neither space nor time, neither perception nor thinking,
       neither light nor darkness, neither east nor west. That is
       the abode of The Eternal where there is everlasting peace
       and bliss.

                                          Sivananda (born 1887)

5. NEGATIVE

4933   The gods play games with men as balls...
       In wondrous ways do the gods make sport with men.

                                           Plautus (B.C. 254-184)

4934   It is fear that first brought gods into the world.

> Petronius (died 66 A.D.)

4935   One atom of the plane where He functions
would shatter the world.

> Ibn Al-'Arabi (1165-1240)

4936   Hath God obliged himself not to exceed the bounds
of our knowledge?

> Montaigne (1533-1592)

4937   As flies are to wanton boys, are we to the gods;
They kill us for their sport.

> Shakespeare (1564-1616)

4938   To believe in God is impossible
not to believe in Him is absurd.

> Voltaire (1694-1778)

4939   Without a God there is for man neither purpose, nor goal,
nor hope, only a wavering future, and an eternal dread of
every darkness.

> Richter (1763-1825)

4940   How did the atheist get his idea of that God whom he denies?

> Samuel Coleridge (1772-1834)

4941   God does not exist...We are precisely on a plane where
nothing exists but men.

> Jean-Paul Sartre (1905-1980)

6. ADVICE

4942   The more we deny ourselves,
the more the gods supply our wants.

> Horace (B.C. 65-8)

4943   Is there any other seat of the Divinity than the earth, sea,
air, the heavens, and virtuous mind? Why do we seek God
elsewhere? He is whatever you see; He is wherever you move.

> Lucan (39-65 A.D.)

4944   It were better to have no opinion of God at all
than such a one as is unworthy of him;
for the one is only belief - the other contempt.

> Plutarch (46-120 A.D.)

4945   We cannot too often think, that there is a never sleeping
eye that reads the heart, and registers our thoughts.

> Bacon (1561-1626)

4946   Acquaint thyself with God, if thou would'st taste
       His works. Admitted once to his embrace,
       Thou shalt perceive that thou was blind before:
       Thine eye shall be instructed; and thine heart
       Made pure shall relish with divine delight
       Till then unfelt, what hands divine have wrought.
                                             Cowper (1731-1800)

4947   You must seek and find God in the heart.
                                             Richter (1763-1825)

4948   You see many stars at night in the sky but find them not
       when the sun rises; can you say that there are no stars
       in the heaven of day? So, O man! because you behold not
       God in the days of your ignorance, say not that there is
       no God.
                                          Ramakrishna (1836-1886)

7. POTPOURRI

4949   I Thy God am the Light and the Mind which were before
       substance was divided from Spirit and darkness from
       Light.
                              The Divine Pymander (BC 2500?-200 AD?)

4950   Who hath stretched forth the heavens with His hand, who hath
       described with His finger the courses of the stars.
                                       Akhenaton? (c. B.C. 1375)

4951   Beyond the senses are their objects, and beyond the objects
       is the mind. Beyond the mind is pure reason, and beyond
       reason is the Spirit in man. Beyond the Spirit in man is
       the Spirit of the universe, and beyond is the Spirit
       Supreme. Nothing is beyond the Spirit Supreme: He is the
       end of the path.
                                       Upanishads (c. B.C. 800)

4952   Nothing is more ancient than God, for he was never created;
       nothing more beautiful than the world, it is the work of
       that same God; nothing more active than thought, for it
       flies over the whole universe; nothing stronger than
       necessity, for all must submit to it.
                                       Thales (B.C. 625?-547?)

4953   ...I am the Father of the Universe and its Mother; I am its
       Nourisher and its Grandfather; I am the Knowable and the
       Pure;...I am the Goal, the Sustainer, the Lord, the Witness,
       the Home, the Shelter, the Lover and the Origin; I am Life
       and Death; I am the Fountain and the Seed Imperishable...
       I am Death and Immortality; I am Being and Non-Being.
                                       Bhagavad Gita (c. B.C. 400)

4954   He is the Ancient of the Ancients, the Mystery of the
Mysteries, the Unknown of the Unknowns...He is seated on a
throne of fiery sparks which He subjects to His will. The
white light emitted by His head illumines four hundred
thousand worlds. This white light becomes the inheritance
of the just in the world to come. Each day sees thirteen
myriads of worlds kindled by His brain...

                                                        Zohar (120?-1200? A.D.)

4955   Blessed be He in whose hand is the Kingdom: and He is
powerful over all; who created death and life to prove
which of you is best in actions, and He is the Mighty,
the Very Forgiving; who hath created seven heavens in
stages.

                                                        Koran (c. 651 A.D.)

4956   Man is certainly stark mad; he cannot make a flea,
and yet he will be making gods by dozens.

                                                 Montaigne (1533-1592)

4957   Under whose feet (subjected to His Grace),
Sit nature, fortune, motion, time, and place.

                                           Torquato Tasso (1544-1595)

4958   At whose sight all the stars
Hide their diminish'd heads.

                                                Milton (1608-1674)

4959   God moves in a mysterious way
  His wonders to perform;
He plants his footsteps in the sea
  And rides upon the storm.

                                         Cowper (1731-1800)

4960   Blessed is he who carries within himself a God, an ideal,
and who obeys it.

                                        Louis Pasteur (1822-1895)

4961   There are scores of thousands of sects who are ready at a
moment's notice to reveal the will of God on every possible
subject.

                                        G. B. Shaw (1856-1950)

4962   The Somewhat which we name but cannot know.
  Even as we name a star and only see
Its quenchless flashings forth, which ever show
  And ever hide him, and which are not he.

                                      William Watson (1858-1935)

4963   We make our friends; we make our enemies;
        but God makes our next-door neighbor.

G. K. Chesterton (1874-1936)

4964   God is subtle but not malicious.

Einstein (1879-1955)

4965   The gods...thousands and ten thousands...are one god.

Chinese Proverb

THOUGHT

Consciousness, Intelligence, Memory and Mind

1. ESSENCE

4966   Thinking is the talking of the soul with itself.
                                            Plato (B.C. 427?-347?)

4967   Memory is the treasury and guardian of all knowledge.
                                            Cicero (B.C. 106-43)

4968   Mind moves matter.
                                            Vergil (B.C. 70-19)

4969   Thought is free.
                                            Shakespeare (1564-1616)

4970   Intellect is brain force.
                                            Schiller (1759-1805)

4971   The power of Thought, the magic of the Mind!
                                            Byron (1788-1824)

4972   Consciousness is what happens to intelligence
        when it is confronted with an object.
                                            Hazrat Inayat Khan (1882-1927)

2. OPPOSITES

4973   Mind is indeed the source of bondage
        and also the source of liberation.
        To be bound to things of this world: this is bondage.
        To be free from them: this is liberation.
                                            Upanishads (c. B.C. 800)

4974   A man must elevate himself by his own mind, not degrade
        himself. The mind is the friend of the conditioned soul,
        and his enemy as well.
                                            Bhagavad Gita (c. B.C. 400)

4975   It is the mind that maketh good or ill,
        That maketh wretch or happy, rich or poor.
                                            Edmund Spenser (1552-1599)

4976   There is one radical distinction between different minds...
        that some minds are stronger and apter to mark the
        differences of things, others mark their resemblances.
                                            Bacon (1561-1626)

4977   There is nothing either good or bad,
        but thinking makes it so.
                                    Shakespeare (1564-1616)

4978   Our thoughts are ours, their ends none of our own.
                                    Shakespeare (1564-1616)

4979   The two offices of memory are collection and distribution.
                                    Johnson (1709-1784)

4980   Few have at once both thought and capacity for action.
        Thought expands, but lames; action animates, but narrows.
                                    Goethe (1749-1832)

4981   In matters of conscience first thoughts are best;
        in matters of prudence last thoughts are best.
                                    Robert Hall (1764-1831)

4982   Of all the faculties of the mind, memory is the first that
        flourishes, and the first that dies.
                                    Colton (1780-1832)

4983   Thought once awakened does not again slumber.
                                    Carlyle (1795-1881)

4984   What is mind? No matter.
        What is matter? Never mind.
                                    Thomas Key (1799-1875)

4985   The revelation of thought takes men out of servitude
        into freedom.
                                    Emerson (1803-1882)

4986   Thoughts come into our minds by avenues which we never left
        open, and thoughts go out of our minds through avenues which
        we never voluntarily opened.
                                    Emerson (1803-1882)

4987   Intellect distinguishes between the possible and the
        impossible; reason distinguishes between the sensible
        and the senseless. Even the possible can be senseless.
                                    Max Born (1872-1970)

3. INSIGHT

4988   The most perfect mind is a dry light.
                                    Heraclitus (B.C. 535-475)

4989   When thy reason has crossed the entanglements of illusion,
        then shalt thou become indifferent both to the philosophies
        thou hast heard and to those thou mayest yet hear.
                                    Bhagavad Gita (c. B.C. 400)

4990   It is the mind that makes the man,
        and our vigour is in our immortal soul.

                                            Ovid (B.C. 43-18 A.D.)

4991   And which of you with taking thought can add to his stature
        one cubit?

                                            Luke (50?-100? A.D.)

4992   Thought, Intelligence, Voice, and Word are one and the same
        thing; that thought is the beginning of all that is, and
        that there can be no break in it. Thought itself is bound
        to Non-Being, and is never parted from it.

                                            Zohar (120?-1200? A.D.)

4993   How fleet is a glance of the mind!
          Compared with the speed of its flight,
        The tempest itself lags behind,
          And the swift-winged arrows of light.

                                            Cowper (1731-1800)

4994   There are two distinct classes of what are called thoughts:
        those that we produce in ourselves by reflection and the act
        of thinking and those that bolt into the mind of their own
        accord.

                                            Paine (1737-1809)

4995   It hinders the creative work of the mind if the intellect
        examines too closely the ideas as they pour in.

                                            Schiller (1759-1805)

4996   The second, sober thought of the people is seldom wrong,
        and always efficient.

                                            Martin Van Buren (1782-1862)

4997   The mind wears the colors of the soul,
        as a valet those of his master.

                                            Anne Swetchine (1782-1857)

4998   Thought will not work except in silence.

                                            Carlyle (1795-1881)

4999   A great memory does not make a mind, any more than a
        dictionary is a piece of literature.

                                            John Henry Newman (1801-1890)

5000   The senses collect the surface facts of matter...It was
        sensation; when memory came, it was experience; when mind
        acted, it was knowledge; when mind acted on it as knowledge,
        it was thought.

                                            Emerson (1803-1882)

5001 Thought is the property of those only who can entertain it.
                                                    Emerson (1803-1882)

5002 What is thought? It is not Matter, nor Spirit. It is not a
      Thing; but a Power and Force. I make upon a paper certain
      conventional marks, that represent that Thought. There is
      no Power or Virtue in the marks I write, but only in the
      Thought which they tell to others. I die, but the Thought
      still lives. It is a Power. The fact that Thought
      continues to exist an instant, after it makes its appearance
      in the soul, proves it immortal: for there is nothing
      conceivable that can destroy it. The spoken words, being
      mere sounds, may vanish into thin air, and the written ones,
      mere marks, be burned, erased, destroyed: but the THOUGHT
      itself lives still, and must live on forever.
                                                    Albert Pike (1809-1891)

5003 A thought often makes us hotter than a fire.
                                                    Longfellow (1807-1882)

5004 Few minds wear out; more rust out.
                                                    Bovee (1820-1904)

5005 Thought has a self-reproductive power, and when the mind is
      held steadily to one idea it becomes coloured by it, and, as
      we may say, all the correlates of that thought arise within
      the mind. Hence the mystic obtains knowledge about any
      object of which he thinks constantly in fixed contemplation.
                                                    H. P. Blavatsky (1831-1891)

5006 It is the mind that makes one wise or ignorant, bound or
      emancipated. One is holy because of his mind, one is
      wicked because of his mind, one is a sinner because of
      his mind, and it is the mind that makes one virtuous. So
      he whose mind is always fixed on God requires no other
      practices, devotion, or spiritual exercises.
                                                    Ramakrishna (1836-1886)

5007 Minds are like parachutes - they only function when open.
                                                    Thomas Dewar (1864-1930)

5008 Consciousness is a state in which a man knows all at once
      everything that he in general knows and in which he can
      see how little he does know and how many contradictions
      there are in what he knows.
                                                    Gurdjieff (1873-1949)

5009 Merely having an open mind is nothing. The object of
      opening the mind, as of opening the mouth, is to shut it
      again on something solid.
                                                    G. K. Chesterton (1874-1936)

5010   I conceive a man's body as a kind of flame, like a candle
       flame, forever upright and yet flowing: and the intellect
       is just the light that is shed on the things around.

                                        D. H. Lawrence (1885-1930)

5011   The mind is a product of experience. It is the result of
       past thinking and is modified by present thinking.

                                        Sivananda (born 1887)

4. POSITIVE

5012   All that we are is the result of what we have thought;
       it is founded on our thoughts. If a man speaks or acts
       with pure thought, happiness follows him, like a shadow
       that never leaves him.

                                        Buddha (B.C. 568-488)

5013   Serenity, simplicity, gravity, self-control and purity of
       thought are the austerities of the mind.

                                        Bhagavad Gita (c. B.C. 400)

5014   A great mind becomes a great fortune.

                                        Seneca (B.C. 3-65 A.D.)

5015   Memory tempers prosperity, mitigates adversity,
       controls youth, and delights old age.

                                        Lactantius (260-340 A.D.)

5016   True thoughts have duration in themselves.
       If the thoughts endure, the seed is enduring;
       if the seed endures, the energy endures;
       if the energy endures, then will the spirit endure.
       The spirit is thought; thought is the heart;
       the heart is the fire; the fire is the Elixir.

                                        Lu Yen (fl. 800 A.D.)

5017   Thoughts are free and are subject to no rule.
       On them rests the freedom of man,
       and they tower above the light of nature.

                                        Paracelsus (1493-1541)

5018   My mind to me a kingdom is,
         Such perfect joy therein I find
       As far exceeds all earthly bliss
         That God or nature hath assigned.

                                        Edward Dyer (1543?-1607)

5019   'Tis the mind that makes the body rich.

                                        Shakespeare (1564-1616)

5020   If a man empties his purse into his head,
        no one can take it from him.

                                            Franklin (1706-1790)

5021   Thinkers are scarce as gold; but he whose thoughts embrace
        all his subject, pursues it uninterruptedly and fearless of
        consequences, is a diamond of enormous size.

                                            Lavater (1741-1801)

5022   He who thinks much says but little in proportion to his
        thoughts. He selects that language which will convey his
        ideas in the most explicit and direct manner.

                                    Washington Irving (1783-1859)

5023   Great men are they who see that spiritual is stronger than
        any material force, that thoughts rule the world.

                                            Emerson (1803-1882)

5024   Thought...quickly tends to convert itself into a power,
        and organizes a huge instrumentality of means.

                                            Emerson (1803-1882)

5025   One man who has a mind and knows it
        can always beat ten men who haven't and don't.

                                            G. B. Shaw (1856-1950)

5026   The empires of the future are the empires of the mind.

                                    Winston Churchill (1874-1965)

5027   The mind...
        Emperor of the body.

                                            Chinese Proverb

5. NEGATIVE

5028   For the imagination of man's heart is evil from his youth.

                                            Genesis (B.C. 1200?)

5029   If a man speaks or acts with an evil thought, pain follows
        him, as the wheel follows the foot of the ox that draws
        the carriage.

                                            Buddha (B.C. 568-488)

5030   It is a man's own mind - not his enemy or his foe that
        lures him into evil ways.

                                            Buddha (B.C. 568-488)

5031   The imagination of water does not quench thirst.
        The thought of fire does not bestow heat.
        And the claim to be seeking does not bring one to the
          Sought.

                                            Tusi (1201-1274)

5032 Nothing fixes a thing so intensely in the memory as the
wish to forget it.

Montaigne (1533-1592)

5033 Men use thought only to justify their wrongdoings,
and speech only to conceal their thoughts.

Voltaire (1694-1778)

5034 He that never thinks never can be wise.

Johnson (1709-1784)

5035 With curious art the brain, too finely wrought,
Preys on herself, and is destroyed by thought.

Charles Churchill (1731-1764)

5036 The rich are too indolent, the poor too weak,
to bear the insupportable fatigue of thinking.

Cowper (1731-1800)

5037 What exile from himself can flee?
  To zones, though more and more remote,
Still, still pursues, where'er I be,
  The blight of life - the demon Thought.

Byron (1788-1824)

5038 Thinking is but an idle waste of thought,
And naught is everything, and everything is naught.

Horace and James Smith (fl. 1800)

5039 Every real thought on every real subject knocks the wind out
of somebody or other.

Oliver Wendell Holmes (1809-1894)

5040 Mind unemployed is mind unenjoyed.

Bovee (1820-1904)

5041 Many a man fails to become a thinker for the sole reason
that his memory is too good.

Nietzsche (1844-1900)

5042 It is remarkable to what lengths people will go to avoid
thought.

Thomas A. Edison (1847-1931)

5043 Thinking is the greatest torture in the world for most
people.

Luther Burbank (1849-1926)

5044   Men fear thought as they fear nothing else on earth -
       more than ruin, more even than death.

> Bertrand Russell (1872-1970)

5045   We have rudiments of reverence for the human body,
       but we consider as nothing the rape of the human mind.

> Eric Hoffer (1902-1983)

6. ADVICE

5046   It is good to tame the mind, which is often difficult to
       hold in and flighty, rushing wherever it listeth; a tamed
       mind brings happiness. Let the wise man guard his thoughts,
       for they are difficult to perceive, very artful, and they
       rush wherever they list: thoughts well guarded bring
       happiness.

> The Dhammapada (c. B.C. 300)

5047   A well-prepared mind hopes in adversity
       and fears in prosperity.

> Horace (B.C. 65-8)

5048   Write down the thoughts of the moment. Those that come
       unsought for are commonly the most valuable.

> Bacon (1561-1626)

5049   All truly wise thoughts have been thought already thousands
       of times; but to make them truly ours, we must think them
       over again honestly, till they take root in our personal
       experience.

> Goethe (1749-1832)

5050   If a man's eye is on the Eternal, his intellect will grow.

> Emerson (1803-1882)

5051   It is well for the heart to be naive
       and for the mind not to be.

> Anatole France (1844-1924)

5052   Thought is a tremendous living force -
       Thought gains strength by repetition,
       Thought moulds your character and shapes your destiny.
       Therefore centre your thoughts on God and sublime Truths.

> Sivananda (born 1887)

5053   If you wish to know the mind of a man,
       listen to his words.

> Chinese Proverb

7. POTPOURRI

5054   I am the Mind - the Eternal Teacher. I am the Father of the
       Word - the Redeemer of all men - and in the nature of the
       wise the Word takes flesh. By means of the Word, the world
       is saved. I, Thought - the Father of the Word, the Mind -
       come only unto men that are holy and good, pure and
       merciful, and that live piously and religiously, and my
       presence is an inspiration and a help to them, for when I
       come they immediately know all things and adore the
       Universal Father. Before such wise and philosophic ones
       die, they learn to renounce their senses, knowing that these
       are the enemies of their immortal souls.
                               The Divine Pymander (BC 2500?-200 AD?)

5055   At the end of the worlds, all things sleep: he alone is
       awake in Eternity. Then from his infinite space new worlds
       arise and awake, a universe which is a vastness of thought.
       In the consciousness of the Eternal One the universe is,
       and into him it returns.
                                              Upanishads (c. B.C. 800)

5056   What a man thinks in his spirit in the world,
       that he does after his departure from the world
       when he becomes a spirit.
                                            Swedenborg (1688-1772)

5057   Lull'd in the countless chambers of the brain,
       Our thoughts are link'd by many a hidden chain;
       Awake but one, and lo, what myriads rise!
       Each stamps its image as the other flies.
                                                   Pope (1688-1744)

5058   The beings of the mind are not of clay;
       Essentially immortal, they create
       And multiply in us a brighter ray
       And more beloved existence.
                                                 Byron (1788-1824)

5059   Thought is the wind, knowledge the sail,
       and mankind the vessel.
                                         August Hare (1792-1834)

5060   Sudden a thought came like a full-blown rose,
       Flushing his brow.
                                                 Keats (1795-1821)

5061   Time to me this truth has taught,
            (Tis a treasure worth revealing)
        More offend from want of thought
            Than from want of feeling.

                                    Charles Swain (1803-1874)

5062   The charm of a deed is its doing;
        the charm of a life is its living;
        the soul of the thing is the thought.

                                    Eugene F. Ware (1841-1911)

5063   Thinking is like loving and dying.
        Each of us must do it for himself.

                                    Josiah Royce (1855-1916)

5064   Few people think more than two or three times a year.
        I have made an international reputation for myself by
        thinking once or twice a week

                                    G. B. Shaw (1856-1950)

5065   Seven Watchmen sitting in a tower,
            Watching what had come upon Mankind,
        Showed the Man the Glory and the Power
            And bade him shape the Kingdom to his mind...
        That a man's mind is wont to tell him more,
            Than Seven Watchmen sitting in a tower.

                                    Kipling (1865-1936)

5066   The difference between intelligence and education is this-
        that intelligence will make you a good living.

                                    Charles Kettering (1876-1958)

5067   The social states of human kinds
        Are made by multitudes of minds,
        And after multitudes of years
        A little human growth appears
        Worth having, even to the soul
        Who sees most plain, it's not the whole.

                                    John Masefield (1878-1967)

5068   The consciousness of man is a veil concealing
        the reality of God in the state of non-manifestation.
        We are ourselves the veil covering God's reality.

                                    Pir Vilayat Inayat Khan (born 1916)

TIME

Duration, Eternity, Past, Present and Future

1. ESSENCE

5069   Our time is a very shadow that passeth away.
Wisdom of Solomon (c. B.C. 200)

5070   Time is a sort of river of passing events, and strong
is its current; no sooner is a thing brought to sight
than it is swept by and another takes its place, and
this too will be swept away.
Marcus Aurelius (121-180 A.D.)

5071   Time has only a relative existence.
Carlyle (1795-1881)

5072   Time is only an illusion produced by the succession of our
states of consciousness as we travel through eternal
duration, and it does not exist where no consciousness
exists in which the illusion can be produced; but "lies
asleep."
H. P. Blavatsky (1831-1891)

2. OPPOSITES

5073   Time destroys the speculations of man,
but it confirms the judgment of nature.
Cicero (B.C. 106-43)

5074   Time will bring to light whatever is hidden; it will cover
up and conceal what is now shining in splendor.
Horace (B.C. 65-8)

5075   A man that is young in years may be old in hours,
if he has lost no time.
Bacon (1561-1626)

5076   What a day may bring, a day may take away.
Thomas Fuller (1608-1661)

5077   Nothing is there to come, and nothing past,
But an eternal Now does always last.
Abraham Cowley (1618-1667)

5078   The past and future are veiled; but the past wears the
widow's veil, the future the virgin's.
Richter (1763-1825)

5079 Time is the most undefinable yet paradoxical of things;
      the past is gone, the future is not come, and the present
      becomes the past, even while we attempt to define it, and,
      like the flash of the lightning, at once exists and expires.
                                           Colton (1780-1832)

5080 Time, the cradle of hope, but the grave of ambition, is the
      stern corrector of fools, but the salutary counsellor of the
      wise, bringing all they dread to the one, and all they
      desire to the other....He that has made it his friend will
      have little to fear from his enemies, but he that has made
      it his enemy will have little to hope from his friends.
                                           Colton (1780-1832)

5081 The future influences the present just as much as the past.
                                           Nietzsche (1844-1900)

5082 We do not know what to do with this short life,
      yet we want another which will be eternal.
                                           Anatole France (1844-1924)

5083 The present contains nothing more than the past,
      and what is found in the effect is already in the cause.
                                           Henri Louis Bergson (1859-1941)

5084 The farther backward you can look,
      the farther forward you are likely to see.
                                           Winston Churchill (1874-1965)

5085 When you sit with a nice girl for two hours,
        you think it's only a minute.
      But when you sit on a hot stove for a minute,
        you think it's two hours.
      That's relativity.
                                           Einstein (1879-1955)

3. INSIGHT

5086 This instant is thine; the next is in the womb of futurity,
      and thou knowest not what it may bring forth;
      maturity of the unborn is in the keeping of the Law.
      Each future state is that thou has created in the present.
                                           Akhenaton? (c. B.C. 1375)

5087 A thousand years in thy sight are but as yesterday when
      it is past, and as a watch in the night.
                                           Psalms 90:4 (B.C. 1000?-300?)

5088 There is a bridge between Time and Eternity; and this
      bridge is the Spirit of man. Neither day nor night cross
      that bridge, nor old age, nor death nor sorrow.
                                           Upanishads (c. B.C. 800)

5089   The velocity with which time flies is infinite,
       as is most apparent to those who look back.
                                   Seneca (B.C. 3-65 A.D.)

5090   In comparison with heaven and earth, man is like a mayfly.
       But compared to the great Way, heaven and earth, too, are
       like a bubble and a shadow. Only the primal spirit and the
       true nature overcome time and space.
                                      Lu Yen (fl. 800 A.D.)

5091   Whether time is long or short, and whether space is broad
       or narrow, depend upon the mind. Those whose minds are at
       leisure can feel one day as a millennium, and those
       whose thoughts are expansive can perceive a small house
       to be as spacious as the universe.
                               Hung Tzu-ch'eng (1593-1665)

5092   The only true time which a man can properly call his own,
          is that which he has all to himself;
       the rest, though in some sense he may be said to live it,
          is other people's time, not his.
                                 Charles Lamb (1775-1834)

5093   Time, whose tooth gnaws away everything else,
       is powerless against truth.
                                Thomas Huxley (1825-1895)

5094   The present is only a mathematical line which divides
       that part of eternal duration which we call the future,
       from that which we call the past.
                               H. P. Blavatsky (1831-1891)

5095   Eternity is the infinite existence of every moment of time.
       If we conceive time as a line, then this line will be
       crossed at every point by the lines of eternity.
       Every point of the line of time will be a line in eternity.
       The line of time will be a plane of eternity.
       Eternity has one dimension more than time.
                                   Gurdjieff (1873-1949)

5096   Time has no divisions to mark its passing.
       There is never a thunderstorm to announce
       the beginning of a new month or year.
                                  Thomas Mann (1875-1955)

5097   The wheels of time are mysterious. Time is a concept of
       mind. Without mind, there is no concept of time.
       Annihilate the mind. You will go beyond time. You will
       enter the realm of Timeless. You will live in the Eternal.
                                   Sivananda (born 1887)

5098   The future comes one day at a time.

Dean Acheson (1893-1971)

5099   In the city, time becomes visible.

Lewis Mumford (born 1895)

4. POSITIVE

5100   Time is the wisest counsellor.

Pericles (B.C. 495-429)

5101   Time discovers truth.

Seneca (B.C. 3-65 A.D.)

5102   Time is the sovereign physician of our passions.

Montaigne (1533-1592)

5103   Time is the greatest of innovators.

Bacon (1561-1626)

5104   One always has time enough, if one will apply it well.

Goethe (1749-1832)

5105   The beautifier of the dead,
       Adorner of the ruin, comforter
       And the only healer when the heart hath bled.

Byron (1788-1824)

5106   Here is a day now before me;
       a day is a fortune and an estate;
       who loses a day loses life.

Emerson (1803-1882)

5. NEGATIVE

5107   Neither will the wave which has passed be called back;
       nor can the hour which has gone by return.

Ovid (B.C. 43-18 A.D.)

5108   Swift speedy time, feathered with flying hours,
       Dissolves the beauty of the fairest brow.

Samuel Daniel (1562?-1619)

5109   What a folly to dread the thought of throwing away
       life at once, and yet have no regard of throwing it away
       by parcels and piecemeal.

John Howe (1630-1705)

5110   We take no note of time but from its loss.

Young (1683-1765)

5111   Tobacco, coffee, alcohol, hashish, prusic acid, strychnine,
       are weak dilutions: the surest poison is time.

Emerson (1803-1882)

5112   In time there is no present,
       In eternity no future,
       In eternity no past.

Alfred Tennyson (1809-1892)

5113   If you lose an hour in the morning, you have to hunt for it
       the rest of the day.

Chinese Proverb

6. ADVICE

5114   Do not dwell in the past. Do not dream of the future.
       Concentrate the mind on the present moment.

Buddha (B.C. 568-488)

5115   Leave the past behind;
       leave the future behind;
       leave the present behind.
       Thou are then ready to go to the other shore.
       Never more shalt thou return to a life that ends in death.

The Dhammapada (c. B.C. 300)

5116   Make use of time, let not advantage slip;
       Beauty within itself should not be wasted:
       Fair flowers that are not gather'd in their prime
       Rot and consume themselves in little time.

Shakespeare (1564-1616)

5117   Enjoy the present smiling hour.
       And put it out of Fortune's power.

Dryden (1631-1700)

5118   If you want the present to be different from the past,
       study the past.

Spinoza (1632-1677)

5119   Know the true value of time; snatch, seize, and enjoy
       every moment of it. No idleness, no laziness, no
       procrastination: never put off till to-morrow what you
       can do to-day.

Chesterfield (1694-1773)

5120   Dost thou love life?
       then do not squander time,
       for that is the stuff life is made of.

Franklin (1706-1790)

5121 Devote each day to the object then in time
and every evening will find something done.

Goethe (1749-1832)

5122 Since time is not a person we can overtake when he is past,
let us honor him with mirth and cheerfulness of heart while
he is passing.

Goethe (1749-1832)

5123 Much may be done in those little shreds and patches of time,
which every day produces, and which most men throw away,
but which nevertheless will make at the end of it no small
deduction from the life of a man.

Colton (1780-1832)

5124 Write it on your heart that every day is the best day
in the year. No man has learned anything rightly, until
he knows that every day is Doomsday.

Emerson (1803-1882)

5125 Make good of every minute that is at thy disposal. Time is
a rat that slowly cuts the thread of life. It may break at
any moment. Believe not that you will be living to enjoy
the objects of life. Death may lay his icy hands on this
body and may shatter it at any time.

Sivananda (born 1887)

7. POTPOURRI

5126 Where Mind and each believing mind are not divided,
And undivided are each believing mind and Mind,
This is where words fail;
For it is not for the past, present, and future.

Seng-T'San (540?-606 A.D.)

5127 Ah, fill the Cup: - what boots it to repeat
How Time is slipping underneath our Feet:
  Unborn To-morrow, and dead Yesterday,
Why fret about them if To-day be sweet!

Omar Khayyam (fl. 1100)

5128 From the beginning of Time, through eternities,
  I was among His hidden treasures.
From Nothing He called me forth, but at the End of Time
  I shall be recalled by the King.

Nahmanides (c. 1300)

5129 All my possessions for a moment of time.

Elizabeth I (1533-1603)

5130   I wasted time, and now doth time waste me.

Shakespeare (1564-1616)

5131   Like as the waves make towards the pebbled shore,
So do our minutes hasten to their end.

Shakespeare (1564-1616)

5132   Time is the king of men;
he is both their parent,
and he is their grave,
and gives them what he will,
not what they crave.

Shakespeare (1564-1616)

5133   Enjoy the present hour,
Be thankful for the past,
And neither fear nor wish
Th' approaches of the last.

Abraham Cowley (1618-1667)

5134   Ever eating, never cloying,
All-devouring, all-destroying,
Never finding full repast,
Till I eat the world at last.

Swift (1667-1745)

5135   Tomorrow is a satire on today,
And shows its weakness.

Young (1683-1765)

5136   Time is a continual over-dropping of moments,
which fall down one upon the other and evaporate.

Richter (1763-1825)

5137   Lost, yesterday, somewhere between sunrise and sunset,
two golden hours, each set with sixty diamond minutes.
No reward is offered, for they are gone forever!

Lydia Sigourney (1791-1865)

5138   Thou shoreless flood, which in thy ebb and flow
claspest the limits of mortality.

Shelley (1792-1822)

5139   So here hath been dawning another blue day:
   Think, wilt thou let it slip useless away?
Out of eternity this new day is born;
   Into eternity at night 'twill return.

Carlyle (1795-1881)

5140   Time is but the stream I go a fishing in.

Thoreau (1817-1862)

5141   Enjoy the spring of love and youth,
          To some good angel leave the rest;
       For time will teach thee soon the truth,
          There are no birds in last year's nest.

Longfellow (1807-1882)

5142   That is the land of lost content,
       I see it shining plain,
       The happy highways where I went
       And cannot come again.

A. E. Housman (1859-1936)

5143   You wake up in the morning, and lo! your purse is magically
       filled with twenty-four hours of the magic tissue of the
       universe of your life. No one can take it from you. No one
       receives either more or less than you receive. Waste your
       infinitely precious commodity as much as you will, and the
       supply will never be withheld from you. Moreover, you
       cannot draw on the future. Impossible to get into debt.
       You can only waste the passing moment. You cannot waste
       tomorrow. It is kept for you.

Arnold Bennett (1867-1931)

5144   Time is breath - try to understand this.

Gurdjieff (1873-1949)

5145   The Future is something which everyone reaches at the rate
       of sixty minutes an hour, whatever he does, whoever he is.

C. S. Lewis (1898-1963)

5146   Hours are Time's shafts,
       and one comes winged with death.

Scottish Clock Motto

TRAVEL
Journey, Path, Wanderlust and Way

1. ESSENCE

5147 The winds and the waves are always on the side of the
ablest navigators.

Gibbon (1737-1794)

5148 To travel hopefully is a better thing than to arrive.

Robert Louis Stevenson (1850-1895)

5149 No road to happiness or sorrow...
Find them in yourself.

Chinese Proverb

2. OPPOSITES

5150 The bright and dark paths out of the world have always
existed. Whoso takes the former, returns not; he who
chooses the latter, returns.

Bhagavad Gita (c. B.C. 400)

5151 It is not fit that every man should travel;
it makes a wise man better, and a fool worse.

Owen Feltham (1602-1668)

5152 Travel is the frivolous part of serious lives,
and the serious part of frivolous ones.

Anne Swetchine (1782-1857)

5153 Thou canst not travel on the path
before thou hast become that Path itself.

H. P. Blavatsky (1831-1891)

5154 The map appears to us more real than the land.

D. H. Lawrence (1885-1930)

3. INSIGHT

5155 They change their sky, not their mind, who cross the sea.
A busy idleness possesses us: we seek a happy life, with
ships and carriages: the object of our search is present
with us.

Horace (B.C. 65-8)

5156 The journey of high honor lies not in smooth ways.

Philip Sidney (1554-1586)

5157   Travel, in the younger sort, is a part of education; in the
       elder, a part of experience. He that travelleth into a
       country before he hath some entrance into the language,
       goeth to school, and not to travel.

                                                Bacon (1561-1626)

5158   Men may change their climate, but they cannot change their
       nature. A man that goes out a fool cannot ride or sail
       himself into common sense.

                                              Addison (1672-1719)

5159   As the Spanish proverb says,
       "He who would bring home the wealth of the Indies
         must carry the wealth of the Indies with him."
       So it is in travelling; a man must carry knowledge with
       him, if he would bring home knowledge.

                                             Johnson (1709-1784)

5160   A good holiday is one spent among people whose notions of
       time are vaguer than yours.

                                      J. B. Priestley (1733-1804)

5161   To see the world is to judge the judges.

                                             Joubert (1754-1824)

5162   Those who visit foreign nations,
       but who associate only with their own countrymen,
       change their climate, but not their customs;
       they see new meridians, but the same men;
       and with heads as empty as their pockets,
       return home with travelled bodies, but untravelled minds.

                                              Colton (1780-1832)

5163   We are all naturally seekers of wonders. We travel far to
       see the majesty of old ruins, the venerable forms of the
       hoary mountains, great waterfalls, and galleries of art.
       And yet the world wonder is all around us; the wonder of
       setting suns, and evening stars, of the magic spring-time,
       the blossoming of the trees, the strange transformations of
       the moth...

                                          Albert Pike (1809-1891)

4. POSITIVE

5164   Nature's way is straight and unerring, foursquare and
       calm, great and tolerant. Everything is accomplished
       without the necessity of fabricated purpose.
         Man's way is equally self-evident. His internal
       principles are correct; his external acts are righteous;
       his results are certain.

                                          I Ching (B.C. 1150?)

5165   Following the Noble Path is like entering a dark room with
        a light in the hand; the darkness will all be cleared away,
        and the room will be filled with light.

                                        Buddha (B.C. 568-488)

5166   As long as you watch the way,
        As long as your steps are steady,
        As long as your wisdom is unimpaired,
        So long will you reap profit.

                                    Nagarjuna (c. 100-200 A.D.)

5167   The world is a great book, of which they who never stir from
        home read only a page.

                                     Augustine (354-430 A.D.)

5168   Good company in a journey makes the way seem shorter.
                                     Izaak Walton (1593-1683)

5169   The use of travelling is to regulate imagination by reality,
        and instead of thinking how things may be, to see them as
        they are.

                                       Johnson (1709-1784)

5170   All travel has its advantages. If the traveler visits
        better countries, he may learn to improve his own; and if
        fortune carries him to worse, he may learn to enjoy his own.

                                       Johnson (1709-1784)

5171   How much a dunce that has been sent to roam
        Excels a dunce that has been kept at home.

                                       Cowper (1731-1800)

5172   Travel is the perfect liberty to think, feel, do just as
        one pleases.

                                       Hazlitt (1778-1830)

5173   The traveled mind is the universal mind educated from
        exclusiveness and egotism.

                                  Amos B. Alcott (1799-1888)

5174   Travel gives a character of experience to our knowledge,
        and brings the figures on the tablet of memory into strong
        relief.

                                     Tuckerman (1813-1871)

5175   One main factor in the upward trend of animal life has been
        the power of wandering.

                           Alfred North Whitehead (1861-1947)

5. NEGATIVE

5176   One may know the world without going out of doors.
        One may see the Way of Heaven without looking through
            the windows.
        The further one goes, the less one knows.
        Therefore the sage knows without going about,
        Understands without seeing,
        And accomplishes without any action.

Lao-Tzu (fl. B.C. 600)

5177   See one promontory, one mountain, one sea, one river, and
        see all.

Socrates (B.C. 469-399)

5178   Everywhere is nowhere.
        When a person spends all his time in foreign travel,
        he ends by having many acquaintances, but no friends.

Seneca (B.C. 3-65 A.D.)

5179   A traveller without observation is a bird without wings.

Saadi (1184-1291)

5180   A traveller! By my faith, you have great reason to be sad.
        I fear you have sold your own lands, to see other men's;
        then to have seen much, and to have nothing,
        is to have rich eyes and poor hands.

Shakespeare (1564-1616)

5181   Never any weary traveller complained that he came too
        soon to his journey's end.

Thomas Fuller (1608-1661)

5182   Usually speaking, the worst-bred person in company is a
        young traveller just returned from abroad.

Swift (1667-1745)

5183   He traveled here, he traveled there-
        But not the value of a hair
        Was heart or head the better.

Wordsworth (1770-1850)

5184   The soul is no traveller; the wise man stays at home...
        Travelling is a fool's paradise.

Emerson (1803-1882)

5185   It is not worth while to go around the world
        to count the cats in Zanzibar.

Thoreau (1817-1862)

5186   Modern travelling is not travelling at all; it is merely
        being sent to a place, and very little different from
        becoming a parcel.
                                            John Ruskin (1819-1900)

5187   The traveller's-eye view of men and women is not satisfying.
        A man might spend his life in trains and restaurants and
        know nothing of humanity at the end. To know, one must be
        an actor as well as a spectator.
                                        Aldous Huxley (1894-1963)

6. ADVICE

5188   The Wanderer finds success through smallness.
        Perseverance brings good fortune to The Wanderer.
                                            I Ching (B.C. 1150?)

5189   As the bee takes the essence of a flower
        and flies away without destroying its beauty and perfume,
        so let the sage wander in this life.
                                    The Dhammapada (c. B.C. 300)

5190   If a traveller does not meet with one who is his better,
        or his equal, let him firmly keep to his solitary journey;
        there is no companionship with a fool.
                                    The Dhammapada (c. B.C. 300)

5191   Walk while ye have the light, lest darkness come upon you.
                                            John (50?-100? A.D.)

5192   If you will be a traveller, have always...two bags very
        full, that is one of patience and another of money.
                                        John Florio (1553?-1625)

5193   Rather see the wonders of the world abroad than,
        living dully sluggardized at home, wear out thy youth
        with shapeless idleness.
                                        Shakespeare (1564-1616)

5194   A traveller must have the back of an ass to bear all,
        a tongue like the tail of a dog to flatter all,
        the mouth of a hog to eat what is set before him,
        the ear of a merchant to hear all and say nothing.
                                        Thomas Nashe (1567-1601)

5195   A wise traveler never despises his own country.
                                        Carlo Goldoni (1707-1793)

5196   A man should know something of his own country, too, before
        he goes abroad.
                                            Sterne (1713-1768)

7. POTPOURRI

5197   One hundred and one subtle ways come from the heart.
One of them rises to the crown of the head.
This is the way that leads to immortality;
the others lead to different ends.

Upanishads (c. B.C. 800)

5198   The great Way is calm and large-hearted,
For it nothing is easy, nothing is hard;
Small views are irresolute,
The more in haste the tardier they go.

Seng-T'San (540?-606 A.D.)

5199   White pebbles just from the river-stream,
Stray leaves red in the cold autumn:
No rain is falling on the mountain path,
But my clothes are damp in the fine green air.

Wang Wei (699-759 A.D.)

5200   When I was at home, I was in a better place;
but travellers must be content.

Shakespeare (1564-1616)

5201   We that acquaint ourselves with every zone
And pass both tropics and behold the poles,
When we come home are to ourselves unknown
And unacquainted still with our own souls.

John Davies (1570-1626)

5202   We sack, we ransack to the utmost sands
Of native kingdoms, and of foreign lands:
We travel sea and soil; we pry, and prowl,
We progress, and we prog from pole to pole.

Quarles (1592-1644)

5203   Let observation with extensive view,
Survey mankind from China to Peru;
Remark each anxious toil, each eager strife,
And watch the busy scenes of crowded life.

Johnson (1709-1784)

5204   I should like to spend the whole of my life in traveling
abroad, if I could anywhere borrow another life to spend
afterwards at home.

Hazlitt (1778-1830)

5205   O'er the glad water of the dark blue sea,
      Our thoughts as boundless, and our souls as free,
      Far as the breeze can bear, the billows foam,
      Survey our empire, and behold our home!

                                   Byron (1788-1824)

5206   Does the road wind up-hill all the way?
        Yes, to the very end.
      Will the day's journey take the whole long day?
        From morn to night, my friend.

                          Christina Rossetti (1830-1894)

5207   There is no unhappiness like the misery of sighting land
      again after a cheerful, careless voyage.

                          Mark Twain (1835-1910)

5208   Down to Gehenna or up to the throne,
      He travels fastest who travels alone.

                          Kipling (1865-1936)

5209   I am fevered with the sunset,
       I am fretful with the bay,
      For the wander-thirst is on me
       And my soul is in Cathay.

                        Richard Hovey (1869-1900)

5210   Life is a pilgrimage. The wise man does not rest by the
      roadside inns. He marches direct to the illimitable domain
      of eternal bliss, his ultimate destination.

                        Sivananda (born 1887)

TRUTH
Honesty and Sincerity

1. ESSENCE

5211   Sincerity and truth are the basis of every virtue.
Confucius (B.C. 551-479)

5212   Truth is always straightforward.
Sophocles (B.C. 495-406)

5213   The language of truth is simple.
Seneca (B.C. 3-65 A.D.)

5214   An honest man is always a child.
Martial (43-104 A.D.)

5215   Abstract truth is the eye of reason.
Rousseau (1712-1778)

5216   Honesty is the first chapter of the book of wisdom.
Thomas Jefferson (1743-1826)

5217   Everything that is possible to be believed
is an image of the truth.
William Blake (1757-1828)

5218   Truth makes on the ocean of nature no one track of light;
every eye, looking on, finds its own.
Bulwer-Lytton (1803-1873)

2. OPPOSITES

5219   Say not unto thyself, Behold, truth breedeth hatred, and
I will avoid it; dissimulation raiseth friends, and I will
follow it. Are not the enemies made by truth, better than
the friends obtained by flattery?
Akhenaton? (c. B.C. 1375)

5220   The Supreme Truth exists both internally and externally,
in the moving and non-moving.
He is beyond the power of material senses to see or know.
Although, far, far away, he is also near to all.
Bhagavad Gita (c. B.C. 400)

5221   They who imagine truth in untruth, and see untruth in truth,
never arrive at truth, but follow vain desires.
They who know truth in truth, and untruth in untruth,
arrive and follow true desires.
The Dhammapada (c. B.C. 300)

5222   The spirits of truth and falsehood
        Struggle within the heart of man;
        Truth born out of the spring of Light,
        Falsehood from the well of darkness.
        And according as man inherits truth
        So will he avoid darkness.
                              Dead Sea Scrolls (c. B.C. 200-680 A.D.)

5223   Truth is confirmed by inspection and delay;
        falsehood by haste and uncertainty.
                                            Tacitus (55-117 A.D.)

5224   The opposite of what is rumored about men and things is
        often the truth.
                                        La Bruyere (1645-1696)

5225   There are two kinds of truth: those of reasoning and those
        of fact. The truths of reasoning are necessary and their
        opposite is impossible; the truths of fact are contingent
        and their opposite is possible.
                                        Leibnitz (1646-1716)

5226   All men wish to have truth on their side;
        but few to be on the side of truth.
                                    Richard Whately (1787-1863)

5227   Every truth is true only up to a point. Beyond that, by way
        of counter-point, it becomes untruth.
                                        Kierkegaard (1813-1855)

5228   As scarce as truth is, the supply has always been in excess
        of the demand.
                                        Josh Billings (1815-1885)

5229   A truth that disheartens because it is true
        is of more value than the most stimulating of falsehoods.
                                    Maurice Maeterlinck (1862-1949)

5230   There are trivial truths and the great truths.
        The opposite of a trivial truth is plainly false.
        The opposite of a great truth is also true.
                                        Niels Bohr (1885-1962)

5231   The essence of Truth is eternal;
        Individual truths wax and wane.
                                    A. L. Linall, Jr. (born 1947)

5232   To know the truth is easy;
        to follow it is difficult.

                                        Chinese Proverb

3. INSIGHT

5233 If the slayer thinks that he kills, and if the slain thinks
that he dies, neither knows the ways of truth. The Eternal
in man cannot kill: the Eternal in man cannot die.
Upanishads (c. B.C. 800)

5234 Absolute truth is indestructible.
Being indestructible, it is eternal.
Being eternal, it is self-existent.
Being self-existent, it is infinite.
Being infinite, it is vast and deep.
Being vast and deep, it is transcendental and intelligent.
Confucius (B.C. 551-479)

5235 Seven years of silent inquiry are needful for a man to
learn the truth, but fourteen in order to learn how to
make it known to his fellowmen.
Plato (B.C. 427?-347?)

5236 Our minds possess by nature an insatiable desire to know
the truth.
Cicero (B.C. 106-43)

5237 There is another old poet whose name I do not now remember
who said, "Truth is the daughter of Time."
Aulus Gellius (117?-180? A.D.)

5238 Children and fools speak true.
John Lyly (1554-1606)

5239 There are three parts in truth:
 first, the inquiry, which is the wooing of it;
 secondly, the knowledge of it, which is the presence of it;
 and thirdly, the belief, which is the enjoyment of it.
Bacon (1561-1626)

5240 Truth emerges more readily from error than from confusion.
Bacon (1561-1626)

5241 Truth is compared in Scripture to a streaming fountain;
if her waters flow not in a perpetual progression,
they sicken into a muddy pool of conformity and tradition.
Milton (1608-1674)

5242 We know the truth, not only by the reason, but also by
the heart.
Pascal (1623-1662)

5243 Truth will be uppermost one time or another, like cork,
though kept down in the water.
William Temple (1628-1699)

5244 Truth comes home to the mind so naturally that when we learn
it for the first time, it seems as though we did no more
than recall it to our memory.
Fontenelle (1657-1757)

5245 The greatest friend of truth is Time,
her greatest enemy is Prejudice,
and her constant companion is Humility.
Colton (1780-1832)

5246 There is nothing so powerful as truth;
and often nothing so strange.
Daniel Webster (1782-1852)

5247 Truth like a torch, the more 'tis shook, it shines.
William Hamilton (1788-1856)

5248 Truth that has merely been learned is like an artificial
limb, a false tooth, a waxen nose; it adheres to us only
because it is put on. But truth acquired by thought of our
own is like a natural limb; it alone really belongs to us.
Schopenhauer (1788-1860)

5249 History has its truth; and so has legend hers.
Victor Hugo (1802-1885)

5250 The nobler the truth or sentiment, the less imports the
question of authorship.
Emerson (1803-1882)

5251 No man thoroughly understands a truth until he has
contended against it.
Emerson (1803-1882)

5252 All truths are Truths of Period, and not truths for
eternity; that whatever great fact has had strength and
vitality enough to make itself real, whether of religion,
morals, government, or of whatever else, and to find place
in this world, has been a truth for the time, and as good
as men were capable of receiving.
Albert Pike (1809-1891)

5253 Truth, like the sun, submits to be obscured;
but like the sun, only for a time.
Bovee (1820-1904)

5254   The stream of time sweeps away errors, and leaves the
        truth for the inheritance of humanity.

                                    Georg Brandes (1842-1927)

5255   Truth must necessarily be stranger than fiction; for
        fiction is the creation of the human mind and therefore
        congenial to it.

                                    G. K. Chesterton (1874-1936)

5256   Facts do not cease to exist because they are ignored.

                                    Aldous Huxley (1894-1963)

4. POSITIVE

5257   O thou who art enamoured with the beauties of Truth,
        and hast fixed thy heart on the simplicity of her charms,
        hold fast thy fidelity unto her, and forsake her not:
        the constancy of thy virtue shall crown thee with honour.

                                    Akhenaton? (c. B.C. 1375)

5258   If you are sincere, you have success in your heart,
        And whatever you do succeeds.

                                    I Ching (B.C. 1150?)

5259   Truth is so great a perfection, that if God would render
        himself visible to men, he would choose light for his
        body and truth for his soul.

                                    Pythagoras (B.C. 582-507)

5260   The King of Truth is the king of kings. His ancestry is
        of the purest and the highest. He not only rules the four
        quarters of the world, but he is also Lord of Wisdom and
        Protector of all Virtuous Teachings.

                                    Buddha (B.C. 568-488)

5261   Truth is always the strongest argument.

                                    Sophocles (B.C. 495-406)

5262   What we have in us of the image of God
        is the love of truth and justice.

                                    Demosthenes (B.C. 384-322)

5263   There is no greater delight than to be conscious of
        sincerity on self-examination.

                                    Mencius (B.C. 371-288)

5264   The gift of Truth conquers all gifts.
        The taste of Truth conquers all sweetness.
        The joy of Truth conquers all pleasures.
        The loss of desires conquers all sorrows.

                                    The Dhammapada (c. B.C. 300)

5265 Truth may be stretched, but cannot be broken, and always
      gets above falsehood, as oil does above water.
                                          Cervantes (1547-1616)

5266 No pleasure is comparable to the standing upon the
      vantage ground of Truth.
                                              Bacon (1561-1626)

5267 No legacy is so rich as honesty.
                                        Shakespeare (1564-1616)

5268 Truth is as impossible to be soiled by any outward touch as
      the sunbeam.
                                             Milton (1608-1674)

5269 Who ever knew truth put to the worse in a free and open
      encounter?
                                             Milton (1608-1674)

5270 An honest man's the noblest work of God.
                                               Pope (1688-1744)

5271 A man who seeks truth and loves it
      must be reckoned precious to any human society.
                                        Frederick II (1712-1786)

5272 Truth and, by consequence, liberty, will always be the
      chief power of honest men.
                                 Germaine De Stael (1766-1817)

5273 Truth is always congruous and agrees with itself;
      every truth in the universe agrees with all others.
                                     Daniel Webster (1782-1852)

5274 One of the sublimest things in the world is plain truth.
                                      Bulwer-Lytton (1803-1873)

5275 The finest and noblest ground on which people can live
      is truth; the real with the real; a ground on which nothing
      is assumed.
                                           Emerson (1803-1882)

5276 Truth is tough. It will not break, like a bubble,
      at a touch; nay, you may kick it about all day,
      like a football, and it will be round and full at evening.
                            Oliver Wendell Holmes (1809-1894)

5277 Truth is the secret of eloquence and virtue, the basis of
      moral authority; it is the highest summit of art and
      of life.
                             Henri Frederic Amiel (1821-1881)

5278   The spirit of truth and the spirit of freedom-
       they are the pillars of society.

                                    Henrik Ibsen (1828-1906)

5279   In the mountains of truth, you never climb in vain.

                                       Nietzsche (1844-1900)

5280   The nearer one approaches the Truth, the happier one
       becomes. For the essential nature of Truth is positive
       Absolute Bliss.

                                     Sivananda (born 1887)

5281   The man who speaks the truth is always at ease.

                                          Persian Proverb

5. NEGATIVE

5282   Truth lies wrapped up and hidden in the depths.

                                  Seneca (B.C. 3-65 A.D.)

5283   Candor and generosity, unless tempered by due moderation,
       lead to ruin.

                                     Tacitus (55-117 A.D.)

5284   There is nothing true anywhere,
       The true is nowhere to be seen;
       If you say you see the true,
       This seeing is not the true one.

                                   Hui-Neng (638-713 A.D.)

5285   Truth, like roses, often blossoms upon a thorny stem.

                                     Hafiz (1325?-1390?)

5286   Take note, take note, O world,
       To be direct and honest is not safe.

                                 Shakespeare (1564-1616)

5287   All truths are not to be told.

                                       Herbert (1593-1632)

5288   Truth does not do so much good in the world,
       as the appearance of it does evil.

                              La Rochefoucauld (1613-1680)

5289   A man that should call everything by its right name,
       would hardly pass the streets without being knocked
       down as a common enemy.

                                      Halifax (1633-1695)

5290   'Tis not enough your counsel still be true;
           Blunt truths more mischief than nice falsehoods do.
                                                  Pope (1688-1744)

5291   There are truths which are not for all men,
           nor for all times.
                                      Voltaire (1694-1778)

5292   Between falsehood and useless truth there is little
             difference.
           As gold which he cannot spend will make no man rich,
           so knowledge which cannot apply will make no man wise.
                                Johnson (1709-1784)

5293   It is easier to perceive error than to find truth,
           for the former lies on the surface and is easily seen,
           while the latter lies in the depth,
           where few are willing to search for it.
                                Goethe (1749-1832)

5294   A truth that's told with bad intent
           Beats all the lies you can invent.
                        William Blake (1757-1828)

5295   Truth is too simple for us; we do not like those who unmask
           our illusions.
                            Emerson (1803-1882)

5296   The dictum that truth always triumphs over persecution is
           one of those pleasant falsehoods which men repeat after one
           another till they pass into commonplace, but which all
           experience refutes.
                      John Stuart Mill (1806-1873)

5297   Sincerity is no test of truth - no evidence of correctness
           of conduct. You may take poison sincerely believing it the
           needed medicine, but will it save your life?
                      Tryon Edwards (1809-1894)

5298   A little sincerity is a dangerous thing,
           and a great deal of it is absolutely fatal.
                      Oscar Wilde (1854-1900)

5299   When truth is buried underground it grows, it chokes, it
           gathers such an explosive force than on the day it bursts
           out, it blows up everything with it.
                      Emile Zola (1840-1902)

5300   The truth is often a terrible weapon of aggression.
           It is possible to lie, and even to murder, with the truth.
                      Alfred Adler (1870-1937)

5301 To speak the truth is the most difficult thing in the world;
and one must study a great deal and for a long time in order
to be able to speak the truth. The wish alone is not
enough. To speak the truth one must know what the truth
is and what a lie is, and first of all in oneself. And
this nobody wants to know.

Gurdjieff (1873-1949)

5302 Sometimes it is easier to see clearly into the liar
than into the man who tells the truth. Truth, like light,
blinds. Falsehood, on the contrary, is a beautiful twilight
that enhances every object.

Albert Camus (1913-1960)

6. ADVICE

5303 Truth is but one; thy doubts are of thine own raising.
He who made virtues what they are, planted also in thee a
knowledge of their pre-eminence. Act as Soul dictates to
thee, and the end shall be always right.

Akhenaton? (c. B.C. 1375)

5304 The high minded man must care more for the truth
than for what people think.

Aristotle (B.C. 384-322)

5305 Honesty is the best policy.

Cervantes (1547-1616)

5306 To thine own self be true,
And it must follow, as the night the day,
Thou canst not then be false to any man.

Shakespeare (1564-1616)

5307 When it is not in our power to determine what is true,
we ought to follow what is most probable.

Rene Descartes (1596-1650)

5308 A man should never be ashamed to own he has been in the
wrong, which is but saying, in other words, that he is
wiser to-day than he was yesterday.

Pope (1688-1744)

5309 Remember, as long as you live, that nothing but strict truth
can carry you through the world, with either your conscience
or your honor unwounded.

Chesterfield (1694-1773)

5310   You need not tell the truth, unless to those who have a
        right to know it all. But let all you tell be truth.
                                                    Horace Mann (1796-1859)

5311   The greatest homage we can pay to truth is to use it.
                                                    Emerson (1803-1882)

5312   When in doubt tell the truth.
                                                    Mark Twain (1835-1910)

7. POTPOURRI

5313   There are four truths in this world:
        first, all living beings rise from ignorance;
        second, all objects of craving desire are impermanent,
            uncertainty and suffering;
        third, all the existing things are also impermanent,
            uncertainty and suffering;
        fourth, there is nothing that can be called an "ego,"
            and there is no such thing as "mine" in all the world.
                                                    Buddha (B.C. 568-488)

5314   Her terrible tale
            You can't assail,
        With truth it quite agrees;
            Her taste exact
            Her faultless fact
        Amounts to a disease.
                                                    William S. Gilbert (1836-1911)

5315   How happy is he born and taught
            That serveth not another's will;
        Whose armour is his honest thought,
            And simple truth his utmost skill.
                                                    Henry Wotton (1568-1639)

5316   For truth is precious and divine;
        Too rich a pearl for carnal swine.
                                                    Samuel Butler (1612-1680)

5317   Truth is the most powerful thing in the world,
        since even fiction itself must be governed by it,
        and can only please by its resemblance.
                                                    Shaftesbury III (1671-1713)

5318   Truth is a good dog; but always beware of barking too close
        to the heels of an error, lest you get your brains kicked
        out.
                                                    Samuel Coleridge (1772-1834)

5319   Truth is a gem that is found at a great depth;
       whilst on the surface of this world,
       all things are weighed by the false scale of custom.
                                            Byron (1788-1824)

5320   Truth crushed to earth shall rise again:
          Th' eternal years of God are hers;
       But Error, wounded, writhes in pain,
          And dies among his worshippers.
                             William Cullen Bryant (1794-1878)

5321   Think truly, and thy thoughts
          Shall the world's famine feed.
       Speak truly, and each word of thine
          Shall be a fruitful seed.
       Live truly, and thy life shall be
          A great and noble creed.
                                  Horatius Bonar (1808-1889)

5322   A vague sense of Nature's Unity, blended with a dim
       perception of an all-pervading Spiritual Essence, has been
       remarked among the earliest manifestations of the Human
       Mind. Everywhere it was the dim remembrance, uncertain
       and indefinite, of the original truth taught by God to the
       first men.
                                     Albert Pike (1809-1891)

5323   I have discovered the art of deceiving diplomats.
       I speak the truth, and they never believe me.
                                Camillo di Cavour (1810-1861)

5324   Get but the truth once uttered, and 'tis like
       A star new-born that drops into its place
       And which, once circling in its placid round,
       Not all the tumult of the earth can shake.
                                   James Lowell (1819-1891)

5325   An eager pursuit of fortune
          is inconsistent with a severe devotion to truth.
       The heart must grow tranquil
          before the thought can become searching.
                                         Bovee (1820-1904)

5326   Lunatics, drunkards and children sometimes give out the
       truth unconsciously, as if inspired by heaven.
                                   Ramakrishna (1836-1886)

5327   I am not struck so much by the diversity of testimony
       as by the many-sidedness of truth.
                                 Stanley Baldwin (1867-1947)

5328   In wartime, truth is so precious that she should always be
        attended by a bodyguard of lies.

                                    Winston Churchill (1874-1965)

5329   Man with the burning soul
        Has but an hour of breath
        To build a ship of truth
        On which his soul may sail -
        Sail on the sea of death,
        For death takes toll
        Of beauty, courage, youth,
        Of all but truth.

                                    John Masefield (1878-1967)

UNDERSTANDING
Instinct, Intuition, Knowledge and Receptive

1. ESSENCE

5330   Knowledge is an infinite series of images in the memory.
Understanding, which penetrates into their significance, is
the power to perceive their essence and interrelationship.
Kabbalah (B.C. 1200?-700? A.D.)

5331   Intuition is the clear conception of the whole at once.
Lavater (1741-1801)

5332   Instinct is the nose of the mind.
Delphine Girardin (1804-1855)

5333   Instinct is intelligence incapable of self-consciousness.
John Sterling (1806-1844)

2. OPPOSITES

5334   In order to contract, It is necessary first to expand.
In order to weaken, It is necessary first to strengthen.
In order to destroy, It is necessary first to promote.
In order to grasp, It is necessary first to give.
This is called subtle light.
The weak and the tender overcome the hard and the strong.
Lao-Tzu (fl. B.C. 600)

5335   To know is not to know, unless someone else has known that
I know.
Lucillius (B.C. 148-103)

5336   Learned men delight in knowledge; the ignorant do not.
Honey bees resort to flowers; not so the fly.
Saskya Pandita (1182-1251)

5337   Sell your cleverness and buy bewilderment;
Cleverness is mere opinion, bewilderment is intuition.
Jalal-Uddin Rumi (1207-1273)

5338   All things I thought I knew; but now confess
The more I know I know, I know the less.
John Owen (1560-1622)

5339   Ignorance is the curse of God;
knowledge is the wing wherewith we fly to heaven.
Shakespeare (1564-1616)

5340   The light of the understanding-
        humility kindleth and pride covereth.

                                            Quarles (1592-1644)

5341   It is a common fault never to be satisfied with our fortune,
        nor dissatisfied with our understanding.
                                    La Rochefoucauld (1613-1680)

5342   Knowledge is proud that he has learned so much;
        Wisdom is humble that he knows no more.

                                            Cowper (1731-1800)

5343   That is indeed twofold knowledge, which profits alike
        by the folly of the foolish, and the wisdom of the wise.
        It is both a shield and a sword; it borrows its security
        from the darkness, and its confidence from the light.
                                            Colton (1780-1832)

5344   Not every end is a goal. The end of a melody is not its
        goal; however, if the melody has not reached its end, it
        would also not have reached its goal. A parable.
                                            Nietzsche (1844-1900)

5345   The noumenal is the real, the phenomenal, the reflection,
        and the wise man seeks the former rather than the latter.
                                    C. Spurgeon Medhurst (born 1850?)

5346   To understand is hard.
        Once one understands, action is easy.
                                            Sun Yat-sen (1866-1925)

3. INSIGHT

5347   At the outset, the man does not comprehend the nature of
        prevailing forces nor does he perceive them as a connected
        whole. This superficial view is acceptable for the masses,
        but the superior man should know better.
                                            I Ching (B.C. 1150?)

5348   He that hath knowledge spareth his words.
                                        Proverbs (B.C. 1000?-200?)

5349   Know thou the self (spirit) as riding in a chariot,
        The body as the chariot.
        Know thou the intellect as the chariot-driver,
        And the mind as the reins.
        The senses, they say, are the horses;
        The objects of sense, what they range over.
        The self combined with senses and mind
        Wise men call "the enjoyer."
                                            Upanishads (c. B.C. 800)

5350   Only by undivided devotional service can The Eternal be
        understood and seen directly. Only in this way can you
        enter into the mysteries of eternal understanding.
                                        Bhagavad Gita (c. B.C. 400)

5351   One part of knowledge consists in being ignorant
        of such things as are not worthy to be known.
                                        Crates (fl. B.C. 320)

5352   Not to know what happened before one was born is always to
        be a child.
                                        Cicero (B.C. 106-43)

5353   Nature has given us the seeds of knowledge,
        not knowledge itself.
                                        Seneca (B.C. 3-65 A.D.)

5354   He who knows one thing, knows all things;
        and he who knows all things, knows one thing.
        He who is careless in all respects, is in danger;
        he who is not careless in all respects, is free from danger.
                                        Nagarjuna (c. 100-200 A.D.)

5355   One man is equivalent to all Creation.
        One man is a World in miniature.
                                        Nathan (fl. 200 A.D.)

5356   Mark well how varied are aspects of the immovable one,
        And know that the first reality is immovable;
        Only when this insight is attained,
        The true working of suchness is understood.
                                        Hui-Neng (638-713 A.D.)

5357   Indeed, the whole world is imagination,
            while He is the Real in Reality.
        Whoever understand this
            knows all the secrets of the Spiritual Path.
                                        Ibn Al-'Arabi (1165-1240)

5358   Whoever acquires knowledge but does not practice it
        is as one who ploughs but does not sow.
                                        Saadi (1184-1291)

5359   The knower and the known are one. Simple people imagine
        that they should see God, as if He stood there and they
        here. This is not so. God and I, we are one in knowledge.
                                        Meister Eckhart (1260-1327)

5360   All our knowledge has its origins in our perceptions.
                                        Leonardo Da Vinci (1452-1519)

5361   The eye of the understanding is like the eye of the sense;
for as you may see great objects through small crannies
or holes, so you may see great axioms of nature through
small and contemptible instances.

Bacon (1561-1626)

5362   Knowledge always desires increase; it is like fire,
which must first be kindled by some external agent,
but which will afterwards propagate itself.

Johnson (1709-1784)

5363   Man is not born to solve the problem of the universe, but
to find out what he has to do; and to restrain himself
within the limits of his comprehension.

Goethe (1749-1832)

5364   The word knowledge, strictly employed, implies three things:
truth, proof, and conviction.

Richard Whately (1787-1863)

5365   The instinctive feeling of a great people is often wiser
than its wisest men.

Louis Kossuth (1802-1894)

5366   To be conscious that you are ignorant is a great step to
knowledge.

Disraeli (1804-1881)

5367   Knowledge comes, but wisdom lingers.

Alfred Tennyson (1809-1892)

5368   To know that we know what we know,
and that we do not know what we do not know,
that is true knowledge.

Thoreau (1817-1862)

5369   Knowledge once gained casts a light beyond its own
immediate boundaries.

John Tyndall (1820-1893)

5370   A man only understands what is akin to something already
existing in himself.

Henri Frederic Amiel (1821-1881)

5371   Knowledge by itself does not give understanding. Nor is
understanding increased by an increase of knowledge alone.
Understanding depends upon the relation of knowledge to
being. Understanding is the resultant of knowledge and
being...It appears only when a man feels and senses what
is connected with it.

Gurdjieff (1873-1949)

5372   There is a great difference between knowing a thing and
       understanding it. You can know a lot about something and
       not really understand it.
                                          Charles Kettering (1876-1958)

5373   Just as rain exists in the clouds, butter in milk, fragrance
       in flowers, so also God is hidden in all these names and
       forms.
                                             Sivananda (born 1887)

4. POSITIVE

5374   Because the Father of all things consists of Life and Light,
       whereof man is made. If, therefore, a man shall learn and
       understand the nature of Life and Light, then he shall pass
       into the eternity of Life and Light.
                                 The Divine Pymander (BC 2500?-200 AD?)

5375   By wisdom a house is built,
         and by understanding it is established;
       by knowledge the rooms are filled
         with all precious and pleasant riches.
       A wise man is mightier than a strong man;
         and a man of knowledge than he who has strength.
                                        Proverbs (B.C. 1000?-200?)

5376   The Valley Spirit never dies.
       It is called the Mysterious Female.
       And the doorway of the Mysterious Female
       Is the base from which Heaven and Earth spring.
       It is there within us all the time.
       Draw upon it as you will, it never runs dry.
                                            Lao-Tzu (fl. B.C. 600)

5377   Amongst all things, knowledge, they say, is truly the best
       thing; from its not being liable ever to be stolen, from
       its not being purchasable, and from its being imperishable.
                                       The Hitopadesa (600?-1100? A.D.)

5378   That jewel knowledge is great riches, which is not plundered
       by kinsmen, nor carried off by thieves, nor decreased by
       giving.
                                          Bhavabhuti (fl. 700 A.D.)

5379   Whatever we well understand we express clearly,
       and words flow with ease.
                                       Nicholas Boileau (1636-1711)

5380 Knowledge is comfortable and a necessary retreat and shelter
for us in advanced age, but if we do not plant it while
young, it will give us no shade when we grow old.
Chesterfield (1694-1773)

5381 Knowledge is more than equivalent to force.
The master of mechanics laughs at strength.
Johnson (1709-1784)

5382 For love is ever the beginning of Knowledge,
as fire is of light.
Carlyle (1795-1881)

5383 Every generation enjoys the use of a vast hoard bequeathed
to it by antiquity, and transmits that hoard, augmented
by fresh acquisitions, to future ages.
Macaulay (1800-1859)

5384 Knowledge is the antidote to fear.
Emerson (1803-1882)

5385 The best part of our knowledge is that which teaches us
where knowledge leaves off and ignorance begins.
Oliver Wendell Holmes (1809-1894)

5386 When we begin to understand we grow polite, happy,
ingenuous.
Nietzsche (1844-1900)

5. NEGATIVE

5387 Of all men's miseries the bitterest is this:
to know so much and to have control over nothing.
Herodotus (B.C. 484-425)

5388 When there is an increase in the mode of ignorance,
madness, illusion, inertia and darkness are manifested.
Bhagavad Gita (c. B.C. 400)

5389 He that increaseth knowledge increaseth sorrow.
Ecclesiastes (B.C. 300?)

5390 To know all things is not permitted.
Horace (B.C. 65-8)

5391 True knowledge is a virtue of the talented,
but harmful to those without discernment.
Spring water free of impurity,
entering the ocean, becomes undrinkable.
Nagarjuna (c. 100-200 A.D.)

5392   The first and wisest of them all professed
       To know this only, that he nothing knew.
                                          Milton (1608-1674)

5393   The defects of the understanding, like those of the face,
       grow worse as we grow old.
                                  La Rochefoucauld (1613-1680)

5394   What we do not understand we do not possess.
                                          Goethe (1749-1832)

5395   The tree of knowledge is not that of life.
                                           Byron (1788-1824)

5396   When a man's knowledge is not in order, the more of it he
       has the greater will be his confusion.
                                  Herbert Spencer (1820-1903)

5397   We do not know one millionth of one percent about anything.
                                  Thomas A. Edison (1847-1931)

5398   Our knowledge is a receding mirage in an expanding desert of
       ignorance.
                                  Will Durant (1885-1981)

6. ADVICE

5399   Know thyself as the pride of His creation, the link
       uniting divinity and matter; behold a part of God Himself
       within thee; remember thine own dignity nor dare descend to
       evil or meanness.
                                  Akhenaton? (c. B.C. 1375)

5400   We must learn not to disassociate the airy flower from the
       earthy root, for the flower that is cut off from its root
       fades, and its seeds are barren, whereas the root, secure
       in mother earth, can produce flower after flower and bring
       their fruit to maturity.
                                  Kabbalah (B.C. 1200?-700? A.D.)

5401   Get wisdom: and with all thy getting get understanding.
                                  Proverbs (B.C. 1000?-200?)

5402   Know thyself.
                                  Chilo (fl. B.C. 560)

5403   When you know a thing,
          hold that you know it;
       when you know not a thing,
          allow that you know it not;
       this is knowledge.

                                  Confucius (B.C. 551-479)

5404   It is well for one to know more than he says.
                                                        Plautus (B.C. 254-184)

5405   This precept descended from Heaven: know thyself.
                                                        Juvenal (40-125 A.D.)

5406   Behold but One in all things;
        it is the second that leads you astray.
                                                        Kabir (1440-1518)

5407   If you have knowledge, let others light their candles
        at it.
                                                        Thomas Fuller (1608-1661)

5408   There is timing in the whole life of the warrior, in his
        thriving and declining, in his harmony and discord.
        Similarly, there is timing in the Way of the merchant, in
        the rise and fall of capital. All things entail rising and
        falling timing. You must be able to discern this.
                                                        Miyamoto Musashi (1584-1645)

5409   There is hardly any place or any company where you may not
        gain knowledge, if you please; almost everybody knows some
        one thing, and is glad to talk about that one thing.
                                                        Chesterfield (1694-1773)

5410   All our progress is an unfolding, like the vegetable bud,
        you have first an instinct, then an opinion, then a know-
        ledge, as the plant has root, bud and fruit. Trust the
        instinct to the end, though you can render no reason.
                                                        Emerson (1803-1882)

5411   The more extensive a man's knowledge of what has been done,
        the greater will be his power of knowing what to do.
                                                        Disraeli (1804-1881)

5412   Better know nothing than half-know many things.
                                                        Nietzsche (1844-1900)

5413   Beware of false knowledge;
        it is more dangerous than ignorance.
                                                        G. B. Shaw (1856-1950)

5414   Scrutinize the mystery underlying all things.
        Seek in higher dimensions of understanding a meaning behind
          all our sufferings.
        Unmask what appears to be the caprice of human destiny -
        How we long to become that which we hardly believe we are!
                                                        Pir Vilayat Inayat Khan (born 1916)

7. POTPOURRI

5415   Two stones build two houses, three stones build six houses, four build twenty-four houses, five build one hundred and twenty houses, six build seven hundred and twenty houses and seven build five thousand and forty houses. From thence further go and reckon what the mouth cannot express and the ear cannot hear.

                              Sepher Yezirah (B.C. 2000?-600 A.D.)

5416   If you love knowledge, you will be a master of knowledge. What you have come to know, pursue by exercise, what you have not learned, seek to add to your knowledge, for it is as reprehensible to hear a profitable saying and not grasp it as to be offered a good gift by one's friend and not accept it. Believe that many precepts are better than much wealth, for wealth quickly fails us, but precepts abide through all time.

                              Isocrates (B.C. 436-338)

5417   As the blazing fire turns firewood to ashes, so does the fire of knowledge burn to ashes all reactions to material activities.

                              Bhagavad Gita (c. B.C. 400)

5418   How can the outpouring of the divine essence flowing out of the essence give you the experience of the essence?... Henceforth there is no need for proof in order to grasp thy reality.

                            al-Hallaj (c. 858-922 A.D.)

5419   Seldom ever was any knowledge given to keep, but to impart; the grace of this rich jewel is lost in concealment.

                            Joseph Hall (1574-1656)

5420   The improvement of the understanding is for two ends: first, for our own increase of knowledge; secondly, to enable us to deliver and make out that knowledge to others.

                            John Locke (1632-1704)

5421   But honest instinct comes a volunteer; Sure never to o'er-shoot, but just to hit, While still too wide or short in human wit.

                            Pope (1688-1744)

5422   Reasoning at every step he treads, Man yet mistakes his way, Whilst meaner things, whom instinct leads, Are rarely known to stray.

                            Cowper (1731-1800)

5423   A goose flies by a chart which the Royal Geographical
       Society could not improve.

                           Oliver Wendell Holmes (1809-1894)

5424   10 is the most perfect number because it includes unity,
       which created everything, and zero, symbol of matter and
       chaos, whence everything emerged. In its figures it
       comprehends the created and the uncreated, the commencement
       and the end, power and force, life and annihilation. By
       the study of this number, we find the relationships of all
       things.

                                   Albert Pike (1809-1891)

5425   If a little knowledge is dangerous, where is the man who
       has so much as to be out of danger?

                               Thomas Huxley (1825-1895)

5426   Knowledge - The small part of ignorance that we arrange and
       classify.

                               Ambrose Bierce (1842-1914?)

5427   I had six honest serving men - They taught me all I knew:
       Their names were Where and What and When - and Why and How
       and Who.

                                   Kipling (1865-1936)

VENGEANCE

Punishment and Revenge

1. ESSENCE

5428   The root of revenge, is in the weakness of the Soul;
the most abject and timorous are the most addicted to it.
Akhenaton? (c. B.C. 1375)

5429   We do not correct the man we hang;
we correct others by him.
Montaigne (1533-1592)

5430   Revenge is an act of passion; vengeance of justice.
Injuries are revenged; crimes are avenged.
Johnson (1709-1784)

2. OPPOSITES

5431   There is nothing so easy as to revenge an offence;
but nothing is so honourable as to pardon it.
Akhenaton? (c. B.C. 1375)

5432   He hurts the good who spares the bad.
Publilius Syrus (fl. B.C. 42)

5433   Punishment, that is the justice for the unjust.
Augustine (354-430 A.D.)

5434   Severities should be dealt out all at once,
   that by their suddenness they may give less offense;
benefits should be handed out drop by drop,
   that they may be relished the more.
Machiavelli (1469-1527)

5435   By taking revenge, a man is but even with his enemy;
but in passing over it, he is superior.
Bacon (1561-1626)

5436   Revenge, at first though sweet, bitter ere long,
back on itself recoils.
Milton (1608-1674)

5437   Crime and punishment grow out of one stem. Punishment is a
fruit that, unsuspected, ripens within the flower of the
pleasure that concealed it.
Emerson (1803-1882)

3. INSIGHT

5438   Why seeketh thou revenge, O man! with what purpose is
it that thou pursuest it? Thinkest thou to pain thine
adversary by it? Know that thou thyself feelest its
greatest torments.

Akhenaton? (c. B.C. 1375)

5439   Before a thunderstorm there is a build-up of tension which
is only relieved by the explosive force of thunder and
lightning. In human affairs there must be a clear
distinction between the penalties for small and great
crimes. Retribution for wrongdoing must be swiftly and
surely applied if greater problems are to be prevented.

I Ching (B.C. 1150?)

5440   If you have committed iniquity, you must expect to suffer;
for vengeance with its sacred light shines upon you.

Sophocles (B.C. 495-406)

5441   Vengeance comes not openly, either upon you or any wicked
man, but steals silently and imperceptibly, placing its
foot on the bad.

Euripides (B.C. 480-406)

5442   We will not punish a man because he hath offended, but that
he may offend no more; nor does punishment ever look to the
past, but to the future; for it is not the result of
passion, but that the same thing be guarded against in time
to come.

Seneca (B.C. 3-65 A.D.)

5443   There's small revenge in words,
but words may be greatly revenged.

Franklin (1706-1790)

5444   There is only one thing worse than Injustice,
and that is Justice without her sword in her hand.
When Right is not Might, it is Evil.

Oscar Wilde (1854-1900)

5445   Revenge upon a wrong-doer brings only one day's pleasure.
For him who bears with patience evil from another,
there will be praise until the world shall end.

Indian Proverb

4. POSITIVE

5446   If there were no strong hand at the service of good in the
world, evil would multiply.

Kabbalah (B.C. 1200?-700? A.D.)

5447 In punishing folly
It does not further one
To commit transgressions.
The only thing that futhers
Is to prevent transgressions.

I Ching (B.C. 1150?)

5448 It (revenge) is sweeter far than flowing honey.

Homer (c. B.C. 700)

5449 Heaven is not always angry when he strikes,
But most chastises those whom most he likes.

John Pomfret (1677-1702)

5450 The work of eradicating crimes is not by making
punishment familiar, but formidable.

Goldsmith (1728-1774)

5451 Revenge is profitable, gratitude is expensive.

Gibbon (1737-1794)

5. NEGATIVE

5452 Think not thou art revenged of thine enemy when thou slayest
him; thou puttest him beyond thy reach, thou givest him
quiet, and takest from thyself all means of hurting him.

Akhenaton? (c. B.C. 1375)

5453 The people are not afraid of death.
Why, then, threaten them with death?...
There is always the master executioner (Heaven) who kills.
To undertake executions for the master executioner is like
  hewing wood for the master carpenter.
Whoever undertakes to hew wood for the master carpenter
  rarely escapes injuring his own hands.

Lao-Tzu (fl. B.C. 600)

5454 Blood stains can not be removed by more blood;
resentment can not be removed by more resentment;
resentment can be removed only by forgetting it.

Buddha (B.C. 568-488)

5455 If the people be led by laws, and uniformity sought to be
given them by punishments, they will try to avoid the
punishment, but have no sense of shame.

Confucius (B.C. 551-479)

5456 Nothing is more common than for great thieves to ride in
triumph when small ones are punished.

Seneca (B.C. 3-65 A.D.)

5457 Revenge is always the weak pleasure
of a little and narrow mind.

Juvenal (40-125 A.D.)

5458 He that studieth revenge keepeth his own wounds green.

Bacon (1561-1626)

5459 Revenge...is like a rolling stone, which, when a man hath
forced up a hill, will return upon him with a greater
violence, and break those bones whose sinews gave it motion.

Jeremy Taylor (1613-1667)

5460 Many without punishment, but none without sin.

John Ray (1627-1705)

5461 Revenge is barren: its delight is murder,
and its satiety, despair.

Schiller (1759-1805)

6. ADVICE

5462 Be always more ready to forgive, than to return an injury;
he that watches for an opportunity of revenge, lieth in
wait against himself, and draweth down mischief on his own
head.

Akhenaton? (c. B.C. 1375)

5463 Punishment should not be meted out in anger. It must fulfill
the purpose of preventing unreasonable excesses by others.

I Ching (B.C. 1150?)

5464 Let the punishment be equal with the offence.

Cicero (B.C. 106-43)

5465 The best sort of revenge is not to be like him who did the
injury.

Marcus Aurelius (121-180 A.D.)

5466 Heat not a furnace for your foe so hot
That it doth singe yourself.

Shakespeare (1564-1616)

5467 To make punishments efficacious, two things are necessary.
They must never be disproportioned to the offence, and they
must be certain.

William Simms (1806-1870)

5468 Distrust all in whom the impulse to punish is powerful.

Nietzsche (1844-1900)

7. POTPOURRI

5469 O think not, bold man, because thy punishment is delayed,
that the arm of God is weakened; neither flatter thyself
with hopes that He winketh at thy doings. His eye pierceth
the secrets of every heart, and He remembereth them for
ever...
Akhenaton? (c. B.C. 1375)

5470 Eye for eye, tooth for tooth, hand for hand, foot for foot.
Deuteronomy (B.C. 1200?-800?)

5471 The ways of the gods are long, but in the end
they are not without strength.
Euripides (B.C. 480-406)

5472 The divine wrath is slow indeed in vengeance,
but it makes up for its tardiness by the severity
of the punishment.
Valerius Maximus (fl. c. 20 A.D.)

5473 The man against whom you feel anger in your heart
Is not to be admonished by mere words.
First, subdue him by force,
And then use your weapon of words.
Nagarjuna (c. 100-200 A.D.)

5474 Had all his hairs been lives, my great revenge had stomach
for them all.
Shakespeare (1564-1616)

5475 If I wished to punish a province, I would have it governed
by philosophers.
Frederick II (1712-1786)

5476 Revenge - A debt in the paying of which the greatest knave
is honest and sincere, and, so far as he is able, punctual.
Colton (1780-1832)

5477 Punishment - The justice that the guilty deal out to those
that are caught.
Elbert Hubbard (1859-1915)

VIRTUE
Innocence and Purity

1. ESSENCE

5478 Virtue is a kind of health, beauty and good habit
of the soul.
Plato (B.C. 427?-347?)

5479 Virtue is the golden mean between two vices,
the one of excess and the other of deficiency.
Aristotle (B.C. 384-322)

5480 Virtue is a habit of the mind,
consistent with nature and moderation and reason.
Cicero (B.C. 106-43)

5481 Virtue consists in avoiding vice, and is the highest wisdom.
Horace (B.C. 65-8)

5482 Virtue is beauty.
Shakespeare (1564-1616)

5483 Virtue, like health, is the harmony of the whole man.
Carlyle (1795-1881)

5484 Virtue is but heroic bravery, to do the thing thought to be
true, in spite of all enemies of flesh or spirit, in despite
of all temptations or menaces.
Albert Pike (1809-1891)

2. OPPOSITES

5485 The man of superior virtue is not conscious of his virtue,
and in this way he really possesses virtue.
The man of inferior virtue never loses sight of his virtue,
and in this way he loses his virtue.
Lao-Tzu (fl. B.C. 600)

5486 The superior man thinks always of virtue;
the common man thinks of comfort.
Confucius (B.C. 551-479)

5487 Virtue is the beauty, and vice the deformity, of the soul.
Socrates (B.C. 469-399)

5488 Holiness is what is loved by all the gods. It is loved
because it is holy, and not holy because it is loved.
Plato (B.C. 427?-347?)

5489   He who dies for virtue, does not perish.

Plautus (B.C. 254-184)

5490   The high-spirited man may indeed die, but he will not stoop
to meanness. Fire, though it may be quenched, will not
become cool.

The Hitopadesa (600?-1100? A.D.)

5491   Virtue is health, vice is sickness.

Francesco Petrarch (1304-1374)

5492   Virtue is persecuted more by the wicked
than it is loved by the good.

Cervantes (1547-1616)

5493   Certainly, virtue is like precious odors,
most fragrant when they are incensed or crushed,
for prosperity doth best discover vice,
but adversity doth best discover virtue.

Bacon (1561-1626)

5494   Some rise by sin, and some by virtue fall.

Shakespeare (1564-1616)

5495   Some people with great virtues are disagreeable,
while others with great vices are delightful.

La Rochefoucauld (1613-1680)

5496   He's armed without that's innocent within.

Pope (1688-1744)

5497   Our virtues and vices spring from one root.

Goethe (1749-1832)

5498   Virtue by calculation is the virtue of vice.

Joubert (1754-1824)

5499   Virtue: Climbing a hill
Vice: Running down.

Chinese Proverb

3. INSIGHT

5500   To produce things and to rear them,
To produce, but not to take possession of them,
To act, but not to rely on one's own ability.
To lead them, but not to master them -
This is called profound and secret virtue.

Lao-Tzu (fl. B.C. 600)

5501 This is the law of God, that virtue only is firm,
and cannot be shaken by a tempest.

Pythagoras (B.C. 582-507)

5502 Just as treasures are uncovered from the earth,
so virtue appears from good deeds,
and wisdom appears from a pure and peaceful mind.
To walk safely through the maze of human life,
one needs the light of wisdom and the guidance of virtue.

Buddha (B.C. 568-488)

5503 Virtue is more to man than either water or fire. I have
seen men die from treading on water and fire, but I have
never seen a man die from treading the course of virtue.

Confucius (B.C. 551-479)

5504 Purity engenders Wisdom, Passion avarice, and Ignorance
folly, infatuation and darkness.

Bhagavad Gita (c. B.C. 400)

5505 Virtue consisteth of three parts, -
temperance, fortitude, and justice.

Epicurus (B.C. 341-270)

5506 Although a man may wear fine clothing, if he lives
peacefully; and is good, self-possessed, has faith
and is pure; and if he does not hurt any living being,
he is a holy man...

The Dhammapada (c. B.C. 300)

5507 Fewer possess virtue, than those who wish us to believe
that they possess it.

Cicero (B.C. 106-43)

5508 God looks with favor at pure, not full, hands.

Publilius Syrus (fl. B.C. 42)

5509 Nature does not bestow virtue; to be good is an art.

Seneca (B.C. 3-65 A.D.)

5510 The holy man, though he be distressed,
Does not eat food mixed with wickedness.
The lion, though hungry,
Will not eat what is unclean.

Saskya Pandita (1182-1251)

5511 I find that the best virtue I have
has in it some tincture of vice.

Montaigne (1533-1592)

5512   Virtue is like a rich stone, best plain set.

Bacon (1561-1626)

5513   Virtue and genuine graces in themselves speak what no words
can utter.

Shakespeare (1564-1616)

5514   We need greater virtues to sustain good fortune than bad.

La Rochefoucauld (1613-1680)

5515   To be innocent is to be not guilty;
but to be virtuous is to overcome our evil inclinations.

William Penn (1614-1718)

5516   There is nothing that is meritorious but virtue and
friendship; and indeed friendship itself is only a part
of virtue.

Pope (1688-1744)

5517   Virtue is everywhere the same, because it comes from God,
while everything else is of men.

Voltaire (1694-1778)

5518   Virtue is the state of war, and to live in it
we have always to combat with ourselves.

Rousseau (1712-1778)

5519   The virtues, like the Muses, are always seen in groups.
A good principle was never found solitary in any breast.

Jane Porter (1776-1850)

5520   Innocence is always unsuspicious.

Haliburton (1796-1865)

5521   The only reward of virtue is virtue.

Emerson (1803-1882)

5522   It has ever been my experience that folks who have no vices
have very few virtues.

Lincoln (1809-1865)

5523   The truly innocent are those who not only are guiltless
themselves, but who think others are.

Josh Billings (1815-1885)

5524   They who disbelieve in virtue because man has never been
found perfect, might as reasonably deny the sun because
it is not always noon.

Hare & Charles (c. 1830)

5525 With virtue you cannot be entirely poor...
Without it you cannot be really rich.

Chinese Proverb

4. POSITIVE

5526 Virtue cannot live in solitude: neighbors are sure to
grow up around it.

Confucius (B.C. 551-479)

5527 The fragrance of the flower is never borne against the
breeze; but the fragrance of human virtue diffuses
itself everywhere.

The Ramayana (B.C. 500?-50?)

5528 The most virtuous of all men is he that contents himself
with being virtuous without seeking to appear so.

Plato (B.C. 427?-347?)

5529 Honor is the reward of virtue.

Cicero (B.C. 106-43)

5530 The glory of riches and of beauty is frail and transitory;
virtue remains bright and eternal.

Sallust (B.C. 86-34)

5531 Virtue knowing no base repulse, shines with untarnished
honour; nor does she assume or resign her emblems of
honour by the will of some popular breeze.

Horace (B.C. 65-8)

5532 Virtue is that perfect good which is the complement of a
happy life; the only immortal thing that belongs to
mortality.

Seneca (B.C. 3-65 A.D.)

5533 Nature has placed nothing so high that virtue can not
reach it.

Curtius-Rufus (fl. 100 A.D.)

5534 Virtue is sufficient of herself for happiness.

Diogenes Laertius (c. 250 A.D.)

5535 For virtue only finds eternal Fame.

Francesco Petrarch (1304-1374)

5536 Of all the benefits that virtue confers upon us,
the contempt of death is one of the greatest.

Montaigne (1533-1592)

5537   Our life is short, but to expand that span to vast eternity
        is virtue's work.

                                               Shakespeare (1564-1616)

5538   A heart unspotted is not easily daunted.

                                               Shakespeare (1564-1616)

5539   Virtue may be assailed, but never hurt,
        Surprised by unjust force, but not enthralled;
        Yea, even that which mischief meant most harm
        Shall in the happy trial prove most glory.

                                                    Milton (1608-1674)

5540   Innocence is like polished armor; it adorns and defends.

                                               Robert South (1634-1716)

5541   Virtue alone is the unerring sign of a noble soul.

                                          Nicholas Boileau (1636-1711)

5542   Sweet are the slumbers of the virtuous man!

                                                  Addison (1672-1719)

5543   Virtue alone outbuilds the pyramids:
        Her monuments shall last, when Egypt's fall.

                                                    Young (1683-1765)

5544   Innocence is its own Defence.

                                                 Franklin (1706-1790)

5545   Virtue, the strength and beauty of the soul,
        Is the best gift of Heaven: a happiness
        That even above the smiles and frowns of fate
        Exalts great Nature's favourites: a wealth
        That never encumbers, nor can be transferred.

                                          John Armstrong (1709-1779)

5546   Riches adorn the dwelling; virtue adorns the person.

                                                       Chinese Proverb

5. NEGATIVE

5547   Those who have virtue always in their mouths, and neglect it
        in practice, are like a harp, which emits a sound pleasing
        to others, while itself is insensible of the music.

                                             Diogenes (B.C. 412-323)

5548   There are some jobs in which it is impossible for a man to
        be virtuous.

                                            Aristotle (B.C. 384-322)

5549   The man who is not virtuous can never be happy.

                                         Epicurus (B.C. 341-270)

5550   That which leads us to the performance of duty by offering
pleasure as its reward, is not virtue, but a deceptive
copy and imitation of virtue.

                                       Cicero (B.C. 106-43)

5551   Although a cloth be washed a hundred times,
How can it be rendered clean and pure
If it be washed in water which is dirty?

                            Nagarjuna (c. 100-200 A.D.)

5552   To purify the heart is like the person ordered to uproot a
tree. However much he reflects and struggles to do so, he
is unable. So he says to himself, "I'll wait until I'm
more powerful and then uproot it." But the longer he waits
and leaves the tree to grow, the larger and stronger it
becomes while he only becomes weaker.

               Abu 'Uthman Al-Maghribi (fl. c. 975 A.D.)

5553   Our virtues are most frequently but vices disguised.

                          La Rochefoucauld (1613-1680)

5554   The smallest speck is seen on snow.

                                    Gay (1688-1732)

5555   Virtue has need of limits.

                            Montesquieu (1689-1755)

5556   Few men have virtue to withstand the highest bidder.

                    George Washington (1732-1799)

5557   Virtue is not hereditary.

                               Paine (1737-1809)

5558   The absence of temptation is the absence of virtue.

                            Goethe (1749-1832)

5559   Innocence is but a poor substitute for experience.

                         Bulwer-Lytton (1803-1873)

5560   Most people are so constituted that they can only be
virtuous in a certain routine; an irregular course of life
demoralizes them.

                      Nathaniel Hawthorne (1804-1864)

5561   Virtue often trips and falls on the sharp-edged rock
of poverty.

                          Marie Sue (1804-1857)

5562   Virtue is insufficient temptation.

G. B. Shaw (1856-1950)

5563   The door to virtue...
        Heavy and hard to push.

Chinese Proverb

6. ADVICE

5564   A noble spirit disdaineth the malice of fortune;
        his greatness of Soul is not to be cast down.

Akhenaton? (c. B.C. 1375)

5565   INNOCENCE. Supreme success.
        Perseverance furthers.
        If someone is not as he should be,
        He has misfortune,
        And it does not further him
        To undertake anything.

I Ching (B.C. 1150?)

5566   Turn yourself not away from three best things:
        Good Thought, Good Word, and Good Deed.

Zoroaster (B.C. 628?-551?)

5567   If he applies The Eternal to himself his virtue will be
            genuine;
        If he applies it to his family his virtue will be abundant;
        If he applies it to his village his virtue will be lasting;
        If he applies it to his country his virtue will be full;
        If he applies it to the world his virtue will be universal.

Lao-Tzu (fl. B.C. 600)

5568   To practice five things under all circumstances constitutes
        perfect virtue; these five are gravity, generosity of soul,
        sincerity, earnestness, and kindness.

Confucius (B.C. 551-479)

5569   The shortest and surest way to live with honor in the world,
        is to be in reality what we would appear to be; all human
        virtues increase and strengthen themselves by the practice
        and experience of them.

Socrates (B.C. 469-399)

5570   One should seek virtue for its own sake and not from hope
        or fear, or any external motive. It is in virtue that
        happiness consists, for virtue is the state of mind which
        tends to make the whole of life harmonious.

Zeno (B.C. 335?-264)

5571   A thankful heart is the parent of all virtues.

                                              Cicero (B.C. 106-43)

5572   Every man has his appointed day; life is brief and
        irrevocable; but it is the work of virtue to extend
        our fame by our deeds.

                                              Vergil (B.C. 70-19)

5573   The only path to a tranquil life is through virtue.
                                              Juvenal (40-125 A.D.)

5574   Virtues are acquired through endeavor,
        Which rests wholly upon yourself.
        So, to praise others for their virtues
        Can but encourage one's own efforts.

                                              Nagarjuna (c. 100-200 A.D.)

5575   Recommend to your children virtue; that alone can make
        happy, not gold.

                                              Beethoven (1770-1827)

5576   No man can purchase his virtue too dear, for it is the only
        thing whose value must ever increase with the price it has
        cost us. Our integrity is never worth so much as when we
        have parted with our all to keep it.

                                              Colton (1780-1832)

5577   He that has energy enough to root out a vice, should go
        further, and try to plant a virtue in its place; otherwise
        he will have his labor to renew. A strong soil that has
        produced weeds may be made to produce wheat.

                                              Colton (1780-1832)

5578   The Lamp burns bright when wick and oil are clean.
                                              H. P. Blavatsky (1831-1891)

5579   Better keep yourself clean and bright; you are the window
        through which you must see the world.
                                              G. B. Shaw (1856-1950)

7. POTPOURRI

5580   One who is to enjoy the purity of both body and mind walks
        the path to enlightenment, breaking the net of selfish,
        impure thoughts and evil desires. He who is calm in mind
        acquires peacefulness and thus is able to cultivate his
        mind day and night with more diligence.

                                              Buddha (B.C. 568-488)

5581   Virtue, dear friend, needs no defence,
The surest guard is innocence:
None knew, till guilt created fear,
What darts or poison'd arrows were.

Horace (B.C. 65-8)

5582   It is the edge and temper of the blade that make a good
sword, not the richness of the scabbard; and so it is
not money or possessions that make man considerable, but
his virtue.

Seneca (B.C. 3-65 A.D.)

5583   There is no ornament like virtue,
There is no misery like worry,
There is no protection like patience,
There is no friend equal to generosity.

Nagarjuna (c. 100-200 A.D.)

5584   Food, sleep, fear, propagation; each is the common property
of men with brutes. Virtue is really their additional
distinction; devoid of virtue, they are equal with brutes.

The Hitopadesa (600?-1100? A.D.)

5585   They fulfill their vows and fear the day whose calamity
shall be far-reaching; and in spite of their own want,
they give food to the poor, and the orphan and the prisoner.

Koran (c. 651 A.D.)

5586   True merit, like a river, the deeper it is,
the less noise it makes.

Halifax (1633-1695)

5587   Shall ignorance of good and ill
Dare to direct the eternal will?
Seek virtue, and of that possest,
To Providence resign the rest.

Gay (1688-1732)

5588   Against the head which innocence secures,
Insidious malice aims her dart in vain;
Turned backwards by the powerful breath of heaven.

Johnson (1709-1784)

5589   And he by no uncommon lot
Was famed for virtues he had not.

Cowper (1731-1800)

5590   One whose heart the holy forms
Of young imagination have kept pure.

Wordsworth (1770-1850)

5591   Blessed is the memory of those
          who have kept themselves unspotted from the world!
        Yet more blessed and more dear the memory of those
          who have kept themselves unspotted in the world.
                                    Anna Jameson (1794-1860)

5592   There is virtue in country houses, in gardens and orchards,
        in fields, streams and groves, in rustic recreations and
        plain manners, that neither cities nor universities enjoy.
                                    Amos B. Alcott (1799-1888)

5593   Of all the virtues necessary to the completion of the
        perfect man, there is none to be more delicately implied
        and less ostentatiously vaunted than that of exquisite
        feeling or universal benevolence.
                                    Bulwer-Lytton (1803-1873)

5594   Ascetic: one who makes a necessity of virtue.
                                    Nietzsche (1844-1900)

5595   The Saints are the Sinners who keep on trying.
                                    Robert Louis Stevenson (1850-1895)

VISION

Discernment, Perception, Prophesy and Sight

1. ESSENCE

5596   Vision - The art of seeing things invisible.

Swift (1667-1745)

5597   The eye sees what it brings the power to see.

Carlyle (1795-1881)

5598   A moment's insight is sometimes worth a life's experience.
Oliver Wendell Holmes (1809-1894)

5599   He who could foresee affairs three days in advance
would be rich for thousands of years

Chinese Proverb

2. OPPOSITES

5600   Men are deceived by what the eyes see,
but the gods are swayed by what the heart conceals.

I Ching (B.C. 1150?)

5601   The easier a matter is reckoned
the more difficult it proves at the last;
for this reason the Sage sees difficulties in everything,
and therefore he encounters no difficulties.

Lao-Tzu (fl. B.C. 600)

5602   If a man take no thought about what is distant,
he will find sorrow near at hand.

Confucius (B.C. 551-479)

5603   Perception is strong and sight weak. In strategy it is
important to see distant things as if they were close and
to take a distanced view of close things.
Miyamoto Musashi (1584-1645)

5604   It is easy to see, hard to foresee.

Franklin (1706-1790)

5605   The future hides in it gladness and sorrow.

Goethe (1749-1832)

5606   And finds with keen, discriminating sight,
Black's not so black - nor white so very white.
George Canning (1770-1827)

5607 Man, if he compare himself with all that he can see,
is at the zenith of power;
but if he compare himself with all that he can conceive,
he is at the nadir of weakness.

Colton (1780-1832)

5608 We are always looking into the future,
but we see only the past.

Anne Swetchine (1782-1857)

5609 Man was created with two eyes, so that with one he may see
God's greatness, and with the other his own lowliness.

Shmuel Yosef Agnon (1888-1970)

3. INSIGHT

5610 When things are going well it is all too easy to become
overconfident and not give proper attention to one's duties.
If this tendency is recognized early it may be corrected and
no harm will be done.

I Ching (B.C. 1150?)

5611 Sound judgement, with discernment, is the best of seers.

Euripides (B.C. 480-406)

5612 One who sees the Supersoul accompanying the individual soul
in all bodies and who understands that neither the soul nor
the Supersoul is ever destroyed, actually sees.

Bhagavad Gita (c. B.C. 400)

5613 I shall always consider the best guesser the best prophet.

Cicero (B.C. 106-43)

5614 Men's minds perceive second causes,
But only prophets perceive the action of the First Cause.

Jalal-Uddin Rumi (1207-1273)

5615 When clouds are seen wise men put on their cloaks.

Shakespeare (1564-1616)

5616 I know of no way of judging the future but by the past.

Patrick Henry (1736-1799)

5617 If the doors of perception were cleansed
every thing would appear to man as it is, infinite.
For man has closed himself up,
till he sees all things thru' narrow chinks of his cavern.

William Blake (1757-1828)

5618   The past cannot be changed,
the future is still in your power.

Hugh White (1773-1840)

5619   The future is not in the hands of fate but in ours.

Jean Jules Jusserand (1855-1932)

5620   Vision looks inward and becomes a duty.
Vision looks outward and becomes aspiration.
Vision looks upward and becomes faith.

Stephen S. Wise (1874-1949)

5621   The only way to predict the future is to have power to shape
the future. Those in possession of absolute power can not
only prophesy and make their prophesies come true, but they
can also lie and make their lies come true.

Eric Hoffer (1902-1983)

5622   The rich man plans for tomorrow...
The poor man for today.

Chinese Proverb

4. POSITIVE

5623   The light of the Spirit is invisible, concealed in all
beings. It is seen by the seers of the subtle, when their
vision is keen and clear.

Upanishads (c. B.C. 800)

5624   Is not he a sage who neither anticipates deceit nor suspects
bad faith in others, yet is prompt to detect them when they
appear?

Confucius (B.C. 551-479)

5625   The eyes are more exact witnesses than the ears.

Heraclitus (B.C. 535-475)

5626   Few things are brought to a successful issue by
impetuous desire, but most by calm and prudent forethought.

Thucydides (B.C. 460-400)

5627   He who lives a hundred years, not seeing the highest law,
a life of one day is better if a man sees the highest law.

The Dhammapada (c. B.C. 300)

5628   The eye of the master will do more work
than both of his hands.

Franklin (1706-1790)

5629 The veil which covers the face of futurity
is woven by the hand of mercy.
Bulwer-Lytton (1803-1873)

5630 A man, foreseeing that another will do a certain act, and
in nowise controlling or even influencing him may use that
action as an instrument to effect his own purposes.
Albert Pike (1809-1891)

5631 The greatest thing a human soul ever does in this world...
To see clearly is poetry, prophecy and religion all in one.
John Ruskin (1819-1900)

5. NEGATIVE

5632 Where there is no vision, the people perish.
Proverbs (B.C. 1000?-200?)

5633 What we look for does not come to pass.
God finds a way for what none foresaw.
Euripides (B.C. 480-406)

5634 You can never plan the future by the past.
Burke (1729-1797)

5635 He who foresees calamities, suffers them twice over.
Porteus (1731-1808)

5636 Forethought we may have, undoubtedly, but not foresight.
Napoleon (1769-1821)

5637 He who anticipates his century is generally persecuted when
living, and is always pilfered when dead.
Disraeli (1804-1881)

5638 All eyes do not see alike. Even the visible creation is
not, for all who look upon it, of one form and one color.
Our brain is a book printed within and without, and the two
writings are, with all men, more or less confused.
Albert Pike (1809-1891)

5639 It is sure to be dark if you shut your eyes.
Tupper (1810-1889)

5640 It is as hard to see one's self as to look backwards
without turning round.
Thoreau (1817-1862)

5641 Among all forms of mistake, prophecy is the most gratuitous.
George Eliot (1819-1880)

5642   I never think of the future. It comes soon enough.
Einstein (1879-1955)

5643   You can only predict things after they've happened.
Eugene Ionesco (born 1912)

6. ADVICE

5644   Study the past if you would divine the future.
Confucius (B.C. 551-479)

5645   With your spirit open and unconstricted,
look at things from a high point of view.
Miyamoto Musashi (1584-1645)

5646   Our grand business is not to see what lies
dimly at a distance, but to do what lies clearly at hand.
Carlyle (1795-1881)

5647   The best preparation for the future,
is the present well seen to, and the last duty done.
George MacDonald (1824-1905)

5648   Before the Soul can see, the Harmony within must be
attained, and fleshly eyes be rendered blind to all
illusion.
H. P. Blavatsky (1831-1891)

5649   It is a mistake to look too far ahead. Only one link in the
chain of destiny can be handled at a time.
Winston Churchill (1874-1965)

5650   To know the road ahead
Ask those coming back.
Chinese Proverb

7. POTPOURRI

5651   The man is quiet, but firm as a rock, yet sensitive to the
first imperceptible signs of impending changes. He does
not delay in taking action.
I Ching (B.C. 1150?)

5652   Behold the universe in the Glory of God; and all that lives
and moves on earth. Leaving the transient, find joy in the
Eternal; set not your heart on another's possession.
Upanishads (c. B.C. 800)

5653   I wonder that a soothsayer doesn't laugh
       whenever he sees another soothsayer.
                                           Cicero (B.C. 106-43)

5654   A wise God shrouds the future in obscure darkness.
                                           Horace (B.C. 65-8)

5655   His eye is ever open and sleepeth not, for it continually
       keepeth watch. And the appearance of the lower is according
       to the aspect of the higher light....His two nostrils like
       mighty galleries, whence His spirit rushes forth over all.
                                           Zohar (120?-1200? A.D.)

5656   There was the Door to which I found no key;
       There was the Veil through which I might not see.
                                           Omar Khayyam (fl. 1100)

5657   The Eternal looked upon me for a moment with his eye of
       power, and annihilated me in his being, and became manifest
       to me in his essence. I saw I existed through him.
                                           Jalal-Uddin Rumi (1207-1273)

5658   Whoe'er thou art, thy master see;
       He was - or is - or is to be.
                                           Voltaire (1694-1778)

5659   The future is purchased by the present.
                                           Johnson (1709-1784)

5660   You can make a better living in the world as a soothsayer
       than as a truthsayer.
                                           Georg Lichtenberg (1742-1799)

5661   To see a World in a Grain of Sand
       And a Heaven in a Wild Flower,
       Hold Infinity in the palm of your hand
       And Eternity in an hour.
                                           William Blake (1757-1828)

5662   The more sand has escaped from the hourglass of our life,
       the clearer we should see through it.
                                           Richter (1763-1825)

5663   Hence in a season of calm weather though inland far we be,
       Our souls have sight of that immortal sea
         which brought us hither,
       Can in a moment travel thither,
       And see the children sport upon the shore,
       And hear the mighty waters rolling evermore.
                                           Wordsworth (1770-1850)

5664 Poets are the hierophants of an unapprehended inspiration; the mirrors of the gigantic shadows which futurity casts upon the present.

> Shelley (1792-1822)

5665 The eye speaks with an eloquence and truthfulness surpassing speech. It is the window out of which the winged thoughts often fly unwittingly. It is the tiny magic mirror on whose crystal surface the moods of feeling fitfully play, like the sunlight and shadow on a still stream.

> Tuckerman (1813-1871)

5666 Prophecy - To observe that which has passed, and guess it will happen again.

> Elbert Hubbard (1859-1915)

5667 The power is yours, but not the sight;
> You see not upon what you tread;
> You have the ages for your guide,
> But not the wisdom to be led.

> Edwin A. Robinson (1869-1935)

5668 I always avoid prophesying beforehand, because it is much better policy to prophesy after the event has already taken place.

> Winston Churchill (1874-1965)

WAR
Destruction and Violence

1. ESSENCE

5669   Speed is the essence of war.
Sun Tzu (fl. c. B.C. 500)

5670   War - the trade of barbarians, and the art of bringing the greatest physical force to bear on a single point.
Napoleon (1769-1821)

5671   War - An act of violence whose object is to constrain the enemy, to accomplish our will.
Carl von Clausewitz (1780-1831)

5672   The essence of war is violence.
Macaulay (1800-1859)

5673   War is the science of destruction.
John Abbott (1805-1877)

5674   War is a series of catastrophes which result in victory.
Sarah Cleghorn (1876-1959)

5675   The essence of war is fire, famine, and pestilence. They contribute to its outbreak; they are among its weapons; they become its consequences.
Dwight D. Eisenhower (1890-1969)

2. OPPOSITES

5676   An ancient strategist has said:
  I dare not take the offensive but I take the defensive;
  I dare not advance an inch but I retreat a foot.
This means:
  To march without formation,
  To stretch one's arm without showing it,
  To confront enemies without seeming to meet them,
  To hold weapons without seeming to have them.
Lao-Tzu (fl. B.C. 600)

5677   Military tactics are like unto water; for water in its natural course runs away from high places and hastens downwards. So in war, the way is to avoid what is strong and to strike what is weak. Like water, taking the line of least resistance.
Sun Tzu (fl. c. B.C. 500)

5678   War leads to peace.

                                Cicero (B.C. 106-43)

5679   In war events of importance are the result of trivial
        causes.

                        Julius Caesar (B.C. 102-44)

5680   War has been prescribed for you and that displeases you,
        it may be you dislike something whilst it is good for you;
        and it may be that you love something that is bad for you,
        because God knows it, and you know it not.

                      Koran (c. 651 A.D.)

5681   In peace the sons bury their fathers
        and in war the fathers bury their sons.

                      Bacon (1561-1626)

5682   There's but a twinkling of a star
        Between a man of peace and war.

                      Samuel Butler (1612-1680)

5683   War its thousands slays,
        Peace its ten thousands.

                      Porteus (1731-1808)

5684   There are only two forces in the world, the sword and the
        spirit. In the long run the sword will always be conquered
        by the spirit.

                      Napoleon (1769-1821)

5685   Defense is the stronger form with the negative object,
        and attack the weaker form with the positive object.

                Carl von Clausewitz (1780-1831)

5686   A war for a great principle ennobles a nation. A war for
        commercial supremacy, upon some shallow pretext, is
        despicable, and more than aught else demonstrates to what
        immeasurable depths of baseness men and nations can descend.

                      Albert Pike (1809-1891)

5687   There was only one virtue, pugnacity;
        only one vice, pacifism.
        That is an essential condition of war.

                      G. B. Shaw (1856-1950)

5688   If a sufficient number of people who wanted to stop war
        really did gather together, they would first of all begin
        by making war upon those who disagreed with them. And it
        is still more certain that they would make war on people
        who also want to stop wars but in another way.

                      Gurdjieff (1873-1949)

5689   An infallible method of conciliating a tiger
       is to allow oneself to be devoured.

                                        Konrad Adenauer (1876-1967)

3. INSIGHT

5690   At the outset, a righteous cause, as well as a proper
       method for conducting the war, is essential for military
       success.

                                        I Ching (B.C. 1150?)

5691   Men grow tired of sleep, love, singing and dancing
       sooner than of war.

                                        Homer (c. B.C. 700)

5692   There is no greater misfortune
       than underestimating the enemy.
       If I underestimate the enemy
       I am in danger of losing my treasure.
       Where two armies confront each other in battle
       the conqueror will be he who wins with a heavy heart.

                                        Lao-Tzu (fl. B.C. 600)

5693   The art of war is of vital importance to the State. It is a
       matter of life and death, a road either to safety or to
       ruin. Hence it is a subject of inquiry which can on no
       account be neglected.

                                        Sun Tzu (fl. c. B.C. 500)

5694   The God of War hates those who hesitate.

                                        Euripides (B.C. 480-406)

5695   Endless money forms the sinews of war.

                                        Cicero (B.C. 106-43)

5696   It is always easy to begin a war, but very difficult to
       stop one, since its beginning and end are not under the
       control of the same man. Anyone, even a coward, can
       commence a war, but it can be brought to an end only with
       the consent of the victors.

                                        Sallust (B.C. 86-34)

5697   To those to whom war is necessary it is just;
       and a resort to arms is righteous in those to whom no means
       of assistance remain except by arms.

                                        Livy (B.C. 59-17 A.D.)

5698   The fortunes of war are always doubtful.

                                        Seneca (B.C. 3-65 A.D.)

5699 For a war to be just three conditions are necessary -
public authority, just cause, right motive.
Thomas Aquinas (1225-1274)

5700 We fight to great disadvantage when we fight with those
who have nothing to lose.
Francesco Guicciardini (1483-1540)

5701 Force and fraud are in war the two cardinal virtues.
Thomas Hobbes (1588-1679)

5702 Most sorts of diversion, in men, children and other animals,
are an imitation of fighting.
Swift (1667-1745)

5703 The Way of strategy is the Way of nature. When you
appreciate the power of nature, knowing the rhythm of
any situation, you will be able to hit the enemy naturally
and strike naturally.
Miyamoto Musashi (1584-1645)

5704 In every heart
Are sown the sparks that kindle fiery war.
Cowper (1731-1800)

5705 Force, that is to say, physical force (for no moral force
exists apart from the conception of a state and law), is the
means; to impose our will upon the enemy is the object. To
achieve this object with certainty we must disarm the enemy,
and this disarming is by definition the proper aim of
military action.
Carl von Clausewitz (1780-1831)

5706 It is an irrepressible conflict between opposing and
enduring forces.
William Henry Seward (1801-1872)

5707 When wars do come, they fall upon the many,
the producing class, who are the sufferers.
Ulysses S. Grant (1822-1885)

5708 Ideas are the great warriors of the world,
and a war that has no idea behind it, is simply a brutality.
James Garfield (1831-1881)

5709 Force is never more operative than when it is known to
exist but is not brandished.
Alfred Thayer Mahan (1840-1914)

5710   War is much too important a matter to be left to the
       generals.
                                    Georges Clemenceau (1841-1929)

5711   As long as war is regarded as wicked it will always have its
       fascinations. When it is looked upon as vulgar, then it
       will cease to be popular.
                                    Oscar Wilde (1854-1900)

5712   The might of the community. Yet, it too, is nothing else
       than violence...it is the communal, not individual, violence
       that has its way.
                                    Sigmund Freud (1856-1939)

5713   There is no such thing as an inevitable war.
       If war comes it will be from a failure of human wisdom.
                                    Andrew Bonar Law (1858-1923)

5714   The increase of armaments that is intended in each nation to
       produce consciousness of strength, and a sense of security,
       does not produce these effects. On the contrary, it
       produces a consciousness of the strength of other nations
       and a sense of fear. Fear begets suspicion and distrust and
       evil imaginings of all sorts.
                                    Edward Grey (1862-1933)

5715   The sinews of war are five - men, money, materials,
       maintenance (food) and morale.
                                    Bernard Baruch (1870-1965)

5716   To destroy is still the strongest instinct in our nature.
                                    Max Beerbohm (1872-1956)

5717   In war, when a commander becomes so bereft of reason and
       perspective that he fails to understand the dependence of
       arms on Divine guidance, he no longer deserves victory.
                                    Douglas MacArthur (1880-1964)

5718   Wars are caused by undefended wealth.
                                    Douglas MacArthur (1880-1964)

5719   Armament is an important factor in war, but not the
       decisive factor...Man, not material, forms the decisive
       factor.
                                    Mao Tse-tung (1893-1976)

5720   Wars occur because people prepare for conflict,
       rather than for peace.
                                    Trygve Lie (1896-1968)

5721 Violence is essentially wordless, and it can begin only
where thought and rational communication have broken down.
Thomas Merton (1915-1968)

4. POSITIVE

5722 The general who advances without coveting fame and retreats
without fearing disgrace, whose only thought is to protect
his country and do good service for his sovereign, is the
jewel of the kingdom.
Sun Tzu (fl. c. B.C. 500)

5723 It is not the object of war to annihilate those who have
given provocation for it, but to cause them to mend their
ways; not to ruin the innocent and guilty alike, but to
save both.
Polybius (B.C. 203?-120)

5724 You need only a show of war to have peace.
Livy (B.C. 59-17 A.D.)

5725 Even war is better than a wretched peace.
Tacitus (55-117 A.D.)

5726 The arms are fair,
When the intent of bearing them is just.
Shakespeare (1564-1616)

5727 The life of states is like that of men.
The latter have the right of killing in self-defense;
the former to make wars for their own preservation.
Montesquieu (1689-1755)

5728 War kills men, and men deplore the loss; but war also
crushes bad principles and tyrants, and so saves societies.
Colton (1780-1832)

5729 It is well that war is so terrible-
we would grow too fond of it.
Robert E. Lee (1807-1870)

5730 Wars, like thunder-storms, are often necessary to purify
the stagnant atmosphere. War is not a demon, without
remorse or reward. It restores the brotherhood in letters
of fire...It is the hurricane that brings the elemental
equilibrium, the concord of Power and Wisdom.
Albert Pike (1809-1891)

5731 So far war has been the only force that can discipline a
whole community, and until an equivalent discipline is
organized, I believe that war must have its way.
William James (1842-1910)

5732 From fear in every guise,
   From sloth, from love of self,
By war's great sacrifice
   The world redeems itself.

John Davidson (1857-1909)

5733 Blood is a cleansing and sanctifying thing, and the nation
that regards it as the final horror has lost its manhood...
There are many things more horrible than bloodshed, and
slavery is one of them!

Padraic Pearse (1879-1916)

5734 The thing constantly overlooked by those hopefuls who talk
about abolishing war is that it is by no means an evidence
of the decay but rather a proof of health and vigor.

H. L. Mencken (1880-1956)

5735 It simply is not true that war never settles anything.

Felix Frankfurter (1882-1965)

5. NEGATIVE

5736 Wherever armies are stationed, briars and thorns grow.
Great wars are always followed by famines.

Lao-Tzu (fl. B.C. 600)

5737 When the army engages in protracted campaigns the resources
of the state will not suffice...For there has never been a
protracted war from which a country has benefited.

Sun Tzu (fl. c. B.C. 500)

5738 Nothing good ever comes of violence.

Martin Luther (1483-1546)

5739 Gentleness succeeds better than violence.

La Fontaine (1621-1695)

5740 All the talk of history is of nothing almost but fighting
and killing, and the honor and renown which are bestowed
on conquerors, who, for the most part, are mere butchers
of mankind, mislead growing youth, who, by these means,
come to think slaughter the most laudable business of
mankind, and the most heroic of virtues.

John Locke (1632-1704)

5741 War! that mad game the world so loves to play.

Swift (1667-1745)

5742 War is the greatest of all crimes; and yet there is no aggressor who does not color his crime with the pretext of justice.

Voltaire (1694-1778)

5743 War is an instrument entirely inefficient toward redressing wrong; and multiplies, instead of indemnifying losses.

Thomas Jefferson (1743-1826)

5744 Preparation for war is a constant stimulus to suspicion and ill will.

James Monroe (1758-1831)

5745 War is nothing less than a temporary repeal of the principles of virtue. It is a system out of which almost all the virtues are excluded, and in which nearly all the vices are included.

Robert Hall (1764-1831)

5746 Nothing except a battle lost can be half so melancholy as a battle won.

Wellington (1769-1852)

5747 If war has its chivalry and its pageantry, it has also its hideousness and its demoniac woe. Bullets respect not beauty. They tear out the eye, and shatter the jaw, and rend the cheek.

John Abbott (1805-1877)

5748 No protracted war can fail to endanger the freedom of a democratic country.

Alexis De Tocqueville (1805-1859)

5749 The ballot is stronger than the bullet.

Lincoln (1809-1865)

5750 War is cruelty, and you cannot refine it.

William T. Sherman (1820-1891)

5751 There is many a boy here today who looks on war as all glory, but boys, it is all hell.

William T. Sherman (1820-1891)

5752 The carnage and suffering which war entails are terrible to contemplate, and constitute an irresistible argument in favor of arbitration.

Lubbock (1834-1913)

5753 Every government has as much of a duty to avoid war as a ship's captain has to avoid a shipwreck.

Guy de Maupassant (1850-1893)

5754   War I abhor, and yet how sweet
The sound along the marching street
Of drum and fife, and I forget
Wet eyes of widows, and forget
Broken old mothers, and the whole
Dark butchery without a soul.

Le Gallienne (1866-1947)

5755   What difference does it make to the dead...whether the mad
destruction is wrought under the name of totalitarianism or
the holy name of liberty or democracy?

Gandhi (1869-1948)

5756   War is only a cowardly escape from the problems of peace.

Thomas Mann (1875-1955)

5757   I know war as few other men now living know it, and nothing
to me is more revolting. I have long advocated its complete
abolition, as its very destructiveness on both friend and
foe has rendered it useless as a method of settling
international disputes.

Douglas MacArthur (1880-1964)

5758   A great war leaves the country with three armies-
an army of cripples, an army of mourners, and
an army of thieves.

German Proverb

6. ADVICE

5759   It is only necessary to make war with five things:
with the maladies of the body,
with the ignorances of the mind,
with the passions of the body,
with the seditions of the city,
with the discords of families.

Pythagoras (B.C. 582-507)

5760   All warfare is based on deception. Therefore, when capable,
feign incapacity; when active, inactivity. When near, make
it appear that you are far away; when far way, that you are
near. Offer the enemy a bait to lure him; feign disorder
and strike him. When he concentrates, prepare against him;
where he is strong, avoid him. Anger his general and
confuse him. Pretend inferiority and encourage his
arrogance. Keep him under a strain and wear him down. When
he is united, divide him. Attack where he is unprepared;
sally out when he does not expect you. These are the
strategist's keys to victory. It is not possible to discuss
them beforehand.

Sun Tzu (fl. c. B.C. 500)

5761   To fight and conquer in all your battles is not supreme
        excellence; supreme excellence consists in breaking the
        enemy's resistance without fighting.
                                    Sun Tzu (fl. c. B.C. 500)

5762   Beware lest in your anxiety to avoid war you obtain a
        master.
                                    Demosthenes (B.C. 384-322)

5763   Wars are to be undertaken in order that it may be possible
        to live in peace without molestation.
                                    Cicero (B.C. 106-43)

5764   Before all else, be armed.
                                    Machiavelli (1469-1527)

5765   Give the enemy not only a road for flight,
        but also a means of defending it.
                                    Rabelais (1490-1553)

5766   Study strategy over the years and achieve the spirit of the
        warrior. Today is victory over yourself of yesterday;
        tomorrow is your victory over lesser men.
                                    Miyamoto Musashi (1584-1645)

5767   To be prepared for war is one of the most effectual means
        of preserving peace.
                                    George Washington (1732-1799)

5768   There are strings in the human heart that had better not be
        vibrated.
                                    Charles Dickens (1812-1870)

5769   The essence of war is violence.
        Moderation in war is imbecility.
                                    John A. Fisher (1841-1920)

5770   Once we have a war there is only one thing to do. It must
        be won. For defeat brings worse things than any that can
        ever happen in war.
                                    Ernest Hemingway (1898-1961)

7. POTPOURRI

5771   Our business in the field of fight
        Is not to question, but to prove our might.
                                    Homer (c. B.C. 700)

5772 And by prudent flight and cunning save
A life, which valour could not, from the grave.
A better shield I can soon regain;
But who can get another life again?

Archilochus (c. B.C. 648)

5773 When discord dreadful bursts her brazen bars,
And shatters locks to thunder forth her wars.

Horace (B.C. 65-8)

5774 Sound trumpets! let our bloody colours wave!
And either victory, or else a grave.

Shakespeare (1564-1616)

5775 Mine eyes have seen the glory of the coming of the Lord:
He is trampling out the vintage where the grapes of wrath
  are stored:
He hath loosed the fateful lightning of his terrible swift
  sword:
His truth is marching on.

Julia Ward Howe (1819-1910)

5776 War, he sung, is toil and trouble;
Honour but an empty bubble.

Dryden (1631-1700)

5777 Everything can collapse. Houses, bodies, and enemies
collapse when their rhythm becomes deranged. In large-
scale battles, when the enemy starts to collapse you must
pursue him without letting the chance go. If you fail to
take advantage of your enemies' collapse, they may recover.

Miyamoto Musashi (1584-1645)

5778 These are the time that try men's souls. The Summer
soldier and the sunshine patriot will, in this crisis,
shrink from the service of their country, but he that stands
now deserves the love and thanks of man and woman.
  Tyranny, like Hell, is not easily conquered; yet we have
this consolation with us - the harder the conflict the more
glorious the triumph.

Paine (1737-1809)

5779 He that fights and runs away,
May turn and fight another day;
But he that is in battle slain,
Will never rise to fight again.

James Ray (fl. 1746)

5780   But Thy most dreaded instrument
In working out a pure intent,
Is man, - arrayed for mutual slaughter,-
Yes Carnage is Thy daughter.

Wordsworth (1770-1850)

5781   The Assyrian came down like the wolf on the fold,
And his cohorts were gleaming in purple and gold.

Byron (1788-1824)

5782   Like the leaves of the forest when summer is green,
That host with their banners at sunset were seen;
Like the leaves of the forest when autumn hath blown,
That host on the morrow lay wither'd and strown!

Byron (1788-1824)

5783   March to the battle-field,
The foe is now before us;
Each heart is Freedom's shield,
And heaven is shining o'er us.

Barry O'Meara (1786-1836)

5784   By the rude bridge that arched the flood,
Their flag to April's breeze unfurl'd;
Here once the embattl'd farmers stood,
And fired the shot heard round the world.

Emerson (1803-1882)

5785   Theirs not to make reply,
Theirs not to reason why,
Theirs but to do and die.

Alfred Tennyson (1809-1892)

5786   For what this whirlwind all aflame?
This thunderstroke of hellish ire,
Setting the universe afire?
While millions upon millions came
Into a very storm of war?
For a scrap of paper.

Charles Loyson (1827-1912)

5787   I hear the hoarse-voiced cannon roar,
the red-mouthed orators of war.

Joaquin Miller (1839-1913)

5788   Yes; quaint and curious war is!
You shoot a fellow down
You'd treat if met where any bar is,
Or help to half-a-crown.

Thomas Hardy (1840-1928)

5789   Naval supremacy is the best security for the peace of the
        world...If...you are ready for instant war, with every unit
        of your strength in the first line and waiting to be first
        in, and hit your enemy in the belly and kick him when he is
        down, and boil your prisoners in oil (if you take any) and
        torture his women and children, then people will keep clear
        of you.

                                        John A. Fisher (1841-1920)

5790   There will one day spring from the brain of science a
        machine or force so fearful in its potentialities, so
        absolutely terrifying, that even man, the fighter, who will
        dare torture and death, will be appalled, and so abandon war
        forever. What man's mind can create, man's character can
        control.

                                    Thomas A. Edison (1847-1931)

WEAKNESS
Cowardice, Servility and Temptation

1. ESSENCE

5791   'Tis one thing to be tempted, another thing to fall.
Shakespeare (1564-1616)

5792   Human brutes, like other beasts, find snares and poison
in the provisions of life, and are allured by their
appetites to their destruction.
Swift (1667-1745)

5793   Weaknesses, so called, are nothing more nor less than
vice in disguise!
Lavater (1741-1801)

2. OPPOSITES

5794   When man is born, he is tender and weak.
At death, he is stiff and hard.
All things, the grass as well as trees,
  are tender and supple while alive.
When dead, they are withered and dried.
Therefore the stiff and hard are companions of death.
The tender and the weak are companions of life.
Lao-Tzu (fl. B.C. 600)

5795   Excessive liberty leads both nations and individuals into
excessive slavery.
Cicero (B.C. 106-43)

5796   God hath chosen the foolish things of the world
  to confound the wise;
and God hath chosen the weak things of the world
  to confound the things that are mighty.
I Corinthians (50?-100? A.D.)

5797   Weakness is more opposite to virtue than is vice itself.
La Rochefoucauld (1613-1680)

5798   All mankind is one of these two cowards:
  to wish to die when he should live,
  to wish to live when he should die.
Robert Howard (1626-1698)

5799   Strength alone knows conflict;
weakness is below even defeat, and is born vanquished.
Anne Swetchine (1782-1857)

5800   Every man has a coward and hero in his soul.

Carlyle (1795-1881)

5801   Strength comes from struggle; weakness from ease.

B. C. Forbes (1880-1954)

3. INSIGHT

5802   Vain and inconstant if thou art, how canst thou but be
        weak? Is not inconstancy connected with frailty? Can
        there be vanity without infirmity? Avoid the danger of
        the one, and thou shalt escape the mischief of the other.

Akhenaton? (c. B.C. 1375)

5803   Instead of solid accomplishments, the man pursues pleasures
        and self-gratification. He will never achieve anything so
        long as he is surrounded by dissipating temptations.

I Ching (B.C. 1150?)

5804   It is a law of nature that faint-hearted men should be the
        fruit of luxurious countries, for we never find that the
        same soil produces delicacies and heroes.

Herodotus (B.C. 484-425)

5805   Things forbidden have a secret charm.

Tacitus (55-117 A.D.)

5806   When a broken tank is filled with water,
        It certainly will leak on every side.
        Weak men who grow rich
        Seldom leave an inheritance.

Saskya Pandita (1182-1251)

5807   How oft the sight of means to do ill deeds
        makes deeds ill done!

Shakespeare (1564-1616)

5808   Many a dangerous temptation comes to us in fine gay colours,
        that are but skin-deep.

Matthew Henry (1662-1714)

5809   Slavery is also as ancient as war,
        and war as human nature.

Voltaire (1694-1778)

5810   The coward only threatens when he is safe.

Goethe (1749-1832)

5811   To sin by silence when they should protest
        makes cowards out of men.

Lincoln (1809-1865)

5812 If you take temptations into account, who is to say that he
is better than his neighbor?

Thackeray (1811-1863)

5813 The man who gives me employment, which I must have or
suffer, that man is my master, let me call him what I will.

Henry George (1839-1897)

5814 Men lie, who lack courage to tell truth - the cowards!

Joaquin Miller (1839-1913)

5815 Not wine...men intoxicate themselves;
Not vice...men entice themselves.

Chinese Proverb

4. POSITIVE

5816 To yield is to be preserved whole.
To be bent is to become straight.
To be empty is to be full.
To be worn out is to be renewed.
To have little is to possess.
To have plenty is to be perplexed.

Lao-Tzu (fl. B.C. 600)

5817 Heaven's eternal wisdom has decreed, that man should
ever stand in need of man.

Theocritus (fl. B.C. 300)

5818 My strength is made perfect in weakness.

II Corinthians (50?-100? A.D.)

5819 Men are in general so tricky, so envious, so cruel,
that when we find one who is only weak, we are happy.

Voltaire (1694-1778)

5820 Even weak men when united are powerful.

Schiller (1759-1805)

5821 Why comes temptation but for man to meet
And master and make crouch beneath his foot,
And so be pedestaled in triumph?

Robert Browning (1812-1889)

5822 No man is matriculated to the art of life till he has been
well tempted.

George Eliot (1819-1880)

5823 There are several good protections against temptation,
but the surest is cowardice.

Mark Twain (1835-1910)

5. NEGATIVE

5824   The dastardly spirit of a timorous man betrayeth him to
        shame. By shrinking under poverty, he stoopeth down to
        meanness; and by tamely bearing insults he inviteth
        injuries....In the hour of danger, he is embarrassed and
        confounded: in the day of misfortune he sinketh and despair
        overwhelmeth his Soul.

                                        Akhenaton? (c. B.C. 1375)

5825   The man is indecisively unable to deal with adversity and
        is oppressed by something which should not oppress him.
        He leans on things like thorns and thistles, which are
        hazardous yet cannot support him.

                                        I Ching (B.C. 1150?)

5826   There is nothing softer and weaker than water,
        And yet there is nothing better for attacking hard and
            strong things.
        For this reason there is no substitute for it.
        All the world knows that the weak overcomes the strong and
            the soft overcomes the hard.
        But none can practice it.

                                        Lao-Tzu (fl. B.C. 600)

5827   To know what is right and not to do it is the worst
        cowardice.

                                        Confucius (B.C. 551-479)

5828   The fire which burned the forest
        Became the companion of the wind.
        But just as the wind extinguished the fire,
        The weak man loses his friends.

                                        Nagarjuna (c. 100-200 A.D.)

5829   Most dangerous is that temptation that doth goad us on to
        sin in loving virtue.

                                        Shakespeare (1564-1616)

5830   To excuse our faults on the ground of our weakness
            is to quiet our fears at the expense of our hopes.
        To be weak is miserable, doing or suffering.

                                        Milton (1608-1674)

5831   Weakness is the only fault that is incorrigible.

                                        La Rochefoucauld (1613-1680)

5832   Temptation is the fire that brings up the scum of the
        heart.

                                        Thomas Boston (1676-1732)

5833   Servitude degrades men even to making them love it.
                                    Vauvenargues(1715-1747)

5834   The concessions of the weak are the concessions of fear.
                                        Burke (1729-1797)

5835   The mortal race is far too weak not to grow dizzy on
        unwonted heights.
                                        Goethe (1749-1832)

5836   The last temptation is the greatest treason:
        To do the right deed for the wrong reason.
                                    T. S. Eliot (1888-1965)

6. ADVICE

5837   If thou wouldst preserve understanding and health to old
        age, avoid the allurements of Voluptuousness, and fly from
        her temptations.... For if thou hearkenest unto the words of
        the Adversary, thou art deceived and betrayed. The joy
        which she promiseth changeth to madness, and her enjoyments
        lead on to diseases and death.
                                    Akhenaton? (c. B.C. 1375)

5838   If you find your mind tempted and entangled in greed,
        you must suppress the greed and control the temptation;
        be the master of your own mind.
                                    Buddha (B.C. 568-488)

5839   The acknowledgement of our weakness is the first step
        toward repairing our loss.
                                    Thomas A. Kempis (1380-1471)

5840   Better shun the bait than struggle in the snare.
                                    Dryden (1631-1700)

5841   Every moment of resistance to temptation is a victory.
                                    Frederick Faber (1814-1863)

5842   Begin to think of this body as nothing better than the house
        you have to live in for a time, and then you will never
        yield to its temptations. Try also with consistent attempts
        to conquer the prominent weaknesses of your nature by
        developing thought in the direction that will kill each
        particular passion.
                                    H. P. Blavatsky (1831-1891)

7. POTPOURRI

5843   A great country is lowly.
Everything under heaven blends with it.
It is like the female, at all times and in every place
overcomes the male by her quietude.
Than quietude there is nothing that is more lowly.
Therefore a great state gains by yielding;
while the smaller state wins the greater by submission.
In the one case lowliness gains adherents,
in the other it procures favors.

Lao-Tzu (fl. B.C. 600)

5844   The cord breaketh at last by the weakest pull.

Bacon (1561-1626)

5845   But Satan now is wiser than of yore,
And tempts by making rich, not making poor.

Pope (1688-1744)

5846   The Sensual and the Dark rebel in vain,
Slaves by their own compulsion! In mad game
They burst their manacles and wear the name
Of Freedom, graven on a heavier chain!

Samuel Coleridge (1772-1834)

5847   Our fellow-countrymen in chains!
   Slaves - in a land of light and law!
Slaves - crouching on the very plains
   Where rolled the storms of Freedom's war!

John Greenleaf Whittier (1807-1892)

5848   The coward wretch whose hand and heart
Can bear to torture aught below,
Is ever first to quail and start
From the slightest pain or equal foe.

Eliza Cook (1818-1889)

5849   They are slaves who fear to speak
For the fallen and the weak;
They are slaves who will not choose
Hatred, scoffing, and abuse,
Rather than in silence shrink
From the truth they needs must think;
They are slaves who dare not be
In the right with two or three.

James Lowell (1819-1891)

5850   To cease smoking is the easiest thing I ever did.
        I ought to know because I've done it a thousand times.

                                            Mark Twain (1835-1910)

5851   Coward - One who in a perilous emergency thinks with his
        legs.

                                        Ambrose Bierce (1842-1914?)

5852   I can resist everything except temptation.

                                        Oscar Wilde (1854-1900)

5853   Temptation - An irresistible force at work on a moveable
        body.

                                        H. L. Mencken (1880-1956)

5854   The Tongue is an instrument yielding and pliant
        Yet safe in the mouth, it ever remains,
        While the teeth are inflexible, hard and defiant,
        And frequently broken to pay for their pains.

                                            Chinese Proverb

WEALTH

Gold, Money, Possessions and Riches

1. ESSENCE

5855 He is richest who is content with the least,
for content is the wealth of nature.

Socrates (B.C. 469-399)

5856 Wealth consists not in having great possessions,
but in having few wants.

Epicurus (B.C. 341-270)

5857 Who gives to friends so much from Fate secures,
That is the only wealth for ever yours.

Martial (43-104 A.D.)

5858 A man's true wealth is the good he does in this world.

Mohammed (570-632 A.D.)

5859 Every man is rich or poor according to the proportion
between his desires and his enjoyments.

Johnson (1709-1784)

5860 Money is human happiness in the abstract.

Schopenhauer (1788-1860)

2. OPPOSITES

5861 Money is a handmaiden, if thou knowest how to use it;
a mistress, if thou knowest not.

Horace (B.C. 65-8)

5862 It is easy at any moment to resign the possession of a
great fortune; to acquire it is difficult and arduous.

Livy (B.C. 59-17 A.D.)

5863 As long as you have wealth, everyone is your friend;
If your fortune declines, everyone is your foe,
An island of precious metals is visited from afar;
When a lake dries up, everyone leaves.

Saskya Pandita (1182-1251)

5864 Great riches have sold more men than they have bought.

Bacon (1561-1626)

5865 If thou art rich, thou art poor;
for, like an ass, whose back with ingots bows,
thou bearest the heavy riches but a journey,
and death unloads thee.

Shakespeare (1564-1616)

5866   He is rich whose income is more than his expenses;
       and he is poor whose expenses exceed his income.
                                        La Bruyere (1645-1696)

5867   Riches exclude only one inconvenience,
       and that is poverty.
                                             Johnson (1709-1784)

5868   Equity money is dynamic and debt money is static.
                                             Burke (1729-1797)

5869   It isn't enough for you to love money -
       it's also necessary that money should love you.
                                    Mayer Rothschild (1743-1812)

5870   Riches amassed in haste will diminish,
       but those collected by little and little will multiply.
                                             Goethe (1749-1832)

5871   Gold, like the sun, which melts wax and hardens clay,
       expands great souls and contracts bad hearts.
                                  Antoine de Rivaroli (1753-1801)

5872   It is far more easy to acquire fortune like a knave
       than to expend it like a gentleman.
                                             Colton (1780-1832)

5873   In this world, it is not what we take up,
       but what we give up, that makes us rich.
                                             Beecher (1813-1878)

5874   With money a dragon
       Without money a worm.
                                             Chinese Proverb

3. INSIGHT

5875   Nature hath hid gold beneath the earth, as unworthy to be
       seen; silver hath she placed where thou tramplest it under
       thy feet. Meaneth she not by this to inform thee, that
       gold is not worthy thy regard, and that silver is beneath
       thy notice?
                                        Akhenaton? (c. B.C. 1375)

5876   Riches certainly make themselves wings;
       they fly away as an eagle toward heaven.
                                    Proverbs (B.C. 1000?-200?)

5877   Money lost is bewailed with unfeigned tears.
                                        Juvenal (40-125 A.D.)

5878   Money is like manure, of very little use except it be
spread.

Bacon (1561-1626)

5879   All wealth is the product of labor.

John Locke (1632-1704)

5880   Much learning shows how little mortals know;
Much wealth, how little worldlings can enjoy.

Young (1683-1765)

5881   When is is a question of money, everybody is of the same
religion.

Voltaire (1694-1778)

5882   If you would know the value of money,
go and try to borrow some.

Franklin (1706-1790)

5883   As wealth is power, so all power will infallibly draw wealth
to itself by some means or other.

Burke (1729-1797)

5884   Many people take no care of their money
till they come nearly to the end of it.
Others do just the same with their time.

Goethe (1749-1832)

5885   Our incomes are like our shoes;
if too small, they gall and pinch us;
but if too large, they cause us to stumble and to trip.

Colton (1780-1832)

5886   If rich men would remember that shrouds have no pockets,
they would, while living, share their wealth with their
children, and give for the good of others, and so know
the highest pleasure wealth can give.

Tryon Edwards (1809-1894)

5887   The use we make of our fortune determines as to its
sufficiency. - A little is enough if used wisely,
and too much if expended foolishly.

Bovee (1820-1904)

5888   Money has little value to its possessor
unless it also has value to others.

Leland Stanford (1824-1893)

5889   Everyone, even the richest and most munificent of men,
       pays much by check more lightheartedly than he pays little
       in cash.

                                           Max Beerbohm (1872-1956)

5890   Earned money - best.
       Inherited money - not so good.
       Brother's money - bad.
       Woman's money - worst.

                                                    Eastern Proverb

4. POSITIVE

5891   Wealth is of all things the most esteemed by men and has the
       greatest power of all things in the world.

                                          Euripides (B.C. 480-406)

5892   A feast is made for laughter, and wine maketh merry;
       but money answereth all things.

                                          Ecclesiastes (B.C. 300?)

5893   There is no fortress so strong that money cannot take it.

                                              Cicero (B.C. 106-43)

5894   Though authority be stubborn as a bear,
       yet he is oft led by the nose with gold.

                                          Shakespeare (1564-1616)

5895   For they say, if money go before, all ways do lie open.

                                          Shakespeare (1564-1616)

5896   There's no fence or fortress against an ass laden with gold.

                                          James Howell (1595-1666)

5897   Money brings honor, friends, conquest, and realms.

                                              Milton (1608-1674)

5898   A heavy purse makes a light heart.

                                                   English Proverb

5899   Let all the learn'd say what they can,
       'Tis ready money makes the man;
       Commands respect where'er we go,
       And gives a grace to all we do.

                                     William Somerville (1675-1742)

5900   Men are seldom more innocently employed
       than when they are honestly making money.

                                              Johnson (1709-1784)

5901   Ready money is Aladdin's lamp.

                                              Byron (1788-1824)

5902   The desire of gold is not for gold.
        It is for the means of freedom and benefit.

                                              Emerson (1803-1882)

5903   Property is desirable, is a positive good in the world.

                                              Lincoln (1809-1865)

5904   Wealth may be an ancient thing, for it means power,
        it means leisure, it means liberty.

                                        James Lowell (1819-1891)

5905   Possession means to sit astride the world
        Instead of having it astride of you.

                                    Charles Kingsley (1819-1875)

5906   It is better to have old secondhand diamonds than none
        at all.

                                          Mark Twain (1835-1910)

5907   When I was young I thought that money was the most important
        thing in life; now that I am old I know that it is.

                                          Oscar Wilde (1854-1900)

5908   Money is the most important thing in the world. It
        represents health, strength, honor, generosity and beauty
        as conspicuously as the want of it represents illness,
        weakness, disgrace, meanness and ugliness.

                                           G. B. Shaw (1856-1950)

5909   Money is like a sixth sense - and you can't make use of the
        other five without it.

                                    Somerset Maugham (1874-1965)

5910   Private property was the original source of freedom.
        It still is its main bulwark.

                                     Walter Lippmann (1889-1974)

5911   In all the world people enjoy salt and money.

                                                  Chinese Proverb

5912   Heat comes equally to all...
        Cold respects the rich man's furs.

                                                  Chinese Proverb

5. NEGATIVE

5913   The earth is barren of good things where she hoardeth up
        treasure; where gold is in her bowels, there no herb
        groweth.
                                    Akhenaton? (c. B.C. 1375)

5914   There is always danger in circumstances of abundance.
        The inferior man pushes forward through excessive ambition,
        thereby losing touch with men of talent and virtue in
        positions below him.
                                    I Ching (B.C. 1150?)

5915   The rich fool is like a pig that is choked by its own fat.
                                    Confucius (B.C. 551-479)

5916   The love of money is the mother of all evil.
                                    Phocylides (fl. B.C. 540)

5917   Wealth is the parent of luxury and indolence, and poverty of
        meanness and viciousness, and both of discontent.
                                    Plato (B.C. 427?-347?)

5918   It is better for you to be free of fear lying upon a pallet,
        than to have a golden couch and a rich table and be full
        of trouble.
                                    Epicurus (B.C. 341-270)

5919   Riches destroy the foolish, if they look not for the other
        shore; by his thirst for riches the foolish man destroys
        himself as if he were his own enemy.
                                    The Dhammapada (c. B.C. 300)

5920   To despise money on some occasions is a very great pain.
                                    Terence (B.C. 185-159)

5921   A great fortune is a great servitude.
                                    Seneca (B.C. 3-65 A.D.)

5922   Riches do not exhilarate us so much with their possession
        as they torment us with their loss.
                                    Gregory I (540-604)

5923   As to those who hoard gold and silver and spend it not in
        God's path, give them, then, the tidings of a painful
        agony: on a day when these things shall be heated in
        hell-fire, and their foreheads, and their sides, and their
        backs shall be branded therewith.
                                    Koran (c. 651 A.D.)

5924   When a man becomes too famous for his riches,
He is destroyed by his wealth.
It is common that rich men are assaulted,
But beggars pass through without harm.
Saskya Pandita (1182-1251)

5925   Great abundance of riches cannot be gathered and kept by any
man without sin.
Erasmus (1466-1536)

5926   A son can bear with equanimity the loss of his father,
but the loss of his inheritance may drive him to despair.
Machiavelli (1469-1527)

5927   Worldly wealth is the Devil's bait; and those whose minds
feed upon riches recede, in general, from real happiness,
in proportion as their stores increase, as the moon,
when she is fullest, is farthest from the sun.
Robert Burton (1576-1640)

5928   He that is proud of riches is a fool. For if he be exalted
above his neighbors because he hath more gold, how much
inferior is he to a gold mine.
Jeremy Taylor (1613-1667)

5929   Gold begets in brethren hate;
Gold in families debate;
Gold does friendship separate;
Gold does civil wars create.
Abraham Cowley (1618-1667)

5930   They who are of the opinion that Money will do everything,
may very well be suspected to do everything for Money.
Halifax (1633-1695)

5931   There is a burden of care in getting riches;
fear of keeping them; temptation in using them;
guilt in abusing them, sorrow in losing them;
and a burden of account at last to be given concerning them.
Matthew Henry (1662-1714)

5932   If Heaven had looked upon riches to be a valuable thing,
it would not have given them to such scoundrels.
Swift (1667-1745)

5933   Gold glitters most where virtue shines no more,
as stars from absent suns have leave to shine.
Young (1683-1765)

5934 Money never made a man happy yet, nor will it.
There is nothing in its nature to produce happiness.
The more a man has, the more he wants.
Instead of its filling a vacuum, it makes one.
Franklin (1706-1790)

5935 If you make money your god,
it will plague you like the devil.
Henry Fielding (1707-1754)

5936 Money and time are the heaviest burdens of life, and the
unhappiest of all mortals are those who have more of either
than they know how to use.
Johnson (1709-1784)

5937 It is only when the rich are sick
that they fully feel the impotence of wealth.
Colton (1780-1832)

5938 The deepest depth of vulgarism is that of setting up
money as the ark of the covenant.
Carlyle (1795-1881)

5939 Money often costs too much.
Emerson (1803-1882)

5940 Money is not required to buy one necessity of the soul.
Thoreau (1817-1862)

5941 It is easier for a camel to go through the eye of a needle,
than for a rich man to enter into the kingdom of God.
Mark 10:25 (50?-100? A.D.)

5942 Money may be the husk of many things, but not the kernel.
It brings you food, but not appetite; medicine, but not
health; acquaintance, but not friends; servants, but not
loyalty; days of joy, but not peace or happiness.
Henrik Ibsen (1828-1906)

5943 It has been said that the love of money is the root of all
evil. The want of money is so quite as truly.
Samuel Butler (1835-1902)

5944 The pride of dying rich raises the loudest laugh in hell.
John Foster (1836-1917)

5945 Misery assails riches, as lightning does the highest towers;
or as a tree that is heavy laden with fruit breaks its
own boughs, so riches destroy the virtue of their possessor.
Richard E. Burton (1861-1940)

5946 The only thing I like about rich people is their money.
Nancy Astor (1879-1964)

5947 Money can help you to get medicines
   but not health.
  Money can help you to get soft pillows,
   but not sound sleep.
  Money can help you to get material comforts,
   but not eternal bliss.
  Money can help you to get ornaments,
   but not beauty.
  Money will help you to get an electric earphone,
   but not natural hearing.
  Attain the supreme wealth, wisdom;
   you will have everything.
Sivananda (born 1887)

6. ADVICE

5948 Neither let prosperity put out the eyes of circumspection,
  nor abundance cut off the hands of frugality;
  he that too much indulgeth in the superfluities of life,
  shall live to lament the want of its necessaries.
Akhenaton? (c. B.C. 1375)

5949 He that trusteth in his riches shall fall.
Proverbs (B.C. 1000?-200?)

5950 Do not lay up for yourselves treasures on earth, where
  moth and rust consume and where thieves break in and
  steal, but lay up for yourself treasures in heaven, where
  neither moth nor rust consumes and where thieves do not
  break in and steal. For where your treasure is, there
  will your heart be also.
Jesus (B.C. 6?-30? A.D.)

5951 Six faults ought to be avoided by a man seeking prosperity
  in this world: sleep, sloth, fear, anger, laziness,
  prolixity.
The Hitopadesa (600?-1100? A.D.)

5952 Money was made, not to command our will,
  But all our lawful pleasures to fulfill.
  Shame and woe to us, if we our wealth obey;
  The horse doth with the horseman away.
Abraham Cowley (1618-1667)

5953   The way to wealth is as plain as the way to market.
       It depends chiefly on two words, industry and frugality;
       that is, waste neither time nor money, but make the best use
       of both. Without industry and frugality, nothing will do;
       and with them, everything.

                                                    Franklin (1706-1790)

5954   Wealth is not his that has it, but his that enjoys it.

                                                    Franklin (1706-1790)

5955   Life is short.
       The sooner that a man begins to enjoy his wealth the better.

                                                    Johnson (1709-1784)

5956   It requires a great deal of boldness and a great deal of
       caution to make a great fortune; and when you have got it,
       it requires ten times as much wit to keep it.

                                            Mayer Rothschild (1743-1812)

5957   Put not your trust in money, but put your money in trust.

                                    Oliver Wendell Holmes (1809-1894)

5958   It's good to have money and the things money can buy. But
       it's good too, to check up once in a while and make sure
       you haven't lost the things that money can't buy.

                                            George Lorimer (1868-1937)

7. POTPOURRI

5959   He that giveth away his treasure wisely, giveth away his
       plagues: he that retaineth their increase, heapeth up
       sorrow.

                                            Akhenaton? (c. B.C. 1375)

5960   Accursed thirst for gold!
       what dost thou not compel mortals to do?

                                                    Vergil (B.C. 70-19)

5961   Truly now is the golden age;
       the highest honour comes by means of gold;
       by gold love is procured.

                                            Ovid (B.C. 43-18 A.D.)

5962   One's desire to be attractive and happy
       And to enjoy the pleasures of wealth,
       Is like the foolishness of a drunken person,
       Who, though healthy, must be carried.

                                        Nagarjuna (c. 100-200 A.D.)

5963   And as for him who is covetous and desirous of riches,
        and denieth the Best, we will speed him onward to trouble;
        and his riches shall not avail him when he falleth down
        into Hell.

                                                    Koran (c. 651 A.D.)

5964   Can wealth give happiness? look round and see
        What gay distress! what splendid misery!
        Whatever fortunes lavishly can pour,
        The mind annihilates, and calls for more.

                                                    Young (1683-1765)

5965   I am indeed rich, since my income is superior to my expense,
        and my expense is equal to my wishes.

                                                    Gibbon (1737-1794)

5966   I have mental joys and mental health,
        Mental friends and mental wealth,
        I've a wife that I love and that loves me;
        I've all but riches bodily.

                                                    William Blake (1757-1828)

5967   Many speak the truth when they say that they despise riches,
        but they mean the riches possessed by other men.

                                                    Colton (1780-1832)

5968   Without a rich heart wealth is an ugly beggar.

                                                    Emerson (1803-1882)

5969   The seven deadly sins...Food, clothing, firing, rent, taxes,
        respectability and children. Nothing can lift those seven
        millstones from man's neck but money; and the spirit cannot
        soar until the millstones are lifted.

                                                    G. B. Shaw (1856-1950)

5970   Money is always there but the pockets change;
        it is not in the same pockets after a change,
        and that is all there is to say about money.

                                                    Gertrude Stein (1874-1946)

5971   Nobody was ever meant
        To remember or invent
        What he did with every cent.

                                                    Robert Frost (1875-1963)

5972   Wealth - any income that is at least one hundred dollars
        more a year than the income of one's wife's sister's
        husband.

                                                    H. L. Mencken (1880-1956)

5973   Money comes like sand scooped with a needle...
        Money goes like sand washed by water.

                                                    Chinese Proverb

WILL

Determination, Resolution, Self-Control and Strength

1. ESSENCE

5974   Will is the dynamic soul-force.

Sivananda (born 1887)

5975   Great souls have wills; feeble ones have only wishes.

Chinese Proverb

2. OPPOSITES

5976   When a man lacks discrimination and
His mind is undisciplined, his senses
Run hither and thither like wild horses,
But they obey the rein like trained horses
When he has discrimination and his
Mind is one-pointed.

Upanishads (c. B.C. 800)

5977   For him who has conquered the mind,
   the mind is the best of friends;
but for one who has failed to do so,
   his mind will be the greatest enemy.

Bhagavad Gita (c. B.C. 400)

5978   There is nothing good or evil save in the will.

Epictetus (50-138 A.D.)

5979   I have known many who could not when they would,
for they had not done it when they could.

Rabelais (1490-1553)

5980   It is the will that makes the action good or ill.

Robert Herrick (1591-1674)

5981   Let not thy Will roar, when thy Power can but whisper.

Thomas Fuller (1608-1661)

5982   All theory is against the freedom of the will,
all experience for it.

Johnson (1709-1784)

5983   Man is made great or little by his own will.

Schiller (1759-1805)

5984   Men are great or small in stature as it pleases God. But
        their nature is great or small as it pleases themselves.
        Men are not born, some with great souls and some with little
        souls. One by taking thought cannot add to his stature, but
        he can enlarge his soul. By an act of the will he can make
        himself a moral giant, or dwarf himself to a pigmy.
                                        Albert Pike (1809-1891)

5985   The only way of setting the will free
        is to deliver it from willfulness.
                                        Hare & Charles (c. 1830)

5986   If knowledge outweighs conscious will a man knows
        but has no power to do. It is useless knowledge.
        On the other hand if conscious life outweighs knowledge
        a man has the power to do, but does not know,
        that is, he can do something but does not know what to do.
                                        Gurdjieff (1873-1949)

5987   Easy to bend the body...
        Not the will.
                                        Chinese Proverb

3. INSIGHT

5988   By steadily disciplining the animal nature, until it becomes
        one pointed, it is possible to establish conscious awareness
        of The Eternal.
                                        Lao-Tzu (fl. B.C. 600)

5989   One who restrains the senses and organs of action, but
        whose mind dwells on sense objects, certainly deludes
        himself and is called a pretender.
                                        Bhagavad Gita (c. B.C. 400)

5990   Every duty is a charge, but the charge of oneself is the
        root of all others.
                                        Mencius (B.C. 371-288)

5991   There are men steady and wise whose body, words and mind are
        self-controlled. They are the men of supreme self-control.
                                        The Dhammapada (c. B.C. 300)

5992   Surely the getting up at night is the strongest way to
        conquer one's self...
                                        Koran (c. 651 A.D.)

5993   The will of man is by his reason swayed.
                                        Shakespeare (1564-1616)

5994 Although men are accused of not knowing their own weakness, yet perhaps as few know their own strength. It is in men as in soils, where sometimes there is a vein of gold which the owner knows not of.

Swift (1667-1745)

5995 Whatever the will commands, the whole man must do; the empire of the will over all the faculties being absolutely over-ruling and despotic.

Sydney Smith (1771-1845)

5996 We deceive ourselves when we fancy that only weakness needs support. Strength needs it far more. A straw or a feather sustains itself long in the air.

Anne Swetchine (1782-1857)

5997 The will is the strong blind man who carries on his shoulders the lame man who can see.

Schopenhauer (1788-1860)

5998 The education of the will is the object of our existence.

Emerson (1803-1882)

5999 Everything in this world depends upon will.

Disraeli (1804-1881)

6000 The strongest man in the world is he who stands most alone.

Henrik Ibsen (1828-1906)

6001 Will is character in action.

William McDougall (1871-1938)

6002 When rendered pure and irresistible, will can work wonders. Will becomes impure and weak through vulgar passions, love of pleasures and desires. Fewer the desires, the stronger the will.

Sivananda (born 1887)

4. POSITIVE

6003 The greatest bounties given to man are, judgment and will; happy is he who misapplieth them not.

Akhenaton? (c. B.C. 1375)

6004 It is an inexorable Law of Nature that bad must follow good, that decline must follow a rise. To feel that we can rest on our achievements is a dangerous fallacy. Inner strength can overcome anything that occurs outside.

I Ching (B.C. 1150?)

6005 To enjoy good health, to bring true happiness to one's
family, to bring peace to all, one must first discipline
and control one's own mind. If a man can control his mind
he can find the way to Enlightenment, and all wisdom and
virtue will naturally come to him.

Buddha (B.C. 568-488)

6006 The army commander of a large State may be carried off,
but the will of even a common man cannot be taken for him.

Confucius (B.C. 551-479)

6007 The man who has the will to undergo all labor
may win to any good.

Menander (B.C. 342-291)

6008 And he who lives a hundred years, idle and weak, a life
of one day is better if a man has attained firm strength.

The Dhammapada (c. B.C. 300)

6009 If you have overcome your inclination and not been
overcome by it, you have reason to rejoice.

Plautus (B.C. 254-184)

6010 Moral conduct, self-restraint,
And control of the mind-
What else does one need
Who perseveres in these?

Nagarjuna (c. 100-200 A.D.)

6011 To rule self and subdue our passions is the more
praiseworthy because so few know how to do it.

Francesco Guicciardini (1483-1540)

6012 He who reigns within himself, and rules passions, desires
and fears, is more than a king.

Milton (1608-1674)

6013 Will opens the door to success, both brilliant and happy.

Louis Pasteur (1822-1895)

6014 Self-control is the best of all vows. Sweetness of speech,
benevolence, absence of malice, anger, and hatred,
forgiveness, patience, forbearance, non-violence, modesty,
courtesy, good behaviour, Truth, straight-forwardness, and
firmness - the combination of all these constitutes self-
control.

Sivananda (born 1887)

5. NEGATIVE

6015   Strength, wanting judgment and policy to rule,
       overturneth itself.

                                                   Horace (B.C. 65-8)

6016   Lawless are they that make their wills their law.
                                            Shakespeare (1564-1616)

6017   Oh! it is excellent to have a giant's strength;
       but it is tyrannous to use it like a giant.
                                            Shakespeare (1564-1616)

6018   What is strength without a double share of wisdom? Vast,
       unwieldy, burdensome, proudly secure, yet liable to fall
       by weakest subtleties; strength's not made to rule, but
       to subserve, where wisdom bears command.
                                                Milton (1608-1674)

6019   Nothing is impossible; there are ways that lead to
       everything, and if we had sufficient will we should
       always have sufficient means. It is often merely for
       an excuse that we say things are impossible.
                                        La Rochefoucauld (1613-1680)

6020   A man can do what he ought to do;
       and when he says he cannot, it is because he will not.
                                                Fichte (1762-1814)

6021   Obstinacy is the result of the will forcing itself into the
       place of the intellect.
                                          Schopenhauer (1788-1860)

6022   Strength is born in the deep silence of long-suffering
       hearts; not amidst joy.
                                        Felicia Hemans (1794-1835)

6023   People do not lack strength, they lack will.
                                           Victor Hugo (1802-1885)

6024   What men want is not talent; it is purpose; in other
       words, not the power to achieve, but the will to labor.
                                        Bulwer-Lytton (1803-1873)

6025   The saddest failures in life are those that come from
       not putting forth the power and will to succeed.
                                        Edwin Whipple (1819-1886)

6. ADVICE

6026   Beware of irresolution in the intent of thy actions, beware
        of instability in the execution; so shalt thou triumph over
        two great failings of thy nature.

                                          Akhenaton? (c. B.C. 1375)

6027   Calmness and irony are the only weapons worthy
        of the strong.

                                               I Ching (B.C. 1150?)

6028   Do God's will as if it were thy will,
        and he will accomplish thy will as if it were his own.

                                          Gamaliel (fl. 100 A.D.)

6029   Because your own strength is unequal to the task,
        do not assume that it is beyond the powers of man;
        but if anything is within the powers and province of man,
        believe that it is within your own compass also.

                                     Marcus Aurelius (121-180 A.D.)

6030   Want of control over the senses is called the road to ruin;
        victory over them, the path to fortune.
        Go then by which you please.

                                   The Hitopadesa (600?-1100? A.D.)

6031   Do not, for one repulse,
        forego the purpose that you resolved to effect.

                                       Shakespeare (1564-1616)

6032   He who is firm in will molds the world to himself.

                                             Goethe (1749-1832)

6033   Reflect upon the defects of your character: thoroughly
        realize their evils and the transient pleasures they give
        you, and firmly will that you shall try your best not to
        yield to them the next time.

                                    H. P. Blavatsky (1831-1891)

7. POTPOURRI

6034   The primal spirit dwells in the square inch between the
        eyes, but the conscious spirit dwells below in the heart...
        The conscious spirit is like a strong, powerful commander
        who despises the heavenly ruler (primal spirit) because of
        his weakness, and takes control of the body. But when the
        primal spirit is fortified and defended (by circulating the
        inner light), then the conscious spirit presents itself like
        an obedient servant ready to take orders.

                                            Lu Yen (fl. 800 A.D.)

6035   The will is a beast of burden.
      If God mounts it, it wishes and goes as God wills;
      if Satan mounts it, it wishes and goes as Satan wills;
      Nor can it choose its rider...
      The riders contend for its possession.

                                          Martin Luther (1483-1546)

6036   And binding nature fast in fate,
      Left free the human will.

                                                      Pope (1688-1744)

6037   In idle wishes fools supinely stay;
      be there a will and wisdom finds the way.

                                          George Crabbe (1754-1832)

6038   To sleep I give my powers away;
      My will is bondsman to the dark.

                                          Alfred Tennyson (1809-1892)

6039   The star of the unconquered will,
        He rises in my breast,
      Serene, and resolute, and still,
        And calm, and self-possessed.

                                          Longfellow (1807-1882)

WISDOM

Enlightenment, Metaphysics, Philosophy and Wonder

1. ESSENCE

6040   A philosopher is one who desires to discern the truth.
Plato (B.C. 427?-347?)

6041   Wisdom is the wealth of the wise.
Ecclesiasticus (B.C. 200?)

6042   Philosophy, rightly defined, is simply the love of wisdom.
Cicero (B.C. 106-43)

6043   Philosophy is the art of living.
Plutarch (46-120 A.D.)

6044   Wise it is to comprehend the whole.
Young (1683-1765)

6045   Metaphysics is the anatomy of the soul.
Boufflers (1738-1815)

6046   Wisdom is only found in truth.
Goethe (1749-1832)

6047   Metaphysics is the attempt of the mind to rise above the mind.
Carlyle (1795-1881)

6048   Philosophy is systematic reflection upon the common experience of mankind.
Robert Maynard Hutchins (1899-1977)

2. OPPOSITES

6049   The childish go after outward pleasures;
They walk into the net of widespread death.
But the wise, knowing immortality,
Seek not the stable among things which are unstable here.
Upanishads (c. B.C. 800)

6050   The sage is as pointed as a square but does not pierce.
He is as acute as a knife but does not cut.
He is as straight as an unbent line but does not extend.
He is as bright as light but does not dazzle.
Lao-Tzu (fl. B.C. 600)

6051   In seeking wisdom thou art wise;
       in imagining that thou hast attained it - thou art a fool.
                                   The Talmud (B.C. 500?-400? A.D.)

6052   He is wise that is wise to himself.
                                       Euripides (B.C. 480-406)

6053   Wise men learn more from fools than fools from the wise.
                                   Cato the Elder (B.C. 234-149)

6054   All philosophy lies in two words, sustain and abstain.
                                       Epictetus (50-138 A.D.)

6055   The career of a sage is of two kinds:
       He is either honored by all in the world,
       Like a flower waving its head,
       Or else he disappears into the silent forest.
                                   Nagarjuna (c. 100-200 A.D.)

6056   A foolish man proclaimeth his qualifications;
       A wise man keepeth them secret within himself;
       A straw floateth on the surface of water,
       But a precious gem placed upon it sinketh.
                                   Saskya Pandita (1182-1251)

6057   We can be knowledgeable with other men's knowledge,
       but we cannot be wise with other men's wisdom.
                                       Montaigne (1533-1592)

6058   Philosophy, when superficially studied, excites doubt;
       when thoroughly explored, it dispels it.
                                       Bacon (1561-1626)

6059   It is easier to be wise for others than for ourselves.
                                   La Rochefoucauld (1613-1680)

6060   To ridicule philosophy is truly philosophical.
                                       Pascal (1623-1662)

6061   A man's wisdom is his best friend;
       folly, his worst enemy.
                                   William Temple (1628-1699)

6062   Revere thyself, and yet thyself despise.
                                       Young (1683-1765)

6063   Wisdom is ofttimes nearer when we stoop than when we soar.
                                   Wordsworth (1770-1850)

6064   The wise only possess ideas;
         the greater part of mankind are possessed by them.

                                     Samuel Coleridge (1772-1834)

6065   By wisdom wealth is won;
         but riches purchased wisdom yet for none.

                                     Bayard Taylor (1825-1878)

6066   The doorstep to the temple of wisdom
         is a knowledge of our own ignorance.

                                   Charles Spurgeon (1834-1892)

6067   One fool can ask more questions in a minute
         than twelve wise men can answer in an hour.

                                   Nikolai Lenin (1870-1924)

3. INSIGHT

6068   When all desires that surge in the heart are
         Renounced, the mortal becomes immortal.
         When all the knots that strangle the heart are
         Loosened, the mortal becomes immortal.
         This sums up the teaching of the Scriptures.

                                   Upanishads (c. B.C. 800)

6069   The sky holds no trace of bird or smoke or storm;
         an evil teaching carries no Enlightenment;
         nothing in this world is stable;
         but an Enlightened mind is undisturbed.

                                   Buddha (B.C. 568-488)

6070   By three methods we may learn wisdom:
         First, by reflection which is noblest;
         second, by imitation, which is the easiest;
         and third, by experience, which is the bitterest.

                                   Confucius (B.C. 551-479)

6071   A short saying oft contains much wisdom.

                                   Sophocles (B.C. 495-406)

6072   He was a wise man who originated the idea of God.

                                   Euripides (B.C. 480-406)

6073   Wonder is the feeling of a philosopher,
         and philosophy begins in wonder.

                                   Plato (B.C. 427?-347?)

6074   True wisdom consists not in seeing what is immediately
         before our eyes, but in foreseeing what is to come.

                                   Terence (B.C. 185-159)

6075 The Beginning of Philosophy...is a Consciousness of your
own Weakness and inability in necessary things.
Epictetus (50-138 A.D.)

6076 He who looks on another's wife as a mother, on another's
goods as a clod of earth, and on all creatures as himself,
is a wise man.
The Hitopadesa (600?-1100? A.D.)

6077 Though by wicked acts one may reach one's aim,
A wise man never resorts to such means.
The wise are not ashamed if they do not reach their goal,
Provided they have righteously endeavored for it.
Saskya Pandita (1182-1251)

6078 The most evident token and apparent sign of true wisdom
is a constant and unconstrained rejoicing.
Montaigne (1533-1592)

6079 A prudent question is one-half of wisdom.
Bacon (1561-1626)

6080 The strongest symptom of wisdom in man is
his being sensible of his own follies.
La Rochefoucauld (1613-1680)

6081 The wisest man is generally he who thinks himself the least
so.
Nicholas Boileau (1636-1711)

6082 The discovery of what is true, and the practice of that
which is good, are the two most important objects of
philosophy.
Voltaire (1694-1778)

6083 Clearness marks the sincerity of philosophers.
Vauvenargues(1715-1747)

6084 Wisdom and goodness are twin-born, one heart
must hold both sisters, never seen apart.
Cowper (1731-1800)

6085 Common sense in an uncommon degree
is what the world calls wisdom.
Samuel Coleridge (1772-1834)

6086 Philosophy is a kind of journey,
ever learning yet never arriving
at the ideal perfection of truth.
Albert Pike (1809-1891)

6087   The philosophy of one century is the common sense of the
        next.
                                                    Beecher (1813-1878)

6088   The art of being wise is the art of knowing what to
        overlook.
                                              William James (1842-1910)

6089   When fruit becomes big, the flower falls down of its own
        accord. Even so, human nature, disappears when divine
        nature sets in.
                                                 Sivananda (born 1887)

4. POSITIVE

6090   The lips of the wise are as the doors of a cabinet; no
        sooner are they opened, but treasures are poured out
        before thee. Like unto trees of gold arranged in beds
        of silver, are wise sentences uttered in due season.
                                            Akhenaton? (c. B.C. 1375)

6091   That which is bright rises twice:
        The image of FIRE.
        Thus the great man, by perpetuating this brightness,
        Illumines the four quarters of the world.
                                               I Ching (B.C. 1150?)

6092   Happy is the man who finds wisdom,
            and the man who gets understanding,
          for the gain from it is better than gain from silver
            and its profit better than gold.
        She is more precious than jewels,
            and nothing you desire can compare with her.
        Long life is in her right hand;
            in her left hand are riches and honor.
        Her ways are ways of pleasantness,
            and all her paths are peace.
        She is a tree of life to those who lay hold of her;
            those who hold her fast are called happy.
                                           Proverbs (B.C. 1000?-200?)

6093   When the wise realize the omnipresent Spirit, who rests
        invisible in the visible and permanent in the impermanent,
        then they go beyond sorrow.
                                            Upanishads (c. B.C. 800)

6094   The sage does not hoard.
        The more he helps others, the more he benefits himself,
        The more he gives to others, the more he gets himself.
        The Way of Heaven does one good but never does one harm.
        The Way of the sage is to act but not to compete.
                                              Lao-Tzu (fl. B.C. 600)

6095   A wise man, recognizing that the world is but an illusion,
       does not act as if it is real, so he escapes the suffering.
                                           Buddha (B.C. 568-488)

6096   Perfect wisdom has four parts: Wisdom, the principle
       of doing things aright. Justice, the principle of doing
       things equally in public and private. Fortitude, the
       principle of not fleeing danger, but meeting it.
       Temperance, the principle of subduing desires and living
       moderately.
                                           Plato (B.C. 427?-347?)

6097   Philosophy is the cultivation of the mental faculties;
       it roots out vices and prepares the mind to receive
       proper seed.
                                           Cicero (B.C. 106-43)

6098   Philosophy is the art and law of life, and it teaches us
       what to do in all cases, and, like good marksmen, to hit
       the white at any distance.
                                           Seneca (B.C. 3-65 A.D.)

6099   Wisdom is the conqueror of fortune.
                                           Juvenal (40-125 A.D.)

6100   Wisdom is to the mind what health is to the body.
                                           La Rochefoucauld (1613-1680)

6101   The weak have remedies, the wise have joys;
       superior wisdom is superior bliss.
                                           Young (1683-1765)

6102   They whom truth and wisdom lead
       Can gather honey from a weed.
                                           Cowper (1731-1800)

6103   His high endeavors are an inward light
       That makes the path before him always bright.
                                           Wordsworth (1770-1850)

6104   The adept may reach one of those rare moments that spell
       illumination - aware of the light of the consciousness
       that illumines our consciousness as the sun dawns on the
       sleeping earth and bathes it in effulgence.
                                           Pir Vilayat Inayat Khan (born 1916)

6105   The pine stays green in winter...
       Wisdom in hardship.
                                           Chinese Proverb

5. NEGATIVE

6106   In youth and beauty wisdom is but rare!

                          Homer (c. B.C. 700)

6107   Enlightenment has no definite form or nature by which it
        can manifest itself, so in Enlightenment itself, there
        is nothing to be enlightened.

                          Buddha (B.C. 568-488)

6108   We become wiser by adversity;
        prosperity destroys our appreciation of the right.

                          Seneca (B.C. 3-65 A.D.)

6109   Philosophy triumphs easily over past and future evils;
        but present evils triumph over it.

                          La Rochefoucauld (1613-1680)

6110   When he to whom one speaks does not understand, and he who
        speaks himself does not understand, this is metaphysics.

                          Voltaire (1694-1778)

6111   Where ignorance is bliss - Tis folly to be wise.

                          Thomas Gray (1716-1771)

6112   Metaphysics is a dark ocean without shores or lighthouse,
        strewn with many a philosophic wreck.

                          Immanuel Kant (1724-1804)

6113   It is easy for men to write and talk like philosophers,
        but to act with wisdom, there is the rub!

                          Antoine de Rivaroli (1753-1801)

6114   The philosophers have only interpreted the world;
        the thing, however, is to change it.

                          Karl Marx (1818-1883)

6115   Philosophy: A route of many roads leading from nowhere
        to nothing.

                          Ambrose Bierce (1842-1914?)

6116   Metaphysics is almost always an attempt to prove the
        incredible by an appeal to the unintelligible.

                          H. L. Mencken (1880-1956)

6. ADVICE

6117   O people of the earth, men born and made of the elements,
        but with the spirit of the Divine Man within you, rise from
        your sleep of ignorance! Be sober and thoughtful. Realize
        that your home is not on the earth but in the Light. Why
        have you delivered yourselves over unto death, having power
        to partake of immortality? Repent, and change your minds.
        Depart from the dark light and forsake corruption forever.
        Prepare to blend your souls with the Eternal Light.
                            The Divine Pymander (BC 2500?-200 AD?)

6118   Presume not in prosperity, neither despair in adversity:
        court not dangers, nor meanly fly from before them:
        dare to despise whatever will not remain with thee.
                                         Akhenaton? (c. B.C. 1375)

6119   Those who know do not talk.
        Those who talk do not know.
        Keep your mouth closed.
        Guard your senses.
        Temper your sharpness.
        Simplify your problems.
        Mask your brightness.
        Be at one with the dust of the earth.
        This is primal union.
        He who has achieved this state
        Is unconcerned with friends and enemies.
        With good and harm, with honor and disgrace.
        This therefore is the highest state of man.
                                         Lao-Tzu (fl. B.C. 600)

6120   Those who seek the true path to Enlightenment must not
        expect an easy task or one made pleasant by offers of
        respect and honor and devotion. And further, they must
        not aim with a slight effort, at a trifling advance in
        calmness or knowledge or insight.
                                         Buddha (B.C. 568-488)

6121   Make thy study of the word of The Eternal a fixed practice;
        say little and do much; and receive all men with a cheerful
        countenance.
                                The Talmud (B.C. 500?-400? A.D.)

6122   Those who are wise lament neither for the living nor the
        dead.
                                 Bhagavad Gita (c. B.C. 400)

6123   To make no mistakes is not in the power of man; but from
        their errors and mistakes the wise and good learn wisdom
        for the future.

                                    Plutarch (46-120 A.D.)

6124   In seeking Wisdom, the first stage is silence, the second
        listening, the third remembrance, the fourth practicing,
        the fifth teaching.

                            Solomon Ibn Gabirol (1021?-1053)

6125   The sublimity of wisdom is to do those things living,
        which are to be desired when dying.

                                Jeremy Taylor (1613-1667)

6126   The clouds may drop down titles and estates, wealth may seek
        us; but wisdom must be sought.

                                    Young (1683-1765)

6127   To act with common sense, according to the moment, is the
        best wisdom; and the best philosophy is to do one's duties,
        to take the world as it comes, submit respectfully to one's
        lot, bless the goodness that has given us so much happiness
        with it, whatever it is.

                                Horace Walpole (1717-1797)

6128   Knowledge dwells in heads replete with thoughts of other
        men; wisdom in minds attentive to their own.

                                    Cowper (1731-1800)

6129   Call him wise whose actions, words, and steps are all a
        clear because to a clear why.

                                    Lavater (1741-1801)

6130   Inspect the neighborhood of thy life;
        every shelf, every nook of thine abode.

                                    Richter (1763-1825)

6131   The sum of wisdom is that time is never lost that is devoted
        to work.

                                    Emerson (1803-1882)

6132   To be a philosopher is not merely to have subtle thoughts;
        but so to love wisdom as to live according to its dictates.

                                    Thoreau (1817-1862)

6133   If thou would'st have that stream of hard-earn'd knowledge,
        of Wisdom heaven-born, remain sweet running waters,
        thou should'st not leave it to become a stagnant pond.

                                H. P. Blavatsky (1831-1891)

6134 Nine-tenths of wisdom consists in being wise in time.

Theodore Roosevelt (1858-1919)

6135 To admit ignorance is to exhibit wisdom.

Ashley Montagu (born 1905)

7. POTPOURRI

6136 The kind man discovers it and calls it kind.
The wise man discovers it and calls it wise.
The people use it day by day and are not aware of it,
for the way of the superior man is rare.

I Ching (B.C. 1150?)

6137 This Self is not realizable by study nor even by intelligence and learning. The Self reveals its essence only to him who applies himself to the Self. He who has not given up the ways of vice, who cannot control himself, who is not at peace within, whose mind is distracted, can never realize the Self, though full of all the learning in the world.

Upanishads (c. B.C. 800)

6138 Attain complete vacuity,
Maintain steadfast quietude.
All things come into being,
And I see thereby their return.
All things flourish,
But each one returns to its root.
This return to its root means tranquility.
It is called returning to its destiny.
To return to destiny is called The Eternal.
To know The Eternal is called enlightenment.
Not to know The Eternal is to act blindly
 which results in disaster.

Lao-Tzu (fl. B.C. 600)

6139 Who, knowing the all in all its parts,
For all its phases hath no lust,
By comprehension of the all
He truly hath escaped all-ill.

Buddha (B.C. 568-488)

6140 The way of a superior man is threefold:
 Virtuous, he is free from anxieties;
 Wise, he is free from perplexities;
 Bold, he is free from fear.

Confucius (B.C. 551-479)

6141   He whose fear of sin takes precedence over his wisdom, his
       wisdom will endure; but he whose wisdom takes precedence
       over his fear of sin, his wisdom will not endure...He whose
       works exceed his wisdom, his wisdom will endure; but he
       whose wisdom exceeds his works, his wisdom will not endure.
                                        The Talmud (B.C. 500?-400? A.D.)

6142   The Ancient oracle said I was the wisest of all the Greeks.
             It is because I alone, of all the Greeks,
                 know that I know nothing.
                                        Socrates (B.C. 469-399)

6143   There are two sentences inscribed upon the Ancient oracle...
       "Know thyself" and "Nothing too much"; and upon these all
       other precepts depend.
                                        Plutarch (46-120 A.D.)

6144   When you strive to gain quiescence by stopping motion,
       The quiescence thus gained is ever in motion;
       As long as you tarry in the dualism,
       How can you realize oneness?
                                        Seng-T'San (540?-606 A.D.)

6145   Old pond:
         frog jump in
           water-sound.
                                        Basho (1644-1694)

6146   The wisdom of the wise and the experience of ages
       may be preserved by quotation.
                                        Disraeli (1804-1881)

6147   The philosopher is Nature's pilot. And there you have our
       difference: to be in hell is to drift: to be in heaven
       is to steer.
                                        G. B. Shaw (1856-1950)

6148   Wisdom alone is true ambition's aim
       Wisdom the source of virtue, and of fame,
       Obtained with labour, for mankind employed,
       And then, when most you share it, best enjoyed.
                                        Alfred North Whitehead (1861-1947)

WORDS

Language, Names and Writing - Books, Literature and Poetry

1. ESSENCE

6149   Books are immortal sons deifying their sires.
                                    Plato (B.C. 427?-347?)

6150   Books are ships which pass through the vast sea of time.
                                    Bacon (1561-1626)

6151   Words are the soul's ambassadors, who go
       Abroad upon her errands to and fro.
                                    James Howell (1595-1666)

6152   Words are but pictures of our thoughts.
                                    Dryden (1631-1700)

6153   Books, the children of the brain.
                                    Swift (1667-1745)

6154   Poetry, the eldest sister of all arts, and parent of most.
                                    William Congreve (1670-1729)

6155   Words are but the signs of ideas.
                                    Johnson (1709-1784)

6156   Prose - words in their best order;
       Poetry - the best words in their best order.
                                    Samuel Coleridge (1772-1834)

6157   All poetry is but a giving of names.
                                    Carlyle (1795-1881)

6158   Poetry is truth dwelling in beauty.
                                    Robert Gilfillan (1798-1850)

6159   Language is the picture and counterpart of thought.
                                    Mark Hopkins (1802-1887)

6160   Language is a city to the building of which every human
       being brought a stone.
                                    Emerson (1803-1882)

6161   Language is the light of the mind.
                                    John Stuart Mill (1806-1873)

6162   Poetry is the rhythmical creation of beauty in words.
                                    Edgar Allan Poe (1809-1849)

6163   Literature is news that stays news.
                                    Ezra Pound (1885-1972)

2. OPPOSITES

6164   Poetry is finer and more philosophical than history;
       for poetry expresses the universal,
       and history only the particular.
                                    Aristotle (B.C. 384-322)

6165   The same words conceal and declare the thoughts of men.
                                    Dionysius Cato (fl. 300 A.D.)

6166   The word is half his that speaks,
       and half his that hears it.
                                    Montaigne (1533-1592)

6167   Men suppose their reason has command over their words;
       still it happens that words in return exercise authority on
       reason.
                                    Bacon (1561-1626)

6168   Words are the counters of wise man, and the money of fools.
                                    Thomas Hobbes (1588-1679)

6169   The last thing that we discover in writing a book
       is to know what to put at the beginning.
                                    Pascal (1623-1662)

6170   It is with books as with men: a very small number play a
       great part, the rest are lost in the multitude.
                                    Voltaire (1694-1778)

6171   The only end of writing is to enable the readers better to
       enjoy life or better to endure it.
                                    Johnson (1709-1784)

6172   Words are the daughters of the earth,
       and things are the sons of heaven.
                                    Johnson (1709-1784)

6173   Words, like eyeglasses, blur everything that they do not
       make more clear.
                                    Joubert (1754-1824)

6174   Books are the best things, well used: abused, among
       the worst.
                                    Emerson (1803-1882)

6175 Words are both better and worse than thoughts, they express
them, and add to them; they give them power for good or
evil; they start them on an endless flight, for instruction
and comfort and blessing, or for injury and sorrow and ruin.
Tryon Edwards (1809-1894)

6176 Poetry puts the infinite within the finite.
Robert Browning (1812-1889)

6177 Words are often seen hunting for an idea,
but ideas are never seen hunting for words.
Josh Billings (1815-1885)

6178 Some words are like rays of sunshine, others like barbed
arrows or the bite of a serpent. And if hard words cut so
deep, how much pleasure can kind ones give?
Lubbock (1834-1913)

6179 Nine times out of ten, the coarse word is the word that
condemns an evil and the refined word the word that excuses
it.
G. K. Chesterton (1874-1936)

6180 Words are potent weapons for all causes, good or bad.
Manly P. Hall (born 1901)

6181 Bitter words are good medicine...
Sweet words carry infection.
Chinese Proverb

3. INSIGHT

6182 This universe is a trinity and this is made of name, form,
and action. The source of all names is the word, for it is
by the word that all names are spoken. The word is behind
all names, even as the Eternal is behind the word.
Upanishads (c. B.C. 800)

6183 Without knowing the force of words,
it is impossible to know men.
Confucius (B.C. 551-479)

6184 Knowledge is the foundation and source of good writing.
Horace (B.C. 65-8)

6185 The desire to write grows with writing.
Erasmus (1466-1536)

6186 The pen is the tongue of the mind.
Cervantes (1547-1616)

6187 Syllables govern the world.

John Selden (1584-1654)

6188 Oaths are but words, and words are but wind.

Samuel Butler (1612-1680)

6189 Poetry is of so subtle a spirit, that in the pouring out of
      one language into another it will evaporate.

John Denham (1615-1668)

6190 The world is satisfied with words.
      Few appreciate the things beneath.

Pascal (1623-1662)

6191 Proper words in proper places,
      make the true definition of a style.

Swift (1667-1745)

6192 Ideas in the mind are the transcript of the world;
      words are the transcript of ideas;
      and writing and printing are the transcript of words.

Addison (1672-1719)

6193 True ease in writing comes from art, not chance,
      As those move easiest who have learn'd to dance.

Pope (1688-1744)

6194 One great use of words is to hide our thoughts.

Voltaire (1694-1778)

6195 Literature is a fragment of a fragment;
      of all that ever happened, or has been said, but a fraction
      has been written, and of this but little is extant.

Goethe (1749-1832)

6196 Language is the armory of the human mind, and at once
      contains the trophies of its past and the weapons of its
      future conquests.

Samuel Coleridge (1772-1834)

6197 Language is not only the vehicle of thought,
      it is a great and efficient instrument in thinking.

Humphrey Davy (1778-1829)

6198 Words are the only things that last forever.

Hazlitt (1778-1830)

6199 There are words which are worth as much as the best actions,
      for they contain the germ of them all.

Anne Swetchine (1782-1857)

6200   But words are things, and a small drop of ink,
      Falling, like dew, upon a thought produces
     That which makes thousands, perhaps millions think.

                              Byron (1788-1824)

6201   A poem is the very image of life
     expressed in its eternal truth.

                              Shelley (1792-1822)

6202   Poetry we will call Musical Thought.

                              Carlyle (1795-1881)

6203   A moment of thinking is an hour of words.

                      Thomas Hood (1798-1845)

6204   By poetry we mean the art of employing words in such a
     manner as to produce an illusion on the imagination;
     the art of doing by means of words,
     what the painter does by means of colors.

                      Macaulay (1800-1859)

6205   It does not need that a poem should be long.
     Every word was once a poem.

                         Emerson (1803-1882)

6206   As shadows attend substances, so words follow upon things.
                         Trench (1807-1886)

6207   The idea, word and writing (of the word), are signs to man
     for a thing, and is not the thing itself, to the Creator,
     however, idea, word and writing (of the word) are the thing
     itself, or as some ancients remarked: "Idea, word and work
     are one and the same to God."

                Isidor Kalisch (1810-1886)

6208   With a knowledge of the name comes a distincter recognition
     and knowledge of the thing.

                        Thoreau (1817-1862)

6209   The oldest books are still only just out to those who have
     not read them.

                  Samuel Butler (1835-1902)

6210   The great art of writing is the art of making people real
     to themselves with words.

                  Logan Smith (1865-1946)

6211   Words are the most powerful drug used by mankind.
                       Kipling (1865-1936)

6212 To write simply is as difficult as to be good.
Somerset Maugham (1874-1965)

6213 Great literature is simply language charged with meaning to
the utmost possible degree.
Ezra Pound (1885-1972)

6214 Many books do not use up words...
Many words do not use up thought.
Chinese Proverb

4. POSITIVE

6215 A word fitly spoken is like apples of gold
in pictures of silver.
Proverbs (B.C. 1000?-200?)

6216 Poetry comes nearer to vital truth than history.
Plato (B.C. 427?-347?)

6217 How forcible are right words!
Job (B.C. 400?)

6218 We see then how far the monuments of wit and learning are
more durable than the monuments of power, or of the hands.
For have not some books continued twenty-five hundred years
or more, without the loss of a syllable or letter; during
which time infinite palaces, temples, castles, and cities
have been decayed and demolished?
Bacon (1561-1626)

6219 Books give not wisdom where none was before,
But where some is, there reading makes it more.
John Harrington (1561-1612)

6220 A good book is the precious lifeblood of a master spirit,
embalmed and treasured up on purpose to a life beyond life.
Milton (1608-1674)

6221 Good words do more than hard speeches, as the sunbeams
without any noise will make the traveller cast off his
cloak, which all the blustering winds could not do, but
only make him bind it closer to him.
Robert Leighton (1611-1684)

6222 Of all those arts in which the wise excel,
Nature's chief masterpiece is writing well.
John Sheffield (1648-1721)

6223 Poetry is the music of the soul, and, above all, of great
and feeling souls.
Voltaire (1694-1778)

6224 The chief glory of every people arises from its authors.
Johnson (1709-1784)

6225 The writings of the wise are the only riches our posterity
cannot squander.
Landor (1775-1864)

6226 That writer does the most, who gives his reader the most
knowledge, and takes from him the least time.
Colton (1780-1832)

6227 Poetry is the record of the best and happiest moments
of the happiest and best minds.
Shelley (1792-1822)

6228 All that Mankind has done, thought, gained or been is
lying as in magic preservation in the pages of Books.
They are the chosen possession of men.
Carlyle (1795-1881)

6229 That is a good book which is opened with expectation and
closed with profit.
Amos B. Alcott (1799-1888)

6230 In the highest civilization the book is still the highest
delight.
Emerson (1803-1882)

6231 Literature is an avenue to glory, ever open for those
ingenious men who are deprived of honours or of wealth.
Disraeli (1804-1881)

6232 With words we govern men.
Disraeli (1804-1881)

6233 A good book is the best of friends,
the same to-day and forever.
Tupper (1810-1889)

6234 A powerful agent is the right word. Whenever we come upon
one of those intensely right words in a book or a newspaper
the resulting effect is physical as well as spiritual...
Mark Twain (1835-1910)

6235 A poem begins in delight and ends in wisdom.
Robert Frost (1875-1963)

6236 But for all their inadequacy and their radical unlikeness to
      the facts to which they refer, words remain the most
      reliable and accurate of our symbols. Whenever we want to
      have a precise report of facts or ideas, we must resort to
      words.

                                            Aldous Huxley (1894-1963)

6237 Words are one of our chief means of adjusting to all the
      situations of life. The better control we have over words,
      the more successful our adjustment is likely to be.

                                            Bergen Evans (born 1904)

6238 One kind word can warm three winter months.

                                                    Japanese Proverb

6239 Words spoken may fly away...
      The writing-brush leaves its mark.

                                                    Chinese Proverb

5. NEGATIVE

6240 To utter pleasant words without practicing them,
      is like a fine flower without fragrance.

                                            Buddha (B.C. 568-488)

6241 If names are not correct, language will not be in accordance
      with the truth of things.

                                            Confucius (B.C. 551-479)

6242 The chief virtue that language can have is clearness, and
      nothing detracts from it so much as the use of unfamiliar
      words.

                                            Hippocrates (B.C. 460-370)

6243 Poets utter great and wise things which they do not them-
      selves understand.

                                            Plato (B.C. 427?-347?)

6244 Words are used to express meaning;
      when you understand the meaning,
      you can forget about the words.

                                            Chuang-tzu (fl. B.C. 350)

6245 It is as easy to draw back a stone thrown with force from
      the hand, as to recall a word once spoken.

                                            Menander (B.C. 342-291)

6246 He utters empty words, he utters sound without mind.

                                            Vergil (B.C. 70-19)

6247   There is no need of words; believe facts.

Ovid (B.C. 43-18 A.D.)

6248   Men of few words are the best men.

Shakespeare (1564-1616)

6249   Obscurity in writing is commonly an argument of darkness in
the mind. The greatest learning is to be seen in the
greatest plainness.

John Wilkins (1614-1672)

6250   A single word often betrays a great design.

Jean Baptiste Racine (1639-1699)

6251   The multitude of books is making us ignorant.

Voltaire (1694-1778)

6252   A successful author is equally in danger of diminution of
his fame, whether he continues or ceases to write.

Johnson (1709-1784)

6253   A very great part of the mischiefs that vex this world
arises from words.

Burke (1729-1797)

6254   Volatility of words is carelessness in actions;
words are the wings of actions.

Lavater (1741-1801)

6255   How many people make themselves abstract to appear profound.
The great part of abstract terms are shadows that hide a
vacuum.

Joubert (1754-1824)

6256   A word too much always defeats its purpose.

Schopenhauer (1788-1860)

6257   An author who speaks about his own books is almost as bad as
a mother who talks about her own children.

Disraeli (1804-1881)

6258   Most books, indeed, are records less
Of fullness than emptiness.

William Allingham (1824-1889)

6259   A thousand words will not leave so deep an impression
as one deed.

Henrik Ibsen (1828-1906)

6260   Actions are the first tragedies in life, words are the
second. Words are perhaps the worst. Words are merciless.
Oscar Wilde (1854-1900)

6261   The difference between journalism and literature is that
journalism is unreadable and literature is not read.
Oscar Wilde (1854-1900)

6262   Water and words...
Easy to pour
Impossible to recover.
Chinese Proverb

6. ADVICE

6263   Use words sparingly,
then all things will fall into place.
A tornado does not last a whole morning.
A downpour of rain does not last a whole day.
And who works these?
Heaven and Earth.
What Heaven and Earth cannot do enduringly:
how much less can man do it?
Lao-Tzu (fl. B.C. 600)

6264   Do not say a little in many words but a great deal in a few.
Pythagoras (B.C. 582-507)

6265   Let your literary compositions be kept from the public
eye for nine years at least.
Horace (B.C. 65-8)

6266   Ye who write, choose a subject suited to your abilities.
Horace (B.C. 65-8)

6267   If you would be a reader, read; if a writer, write.
Epictetus (50-138 A.D.)

6268   When words are scarce they're seldom spent in vain.
Shakespeare (1564-1616)

6269   In words, as fashions, the same rule will hold;
Alike fantastic, if too new, or old:
Be not the first by whom the new are tried,
Nor yet the last to lay the old aside.
Pope (1688-1744)

6270   A good writer does not write as people write,
but as he writes.
Montesquieu (1689-1755)

6271 It is in books the chief of all perfections
to be plain and brief.

Joseph Butler (1692-1752)

6272 If you be pungent, be brief; for it is with words as with
sunbeams - the more they are condensed the deeper they burn.

Robert Southey (1774-1843)

6273 Make the same use of a book that the bee does of a flower:
she steals sweets from it, but does not injure it.

Colton (1780-1832)

6274 Master books, but do not let them master you. -
Read to live, not live to read.

Bulwer-Lytton (1803-1873)

6275 In science, read, by preference, the newest works;
in literature, the oldest.
The classic literature is always modern.

Bulwer-Lytton (1803-1873)

6276 An orator or author is never successful till he has
learned to make his words smaller than his ideas.

Emerson (1803-1882)

6277 The writer must earn money in order to be able to live and
to write, but he must by no means live and write for the
purpose of making money.

Karl Marx (1818-1883)

6278 A book should be luminous, but not voluminous.

Bovee (1820-1904)

7. POTPOURRI

6279 The word which appeared as a pillar of flame out of the
darkness is the Son of God, born of the mystery of the Mind.
The name of that Word is Reason. Reason is the offspring of
Thought and Reason shall divide the Light from the darkness
and establish Truth in the midst of the waters.

The Divine Pymander (BC 2500?-200 AD?)

6280 Twenty-two letters: He drew them, hewed them, combined
them, weighed them, interchanged them, and through them
produced the whole creation and everything that is destined
to come into being.

Sepher Yezirah (B.C. 2000?-600 A.D.)

6281 The paper burns, but the words fly away.

Ben Joseph Akiba (40?-135 A.D.)

6282   It is not possible to attain to an understanding of the
creation of man, except by the mystery of letters; and in
these worlds of The Infinite is nothing, except the letters
of the Alphabet and their combinations. All the worlds are
Letters and Names; but He Who is the Author of all, has no
name.

> Zohar (120?-1200? A.D.)

6283   What do you read, my lord?
    Words, words, words.

> Shakespeare (1564-1616)

6284   One merit of poetry few persons will deny:
it says more and in fewer words than prose.

> Voltaire (1694-1778)

6285   Your manuscript is both good and original;
but the part that is good is not original,
and the part that is original is not good.

> Johnson (1709-1784)

6286   How pure the joy when first my hands unfold
The small, rare volume, black with tarnished gold.

> John Ferriar (1761-1815)

6287   O! many a shaft, at random sent,
Finds mark the archer little meant!
And many a word, at random spoken,
May soothe or wound a heart that's broken!

> Walter Scott (1771-1832)

6288   The world is full of poetry. - The air is living with its
spirit; and the waves dance to the music of its melodies,
and sparkle in its brightness.

> James Percival (1795-1856)

6289   In books lies the soul of the whole Past Time;
the articulate audible voice of the Past,
when the body and material substance of it
has altogether vanished like a dream.

> Carlyle (1795-1881)

6290   For no man can write anything who does not think that what
he writes is, for the time, the history of the world.

> Emerson (1803-1882)

6291   He who writes prose builds his temple to Fame in rubble;
he who writes verses builds it in granite.

> Bulwer-Lytton (1803-1873)

6292   The Word of God is the universal and invisible Light,
       cognizable by the senses, that emits its blaze in the Sun,
       Moon, Planets, and other Stars.

                                        Albert Pike (1809-1891)

6293   There is probably no hell for authors in the next world-
       they suffer so much from critics and publishers in this.

                                        Bovee (1820-1904)

6294   A definition encloses a wilderness of idea
       within a wall of words.

                                        Samuel Butler (1835-1902)

6295   But from sharp words and wits men pluck no fruit;
       And gathering thorns they shake the tree at root;
       For words divide and rend,
       But silence is most noble till the end.

                                        Swinburne (1837-1909)

6296   And while the great and wise decay,
       And while their trophies pass away,
       Some sudden thought, some careless rhyme,
       Still floats above the wrecks of time.

                                        William Lecky (1838-1903)

6297   God wove a web of loveliness,
       of clouds and stars and birds,
       but made not anything at all
       so beautiful as words.

                                        Anna Hempstead Branch (1874-1937)

WORK
Labor and Profession

1. ESSENCE

6298   Labor is life.

Carlyle (1795-1881)

6299   The essence of work is concentrated energy.

Walter Bagehot (1826-1877)

2. OPPOSITES

6300   If you pursue good with labor,
       the labor passes away but the good remains;
    if you pursue evil with pleasure,
       the pleasure passes away and the evil remains.

Cicero (B.C. 106-43)

6301   Men of lofty genius when they are doing the least work are
most active.

Leonardo Da Vinci (1452-1519)

6302   A man is not idle because he is absorbed in thought.
There is a visible labor and there is an invisible labor.

Victor Hugo (1802-1885)

6303   Business despatched is business well done,
but business hurried is business ill done.

Bulwer-Lytton (1803-1873)

6304   The highest excellence is seldom attained in more than one
vocation. The roads leading to distinction in separate
pursuits diverge, and the nearer we approach the one, the
farther we recede from the other.

Bovee (1820-1904)

6305   Work consists of whatever a body is obliged to do,
and Play consists of whatever a body is not obliged to do.

Mark Twain (1835-1910)

6306   The finest eloquence is that which gets things done;
the worst is that which delays them.

Lloyd George (1863-1945)

6307   Work is work if you're paid to do it,
and it's pleasure if you pay to be allowed to do it.

Finley P. Dunne (1867-1936)

3. INSIGHT

6308   Better is a man of humble standing who works for himself
        than one who plays the great man but lacks bread.
                                        Proverbs (B.C. 1000?-200?)

6309   He whose wisdom exceeds his works, to what may he be
        likened? To a tree whose branches are numerous but whose
        roots are few. The wind comes along and uproots it and
        sweeps it down.
                                        The Talmud (B.C. 500?-400? A.D.)

6310   Work divided is in that manner shortened.
                                        Martial (43-104 A.D.)

6311   Each natural agent works but to this end,
        To render that it works on like itself.
                                        George Chapman (1557-1634)

6312   Excellence, in any department,
        can only be attained by the labor of a lifetime.
        It is not purchased at a lesser price.
                                        Johnson (1709-1784)

6313   Labour was the first price, the original purchase-money that
        was paid for all things. It was not by gold or by silver,
        but by labour, that all wealth of the world was originally
        purchased.
                                        Adam Smith (1723-1790)

6314   It is the first of all problems for a man to find out
        what kind of work he is to do in this universe.
                                        Carlyle (1795-1881)

6315   Without ambition one starts nothing. Without work one
        finishes nothing. The prize will not be sent to you. You
        have to win it. The man who knows how will always have a
        job. The man who also knows why will always be his boss. As
        to methods there may be a million and then some, but
        principles are few. The man who grasps principles can
        successfully select his own methods. The man who tries
        methods, ignoring principles, is sure to have trouble.
                                        Emerson (1803-1882)

6316   Labor is prior to and independent of capital. Capital is
        only the fruit of labor, and could never have existed if
        labor had not first existed.
                                        Lincoln (1809-1865)

6317   The moment a man can really do his work, he becomes
speechless about it; all words are idle to him;
all theories. Does a bird need to theorize about building
its nest, or boast of it when built? All good work is
essentially done that way; without hesitation; without
difficulty; without boasting.

John Ruskin (1819-1900)

6318   A man who has no office to go to - I don't care who he is -
confronts a trial of which you can have no conception.

G. B. Shaw (1856-1950)

6319   The effectiveness of work increases according to geometric
progression if there are no interruptions.

Andre Maurois (1885-1967)

6320   Work and love - these are the basics.
Without them there is neurosis.

Theodor Reik (born 1888)

6321   Firewood alone will not start a fire.

Chinese Proverb

4. POSITIVE

6322   Nothing is impossible to industry.

Periander (fl. c. B.C. 570)

6323   One who works in devotion, who is a pure soul,
and who controls his mind and senses,
is dear to everyone, and everyone is dear to him.
Though always working, such a man is never entangled.

Bhagavad Gita (c. B.C. 400)

6324   As from a large heap of flowers many garlands and wreaths
can be made, so by a mortal in this life there is much good
work to be done.

The Dhammapada (c. B.C. 300)

6325   Any man who strives to do his best
Whether his work be great or small
Is considered to be doing the work of a lion.

Nagarjuna (c. 100-200 A.D.)

6326   The labor of the body relieves us from the fatigues of the
mind; and it is this which forms the happiness of the poor.

La Rochefoucauld (1613-1680)

6327   Work keeps at bay three great evils:
boredom, vice, and need.

Voltaire (1694-1778)

6328 No man ever was glorious, who was not laborious.
Franklin (1706-1790)

6329 Nothing is denied to well-directed labor,
and nothing is ever to be attained without it.
Joshua Reynolds (1723-1792)

6330 From labor, health; from health, contentment springs.
James Beattie (1735-1803)

6331 Labor is the great producer of wealth;
it moves all other causes.
Daniel Webster (1782-1852)

6332 The work an unknown good man has done is like a vein of
water flowing hidden underground, secretly making the
ground green.
Carlyle (1795-1881)

6333 Every man's task is his life-preserver.
Emerson (1803-1882)

6334 To work with the hands or brain, according to our require-
ments and our capacities, to do that which lies before us
to do, is more honorable than rank and title.
Albert Pike (1809-1891)

6335 Good for the body is the work of the body,
good for the soul is the work of the soul,
and good for either the work of the other.
Thoreau (1817-1862)

6336 For his heart was in his work, and the heart
Giveth grace unto every Art.
Longfellow (1807-1882)

6337 As a remedy against all ills - poverty, sickness, and
melancholy - only one thing is absolutely necessary:
a liking for work.
Baudelaire (1821-1867)

6338 Work is the inevitable condition of human life,
the true source of welfare.
Leo Tolstoy (1828-1910)

6339 We work to become, not to acquire.
Elbert Hubbard (1859-1915)

6340 Work is a high human function...the most dignified thing in
the life of man.
David Ben-Gurion (1886-1973)

5. NEGATIVE

6341   It is honour to thy nature when worthily employed;
       when thou directeth it to wrong purposes,
       it shameth and destroyeth thee.
                                  Akhenaton? (c. B.C. 1375)

6342   Without labor nothing prospers.
                                  Sophocles (B.C. 495-406)

6343   No labour bestowed upon a worthless thing can be productive
       of fruit; even by a hundred efforts a crane cannot be made
       to talk like a parrot.
                            The Hitopadesa (600?-1100? A.D.)

6344   All work and no play makes Jack a dull boy.
                                  James Howell (1595-1666)

6345   Hard labor is not whenever you are very actively employed,
       but when you must be.
                              Richard Whately (1787-1863)

6346   In time a profession is like a marriage,
       we cease to note anything but its inconveniences.
                                      Balzac (1799-1850)

6347   Work is the curse of the world, and nobody can meddle with
       it without becoming proportionately brutified.
                            Nathaniel Hawthorne (1804-1864)

6348   Men without duties to do, are like trees planted on
       precipices; from the roots of which all the earth has
       crumbled...and yet there are men who pride themselves that
       they and theirs have done no work. So neither have the
       swine.
                                  Albert Pike (1809-1891)

6349   Work is the refuge of people who have nothing better to do.
                                  Oscar Wilde (1854-1900)

6350   Folks who never do any more than they get paid for,
       never get paid for any more than they do.
                               Elbert Hubbard (1859-1915)

6351   Work expands so as to fill the time available for its
       completion (and) the thing to be done swells in importance
       and complexity in a direct ratio with the time to be spent.
                            C. Northcote Parkinson (born 1909)

6352   That man who knows too many trades...
        his family starves.

Chinese Proverb

6. ADVICE

6353   All are not called to the guiding of the helm of state;
        neither are there armies to be commanded by every one;
        do well in that which is committed to thy charge,
        and praise shall remain upon thee.

Akhenaton? (c. B.C. 1375)

6354   When you are laboring for others let it be with the same
        zeal as if it were for yourself.

Confucius (B.C. 551-479)

6355   It is better to do one's own duty, however defective it may
        be, than to follow the duty of another, however well one may
        perform it. He who does his duty as his own nature reveals
        it, never sins.

Bhagavad Gita (c. B.C. 400)

6356   Nothing can be done at once hastily and prudently.

Publilius Syrus (fl. B.C. 42)

6357   Begin; to begin is half the work. Let half still remain;
        again begin this, and thou wilt have finished.

Ausonius (310-395 A.D.)

6358   When occupations come to us we must accept them; when things
        come to us we must understand them from the ground up.

Lu Yen (fl. 800 A.D.)

6359   Apply yourself both now and in the next life.
        Without effort, you cannot be prosperous.
        Though the land be good,
        You cannot have an abundant crop without cultivation.

Saskya Pandita (1182-1251)

6360   Whatever is worth doing at all is worth doing well.

Chesterfield (1694-1773)

6361   Plough deep while sluggards sleep.

Franklin (1706-1790)

6362   If you intend to work, there is no better place than right
        where you are; if you do not intend to go to work, you
        cannot get along anywhere. Squirming and crawling from
        place to place can do no good.

Lincoln (1809-1865)

6363   When your work speaks for itself, don't interrupt.

Henry J. Kaiser (1882-1967)

7. POTPOURRI

6364   The first creature of God, in the works of the days,
was the light of the sense: the last was the light of
reason: and his sabbath work ever since is the illumination
of his Spirit.

Bacon (1561-1626)

6365   Begin, be bold, and venture to be wise;
He who defers his work from day to day,
Does on a river's bank expecting stay;
Till the whole stream which stopped him should be gone,
That runs, and as it runs, for ever will run on.

Abraham Cowley (1618-1667)

6366   All work of man is as the swimmer's. A vast ocean threatens
to devour him; if he front it not bravely, it will keep its
word. By incessant wise defiance of it, lusty rebuke and
buffet of it, behold how it loyally supports him, bears him
as its conqueror along! It is so with all things that man
undertakes in this world.

Goethe (1749-1832)

6367   The Prime Material of the Great Work, in the Superior World,
is enthusiasm and activity; in the intermediate world,
intelligence and industry; in the lower world, labor...
The Great Work is, above all things, the creation of man by
himself; that is to say, the full and entire conquest which
he effects of his faculties and his future.

Albert Pike (1809-1891)

6368   Work for some good, be it ever so slowly;
Cherish some flower, be it ever so lowly;
Labour - all labour is noble and holy.

Frances Osgood (1811-1850)

6369   I never did anything worth doing by accident,
nor did any of my inventions come by accident;
they came by work.

Thomas A. Edison (1847-1931)

6370   Work thou for pleasure - paint or sing or carve
The thing thou lovest, though the body starve -
Who works for glory misses oft the goal;
Who works for money coins his very soul.
Work for the work's sake, then, and it may be
That these things shall be added unto thee.

Kenyon Cox (1856-1919)

6371   I like work; it fascinates me. I can sit and look at it
       for hours. I love to keep it by me: the idea of getting
       rid of it nearly breaks my heart.

                                    Jerome K. Jerome (1859-1927)

6372   But till we are built like angels,
          with hammer and chisel and pen,
       We will work for ourself and a woman,
          for ever and ever, Amen.

                                            Kipling (1865-1936)

6373   By working faithfully eight hours a day, you may even-
       tually get to be a boss and work twelve hours a day.
                                       Robert Frost (1875-1963)

6374   Work is love made visible. And if you cannot work with love
       but only with distaste, it is better that you should leave
       your work and sit at the gate of the temple and take alms of
       those who work with joy.

                                      Kahlil Gibran (1883-1931)

6375   Anyone can do any amount of work provided it isn't
       the work he is supposed to be doing at that moment.
                                    Robert Benchley (1889-1945)

WORLD

Earth, Foundation, Order, Plans and Universe

1. ESSENCE

6376   The world is God's epistle to mankind -
his thoughts are flashing upon us from every direction.
Plato (B.C. 427?-347?)

6377   The world is but a perpetual see-saw.
Montaigne (1533-1592)

6378   The world is a wheel, and it will all come round right.
Isaac D'Israeli (1766-1848)

6379   That one vast thought of God which we call the world.
Bulwer-Lytton (1803-1873)

6380   The Universe is the periodical manifestation of the unknown
Absolute Essence.
H. P. Blavatsky (1831-1891)

2. OPPOSITES

6381   The Laws of Nature are such that things at their peak must
decline and those at their lowest point must rise up, just
as the sun and moon follow one another ceaselessly through
the skies. Man also follows these Laws.
I Ching (B.C. 1150?)

6382   The Heavens seemed to men to fulfill the functions of
father, and the Earth of mother. The former impregnated
the earth with its fertilizing rains, and the earth,
receiving them, became fruitful and brought forth.
Plutarch (46-120 A.D.)

6383   The entire lower world was created in the likeness of the
higher world. All that exists in the higher world appears
like an image in this lower world; yet all this is but One.
Zohar (120?-1200? A.D.)

6384   Like an image in a dream the world is troubled by love,
hatred, and other poisons. So long as the dream lasts,
the image appears to be real; but on awaking it vanishes.
Sankara (c. 900 A.D.)

6385   The world in all does but two nations bear,
The good, the bad, and these mixed everywhere.
Andrew Marvell (1621-1678)

6386   But as the world, harmoniously confused,
       Where order in variety we see;
       And where, tho' all things differ, all agree.

                                                    Pope (1688-1744)

6387   This world is a comedy to those who think,
       a tragedy to those who feel.

                                            Horace Walpole (1717-1797)

6388   The world is seldom what it seems; to man, who dimly sees,
       realities appear as dreams, and dreams realities.
                                            Thomas Moore (1779-1852)

6389   There are two worlds; the world that we can measure with
       line and rule, and the world that we feel with our hearts
       and imaginations.
                                                Leigh Hunt (1784-1859)

6390   A piece of wood may be saturated with water,
       water may in its turn be filled with gas.
       Exactly the same relation between different kinds of
       matter may be observed in the whole of the universe:
       the finer matters permeate the coarser ones.
                                                Gurdjieff (1873-1949)

6391   The world is like a grand staircase,
       some are going up and some are going down.

                                                        Italian Proverb

6392   Water floats a ship
       Water sinks a ship.

                                                      Chinese Proverb

3. INSIGHT

6393   The three mothers in the world are: air, water and fire.
       Heaven was created from fire or ether; the earth
       (comprising sea and land) from the elementary water;
       and the atmospheric air from the elementary air, or spirit,
       which establishes the balance among them.
                                   Sepher Yezirah (B.C. 2000?-600 A.D.)

6394   How Heaven and Earth are like a bellows!
       While vacuous, it is never exhausted.

                                              Lao-Tzu (fl. B.C. 600)

6395   One generation passeth away, and another generation cometh:
       but the earth abideth for ever.
                                            Ecclesiastes (B.C. 300?)

6396   The universal order and the personal order are nothing but
       different expressions and manifestations of a common
       underlying principle.
                                    Marcus Aurelius (121-180 A.D.)

6397   The wave, the sea, and the bubbles are all one.
       All is one, nothing else, whether less or more.
                                    Ni'matullah Wali (1331-1431?)

6398   The world's a theatre, the earth a stage,
       Which God and nature do with actors fill.
                                    John Heywood (1497?-1580?)

6399   All the world's a stage, and all the men and women in it
       merely players. They have their exits and their entrances;
       and one man in his time plays many parts.
                                    Shakespeare (1564-1616)

6400   My soul, what's lighter than a feather? Wind.
       Than wind? The fire. And what than fire? The Mind.
       What's lighter than the mind? A thought. Than thought?
       This bubble world. What than this bubble? Nought.
                                    Quarles (1592-1644)

6401   The created world is but a small parenthesis in eternity,
       and a short interposition for a time, between such a state
       of duration as was before it, and may be after it.
                                    Thomas Browne (1605-1682)

6402   The world is a beautiful book, but of little use to him
       who cannot read it.
                                    Carlo Goldoni (1707-1793)

6403   Whoever has seen the masked at a ball dance amicably
       together, and take hold of hands without knowing each other,
       leaving the next moment to meet no more, can form an idea of
       the world.
                                    Vauvenargues(1715-1747)

6404   The world is a great ocean, upon which we encounter more
       tempestuous storms than calms.
                                    Edgar Allan Poe (1809-1849)

6405   The first fundamental law of the universe is the law of
       three forces, or three principles, or, as it is often
       called, the law of three. According to this law every
       action, every phenomenon in all worlds without exception,
       is the result of a simultaneous action of three forces-
       the positive, the negative, and the neutralizing.
                                    Gurdjieff (1873-1949)

6406   This world which consists of friends, enemies and neutrals, which affects you with pleasure and pain, is only a creation of your mind which is a product of ignorance.

                                                   Sivananda (born 1887)

6407   Man has a thousand plans...
Heaven but one.

                                                   Chinese Proverb

4. POSITIVE

6408   By three things is the world sustained: by justice, by truth, and by peace.

                               The Talmud (B.C. 500?-400? A.D.)

6409   Beauty from order springs.

                                     William King (1663-1712)

6410   Everything is for the best in the best of all possible worlds.

                                     Voltaire (1694-1778)

6411   O Earth! all bathed with blood and tears, yet never Hast thou ceased putting forth thy fruit and flowers.

                             Germaine De Stael (1766-1817)

6412   Long have I loved what I behold.
The night that calms, the day that cheers;
The common growth of mother-earth
Suffices me.

                                   Wordsworth (1770-1850)

6413   This world, after all our science and sciences, is still a miracle; wonderful, inscrutable, magical and more, to whosoever will think of it.

                                   Carlyle (1795-1881)

6414   The Universe should be deemed an immense Being, always living, always moved and always moving in an eternal activity inherent in itself, and which, subordinate to no foreign cause, is communicated to all its parts, connects them together, and makes the world of things a complete and perfect whole.

                                   Albert Pike (1809-1891)

6415   For every man the world is as fresh as it was at the first day, and as full of untold novelties for him who has the eyes to see them.

                                   Thomas Huxley (1825-1895)

6416   The grand show is eternal. It is always sunrise somewhere;
the dew is never all dried at once; a shower is forever
falling; vapor is ever rising. Eternal sunrise, eternal
sunset, eternal dawn and gleaming, on sea and continents and
islands, each in its turn, as the round earth rolls.

                                           John Muir (1838-1914)

5. NEGATIVE

6417   The world has no self-substance of its own. It is simply
a vast concordance of causes and conditions that have had
their origin, solely and exclusively, in the activities of
the mind as it has been stimulated by ignorance, false
imagination, desires and infatuation.

                                   Buddha (B.C. 568-488)

6418   Trust not the world, for it never payeth that it promiseth.

                            Augustine (354-430 A.D.)

6419   The world is but a large prison,
out of which some are daily selected for execution.

                         Walter Raleigh (1552-1618)

6420   The more a man drinketh of the world,
the more it intoxicateth.

                              Bacon (1561-1626)

6421   The world is all a carcass and vanity,
The shadow of a shadow, a play
And in one word, just nothing.

                       Owen Feltham (1602-1668)

6422   What is this world? Thy school, O misery!
Our only lesson is to learn to suffer.

                            Young (1683-1765)

6423   The world, in its best state, is nothing more than a larger
assembly of beings, combining to counterfeit happiness
which they do not feel.

                           Johnson (1709-1784)

6424   Believe everything you hear said of the world;
nothing is too impossibly bad.

                          Balzac (1799-1850)

6425   This earth is but the dismal entrance leading to the
twilight that precedes the valley of true light,
that light which no wind can extinguish,
that light which burns without a wick or fuel.

                       H. P. Blavatsky (1831-1891)

6426   The world rolls round forever like a mill;
        It grinds out deaths and life and good and ill;
        It has no purpose, heart or mind or will.
                                        James B. V. Thomson (1834-1882)

6427   Man has lost the capacity to foresee and to forestall.
        He will end by destroying the earth.
                                        Albert Schweitzer (1875-1965)

6428   The world is an illusion. Friends are hypocritical cheats.
        Relatives are selfish bugs. There is none on whom you can
        depend except God.
                                        Sivananda (born 1887)

6429   Though a tree grow a thousand feet...
        The fruits will fall to earth again.
                                        Chinese Proverb

6430   Heaven lent you a soul
        Earth will lend a grave.
                                        Chinese Proverb

6. ADVICE

6431   This world is like a foyer leading into the world to come -
        prepare thyself in the foyer so that thou mayest enter into
        the inner chamber.
                                        The Talmud (B.C. 500?-400? A.D.)

6432   The world is a looking glass, and gives back to every
        man the reflection of his own face. Frown at it and it
        will in turn look sourly upon you; laugh at it and with
        it, and it is a jolly kind companion.
                                        Thackeray (1811-1863)

6433   You and I must not complain if our plans break down if we
        have done our part. That probably means that the plans of
        One who knows more than we do have succeeded.
                                        Edward E. Hale (1822-1909)

6434   Be sure of the foundation of your life. Know why you live
        as you do. Be ready to give a reason for it. Do not, in
        such a matter as life, build it on opinion or custom or what
        you guess is true. Make it matter of certainty and science.
                                        T. Starr King (1824-1864)

6435   The most efficient way to live reasonably is every morning
        to make a plan of one's day and every night to examine the
        results obtained.
                                        Alexis Carrel (1873-1944)

6436   Your life will be no better than the plans you make and the
        action you take. You are the architect and builder of your
        own life, fortune, destiny.

                                    Alfred A. Montapert (born 1910?)

7. POTPOURRI

6437   In a vision he asked the Dragon (symbol of universal light)
        to disclose the nature of the universe and the constitution
        of the gods...The Dragon acquiesced...Immediately the form
        of the Spirit changed. Where it had stood there was a
        glorious and pulsating Radiance. This Light was the
        spiritual nature of the Great Dragon itself. The universe
        of material things faded from his consciousness. Presently
        a great darkness descended and expanding, swallowed up the
        Light. Everything was troubled. About Him swirled a
        mysterious watery substance which gave forth a smokelike
        vapor. The air was filled with inarticulate moanings and
        sighings which seemed to come from the Light swallowed up in
        darkness. His mind told Him that the Light was the form of
        the spiritual universe that the swirling darkness which had
        engulfed it represented material substance. Then out of the
        imprisoned Light a mysterious and Holy Word came forth and
        took its stand upon the smoking waters. This Word - the
        Voice of the Light - rose out of the darkness as a great
        pillar, and the fire and the air followed after it, but the
        earth and the water remained unmoved below. Thus Light was
        divided from darkness, and from the waters of Light were
        formed the worlds above and from...darkness...worlds below.

                                    The Divine Pymander (BC 2500?-200 AD?)

6438   The question of whether the universe has limits or is
        eternal can wait until some way is found to extinguish the
        fires of birth, old age, sickness and death; in the presence
        of lamentation, sorrow, suffering, and pain; one should
        first search for a way to solve these problems and then
        devote oneself to the practice of that way.

                                    Buddha (B.C. 568-488)

6439   Beauty, strength, youth, are flowers but fading seen;
        Duty, faith, love, are roots, and ever green.

                                    George Peele (1558?-1597?)

6440   Confusion heard his voice, and wild uproar
        Stood ruled, stood vast infinitude confined;
        Till at his second bidding darkness fled,
        Light shone, and order from disorder sprung.

                                    Milton (1608-1674)

6441   As beauteous is the world, and many a joy
       Floats through its wide dominion. But, alas,
       When we would seize the winged good, it flies,
       And step by step, along the path of life,
       Allures our yearning spirits to the grave.

                                                Goethe (1749-1832)

6442   This world is all a fleeting show,
           For man's illusion given;
       The smiles of joy, the tears of woe,
       Deceitful shine, deceitful flow,-
           There's nothing true but Heaven.

                                          Thomas Moore (1779-1852)

6443   For the world was built in order
           And the atoms march in tune;
       Rhyme the pipe, and Time the warder,
           The sun obeys them, and the moon.

                                             Emerson (1803-1882)

6444   The Universe, which is the uttered Word of God, is infinite
       in extent. There is no empty space beyond creation on any
       side. The Universe, which is the Thought of God pronounced,
       never was not, since God never was inert; nor was, without
       thinking and creating. The forms of creation change, the
       suns and worlds live and die like the leaves and the
       insects, but the Universe itself is infinite and eternal,
       because God Is, Was, and Will forever Be, and never did
       not think and create.

                                          Albert Pike (1809-1891)

6445   Earth took her shining station as a star,
       In Heaven's dark hall, high up the crowd of worlds.

                                             Bailey (1816-1902)

6446   Love to his soul gave eyes; he knew things are not
           as they seem.
       The dream is his real life; the world around him
           is the dream.

                                       Francis Palgrave (1824-1897)

6447   The chess-board is the world,
           the pieces are the phenomena of the universe,
           the rules of the game are what we call the laws of Nature.
       The player on the other side is hidden from us.

                                          Thomas Huxley (1825-1895)

6448   This world is full of beauty, as other worlds above,
And if we did our duty, it might be as full of love.

Gerald Massey (1828-1907)

6449   A man said to the universe:
"Sir, I exist!"
"However," replied the universe,
"That fact has not created in me
A sense of obligation."

Stephen Crane (1871-1900)

WORSHIP
Prayer, Religion and Symbolism

1. ESSENCE

6450   Prayer is the contemplation of the facts of life
from the highest point of view.

Emerson (1803-1882)

6451   Prayer is the spirit speaking truth to Truth.

Bailey (1816-1902)

6452   Superstition is...religion which has grown incongruous with
intelligence.

John Tyndall (1820-1893)

6453   All religions are therapies for the sorrows and disorders of
the soul.

C. G. Jung (1875-1961)

6454   Religion is essentially the art and the theory of the
remaking of man. Man is not a finished creation.

Sivananda (born 1887)

6455   Religion is the intellectual resolution of the unknown.

Buckminster Fuller (1895-1983)

2. OPPOSITES

6456   The gods are the creations of the created. They are not
emanations of The Eternal. They are made by the adoration
of their worshippers. It is not the gods that do the work
of creation. This is done by the great natural forces
working each according to its nature; the gods come into
their procession after the egg of manifestation has been
laid in the darkness of the cosmic night.

Kabbalah (B.C. 1200?-700? A.D.)

6457   He who pursues learning will increase every day;
He who pursues The Eternal will decrease every day.
He will decrease and continue to decrease,
Till he comes at non-action;
By non-action everything can be done.

Lao-Tzu (fl. B.C. 600)

6458   Trouble and perplexity drive me to prayer,
and prayer drives away perplexity and trouble.

Philip Melanchton (1497-1560)

6459 My words fly up, my thoughts remain below:
Words without thoughts never to heaven go.
Shakespeare (1564-1616)

6460 Heaven is never deaf but when man's heart is dumb.
Quarles (1592-1644)

6461 Religion is the best armor in the world,
but the worst cloak.
John Bunyan (1628-1688)

6462 In prayer it is better to have a heart without words,
than words without a heart.
John Bunyan (1628-1688)

6463 Religion is too often talked of, but too little known.
Swift (1667-1745)

6464 In religion as in friendship,
they who profess most are ever the least sincere.
Richard Sheridan (1751-1816)

6465 In earlier religions the spirit of the time was expressed
through the individual and confirmed by miracles.
In modern religions the spirit is expressed through the many
and confirmed by reason.
Heine (1797-1856)

6466 Prayer does not change God, but changes him who prays.
Kierkegaard (1813-1855)

6467 The hands and feet of the man of God are nailed on earth
and free in the heavens.
The hands and feet of most are free on earth
and nailed in the heavens.
Hazrat Inayat Khan (1882-1927)

3. INSIGHT

6468 Devotion is love for something higher than ourselves;
something that evokes our idealism;
which, while we despair becoming equal to it,
yet makes us aspire to become like it.
Kabbalah (B.C. 1200?-700? A.D.)

6469 Not by speech, not by mind,
Not by sight can He be apprehended.
How can He be comprehended
Otherwise than by one's saying "He is"?...
Upanishads (c. B.C. 800)

6470   The greatest prayer is patience.
                                                    Buddha (B.C. 568-488)

6471   Prayer is the wing wherewith the soul flies to heaven,
        and meditation the eye wherewith we see God.
                                                    Ambrose (340-397 A.D.)

6472   Mystical union consists in this: That you reduce yourself
        to your unity in proclaiming the unity of God - and thus God
        makes you the witness of yourself.
                                                    al-Hallaj (c. 858-922 A.D.)

6473   It is God whom every lover loves in every beloved.
                                                    Ibn Al-'Arabi (1165-1240)

6474   The fewer words the better prayer.
                                                    Martin Luther (1483-1546)

6475   Any system of religion that has anything in it that shocks
        the mind of a child, cannot be a true system.
                                                    Paine (1737-1809)

6476   Prayer is to religion what thinking is to philosophy.
        To pray is to make religion.
                                                    Novalis (1772-1801)

6477   There is but one temple in the universe, and that is the
        body of man. Nothing is holier than that high form...We
        touch heaven when we lay our hand on a human body...We are
        the miracle of miracles, - the great inscrutable Mystery.
                                                    Carlyle (1795-1881)

6478   Symbols were the almost universal language of ancient
        theology. They were the most obvious method of instruction;
        for, like nature herself, they addressed the understanding
        through the eye...
                                                    Albert Pike (1809-1891)

6479   A prayer, in its simplest definition, is merely a wish
        turned heavenward.
                                                    Phillips Brooks (1835-1893)

6480   As one can ascend to the top of a house
        by means of a ladder or a tree or a staircase or a rope,
        so diverse are the ways and means to approach God,
        and every religion in the world shows one of these ways.
                                                    Ramakrishna (1836-1886)

6481   Every name of God and each attribute are but shadows of the
       Reality, limited manifestations of the Limitless, as time is
       an attribute of Eternity, mind an attribute of
       Consciousness, flame an attribute of Fire.

                                        C. Spurgeon Medhurst (born 1850?)

6482   Prayer is a force as real as terrestrial gravity...It is not
       only worship; it is also an invisible emanation of man's
       worshipping spirit - the most powerful form of energy that
       one can generate.

                                              Alexis Carrel (1873-1944)

6483   Every real religion, that is, one that has been created by
       learned people for a definite aim, consists of two parts.
         One part teaches what is to be done. This part becomes
       common knowledge and in the course of time is distorted and
       departs from the original.
         The other part teaches how to do what the first part
       teaches. This part is preserved in secret in special
       schools and with its help it is always possible to rectify
       what has been distorted in the first part or to restore what
       has been forgotten.

                                                Gurdjieff (1873-1949)

6484   The unconscious can be reached and expressed only by
       symbols, which is the reason why the process of
       individuation can never do without the symbol. The
       symbol is the primitive expression of the unconscious,
       but at the same time it is also an idea corresponding
       to the highest intuition produced by consciousness.

                                              C. G. Jung (1875-1961)

6485   Man's ultimate concern must be expressed symbolically,
       because symbolic language alone is able to express the
       ultimate.

                                             Paul Tillich (1886-1965)

6486   Religion is the most rational science of life, the science
       of man as he essentially is, the science which shows him how
       he is a part of Cosmos, how he ought to abide by the law of
       the Cosmos, and aim at the fulfillment
       process of the Cosmos.

                                            Sivananda (born 1887)

6487   The word "prayer" is applied to at least four distinct
       procedures: petition, intercession, adoration, and
       contemplation.

                                         Aldous Huxley (1894-1963)

6488   If in the dark he kneels to pray...
He really prays.

                          Chinese Proverb

4. POSITIVE

6489   When the wisest rests his mind in contemplation on our God
beyond time, who invisibly dwells in the mystery of things
and the heart of man, then he rises above pleasures and
sorrow.

                       Upanishads (c. B.C. 800)

6490   But the hour cometh, and now is, when the true worshippers
shall worship the Father in spirit and in truth: for the
Father seeketh such to worship him. God is a spirit: and
they that worship him must worship him in spirit and in
truth.

                       Jesus (B.C. 6?-30? A.D.)

6491   The worship most acceptable to God comes from a thankful and
cheerful heart.

                       Plutarch (46-120 A.D.)

6492   By association with the exalted,
Who would not become uplifted?
The thread which strings the flowers
Becomes a garland for the head.

                   Nagarjuna (c. 100-200 A.D.)

6493   Prayer is a virtue that prevaileth against all temptations.
                 Bernard of Clairvaux (1090-1153)

6494   Truth is what prays in man, and a man is continually at
prayer when he lives according to the truth.
                    Swedenborg (1688-1772)

6495   True religion is the poetry of the heart;
it has enchantments useful to our manners;
it gives us both happiness and virtue.

                     Joubert (1754-1824)

6496   Prayer purifies; it is a self-preached sermon.

                     Richter (1763-1825)

6497   Between the humble and contrite heart and the majesty of
heaven there are no barriers; the only password is prayer.
                   Hosea Ballou (1771-1852)

6498   Religion is a necessary, an indispensable element in any
        great human character. There is no living without it.
        Religion is the tie that connects man to his Creator, and
        holds him to his throne.
                                        Daniel Webster (1782-1852)

6499   Is not prayer a study of truth, a sally of the soul into
        the unfound infinite? - No man ever prayed heartily without
        learning something.
                                        Emerson (1803-1882)

6500   Light was the first Divinity worshipped by men. To it
        they owed the brilliant spectacle of Nature. It seems an
        emanation from the Creator of all things, making known to
        our senses the Universe which darkness hides from our eyes,
        and, as it were, giving it existence.
                                        Albert Pike (1809-1891)

6501   True prayer is the contemplation of all sacred things, of
        their application to ourselves, our daily life and actions,
        accompanied by the most heartfelt and intense desire to make
        their influence stronger and our lives better and nobler...
                                        H. P. Blavatsky (1831-1891)

6502   A generous prayer is never presented in vain; the petition
        may be refused, but the petitioner is always, I believe,
        rewarded by some gracious visitation.
                                        Robert Louis Stevenson (1850-1895)

6503   All religions are equally good. God is the fruit of any
        religion truly practised. Make no mistake about it. God
        is one. Truth is one. The colour of the cow may be
        different, but milk is white.
                                        Sivananda (born 1887)

6504   Rites, sacraments, and ceremonials are valuable to the
        extent that they remind those who take part in them of the
        true Nature of Things.
                                        Aldous Huxley (1894-1963)

6505   There is no greater intoxication than that of love
        when it transcends the human object and is directed
        towards the divine being.
                                        Pir Vilayat Inayat Khan (born 1916)

5. NEGATIVE

6506 If one profanes the name of heaven in secret he shall be
punished in broad daylight: unwittingly or wittingly, it
is all one in profaning the name.

The Talmud (B.C. 500?-400? A.D.)

6507 Cease to think that the decrees of the gods can be
changed by prayers.

Vergil (B.C. 70-19)

6508 Nothing costs so much as what is bought by prayers.

Seneca (B.C. 3-65 A.D.)

6509 The saviour of wandering in the ocean of deathless life
has rid me of all my asking;
As the tree is in the seed,
so all diseases are in this asking.

Kabir (1440-1518)

6510 Religion, which should most distinguish us from beasts, and
ought most peculiarly to elevate us, as rational creatures,
above brutes, is that wherein men often appear most
irrational, and more senseless than beasts themselves.

John Locke (1632-1704)

6511 The notion of the Trinity of Gods has enfeebled the belief
in one God. A multiplication of beliefs acts as a division
of belief; and in proportion as anything is divided it is
weakened.

Paine (1737-1809)

6512 A religion that requires persecution to sustain it is of the
devil's propagation.

Hosea Ballou (1771-1852)

6513 Men will wrangle for religion; write for it; fight for it;
die for it; anything but - live for it.

Colton (1780-1832)

6514 The world would be astonished if it knew how great a
proportion of its brightest ornaments, of those most
distinguished even in popular estimation for wisdom and
virtue, are complete skeptics in religion.

John Stuart Mill (1806-1873)

6515 Men are idolaters, and want something to look at and kiss
and hug, or throw themselves down before; they always did,
they always will, and if you don't make it of wood, you must
make it of words.

Oliver Wendell Holmes (1809-1894)

6516   People of this age care for the essence of everything.
        They will accept the essential of religion and not its
        non-essentials (that is, the rituals, ceremonials, dogmas
        and creeds).
                                        Ramakrishna (1836-1886)

6517   Prayer - to ask that the laws of the universe be annulled in
        behalf of a single petitioner confessedly unworthy.
                                        Ambrose Bierce (1842-1914?)

6518   Religion is a monumental chapter in the history of human
        egotism.
                                        William James (1842-1910)

6519   There is not even enough religion in the world to destroy
        the world's religions.
                                        Nietzsche (1844-1900)

6520   When the gods wish to punish us they answer our prayers.
                                        Oscar Wilde (1854-1900)

6521   My debts are large, my failures great, my shame secret and
        heavy; yet when I come to ask for my good, I quake in fear
        lest my prayer be granted.
                                        Rabindranath Tagore (1861-1941)

6522   Religion is the last refuge of human savagery.
                                        Alfred North Whitehead (1861-1947)

6523   Religion without myth not only fails to work, it also fails
        to offer man the promise of unity with the transpersonal and
        eternal.
                                        C. G. Jung (1875-1961)

6524   Priests are no more necessary to religion
        than politicians to patriotism.
                                        John H. Holmes (born 1879)

6525   An atheist is a man who has no invisible means of support.
                                        Fulton J. Sheen (1895-1979)

6. ADVICE

6526   One should worship with the thought that he is just one's
        self, for therein all these become one. That same thing,
        namely this self, is the trace of this All, for by it one
        knows this All... He finds fame and praise who knows this...
                                        Upanishads (c. B.C. 800)

6527 Our prayers should be for blessings in general,
for God knows best what is good for us.

Socrates (B.C. 469-399)

6528 Pray to God, at the beginning of all thy works,
so that thou mayest bring them all to a good ending.

Xenophon (B.C. 430-355)

6529 Seek not the law in your scriptures, for the law is life,
whereas the scripture is dead...The law is living word of
living God to living prophets for living men. In everything
that is life is the law written. You find it in the grass,
in the tree, in the river, in the mountain, in the birds of
heaven, in the fishes of the sea; but seek it chiefly in
yourselves.

Jesus (B.C. 6?-30? A.D.)

6530 The first petition that we are to make to Almighty God is
for a good conscience, the next for health of mind, and then
of body.

Seneca (B.C. 3-65 A.D.)

6531 Unless we place our religion and our treasure in the same
thing, religion will always be sacrificed.

Epictetus (50-138 A.D.)

6532 'Release is in the eye.'... 'The seed-blossoms (spiritual
embryo) of the human body must be concentrated upward in the
empty space (the heavenly heart between the eyes).'
 Immortality is contained in this sentence and also the
overcoming of the world is contained in it. This is the
common goal of all religions.

Lu Yen (fl. 800 A.D.)

6533 An individual should hold an awareness of God and His love
all the time. He should not separate his consciousness from
the Divine while he journeys on the way, nor when he lies
down nor when he rises up.

Nahmanides (c. 1300)

6534 A good life is the only religion.

Thomas Fuller (1608-1661)

6535 All religions must be tolerated...for...every man must get
to heaven in his own way.

Frederick II (1712-1786)

6536 O you who are seeking God,
 know this:
Know that we are the mirror of God,
 the Absolute Truth.

Nur 'Ali Shah (died 1797)

6537   He prayeth best who loveth best
        All things, both great and small.

                              Samuel Coleridge (1772-1834)

6538   Practice in life whatever you pray for,
        and God will give it to you more abundantly.

                              Edward Pusey (1800-1882)

6539   To worship rightly is to love each other,
        each smile a hymn, each kindly deed a prayer.

                              John Greenleaf Whittier (1807-1892)

6540   Pray as if everything depended on God,
        and work as if everything depended upon man.

                              Francis J. Spellman (1889-1967)

7. POTPOURRI

6541   O praise His goodness with songs for thanksgiving,
        and meditate in silence on the wonders of His love;
        let thy heart overflow with gratitude and acknowledgment,
        let the language of thy lips speak praise and adoration,
        let the actions of thy life show thy love to His law.

                              Akhenaton? (c. B.C. 1375)

6542   Sacrifice is the transmutation of force.
        Cosmic archetypes shape this force into spiritual energy,
        which can then reappear on the planes of form as an entirely
        different type of force to that as which it started.

                              Kabbalah (B.C. 1200?-700? A.D.)

6543   To him who hearkens to the gods, the gods give ear.

                              Homer (c. B.C. 700)

6544   In all thou dost first let thy Prayers ascend,
        And to the Gods thy Labours first commend,
        From them implore Success, and hope a prosperous End.

                              Pythagoras (B.C. 582-507)

6545   God is not to be worshipped with sacrifices and blood; for
        what pleasure can He have in the slaughter of the innocent?
        but rather with a pure mind, a good and honest purpose.
        Temples are not to be built for Him with stones piled high;
        God is to be consecrated in the breast of each.

                              Seneca (B.C. 3-65 A.D.)

6546 If we traverse the world, it is possible to find cities
without walls, without letters, without kings, without
wealth, without coin, without schools and theatres; but a
city without a temple, or that practiseth not worship,
prayer, and the like, no one ever saw.

Plutarch (46-120 A.D.)

6547 It isn't anything manly to go to the mountains. A man ought
to be able to live in the city among people while being so
occupied with God that not for a single moment is he empty
of Him.

Sari al-Saqati (fl. c. 850 A.D.)

6548 For those who have been lost in the contemplation of the
    divine immanence, God reveals his transcendence.
And for those who are lost in the contemplation of God's
    transcendence, God reveals his immanence.

Jalal-Uddin Rumi (1207-1273)

6549 Even as the needle that directs the hour,
(Touched with the loadstone) by the secret power
Of hidden Nature, points upon the pole;
Even so the wavering powers of my soul,
Touched by the virtue of Thy spirit, flee
From what is earth, and point alone to Thee.

Quarles (1592-1644)

6550 If I am right, Thy grace impart,
    Still in the right to stay;
If I am wrong, O teach my heart
    To find that better way!

Pope (1688-1744)

6551 Prayer is the soul's sincere desire,
    Uttered or unexpressed,
The motion of a hidden fire
    That trembles in the breast.

James Montgomery (1771-1854)

6552 Such love of all our virtues is the gem;
    We bring with us the immortal seed at birth;
Of heaven it is, and heavenly; woe to them
    Who make it wholly earthly and of earth!

Robert Southey (1774-1843)

6553 I ask and wish not to appear
    More beauteous, rich or gay:
Lord, make me wiser every year,
    And better every day.

Charles Lamb (1775-1834)

6554 As down in the sunless retreats of the ocean
 Sweet flowers are springing no mortal can see,
So deep in my soul the still prayer of devotion
 Unheard by the world, rises silent to Thee.
Thomas Moore (1779-1852)

6555 Father! no prophet's laws I seek,-
 Thy laws in Nature's works appear;-
I own myself corrupt and weak,
 Yet will I pray, for thou wilt hear.
Byron (1788-1824)

6556 Speak to Him thou for He hears,
 and spirit with spirit can meet-
Closer is He than breathing,
 and nearer than hands and feet.
Alfred Tennyson (1809-1892)

6557 Kneeling in prayer, and not ashamed to pray,
 The tumult of the time disconsolate
To inarticulate murmurs dies away,
 While the eternal ages watch and wait.
Longfellow (1807-1882)

6558 Religion is a great force - the only real motive force in
the world; but you must get a man through his own religion,
not through yours.
G. B. Shaw (1856-1950)

6559 We dance around in a ring and suppose,
But the Secret sits in the middle and knows.
Robert Frost (1875-1963)

6560 Let my imperfect self advance towards thy perfect being Lord
as the crescent rises to fullness.
Hazrat Inayat Khan (1882-1927)

6561 O God, give us serenity to accept what cannot be changed;
courage to change what should be changed,
and wisdom to distinguish one from the other.
Reinhold Niebuhr (1892-1971)

Subject Finder Index

The **WISDOM OF THE AGES** has 81 different subjects. Each subject includes minor subjects and subtitles.   This alphabetical index of over 400 subtitles will help you locate a subject.

SUBTITLE	-will be found in-	SUBJECT
Absence		Separation
Action		Activity
Activity		Activity
Adversity		Opposition
Aging		Decrease
Ambition		Enthusiasm
Ancestry		Family
Anger		Anger
Anxiety		Fear
Appreciation		Taste
Argument		Strife
Arrogance		Pride
Art		Creation
Authority		Power
Autumn		Decrease
Beauty		Beauty
Becoming		Realization
Being		Life
Belief		Hope
Boasting		Pride
Books		Words
Boredom		Inertia
Bravery		Courage
Calamity		Ruin

AUTHOR INDEX

Abbott, John S. C. --- American Theologian -- 1805-1877

Abbott, Lyman --- American Clergyman, Author, and Editor -- 1835-1922

Acheson, Dean Gooderham --- American Statesman and Lawyer -- 1893-1971

Adams, Brooks --- American Historian -- 1848-1927

Adams, Franklin P. --- American Journalist and Humorist -- 1881-1960

Adams, John --- American - 2nd President of the United States -- 1735-1826

Adams, John Quincy --- American - 6th President of the U.S. -- 1767-1848

Addison, Joseph --- English Essayist, Poet, and Statesman -- 1672-1719

Adenauer, Konrad --- German Statesman -- 1876-1967

Adler, Alfred --- Austrian Psychologist -- 1870-1937

Adler, Mortimer --- American Philosopher, Educator, and Editor -- born 1902

Aeschylus, --- Greek Tragic Poet -- B.C. 525-456

Agassiz, Jean Louis --- Swiss-American Zoologist and Geologist -- 1807-1883

Agnon, Shmuel Yosef --- Israeli Author -- 1888-1970

Akhenaton, --- Egyptian King and Monotheist -- c. B.C. 1375

Akiba, Ben Joseph --- Palestinian Rabbi and Sage -- 40?-135 A.D.

Alarcon, Ruiz de --- Spanish Dramatic Poet -- 1581-1639

Alberti, Leon Battista --- Italian Artist and Musician -- 1404-1472

Alcott, Amos Bronson --- American Teacher and Philosopher -- 1799-1888

Aldrich, Thomas Bailey --- American Poet, Writer, and Editor -- 1836-1907

Alfieri, Vittorio --- Italian Poet and Dramatist -- 1749-1803

Alger, William R. --- American Writer and Theologian -- 1822-1905

Ali, --- Arabian Caliph - Son-In-Law of Mohammed -- 600-661 A.D.

Allen, James L. --- American Novelist and Short-Story Writer -- 1849-1925

Allingham, William --- Irish Poet -- 1824-1889

Ambrose, Saint --- Roman - Bishop of Milan -- 340-397 A.D.

Amiel, Henri Frederic --- Swiss Philosopher and Critic -- 1821-1881

Anacharsis, --- Scythian Philosopher -- fl. B.C. 600

Anderson, Hans C. --- Danish Poet, Novelist, and Dramatist -- 1802-1875

Antiphanes, --- Greek Playwright -- c.B.C. 388-311

Antisthenes, --- Greek Cynic and Philosopher -- fl. B.C. 444

Apollonius, --- Greek Mathematician and Epic Poet -- B.C. 247-205

Aquinas, St. Thomas --- Italian Theologian and Philosopher -- 1225-1274

Arabian Proverb, --- Anonymous Saying of Arabian Origin -- 1707-1788

Archilochus, --- Greek Poet -- c. B.C. 648

Arendt, Hannah --- American-German Political Scientist -- 1906-1975

Aristophanes, --- Greek Comic Poet and Satirist -- B.C. 448-380

Aristotle, --- Greek Philosopher -- B.C. 384-322

Armstrong, John --- Scottish Poet and Physician -- 1709-1779

Arnold, Edwin --- English Poet and Author -- 1832-1904

Arnold, Matthew --- English Poet and Critic -- 1822-1888

Astor, Lady Nancy --- English Parliament Member -- 1879-1964

Auden, Wynstan Hugh --- Anglo-American Poet -- 1907-1973

Auerbach, Berthold --- German Novelist -- 1812-1882

Augustine, Saint --- Numidian Philosopher - Bishop of Hippo -- 354-430 A.D.

Aurelius, Marcus --- Roman Emperor and Philosopher -- 121-180 A.D.

Ausonius, Decimus Magnus --- Latin Poet and Man of Letters -- 310-395 A.D.

Babson, Roger --- American Statistician and Columnist -- 1875-1967

Bacon, Francis --- English Philosopher, Essayist, and Statesman -- 1561-1626

Bagehot, Walter --- English Economist and Journalist -- 1826-1877

Bailey, Philip James --- English Poet -- 1816-1902

Baillie, Joanna --- Scottish Dramatist and Poet -- 1762-1851

Bakunin, Mikhail A. --- Russian Anarchist and Writer -- 1814-1876

Baldwin, Stanley --- English Statesman and Prime Minister -- 1867-1947

Ballou, Hosea --- American Clergyman, Founder of "Universalism" -- 1771-1852

Balzac, Honore de --- French Novelist -- 1799-1850

Bancroft, George --- American Historian -- 1800-1891

Banks, George L. --- English Writer -- 1821-1881

Barbauld, Anna Letiti --- English Poet and Editor -- 1743-1825

Barbour, John --- Scottish Poet -- 1320-1395

Barrie, James Matthew --- British Playwright and Novelist -- 1860-1937

Barrow, Isaac --- English Mathematician and Theologian -- 1630-1677

Barton, Bruce --- American Author and Advertising Executive -- 1886-1967

Baruch, Bernard M. --- American Financier and Statesman -- 1870-1965

Basho, --- Japanese Poet -- 1644-1694

Basil, Saint --- Cappadocian Religious Leader -- 329-379 A.D.

Baudelaire, Pierre Charles --- French Poet and Critic -- 1821-1867

Baxter, Richard --- English Nonconformist Theologian -- 1615-1691

Beard, Mary --- American Historical Writer -- 1876-1958

Beattie, James --- English Poet and Essayist -- 1735-1803

Beaumarchais, Pierre --- French Dramatist and Writer -- 1732-1799

Beaumont, Francis --- English Dramatist -- 1584-1616

Beaverbrook, Lord --- British Politician/Publisher -- 1879-1964

Beecher, Henry Ward --- American Preacher, Orator, and Writer -- 1813-1878

Beerbohm, Sir Max --- English Essayist, Caricaturist, and Parodist -- 1872-1956

Beethoven, Ludwig Van --- German Composer -- 1770-1827

Ben-Gurion, David --- Israeli Prime Minister and Founding Father -- 1886-1973

Benchley, Robert --- American Humorist and Critic -- 1889-1945

Bennett, Arnold --- English Novelist and Dramatist -- 1867-1931

Bentham, Jeremy --- English Jurist and Philosopher -- 1748-1832

Berdyaev, Nicholas --- Russian Philosopher -- 1874-1948

Bergson, Henri Louis --- French Philosopher -- 1859-1941

Berlioz, Hector --- French Romantic Composer -- 1803-1869

Bernanos, Georges --- French Novelist and Polemicist -- 1888-1948

Bernard, Saint --- French Theologian and Mystic -- 1090-1153

Bhagavad Gita, --- Sanskrit Poem Incorporated into the Mahabharata -- a. B.C. 400

Bhavabhuti, --- Indian Dramatist and Poet -- fl. 700 A.D.

Bias, --- Greek Sage and Maxim Writer -- fl. B.C. 600

Bierce, Ambrose --- American Journalist and Author -- 1842-1914?

Bigelow, Jacob --- American Physician and Botanist -- 1786-1879

Billings, Josh --- American Humorist and Lecturer -- 1815-1885

Blacker, Colonel --- British Officer -- 1778-1823

Blackstone, Sir William --- English Writer and Jurist -- 1723-1780

Blair, Hugh --- Scottish Theologian and Rhetoric Professor -- 1718-1800

Blake, William --- English Poet and Artist -- 1757-1828

Blavatsky, Helena Petrova --- Russian Author and Theosophist -- 1831-1891

Blessington, Marguerite --- English Author and Countess -- 1789-1849

Bodin, Jean --- French Political Philosopher -- 1530-1596

Boethius, --- Roman Philosopher -- 480?-524

Bohr, Niels Henrik D. --- Danish Physicist and Professor -- 1885-1962

Boileau, Nicholas --- French Literary Poet and Critic -- 1636-1711

Bolingbroke, Henry St. John --- English Statesman -- 1678-1751

Bonar, Horatius --- Scottish Clergyman and Hymn Writer -- 1808-1889

Bonnard, Bernard De --- French Poet -- 1744-1784

Born, Max --- German Theoretical Physicist -- 1872-1970

Bossuet, Jacques Benigue --- French Prelate and Orator -- 1627-1704

Boston, Thomas --- Scottish Theologian -- 1676-1732

Boufflers, --- French Author -- 1738-1815

Bourdillon, Francis W. --- English Poet -- 1852-1921

Bourne, Randolph S. --- American Author -- 1886-1918

Bovee, Christian N. --- American Author and Editor -- 1820-1904

Bowring, Sir John --- British Statesman and Linguist -- 1792-1872

Branch, Anna Hempstead --- American Lyric and Mystical Poet -- 1874-1937

Brandeis, Louis Dembitz --- American - U.S. Supreme Court Justice -- 1856-1941

Brandes, Georg --- Danish Literary Critic -- 1842-1927

Bret, Antoine --- French Writer and Poet -- 1717-1792

Bridges, Madeline --- American Poet -- 1844-1920

Brooke, Henry --- Irish Author -- 1703-1783

Brooke, Rupert --- English Poet -- 1887-1915

Brooks, Phillips --- American Episcopalian Bishop -- 1835-1893

Browne, Sir Thomas --- English Author, Physician, and Philosopher -- 1605-1682

Browning, Elizabeth --- English Poet -- 1806-1861

Browning, Robert --- English Poet -- 1812-1889

Bruce, Michael --- Scottish Poet and Schoolmaster -- 1746-1767

Bruno, Giordano --- Italian Philosopher -- 1548-1600

Bryant, William Cullen --- American Poet and Newspaper Editor -- 1794-1878

Buchan, Sir John --- Scottish Author and Administrator -- 1875-1940

Buddha, Gotama --- Indian - Founder of Buddhism -- B.C. 568-488

Bulwer-Lytton, Edward George --- English Novelist and Poet -- 1803-1873

Bunyan, John --- English Author -- 1628-1688

Burbank, Luther --- American Horticulturist -- 1849-1926

Burke, Edmund --- English Political Writer and Statesman -- 1729-1979

Burns, Robert --- Scottish Poet -- 1759-1756

Burr, Aaron --- American Political Leader -- 1756-1836

Burroughs, John --- American Naturalist and Author -- 1837-1921

Burton, Richard E. --- American Poet, Journalist, and Critic -- 1861-1940

Burton, Robert --- English Clergyman and Scholar -- 1576-1640

Bushnell, Horace --- American Congregational Minister -- 1802-1876

Butler, Joseph --- English Bishop, Theologian, and Moralist -- 1692-1752

Butler, Samuel --- English Poet and Satirist -- 1612-1680

Butler, Samuel. --- English Author and Philosopher -- 1835-1902

Buxton, Charles --- English Author -- 1823-1871

Byrnes, James Francis --- American Politician -- 1879-1972

Byrom, John --- English Poet and Shorthand Developer -- 1692-1763

Byron, George Gordon N --- English Poet -- 1788-1824

Chrysostom, Saint John --- Greek Archbishop -- 347-407 A.D.

Chuang-tzu, --- Chinese Philosopher -- fl. B.C. 350

Churchill, Charles --- English Poet and Satirist -- 1731-1764

Churchill, Sir Winston --- British Statesman, Soldier, and Author -- 1874-1965

Ciano, Galeazzo --- Italian Politician and Fascist Leader -- 1903-1944

Cibber, Colley --- English Dramatist and Actor -- 1671-1757

Cicero, Marcus Tullius ---Roman Orator, Politician, and Philosopher -- B.C. 106-43

Clarke, James F. --- American Unitarian Clergyman and Author -- 1810-1888

Claudianus, --- Latin Classic Poet -- 365?-408? A.D.

Clausewitz, Carl von --- Prussian Officer and Military Strategist -- 1780-1831

Cleghorn, Sarah N. --- American Poet -- 1876-1959

Clemenceau, Georges --- French Politician -- 1841-1929

Clough, Arthur Hugh --- English Poet -- 1819-1861

Coke, Sir Edward --- English Jurist -- 1552-1633

Coleridge, Hartley --- English Poet -- 1796-1849

Coleridge, Samuel T. --- English Poet, Critic, and Philosopher -- 1772-1834

Collier, Jeremy --- English Clergyman -- 1650-1726

Collingwood, Robin George --- English Historian and Philosopher -- 1889-1943

Colman, George --- English Dramatist and Theater Manager -- 1762-1836

Colton, Caleb Charles --- English Sportsman and Writer -- 1780-1832

Conant, James B. --- American Educator and Diplomat -- 1893-1978

Confucius, --- Chinese Ethical Teacher - Founder of Confucianism -- B.C. 551-479

Congreve, William --- English Dramatist -- 1670-1729

Conrad, Joseph --- English Novelist -- 1857-1934

Cook, Eliza --- English Poet -- 1818-1889

Coolidge, Calvin --- American - 30th President of the U.S. -- 1872-1933

Coolidge, Susan --- American Writer -- 1845-1905

Cooper, Thomas --- American Scientist, Educator, and Philosopher -- 1759-1839

Cordouero, Moses --- Spanish Metaphysician and Kabbalist -- 1522-1570

Corneille, Pierre --- French Dramatist -- 1606-1684

Cornford, Frances C. --- English Poet -- 1886-1960

Cornuel, A.M. Bigot De --- French Writer -- 1614-1694

Cornwall, Barry --- English Poet -- 1787-1874

Cotton, Nathaniel --- English Physician and Poet -- 1705-1788

Cowley, Abraham --- English Metaphysical Poet -- 1618-1667

Cowley, Malcolm --- American Poet, Writer, and Critic -- born 1898

Cowper, William --- English Poet -- 1731-1800

Descartes, Rene --- French Philosopher and Scientist -- 1596-1650

Deuteronomy, --- Jewish - Old Testament - Torah -- BC 1200?-800?

Dewar, Lord Thomas --- British Distiller, Writer, and Wit -- 1864-1930

Dewey, John --- American Educator and Philosopher -- 1859-1952

Dhammapada, --- Buddhist Collection of Moral Aphorisms -- c. B.C. 300

Dickens, Charles --- English Novelist -- 1812-1870

Dickinson, Emily --- American Poet -- 1830-1886

Diderot, Denis --- French Encyclopedist and Philosopher -- 1713-1784

Diogenes, --- Greek Cynic Philosopher -- B.C. 412-323

Disraeli, Benjamin --- English Statesman and Author -- 1804-1881

Doddridge, Philip --- English Minister and Hymn Writer -- 1702-1751

Donne, John --- English Metaphysical Poet -- 1572-1631

Dorr, Julia C. R. --- American Poet and Novelist -- 1825-1931

Douglas, William O. --- American Supreme Court Justice -- 1898-1980

Dowden, Edward --- Irish Critic -- 1843-1913

Doyle, Arthur Conan --- British Writer and Physician -- 1859-1930

Drake, Joseph Rodman --- American Poet and Satirist -- 1795-1820

Dreiser, Theodore --- American Novelist -- 1871-1945

Drucker, Peter F. --- American-Austrian Management Consultant -- born 1909

Drummond, Henry --- English Scientist and Theological Writer -- 1851-1897

Drummond, William --- Scottish Poet -- 1585-1659

Dryden, John --- English Poet, Dramatist, and Critic -- 1631-1700

Dumas, Alexandre --- French Novelist and Dramatist -- 1802-1870

Dunne, Finley Peter --- American Humorist and Journalist -- 1867-1936

Durant, William J. --- American Historian and Essayist -- 1885-1981

Dyer, Edward --- English Poet -- 1543?-1607

Dyer, John --- English Nature Poet -- 1700-1758

Dzyan, Book of --- Claimed Antediluvian Manuscript in Sen-Zar -- B.C. 3000?

EbnerEschenbach, Marie von --- Austrian Novelist -- 1830-1916

Ecclesiastes, --- Jewish - Old Testament - Scrolls -- c. B.C. 300?

Ecclesiasticus, --- Jewish - Apocrypha - Old Testament -- c. B.C. 200?

Eckhart, Meister --- German Mystic -- 1260-1327

Eddy, Mary Baker --- American Founder of Christian Science -- 1821-1910

Edgeworth, Maria --- English Novelist -- 1767-1849

Edison, Thomas A. --- American Inventor -- 1847-1931

Edwards, Jonathan --- American Theologian and Metaphysician -- 1703-1758

Foch, Ferdinand --- French Field Marshal -- 1851-1929

Fontenelle, Bernard L.B. De --- French Author -- 1657-1757

Forbes, Bertie Charles --- American Publisher -- 1880-1954

Ford, John --- English Dramatist -- 1586-1640

Forster, John --- English Biographer and Critic -- 1812-1876

Foster, John --- Englishman Clergyman and Essayist -- 1770-1843

Foster, John. --- American Diplomat -- 1836-1917

France, Anatole --- French Novelist -- 1844-1924

Francis de Sales, St. --- French Prelate -- 1567-1622

Frankfurter, Felix --- American - U.S. Supreme Court Justice -- 1882-1965

Franklin, Benjamin --- American Statesman, Scientist and Writer -- 1706-1790

Frederick II, "The Great" --- King of Prussia -- 1712-1786

French Proverb, --- Anonymous Saying of French Origin -- fl. B.C. 260

Freud, Sigmund --- Austrian Physician - Founder of Psychoanalysis -- 1856-1939

Fromm, Erich --- German Born American Psychoanalyst -- 1900-1980

Frost, Robert --- American Poet -- 1875-1963

Froude, James Anthony --- English Historian -- 1818-1894

Fuller, Margaret --- American Writer and Lecturer -- 1810-1850

Fuller, R. --- American Inventor and Philosopher -- 1895-1983

Fuller, Thomas --- English Clergyman and Author -- 1608-1661

Galileo, --- Italian Astronomer and Mathematician -- 1564-1642

Gallus, Gaius Cornelius --- Roman Poet and Soldier -- B.C. 70-26

Gamaliel, Rabbi --- Hebrew Scholar -- fl. 100 A.D.

Gambetta, Leon --- French Statesman and Orator -- 1838-1882

Gandhi, Mohandas K. --- Indian Political Leader -- 1869-1948

Garfield, James Abram --- American - 20th U.S. President -- 1831-1881

Garrick, David --- English Actor, Manager, and Dramatist -- 1716-1779

Garrison, William Lloyd --- American Abolitionist -- 1805-1879

Garth, Sir Samuel --- English Poet and Physician -- 1670-1719

Gay, John --- English Playwright and Poet -- 1688-1732

Gaynor, William J. --- American Politician -- 1849-1913

Gellius, Aulus --- Roman Writer -- 117?-180? A.D.

Genesis, --- Jewish - Old Testament - Torah -- c. B.C. 1200?

George, Henry --- American Writer and Lecturer -- 1839-1897

German Proverb, --- Anonymous Saying of German Origin -- 1797-1839

Gibbon, Edward --- English Historian -- 1737-1794

Hamilton, Alexander --- American Statesman and Founding Father -- 1757-1804

Hamilton, Andrew --- American Lawyer -- 1676-1741

Hamilton, Sir William --- Scottish Philosopher -- 1788-1856

Hammerstein, Oscar --- American Lyricist and Musical Producer -- 1895-1960

Hand, Learned --- American Jurist -- 1872-1961

Hardy, Thomas --- English Novelist and Poet -- 1840-1928

Hare, August W. --- English Divine -- 1792-1834

Hare & Charles, --- English Theological Literary Collaborators -- c. 1830

Harrington, Sir John --- English Writer -- 1561-1612

Harte, F. Bret --- American Writer of Short Stories -- 1836-1902

Hastie, William Henry --- American Judge -- 1904-1976

Hauff, Wilhelm --- German Novelist and Short-Story Writer -- 1802-1825

Havergal, Frances R. --- English Poet -- 1836-1879

Hawkins, Anthony H. --- English Novelist and Playwright -- 1863-1933

Hawthorne, Nathaniel --- American Novelist and Short Story Writer -- 1804-1864

Hazlitt, William --- English Essayist -- 1778-1830

Heber, Reginald --- English Clergyman and Hymn Writer -- 1783-1826

Hebrews, --- Christian - New Testament - Pauline Epistle -- 50?-100? A.D.

Hedge, Frederick H. --- American Unitarian Clergyman and Author -- 1805-1890

Hegel, Georg W. F. --- German Philosopher -- 1770-1831

Heine, Heinrich --- German Poet -- 1797-1856

Helps, Sir Arthur --- English Historian and Author -- 1813-1875

Hemans, Felicia D. --- English Poet -- 1794-1835

Hemingway, Ernest Miller --- American Writer -- 1898-1961

Henley, William Ernest --- English Writer, Poet, and Critic -- 1849-1903

Henry, Matthew --- English Theologian -- 1662-1714

Henry, Patrick --- American Orator and Patriot -- 1736-1799

Heraclitus, --- Greek Philosopher -- B.C. 535-475

Herbert, George --- English Metaphysical Poet -- 1593-1632

Herford, Oliver --- American Humorist, Poet, and Illustrator -- 1863-1935

Herod, "The Great" --- Palestinian - King of Judea -- B.C. 73-4

Herodotus, --- Greek Historian -- B.C. 484-425

Herrick, Robert --- English Poet -- 1591-1674

Hesiod, --- Greek Poet -- B.C. 800?

Hesse, Hermann --- German Novelist and Poet -- 1877-1962

Heywood, John --- English Dramatist and Proverb Collector -- 1497?-1580?

Higginson, Thomas W. --- American Author -- 1823-1911

Kafka, Franz --- Austrian Writer -- 1883-1924

Kaiser, Henry John --- American Industrialist -- 1882-1967

Kalidasa, --- Indian Dramatist -- fl. c. 450 AD

Kalisch, Isidor --- Russian Rabbi and Author -- 1810-1886

Kant, Immanuel --- German Metaphysician -- 1724-1804

Karr, Jean --- French Author -- 1808-1890

Katib, Abu Ali --- Iraqi Sufi Leader -- fl. 940 A.D.

Kazinczy, Francis --- Hungarian Author and Critic -- 1759-1831

Keats, John --- English Poet -- 1795-1821

Keller, Helen Adams --- American Author and Lecturer -- 1880-1968

Kemble, Francis Anne --- English Actress and Poet -- 1809-1893

Kempis, Thomas A. --- German Ecclesiastic and Mystic -- 1380-1471

Kennedy, John F. --- American - 35th President of the United States -- 1917-1963

Kettering, Charles F. --- American Engineer and Inventor -- 1876-1958

Key, Thomas Hewitt --- English Philologist -- 1799-1875

Khan, Hazrat --- Indian - Sufi Teacher and Musician -- 1882-1927

Khan, Pir Vilayat --- Western Sufi Master/Teacher -- born 1916

Khayyam, Omar --- Persian Poet and Mathematician -- fl. 1100

Kierkegaard, Soren --- Danish Philosopher and Writer -- 1813-1855

King, Martin L. --- American Clergyman and Civil Rights Leader -- 1929-1968

King, T. Starr --- American Unitarian Clergyman and Author -- 1824-1864

King, William --- English Poet -- 1663-1712

Kingsley, Charles --- English Author and Clergyman -- 1819-1875

Kipling, Rudyard --- English Author of Prose and Verse -- 1865-1936

Klee, Paul --- Swiss Painter -- 1879-1940

Kleiser, Grenville --- American Author -- 1868-1953

Klopstock, Friedrich G. --- German Poet -- 1724-1803

Koestler, Arthur --- Hungarian Born British Writer -- 1905-1983

Koran, The --- Arabic - Sacred Book of Islam -- c. 651 A.D.

Kossuth, Louis --- Hungarian Revolutionary Hero -- 1802-1894

L'Enclos, Ninon de --- French Courtesan -- 1620-1705

L'Estrange, Sir Roger --- English Journalist and Writer -- 1616-1704

La Bruyere, Jean de --- French Classical Writer -- 1645-1696

La Fontaine, Jean de --- French Poet -- 1621-1695

La Rochefoucauld, Francois de --- French Classical Writer -- 1613-1680

Lacordaire, --- French Catholic Priest and Liberal -- 1802-1861

Lactantius, Lucius C. --- Latin Author and Apologist -- 260-340 A.D.

Laertius, Diogenes --- Greek Author -- c. 250 A.D.

Lamartine, Alphonse de --- French Poet -- 1790-1869

Lamb, Charles --- English Essayist -- 1775-1834

Landon, Letitia E. --- English Poet and Novelist -- 1802-1838

Landor, Walter Savage --- English Poet and Essayist -- 1775-1864

Lao-Tzu, --- Chinese Philosopher - Founder of Taoism -- fl. B.C. 600

Lardner, Ring Wilmer --- American Humorist and Short-Story Writer -- 1885-1933

Lauder, Sir Harry --- Scottish Song Writer -- 1870-1950

Lavater, John Caspar --- Swiss Theologian and Mystic -- 1741-1801

Law, Andrew --- Canadian Born Scottish Politician -- 1858-1923

Lawrence, David H. --- English Author -- 1885-1930

Le Gallienne, Richard --- English Author -- 1866-1947

LeBon, Gustave --- French Physician and Social Psychiatrist -- 1841-1931

Lecky, William E. H. --- British Historian -- 1838-1903

Lee, Robert E. --- American - Confederate Army Commander -- 1807-1870

Leibnitz, Gottfried --- German Philosopher -- 1646-1716

Leighton, Robert --- Scottish Prelate and Classical Scholar -- 1611-1684

Leland, Charles G. --- American Author -- 1824-1903

Lenin, Nikolai --- Russian Revolutionary and Statesman -- 1870-1924

Lessing, Gotthold E. --- German Philosopher, Dramatist, and Critic -- 1729-1781

Lewis, Clive Staples --- English Author and Scholar -- 1898-1963

Lichtenberg, Georg C. --- German Physicist and Satirist -- 1742-1799

Lie, Trygve Halvdan --- Norwegian Statesman -- 1896-1968

Liebig, Justus von F. --- German Chemist and Professor -- 1803-1873

Linall, Jr., A. L. --- American Editor --

Lincoln, Abraham --- American - 16th President of the U.S. -- 1809-1865

Lippmann, Walter --- American Author and Editor -- 1889-1974

Livy, Titus --- Roman Historian -- B.C. 59-17A.D.

Lloyd George, David --- English Statesman -- 1863-1945

Locke, John --- English Philosopher -- 1632-1704

Longfellow, Henry W. --- American Poet -- 1819-1892

Lorenz, Konrad --- Austrian Zoologist and Writer -- b. 1903

Lorimer, George Horace --- American Editor -- 1868-1937

Lovelace, Richard --- English Poet -- 161-16557

Lover, Samuel --- Irish Novelist and Song Writer -- 1797-1868

Lowell, Amy --- American Poet and Critic -- 1874-1925

Lowell, James R. --- American Poet, Critic and Editor -- 1819-1891

Loyson, Charles --- French Preacher -- 1827-1912

Lubbock, Sir John --- English Statesman, Banker, and Naturalist -- 1834-1913

Lucan, --- Roman Epic Poet -- 39-65 A.D.

Lucas, Edward Verrall --- English Author and Critic -- 1868-1938

Lucillius, Gaius --- Roman Satiric Poet -- B.C. 148-103

Lucretius, --- Italian Philosophical Poet -- B.C. 99-55

Luke, --- Christian - New Testament - Gospels -- 50?-100? A.D.

Luther, Martin --- German Leader of the Protestant Reformation -- 1483-1546

Lyly, John --- English Dramatist and Prose Writer -- 1554-1606

Lynch, Thomas --- American Revolutionary Patriot -- 1749-1779

Ma'Arri, --- Arabian Poet -- 973-1057 A.D.

MacArthur, Douglas --- American General -- 1880-1964

Macaulay, Thomas B. --- English Historian and Author -- 1800-1859

MacDonald, George --- Scottish Novelist -- 1824-1905

Machiavelli, Niccolo --- Italian Author and Statesman -- 1469-1527

Mackay, Charles --- Scottish Poet and Song Writer -- 1814-1889

Maeterlinck, Maurice --- Belgian Author -- 1862-1949

Maghribi, Abu 'Uthman Al- --- North African Sufi Leader -- fl. 975 A.D.

Mahabharata, --- Indian Epic Poem -- c. B.C. 400

Mahan, Alfred Thayer --- American Naval Historian and Theorist -- 1840-1914

Maintenon, Francoise de — French - Second Wife of Louis XIV of France — 1635-1719

Malherbe, Francois de --- French Poet and Critic -- 1555-1628

Malone, Walter --- American Jurist -- 1866-1915

Malraux, Andre --- French Writer, Critic, and Politician -- 1901-1976

Manilius, Marcus --- Latin Poet -- fl. 100 A.D.

Mann, Horace --- American Educator -- 1796-1859

Mann, Thomas --- German Novelist and Essayist -- 1875-1955

Mansfield, Lord --- English Jurist -- 1705-1793

Manu, --- Hindu - Semi-Legendary Lawgiver and Poet -- c. B.C. 200

Margaret, de Valois --- French Author - Wife of Henry IV -- 1553-1615

Mark, --- Christian - New Testament - Gospel -- 50?-100? A.D.

Markham, Edwin --- American Poet -- 1852-1940

Marlowe, Christopher --- English Dramatist and Poet -- 1564-1593

Marquis, Donald --- American Author -- 1878-1937

Marryat, Frederick --- English Novelist -- 1792-1848

Martial, Marcus Valerius --- Roman Epigrammatic Poet -- 43-104 A.D.

Martineau, Harriet --- English Author -- 1802-1876

Marvel, Ik --- American Author -- 1822-1908

Marvell, Andrew --- English Metaphysical Poet -- 1621-1678

Marx, Karl --- German Social Philosopher and Radical Leader -- 1818-1883

Masefield, John --- English Novelist, Poet, and Playwright -- 1878-1967

Massey, Gerald --- English Poet -- 1828-1907

Massillon, Jean Baptiste --- French Clergyman -- 1663-1742

Massinger, Philip --- English Dramatist -- 1583-1640

Masters, Edgar Lee --- American Poet and Biographer -- 1869-1950

Mathers, Samuel L. --- English Metaphysician -- 1850?-1918

Matthew, --- Christian - New Testament - Gospel -- 50?-100? A.D.

Maugham, Wm. Somerset --- English Novelist and Playwright -- 1874-1965

Maupassant, Guy de --- French Writer -- 1850-1893

Maurois, Andre --- French Writer -- 1885-1967

Maximus, Valerius --- Roman Writer -- fl. c. 20 A.D.

Maxwell, William --- English - 5th Earl of Nithsdale -- 1676-1744

Mazzini, Giuseppe --- Italian Patriot and Writer -- 1805-1872

McCreery, John Luckey --- American Journalist -- 1835-1906

McDougall, William --- American Psychologist -- 1871-1938

Medhurst, C. Spurgeon --- English Translator, and Missionary -- born c. 1850?

Melanchthon, Philip --- German Scholar and Humanist -- 1497-1560

Melville, Herman --- American Writer -- 1819-1891

Menander, --- Greek Dramatic Poet -- B.C. 342-291

Mencius, --- Chinese Mandarin Philosopher -- B.C. 371-288

Mencken, Henry L. --- American Editor, Author, and Critic -- 1880-1956

Mendelssohn, Felix --- German Composer -- 1809-1847

Meredith, George --- English Novelist and Poet -- 1828-1909

Meredith, Owen --- English Politician & Poet -- 1831-1891

Merton, Thomas --- American Religious and Writer -- 1915-1968

Metastasio, --- Italian Poet and Dramatist -- 1698-1782

Michelangelo, --- Italian Renaissance Painter and Sculptor -- 1474-1564

Michelet, Jules --- French Writer -- 1798-1874

Mill, John Stuart --- English Philosopher and Economist -- 1806-1873

Millay, Edna --- American Poet -- 1892-1950

Miller, Henry --- American Author -- 1891-1980

Miller, Joaquin --- American Poet -- 1839-1913

Milman, Rev. Henry H. --- English Clergyman, Poet, and Historian -- 1791-1868

Milnes, Richard M. --- English Politician, Poet, and Writer -- 1809-1885

Milton, John --- English Poet -- 1608-1674

Mirabeau, Honore Gabriel --- French Statesman -- 1749-1791

Mitford, William --- English Historian and Writer -- 1744-1827

Mohammed, --- Arabian Prophet - Founder of Islam -- 570-632 A.D.

Moliere, --- French Dramatist and Actor -- 1622-1673

Monroe, James --- American - 5th President of the United States -- 1758-1831

Montagu, Ashley --- American Anthropologist and Social Biologist -- born 1905

Montaigne, Michel de --- French Philosopher and Essayist -- 1533-1592

Montalvo, Juan --- Ecuadorian Writer -- 1832-1889

Montapert, Alfred A. --- American Inventor, Industrialist, and Writer -- born 1910?

Montesquieu, --- French Jurist and Political Philosopher -- 1689-1755

Montgomery, James --- Scottish Poet and Editor -- 1771-1854

Moore, Thomas --- Irish Poet -- 1779-1852

More, Hannah --- English Author -- 1745-1833

Morgan, Lady Sidney --- Irish Writer -- 1789-1859

Morgenstern, Christian --- German Poet -- 1871-1914

Morley, Christopher --- American Editor and Author -- 1890-1957

Morris, Lewis --- Welsh Lawyer and Writer of English Verse -- 1835-1907

Mosheim, Johann L. Von --- German Theologian and Professor -- 1694-1755

Motokiyo, Seami --- Japanese Playwright -- 1363-1444

Muir, John --- Scottish Born American Naturalist -- 1838-1914

Mumford, Lewis --- American Social Critic and Historian -- born 1895

Murray, Gilbert --- English Classical Scholar -- 1866-1957

Musashi, Miyamoto --- Japanese Samurai Warrior and Strategist -- 1584-1645

Musset, Alfred de --- French Poet, Dramatist, and Fiction Writer -- 1810-1857

Nagarjuna, Siddha --- Indian/Tibetan Father of Mahayana Buddhism -- c. 100-200 AD

Nahmanides, Rabbi --- Spanish Rabbi -- c. 1300

Napoleon, --- French Emperor -- 1769-1821

Nash, Ogden --- American Humorous Poet -- 1902-1971

Nashe, Thomas --- English Satirist -- 1567-1601

Nathan, Rabbi --- Palestinian Rabbi -- fl. 200 A.D.

Navajo, Edward A. --- Navajo -- 1860-1937

Neale, John Mason --- English Clergyman and Hymn Writer -- 1818-1866

Necker, Suzanne --- Swiss Writer -- 1739-1794

Nehru, Jawaharial --- Indian Nationalist and Statesman -- 1889-1964

Newman, John Henry --- English Religious Leader and Writer -- 1801-1890

Ni'matullah, Shah --- Persian Sufi Mystic and Master -- 1331-1431?

Niebuhr, Reinhold --- American Clergyman and Theologian -- 1892-1971

Nietzsche, Friedrich W. --- German Philosopher -- 1844-1900

Novalis, --- German Poet -- 1772-1801

Noyes, Alfred --- English Poet and Writer -- 1880-1958

Nur 'Ali Shah, --- Persian Sufi Master -- died 1797

O'Meara, Barry E. --- Irish Physician -- 1786-1836

O'Neill, Eugene G. --- American Playwright -- 1888-1953

O'Reilly, John Boyle --- Irish Born American Writer -- 1844-1890

O'Shaughnessy, Arthur --- English Poet and Naturalist -- 1844-1881

Opie, John --- English Portrait and Historical Painter -- 1761-1807

Oppenheim, James --- American Free Verse Poet and Fiction Writer -- 1882-1932

Oppenheimer, J. Robert --- American Physicist -- 1904-1967

Osgood, Frances S. --- American Poet -- 1811-1850

Osler, Sir William --- Canadian Physician and Professor -- 1849-1919

Otway, Thomas --- English Dramatist -- 1652-1685

Ouida, --- English Novelist -- 1839-1908

Overbury, Sir Thomas --- English Author and Courtier -- 1581-1613

Ovid, --- Latin Poet -- B.C.43-18A.D.

Owen, John --- Welsh Epigrammatist -- 1560-1622

Paine, Thomas --- American Political Theorist and Writer -- 1737-1809

Paley, William --- English Theologian -- 1743-1805

Palgrave, Francis Turner --- English Poet and Anthologist -- 1824-1897

Pandita, Saskya --- Tibetan Grand Lama of Saskya -- 1182-1251

Paracelsus, --- Swiss Medical Philosopher -- 1493-1541

Parkinson, C. Northcote --- English Historian and Author -- born 1909

Parnell, Thomas --- English Poet -- 1679-1717

Pascal, Blaise --- French Scientist and Religious Philosopher -- 1623-1662

Pasteur, Louis --- French Chemist -- 1822-1895

Patanjali, --- Hindu Raja - Yoga Master -- c. B.C. 500?

Pater, Walter --- English Essayist and Critic -- 1839-1894

Patton, George Smith --- American Army Officer -- 1885-1945

Pavese, Cesare --- Italian Writer -- 1908-1950

Pollard, Josephine --- American Poet -- 1843-1892

Pollok, Robert --- Scottish Religious Poet -- 1798-1827

Polybius, --- Greek Historian -- B.C. 203?-120

Pomfret, John --- English Poet and Cleric -- 1677-1702

Pope, Alexander --- English Poet, Critic, and Translator -- 1688-1744

Porter, Jane --- Scottish Novelist -- 1776-1850

Porteus, Beilby --- English Writer and Bishop -- 1731-1808

Pound, Ezra Loomis --- American Poet, Critic, and Editor -- 1885-1972

Powys, John Cowper --- English Author -- 1872-1963

Preston, Margaret J. --- American Writer -- 1820-1897

Priestley, Joseph B. --- English Theologian and Scientist -- 1733-1804

Prior, Matthew --- English Poet and Diplomat -- 1664-1721

Procter, Adelaide --- English Poet -- 1825-1864

Propertius, Sextus --- Roman Elegiac Poet -- B.C. 50-16

Proust, Marcel --- French Novelist -- 1871-1922

Proverbs, --- Jewish - Old Testament -- BC 1000?-200?

Psalms, --- Jewish - Old Testament -- B.C. 1000?-300

Pusey, Edward B. --- English Clergyman -- 1800-1882

Pymander, The Divine --- Egyptian - Extant Work of Hermes Trismegistus – BC 2500?-200AD

Pythagoras, --- Greek Philosopher and Mathematician -- B.C. 582-507

Quarles, Francis --- English Poet -- 1592-1644

Quincey, Thomas De --- English Essayist -- 1785-1859

Quintilian, Marcus Fabius --- Roman Rhetorician -- 35-90 A.D.

Rabelais, Francois --- French Writer and Physician -- 1490-1553

Racine, Jean Baptiste --- French Dramatist -- 1639-1699

Raleigh, Sir Walter --- English Statesman and Man of Letters -- 1552-1618

Ramakrishna, Sri --- Hindu Mystic -- 1836-1886

Ramayana, The --- Sanskrit Epic -- c. B.C. 500-50

Rathenau, Walter --- German Industrialist and Statesman -- 1867-1922

Ray, James --- English Historian -- circa 1746

Ray, John --- English Naturalist -- 1627-1705

Reade, Charles --- English Novelist and Dramatist -- 1814-1884

Reagan, Ronald --- American - 40th President of the U.S. -- b. 1911

Regnard, Jean Francois --- French Comic Dramatist -- 1655-1709

Regnier, Mathurin --- French Poet -- 1573-1613

Reik, Theodor --- American-Austrian Psychologist and Author -- born 1888

Revelation, --- Christian - New Testament -- c. 85 A.D.

Reynolds, Sir Joshua --- English Portrait Painter -- 1723-1792

Rice, Grantland --- American Journalist and Author -- 1880-1954

Richter, Jean Paul F. --- German Novelist -- 1763-1825

Rickenbacker, Edward --- American War Hero and Airline Executive -- 1890-1973

Rig Veda, --- Collection of Indian Mythological Hymns -- B.C. 1200-900?

Rilke, Rainer Maria --- German Lyric Poet -- 1875-1926

Rinehart, Mary Roberts --- American Novelist and Dramatist -- 1876-1958

Rittenhouse, Jessie B. --- American Poet and Anthologist -- 1869-1948

Rivaroli, Antoine de --- French Journalist -- 1753-1801

Robinson, Edwin A. --- American Poet -- 1869-1935

Roche, James J. --- American Editor -- 1847-1908

Rogers, Samuel --- English Poet and Conversationalist -- 1763-1855

Rogers, Will --- American Humorist -- 1879-1935

Rojas, Fernando --- Spanish Writer -- 1465?-1541?

Romans, --- Christian - New Testament - Pauline Epistle -- c. 56 A.D.

Roosevelt, Franklin D. --- American - 32nd President of the U.S. -- 1882-1945

Roosevelt, Theodore --- American - 26th President of the U.S. -- 1858-1919

Root, Elihu --- American Statesman -- 1845-1937

Roscommon, Wentworth D. --- English Poet and Scholar -- 1633?-1685

Rossetti, Christina G. --- English Poet -- 1830-1894

Rothschild, Mayer A. --- German Banker -- 1743-1812

Rousseau, Jean Jacques --- French Philosopher, Author and Composer -- 1712-1778

Rowe, Nicholas --- English Dramatist -- 1674-1718

Roy, Pierre Charles --- French Satirist and Dramatic Poet -- 1683-1764

Royce, Josiah --- American Philosopher -- 1855-1916

Ruffini, Giovanni --- Italian Writer -- 1807-1881

Rumi, Jalal-Uddin --- Persian Sufi Mystic Poet -- 1207-1273

Rusk, Dean --- American Secretary of State -- b. 1909

Ruskin, John --- English Critic and Social Theorist -- 1819-1900

Russell, Bertrand --- British Philosopher, Mathematician, and Essayist -- 1872-1970

Russell, George W. --- Irish Man of Letters -- 1867-1936

Russell, Lord John --- British Statesman -- 1792-1858

Ryunosuke, Akutagawa --- Japanese Author -- 1892-1927

Saadi, Moslih Eddin --- Persian Poet -- 1184-1291

Stael, Germaine de --- French-Swiss Novelist -- 1766-1817

Stanford, Leland --- American Politician - U.S. Senator -- 1824-1893

Stanislaus, Leszczynski --- Polish King -- 1677-1766

Steele, Sir Richard --- English Essayist and Playwright -- 1672-1729

Steffens, Lincoln --- American Editor and Author -- 1866-1936

Stein, Gertrude --- American Author and Patron of the Arts -- 1874-1946

Steinmetz, Charles P. --- American Electrical Engineer -- 1865-1923

Stendhal, Henri B. --- French Writer -- 1783-1842

Stephens, James --- Irish Poet and Fiction Writer -- 1882-1950

Sterling, John --- English Poet and Critic -- 1806-1844

Sterne, Laurence --- English Author -- 1713-1768

Stevenson, Adlai E. --- American Lawyer and Politician -- 1900-1965

Stevenson, Robert L. --- Scottish Essayist, Poet, and Novelist -- 1850-1895

Stirner, Max --- German Satiric Philosopher -- 1806-1856

Stoddard, Richard Henry --- American Critic and Poet -- 1825-1903

Stowe, Harriet Beecher --- American Humanitarian and Novelist -- 1811-1896

Struther, Jan --- English Poet and Novelist -- 1901-1953

Suckling, Sir John --- English Poet -- 1609-1642

Sue, Marie J. E. --- French Novelist -- 1804-1857

Sun Yat-sen, --- Founder of the Kuomintang -- 1866-1925

Swain, Charles --- English Poet -- 1803-1874

Swedenborg, Emanuel --- Swedish Scientist, Religious Teacher, and Mystic – 1688-1772

Swetchine, Anne Sophie --- Russian Author -- 1782-1857

Swift, Jonathan --- English Author -- 1667-1745

Swinburne, Algernon --- English Poet -- 1837-1909

Swing, Raymond G. --- American Journalist -- 1887-1968

Syrus, Publilius --- Syrian Born - Roman Writer of Aphorisms -- fl. B.C. 42

Tacitus, --- Roman Historian -- 55-117 A.D.

Tagore, Rabindranath --- Indian Author -- 1861-1941

Talmage, Thomas De Witt --- American Clergyman -- 1832-1902

Talmud, The --- Jewish Archive of Oral Tradition -- BC 500?-400?AD

Tancred, --- Norman Crusader -- 1076-1112

Tasso, Torquato --- Italian Poet -- 1544-1595

Tate, Nahum --- English Poet and Dramatist -- 1652-1715

Taylor, Anne --- English Writer of Children's Verse -- 1782-1866

Taylor, Bayard --- American Journalist, Traveler, and Author -- 1825-1878

Valery, Paul --- French Poet and Philosopher -- 1871-1945

Van Buren, Martin --- American - 8th President of the U.S. -- 1782-1862

Van Dyke, Henry --- American Clergyman, Educator, and Author -- 1852-1933

Van Gogh, Vincent --- Dutch Postimpressionist Painter -- 1853-1890

Van Loon, Hendrik Willem --- American Historian and Writer -- 1882-944

Vanbrugh, Sir John --- English Dramatist and Architect -- 1666-1726

Vauvenargues, --- French Moralist -- 1715-1747

Vergil, --- Roman Epic, Didactic, and Idyllic Poet -- B.C. 70-19

Villiers, George --- English Wit, Poet, and Statesman -- 1628-1687

Voiture, Vincent --- French Man of Letters -- 1597-1648

Voltaire, --- French Historian and Writer -- 1694-1778

Wallace, Lew --- American Novelist and Diplomat -- 1827-1905

Walpole, Horace --- English Author -- 1717-1797

Walton, Izaak --- English Writer -- 1593-1683

Ware, Eugene F. --- American Lawyer and Verse Writer -- 1841-1911

Warhol, Andy --- American Artist and Filmmaker -- b. 1930

Warren, Earl --- American - Chief Justice - U.S. Supreme Court -- 1891-1974

Washington, Booker T. --- American Educator -- 1856-1915

Washington, George --- American Soldier & Statesman - 1st U.S. President – 1732-1799

Watson, Thomas E. --- English Poet and Scholar -- 1557-1592

Watson, William --- English Poet -- 1858-1935

Webster, Daniel --- American Statesman, Lawyer, and Orator -- 1782-1852

Webster, John --- English Dramatist -- 1580?-1634

Wei, Wang --- Chinese Poet and Painter -- 699-759 A.D.

Weiss, John --- American Unitarian Minister -- 1818-1879

Wellington, Duke Arthur W. --- British Soldier and Statesman -- 1769-1852

Wesley, John --- English Preacher and Founder of Methodism -- 1703-1791

Whately, Richard --- English Prelate and Writer -- 1787-1863

Whipple, Edwin Percy --- American Lecturer and Critic -- 1819-1886

White, Hugh Lawson --- American Political Leader -- 1773-1840

Whitehead, Alfred North --- English Mathematician and Philosopher -- 1861-1947

Whitman, Walt --- American Poet -- 1819-1892

Whittier, John Greenleaf --- American Poet, Reformer, and Author -- 1807-1892

Wilcox, Ella Wheeler --- American Poet and Journalist -- 1855-1919

Wilde, Oscar --- British Author and Wit -- 1856-1900